Student Assessment and Learning Guide

for

Understanding Business

Ninth Edition

William G. Nickels
University of Maryland

James M. McHugh
St. Louis Community College – Forest Park

Susan M. McHugh
Applied Learning Systems

Prepared by
Barbara Barrett
St. Louis Community College – Meramec

McGraw-Hill
Irwin

Student Assessment and Learning Guide for
UNDERSTANDING BUSINESS
William G. Nickels, James M. McHugh, and Susan M. McHugh

Published by McGraw-Hill/Irwin, an imprint of The McGraw-Hill Companies, Inc., 1221 Avenue of the
Americas, New York, NY 10020. Copyright © 2010, 2008, 2005, 2002, 1999, 1996, 1993, 1990, 1987 by The McGraw-Hill
Companies, Inc. All rights reserved.

1 2 3 4 5 6 7 8 9 0 QWD/QWD 0 9

ISBN: 978-0-07-726842-8
MHID: 0-07-726842-3

www.mhhe.com

Table of Contents

TO OUR STUDENTS

This study guide is designed to give you, the Introduction to Business student, every advantage in mastering the concepts presented in *Understanding Business,* ninth edition, by Bill Nickels, Jim McHugh and Susan McHugh.

Using this study guide will give you an edge; you will go beyond just memorizing terms, to developing and using the critical thinking and creative problem solving skills that are so important in today's dynamic business environment.

Using The Study Guide

There are many different ways to learn, so I can only make suggestions about how to use this guide more effectively. You may find a different way, which suits you better.

First, this study guide is not designed to replace reading the text! In fact, reading the text is an integral part of using this study guide. You can use the guide to help point out places where you need more work, or need to review. The guide is very detailed, and requires you not only to remember facts, but also to apply concepts in a way that will help you to develop a better understanding of today's business environment.

You will find that there is a lot of writing in completing these exercises. Writing the answers to the questions, rather than just choosing a number or matching a term with a letter, will help to reinforce the material. You will also be better prepared to answer essay or short answer questions when you have studied by writing out answers in your own words.

Finally, to make effective use of this study guide, I suggest that you:

- Read the text before each class period, and outline important concepts. You will probably have a syllabus that outlines the reading assignments for each class.
- Attend class and take good, detailed notes. Ask questions in class; get involved!
- Do the exercises in the study guide *after* you have completed the first two steps. I would suggest that you do the exercises in stages, and not try to do the whole chapter at one sitting. For example, if there are 6 learning goals, do the exercises pertaining to the first three learning goals on one day, and then complete the remaining exercises the next day. Or, do the factual based exercises one day, the critical thinking exercises the next, and so on.
- Do *all* the exercises in the guide, not just the ones that take less time!
- Review your answers, and mark the questions you had problems answering. Then, reread the section of the text that deals with those areas.
- Before a test, review your class notes, the text and the study guide material.
- Remember, your instructor may add material in class that is not in the text, and the study guide won't cover that material. That takes us back to the first suggestions: read the book before class, attend every class, take notes, and get involved!

Design Of This Study Guide

Each chapter in this guide contains the following sections to help you be successful in this Introduction to Business course.

- *Learning goals:* Each learning goal is listed in the order in which it appears in the text. This is to help you focus on what is important throughout the chapter. The appropriate learning goal for each exercise is also noted in the side margin as you go through the chapter.

- *Learning the Language:* This section identifies the key terms and definitions from the chapter. This is a matching section, in which you read the definition then choose the appropriate term. Many of the definitions will be direct quotes from the chapter, or a slight variation.

- *Assessment Check:* These exercises help you to learn the facts of the material from the text. You will be writing answers to factually based questions from the chapter, organized by learning goals. This section is designed to develop your knowledge of the text material. I suggest you keep the book nearby while doing these exercises, but do as much as you can without opening the book. This will help you to determine the areas where you need to review.

- *Critical Thinking Exercises:* Business people need a variety of skills. Among the most important skills you can bring to a job is the ability to think for yourself, analyze problems, develop solutions based upon your analysis, and present the solutions in written form. There are many opportunities to hone these skills with this text. In this section of the study guide, the questions will require you to think and apply the material from the chapter to come up with a solution to the situation presented. These application questions are designed to provide you with the opportunity to enhance your decision-making skills and understanding of the material. In some cases, there are no definitive answers, only suggested answers.

- *Practice Test:* In all likelihood, you will be required to take some objective exams. The practice test is divided into two sections, multiple choice, and true false. Keep in mind this is only a sample of the types of questions you could see on an exam, and these are not the actual questions you will see on a classroom test! The practice exam will give you the chance to find out what areas of the chapters you need to take some extra time with before your classroom exam.

- *You Can Find It On The Net:* Business research is an integral part of being a successful businessperson. These Internet exercises provide an opportunity to practice your research skills on the Internet. The web addresses listed are only an entry to the information available. The web sites were valid at the time of this writing. Please understand that the Internet changes daily, and not all the web sites may be available when you are completing the exercise. If a web site referenced in an exercise is no longer available, demonstrate your research skills by finding a similar site that answers the exercise questions.

- *Answers:* The answers to all the Retention Check, Critical Thinking Exercises, and Practice Tests are at the end of each chapter.

There is no substitute for just plain hard work. To be successful in tomorrow's work world, you will need to work hard today to develop the skills employers are looking for. The text, *Understanding Business,* and this study guide are designed to help you to be successful by starting you on the road to developing those skills. The rest is up to you. Good Luck!

Acknowledgments

Many thanks are due, and I will be brief. First, thanks to Bill Nickels, Susan McHugh and Jim McHugh, and to McGraw-Hill/Irwin for allowing me to continue my involvement with this wonderful text. To Ryan and Chad, thank you for your support, understanding, and computer consultation! And to all my colleagues at the Meramec campus of St. Louis Community College, thanks for your support and encouragement.

Barbara Barrett

CHAPTER 1 – MANAGING WITHIN THE DYNAMIC BUSINESS ENVIRONMENT

LEARNING GOALS

After you have read and studied this chapter, you should be able to:

1. Describe the relationship of businesses' profit to risk assumption and discuss how businesses and nonprofit organizations add to the standard of living for all.
2. Compare and contrast being an entrepreneur and working for others.
3. Examine how the economic environment and taxes affect businesses.
4. Describe the effect of technology on business.
5. Demonstrate how businesses can meet and beat competition.
6. Analyze the social changes affecting businesses.
7. Identify what businesses must do to meet the global challenge, including war terrorism.
8. Review how trends from the past are being repeated in the present and what they mean for tomorrow's college graduate.

LEARNING THE LANGUAGE

Listed below are important terms found in the chapter. Choose the correct term for each definition and write it in the space provided.

Business	Goods	Revenue
Business environment	Identity theft	Risk
Database	Loss	Services
Demography	Nonprofit organization	Stakeholders
E-commerce	Outsourcing	Standard of living
Empowerment	Productivity	Technology
Entrepreneur	Profit	
Factors of production	Quality of life	

1. Land, labor, capital, entrepreneurship and knowledge are known as _____.

2. Otherwise known as _____ this refers to buying and selling products and services over the Internet.

3. _____ refers to the general well-being of a society in terms of freedom, a clean natural environment, education, health care, safety, free time, and rewards that add to the satisfaction and joy that other goods and services provide.

4. An _____ is the person who risks time and money to start and manage a business.

5. Products that are intangible, such as education, heath care, insurance, recreation and travel and tourism are known as _____.

6. A _____ is any activity which seeks to provide goods and services to others while operating at a profit.

7. When a business's expenses are more than its revenues a _____ has occurred.

8. Entrepreneurs take a _____ when they take the chance that they will lose time and money on a business that may not prove to be profitable.

9. A society's _____ is the amount of goods and services people can buy with the money they have.

10. A _____ is an organization whose goals do not include making a personal profit for its owners or organizers.

11. An electronic storage file where information is kept is known a(n) _____.

12. When we study _____, we are looking at a statistical study of the human population with regard to its size, density and other characteristics such as age, race, gender and income.

13. Known as _____, this means giving frontline workers the responsibility, authority, and freedom to respond quickly to customer requests.

14. Computers, food, clothing, cars, and appliances are tangible products known as _____.

15. _____ is the amount of money a business earns above and beyond what it spends for salaries and other expenses.

16. A business's_____ are all the people who stand to gain or lose by its policies and activities and whose concerns the business needs to address.

17. The total amount of money a business takes in during a given period by selling goods and services is called _____.

18. _____ is considered to be everything that makes business processes more effective, efficient and productive, such as phones, copiers, computers, medical imaging devices, personal digital assistants and various software programs.

19. The surrounding factors of the _____ either help or hinder the development of businesses.

20. The amount of output you generate given the amount of input such as hours worked is called _____.

21. Contracting with other companies to do some or all of the functions of a firm such as accounting or production is known as _____.

22. _____ is obtaining private information about a person, such as Social Security number and credit card numbers, and using that information for illegal purposes.

23. The trend known as _____ refers to the trend of saving energy and producing products that cause less harm to the environment.

24. A _____ is the movement of the temperature of the planet up or down over time.

ASSESSMENT CHECK

Learning Goal 1

Entrepreneurship and Wealth Building

1. What could be the result, for you, of successfully filling a market need?

2. Describe the difference between revenue and profit.

3. When does a company experience a loss? Over time, what will likely result from business losses?

4. What is the relationship between risk and profit?

5. How do the taxes paid by businesses and their employees benefit everyone in their communities?

6. How is it that a person in one country, such as Germany, can buy fewer goods with the same amount of money as a person who lives in the United States, for example? How does this affect our standard of living?

7. Describe the challenges businesses of the 21st century will face with regard to stakeholders and profitability.

8. What is "insourcing" and what are the benefits?

9. How do nonprofits use financial gains?

10. What are "social entrepreneurs"?

Learning Goal 2

Entrepreneurship Versus Working for Others

11. What are two ways to succeed in business, according to the text? What are the advantages of each way?

12. How have individuals, members of minority groups, and women business owners in the United States participated in entrepreneurship?

13. List the 5 factors of production.

    a. _____   d. _____

    b. _____   e. _____

    c. _____

14. What combination of the factors of production distinguishes rich countries from poor countries?

Learning Goal 3

The Business Environment

15. What are the 5 factors that make up the business environment?

    a. _____   d. _____

    b. _____   e. _____

    c. _____

The Economic and Legal Environment

16. What are six ways governments can reduce the risk of starting businesses and thus increase entrepreneurship?

    a. _____

    b. _____

    c. _____

    d. _____

    e. _____

    f. _____

17. According to the text, what "failures" contributed to the faltering economy of 2006–2009?

Learning Goal 4

The Technological Environment

18. Describe the difference between "effectiveness" and "efficiency".

19. What are the two major types of e-commerce transactions?

    a. _____

    b. _____

20. How do businesses make use of bar codes and the resulting databases?

21. What are some ways you can prevent identify theft, according to the text?

Learning Goal 5

The Competitive Environment

22. What must companies offer in order to stay competitive in today's world markets?

23. What is meant by the phrase: "Competing by Exceeding Customer Expectations"?

24. Describe the concept of Competing by Restructuring and Empowerment.

Learning Goal 6

The Social Environment

25. What are three general ways in which the social environment is changing?

  a. _____

  b. _____

  c. _____

26. How has the meaning of diversity changed?

27. What kinds of business opportunities are presented by the increase in the number of older Americans?

28. What will be the impact of an increasing population of older Americans on Social Security and what are the options for fixing the problem?

29. What effect has the growth in single-parent families had on businesses?

Learning Goal 7

The Global Environment

30. Two important global environmental changes have been:

  a. _____

  b. _____

31. Another name for global trade is _____

32. World trade has grown thanks to:

   a. _____

   b. _____

33. How has world trade affected living standards around the world?

34. Describe the effects of war and terrorism on business.

35. How will these global changes affect you?

Learning Goal 8

The Evolution of American Business

36. How has the agricultural industry and farm employment changed in the last century?

37. What has been the consequence of increased productivity in the manufacturing sector regarding jobs? Where have workers found jobs as a result?

38. How important is the services industry to our economy and to job creation?

39. As the service sector era seems to be coming to a close, what is the next new era expected to be?

CRITICAL THINKING EXERCISES

Learning Goal 1

1. Monika lives in Germany, works for the Mercedes plant in her hometown and makes the equivalent of $65/hour American. Her cousin Joe lives in the United States and works for the Honda plant in his hometown. When Monika visits Joe she is amazed at how big his house is compared to where she lives, his sound system and how well he seems to live. "Boy," says Monika, "I sure can't live like this at home. Why not?"

Learning Goal 2

2. Revelle Industries is a small company located in an area of the country where unemployment has been very high for the last several years. In 2009, Revelle was struggling. There were only 20 employees, and profits were low. As the economy improved, and with new management, things began to turn around, and now Revelle employs almost 75 people. This year they sold 120,000 units of their only product line, a component part used in the manufacture of industrial ventilation systems. The price of their product is $20/unit. The cost of salaries, expenses and other items was $2,050,000. Sales forecasts look good for the next several years, as Revelle has customers world wide and will be expanding their product line in the next 18 months.

    a. What are Revelle's revenues?

    b. What are Revelle's profits?

    c. How has the company generated wealth and created a higher standard of living?

Learning Goal 3

3. Eastern Europe has experienced dramatic changes during the last 20 years, with changes in both government and economic policies. The newly formed countries have struggled for the last decade with questions about how to be successful in the 21st century. What will be the key to developing the economies of these countries?

4. Schnucks is a large grocery retailer located in the St. Louis, Missouri area. The company is expanding, and continually improving the technology in their stores. How can a database help Schnucks better serve its customers? How do you think a grocery store such as Schnucks will compete in the area of e-commerce?

Learning Goal 5

5. Consider your college or university, or, if you are employed, consider the company for which you work:

   a. Who are its competitors?

   b. How does the organization meet and (hopefully) exceed their customers' expectations?

   c. Who are the organization's stakeholders? Does it meet the needs of the stakeholders? Why or why not?

   d. How has the organization restructured to empower its workers?

Learning Goals 4, 5, 6, 7

6. Consider a company with which you are familiar. For example, evaluate the company where you or one of your family members is currently employed.

   a. How are various technologies implemented in the business? Does the company sell their products on a website? Evaluate the website. Is it customer friendly?

   b. What kinds of programs has the company implemented to meet the needs of single parents and other employees?

   c. Does the company appear to be competing in the manner described by your text, by meeting the needs of its employees and its customers?

   d. How diverse is the company's workforce?

   e. How important is the global marketplace to this business?

7. How do the changes and programs companies have implemented to meet the needs of single parent families help these companies to be more competitive?

Learning Goal 7

8. How can increased global competition benefit the United States and U.S. workers?

Learning Goal 8

9. How are the changes we are experiencing in manufacturing and services similar to the changes in the farming industry we saw in previous centuries?

PRACTICE TEST

MULTIPLE CHOICE — Circle the best answer.

Learning Goal 1

1. A loss occurs when a company
   a. has revenues greater than expenses.
   b. hires too many new workers.
   c. has expenses greater than revenues.
   d. has taken a risk.

2. In general, the _____ the risk, the _____ the profit.
   a. higher/higher
   b. lower/higher
   c. higher/lower
   d. faster/quicker

3. Taxes would not be used to support which of the following activities?
   a. Build a new school
   b. Support people in need
   c. Keep a clean environment
   d. Help run a privately owned day care center

4. A clean environment, safety, free time and health care are elements which contribute to our:
    a. standard of living.
    b. quality of life.
    c. economic environment.
    d. factors of production.

5. A list of stakeholders of an organization would include:
    a. customers.
    b. employees.
    c. stockholders.
    d. all of the above are stakeholders.

6. Insourcing is:
    a. contracting with other companies to do some or all of the functions of a firm.
    b. keeping all essential functions within the firm.
    c. when a foreign company sets up design and production facilities in the United States.
    d. providing in-house consulting services for employees.

Learning Goal 2

7. The number of businesses owned by immigrants, minority groups, and women has _____ in recent years.
    a. declined
    b. stabilized
    c. grown
    d. been dramatically reduced

8. Which of the following is (are) not considered a factor of production?
    a. Knowledge
    b. Capital
    c. Labor
    d. Taxes

9. The two factors of production that contribute most to making countries rich are:
    a. land and labor.
    b. capital and land.
    c. entrepreneurship and use of knowledge.
    d. use of knowledge and taxes.

Learning Goal 3

10. To foster entrepreneurial growth governments must:
    a. pass laws that enable business people to write contracts that are enforceable in court.
    b. establish a high tax rate to support loans for small businesses.
    c. take over ownership of small businesses when they are first getting started.
    d. reduce the value of their currency to encourage foreign investment.

11. When corruption is evident in governments:
    a. the news media attempts to keep it quiet in order to minimize bad publicity.
    b. it's easier to open a store without a permit.
    c. minimum wages are lower.
    d. factories are more difficult to build without obtaining a permit through bribery of public officials.

12. One of the most serious negative results of the increased use of databases by companies has been:
    a. an decrease in the amount of "junk mail" received by consumers.
    b. an increase in identity theft.
    c. increased failure rates by Internet companies.
    d. changes in the organizational structures of companies leading to loss of jobs.

13. Efficiency means
    a. producing items using the least amount of resources.
    b. the amount of output you generate in a given amount of time.
    c. using high tech equipment to do a job.
    d. producing as much as you can as fast as you can, regardless of cost.

Learning Goal 5

14. What must companies do to be competitive in today's market?
    a. offer high quality products and outstanding service at competitive prices.
    b. create innovative and high quality marketing programs.
    c. create alliances with competitors.
    d. focus on those activities that will create the most profit.

Learning Goal 6

15. One of the results of the increase in the older population of the United States is:
    a. a future problem for the Social Security system.
    b. fewer opportunities for new businesses as the population declines.
    c. a decline in the economy, as this segment of the population tends to be poorer.
    d. less focus on technology as the older population will be less interested in technology related products.

16. Increased diversity of the population of the United States has
    a. led to companies with more diverse workforces.
    b. much narrower definition of the meaning of diversity.
    c. fewer conflicts between groups at work as they learn to work with one another.
    d. declining need for dual language signs and brochures as the immigrant population learns English.

Learning Goal 7

17. Among the changes resulting from increased global trade are:
    a. less need for efficient distribution systems.
    b. less global competition as companies set up manufacturing systems in foreign countries.
    c. less need for employees to update skills as workers conform to U.S. standards.
    d. improved living standards around the world.

18. The impact of war and terrorism on U.S. business is that:
    a. fewer jobs will be created in the United States.
    b. companies have grown more slowly as money has been diverted to the war effort in Iraq.
    c. there is less global trade.
    d. lower organizational costs for security personnel and equipment as firms are depending upon the government to provide those items.

19. Since the mid-1980s, the _____ has generated most of the increases in employment in the United States.
    a. manufacturing sector
    b. agricultural sector
    c. service sector
    d. goods producing sector

20. The new era of business will:
    a. probably see a major decline in productivity.
    b. be an information based global revolution that will impact all sectors of the economy.
    c. be dominated by an increase in the manufacturing sector as global markets grow.
    d. see a rise in the agricultural sector.

TRUE–FALSE

Learning Goal 1

1. _____ A social entrepreneur is an individual who uses business principles to start and manage not-for-profit organizations, and help address social issues.

2. _____ As a potential business owner, you may want to invest your money in a company with a lot of risk, in order to earn a lot of money quickly.

3. _____ There is basically no difference between "goods" and "services".

4. _____ Mariko, who lives in Tokyo, makes the equivalent of approximately $35,000 per year, while Donada, living in the United States makes only $25,000. From this you can assume Mariko has a higher standard of living than Donada.

5. _____ Business skills are useful and necessary in non-profit institutions.

Learning Goal 2

6. _____ In analyzing factors of production that make a country "rich," it has been observed that some relatively poor countries often have plenty of land and natural resources.

7. _____ While knowledge is an important factor in business success, it is not considered to be one of the factors of production.

Learning Goal 3

8. _____ Governments can reduce the risk of starting businesses and increasing entrepreneurship by keeping taxes and regulations to a minimum.

9. _____ One of the causes of the economic downturn of 2006-2009 was the failure of many mortgage lenders to do the research necessary to ensure their borrowers creditworthiness.

Learning Goal 4

10. _____ Few technological changes have had a greater impact on business than the emergence of information technology, such as computers, cell phones, and the Internet.

11. _____ Technology really only affects companies involved in manufacturing.

12. _____ Successful organizations must listen to the needs of consumers and adjust products, policies and practices to meet customer needs.

13. _____ One of the ways a company can compete is to empower frontline workers.

Learning Goal 6

14. _____ Population shifts are leading to many new business opportunities.

15. _____ Social Security has become a major issue as older Americans drain the system.

Learning Goal 7

16. _____ Improvements in distribution and in communication have led to more global trade.

17. _____ Threats of war and terrorism have had little impact on businesses either in the U.S. or anywhere in the world.

Learning Goal 8

18. _____ When workers in the industrial sector were laid off, many of them went back to work in the agricultural sector.

You Can Find It On The Net

These are additional exercises for your own exploration and information. The answers for this section aren't provided.

A. The "green" initiative in business is "big business" today. Take a look at the website listed below: http://www.greenatworktoday.com/

What's the latest news?

What companies can you find that have "green initiatives"? What steps are these companies taking to become more environmentally friendly?

Do a search to discover "green" products, either by manufacture, or because they are less harmful to the environment.

B. The purpose of this exercise is to gather data regarding trends in occupations and in the population and the social environment and to analyze how these changes affect Americans and American businesses. To answer these questions, begin with the Census Bureau homepage on the Internet at www.census.gov

Select the population Clock from the Census bureau's homepage. Record the time and population of the United States. Try to find the population of the world. What proportion of the world's population is represented by the United States?

What is the fastest growing occupation? What could contribute to the increase in this profession? The Bureau of Labor Statistics is a good place to search for occupational growth stats.

What is the population of your home state? What percentages of the population of your home state are from minority groups?

What are the average salaries for individuals with high school degrees, college degrees, master's degrees, and professional degrees? What is the trend, and what does that indicate about incomes in the United States for the future?

Return to the Census Bureau's homepage. What is the population of the country now? If you come back to the homepage for three consecutive days, you will see how quickly the population is growing. How can businesses use this information?

ANSWERS

LEARNING THE LANGUAGE

1. Factors of production	9. Standard of living	17. Revenue
2. E-commerce	10. Nonprofit organization	18. Technology
3. Quality of life	11. Database	19. Business environment
4. Entrepreneur	12. Demography	20. Productivity
5. Services	13. Empowerment	21. Outsourcing
6. Business	14. Goods	22. Identity theft
7. Loss	15. Profit	23. Greening
8. Risk	16. Stakeholders	24. Climate change

ASSESSMENT CHECK

Learning Goal 1

Entrepreneurship and Wealth Building

1. One result of successfully filling a market need is that you can make money for yourself by giving customers what they want.

2. Revenue is money generated by selling goods, while profit is the money left over after a business has paid its expenses.

3. A company will have a loss when expenses of doing business are greater than the revenues generated. If a business loses money over time, it will likely have to close, putting people out of work.

4. In general, the companies that take the most risk can make the most profit. According to the text, the more risk you take, the higher the rewards may be.

5. Taxes are used by the federal government and local communities to build hospitals, schools, libraries, playgrounds and other facilities. Taxes are also used to keep the environment clean to support people in need and to pay for police and fire protection.

6. Prices for goods and services in other countries such as Germany and Japan are higher than they are here in the United States. So people living in those countries can buy less than what a person who lives in the U. S. can buy, with the same amount of money. So, our standard of living is higher here than in other countries where prices are higher.

7. The challenge for the 21st century will be for organizations to remain profitable while trying to maintain a balance between the needs and wants of all stakeholders. For example, the need for a business to make a profit may be balanced against the needs of employees for sufficient income or the need to protect the environment. The need to stay competitive may require businesses to outsource jobs to other countries which could do great harm to a community from the loss of jobs.

8. Insourcing refers to the fact that some foreign companies are setting up design and production facilities here in the United States. This creates many new jobs and helps to offset the loss of jobs created by outsourcing.

9. Nonprofit organizations use financial gains to benefit the stated social or educational goals of the organization rather than profit.

10. Social entrepreneurs are people who use business principles to start and manage not-for-profits that help address social issues.

Learning Goal 2

Entrepreneurship Versus Working for Others

11. The two main ways to succeed in business according to the text are to rise up through the ranks of a business, and to start your own business.
The advantage of working for others is that someone else assumes the risk and provides you with benefits.
The advantage of starting your own business is that you can reap the profits. The down side of owning your own business is that many small businesses fail each year, and you don't receive any benefits. You have to provide them for yourself.

12. The number of Hispanic-owned businesses has increased considerably, as have the number of businesses owned by members of other groups such as Asians, American Indians, Pacific Islanders, Alaskan Natives and African Americans. Women now own over a third of all businesses.

13. The five factors of production are:
    a. land and other natural resources.
    b. labor.
    c. capital, such as, machines tools, and buildings. It does NOT include money.
    d. entrepreneurship.
    e. knowledge.

14. If you were to analyze rich countries versus poor countries the factors of production that makes countries rich today is a combination of entrepreneurship and effective use of knowledge. Many countries have labor but continue to be poor, like Mexico, while others have a lack of resources, but are rich, such as Japan. A lack of entrepreneurship and the absence of knowledge among workers, along with a lack of economic and political freedom contribute to keeping poor countries poor.

Learning Goal 3

The Business Environment

15. The five factors in the business environment are:
    a. the economic and legal environment.
    b. the technological environment.
    c. the competitive environment.
    d. the social environment.
    e. the global business environment.

The Economic and Legal Environment

16. Governments can increase entrepreneurship by:
    a. keeping taxes and regulations to a minimum.
    b. allowing private ownership of businesses.
    c. minimizing interference with the free exchange of goods and services.
    d. passing laws that enable business people to write contracts that are enforceable in court.
    e. establishing a currency that is tradable on world markets.
    f. minimizing corruption.

17. Failures of the fundamental principles of honesty, integrity and high ethical standards weakened the economy from 2006-2009. Some mortgage lenders failed to ensure borrower's creditworthiness, and many subprime borrowers defaulted on their loans as a result. As a result, housing values declined, and it was more difficult for new borrowers to get loans.

Learning Goal 4

The Technological Environment

18. Effectiveness means producing the desired result. Efficiency means producing goods and services using the least amount of resources.

19. The two major types of e-commerce transactions are:
    a. business-to-consumer (B2C)
    b. business-to-business (B2B).

20. Bar codes identify the product being purchased and can be used by retailers to tell what size you have purchased, in what color, and at what price. The scanner at the checkout counter reads that information and puts it into a database.

    Once information from bar codes is in a database, companies can send you catalogs and other direct mail that offers the kind of products you might want, as indicated by past purchases. The use of the database enables stores to carry the merchandise that the local population wants.

21. The text suggests that to prevent identity theft, you should limit those to whom you give information such as credit card numbers and your social security number. You should also install antivirus software on your computer, as well as a firewall and anti-spyware software, and monitor your credit report.

Learning Goal 5

The Competitive Environment

22. To be competitive in today's world markets, a company must offer quality products and outstanding service at competitive prices.

23. "Competing by Exceeding Customer Expectations" means that businesses today must be customer driven, and that customer's wants and needs must come first. Successful organizations must listen more closely to their customers and adjust the firm's products, policies, and practices to meet the needs of their customers.

24. In order to meet the needs of customers front line workers such as office clerks, front-desk people, salespeople, for example must be empowered. This means giving those workers the responsibility, authority, freedom, training, and equipment they need to respond quickly to customer requests and to make decisions essential to providing high quality goods and services. This can require restructuring an organization so that managers are willing to give up authority and employees are willing to assume more responsibility.

Learning Goal 6

The Social Environment

25. The social environment is changing through:
    a. increased diversity.
    b. an increase in the number of older Americans.
    c. more single parent families.

26. Diversity has come to mean more than minorities and women. Many groups are now included in diversity efforts, including seniors, the disabled, homosexuals, extroverts, introverts, married, singles, and the devout. It also means dealing with workers and cultures around the world with sensitivity.

27. People aged 65-74 are currently the richest demographic group in the United States. They represent a lucrative market for many types of businesses. The increase in the number of older Americans will provide many business opportunities in travel, medicine, nursing homes, assisted-living facilities, adult day care, home health care, recreation, and others.

28. There are fewer workers per retiree paying into the Social Security System. By the year 2017 less money will be going into Social Security that going out, and the government will have to do something about the shortfall. The options to fix the problem are not popular: raise taxes, cut benefits, reduce spending elsewhere or borrow.

29. Single parents have encouraged businesses to implement programs such as family leave and flextime.

Learning Goal 7

The Global Environment

30. Two important global environmental changes have been:
    a. the growth of international competition.
    b. the increase of free trade among nations.

31. Another name for global trade is globalization.

32. World trade has grown thanks to:
    a. more efficient distribution systems.
    b. communication advances such as the Internet.

33. Living standards around the world have improved due to globalization, and China and India have become major competitors of the U.S.

34. The wars in Iraq and Afghanistan drawn billions of dollars out of the American economy. Some companies have benefited but most have not, and have grown more slowly as money has been diverted to the war effort.
    The threat of terrorism adds to organizational costs including the cost of security personnel and equipment and insurance.

35. Global changes will affect you in a number of ways. New jobs will be created as businesses expand to serve global markets. Students must be prepared to compete in a rapidly changing world-wide environment that necessitates continuous learning to stay competitive.

Learning Goal 8

The Evolution of American Business

36. The farming industry became so efficient through the use of technology that the number of farmers had dropped considerably over the last century. The millions of small farms that used to exist have been replaced by some huge farms and some large farms. The resulting loss of farm jobs has not been a negative sign. Today U.S. agricultural workers are the most productive in the world. Most farm workers who lost their jobs in the previous century went to work in manufacturing.

37. The manufacturing industry, like the farming industry, has used technology to become more productive. As a consequence, many jobs were eliminated. Many of these workers found jobs in the service sector.

38. Today, the leading firms in the U.S. are in services. Since the mid-1980s the service industry has generated almost all of the U.S. economy's increases in employment. Although service-sector growth has slowed, it remains the largest area of growth.

39. As the service era comes to a close, we are in the middle of an information-based global revolution that will affect all areas of the economy—agricultural, industrial and service.

CRITICAL THINKING EXERCISES

Learning Goal 1

1. Monika is surprised at the standard of living Joe seems to have attained compared to hers, while working at a similar job. While Monika makes more per hour (equivalent U.S. dollars) than Joe, the cost of food, housing and other services is probably much higher for her. Therefore she can't buy as much with her money as Joe can - it simply costs too much. A similar situation exists in the United States when you compare one region to another. Compare average housing prices for example in San Francisco, California to those in St. Louis, Missouri. When you compare per capita income for those areas, you will also find a difference.

Learning Goal 2

2. a. $2,400,000 in revenue
   b. Profit is $350,000 after taking expenses of $2,050,000.
   c. Companies like Revelle generate wealth and create a higher standard of living in many ways. Workers pay taxes that federal and local governments use to build hospitals, schools, roads and playgrounds. Tax money is also used to keep the environment clean. Businesses also pay taxes to the federal government and the local community. Standards of living go up because people can buy goods and services with the money they earn from being employed. When businesses start, grow and prosper, and generate wealth, our quality of life improves as the taxes the workers and the business pay provide for good schools, good health care, a clean environment and so on.

3. In the analysis of the factors of production, the most important factor is not capital, natural resources or labor. Countries in Eastern Europe have land and labor, but they are still poor countries. The key to developing an economy is entrepreneurship and the effective use of information and knowledge entrepreneurship and provide the information necessary to help people to move ahead.

   These countries must pass laws that enable companies to write enforceable contracts, necessary to do business. They must create a currency that is tradable, which allows their citizens to buy and sell goods and services anywhere in the world. Governments must also work to minimize corruption.

4. The new retailing technology allows a retailer to determine what kind of products customers purchase, in what amount, in what size and at what price. That information, plus information such as the name, address and family information about a customer will go into a database.

   With that information Schnucks can send direct mail pieces to customers offering exactly what they want. It will allow Schnucks to carry inventory specifically for a customer base in different areas around the city.   For example, if there is an area with a large Italian population, the Schnucks store in that area will carry more of the type of products those customers might buy. If there is a large Jewish population in another area of the city, the store serving that area may carry fewer of the Italian products, and more for the dietary needs of the Jewish customer, and so on. These stores will also be able to replace the items quickly through contact with the suppliers, who also have the bar code information. If Schnucks is interested in developing direct mail pieces or other types of services, this technology will help decision makers to know exactly what to feature, and mailing lists will be readily available.

5. a. Competitors for some schools will be the other colleges and universities in the local community. For others it may be other schools in the region or the nation.

   b. A college or university may please its customers (students, in a way) by offering classes at convenient times (many schools offer weekend college programs for example), in convenient locations (off site locations), encouraging faculty to be accessible to student through designated office hours or mentoring programs, offering a variety of programs, offering Internet or other technology based courses, establishing a format for easy access to faculty and assignments through the Internet, and, of course, having winning sports teams!

   c. The stakeholders are students, parents of students, employees, taxpayers, the community in which the school is located and alumni for example. How schools meet the needs of its stakeholders may be through a variety of course offerings, tuition and rate of tuition increases, level of community involvement by the school's administrators, responsiveness to student organizations, cooperation with alumni groups, and so on.

   d. Students may have difficulty answering how the school meets the needs of employees. You may find out if there is a structure for faculty and staff to communicate openly with their manager, for example, or how employees view the administration and the school's policies.

Learning Goals 4,5,6,7

6.   Answers to this question will vary. Most companies have computerized everything from inventory management to payroll to customer checkout. Students will find that companies are using technology in hundreds of different ways. Most companies will have a Web site. Some offer their products for sale, others will direct customers to local retailers that carry their products. Many companies today are offering benefits such as time off to work as a volunteer, on-site day care centers and more. Most will also find that the company is involved in some way in the international area, even if it is just selling or buying a few products imported from overseas. Many of these companies will have a diverse workforce, and employ a variety of international workers at all levels.

Learning Goal 6

7.   By developing programs such as flextime and family leave, companies better meet employee needs. This can make a company more competitive by fostering a positive environment with satisfied workers who may then be more productive. Further, these programs can be used to attract the kinds of skilled workers companies will need in the future to remain competitive.

Learning Goal 7

8.   If U.S. firms want to be competitive in today's global environment, they must continue to focus on quality issues in the same way that countries like China and India have done. U.S. firms have begun to serve the growing global markets with the highest quality products and services at the lowest possible prices. This has provided U.S. workers with jobs by expanding our global marketplace.

Learning Goal 8

9.   As the agricultural industry became more productive through advances in technology, fewer people were needed to produce the same or greater volume. Agricultural workers had to find jobs elsewhere, in other industries, and learn new skills. Many of these people went to work in manufacturing, helping to make the United States a world manufacturing power in the first half of this century.

The same trend has occurred today in the industrial or manufacturing sector. As factories have been able to improve productivity through technology, fewer workers are needed to produce the same or greater volume of high quality products. Factory workers today have found new employment in the service industries, which have generated almost all of the employment growth increases since the mid-1980s.

PRACTICE TEST

MULTIPLE CHOICE   **TRUE–FALSE**

1.	c	11.	d
2.	a	12.	b
3.	d	13.	a
4.	b	14.	a
5.	d	15.	a
6.	c	16.	a
7.	c	17.	d
8.	d	18.	b
9.	c	19.	c
10.	a	20.	b

1.	T	10.	T
2.	F	11.	F
3.	F	12.	T
4.	F	13.	T
5.	T	14.	T
6.	T	15.	T
7.	F	16.	T
8.	T	17.	F
9.	T	18.	F

CHAPTER 2 – HOW ECONOMICS AFFECTS BUSINESS: THE CREATION AND DISTRIBUTION OF WEALTH

LEARNING GOALS

After you have read and studied this chapter you should be able to:

1. Explain basic economics.
2. Explain what capitalism is and how free markets work.
3. Compare socialism and communism.
4. Analyze the trend toward mixed economies.
5. Describe the economic system of the United States including the significance of key economic indicators (especially GDP), productivity, and the business cycle.
6. Contrast fiscal policy and monetary policy and explain how each affects the economy.

LEARNING THE LANGUAGE

Listed below are important terms found in this chapter. Choose the correct term for each definition below and write it in the space provided.

Brain Drain	Free market economies	Monopoly
Business cycles	Gross domestic product	National debt
Capitalism	Inflation	Oligopoly
Command economies	Invisible hand	Perfect competition
Communism	Keynesian economic theory	Producer price index
Consumer price index	Macroeconomics	Recession
Deflation	Market price	Resource development
Demand	Microeconomics	Socialism
Depression	Mixed economies	Stagflation
Disinflation	Monetary policy	Supply
Economics	Monopolistic competition	Unemployment rate
Fiscal policy		

1. The quantity of products that manufacturers or owners are willing to sell at different prices at a specific time is known as _____.

2. The part of economic study that looks at the behavior of people and organizations in particular markets is called_____.

3. The country is in a _____when GDP has declined for two consecutive quarters.

4. The economic system known as _____ is one in which all or most of the factors of production and distribution are privately owned and operated for profit.

5. _____ is the quantity of products that people are willing to buy at different prices at a specific time.

6. We define the _____ as the number of civilians at least 16 years old who are unemployed and tried to find a job within the prior four weeks.

7. In economic systems considered _____ the market largely determines what goods and services get produced, who gets them, and how the economy grows.

8. The _____ consists of monthly statistics that measure the pace of inflation or deflation.

9. The sum of government deficits over time is called the _____.

10. A course in _____ will teach us how society chooses to employ resources to produce goods and services and to distribute them for consumption among various competing groups and individuals.

11. Government economists keep a close watch on _____, which is the general rise in the price level of goods and services over time.

12. One key economic indicator is _____, the total value of goods and services produced in a country in a given year.

13. Some countries operate under _____, economic systems in which the government largely decides what goods and services will be produced, who will get them, and how the economy will grow.

14. In developing _____ the government is managing the money supply and interest rates.

15. _____ is a situation in which price increases are slowing (the rate of inflation is slowing.

16. A severe recession is known as a(n)_____, and is usually accompanied by disinflation.

17. _____ is an economic system based on the premise that some, if not most basic businesses should be owned by the government so that profits can be evenly distributed among the people.

18. When the federal government makes an effort to keep the economy stable, it may use _____, by increasing or decreasing taxes or government spending.

19. _____are economic systems where some allocation of resources is made by the market and some by the government.

20. The economy is experiencing _____ when prices are actually declining.

21. A _____ is a market in which only one seller controls the total supply of a product or service and sets the price.

22. The market situation known as _____ is where there are many sellers in a market and no seller is large enough to dictate the price of the product.

23. Adam Smith coined the term _____ to describe the process that turns self-directed gain into social and economic benefits for all.

24. A form of competition where the market is dominated by just a few sellers is called a(n)_____.

25. The part of economic study called _____ looks at the operation of a nation's economy as a whole.

26. The study of _____ focuses on how to increase resources and to create the conditions that will make better use of those resources.

27. The _____ is the price determined by supply and demand.

28. _____ is the market situation in which there are a large number of sellers that produce similar products, but the products are perceived by buyers as different.

29. The economic and political system called _____ is one in which the state (the government) makes all economic decisions and owns almost all the major factors of production.

30. The index that measures prices at the wholesale level is the _____.

31. _____ describe the periodic rises and falls that occur in all economies over time.

32. The loss of the best and brightest people to other countries is called the _____.

33. A situation known as _____ is occurring when the economy is slowing, but prices are still going up.

34. An economic theory called _____ is the theory that a government policy of cutting taxes and increasing spending could stimulate the economy in a recession.

ASSESSMENT CHECK

Learning Goal 1

How Economic Conditions Affect Businesses

1. How is macroeconomics different from microeconomics?

2. How can businesses contribute to an economic system through resource development?

3. What do followers of Thomas Malthus (neo Malthuasians) believe? How do their views differ from other economists?

4. What kinds of freedom did Adam Smith believe were vital to the survival of any economy? Why?

5. Describe Adam Smith's theory of the invisible hand and how wealth would be created.

Learning Goal 2

Understanding Free-Market Capitalism

6. In a capitalist system, who/what owns the businesses and decides what to produce, how much to produce, how much to pay workers and how much to charge for goods?

7. The foundation of the U.S. economic system is: _____

8. What are the four basic rights of a free market (capitalist) system?

   a. _____   c. _____

   b. _____   d. _____

9. Describe how decisions about what to produce, and in what quantities are made in a free market system.

10. What is "supply" in economic terms, and what happens to quantity supplied as price goes up?

11. What is "demand" in economic terms and what happens to demand as price goes up?

12. The key factor in determining quantity supplied and quantity demanded is: _____

13. Label the graph

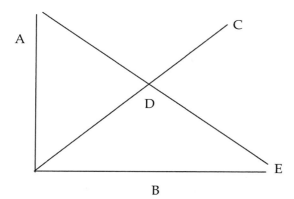

14. What is the equilibrium point and what is its relationship to price?

15. Describe what proponents of a free market system say about government involvement in a free market system.

16. What happens in countries where there is no mechanism, such as a free market, for businesses to determine what and how much to produce?

17. Describe, including examples:

   a. perfect competition: _____

   _____

   b. monopolistic competition: _____

   _____

   c. oligopoly: _____

   _____

   d. monopoly: _____

   _____

18. What has been the benefit of the free market system for industrialized countries?

19. The text describes the limitation of the free market system as inequality. What does that mean?

20. How have ethics been compromised by the free market system?

Learning Goal 3

Understanding Socialism

21. What is the basic premise of socialism?

22. Describe the major benefits of socialism.

23. What are the negative consequences of socialism?

Understanding Communism

24. In a communist system, how are economic decisions made?

25. What are two problems associated with communism, and what have been the results?

Learning Goal 4

The Trend Toward Mixed Economies

26. What is the major principle of each of the two major economic systems in the world?

    a. Free market economies: _____

    _____

    b. Command economies: _____

    _____

27. Experience has shown that neither capitalism nor socialism has had optimal results in terms of the economy. What are the problems with:

    a. A free market system (Capitalism) _____

    _____

    b. Socialism/communism: _____

    _____

    c. As a result of those problems, the trends in free market economies and in socialist and communist countries has been: _____

    _____

28. What kind of economic system do we have in the United States? Why is it considered to be this type of system?

Learning Goal 5

Understanding the Economic System of the United States

29. What are three major indicators of economic health?

    a. _____

    b. _____

    c. _____

30. Is the production output for foreign companies, such as Honda, included in GDP figures?

31. What is one major influence on the growth of GDP?

32. Describe the four types of unemployment.

    a. _____

    b. _____

    c. _____

    d. _____

33. What is the difference between inflation and disinflation?

34. What is the difference between inflation and deflation?

35. What is happening during a period of stagflation?

36. List two measures of price changes over time.

    a. _____   b. _____

37. The CPI is an important figure because: _____

    _____

38. Describe the C-CPI.

39. In addition to the Producer Price Index, what other measures are included in the indicators of the economy's condition?

    a. _____

    b. _____

    c. _____

40. Why are business people eager to increase productivity?

41. What is a problem with regard to measuring productivity in the service sector?

42. The four phases of long-term business cycles are:

   a. _____   c. _____

   b. _____   d. _____

43. What is the difference between a "boom" and a recovery?

44. What three things happen when a recession occurs?

   a. _____

   b. _____

   c. _____

45. Identify three negative consequences of a recession.

   a. _____

   b. _____

   c. _____

Learning Goal 6

Stabilizing the Economy Through Fiscal Policy

46. What 2 areas are addressed with fiscal policy?

   a. _____   b. _____

47. Theoretically, high tax rates could: _____

   _____

48. What is meant by the term "national deficit"? How is the national deficit related to the national debt?

49. One way to reduce annual deficits is to _____

50. Describe the basic ideas of Keynesian economic theory.

Using Monetary Policy to Keep the Economy Growing

51. What is the Federal Reserve Bank (The Fed)?

52. What are two areas managed by monetary policy?

    a. _____

    b. _____

53. What action does the Fed take when the economy is booming? What happens in the economy as a result?

54. What happens when the Fed lowers interest rates?

CRITICAL THINKING EXERCISES

Learning Goal 1

1. They're everywhere! McDonald's hamburgers can be purchased in cities and suburbs, on riverfronts, in college football stadiums and in discount stores. There are fast food restaurants at most major road intersections, and billions of dollars are spent annually to advertise everything from fast food frozen yogurt to kid's meals. Grocery stores have even gotten into the act with their own versions of fast food restaurants.

   Families with sick children can stay in Ronald McDonald houses located close to the hospital where the children are receiving treatment, and businesses routinely come to the aid of disaster victims.

   How does the founding and growth of entrepreneurial ventures like McDonald's and the resulting growth in other, similar businesses illustrate Adam Smith's invisible hand theory?

Learning Goal 2

2. There are four basic rights under the capitalist economic system;

   Private property   Competition
   Profit   Freedom of choice

   Read the situations below and determine which of these is being demonstrated.

   a. _____   The owners of Pro Performance, Inc. make a profit for the owners for the first time in their history and decide to pay themselves a dividend.

   b. _____   The owners of Pro Performance, Inc. bought a piece of land for investment purposes.

   c. _____   Proctor and Gamble spends over $5 billion a year on advertising to keep their brand names at the top of the consumer mind.

   d. _____   Tom Oswalt decided to take a job as manager of an insurance agency after he graduated from college.

   e. _____   Arthur Tower receives a patent for a new method he devised to make metal springs

   f. _____   Alfred Rockwood, after he retired, decided to move to northern Michigan and start his own fly-tying business.

g. _____ Nintendo introduces a new video game console, the Wii, and many games to accompany the console in order to grab a larger share of the toy market.

h. _____ The Andersens, a young, dual income couple, draw up a will, making their children their beneficiaries of their home, property and other assets.

3. Plot a supply curve using the information below:

Unit price (dollars)	Amount supplied (units)
$125	500
100	400
75	300
50	200
25	100

On the same graph, plot the demand curve using the information listed below.

Unit Price (dollars)	Amount Demanded (units)
$125	100
100	200
75	300
50	400
25	500

a. What is the equilibrium price? _____

b. How many units will be supplied and purchased at that price? _____

4. Indicate whether the market price of a product will most likely go up or down in the following situations:

a. _____ There is a drought in the Midwest (bushel of wheat)

b. _____ Strawberries are in season with an abundant crop.

c. _____ It's the ski season (price of motel rooms in ski areas).

d. _____ A nutrition study indicates that red meat should be eaten only in moderation, if at all. (price of red meat)

e. _____ A major corporation announces that it has to borrow money from the government in order to stay in business. (price of its stock)

5. There are four degrees of competition:

perfect competition   oligopoly
monopolistic competition   monopoly

Match the type of competition to the situation described below

a. _____ Murray Barnard takes his soybean crop to the grain elevator in Decatur Illinois. He found that because of government price supports he would make a nice profit this year.

b. _____ Because it is the only provider of electrical service in the area, AmerenUE is carefully regulated by the Missouri Public Service Commission.

c. _____ Cheer cleans in all temperatures. Ivory Snow is gentle enough to launder a baby's clothes and Tide cleans the dirtiest clothes. Procter and Gamble makes these brands, as well as several others, which all appear to be different. Procter and Gamble competes with many other manufacturers and retains control over advertising, branding and packaging.

d. _____ The purchasing agent for a steel specialty products company says that he buys the steel the company uses to make their sign posts primarily on the basis of the best delivery date and the highest quality, rather than price, since all of his suppliers charge the same dollar amount per ton. The company has very few competitors.

Learning Goals 2, 3

6. Julie Marshall's first cousin, Jean-Paul, lives and works in Belgium. They have had long "discussions" via e-mail about the benefits and drawbacks of living in the U.S., a capitalist system, vs. living in Belgium a socialist economic system. Both Julie and Jean-Paul defend their country's system. What do you think Julie would say about the benefits of living in the U.S. and the drawbacks of living in Belgium, and how would Jean-Paul respond?

Learning Goals 2, 3, 4

7. Four basic economic systems are:

Capitalism   Socialism
Mixed Economy   Communism

Read the following examples and using the table in the text as well as other material in the text determine which system is MOST likely being described:

a. _____ John works for a large business in a major industry which is owned by the government (public ownership) of the country in which he lives. He is considered to be a government employee. John's brother owns his own small printing business, and John is thinking of opening a small business of his own. The problem is the tax rate he knows he has to pay on his earnings.

b. _____ Because the market is "ruled" by supply and demand with little government involvement, Maria has a wide variety of goods and services available for purchase where she lives and there are rarely shortages of goods and services.

c. _____ Many of the products Maria purchases have been made or assembled outside her country. These products are available because the government of her country does not control or interfere with trade with other countries.

d. _____ Although he disagrees with many of his government's policies, Ahmo cannot protest any of the government actions, and he is unable to buy the home he would like for his family.

e. _____ Hong's uncle works for a large corporation where promotions and raises are given to those who work hard and do a good job. The only problem is, the tax rate is so high there is little incentive for anyone to work that hard. Hong is a teacher in a public school, and the government controls his wages.

f. _____ Sam is a farmer in his country, and is being paid government subsidies so that over supply of the crops he grows is controlled.

g. _____ Ramon works hard at his job because where he lives and works, profits are kept by the owners of the company, and he is one of the owners. The government controls the pricing in his company because he works in an industry that is a monopoly.

h. _____ Enrique has a cousin in another country who tries to supply him with blue jeans and other products which are in very short supply in his country. Enrique often finds that some basic things, such as some food and clothing products are in short supply.

Learning Goal 5

8. Discuss the relationship between productivity and price levels. What is the relationship between productivity and Gross Domestic Product?

9. There are four types of unemployment:

frictional   cyclical
structural   seasonal

Match the situation being described to the type of unemployment

a. _____ As sales of new homes decline, the constructions industry lays off thousands of workers.

b. _____ A migrant worker, finished with his job in the potato fields in Idaho, travels to Michigan to look for a job harvesting fruit.

c. _____ A middle manager is laid off. His job has been eliminated with the installation of high tech information processing equipment.

d. _____ A businessman quits his job over a major disagreement with company policy.

Learning Goal 6

10. Determine whether fiscal policy or monetary policy is being discussed:

    a. _____ Congress debates a major income tax revision.

    b. _____ The Federal Reserve raises interest rates to combat inflation.

    c. _____ A candidate for major political office promises to cut spending for social programs to reduce the national debt.

    d. _____ Major government programs lose federal funding.

    e. _____ In an attempt to ease unemployment, the Fed increases the money supply.

    f. _____ A proposal is made to cut defense spending, but to raise taxes to fund defense spending.

    g. _____ American taxpayers express concern over tax loopholes for the rich.

    h. _____ A debate centers on whether to lower the national debt through an increase in the tax rate, less spending, or both.

11. Political campaigns often revolve around the issue of taxes and how an increase or a decrease will affect government spending and revenues. Since government revenues come from collecting taxes, discuss how a tax *decrease* <u>could</u> have the effect of *raising* government revenues. (Some of this answer will come from what you learned in Chapter 1)

PRACTICE TEST

MULTIPLE CHOICE — Circle the best answer

Learning Goal 1

1. _____ is the study of how to increase resources and to create conditions that will make better use of those resources.
   a. Economics
   b. Macroeconomics
   c. Microeconomics
   d. Resource development

2. The foundation of the U.S. economic system is considered to be:
   a. capitalism.
   b. socialism.
   c. a command economy.
   d. a mixed economy.

3. Adam Smith's theory of the "invisible hand" means that
   a. people should work in order to provide funding for charitable causes.
   b. through working for their own prosperity, people will actually help the economy grow and prosper.
   c. governments should own major businesses so that resources are equally distributed.
   d. the government manages the economy through monitoring government taxes and government spending.

Learning Goal 2

4. One of the problems with_____ is that it naturally leads to unequal distribution of wealth.
   a. communism
   b. socialism
   c. a command economy
   d. capitalism

5. Willie Hayes owns his own landscaping business, including all the land on which they grow their nursery plants, and all the equipment. Willie's son Josh has just graduated from college with an architectural landscaping degree. Willie hopes to retire in a few years and turn the business over to Josh, and Josh will inherit the business when Willie dies. This is an example _____ in a capitalist system.
   a. The right to have a job.
   b. The right to private property.
   c. The right to compete.
   d. The right to freedom of choice.

6. Typically, the quantity of products that manufacturers are willing to supply will _____ when prices _____.
   a. increase/increase
   b. decrease/increase
   c. stay the same/increase
   d. increase/stay the same

7. One holiday season a few years ago, there was a toy called Tickle My Elbow that was all the rage. Demand for this toy was so high that stores couldn't keep them on the shelf! There was quite a shortage of Tickle My Elbow that year. When a shortage such as this exists, what generally happens?
   a. the price goes up
   b. the price stays the same, and mothers everywhere fight for the last toy
   c. the government intervenes, and forces the manufacturer to make more of the toy
   d. when customers realize they can't get the toy, they give up, and the price goes down

8. A(n)_____shows the amount people are willing to buy at the prices at which sellers are willing to sell.
   a. supply curve
   b. demand curve
   c. marginal revenue point
   d. equilibrium point

9. What's going on here? As soon as Dewey Cheatum and Howe Motors increases the prices on their sport utility vehicle, then so does their only competitor, You Betcha Motors! Their prices are basically the same for similar vehicles, although their advertising says their products are really very different. What kind competition exists here?
   a. perfect competition
   b. monopoly
   c. oligopoly
   d. monopolistic competition

Learning Goal 3

10. Citizens of socialist nations can rely on the government to provide all of the following except:
    a. education.
    b. health care.
    c. unemployment and retirement benefits.
    d. money to start a business.

11. Socialist systems tend to:
    a. encourage innovation.
    b. keep up with countries like the U.S. in the areas of job and wealth creation.
    c. discourage the best from working as hard as they can.
    d. have relatively low tax rates.

12. What kind of a system exists when the government largely determines what goods and services get produced, who gets them and how the economy grows?
    a. Capitalist economy
    b. Socialist economy
    c. Free market economy
    d. Communist economy

Learning Goal 4

13. For the last several years, the country of Amerensk has been moving from a communist country to a more mixed economic system. Which of the following most likely would NOT occur in Amerensk?
    a. An increase in the level of government involvement in trade.
    b. Private ownership of business.
    c. An increase in the rate at which jobs are created.
    d. More incentives for workers to work harder.

14. In terms of economic systems, the trend has been for:
    a. countries that are mostly socialist to move toward communist systems.
    b. countries that are mostly capitalist to move toward more socialism.
    c. countries that are capitalist to move toward communism.
    d. countries to remain primarily within the economic system the country has in place.

Learning Goal 5

15. Which of the following would not be considered a key economic indicator?
    a. GDP
    b. The unemployment rate
    c. The tax rate
    d. The price indexes

16. Juan Valdez was laid off from his job at the coffee factory, because the demand for coffee has weakened. The kind of unemployment Juan is experiencing would be:
    a. frictional.
    b. seasonal.
    c. structural.
    d. cyclical.

17. When the economy in the United States began to slow, price increases, while still measurable, began to slow. This situation is known as:
    a. inflation.
    b. disinflation.
    c. deflation.
    d. fiscal policy.

18. Which of the following won't occur during a recession?
    a. high unemployment
    b. increase in business failures
    c. drop in the standard of living
    d. increase in interest rates

19. The nation of Finlandia is experiencing an economic crisis. The country has seen prices rise with increases in the price of oil and petroleum related products. At the same time, many businesses are experiencing profit problems because of the rising prices, and have begun to lay people off in order to cut costs. So, unemployment is rising. Finlandia is experiencing:
    a. a depression
    b. a period of stagflation
    c. disinflation
    d. deflation

Learning Goal 6

20. Fiscal policy is at issue when:
    a. The Federal Reserve raises interest rates.
    b. The Federal Reserve debates combating inflation by cutting the money supply.
    c. Congress debates a proposal to cut defense spending, and raising taxes to support spending for education.
    d. Unemployment goes up as the country slides into a recession.

21. Which of the following is not a part of the business cycles that occur in economics over time?
    a. Economic boom
    b. Depression
    c. Structural unemployment
    d. Recovery

22. When President Barack Obama was elected, the economy of the United States was in trouble, and had slid into a recession. Consumer spending was low and getting worse. In an effort to stop the decline, President Obama proposed an economic stimulus package which included government spending on roads, bridges, schools among other things, and a tax cut that each U.S. worker would see in their paycheck. Apparently, President Obama was a proponent of:
    a. Malthusian economics.
    b. Monetary policy.
    c. Keynesian economic theory.
    d. Communist economic theory.

23. The sum of all the federal deficits over time is known as the:
    a. national debt.
    b. gross national debt.
    c. fiscal policy.
    d. aggregate demand for money.

TRUE–FALSE

Learning Goal 1

1. _____ The world's population is growing more slowly than expected, and there are some industrial countries in which growth may be so slow that there will be too many old people and too few young people to support them.

2. _____ Today many U.S. businesspeople are becoming more concerned about social issues and their obligation to return to society.

3. _____ Microeconomics looks at the operation of a nation's economy as a whole.

Learning Goal 2

4. _____ In a free market system, price is determined through negotiation between buyers and sellers.

5. _____ When there is a surplus of products, manufacturers will tend to raise the price so that they will make a profit from those products they are able to sell.

6. _____ Monopolistic competition exists when just a few sellers dominate a market.

7. _____ As capitalist systems have evolved in the United States and other parts of the world, wealth has become more equally distributed.

Learning Goal 3

8. _____ One of the consequences of a socialist system is a high tax rate on those who do work, in order to pay for services for those that don't, or can't, work.

9. _____ A negative consequence of socialism has been brain drain.

10. _____ Socialism and communism are popular terms used to describe free market economies.

11. _____ A communist system is based upon the premise that the government owns all major forms of production and all economic decisions are made by the government

Learning Goal 4

12. _____ The United States is a purely free market economy.

13. _____ Mixed economies exist where some allocation of resources is made by the marketplace, and some by the government.

Learning Goal 5

14. _____ Production from a foreign company located in the U.S., like Honda, is not included in calculating GDP.

15. _____ Betty Bixler worked for Chrysler for 20 years before being laid off when her job was eliminated because updated technology made her job obsolete. Betty is structurally unemployed.

16. _____ The PPI is important because some government benefits, wages and salaries, rents and leases, tax brackets, and interest rates are all based upon this figure.

17. _____ It has become relatively easy to measure productivity in the service sector due to the influx of machinery.

18. _____ An increase in productivity means the same worker produces more in the same amount of time.

19. _____ During a recession, we could experience an overall drop in our standard of living, high unemployment, and increased business failures.

20. _____ During a period of disinflation, prices are actually going down.

Learning Goal 6

21. _____ When a political candidate indicates that the only way to cut the deficit is to cut spending and raise taxes, the candidate is addressing fiscal policy.

22. _____ High tax rates are encouraged by small business owners because the increase in government revenues from higher taxes will be used by the government for small business loans.

You Can Find It on The Net

Many economic statistics can be found on government sites. Visit the Bureau of Labor Statistics at www.bls.gov.

What is the most recent change in the Consumer Price Index?

Use the inflation calculator to determine the cost of tuition at your school in 10 years. What would tuition have been 10 years ago?

What is the most recent unemployment rate for the United States?

Go to the International Statistics link. How do the unemployment rate and the changes in the Consumer Price Index in the United States compare to other major countries such as Canada, Japan and parts of Europe?

Click on the map of the United States on your state. What is the unemployment rate in your state?

What is the trend over 6 months, indicated on this web page?

ANSWERS

LEARNING THE LANGUAGE

1.	Supply	12.	Gross Domestic Product	23.	Invisible hand
2.	Microeconomics	13.	Command economies	24.	Oligopoly
3.	Recession	14.	Monetary policy	25.	Macroeconomics
4.	Capitalism	15.	Disinflation	26.	Resource development
5.	Demand	16.	Depression	27.	Market price
6.	Unemployment rate	17.	Socialism	28.	Monopolistic competition
7.	Free market economies	18.	Fiscal policy	29.	Communism
8.	Consumer price index	19.	Mixed economies	30	Producer Price Index
9.	National debt	20.	Deflation	31.	Business cycles
10.	Economics	21.	Monopoly	32.	Brain drain
11.	Inflation	22.	Perfect competition	33.	Stagflation
				34.	Keynsian economic theory

ASSESSMENT CHECK

Learning Goal 1

How Economic Conditions Affect Business

1. Macroeconomics looks at the operation of a nation's economy as a whole, and microeconomics looks at the behavior of people and organizations in particular markets.

2. Businesses contribute to an economic system and resource development by inventing products that increase available resources. Businesses may discover new energy sources or new ways of growing food.

3. Followers of Thomas Malthus believe that there are too many people in the world and that the solution to poverty is birth control. However, statistics show that populations in some countries are growing so slowly that there may be too many old people and too few young people to care for them.
   These views differ from other economists because there are macroeconomists who believe that a large population can be a valuable resource, especially if the people are educated. They believe that one of the keys to economic growth in the world is to educate people better.

4. Adam Smith believed that freedom was vital to the survival of any economy, especially the freedom to own land or property and the freedom to keep the profits from working the land or running a business. He believed people will work hard if they have the incentive to do so. People have a desire to improve their "condition in life", and as long as workers can see economic reward for their efforts they will work long hours and work hard. As a result of those efforts the economy would prosper.

5. The "invisible hand" is how Smith believed an economy grows and prospers, through the production of needed goods and services. The idea is that people working for their own benefit will provide goods and services, which are needed by others. To become wealthy business owners have to hire workers to produce those goods and services. As a consequence, an area has plenty of goods and services, and many people have jobs.

Understanding Free-Market Capitalism

6. In a capitalist system, all or most of the factors of production and distribution are owned by individuals, and are operated for profit. So, in a capitalist system, business people decide what to produce, how much to pay workers, how much to charge for goods and services, whether to produce certain goods domestically, import them, or contract to have them made in other countries, and so on.

7. The foundation of the U.S. economic system is capitalism

8. The four basic rights of a free market (capitalist) system are:
   a. The right to own private property.
   b. The right to own a business and keep the profits.
   c. The right to freedom of competition.
   d. The right to freedom of choice.

9. In a free market system decisions about what to produce and in what quantities are made by the market. Consumers in a free market economy send signals to producers that tell the producers what and how much to make by choosing to buy, or not to buy, products and services, at the price we are charged in the store.

10. Supply refers to the quantity of products that manufacturers or owners are willing to sell at different prices at a specific time. In general, as price goes up, the quantity supplied will go up because sellers can make more money with a higher price.

11. Demand refers to the quantity of products that people are willing to buy at different prices at a specific time. In general, as price goes down, quantity demanded will go up.

12. The key factor in determining the quantity supplied and the quantity demanded is price.

13. A. Price   D. Equilibrium point
    B. Quantity   E. Demand curve
    C. Supply curve

14. The equilibrium point, or equilibrium price, is the point on a graph where the quantity supplied is equal to the quantity demanded. In the long run, that price becomes the market price.

15. Proponents of a free market system argue that there is no need for government to set price. When quantity supplied exceeds quantity demanded, a signal is sent to sellers to lower the price. If shortages develop, when quantity demanded exceeds quantity supplied, a signal is sent to sellers to increase the price. Eventually supply and demand will again be equal, if nothing interferes with the market forces.

16. In countries where there is no mechanism for businesses to determine what and how much to produce there are often shortages or surpluses. In these countries the government decides what to produce and in what quantities, but without the price signals, the government has no way of knowing proper quantities.

17. a. Perfect competition exists when there are many sellers in a market and no one producer is big enough to dictate the price of a product. Sellers produce products that appear to be identical. An example would be agricultural products.

b. Monopolistic competition exists when a large number of sellers produce products that appear similar, but are perceived as being different by the buyers. Product differentiation is the key to success in this type of competitive situation. Examples are personal computers and T-shirts.

c. In an oligopoly, just a few sellers dominate the market, as is the case in the tobacco, gasoline, and aircraft industry for example. The initial investment to enter an oligopoly is very high, and prices are similar. Product differentiation is usually the main factor in market success.

d. A monopoly exists where there is only one seller for a product or service. One seller controls supply, and so could raise prices dramatically. For this reason laws in the United States prohibit monopolies, except for approved monopolies such as utility service.

18. The benefit of the free market system for industrialized countries is that it was a major factor in creating the wealth these countries now enjoy. Capitalism encourages businesses to be more efficient so they can successfully compete on price and quality.

19. Even as the free market system has brought prosperity to the United States and many other parts of the world, it has brought inequality at the same time. A free market economy leads to inequality of wealth because business owners and managers will make more money and have more wealth than workers. Further, there will be people who are unable or unwilling to work or start a business. Others may not have the talent or drive to do so. So there is an unequal distribution of wealth.

20. One of the dangers of a free market system is that business people may let greed dictate how they act in order to increase personal assets. There are many examples of corruption in may different industries. To overcome this limitation of capitalism some countries have adopted socialism.

Learning Goal 3

Understanding Socialism

21. The basic premise of socialism is that most basic businesses, such as steel mills, coal mines, and utilities, should be owned by the government so that profits can be evenly distributed among the people. Entrepreneurs often own and run small businesses, but private businesses and individuals are taxed steeply to pay for social programs. Socialists believe the government should carry out the distribution of wealth and be more involved in protecting the environment and providing for the poor.

22. The major benefit of socialism is social equality, because income is taken from the wealthier people through taxes and redistributed to the poorer members of the population though government programs. Benefits include free education through college, free health care, free childcare, longer vacations, shorter workweeks, and more generous employee benefits.

23. One of the negative consequences of socialism is brain drain. Brain drain is the term used to describe the trend for professionals like doctors and lawyers, and business people and others with high incomes, to leave socialist countries for more capitalistic countries with lower tax rates. Socialism also results in fewer inventions and less innovation because those who come up with the ideas usually don't receive as much reward as they would in a capitalist system.

Understanding Communism

24. In a communist system all economic decisions are made by the government and the government owns all the major factors of production.

25. One problem with a communist system is that a government doesn't always know the right amount to produce because prices don't reflect supply and demand. As a result, there can be shortages of many goods, even basics such as food. Another problem with communism is that it doesn't inspire businesspeople to work hard because there are no incentives. Therefore communism is slowly disappearing as an economic form. Communist countries today are suffering severe economic depression and some people are starving.

Learning Goal 4

The Trend Toward Mixed Economies

26. a. <u>Free market economies</u> exist when the marketplace largely determines what goods and services get produced, who gets them and how the economy grows.
    The popular term for this system is capitalism.
    b. <u>Command economies</u> exist when the government largely decides what goods and services to produce, who will get them and how the economy will grow.
    Socialism and communism are terms used to describe this type of system.

27. a. Many believe that a free market system is not responsive enough to the needs of the old, the disabled, the poor. Many believe businesses in free market economies have not done enough to protect the environment.
    b. Socialism and communism have not created enough jobs or wealth to keep economies growing fast enough. Communist governments are disappearing and socialist governments are cutting back on services.
    c. The results of these problems have been a trend for free market economies, such as the United States, to move toward socialism and for socialist countries to move toward capitalism.

28. The United States is a mixed economy because of government involvement in the economy. The government is now the largest employer in the United States.

Learning Goal 5

Understanding the Economic System of the United States

29. Three major indicators of economic health are:
    a. the gross domestic product.
    b. the unemployment rate.
    c. the price indexes.

30. Production values from foreign manufacturers are included in the U.S. GDP as long as the company is located within the country's boundaries.

31. A major influence on the growth of GDP is the productivity of the workforce.

32. a. *Frictional unemployment* refers to those people who have quit work, and who haven't yet found a new job.
     b. *Structural unemployment* refers to unemployment caused by the restructuring of firms or by a mismatch between the skills or location of job seekers and the requirements or location of available jobs.
     c. *Cyclical unemployment* refers to unemployment caused because of a recession or similar downturn in the business cycle.
     d. *Seasonal unemployment* occurs where demand for labor varies over the year.

33. Inflation is a rise in prices, and disinflation is a condition where the rise in prices is slowing, or in other words, the inflation rate is declining.

34. Inflation is a rise in prices of goods and services over time, and deflation is a situation where prices are actually declining.

35. During a period of stagflation, the economy is slowing, but prices are still going up.

36. Two measures of prices changes over time are:
     a. consumer price index.
     b. producer price index.

37. The CPI is an important figure because some government benefits, wages and salaries, rents and leases, tax brackets, and interest rates are all based on the CPI.

38. The C-CPI is also known as the Chained Consumer Price Index. It is a new index created by the government because the CPI failed to take into account that consumers would shift their purchases as prices went up or down. So, if the price of beef went up, consumers may switch to chicken which is less expensive. The C-CPI factors in those decisions.

39. Other indicators of the economic conditions are:
     a. housing starts.
     b. retail sales.
     c. changes in personal income.

40. Business people are eager to increase productivity because an increase in productivity means that a worker can produce more goods and services than before. Higher productivity means lower costs in producing goods and services and lower prices. This can help to make a firm more competitive.

41. Measuring productivity is a problem in the service industry because technology may add to the *quality* of the service provided, but not to the *output per worker*, which is defined as productivity.

42. The four phases of long-term business cycles are:
     a. boom.
     b. recession.
     c. depression.
     d. recovery.

43. A boom is a time when businesses are doing well. When we are in a recovery, we are coming out of a recession, and the economy is stabilizing and starting to grow. This will eventually lead to a boom, starting the cycle over again.

44. When a recession occurs:
    a. prices fall.
    b. people purchase fewer products.
    c. more businesses fail.

45. Three negative consequences of a recession are:
    a. high unemployment.
    b. increased business failures.
    c. overall drop in living standards.

Learning Goal 6

Stabilizing the Economy Through Fiscal Policy

46. Two areas addressed by fiscal policy are:
    a. taxes.   b. government spending.

47. Theoretically, high tax rates could slow the economy because they draw money away from the private sector and put it into the government. High tax rates also may discourage small-business ownership.

48. The national deficit is the amount of money that the federal government spends over and above the amount it gathers in taxes. The national debt is the sum of the deficits over time.

49. One way to reduce annual deficits is to cut government spending.

50. The idea of Keynesian economic theory suggest that increased government spending, for example on roads, bridges, schools and utilities (infrastructure), and a cut in taxes will stimulate the economy in a recession.
    When the economy is growing too fast, this idea is to cut back government spending or increase taxes, which is fiscal policy. These are supposed to be short term solutions to wide swings in the business cycles.

Using Monetary Policy to Keep the Economy Growing

51. The Federal Reserve Bank, or the Fed, is a semi-private organization that is not under the direct control of the government, but its members are appointed by the President.

52. Two areas managed by monetary policy are:
    a. money supply.
    b. interest rates.

53. When the economy is booming, the Fed tends to raise interest rates. This makes money more expensive to borrow. Businesses borrow less, and the economy slows. Businesspeople spend less money on everything they need to grow, including labor and machinery.

54. In theory when the Fed lowers interest rates businesses tend to borrow more and the economy takes off.

CRITICAL THINKING EXERCISES

Learning Goal 1

1. Adam Smith believed that an economy would prosper when people were allowed to produce needed goods and services and keep the profit in an attempt to improve their own standard of living. When people saw the potential gain from working hard and hiring others to help work, Smith argued that new businesses would be created, fueled by a desire for wealth. The invisible hand turned individual gain into social and economic benefits. Ray Kroc, the founder of McDonald's saw a need for fast food in the marketplace. He took an idea and developed it into a multibillion-dollar corporation. He became a self-made millionaire, and spawned several companies along the way.

   These companies have provided jobs for thousands of people, from high school kids working the counter after school to the franchisee who owns twenty restaurants to the advertising executive in charge of the McDonald's account. The companies benefiting from McDonalds' success provide a service U.S. consumers need and want, make a living providing goods and services and give people jobs. McDonald's also goes beyond jobs and other tangible economic benefits, with Ronald McDonald Houses providing a social benefit beyond economic measure.

Learning Goal 2

2.
   a. Profit
   b. Private property
   c. Competition
   d. Freedom of choice

   e. Private property
   f. Freedom of choice
   g. Competition
   h. Private property

3.

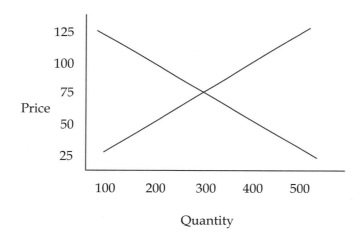

   a. The equilibrium price is $75.
   b. 300 units will be supplied at that price.

4.
   a. up
   b. down
   c. up

   d. down
   e. down

5.
   a. perfect competition
   b. monopoly

   c. monopolistic competition
   d. oligopoly

Learning Goals 2, 3

6. In her discussions with Jean-Paul, Julie might defend capitalism by saying that one benefit of the free-market system is that it allows open competition among companies. Businesses must provide customers with quality goods and services at fair prices with good service or they will lose customers to other companies that do just that. She might also say that in the U.S. there is a benefit to working hard because we have the incentive of being able to keep the rewards of our work – i.e. profits.

    Julie might say further that the drawback of living in a socialist system is that the tax rate is so high that there is little incentive to work hard, be innovative and create new products because the government takes away so much of what you earn. Consequently, there are fewer inventions and less innovation because those who come up with new ideas usually don't receive as much reward as they would in a capitalist system.

    Jean-Paul may respond that a major limitation of capitalism is the inequality of wealth distribution in a capitalist system. Business owners make more money than the workers, and some people who are old, disabled or don't have the talent to run a business can't create wealth for themselves. A major benefit of socialism is social equality. There is more equality because income is taken from the richer people in the form of taxes and redistributed to the poorer members of the population through various government programs such as free education, free health care, and free child care. Workers in these countries get longer vacations and tend to work fewer hours per week and have more employee benefits than workers in capitalist countries.

Learning Goals 2, 3, 4

7. a. Socialism
    b. Capitalism
    c. Capitalism
    d. Communism
    e. Socialism
    f. Mixed economy
    g. Could be either capitalism or mixed economy
    h. Communism

Learning Goal 5

8. Increases in productivity mean that the same amount of labor is able to produce a greater output. Costs are thus lower in producing goods and services, and so prices can be lower. So, efficiency in both manufacturing and the service sector can help to hold down inflation. If productivity slows, GDP growth could also slow. This would have a negative effect on the economy.

9. a. cyclical
    b. seasonal
    c. structural
    d. frictional

Learning Goal 6

10. a. Fiscal policy
    b. Monetary policy
    c. Fiscal policy
    d. Fiscal policy
    e. Monetary policy
    f. Fiscal policy
    g. Fiscal policy
    h. Fiscal policy

11. Small business owners, who create many of the jobs and much of the wealth for the economy, are often severely affected by changes in the tax rates. In theory, these business owners may add jobs and hire more people when they know their tax liability will be lower as a result of a tax reduction. Consequently, while tax rates may be lower, a greater number of people will be paying in to the system, and this could have the effect of increasing government tax revenues.

PRACTICE TEST

MULTIPLE CHOICE

1.	d	13.	a
2.	a	14.	b
3.	b	15.	c
4.	d	16.	d
5.	b	17.	b
6.	a	18.	d
7.	a	19.	b
8.	d	20.	c
9.	c	21.	c
10.	d	22.	c
11.	c	23.	a
12.	d		

TRUE-FALSE

1.	T	12.	F
2.	T	13.	T
3.	F	14.	F
4.	T	15.	T
5.	F	16.	F
6.	F	17.	F
7.	F	18.	T
8.	T	19.	T
9.	T	20.	T
10.	F	21.	T
11.	T	22.	F

CHAPTER 3 – COMPETING IN GLOBAL MARKETS

LEARNING GOALS

After you have read and studied this chapter, you should be able to:

1. Discuss the importance of the global market and the roles of comparative advantage and absolute advantage in global trade.
2. Explain the importance of importing and exporting, and understand key terms used in global business.
3. Illustrate the strategies used in reaching global markets and explain the role of multinational corporations in global markets.
4. Evaluate the forces that affect trading in global markets.
5. Debate the advantages and disadvantages of trade protectionism.
6. Discuss the changing landscape of the global market and the issue of offshore outsourcing.

LEARNING THE LANGUAGE

Listed below are important terms found in this chapter. Choose the correct term for each definition and write it in the space provided.

Absolute advantage	Embargo	Joint venture
Balance of payments	Exchange rate	Licensing
Balance of trade	Exporting	Multinational corporation
Common market	Foreign direct investment	North American Free Trade Agreement (NAFTA)
Comparative advantage theory	Foreign subsidiary	Strategic alliance
Contract manufacturing	Free trade	Tariff
Countertrading	General Agreement on Tariffs and Trade (GATT)	Trade deficit
Devaluation	Importing	Trade protectionism
Dumping	Import quota	World Trade Organization (WTO)

1. A long-term partnership between two or more companies, a _____ is established to help each company build competitive market advantages.

2. A tax known as a _____ is imposed on imports.

3. The practice of selling products in foreign countries at lower prices than you charge for the same products in the producing country is known as _____.

4. A country has a(n) _____ when it has a monopoly on the production of a specific product or is able to produce it more efficiently than all other countries.

5. The difference between money coming into a country and money leaving the country plus money-flows from other factors such as tourism, foreign aid, military expenditures and foreign investment is the _____.

6. A(n) _____ is a complete ban on the import or export of a certain product or when all trade with a particular country has been stopped.

7. When there is a limit on the number of products in certain categories that a nation can import, a(n) _____ has been established.

8. An unfavorable balance of trade, or _____ occurs when the value of a country's imports exceeds that of its exports.

9. A nation's _____ is the total value of a nation's exports compared to its imports measured over a period of time.

10. The _____ is the value of one currency relative to the currencies of other countries.

11. A country is involved in _____ when it is buying products from another country.

12. In a _____ a partnership has been formed in which two or more companies, often from different countries, have joined to undertake a major project.

13. A global strategy known as _____ is one in which a firm allows a foreign company to produce its product in exchange for a fee (a royalty).

14. The European Union is an example of a _____ , a regional group of countries that have no internal tariffs, a common external tariff and a coordination of laws to facilitate exchange between countries. It is also known as a trading bloc.

15. A company is involved in _____ when it is selling products to another country.

16. An organization that manufactures and markets products in many different countries and has multinational stock ownership and multinational management is a(n) _____.

17. The theory of _____ states that a country should sell to other countries those products that it produces most effectively and efficiently, and buy from those other countries those products that it cannot produce as effectively and efficiently.

18. _____ occurs when a foreign country produces private-label goods to which a domestic company then attaches its brand name or trademark.

19. Lowering the value of a nation's currency relative to other currencies is known as _____.

20. There is _____ when the movement of goods and services among nations occurs without political or economic barriers.

21. The use of government regulations to limit the import of goods and services is considered to be _____.

22. A complex form of bartering known as _____ occurs when several countries each trade goods for goods or services for services.

23. Many countries today are involved in _____ , which is the buying of permanent property and businesses in foreign nations.

24. A _____ is a company that is owned in a foreign country by another company called the parent company.

25. This organization, known as the _____ , replaced the GATT agreement and was assigned the duty to mediate trade disputes among nations.

26. The agreement known as the _____ created a free trade agreement between the United States, Canada, and Mexico.

27. The agreement signed in 1948 called the _____ established an international forum for negotiating mutual reductions in trade restrictions.

ASSESSMENT CHECK

Learning Goal 1

The Dynamic Global Market

1. What are three reasons why countries trade with each other?

   a. _____

   b. _____

   c. _____

2. What are the pros and cons of free trade?

   <u>Pros</u>   <u>Cons</u>

   a. _____   a. _____

   b. _____   b. _____

   c. _____   c. _____

   d. _____   d. _____

   e. _____

3. How does the comparative advantage theory benefit the United States and its trading partners?

Getting Involved in Global Trade

4.   Where may the real job potential be when evaluating global markets?

5.   Explain how many individuals and entrepreneurs have become involved in the global marketplace through importing and exporting.

6.   How would you describe the impact exporting has had on the U.S. economy?

Measuring Global Trade

7.   What is the difference between a favorable balance of trade and an unfavorable balance of trade?

8.   Why do countries prefer to have a favorable balance of trade?

9.   Explain the difference between the balance of trade and the balance of payments. What is the goal regarding the balance of payments?

   Balance of trade is: _____

   Balance of payment is: _____

   The goal is: _____

10.   Does the United States have a favorable or unfavorable balance of trade?

11.   How can we explain that while the U.S. has an unfavorable balance of trade (trade deficit) the U.S. is still one of the world's largest exporters?

12. Why do countries use the tactic of dumping?

Learning Goal 3

Strategies for Reaching Global Markets

13. List six strategies for reaching global markets

   a. _____   d. _____

   b. _____   e. _____

   c. _____   f. _____

14. What are the advantages and disadvantages of licensing?

   Advantages: a. _____

   b. _____

   c. _____

   Disadvantages: a. _____

   b. _____

   _____

15. What is an Export Assistance Center? What are export-trading companies?

16. When they go global, franchisers must be careful to:

17. Describe the benefits of contract manufacturing.

   a. _____

   b. _____

18. What are the reasons companies enter into international joint ventures?

19. What are the benefits and drawbacks of international joint ventures?

Benefits   Drawbacks

a. _____   a. _____

b. _____   b. _____

c. _____   c. _____

20. What do strategic alliances provide for participating companies? How is a strategic alliance different from a joint venture?

21. How does a foreign subsidiary operate? What is the advantage of a subsidiary? What is the major disadvantage?

22. Describe sovereign wealth funds.

Learning Goal 4

Forces Affecting Trading in Global Markets

23. Four forces affecting trading in global markets are:

a. _____

b. _____

c. _____

d. _____

24. What elements are included in a description of the term "culture"?

25. What is meant by the term "ethnocentricity" and how does it relate to U.S. businesspeople?

26. Identify two major elements of the socio-cultural environment that have significant impact on business operations, according to the text. Give examples

27. A sound philosophy to adopt in global markets is _____

    _____

28. Give examples of how economic conditions will affect consumption of goods that might seem to have great global opportunity.

29. What is meant by a "high value of the dollar"? What impact does a "high value of the dollar" have on U.S. businesses?

30. What is meant by a "low value of the dollar"? What impact does this have on U.S. businesses?

31. What is a "floating exchange rate"? How is supply and demand for currencies created?

32. Why would a country devalue its currency?

33. When a country has an especially weak currency the only possibility of trade is often through *bartering*, which is: _____

34. What characteristics of legal and regulatory forces make conducting global business so difficult?

35. What does the Foreign Corrupt Practices Act prohibit? What is the impact on American firms?

36. Give some examples in the area of technology that pose challenges for doing business in global markets.

Learning Goal 5

Trade Protectionism

37. According to the text, advocates believe trade protectionism allows_____

_____

Countries often use trade protectionism measures to_____

_____

38. Describe the economic philosophy that led governments to impose tariffs.

39. List five forms of trade protectionism

   a. _____   d. _____

   b. _____   e. _____

   c. _____

40. Distinguish between a revenue tariff and a protective tariff.

41. What are non-tariff barriers? Provide examples of non-tariff barriers.

42. What was the purpose of the GATT? What two areas are covered by the Uruguay round of the GATT, passed in 1994?

43. How was the World Trade Organization created, and what is the primary task of the WTO?

44. What are some of the continuing problems and challenges faced by the WTO?

    a. _____

    b. _____

45. What is the EU?

46. The euro is: _____

47. What countries are parts of the Mercosur?

48. What countries are parts of the ASEAN?

    a. _____   f. _____

    b. _____   g. _____

    c. _____   h. _____

    d. _____   i. _____

    e. _____   j. _____

49. What does NAFTA stand for? What three countries are parts of the NAFTA agreement?

50. The objectives of NAFTA were:

    a. _____

    b. _____

    c. _____

    d. _____

    e. _____

    f. _____

51. Has NAFTA been successful?

52. Describe the CAFTA? What are the issues surrounding this agreement?

Learning Goal 6

The Future of Global Trade

53. Describe the importance of the Chinese market in today's global trade environment.

54. What is meant by the term "China price"?

55. What are some concerns about entering the Chinese market?

a. _____

b. _____

c. _____

d. _____

56. What is the potential for markets in India and Russia and other parts of Asia? What are the concerns?

57. What is "offshore outsourcing" and why has it become a major issue?

58. What are the concerns regarding outsourcing, other than loss of jobs?

CRITICAL THINKING EXERCISES

Learning Goal 1

1. How does the theory of comparative advantage relate to the development of free trade agreements around the world, such as NAFTA and the EU?

Learning Goal 2

2. Re-read the example of the ice factory in Africa, and the other examples of opportunities found in international markets. How do they illustrate the importance of entrepreneurship, capitalism and Adam Smith's "invisible hand" theory in the international market? How can you take advantage of the opportunities?

3. There are several terms used in global trade:
   a. Balance of trade.
   b. Trade deficit.
   c. Balance of payments.
   d. Dumping.

   Match the term with the description below:

   _____ An unfavorable one means that there is more money flowing into the country than flowing out of the country.

   _____ Japan, Brazil, Russia and Canada have all been accused of this in the U.S. market.

   _____ A favorable one occurs when the value of the country's exports exceeds the value of the country's imports.

   _____ Another name for this is an unfavorable balance of trade.

Learning Goals 2, 3

4. There are several strategies to reach global markets:

    Licensing   Contract manufacturing
    Exporting   International Joint ventures
    Franchising   Foreign Direct Investment

Match the term with the situations below:

a. _____ This partnership with a Japanese food concern gave Campbell Soup a chance to increase its low market share in Japan's soup market, which is very difficult to enter.

b. _____ In this kind of agreement, also known as outsourcing, Nike gives it's name to shoes manufactured overseas and distributed in the United States.

c. _____ Companies such as Subway, McDonalds, and Dunkin Donuts have agreements to operate in foreign markets using this form of arrangement, after allowing the local operators to change their product to suit local tastes.

d. _____ In 2007, a French firm purchased Lucent Technologies, a U.S. based firm. The new firm was named Alcatel-Lucent.

e. _____ GE has a number of bilingual workers with advanced degrees in its trading department to help the corporation with this kind of international trade, selling their product to foreign markets.

f. _____ Coke and Pepsi often enter foreign markets by allowing a foreign manufacturer to use its trademark and pay them (Coke and Pepsi) a royalty for that right.

Learning Goal 4

5. Discuss the issues of the value of the dollar relative to other currencies. What is the impact of a lower value of the dollar? How would American businesses be affected if the dollar were devalued, as the Mexican peso was a few years ago?

6. The everyday difficulties of doing business at home are compounded by a variety of differences between U.S. and foreign markets. Difficulties can stem from cultural and social differences, economic problems, legal and political regulations and physical and environmental forces such as technology. Keep those ideas in mind in completing the following.

You have a successful ice cream/frozen yogurt business in the United States, and are especially interested in opening a store in South America, probably Argentina or Chile. You market your product thorough free- standing buildings in the U.S., but are unsure of how to start up in South America. You have begun to seriously think about the possibility, but are concerned about some of the problems you may encounter. What are forces affecting trade in global markets will you need to consider before going ahead with your plan?

Learning Goal 5

7. Governments have developed a number of ways to protect their domestic industries from what they would consider the potentially negative impact of foreign trade:

Protective tariffs   Embargoes
Revenue tariffs   Non-tariff barriers
Import quotas

Match the correct type of trade protectionism to each of the following:

_____ a. The amount of Argentine beef brought into the United States is limited by this form of agreement

_____ b. Mexico has several of this type of tariff, designed to raise money for its government.

_____ c. The U.S. imposed this type of "restriction" on Chinese textiles, in retaliation for the pirating of U.S. made products by Chinese manufacturers. The effect of this "restriction" was an increase in the cost of Chinese textiles sold in the United States.

_____ d. The U.S. has refused to allow the products of Cuba and some other countries to be sold in the U.S. under one of these programs.

_____ e. Denmark requires margarine to be sold in cubes, cutting off those companies that manufacture margarine in tubs.

8. Look at the website for Coca-Cola (www.coke.com). How has today's technology enabled this company to reach a much larger marketplace? What has this company done to address the issues involved in taking an "American" company global?

Learning Goal 6

9. Visit this website http://www.chinadaily.com.cn/index.html
Search the paper for business articles. What does it indicate about the current market conditions in China? Is the market growing? Are foreign companies still finding China to be an attractive market?

PRACTICE TEST

MULTIPLE CHOICE — Circle the best answer

Learning Goal 1

1. Buying products produced in another country is known as:
   a. importing.
   b. trade protectionism.
   c. comparative advantage.
   d. exporting.

2. All of the following are reasons for countries to participate in foreign trade except
   a. it is just as easy to start a business overseas as it is in the U.S.
   b. no nation can produce all of the products its people want and need.
   c. even if a country were self-sufficient, other nations would seek to trade with that country in order to meet the needs of its own people.
   d. some nations have resources, but not technological know-how; while others have know-how, but lack resources.

3. Many clothing items sold in the U. S. are imported from Asia because workers there can produce the items more efficiently than we can in the United States. This is an example of:
   a. absolute advantage.
   b. free trade.
   c. international marketing.
   d. comparative advantage theory.

Learning Goal 2

4. When the value of exports from a country exceeds the value of imports into that country, there is a _____
   a. trade deficit.
   b. balance of payments.
   c. favorable balance of trade.
   d. unfavorable balance of trade.

5. The difference between money coming into a country from exports and money leaving a country due to imports, plus money flows from other factors, is known as the:
   a. balance of trade.
   b. free trade.
   c. balance of payments.
   d. trade deficit.

6. The United States exports:
   a. less volume, but a greater percentage of our products than other countries.
   b. greater volume than other countries, and a greater percentage of our products.
   c. about the same volume as other countries, but a lower percentage of our products.
   d. a greater volume than other countries, but a lower percentage of our products.

7. In global trade, the term "dumping" refers to:
   a. a situation that exists when a country exports more than it imports.
   b. the buying of permanent property and businesses in foreign nations.
   c. the practice of selling products in a foreign country at lower prices than those charged in the producing country.
   d. a foreign company's production of private-label goods to which a domestic company attaches its own brand name.

Learning Goal 3

8. In recent years the Nestle Company has acquired several U.S. firms, such as Carnation. Carnation now operates in the U.S. as a(n):
   a. exporter.
   b. subsidiary.
   c. licensing agent.
   d. franchise.

9. Coke and Pepsi often enter foreign markets by allowing a foreign manufacturer to use their trademark and pay them (Coke or Pepsi) a royalty for that right. This is an example of:
   a. a joint venture.
   b. exporting.
   c. licensing.
   d. a strategic alliance.

10. In franchising to foreign markets, companies such McDonald's and KFC have had to:
    a. be careful to adapt to the countries they are attempting to enter.
    b. find franchisees with money they can afford to lose if the franchise fails.
    c. be sure not to alter their products for the foreign countries, so that consumers know exactly what they are getting.
    d. find opportunities for joint ventures, as franchising doesn't seem to work in foreign markets.

11. Multinational corporations:
    a. are typically extremely large corporations.
    b. are companies that simply export everything they produce.
    c. do not necessarily have manufacturing capacity in other nations.
    d. are predominantly small companies that export their products to many different countries.

12. Americans are often been accused of ethnocentricity. This means that:
    a. Americans feel their culture is superior to others.
    b. Americans welcome diversity in their workforce.
    c. U.S. firms are actively seeking international markets.
    d. U.S. businesses are pursuing a policy of multiculturalism.

13. Guillermo Martinez was concerned that his new boss Donald Darr didn't know his job very well. Donald is continually asking Guillermo and the other workers in the company's plant in Mexico City to give him their opinions before he makes a final decision. Guillermo's concern stems from _____ differences between Donald and him.
    a. economic
    b. cultural
    c. language
    d. regulatory

14. The makers of Whirlpool washers and other electrical appliance manufacturers need to be concerned about the kind and availability of electricity in the global marketplace. If there were a compatibility problem, it would be the result of a _____ difference.
    a. cultural
    b. technological
    c. economic
    d. societal

15. The law that specifically prohibits "questionable" or "dubious" payments to foreign officials in an effort to secure business contracts is called the:
    a. North American Free Trade Agreement
    b. General Agreement on Tariffs and Trade
    c. Securities and Exchange Act
    d. Foreign Corrupt Practices Act

16. A low value of the dollar would mean:
    a. your American dollar is worth more when purchasing a foreign made good.
    b. a dollar could be traded for less foreign currency than normal.
    c. you could trade in your money for gold.
    d. costs of foreign manufacturing would be higher.

17. When Mexico devalued the peso, the peso became _____ valuable relative to other currencies.
    a. more
    b. less
    c. equally
    d. significantly more

Learning Goal 5

18. Using government regulations to limit the import of goods and services is called:
    a. mercantilism.
    b. regulating the balance of trade.
    c. global marketing.
    d. trade protectionism.

19. When the Vietnamese government imposes a tax on imported electronics products to help their relatively young electronics industry compete in the global marketplace, a(n) _____ is being levied.
    a. protective tariff
    b. import quota
    c. embargo
    d. revenue tariff

20. The EU is an example of a trading bloc, or a_____, which has a common external tariff, no internal tariffs and the coordination of laws to facilitate trade between member countries.
    a. strategic alliance
    b. common market
    c. joint venture
    d. multinational export assistance center

21. The _____ is assigned the task of mediating trade disputes.
    a. WTO
    b. EU
    c. GATT
    d. NAFTA

22. NAFTA has:
    a. been totally successful, with no difficulties.
    b. decreased exports from the U.S. to its NAFTA partners by 25%.
    c. greatly increased trade flows between the member nations.
    d. reduced concerns about illegal immigration.

23. There are those who hope that the _____ is a stepping stone to the creation of a Free Trade Area of the Americas. The agreement is between the United States and several Central American countries.
    a. NAFTA
    b. EU
    c. Mercosur
    d. CAFTA

24. Which of the following is not considered to be a concern when evaluating trade with China?
    a. The one-party political system
    b. Human rights policies
    c. A shrinking market
    d. A growing trade imbalance

25. The term "China price" means:
    a. the price that would be charged in China for a good sold there.
    b. the price that China charges it's U.S. manufacturers.
    c. the price that companies think customers will want to pay.
    d. the lowest price possible.

TRUE–FALSE

Learning Goal 1

1. _____ One reason that companies trade is because no nation, not even a technologically advanced nation, can produce all the products it's people need.

Learning Goal 2

2. _____ Many foreign firms find it hard to sell their products in the United States because most U.S. firms produce products more efficiently that most foreign firms.

3. _____ When the country of Monrovia is buying less from the United States than it is selling to the United States, a favorable balance of trade exists for Monrovia.

4. _____ Even today, most large businesses are not involved in global trade.

5. _____ Exporting does not provide a big boost to the U.S. economy, because we still have a balance of trade deficit.

Learning Goal 3

6. _____ An example of contract manufacturing is when Dell contracts with a computer company to manufacture PCs, on which Dell puts the Dell name.

7. _____ One disadvantage of licensing is the cost to the company of licensing its product or trademark (the licensor) to the foreign firm (the licensee).

8. _____ Export Assistance Centers serve the role of matching buyers and sellers from different countries and of providing other services to ease the process of exporting.

Learning Goal 4

9. _____ Religion is an important element of a society's culture and should be considered in making many business decisions.

10. _____ Economic differences between countries can affect purchasing patterns, such as quantity purchased at a given time.

11. _____ A sound global philosophy is "always assume that what works in one country will work in another".

12. _____ E-commerce in some developing nations is difficult because computer and Internet use is negligible.

Learning Goal 5

13. _____ Trade protectionism is based upon the idea that barriers will help domestic producers grow and create more jobs.

14. _____ Non-tariff barriers can be just as detrimental to free trade as tariffs.

15. _____ The WTO totally eliminated the internal national laws that impeded global trade expansion.

16. _____ The official monetary unit of the EU is the euro.

17. _____ Investment in China is still considered to be too risky to invest a great deal of money.

18. _____ India and Russia are considered to be potentially lucrative markets for the future.

<u>You Can Find It On The Net</u>

Find the most recent trade statistics for

    a.   The United States   Exports/Imports/Balance of Trade (deficit) (surplus)

    b.   Your state   Exports/Imports/Balance of Trade

What are the top ten countries with which your state trades? What is the largest category of foreign sales? How does this affect businesses and jobs, in your area?

These statistics can be found on the Internet with just a bit of looking around. A good place to start for the information regarding the U.S Trade Statistics is <u>www.census.gov</u>.

For the state data, use a search engine with the key words "exports" and the name of your state. Several websites should appear, including your state's department of economic development.

ANSWERS

LEARNING THE LANGUAGE

1.	Strategic alliance	10.	Exchange rate	19.	Devaluation
2.	Tariff	11.	Importing	20.	Free trade
3.	Dumping	12.	Joint venture	21.	Trade protectionism
4.	Absolute advantage	13.	Licensing	22.	Countertrading
5.	Balance of payments	14.	Common market	23.	Foreign direct investment
6.	Embargo	15.	Exporting	24.	Foreign subsidiary
7.	Import quota	16.	Multinational corporation (MNC)	25.	World Trade Organization (WTO)
8.	Trade deficit	17.	Comparative advantage theory	26.	North American Free Trade Agreement (NAFTA)
9.	Balance of trade	18.	Contract manufacturing	27.	General Agreement on Tariffs and Trade (GATT)

ASSESSMENT CHECK

Learning Goal 1

The Dynamic Global Market

1. a. No nation can produce all of the products its people need and want.
    b. Even if a given country were self-sufficient, other nations would want to trade with that country to meet the needs of its people.
    c. Some nations have many natural resources but limited technological know how, while other countries have sophisticated technology but few resources. Trade allows nations to produce what they are capable of producing and to buy what they need from others.

2. Pros
    a. Global market has over 6.7 billion customers.
    b. Productivity grows with comparative advantage.
    c. Global competition and lower-cost imports keep prices down.
    d. Free trade encourages innovation.
    e. Interest rates lower due to uninterrupted flow of capital.

    Cons
    a. Domestic workers in manufacturing could lose jobs.
    b. Workers face pay-cut demands from employers.
    c. Competitive pressure makes some jobs vulnerable to operations moving overseas.
    d. Domestic companies can lose comparative advantage when competitors build operations in low wage countries.

3. The theory <u>of comparative advantage</u> states that a country should produce and sell to other countries those products that it produces most effectively and efficiently, and should buy from other countries those products it cannot produce as effectively or efficiently. The United States has a comparative advantage in producing goods and services such as software and engineering services. But we lack a comparative advantage in other areas such as growing coffee or making shoes, so we import those goods. Through specializing in certain areas, the U.S. and its trading partners can realize mutually beneficial exchanges.

Learning Goal 2

Getting Involved in Global Trade

4. The greatest job potential in global markets may be with small businesses. Today in the U.S. small businesses generate about half of the private-sector commerce, but account for only 30 percent of exports.

5. Exporting and importing products have created a number of opportunities for individuals and entrepreneurs. Foreign students have noticed that some products widely available in their countries are not available in the U.S. Some people see a lack in the U.S. of a particularly appealing product from elsewhere, such as that which Howard Schultz of Starbucks saw in Italy.

   Also, just about any good or service that is used in the U.S. can be used in other countries as well, and the competition abroad is often not nearly as intense for most providers of these products as it is at home.

6. Exporting has been a terrific boost to the U.S. economy. The Institute for International Economics estimates that every $1 billion in U.S. exports generates 20,000 jobs at home.

Measuring Global Trade

7. A favorable balance of trade exists when the value of exports exceeds the value of imports. An unfavorable balance of trade occurs when the value of the country's imports exceeds that of its exports.

8. Countries prefer to export more than they import, or have a favorable balance of trade, because the country will retain more of its money to buy other goods and services. As the example in the text illustrates, if I sell you $200 worth of goods, and only buy $100, I have an extra $100 available to buy other things.

9. The balance of trade is a nation's relationship of exports to imports.
   The balance of payments is the difference between money coming into a country from exports and money leaving a country for imports, plus money flows from other factors.
   The goal is always to have more money flowing into the country than flowing out of the country; in other words, a favorable balance of payments.

10. The United States has bought more goods from other nations than it has sold to other nations every year since 1975. So, the U.S. has an unfavorable balance of trade.

11. Even though the U.S. exports the largest volume of goods globally, it exports a much lower percentage of its products than other countries do.

12. Dumping is sometimes used to reduce surplus products in foreign markets or to gain a foothold in a new market by offering products for lower prices than domestic competitors.

Learning Goal 3

Strategies for Reaching Global markets

13. a. Licensing   d. Contract manufacturing
    b. Exporting   e. International joint ventures and strategic alliances
    c. Franchising   f. Foreign direct investment

14. Advantages of licensing are:
    a. Additional revenue from a product that would not have generated in its home market.
    b. Start-up supplies, materials and consulting services must be purchased from the licensing firm, which generates even more revenue and reduces costs of entering a foreign market.
    c. Licensors spend little or no money to produce and market their products. Most costs are borne by the licensee.

    Disadvantages with licensing include:
    a. A firm often must grant licensing rights to its product for as long as 20 years. Revenue from an especially successful product would then go to the licensee.
    b. If a foreign licensee learns the technology, it could break its agreement and begin to produce the product on its own. The licensing company loses trade secrets and royalties.

15. An Export Assistance Center (EAC) provides hands-on exporting assistance and trade finance support for small and medium sized businesses that choose to export.
    Export trading companies are specialists in matching buyers and sellers from different countries and providing services to ease the process of entering foreign markets.

16. When going global, franchisers must be careful to adapt to the customs and tastes of the countries they serve.

17. Through contract manufacturing:
    a. A company can experiment in a new market without heavy start-up costs, which reduces risk.
    b. A firm can also use contract manufacturing temporarily to meet an unexpected increase in orders.

18. There are many business reasons that joint ventures are developed, such as the opportunity to expand low market share in participating countries.

19. Benefits of international joint ventures include:
    a. Shared technology and risk.
    b. Shared marketing and management expertise.
    c. Entry into markets where foreign companies are not allowed unless their goods are produced locally.

    Drawbacks are:
    a. One partner can learn the other's technology and go off on its own as a competitor.
    b. Shared technology may become obsolete.
    c. Joint venture may become too large to be flexible.

20. Strategic alliances can provide access to markets, capital and technical expertise, but unlike joint ventures, they do not involve sharing costs, risk, management or profits. Strategic alliances can be flexible and they can effectively link firms of different sizes.

21. A foreign subsidiary operates much like a domestic firm, with production, distribution, promotion, pricing, and other business functions under the control of the foreign subsidiary's management.

   The primary advantage of a subsidiary is that the company maintains complete control over any technology or other expertise it may possess.

   The major disadvantage of creating a subsidiary is that the parent company is committing a large amount of funds and technology within foreign boundaries. If relations with the host country take a downturn, the firm's assets could be taken over by the foreign government. That kind of takeover is called an expropriation.

22. Sovereign wealth funds are investment funds controlled by governments holding large stakes in foreign companies. These SWFs have purchased significant portions of many U.S. companies, and controlled $3 trillion in U.S. firms as of 2008.

Learning Goal 4

Forces Affecting Trading in Global Markets

23. Four forces affecting trading in global markets are:
   a. Socio-cultural
   b. Economic and financial
   c. Legal and regulatory
   d. Physical and environmental

24. Culture refers to the set of values, beliefs, rules, and institutions held by a specific group of people. The term culture can include social structure, religion, manners and customs, values and attitudes, language, and personal communication.

25. Many American businesspeople have been accused of ethnocentricity, the feeling that one's own culture is superior to all others. By contrast, foreign business people are very good at adapting to U.S. culture.

26. Two socio-cultural elements of which it is important to be aware when working with individuals from other cultures are religion and religious customs, and management of employees.
   An example of how religious customers can impact business operations is when McDonald's and Coca-Cola put the image of the Saudi Arabian flag on their packaging, which offended the Muslim communities.
   It is also important to be aware of customs when managing employees. In Latin American countries, workers believe managers are in positions of authority to make decisions. A U.S. manager in Peru, who was unaware of this cultural characteristic believed he could motivate his workers to more productivity by including them in decisions. When he instituted a more democratic way of managing, workers began to quit, believing that this manager was incompetent.

27. A sound philosophy to adopt in global markets is "Never assume that what works in one country will work in another."

28. The text cites examples such as in Haiti, where customers can only buy small quantities of gum, for example because of their low incomes. Cultural conditions as well as economic conditions affect companies like Hershey's, Skippy peanut butter and Coca-Cola. Indians only consume three soft drinks per person per year because they drink tea, and most people can't afford chocolate or peanut butter.

29. A high value of the dollar means that the dollar can be traded for more foreign currency than previously. When the dollar is high the products of foreign producers become cheaper, because it takes fewer dollars to buy them. The cost of U.S.-produced goods, on the other hand, becomes more expensive to foreign buyers, because of the dollar's high value.

30. A low value of the dollar means that the dollar will buy or can be traded for less foreign currency than normal. Therefore, foreign goods become more expensive in the U.S. because it takes more dollars to buy them; but American goods become cheaper to foreign buyers because it takes less foreign currency to buy American goods.

31. The floating exchange rate is a system in which currencies "float" according to the supply and demand in the market for the currency. The supply and demand for currencies is created by global currency traders, who create a market for a nation's currency based on the perceived trade and investment potential of the country.

32. A country may devalue its currency in order to increase the export potential of its products.

33. Bartering is the exchange of merchandise for merchandise or service for service with no money involved.

34. Some of the legal and regulatory difficulties in the global market stem from the fact that in global markets no central system of law exists, so different systems of laws and regulations may apply. Laws and regulations in global markets are often inconsistent. Legal questions related to antitrust rules, labor relations, patents, copyrights, trade practices, taxes, product liability, child labor, prison labor, and other issues are governed differently country by country.

35. The Foreign Corrupt Practices Act specifically prohibits "questionable" or "dubious" payments to foreign officials to secure business contracts. This type of legislation can create hardships for American businesses in competing with foreign competitors, because in some countries actions such as corporate bribery are acceptable, and sometimes the only way to secure a lucrative contract.

36. Technological constraints may make it difficult to conduct business in developing countries. Some developing countries have outdated transportation and storage systems that make international distribution ineffective. Technological differences also affect the nature of exportable products, such as electrical appliances. Computer and Internet usage in many developing countries is also a concern, because it can be spotty or even non-existent in some countries. This would make doing business and conducting e-commerce difficult.

Learning Goal 5

Trade Protectionism

37. Advocates of trade protectionism believe it allows domestic producers to survive and grow, producing more jobs.

    Countries often use protectionist measures to guard against such practices as dumping. Many countries are wary of foreign competition in general.

38. Tariffs basically came out of the economic belief called mercantilism. The primary idea behind mercantilism is for a nation to sell more goods to other nations than it bought from them, or, to have a favorable balance of trade. This should result in a flow of money to the country that sells the most globally. This led to government's imposing tariffs, or taxes on imports, which makes imported goods more expensive to buy.

39. Forms of trade protectionism are:
   a. Protective tariffs
   b. Revenue tariffs
   c. Import quotas
   d. Embargoes
   e. Non-tariff barriers

40. A protective tariff is designed to raise the retail price of an imported good so the domestic product will be more competitive. The revenue tariff is designed to raise money for the government and to help infant industries compete in global markets.

41. Nontariff barriers take a variety of forms. They are not as specific as other forms of protectionism but can be as detrimental to free trade. Countries have imposed restrictive standards that detail exactly how a product must be sold in a country, such as Denmark, which requires companies to sell butter in cubes. Japan for many years used the keiretsu as a way to keep out foreign manufacturers. The Japanese tradition of keiretsu was one in which corporate families forged semi-permanent ties with suppliers, customers, and distributors with the support of the government.

42. The GATT established an international forum for negotiating mutual reductions in trade restrictions. Countries agreed to negotiate to create monetary and trade agreements that might facilitate the exchange of goods, services, ideas, and cultural programs.

   The Uruguay round of the GATT lowered tariffs by 38 percent worldwide and extended GATT rules to new areas such as agriculture, services and the protection of patents.

43. The World Trade Organization (WTO) was created by the Uruguay round of the GATT to assume the task of mediating trade disputes. The WTO acts as an independent entity that oversees key cross-border trade issues and global business practices.

44. Challenges faced by the WTO are
   a. the legal and regulatory problems which impede trade expansion.
   b. the wide gap which separates developing nations, 80% WTO membership, and industrialized nations such as the United States.

45. The EU is a group of 27 nations in Europe that united economically and formed a common market.

46. The euro is the currency commonly used in most member countries of the EU.

47. The Mercosur consists of the countries of Brazil, Argentina, Paraguay, Uruguay and associate members Chile and Bolivia.

48. The counties that are part of ASEAN are:
   a. Indonesia
   b. Malaysia
   c. Philippines
   d. Singapore
   e. Thailand
   f. Brunei
   g. Cambodia
   h. Lao PDR
   i. Myanmar
   j. Vietnam

49. NAFTA stands for the North American Free Trade Agreement. The three countries that are part of NAFTA are the United States, Canada and Mexico.

50. The objectives of NAFTA were to:
    a. eliminate trade barriers and facilitate cross-border movement of goods and services between the three member countries.
    b. promote conditions of fair competition in the free trade area.
    c. increase investment opportunities.
    d. provide effective protection and enforcement of intellectual property rights.
    e. establish a framework for further regional trade cooperation.
    f. improve working conditions in North America.

51. NAFTA has had positive and negative consequences. The value of U.S. exports to NAFTA partners, and trade have increased significantly since the agreement was signed.
    On the down side, it is estimated that the U.S. has lost 500,000 job, and some believe the number is much higher. Per capita income in Mexico still lags behind the U.S. causing illegal immigration to be a continuing problem. Critics argue that working conditions in Mexico are less safe than before NAFTA.

52. CAFTA is an agreement which created a free trade zone with the U.S. and several Central American nations – Costa Rica, the Dominican Republic, El Salvador, Guatemala, Honduras, and Nicaragua. Supporters claim that the agreement will open new markets, lower tariffs, and ease regulations. Critics argue that the agreement will cost American jobs in textiles and sugar industries.

Learning Goal 6

The Future of Global Trade

53. China is the world's third largest exporter, behind Germany and the United States. China attracts more foreign investment than the United States. China is the largest global consumer of steel, copper, coal, and cement, and is second only the U.S. in consumption of oil. Companies such as General Motors and Wal-Mart have invested heavily in the Chinese market.

54. The term China price is used by manufacturer to mean the lowest price possible.

55. Concerns remain about
    a. China's one-party political system.
    b. its human rights policies.
    c. increasing urban population growth.
    d. product piracy and counterfeiting.

56. India and Russia represent enormous opportunities because of their large populations. The concerns stem from poverty, difficult trade laws, political, currency and social problems.

    Developing nations of Indonesia, Thailand, Singapore, the Philippines, Korea, Malaysia and Vietnam also offer potential for U.S. businesses.

57. Offshore outsourcing refers to the shift in outsourcing manufacturing and services from domestic businesses to countries with much lower wage rates. The "second wave" of offshore outsourcing involves large numbers of skilled, well-educated, middle-income workers in service sector jobs such as accounting, law, financial and risk management, health care, and information technology that were thought to be safe from foreign market competition. This process is proving more disruptive to the U.S. job market, which primarily affected manufacturing.

58. The concerns include the fact that China has a spotty safety record in manufacturing some products. Also concerns are mounting that companies are shifting production of sensitive medical devices to China, and airlines are shifting maintenance to other countries. Medical providers are shifting surgical procedures to India and other nations, and India is also able to provide more sophisticated services because of a large talent pool.

CRITICAL THINKING EXERCISES

Learning Goal 1

1. The theory of comparative advantage states that a country should sell to other countries those products that it produces most effectively and efficiently, and buy from other countries those products it cannot produce as effectively or efficiently. The development of free trade agreements such as NAFTA and the EU can enable trading partners not only to reduce prices of traded products within those countries, but enables these trading blocs to use comparative advantage to their benefit to realize mutually beneficial exchanges for all members by focusing their efforts on those products and services in which each member has a comparative advantage. The trading blocs have an economic advantage that can make them a strong competitor in the global market, better able to take advantage of the theory of comparative advantage.

Learning Goal 2

2. It was stated in chapter 2 that developing countries must allow entrepreneurship to flourish if their economies are to develop and become active participants in the global market. The same can be said for any part of the world. Adam Smith's idea of the invisible hand was simply that when an individual is allowed the incentive to work hard by being allowed to keep the profits from his business, society will benefit by getting needed goods or services. The story of the ice factory illustrates the invisible hand theory - the entrepreneur started the factory and gained a considerable return on his idea, the people in the country have a needed product and more jobs.

    The way to take advantage of these ideas is by doing research, traveling, finding a need either in the United States for a product that can be imported, or overseas for a product that can be exported. The key is to <u>be creative</u>.

3. c – Balance of payments
   d – dumping
   a – balance of trade
   b – trade deficit

Learning Goals 2, 3

4. a.   International Joint venture.
   b.   Contract Manufacturing
   c.   Franchising

   d.   Foreign direct investment
   e.   Exporting
   f.   Licensing

5. A lower value of the dollar means that a dollar is traded for less foreign currency than normal. Foreign goods would become more expensive because it would take more dollars to buy them. It also makes American goods cheaper to foreign buyers because it would take less foreign currency to buy them. In the long run, this could benefit U.S. firms in foreign markets. Devaluing a currency means lowering the value of a nation's currency relative to other currencies. This can cause problems with changes in labor costs, material costs and financing.
American businesses would find their products less expensive in foreign countries, which could be beneficial for sales, but their cost of doing business in foreign countries could be negatively affected by devaluation.

6. One of the first things that should be considered is how the South Americans feel about ice cream/frozen yogurt as a product. How it's eaten, their views on dairy products (some religions have different views on dairy products and how they should be handled), where it can be marketed (do they have the same kind of grocery stores? do you open a free standing store?), even their familiarity with the product are all issues that must be addressed. There is a possibility that this may be a totally new product concept and you as a seller of the product will need to be aware of how to convince the South American people that this is a viable and acceptable product.

Social and economic differences from the American market must also be considered. In the U.S. frozen yogurt and ice cream may be purchased on a trip to the grocery store, and stored at home in the refrigerator. Is that a similar life style to the South Americans? Is the type of equipment available which is needed to store the product before it is purchased? Does a typical South American home have the type of storage needed, i.e. a freezer? American families may go to an ice cream or frozen yogurt stand as a family outing. Would that be true of a typical South American family? We eat ice cream or frozen yogurt as a dessert or sometimes as a snack. How would the South American population view the product? When might they choose to eat it?

Although Argentina, for example, as a nation may be wealthy, does the average Argentinean have the money to buy a nonessential item like this?

Further questions to be answered revolve around legal and regulatory differences. The way of doing business in South America is quite different from that of the U.S. Laws and regulations will vary, and practices will be different there than at home. The manner of entering business in South America will be different from the U.S.

Additionally, will it be economically feasible to invest in South America? How is the American dollar against the currency of the country you choose? That may affect the ability and willingness of the South Americans to try your product should you simply decide to export your product to the country. Should you decide to attempt to produce and sell your product in South America, the value of the U.S. dollar will take on even more significance in light of the greater investment?

7. a. Import quotas
   b. Revenue tariffs
   c. Protective tariffs
   d. Embargoes
   e. Non-tariff barriers

Learning Goals 4, 6

8. Coca-Cola has been able to reach their international markets conveniently through their website. A website allows them to "advertise", or promote, their product internationally because it is easily accessible to anyone with access to the Internet. It also allows Americans to see how their counterpart soft drink fans are slightly different. The website has geared its various sites to local markets by using the native language and modifying the content of the page for the "local" international market. Each page is different as they have modified each country's page to fit to individual cultures.

Learning Goal 6

9. Your findings for this exercise will depend upon what conditions are at the time you search. When this book was being written, an article about U.S. firms investment in China indicated that U.S. firms were still finding the country to be an attractive investment, even in light of the global economic recession that was occurring at the time.

PRACTICE TEST

MULTIPLE CHOICE

1.	a	14.	b
2.	a	15.	d
3.	d	16.	b
4.	c	17.	b
5.	c	18.	d
6.	d	19.	a
7.	c	20.	b
8.	b	21.	a
9.	c	22.	c
10.	a	23.	d
11.	a	24.	c
12.	a	25.	d
13.	b		

TRUE–FALSE

1.	T	10.	T
2.	F	11.	F
3.	T	12.	T
4.	F	13.	T
5.	F	14.	T
6.	T	15.	F
7.	F	16.	T
8.	F	17.	F
9.	T	18.	T

CHAPTER 4 – DEMANDING ETHICAL BEHAVIOR AND SOCIALLY RESPONSIBLE BEHAVIOR

LEARNING GOALS

After you have read and studied this chapter, you should be able to:

1. Explain why obeying the law is only the first step in behaving ethically.
2. Ask the three questions one should answer when faced with a potentially unethical action.
3. Describe management's role in setting ethical standards.
4. Distinguish between compliance-based and integrity-based ethics codes, and list the six steps in setting up a corporate ethics code.
5. Define corporate social responsibility and examine corporate responsibility to various stakeholders.
6. Analyze the role of U.S. businesses in influencing ethical behavior and social responsibility in global markets.

LEARNING THE LANGUAGE

Listed here are important terms found in this chapter. Choose the correct term for each definition and write it in the space provided.

Compliance-based ethics codes	Ethics
Corporate philanthropy	Insider trading
Corporate policy	Integrity-based ethics codes
Corporate responsibility	Social audit
Corporate social initiatives	Whistleblowers
Corporate social responsibility	

1. Ethical standards emphasize preventing unlawful behavior by increasing control and by penalizing wrongdoers are called _____.

2. A _____ is a systematic evaluation of an organization's progress toward implementing programs that are socially responsible and responsive.

3. The dimension of social responsibility knows as a(n) _____ refers to the position a firm takes on social and political issues.

4. Standards of moral behavior, or _____, is behavior that is accepted by society as right or wrong.

5. In a corporation, a(n) _____ refers to ethical standards that define the organization's guiding values, create an environment that supports ethically sound behavior, and stress a shared accountability among employees.

6. _____ is the dimension of social responsibility that includes charitable donations.

7. A business's concern for the welfare of a society as a whole is called _____.

8. A dimension of social responsibility known as _____ includes everything from hiring minority workers to making safe products.

9. An unethical activity called _____ occurs when insiders use private company information to further their own fortunes or those of their family and friends.

10. People who report illegal or unethical behavior are known as _____.

11. Enhanced forms of corporate philanthropy called _____ are more directly related to the company's competencies.

ASSESSMENT CHECK

Learning Goal 1

Ethics Is More Than Legality

1. What are some things that could be done to restore trust in the free market system and in corporate leaders?

   a. _____

   b. _____

   c. _____

2. What is the danger in simply writing new laws to correct behavior?

3. What is the difference between being "ethical" and being "legal"?

4. What is meant by the statement "Many Americans today have no moral absolutes."?

5. The common themes from the Bible, Aristotle, Shakespeare, the Koran and Confucius are:

6. How "socially minded" are Americans in general? What information does the text cite to support that claim?

7. What is an "ethical dilemma"?

Learning Goal 2

Ethics Begins with Each of Us

8. How did teams respond when they were asked about making ethical decisions?

9. Describe an ethical dilemma.

10. What are three questions to ask yourself when faced with an ethical dilemma?

    a. _____

    b. _____

    c. _____

Learning Goal 3

Managing Businesses Ethically and Responsibly

11. Organizational ethics begin at _____

    People learn their standards and values from _____

12. What are the reasons to manage ethically?

    a. _____

    b. _____

    c. _____

    d. _____

    e. _____

    f. _____

    g. _____

    h. _____

Setting Corporate Ethical Standards

13. Identify the difference between a compliance-based ethics code and an integrity-based ethics code.

14. What are six steps to follow for a long-term improvement of America's business ethics?

   a. _____

   b. _____

   c. _____

   d. _____

   e. _____

   f. _____

15. What is the most important factor to the success of enforcing an ethics code? What makes that person effective?

Learning Goal 5

Corporate Social Responsibility

16. Corporate social responsibility is based on:

17. Critics of corporate social responsibility (CSR) believe:

18. Defenders of CSR believe:

19. Identify the four dimensions of corporate social responsibility.

   a. _____

   b. _____

   c. _____

   d. _____

20. Describe the USA Freedom Corps.

21. Identify three web-based volunteer services that link volunteers with nonprofit and public sector organizations.

22. What are four groups that comprise the stakeholders to whom businesses are responsible?

   a. _____   c. _____

   b. _____   d. _____

23. President John F. Kennedy proposed these four basic rights of consumers:

   a. _____   c. _____

   b. _____   d. _____

24. One of the surest ways of failing to please customers is_____

25. How does Bagel Works, a New England based chain of bagel stores, demonstrate a two-way, or dual approach to social responsibility?

26. Is it only company executives that participate in insider trading?

27. What is required by Regulation FD, adopted by the SEC in the early 2000s?

28. What responsibilities do businesses have toward employees?

    a. _____

    b. _____

    c. _____

29. What are "contented cow"companies, vs. "common cow" companies?

30. How does offering employees good salaries and benefits help companies?

31. What actions might disgruntled employees take?

    a. _____

    b. _____

    c. _____

    d. _____

    e. _____

    f. _____

    g. _____

32. Some companies feel responsible for promoting social justice and believe they have a role in giving back. What kinds of social contributions have companies made to go beyond charity?

33. What is a product's carbon footprint?

34. What is the potential financial impact of environmental strategies?

35. Describe the impact of the green movement on the U.S. labor force.

36. A major problem of conducting a social audit is _____

_____

37. Many consider that a workplace audit should measure:

a. _____

b. _____

c. _____

d. _____

e. _____

f. _____

38. How is a "net social contribution" calculated?

39. Describe the four types of "watch-dog" groups that monitor how well companies enforce ethical and social responsibility policies.

a. _____

b. _____

c. _____

d. _____

Learning Goal 6

International Ethics and Social Responsibility

40. Are ethical problems unique to the United States? What is new about the ethical standards used to judge government leaders?

41.	What are many American businesses demanding from their international suppliers in terms of social responsibility?

42.	Describe the Joint Initiative on Corporate Accountability and Workers' Rights.

43.	What questions surround the issue of American ethical standards and international suppliers?

44.	Is it likely that there will be a single set of international rules governing multinational corporations? Why or why not?

CRITICAL THINKING EXERCISES

Learning Goal 1

1.	You are a buyer for a major manufacturer of automotive parts and have control over multi-million dollar contracts. You were recently talking with one of your suppliers and mentioned that you were planning a pleasure trip to Los Angeles with your family, and weren't sure yet where you would be staying. "It's so expensive in L.A. I'm afraid we won't find a decent place to stay." The supplier said that he has contacts in L.A. in the hotel industry, and that he would not only make the reservation for you, but would pay for the hotel stay for you and your family.

	Your company's policy regarding "gifts" from suppliers is not entirely clear. Tangible gifts with a value over $50 are not to be accepted. Other things such as dinners, and other intangibles, are to be evaluated on a case-by-case basis, and acceptance is left up to the discretion of the employee. Any employee who violates the policy could face severe penalties, including dismissal.

	Is this an ethical dilemma? Why or why not? What ethical issues are involved? Is there a question of "legal versus ethical"? What would you do?

2. Refer to the ethics check questions in your text and determine how you would handle the following situation.

    Daryl, the general supervisor of a marketing department of a mid-sized Midwestern corporation, is an ambitious young man. He is writing a book that he hopes will make a name for himself in the business community. Because the typing for the actual text is very time-consuming, Daryl is using the secretary he shares with 2 other managers, as well as some of his market research interns to both do research and to type the book while they're at work. Because they are often busy doing his book, people from the other departments are finding they can't get their work-related business done. The secretary and interns feel they have to do what Daryl says because he is their direct supervisor. You are Daryl's peer in another department and you also have outside work you need to have typed. You're annoyed at Daryl's actions, but would rather not inform your boss, (who is also Daryl's boss) about what's going on because you want to maintain a friendly working relationship with Daryl. Besides, you never know how "the boss" is going to react. Sometimes you begin to think that if Daryl can get away with using company equipment, personnel, and time for his personal projects, why can't you? Discuss what you believe are the ethical issues in this situation, and determine how you would handle this situation.

3. You work for a major car manufacturer as a district manager, calling on car dealerships as a representative of the manufacturer. It is three days before the end of a sales incentive contest, and one of your dealers is close to winning a trip to Hawaii. If your dealer wins the contest for your area, you get a lot of recognition and a good chance for a promotion, which will enable you to stop traveling so much during the week. The dealer wants you to report as "sold" eight cars that he has not yet sold but will have deals on next week, several days after the end of the contest. Those eight cars will put him over the top and enable him to win the contest. You just received a directive from the corporate headquarters on this practice of pre-reporting sales, indicating that the company would take strong action against anyone discovered taking such steps. Your boss and his superior have taken you aside and encouraged you to take whatever action is necessary to win the contest. You think you could get by with it and not get caught. An added problem is that the customer warranty starts the day the car is reported sold, so whoever purchases the car would lose several days of warranty service. What is your manager's role in this situation? What would you do?

4. Ethics codes can be classified into two major categories:
   Compliance-based   Integrity-based

   Read the following examples of corporate behavior, and determine which kind of ethical code the company may be using.

   a. _____ At Mary's Flowers employees are encouraged to be active in community affairs, and to be aware of their obligation to society. The company stresses honesty, provides seminars   on making ethical choices, and has a commitment to hire an ethnically diverse workforce.

   b. _____ At Pro-Tec, management has developed and distributed a code of ethics for employees. It defines what is acceptable behavior, and states that "behavior deemed to be unethical will not be tolerated." The policy does not define behavior that would be considered unethical, but does say that if there is a question a manager should be consulted.

5. You have just been hired as Pro-Tech's first Ethics officer. You feel that your first project should be to set up the company's corporate code of ethical conduct. How would you start, and what steps would you take?

Learning Goal 5

6. ". . . corporate social responsibility is the concern businesses have for the welfare of society." Read the situation described below and answer the questions that follow:

   MUMC is a successful medium-sized firm that supplies parts for electric motors.
   Dan Furlong, the president, was being interviewed by the business features writer of the local newspaper. The reporter asked Dan his views on social responsibility, and how MUMC reflected a socially responsive position. Dan replied that although he had never done a so-called social audit (as the textbooks call it) he did figure that the firm was a good corporate citizen. He said, "We pay our employees a good salary, and the guys in the shop are getting paid above hourly wages for this area. We make a profit, and give everyone a bonus at the holidays. We take a lot or precautions in the shop, and no one has had an accident to speak of in several years. A few cuts or bruises, but that's part of that kind of job. Whenever we have customer complaints, I make sure someone handles them right away. We charge what I think is a fair price for our product, which I think is higher quality than most of my competitors. I pay my bills on time and don't cheat on my taxes. I guess you could say that we are a pretty socially responsible company."

   a. In keeping with the idea of social audits and socially responsible business activities, is Mr. Furlong running the business in a socially responsible manner?

   b. Who are Mr. Furlong's stakeholders?

   c. What suggestions can you make to improve MUMC's social responsibility position?

7. Who are four stakeholders to whom businesses are responsible? What does "being responsible" to each of these groups require?

Learning Goal 6

8. How does the increasingly global nature of U.S. business impact the issue of social responsibility and ethics?

PRACTICE TEST

MULTIPLE CHOICE—Circle the best answer

Learning Goal 1

1. Which of these actions is least likely to restore the trust of the American public in the free market system?
   a. Pass new accounting laws.
   b. Punish those who have broken the law.
   c. Define the concept of ethics more narrowly, and make the definition closer to the definition of legality.
   d. Pass new laws making business, religious and government leaders more accountable for their actions.

2. The difference between ethics and legality is that:
   a. Legality reflects how people should treat each other, while ethics is more limiting.
   b. Ethics refers to ways available to us to protect ourselves from theft, violence, and fraud.
   c. Legality is narrower than ethics and refers to laws written to protect ourselves.
   d. Ethics refers to a narrower range of behavior than legality.

3. A survey revealed that:
   a. many Americans decide what's ethical behavior based upon the situation in which they find themselves.
   b. most Americans give a considerable amount of time to their communities.
   c. employees rarely violate safety standards or "goof off" at work.
   d. most Americans have an absolute sense of what is moral.

Learning Goal 2

4. According to the text, ethical behavior begins with:
   a. Corporate leaders.
   b. Government leaders.
   c. Religious leaders.
   d. You and me.

5. Sometimes an obvious choice from an ethical standpoint has personal or professional drawbacks. An example might be when a supervisor asks you to do something unethical, and you face negative consequences if you refuse. When you are in such a situation you are faced with:
   a. two lousy choices.
   b. an ethical dilemma.
   c. deciding the legality of your choice.
   d. a social responsibility issue.

6. Which of the following is not included as one of the questions we must ask when faced with an ethical dilemma?
   a. Is it legal?
   b. Is it balanced?
   c. How will it make me feel about myself?
   d. Is it okay if everyone else is doing it?

7. The most basic step in an ethics based management system is asking the question:
   a. Is it legal?
   b. Who will know?
   c. Is it balanced?
   d. Has it been done before?

Learning Goal 3

8. Which of the following is the best reason for a business to be managed ethically?
   a. Business leaders don't want to get caught behaving unethically.
   b. An ethically managed business can reduce employee turnover.
   c. If the company is engaged in a lawsuit, it can use the ethics code as a legal defense.
   d. So that new customers will not be able to complain about the ethical behavior of the company.

9. Organizational ethics begin
   a. at the top levels of management.
   b. only with employees.
   c. with the unions.
   d. with mid level managers.

Learning Goal 4

10. Which of the following is not a part of an integrity-based ethics code?
    a. stresses shared accountability
    b. emphasizes penalizing of wrong-doers
    c. supports ethically sound behavior
    d. defines an organization's guiding principles

11. According to the text, which of the following actions is probably most critical In establishing an effective ethics program?
    a. Managers must be trained to consider ethical implications of all decisions.
    b. Outsiders such as suppliers, distributors, and customers must be told about the program.
    c. The ethics code must be enforced with timely action if any rules are broken.
    d. An ethics office must be set up.

12. A logistics company, TNT keeps an emergency response team on standby to go anywhere in the world at 48 hours notice. This is an example of:
    a. corporate philanthropy.
    b. corporate social initiatives.
    c. corporate policy.
    d. corporate responsibility.

13. Defenders of corporate social responsibility (CSR) believe:
    a. It is being socially responsible to make money for stockholders and return that money to those investors.
    b. spending money on CSR is moving toward socialism.
    c. in Milton Friedman's view that the main CSR of businesses is to make money.
    d. businesses owe their existence to the societies they serve.

14. Being energy conscious, ensuring that employees have a safe working environment, and monitoring corporate hiring policies to prevent discrimination is part of:
    a. corporate responsibility.
    b. corporate philanthropy.
    c. corporate policy.
    d. corporate legal standards.

15. In terms of social responsibility, many people believe that
    a. it does not make good financial sense for companies to be "up front" about potential product problems.
    b. it makes financial and moral sense to invest in companies that plan ahead to create a better environment.
    c. businesses have no responsibility to create jobs.
    d. businesses have no responsibility to social causes.

16. In terms of social responsibility, the "contented cow" idea states that
    a. it is important to provide cafeteria style benefits to employees.
    b. corporations have a responsibility to provide aid to struggling American farmers.
    c. companies that treat employees with respect will make a difference in the bottom line.
    d. corporations owe a responsibility to the environment and to make the physical environment so good that it would create "contented cows."

17. Maria Hernandez is a secretary at Big Bud's Brewery a major U.S. brewer of specialty beers. Maria was at lunch with her friend Olga, who is the Administrative Assistant to the president of the Brewery, January Flower. Olga mentioned that she overheard her boss talking to a potential buyer of Big Bud's Brewery. Maria began thinking that perhaps she should buy some extra stock in the company, as the price was most likely to go up if the company was going to be sold. If Maria does buy the stock before the sale of Big Bud's is publicly announced, she:
    a. could be seen as a really smart investor.
    b. could be accused of insider trading.
    c. should be sure her stockbroker knows how she got the information.
    d. could be considered to be stealing from Big Bud's.

18. Which of the following is not one of the watchdog groups that evaluate how well companies enforce their ethical and social responsibility policies?
    a. Socially conscious investors and consumers
    b. Environmentalists
    c. Union officials
    d. Employees

Learning Goal 6

19. Government and business leaders are being held to:
    a. lower ethical standards than in the past.
    b. ethical standards in the United States, but foreign leaders are not being subjected to ethical scrutiny.
    c. higher ethical standards than in the past.
    d. ethical standards that cannot be met by most leaders.

20. American businesses are:
    a. demanding socially responsible behavior from international suppliers, particularly in the areas of environmental standards and human rights issues.
    b. holding international suppliers to different standards than American companies must adhere to in the United States.
    c. not concerned with the ethical or socially responsible behavior of their international suppliers.
    d. are demanding that international suppliers adhere to higher standards than their American counterparts.

TRUE–FALSE

Learning Goal 1

1. _____ One danger in writing new laws to correct behavior is that people may begin to think that any behavior that is within the law is also ethically acceptable.

2. _____ Ethics and legality are basically the same thing.

Learning Goal 2

3. _____ Solutions to ethical problems are usually easily determined.

4. _____ In an organization, ethics begin at the top.

Learning Goal 3

5. _____ One of the reasons for ethical management is to avoid lawsuits.

Learning Goal 4

6. _____ Compliance-based ethics codes define an organization's guiding values, create an environment that supports ethical behavior and stresses shared accountability.

7. _____ One step to the success of enforcing an ethics code is the selection of an ethics officer.

8. _____ It's not important for employees to be given a specific ethics code. They should be aware of what constitutes ethical behavior without being told.

9. _____ Whistleblowers are individuals who report unethical or illegal behavior in an organization.

10. _____ Corporate social responsibility is the concern businesses have for their profitability.

11. _____ In reality, it appears that even people who want to be socially responsible can't define what being socially responsible means.

12. _____ One of the best ways to please customers is to hide product defects from them.

13. _____ Insider trading involves employees buying and selling the stock of the company by which they are employed.

14. _____ Businesses have a responsibility to employees to create jobs.

15. _____ A carbon footprint can be defined as the amount of carbon released during the production, distribution, consumption and disposal of a product.

Learning Goal 6

16 _____ Ethical problems and issues of social responsibility are unique to the United States.

17. _____ Nike has been accused of treating workers in some parts of the world unfairly, and has begun an effort to improve its reputation.

You Can Find It On the Net

Go to the Ben and Jerry's website www.benjerry.com and find the company's mission statement.

What three areas are included in their mission statement?

What is Ben and Jerry's social mission?

What campaigns and causes does Ben and Jerry's support?

What is the purpose of the Ben and Jerry's Foundation?

Check out the most recent Social and Environmental Assessment. In this document the company reports their activities in a number of areas, regarding their social responsibility behavior. What has Ben and Jerry's been up to?

ANSWERS

LEARNING THE LANGUAGE

1.	Compliance based ethics codes	7.	Corporate social responsibility
2.	Social audit	8.	Corporate responsibility
3.	Corporate policy	9.	Insider trading
4.	Ethics	10.	Whistleblowers
5.	Integrity based ethics codes	11.	Corporate social initiatives
6.	Corporate philanthropy		

ASSESSMENT CHECK

Learning Goal 1

Ethics Is More Than Legality

1. In order to restore trust in the free market system and in corporate leaders, we need to
   a. punish those who have broken the law. No one should be above those laws.
   b. pass new laws making accounting records easier to read and understand.
   c. pass more laws making business people and others more accountable.

2. The danger in writing new laws to correct behavior is that people may begin to think that any behavior that is within the law is also acceptable. When people consider only what is illegal, and not what is ethical, a society gets into trouble.

3. Ethics and legality are very different things. Being legal means following the laws written to protect ourselves from fraud, theft and violent acts. It is narrower than ethical behavior. Ethical behavior requires more than simply following the law and looks at behavior in terms of people's relations with one another.

4. This statement means that many Americans decide whether it's o.k. to steal, lie, or drink and drive based on the situation. He or she thinks that what is right is whatever works best for the individual, and that each person has to work out for himself or herself the difference between right and wrong.

5. The common themes from the Bible, Aristotle, Shakespeare, the Koran and Confucius are basic moral values such as integrity, respect for human life, self-control, honesty, courage, and self-sacrifice are right; cheating, cowardice and cruelty are wrong.

6. A recent study revealed that a majority of the American population reported never giving any time to their community. One third reported never giving to a charity. Business managers and workers cited low managerial ethics as a major cause of competitive woes for American businesses. Employees report violating safety standards and many students report cheating on exams. In other words, Americans are not especially "socially minded." The text cites examples from college classrooms and from corporate leaders' behavior as examples.

7. An ethical dilemma is a situation in which you must choose between equally unsatisfactory alternatives when making a decision.

Learning Goal 2

Ethics Begins with Each of Us

8. Most teens said they were prepared to make ethical decision in the workforce, but 38% felt lying, cheating, plagiarizing, or behaving violently is sometimes necessary.

9. An ethical dilemma is a situation in which a person must choose between two equally unsatisfactory alternatives.

10. Three questions to ask are:
    a. Is it legal? (Am I violating any law or company policy?)
    b. Is it balanced? (Am I acting fairly?)
    c. How will it make me feel about myself? (Would I feel proud if my family learned of my decision?)

Learning Goal 3

Managing Businesses Ethically and Responsibly

11. Organizational ethics begin at the top.

    People learn their standards and values from observing what others do.

12. Reasons to manage ethically are:
    a. to maintain a good reputation.
    b. to keep existing customers.
    c. to attract new customers.
    d. to avoid lawsuits.
    e. to reduce employee turnover.
    f. to avoid government intervention.
    g. to please customers, employees, and society.
    h. it's the right thing to do.

Learning Goal 4

Setting Corporate Ethical Standards

13. *Compliance based* ethics codes emphasize preventing unlawful behavior by increasing control and by penalizing wrongdoers. This type of ethics code is based on avoiding legal punishment. *Integrity based* ethics codes define the organization's guiding values, create an environment that supports ethically sound behavior, and stress a shared accountability among employees.

14. a. Top management must adopt and support an explicit code of conduct.
    b. Employees must understand that top management expects ethical behavior.
    c. Managers and employees must be trained to consider ethical implications of business decisions.
    d. Companies must set up an ethics office for employees to communicate about ethical matters anonymously.
    e. Outsiders must be told about the ethics program.
    f. The ethics code must be enforced.

15. An important factor to the success of enforcing an ethics code is to select an ethics officer. The effective ethics officer will set a positive tone, communicate effectively, and relate well with employees at every level. It is important the ethics officers have strong communications skills.

Learning Goal 5

Corporate Social Responsibility

16. Corporate social responsibility is based on a company's concern for the welfare of all its stakeholders, not just owners and on a commitment to the principles of integrity, fairness, and respect.

17. Critics of corporate social responsibility believe a manager's role is to compete and win in the marketplace. Some believe managers who pursue CSR are doing so with other people's money, which they invest to make more money, not to improve society.

18. Defenders of CSR believe businesses owe their existence to the societies they serve. Firms have access to society's labor pool and natural resources, in which every member of society has a stake. CSR defenders believe that businesses have obligations to investors and that CSR makes more money for investors in the long run.

19. a. *Corporate philanthropy* includes charitable donations to nonprofit groups.
    b. *Corporate social initiatives* include enhanced forms of traditional philanthropy. These initiatives differ from traditional philanthropy in that they are directly related to the company's competencies.
    c. *Corporate responsibility* includes responsibility in all business decisions, such as hiring, pollution control, product decisions, responsible use of energy, and providing a safe work environment.
    d. *Corporate policy* refers to the position taken on social and political issues

20. The USA Freedom Corps was established to oversee Citizen Corps, a program designed to strengthen homeland security efforts through the use of volunteers. Volunteers handle administrative work at local police departments and spread antiterrorism information as part of expanded Neighborhood Watch programs.

21. NetworkforGood.org
    1-800-Volunteer.org
    VolunteerMatch.org

22. Four stakeholder groups are:
    a. Customers   c. Employees
    b. Investors   d. Society and the environment

23. President John F. Kennedy proposed these four basic rights of consumers:
    a. the right to safety.   c. the right to choose.
    b. the right to be informed.   d. the right to be heard.

24. One of the surest ways of failing to please customers is not being totally honest with them.

25. Bagel Works approach to social responsibility focuses on the well being of the planet in addition to profits. Each store employs environmentally protective practices, and donates to community causes.

26. Insider trading isn't limited to company executives. An IBM secretary told her husband about a takeover of Lotus Development before it was publicly known. Her husband told two co-workers, who told friends, relatives, business associates, and others. In all, 25 people traded illegally on this tip. These people ended up with significant fines as a result.

27. Regulation FD (for fair disclosure) requires that companies which release any information share it with everyone, not just a few select people. If companies tell anyone, they must tell everyone, at the same time.

28. Business' responsibility to employees includes:
    a. a responsibility to create jobs.
    b. an obligation to fairly reward hard work and talent.
    c. treating employees with respect.

29. "Contented cow" companies are companies with contented employees. These companies outgrew and out earned their "common cow" companies by a significant amount. The difference in performance is attributed to the commitment and caring the outstanding companies demonstrated for their employees.

30. Offering good salaries and benefits reduces employee turnover. This saves the company money, so retaining workers is good for morale and is good for business.

31. When employees feel they have been treated unfairly they will strike back, and get even in such ways as:
    a. blaming mistakes on others.
    b. not accepting responsibility for decision making.
    c. manipulating budgets and expenses.
    d. making commitments they intend to ignore.
    e. hoarding resources.
    f. doing the minimum needed to get by.
    g. making results look better than they are.

32. When companies play a role in building a community, their contributions can include cleaning up the environment, providing computer lessons, supporting the elderly and children from low-income families, and building community facilities.

33. A product's carbon footprint is the amount of carbon released during production, distribution, consumption and disposal. This can include such items as the carbon released by the fertilizer used to grow agricultural products, including the carbon in the fertilizer itself, the gas used to run farm equipment and to transport the agricultural product, electricity and so on.

34. Some environmental efforts can allow a company to charge higher prices or to increase market share. Other times the efforts fail, when customers aren't willing to pay a premium for products which are environmentally responsible.

35. The green movement has had a positive impact on the U.S. labor force. Emerging renewable-energy and energy-efficient industries account for 8.5 million jobs and by 2030 will create as many as 40 million more in a variety of industries.

36. A major problem of conducting a social audit is establishing procedures for measuring a firm's activities and their effects on society. The question is: what should be measured?

37. Many consider that a workplace audit should measure:
    a. workplace issues.
    b. the environment.
    c. product safety.
    d. community relations.
    e. military weapons contracting.
    f. international operations and human rights.
    g. respect for the rights of local people.

38. A "net social contribution" is calculated by adding all positive social actions, and then subtracting negative effects such as layoffs and pollution.

39. Four watchdog groups are:
    a. Socially conscious investors, who insist that companies extend the company's high standards to all their suppliers.
    b. Environmentalists, who apply pressure by naming companies that don't abide by environmentalists' standards.
    c. Union officials, who force companies to comply with standards to avoid negative publicity.
    d. Customers who make buying decisions based on their social conscience.

Learning Goal 6

International Ethics and Social Responsibility

40. No, ethical problems are not unique to the U.S. What is new about the moral and ethical standards by which government leaders are being judged is that the standards are much stricter now. In other words, government leaders are now being held to a higher standard than in the past.

41. Many American businesses are demanding socially responsible behavior from their international suppliers by making sure their suppliers do not violate U.S. human rights and environmental standards.

42. The Joint Initiative on Corporate Accountability and Workers' Rights is a project that is designed to create a single set of labor standards with a common factory inspection system. The goal is to replace the current system of multiple approaches with something that is easier and cheaper to use. If it works, one of the outcomes is that the common guidelines will keep companies from undercutting one another on labor standards. A major issue is what constitutes a living wage in different areas of the world.

43. Examples of the questions surrounding the issues of international ethics are:
    Is it always ethical for American companies to demand compliance with our moral standards?
    What about countries where child labor is an accepted part of society?
    What about foreign companies doing business in the U.S.?
    Should foreign companies doing business in the U.S. expect American companies to comply with their ethical standards?
    To what country's standards should multinational companies adhere?

44. It is unlikely that there will be a single set of international rules governing multinational corporations in the near future. There are too many differing opinions about what is ethical and socially responsible. Most standards set by various international bodies are advisory only.

CRITICAL THINKING EXERCISES

Learning Goal 1

1. In many people's opinion, this situation would be an ethical dilemma because you are deciding between essentially violating company policy and not having a nice place for you and your family to stay in L.A. Both of these are unsatisfactory options. At issue are the ethical dilemma of violation of company policy, and the "ethics questions" checklist. The sense of "legal" versus "ethical" comes from company policy, which isn't very well defined.

Learning Goals 1, 2

2. This is a difficult problem, but ethically it's not really too hard to figure out what to do. The decision about going to the boss is an individual one, but using the secretary and the interns for personal business, particularly to the extent that Daryl is using, is probably unethical. To answer the ethics questions: a) Is it legal? Daryl's actions are most likely violating some company policy.
b) Is it balanced? This seems to be a win-lose situation, because while Daryl is getting what he needs, the typing, others in the company are not able to get their work done because of Daryl's actions. c) How will it make me feel about myself? This is a personal question that only the individual can answer.

Learning Goals 2, 3

3. There is no "correct" answer to this question although there is probably a "most appropriate" mode of behavior. In this era of customer service and quality products in a competitive marketplace, these kinds of decisions are likely to come up frequently. Now is the time to think about how you would act. A helpful guide would be to ask yourself the questions the text proposes: a. Is it legal? b. Is it balanced? Would I want to be treated this way? Do I win at the expense of someone else? c. How will it make me feel about myself?

Learning Goal 4

4. a. Integrity-based ethics code
   b. Compliance-based ethics code

5. As a company's Ethics Officer, the first step you would probably take is to set up a meeting with the company's top executives to ensure their support of any actions you want to take regarding setting up a code of conduct. The unconditional support of top management is vital to the success of a corporate ethics code. The next step most likely is to develop a set of standards of acceptable behavior, and to make sure that employees understand the expectations of those standards. Employees must be trained to consider the ethical implications of their decisions, so there must be explicit standards and guidelines to follow.

   Further, as the Ethics Officer, your office must set up a system so that employees can report and discuss ethical issues anonymously, and whistleblowers must feel protected. Your office must also inform outsiders such as suppliers, subcontractors, distributors, and customers of the ethics code. This can be done easily on your company's web site.

   Lastly, the ethics code must be enforced by taking timely action when a violation has occurred.

6. a. Social responsibility includes providing a safer work environment, good benefits, a safe, high quality product line, prompt complaint handling, and honest pricing policies. The result of a social audit would indicate that Mr. Furlong is running his business in a socially responsible manner, as far as he goes.

    b. Mr. Furlong's stakeholders would be his boss, the stockholders, employees, customers, competitors, suppliers and the general public.

    c. Although he would get fairly high scores from his employees in the area of social responsibility, Mr. Furlong doesn't appear to have any involvement with the community in which he operates. Of the four dimensions of corporate social performance, he addresses only the corporate responsibility issue; those of corporate philanthropy, corporate social initiatives and corporate policy appear to be ignored. He could improve community relations (and even increase his customer base) by encouraging his employees to get involved in community related projects, donating time and/or money to local charities, developing a stand on local issues, improving employee-related benefits with job enrichment and employee development, and making opportunities for members of ethnic and minority groups.
    Mr. Furlong also did not address the impact his company has on the environment. Many studies have shown that customers are willing to pay more for products that are environmentally friendly.

7. Businesses are responsible to four general stakeholder groups: customers, investors, employees, and society in general. Being responsible to *customers* means offering them goods and services of real value. This includes being honest with customers about problems with products, and committing resources to solve the problems.

    Responsibility to *investors* means making money for stockholders. This includes financial ethical behavior. Many believe that it makes financial as well as moral sense to invest in companies that are planning ahead to create a better environment.

    Responsibility to *employees* means creating jobs, making sure that hard work and talent are fairly rewarded, and demonstrating respect for employees by treating them fairly. This includes giving employees salaries and benefits that help them reach their personal financial goals.

    Responsibility to *society* means creating wealth, promoting social justice, giving back to communities, and helping to make the environment a better place.

8. In the past, officials of foreign firms have been judged by standards that were less harsh than those used in the United States. More recently, it seems that top leaders in some parts of the world are being judged by stricter standards. This could stem from the fact that American businesses have begun to demand more socially responsible behavior from international suppliers. As the business sector becomes increasingly globalized, international suppliers will be expected to conform to U.S. standards concerning ethics, human rights codes and the environment.

    The justness of requiring international suppliers to adhere to American ethical standards is not clear-cut. There are questions such as: Is it always ethical for companies to demand compliance with the standards of their own countries? What about countries where child labor is an accepted part of the society and families depend on the children's earnings for survival? Should foreign companies doing business in the United States expect American companies to comply with their ethical standards? To which society's standards should multinational companies conform? None of these questions have easy answers, but demonstrate the complexity of social responsibility issues in international markets.

PRACTICE TEST

MULTIPLE CHOICE

1.	c	11.	c
2.	c	12.	b
3.	a	13.	d
4.	d	14.	a
5.	b	15.	b
6.	d	16.	c
7.	a	17.	b
8.	b	18.	d
9.	a	19.	c
10.	b	20.	a

TRUE–FALSE

1.	T	10.	F
2.	F	11.	T
3.	F	12.	F
4.	T	13.	F
5.	T	14.	T
6.	T	15.	T
7.	T	16.	F
8.	F	17.	T
9.	T		

CHAPTER 5 – HOW TO FORM A BUSINESS

LEARNING GOALS

After you have read and studied this chapter, you should be able to:

1. Compare the advantages and disadvantages of sole proprietorships.
2. Describe the differences between general and limited partnerships and compare the advantages and disadvantages of partnerships.
3. Compare the advantages and disadvantages of corporations and summarize the differences between C corporations, S corporations and limited liability companies.
4. Define and give examples of three types of corporate mergers and explain the role of leveraged buyouts and taking a firm private.
5. Outline the advantages and disadvantages of franchises and discuss the opportunities for diversity in franchising and the challenges of global franchising.
6. Explain the role of cooperatives.

LEARNING THE LANGUAGE

Listed below are important terms found in this chapter. Choose the correct term for each definition and write it in the space provided.

Acquisition	General partner	Limited partnership
Conglomerate merger	General partnership	Master limited partnership
Conventional corporation (C)	Horizontal merger	Merger
Cooperative	Leveraged buyout (LBO)	Partnership
Corporation	Limited liability	S Corporation
Franchise	Limited Liability company (LLC)	Sole proprietorship
Franchise agreement	Limited Liability partnership (LLP)	Unlimited liability
Franchisee	Limited partner	Vertical merger
Franchisor		

1. A _____ joins two firms in the same industry.

2. A legal form of business with two or more owners is a _____.

3. A _____ is an arrangement whereby someone with a good idea for a business sells the rights to use the business name and to sell a product or service to others in a given territory.

4. In a(n)_____ one company purchases the property and obligations of another company.

5. Limited partners and shareholders have _____ because they are only responsible for the losses of a business up to the amount they invest.

6. This unique government creation called a(n) _____ looks like a corporation but is taxed like sole proprietorships and partnerships.

7. A _____ is a company that develops a product concept and sells others the rights to make and sell the products.

8. A business proposition that joins firms in completely unrelated industries is called a(n) _____.

9. An agreement such as a(n) _____ is a partnership with one or more general partners and one or more limited partners.

10. A(n) _____ looks much like a corporation in that it acts like a corporation and is traded on a stock exchange but is taxed like a partnership and thus avoids corporate income tax.

11. A legal entity with authority to act, a(n) _____ has liability separate from its owners.

12. The result of two firms forming one company is a _____.

13. A _____ is a person who buys a franchise.

14. A partner is called a _____ when she has invested money in a business but does not have any management responsibility or liability for losses beyond the investment.

15. A company that is similar to an S corporation, but without the special eligibility requirement is called a (n) _____.

16. A partner who has unlimited liability is called a _____ and is active in managing the firm.

17. A _____ is a business that is owned and controlled by the people who use it – producers, consumers or workers with similar needs who pool their resources for mutual gain.

18. A partnership is called a(n) _____when all owners share in operating the business and in assuming liability for the business's debts.

19. An attempt by employees, management, or a group of investors to purchase an organization primarily through borrowing is called a(n) _____.

20. A _____ is the right to use a business name and to sell a product or service in a given territory.

21. In the business venture known as a(n) _____, two companies which are involved in different stages of related businesses join together.

22. A business that is owned, and usually managed, by one person is a(n) _____.

23. The concept of _____ means that business owners are responsible for all of the debts of a business.

24. A(n) _____ is one that limits partners' risk of losing their personal assets to only their own acts and omissions and to the acts and omissions of people under their supervision.

25. A state-chartered legal entity with authority to act and have liability separate from its owners is a(n) _____.

ASSESSMENT CHECK

Learning Goal 1

Basic Forms of Business Ownership

1. What are three general forms of business ownership? Which is the most common form of business ownership?

   a. _____

   b. _____

   c. _____

2. Which form of ownership is separate from its owners?

3. What are the advantages of a sole proprietorship?

   a. _____

   b. _____

   c. _____

   d. _____

   e. _____

   f. _____

4. What do you have to do to start a sole proprietorship?

5. How are profits taxed in a sole proprietorship?

6. The disadvantages of sole proprietorships are:

   a. _____

   b. _____

   c. _____

   d. _____

   e. _____

   f. _____

   g. _____

7. How are the debts of a sole proprietorship handled?

8. The forms of ownership that have a greater probability of obtaining needed financial backing are:

   _____

Learning Goal 2

Partnerships

9. What are the forms of partnerships?

   a. _____

   b. _____

   c. _____

10. What is the difference between a general partnership and a limited partnership? What is the minimum number of general partners required?

11. What is the difference between a general partner and a limited partner?

12. Describe the characteristics of a master limited partnership.

13. Describe the characteristics of a limited liability partnership (LLP).

14. The Uniform Partnership Act (UPA) identifies what three key elements of a general partnership?

   a. _____

   b. _____

   c. _____

15. What are the advantages of a partnership?

   a. _____

   b. _____

   c. _____

   d. _____

16. What are the disadvantages of a partnership?

   a. _____

   b. _____

   c. _____

   d. _____

17. In a partnership, who is responsible for the debts of the firm and has unlimited liability?

18. Because of potential conflict between partners, all terms of the partnership should: _____

   _____

Learning Goal 3

Corporations

19. Explain the following statement. "A corporation is separate from its owners". What is another name for the owners of a corporation?

20. What are the advantages of conventional "C" corporations?

   a. _____

   b. _____

   c. _____

   d. _____

   e. _____

   f. _____

   g. _____

21. What are three ways a corporation can raise money?

   a. _____

   b. _____

   c. _____

22. What is the benefit of the size of a large corporation? Does a company have to be large to be a corporation?

23. How do the owners of a corporation (stockholders) influence how a business is managed?

24. What are the disadvantages of conventional "C" corporations?

a. _____

b. _____

c. _____

d. _____

e. _____

f. _____

g. _____

25. What is meant by two tax returns and "double taxation"?

26. How can size be a disadvantage of a large corporation?

27. Illustrate the basic structure of a corporation.

28. What are the advantages for individuals when they incorporate?

29. In order to qualify as an "S" corporation a company must:

a. _____

b. _____

c. _____

d. _____

30. Compare and contrast S corporations with conventional C corporations.

31. What are the types of corporations, other than an "S"?

a. _____   f. _____

b. _____   g. _____

c. _____   h. _____

d. _____   i. _____

e. _____

32. What are the advantages of limited liability companies?

a. _____

b. _____

c. _____

d. _____

e. _____

33. List the disadvantages of an LLC:

a. _____

b. _____

c. _____

d. _____

e. _____

34. How is ownership transferred in an LLC?

35. What could happen to an LLC in the event of a member's death?

Learning Goal 4

Corporate Expansion: Mergers and Acquisitions

36. What is the difference between a merger and an acquisition?

37. Describe:
    a. vertical mergers: _____

        _____

    b. horizontal mergers: _____

        _____

    c. conglomerate mergers: _____

        _____

38. What is involved in "taking a firm private"?

39. How are the funds in a leveraged buyout (LBO) used? Who become the owners of the firm?

40. Are business acquisitions limited to U.S. buyers?

Learning Goal 5

Special Forms of Ownership

41. Describe the difference between a franchisor and a franchisee.

42. List the advantages of owning a franchise

    a. _____   d. _____

    b. _____   e. _____

    c. _____

43. What are the reasons that a franchisee has a greater chance of succeeding in business?

44. List the disadvantages of owning a franchise.

a. _____   d. _____

b. _____   e. _____

c. _____   f. _____

45. Describe the coattail effect.

46. How have women been involved in franchising?

47. How has minority involvement in franchising changed?

48. What government agency provides training for minorities in franchising?

49. Identify four advantages of home franchising.

a. _____   c. _____

b. _____   d. _____

50. What are the ways in which e-commerce is affecting franchising?

51. How are franchisors using technology?

52. Some areas of the world that are popular targets for international franchising include:

_____   _____

_____   _____

_____   _____

_____   _____

_____   _____

_____   _____

53. The characteristics that make franchising successful in international markets are _____

_____

Learning Goal 6

Cooperatives

54. Describe the two kinds of cooperatives mentioned in the text.

a. _____

_____

b. _____

_____

55. Give some examples of successful cooperatives in the United States.

CRITICAL THINKING EXERCISES

Learning Goal 1

1. Jeff Baker has his own business as the owner of a tanning salon in his hometown. He is talking with a good friend, Bill Jacobs, who is interested in going into business for himself. "After I had purchased the necessary equipment, all I had to do was fill out a form for the county and open my doors, easy as that," Jeff mentioned, over lunch one day. "The only problem is, now I owe a lot of money for this tanning equipment. I'll be in rough shape if we go under!" "You know", said Bill "I have company- paid life and health insurance where I work now. I'm a little concerned about losing that." "Yeah, that's a concern," replied Jeff," but I can try things with this business that my old bosses would never have let me try. I can be really creative. I think we earned enough this year to open a second facility after we pay off the loans we have now. We're at our limit at the bank. But at least I can do what I want to with the money and not share it with anyone else." "What about the amount of time you spend at work? Any problem?" asked Bill. "Well... I usually get to the salon at 8 a.m. and don't leave until 10 or 11 p.m., if that's what you're asking," answered Jeff, "but you know, I don't mind, because this business is all mine, and it has been worth the hard work. Right now, though, I am having some problem finding a good person to help me out." "Listen", he continued," I have to go. I've got an appointment with the accountant in 20 minutes. He saved me a lot of money last year, and I didn't owe anything on my taxes. Great guy! My lawyer needs some information from him, too. I 'm making a will to make sure the kids will get the business if anything happens to me. Hey Bill, good luck!"

Identify the advantages and disadvantages Jeff mentioned regarding a sole proprietorship.

Learning Goal 2

2. There are four basic types of partnerships

| General partnership | Master limited partnership |
| Limited partnership | Limited liability partnership |

Using the information below, distinguish between each type of partnership

a. _____ Sunoco Logistics is a type of partnership that is traded on a stock exchange.

b. _____ Joe Allen invested in his friend Jose's business, but he doesn't have any management responsibilities.

c. _____ Dave Pardo and his partner Bettina Gregory both stand to lose a lot of money if their business goes under, as they are both responsible for the debt the business has undertaken.

d. _____ Even though any of us could buy stock in Perkins Family Restaurant, the company is taxed like a partnership.

e. _____ When Terry Esser invested in Dave and Bettina's company, she figured it was a minimal risk, because she (Terry) isn't active in the business and would only stand to lose what she invested if the company didn't make it.

f. _____ Randy Ford and Marty Dietrich have agreed to spend all their time managing the business they have just started.

g. _____ Partners in the now defunct Arthur Andersen who were not involved in the Enron scandal could expect to be exempt from losses incurred by guilty partners because Arthur Andersen is this type of partnership.

3. After some consideration, Bill Jacobs decided he would ask Jeff Baker if he could become a partner in Jeff's business. "After all," Bill said to himself, "I've got some money, and Jeff does want to expand, and he's looking for someone to work for him. I'll just work with him, give him some free time. I'm a little nervous about taking on the debt, but the statistics say we're more likely to stay in business than a sole proprietorship is, so it shouldn't be too bad."

Bill went to Jeff and began to discuss becoming a partner in the business.

"Whoa . . . wait a minute," interrupted Jeff when he heard Bill's offer. "I have to think about this. I like making my own decisions, and I like keeping my profits! How do I know you'll work as hard as I do? Who will work when? What happens when I want to borrow money for some new equipment and you don't want to?" Bill had to admit these were things he hadn't thought of. "Well . . . if it doesn't work out, we can just split up, can't we?" said Bill. "It's just not that simple, Bill." What advantages and disadvantages of partnerships did Bill and Jeff discuss? How could Bill and Jeff overcome some of the disadvantages?

Learning Goal 3

4. Bill and Jeff eventually did form a partnership. Business has been very good. They have expanded their facility, rented some space to several hair stylists, and added several product lines that compliment the tanning and hair salon area. They now have a total of three facilities and are wondering if they should incorporate their business, as they would like to expand even further, perhaps one day franchising their idea. What can you tell them about the advantages and disadvantages of incorporation, and what would you suggest for them?

5. What benefit does a corporation have over partnerships and sole proprietorships, for a small business owner?

6. There are several terms used to describe different types of corporations

alien   quasi-public
domestic   professional
foreign   nonprofit
closed (private)   multinational
open (public)

Match the type of corporation to each of the following:

a. _____   The stock of Maritz, Inc. is held by a small number of people and is not listed on a stock exchange.

b. _____   Proctor and Gamble has sold more than 200 million shares of stock.

c. _____   General Motors is incorporated in Delaware, but has its headquarters in Detroit, Michigan.

d. _____   You can have a Big Mac and fries in Three Rivers, Michigan, Paris, France, Sydney, Australia and Moscow, and expect the same quality.

e. _____   Toyota is incorporated in Japan, but has corporate offices located in the United States.

f. _____   Mainini Home Improvement is incorporated in Missouri, has its headquarters in Ellisville, Missouri, and only does business in Missouri.

g. _____   The Red Cross sponsors a classic car show and auction every year to raise funds for disaster relief.

h. _____   Ameren U.E., an electrical service provider, must apply to a government agency when it wants to raise rates to its customers.

i. _____   Dr. Kory and Dr. Schoenwalder have incorporated their practice of internal medicine in order to benefit from the advantages of incorporation, however their stock won't be traded on a exchange.

7. Two forms of business ownership have received some attention recently:

"S" corporations   Limited liability companies.

Which one is being described in the following?

a. _____   This offers flexible ownership rules and personal asset protection.

b. _____   This type can tell the IRS how it wants to be taxed.

c. _____   Looks like a corporation but is taxed like sole proprietorships and partnerships.

d. _____   If the company loses its status as this type of company, it can't reelect this status for five years.

e. _____   This business may have no more than 100 shareholders.

f. _____   With this form of ownership, there are fewer incentives available, and since there is no stock, stock options can't be used as an employee incentive.

Learning Goal 4

8. There are several types of corporate mergers and buyouts. Match the situation being described to the correct term:

Acquisition   Conglomerate merger
Vertical merger   Leveraged buyout
Horizontal merger   Taking a firm private

a. _____   Tommy Hilfilger bought its Canadian distributor and its American licensee, Pepe Jeans USA, in order to own manufacturing and distribution rights.

b. _____   When InBev bought Anheuser-Busch, they borrowed billions of dollars.

c. _____   The Boeing Company bought McDonnell Douglas. Subsequently, the McDonnell–Douglas Corporation ceased to exist.

d. _____   Two drug companies, Glaxo Wellcome PLC and SmithKline Beecham PLC began talks to merge their companies.

e. _____   Berkshire-Hathaway, which owns Dexter Shoe Company and International Dairy Queen, bought Helzberg Diamonds, a jewelry store chain in the Midwest.

f. _____   JLM founder John Macdonald and shareholder Philip Sassower, paid $1.40 per share for each of the roughly 5.3 million shares owned by other JLM investors and are now the sole owners of the business.

9. KFC is a nationwide fast-food franchise. All prospective KFC franchise owners must go through an evaluation process, during which they must submit an application and site proposal for approval and submit to a personal interview in Louisville, KY, KFC's headquarters. Upon approval, KFC offers the franchisee a training program covering management functions such as accounting, sales, advertising and purchasing. KFC pays a portion of this training program. KFC makes an advertising and promotion kit available to the franchisee as well as opening assistance, equipment layout plans, and a choice of interior decor from a list they provide. In addition to standard menu items, a franchisee may offer other items upon approval from KFC management. KFC outlines the estimated cash requirements for opening for such things as equipment, insurance payments, utility down payments, as well as for the facility itself to give franchisees an idea of their cash needs. The franchise fee and the costs of the building and land are the responsibility of the franchisee. There is a royalty rate based on a percentage of gross sales, which is paid on a regular basis to KFC for continuing franchises.

    KFC advertises on nationwide television on behalf of its franchisees, so local owners do not have to develop their own television advertising. The local owners do pay a percentage of their gross sales to KFC as a national advertising fee, and each franchisee is required to spend an additional percentage for local advertising.

    Based on this description, identify some of the benefits and drawbacks of owning a franchise.

10. There are many choices for business ownership. What would be the best choices for the following types of businesses? Why?

    a. Landscape/lawn care service

    b. Small manufacturer of a component part for automobiles

    c. Fast food restaurant

    d. Construction/Remodeling firm

Learning Goal 6

11.   Visit www.oceanspray.com and click on the "about us" link. What kind of cooperative is Ocean Spray, based on the description in the text?

PRACTICE TEST

MULTIPLE CHOICE—Circle the best answer

Learning Goal 1

1.   Which form of ownership is the most common?
    a.   Corporations
    b.   Master limited partnerships
    c.   General partnerships
    d.   Sole proprietorships

2.   One of the problems with a _____ is that there is no one with whom to share the burden of management
    a.   sole proprietorship
    b.   limited partnership
    c.   S corporation
    d.   limited liability company

3.   If you are interested in starting your own business, you want to minimize the hassle and you don't want to have anyone tell you what to do, you should organize your business as a (n):
    a.   S corporation.
    b.   limited partnership.
    c.   sole proprietorship.
    d.   closed corporation.

Learning Goal 2

4.   At Sound Off!, a store that buys and sells used c.d.'s, there is only one owner, Sonia.
    She spends all her time running the business, and makes all the decisions. Sonia's mother and brother put up money for her to buy the store, but they work full time at other jobs and have no management say in the running of Sound Off! This is an example of a:
    a.   general partnership.
    b.   master limited partnership.
    c.   S corporation.
    d.   limited partnership.

5.   When going into a partnership, you should always:
    a.   put all terms of the partnership into writing, in a partnership agreement.
    b.   make sure that you have limited liability while you are in charge.
    c.   make sure all the profits are reinvested into the company.
    d.   divide the profits equally.

6. A new form of business ownership looks like a corporation in that it is traded on the stock exchanges like a corporation, but it is taxed like a partnership and avoids the corporate income tax. This is known as a(n):
   a. sole proprietorship.
   b. master limited partnership.
   c. "S" corporation.
   d. general partnership.

7. One of the benefits a general partnership has over a sole proprietorship is:
   a. limited liability.
   b. more financial resources.
   c. easy to start.
   d. a board of directors to help with decisions.

8. Which form of partnership limits your liability to only your actions, or those of your subordinates, so that you can operate without fear that one of your partners might commit an action of malpractice that could cause you to lose your personal assets?
   a. General partnership
   b. Limited partnership
   c. Master Limited Partnership
   d. Limited Liability Partnership

Learning Goal 3

9. The owners of a corporation are called:
   a. general partners.
   b. stockholders.
   c. limited partners.
   d. proprietors.

10. A _____ is one whose stock is not available to the general public through a stock exchange.
    a. alien corporation
    b. domestic corporation
    c. public corporation
    d. closed corporation

11. Joe and Mark would like to start a new business selling a product new to the United States, the Peraves Monotracer. This is a motorcycle type vehicle that is encased in a sort of shell, so that the rider can ride this product in any kind of weather. Joe and Mark have done a considerable amount of research on this product, and think it would be successful in the U.S. However they are still concerned about the risk of a new venture and would like to avoid losing personal assets by organizing their firm as a:
    a. corporation.
    b. limited partnership.
    c. general partnership.
    d. sole proprietorship.

12. A form of ownership which can have only 100 shareholders, who must be permanent residents of the United States, is called a(n):
    a. conventional C corporation.
    b. closed corporation.
    c. limited liability partnership.
    d. S corporation.

13. _____ can be both an advantage and a disadvantage of a conventional corporation, as they have the ability to raise large amounts of money and hire experts, but can become inflexible and tied down in red tape.
    a. Size
    b. Tax returns
    c. Termination
    d. Limited liability

14. Which of the following is not considered an advantage of a limited liability company?
    a. limited number of shareholders
    b. personal asset protection
    c. choice of how to be taxed
    d. flexible ownership rules

15. When Jeanne-Marie Delacourt was born, her American grandmother bought her 10 shares of Disney stock. As Jeanne-Marie grows, so will her investment. However, if Disney should happen to go out of business:
    a. Jean-Marie will be responsible for some of the debt of Disney.
    b. Jean-Marie will have to go to court to show she has no involvement in the firm.
    c. Jean-Marie will only lose the value of her shares.
    d. Jean-Marie will have to borrow money from her grandmother to pay for the value of her shares.

16. In a corporation, the Board of Directors:
    a. consists of a group of major shareholders who want a say in running the business.
    b. is elected by the owners/stockholders.
    c. is made up of lenders to the corporation.
    d. has unlimited liability.

Learning Goal 4

17. When the Federated Department Stores, which owns several department store chains, bought the May Company, another department store chain, so Federated could expand their product offerings, it was a:
    a. vertical merger.
    b. horizontal merger.
    c. conglomerate merger.
    d. cooperative merger.

18. The main reason for a conglomerate merger is that:
    a. the investors want more for their money.
    b. it ensures a constant supply of materials needed by other companies.
    c. it allows for a firm to offer a variety of related products.
    d. the business can diversify its business operations and investments.

19. When a major national bakery bought out a smaller more regional bakery in the east, it took over all their assets and their debt and the smaller bakery ceased to exist. This is an example of a(n):
    a. acquisition.
    b. merger.
    c. nationalization.
    d. appropriation.

20. In order to avoid a hostile takeover by a Kollmorgaen, managers at Pacific Scientific considered making a bid for all the company's stock themselves and taking it off the open market. The term to describe this action is:
    a. a leveraged buyout.
    b. a conglomerate merger.
    c. taking the firm private.
    d. forming a master limited partnership.

Learning Goal 5

21. When Pat Sloane bought a Tidy Maid franchise, she became a:
    a. franchisor.
    b. stockholder.
    c. venture capitalist.
    d. franchisee.

22. One of the advantages of a franchise is:
    a. receiving management and marketing expertise from the franchisor.
    b. fewer restrictions on selling than in other forms of businesses.
    c. lower start up costs than other businesses.
    d. you get to keep all the profits of your business after taxes.

23. When your profitable franchise fails simply because other franchisees have failed, this is known as the:
    a. royalty rate.
    b. coattail effect.
    c. failure rate.
    d. green ceiling.

24. International franchising is:
    a. a successful area for both small and large franchises.
    b. costs about the same as domestic franchising.
    c. becoming increasingly difficult, and so is not growing.
    d. easy, because you really do not have to adapt your product at all.

Learning Goal 6

25. In a _____ , members democratically control the business by electing a board of directors that hires professional management.
    a. corporation
    b. cooperative
    c. franchise
    d. master limited partnership

TRUE–FALSE

Learning Goal 1

1. _____ One of the benefits of a sole proprietorship is that you have easy availability of funds from a variety of sources.

2. _____ It is relatively easy to get in and out of business when you are a sole proprietor.

3. _____ A common complaint among sole proprietors is that good workers are hard to find because they can't afford to pay competitive salaries and fringe benefits.

Learning Goal 2

4. _____ It is best to form a limited partnership because then there is no one individual who takes on the unlimited liability.

5. _____ In a partnership, one of the major disadvantages is the potential for disagreements among the partners.

6. _____ A master limited partnership is much like a corporation because its stock is traded on a stock exchange.

Learning Goal 3

7. _____ Individuals are not permitted to incorporate.

8. _____ Corporations are the easiest form of ownership to start and terminate.

9. _____ One advantage of a corporation is the limited liability of the owners.

10. _____ An S corporation avoids the double taxation of a conventional C corporation.

11. _____ A disadvantage of incorporation is the possibility of conflict between the officers of the corporation and the stockholders and/or the board of directors.

12. _____ A limited liability company can choose to be taxed either as a corporation or as a partnership.

Learning Goal 4

13. _____ An example of a vertical merger was the merger between Daimler, a German automaker, and Chrysler, an American automotive manufacturer.

14. _____ In a leveraged buyout the managers of a company buy all of the stock of a firm and take it off the open market.

Learning Goal 5

15. _____ A franchise can be formed as a sole proprietorship, a partnership, or a corporation.

16. _____ As a franchisee, you are entitled to financial advice and assistance from the franchisor.

17. _____ One of the disadvantages of a franchise is that if you want to sell, the franchisor must approve the new owner.

18. _____ Female participation in franchising grows as the cost of the franchise increases.

19. _____ One of the advantages that a home based franchisee has over a business owner based at home is that the franchisee feels less isolated.

Learning Goal 6

20. _____ One common element of a cooperative is for members to work a few hours a month as part of their duties.

You Can Find It On the Net

INC Magazine is dedicated to helping small businesses get off the ground. Visit their website at www.inc.com

What special hints are available to small business owners?

What kinds of advice does INC make available to entrepreneurs and small business owners?

What kinds of resources are offered to buyers and sellers of businesses?

Go back to the home page. What information is offered about franchising?

If you are interested in obtaining a specific franchise, you can click onto the Buying a Franchise page and download the franchise evaluation form provided by this site. Use it to evaluate your potential business.

Now, visit www.betheboss.com

What are the most popular franchise opportunities?

Click on the Resources link, then on the Introduction to Franchising.

What are the four types of franchises?

What are the 5 steps of franchising, according to this site?

Take the Interactive Self-Test – Are you a good candidate to buy a franchise?

There are also a number of helpful guides on this site to determine the financial requirements of a franchise you might be interested in acquiring.

ANSWERS

LEARNING THE LANGUAGE

1.	Horizontal merger	10.	Master limited partnership (MLP)	18.	General partnership
2.	Partnership	11.	Corporation	19.	Leveraged buyout (LBO)
3.	Franchise agreement	12.	Merger	20.	Franchise
4.	Acquisition	13.	Franchisee	21.	Vertical merger
5.	Limited liability	14.	Limited partner	22.	Sole proprietorship
6.	S Corporation	15.	Limited liability company	23.	Unlimited liability
7.	Franchisor	16.	General partner	24.	Limited liability partnership
8.	Conglomerate merger	17.	Cooperative	25.	Conventional corporation
9.	Limited partnership				

ASSESSMENT CHECK

Learning Goal 1

Basic Forms of Business Ownership

1. a. sole proprietorship
    b. partnership
    c. corporation

    The sole proprietorship is the most common form of business ownership

2. A corporation is the only form of ownership where the business is separate from the owners.

3. a. Ease of starting and ending business
    b. Being your own boss
    c. Pride of ownership
    d. Leaving a legacy
    e. Retention of company profit
    f. No special taxes

4. All you have to do to start a sole proprietorship is buy or lease the needed equipment and put up some announcements indicating that you are in business. You may have to get a permit or license from the local government.

5. Profits of a sole proprietorship are taxed as the personal income of the owner.

6. a. Unlimited liability and the risk of losses
    b. Limited financial resources
    c. Management difficulties
    d. Overwhelming time commitment
    e. Few fringe benefits
    f. Limited growth
    g. Limited life span

7. With a sole proprietorship, the debts or damages incurred by the business are your debts and you must pay them, even if it means selling your personal assets.

8. The forms of ownership that have a greater probability of obtaining the needed financial backing are partnerships and corporations.

Learning Goal 2

Partnerships

9. Four forms of partnerships agreements are:
   a. general partnership.   c. master limited partnership.
   b. limited partnership.

10. In a *general partnership* agreement, the partners agree to share in the operation of the business and assume unlimited liability for the company's debts. In a *limited partnership*, the limited partners do not have an active role in managing the business, and have liability only up to the amount invested in the firm. That is called limited liability.
    There must be at least one general partner in any partnership.

11. A general partner is active in managing the firm and has unlimited liability. A limited partner invests money in the business, but doesn't have any management responsibilities.

12. A master limited partnership looks much like a corporation and is traded on the stock exchange like a corporation, but is taxed like a partnership and so avoids the corporate income tax.

13. An LLP limits partners' risk of losing their personal assets to only their own acts and to the acts of the people under their supervision. Thus, an LLP allows you to operate without the fear that one of your partners might commit an act of malpractice that would result in a judgment that takes away your assets. This protection may not extend to liabilities such as bank loans and other financial obligations.

14. The Uniform Partnership Act identifies these elements as key to a general partnership
    a. Common ownership.
    b. Shared profits and losses.
    c. The right to participate in managing the operations of the business.

15. Advantages of partnerships include:
    a. More financial resources.
    b. Shared management/pooled skills and knowledge.
    c. Longer survival.
    d. No special taxes.

16. Disadvantages of partnerships include:
    a. Unlimited liability.
    b. Division of profits.
    c. Disagreements among partners.
    d. Difficult to terminate.

17. In a partnership each general partner is liable for the debts of the firm, no matter who was responsible for causing the debts. You, as a partner, are responsible for your partner's mistakes as well as your own.

18. Because of potential conflict between partners, all the terms of the partnership should be spelled out in writing in a partnership agreement.

Learning Goal 3

Corporations

19. The fact that a corporation is separate from its owners means that the owners are not liable for the debts or any other problems of the corporation beyond the money they invest. Another name for the owners of a corporation is a stockholder.

20. The advantages of a "C" corporation include:
     a. Limited liability.
     b. More money for investment.
     c. Size.
     d. Perpetual life.
     e. Ease of ownership change.
     f. Ease of drawing talented employees.
     g. Separation of ownership from management.

21. A corporation can raise money by:
     a. selling stock, or ownership, to anyone who is interested.
     b. borrowing money from individual investors through issuing bonds.
     c. obtaining loans from financial institutions.

22. Because large corporations have the ability to raise large amounts of money to work with, corporations can build modern factories or software development firms with the latest equipment. They can hire experts or specialists, and buy other corporations to diversify their risk. In other words, they have the size and resources to take advantage of opportunities anywhere in the world. However, a company does not have to be large to be a corporation. Individuals and small companies can also incorporate.

23. The owners have an influence on how a business is managed by electing the board of directors. The directors hire the officers of the corporation and oversee major policy issues. The owners/stockholders thus have some say in who runs the corporation but they have no control over the daily operations.

24. The disadvantages of a "C" corporation include:
     a. Initial cost.
     b. Paperwork.
     c. Double taxation.
     d. Two tax returns.
     e   Size.
     f. Difficulty of termination.
     g. Possible conflict with stockholders and board of directors.

25.   Corporate income is taxed twice, because the corporation pays tax on income before it can distribute any to stockholders, then the stockholder pays tax on the income they receive from the corporation. If an individual incorporates, he or she must file a corporate return and an individual tax return.

26. Size can be a disadvantage because large corporations sometimes become too inflexible and too tied down in red tape to respond quickly to market changes.

27. The structure of a corporation looks like this:

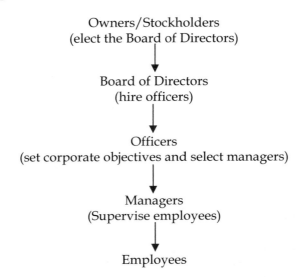

Owners/Stockholders
(elect the Board of Directors)

Board of Directors
(hire officers)

Officers
(set corporate objectives and select managers)

Managers
(Supervise employees)

Employees

28. The major advantages to individuals incorporating are limited liability and possible tax benefits.

29. a. Have no more than 100 shareholders.
    b. Have shareholders that are individuals or estates and are citizens or permanent residents of the United States.
    c. Have only one class of outstanding stock.
    d. Not have more than 25% of income derived from passive sources such as rents, royalties, interest etc.

30. The paperwork and some details of the S corporation are similar to those of conventional C corporations. S corporations have shareholders, directors, and employees and have the benefit of limited liability.
    However, S corporations are taxed as the personal income of the shareholders so the owners avoid double taxation.

31. The types of corporations other than "S" include:
    a. Alien
    b. Domestic
    c. Foreign
    d. Closed (private)
    e. Open (public)
    f. Quasi-public
    g. Professional
    h. Nonprofit
    i. Multinational

32. The advantages of limited liability companies are:
    a. Limited liability.
    b. Choice of taxation.
    c. Flexible ownership rules.
    d. Flexible distribution of profit and losses.
    e. Operating flexibility.

33. The disadvantages of an LLC include:
    a. No stock – so LLC ownership is not transferable.
    b. Limited life span – dissolution dates must be identified, and in some states can be no more than 30 years.
    c. Fewer incentives – benefits can't be deducted and there are no stock options.
    d. Taxes – must pay self-employment taxes on profits.
    e. Paperwork – more than for a sole proprietorship.

34. LLC ownership is not transferable. LLC members need the approval of other members in order to sell their interests.

35. The death of an LLC member can cause the company to dissolve automatically.

Learning Goal 4

Corporate Expansion: Mergers and Acquisitions

36. An acquisition is one company buying the property and obligations of another company, while a merger is when two companies join and create one company. It's like the difference between a marriage (merger) and buying a house (acquisition).

37. a. A vertical merger joins two firms involved in different stages of related businesses, like a merger between a soft drink company and a company that produces artificial sweeteners.
    b. A horizontal merger joins two firms in the same industry and allows them to diversify or expand their products, like a soft drink company and a mineral water company.
    c. A conglomerate merger unites firms in completely unrelated industries, like a soft drink company and a food company. The primary purpose of a conglomerate merger is to diversify business operations and investments.

38. When taking a firm private, a group of stockholders or management obtains all a firm's stock for themselves.

39. A leveraged buyout is an attempt by employees, management, or a group of investors to purchase an organization primarily through borrowing. The funds borrowed are used to buy out the stockholders in the company. The employees, managers, or investors now become the owners of the firm.

40. No, business acquisitions are not limited to U. S. buyers. In 2007 foreign investors poured $414 billion into U. S. companies.

Learning Goal 5

Special Forms of Business Ownership

41. A *franchisor* is someone with a good idea for a business who sells the right to use the business name to someone else, the *franchisee.*

42. The advantages of a franchise are:
    a. Management and marketing assistance.   d. Financial advice and assistance.
    b. Personal ownership.   e. Lower failure rate.
    c. Nationally recognized name.

43. A franchisee has a greater chance of succeeding because he or she has an established product, help with choosing a location, help with promotion, and assistance in all phases of operation.

44. The disadvantages of franchising are:
    a. High start up costs.
    b. Shared profit.
    c. Management regulation.
    d. Coattail effects.
    e. Restrictions on selling.
    f. Fraudulent franchisors.

45. The coattail effect is a term used to describe the fact that if other franchisees fail, you could be forced out of business even if your particular franchise has been profitable.

46. Studies show that as the cost of a franchise increases, female ownership decreases and women receive little venture capital money. As a result, women are becoming franchisors as well as franchisees when they have trouble obtaining financing to expand their business.

47. Minority owned businesses are increasing rapidly, and franchisors are becoming focused on recruiting minority franchisees.

48. The U.S. Commerce Department's Federal Minority Business Development Agency provides minorities with training in how to run a franchise.

49. Four advantages of home franchising are:
    a. Relief from the time and stress of commuting.
    b. Extra time for family activities.
    c. low overhead expenses.
    d. home based franchisees feel less isolated than other home based business owners.

50. Many franchisees with existing brick-and-mortar stores are expanding their businesses online. Franchisees that started with a limited territory are branching out to customers throughout the world. Many franchisors prohibit franchisee-sponsored websites. Conflicts between franchisors and franchisees can erupt if the franchisor then creates its own website. The franchisees may be concerned that the site will pull sales from their brick and mortar locations.

51. Franchisors are using technology to meet the needs of both their customers and their franchisees. Technology can streamline communication, give immediate access to subjects involving the franchise operation, including forms to complete. Franchisees can be kept up to date on company news via e-mail.

52. Some areas of the world which are popular for international franchising include:

Canada	Malaysia
South Africa	Indonesia
the Philippines	Singapore
the Caribbean	Japan
the Middle East	Venezuela
	Thailand

The United States has become a popular market for foreign franchisors.

53. The characteristics that make franchising successful in international markets are convenience and a predictable level of service and quality. Franchisors must also be careful to adapt to the region.

Cooperatives

54. Two kinds of cooperatives can be described as:

    a. A cooperative in which members/customers work at the cooperative for a number of hours a month as part of their duties. Members control these businesses by electing a board of directors that hires professional management.

    b. Another kind of cooperative is formed to give members more economic power as a group than they would have as individuals. These are often farm cooperatives, which now buy and sell fertilizer, farm equipment, seed, and other products needed on the farm. These cooperatives now own many manufacturing facilities. Farm cooperatives do not pay the same kind of taxes as corporations and so have an advantage in the marketplace.

55. Some successful cooperatives include Land O Lakes, Sunkist, Ocean Spray, Blue Diamond, Associated Press, Ace Hardware, True Value Hardware, Riceland Foods and Welch's.

CRITICAL THINKING EXERCISES

Learning Goal 1

1. Jeff and Bill covered most of the advantages and disadvantages of owning a sole proprietorship. Jeff mentioned the ease of starting the business, the fact that you are your own boss and how proud he seemed to be of what he had accomplished with his hard work. He also mentioned that his tax liability was reasonable (in other words, he didn't have to pay any special taxes), and that he was making a profit that was his to keep and do with as he pleased. Some of the disadvantages Jeff mentioned were that he worked long hours, and had some difficulty in finding financial sources beyond the bank. He was nervous about the unlimited financial liability, and agreed that few fringe benefits was a concern. He also noted that he's having a problem finding a good person to work for him as is common with sole proprietorships. Lastly, he noted one final disadvantage of sole proprietorship, the limited life span. He is making arrangements for his children to inherit the business and continue with it if something happens to him.

Learning Goal 2

2. a. Master Limited Partnership (MLP)
   b. Limited partnership
   c. General partnership
   d. MLP
   e. Limited partnership
   f. General partnership
   g. Limited Liability partnership

3. It appears that Bill thought of most of the advantages and Jeff could only find disadvantages! Bill realized that he could give Jeff the financial resources he needed, and could relieve Bill of the long hours he was spending at the business. He also recognized that statistics indicate that partnerships have a longer survival rate than sole proprietorships. The one disadvantage Bill mentioned was the unlimited liability taken on by a general partner. Jeff was quick to point out the disadvantages of shared profits, potential disagreements and the difficulty of terminating a partnership.

   One way that Bill and Jeff could overcome some of these problems is to put all of the conditions of the partnership in writing, in the form of a partnership agreement.

4. There are a number of things to consider before Bill and Jeff decide to incorporate. If they are interested in expanding even further, incorporating would give them a wider source of funds for investment, because they could sell stock and keep the investors out of management for the most part. However, their business is small, and there is a question of how "marketable" their stock would be. A major advantage for them both is the aspect of limited liability. Expansion may require going into debt, and if they incorporate, Bill and Jeff would not be liable should something happen to the business. Another advantage for both of the partners is the perpetual life of a corporation. If something should happen to either Bill or Jeff, the remaining owners could still continue with the business. Further, if one of them decided to get out of the business, it is relatively easy, as they would simply have to sell their stock to the remaining owners.

    One major disadvantage of incorporating is the initial cost, which can be very high. It also requires a lot of additional paperwork, particularly regarding the accounting records. Bill and Jeff would have to file more tax returns, and they would be taxed twice, once on their earned income and additionally on the income they received from dividends.

    It appears that Bill and Jeff should incorporate, as it looks like the advantages may outweigh the disadvantages. Because they are a small company, they will become a closed corporation. That will eliminate the problem of having a market for their stock. They may also want to consider becoming an "S" corporation.

5. One of the primary advantages of a corporation over proprietorships and partnerships is unlimited liability for the owners. There are additional sources of revenue for a corporation and many times it is easier to attract talented employees because a corporation may be able to offer better benefits. Some corporations are very large, and so size becomes a distinct advantage in terms of facilities and the ability to hire specialties. For a small business owner, the primary advantages would seem to be the unlimited liability, perpetual life, and ease of ownership change.

6.
a.	Closed	f.	Domestic
b.	Open	g.	Nonprofit
c.	Foreign	h.	Quasi public
d.	Multinational	i.	Professional
e.	Alien		

7.
a.	Limited liability	d.	"S" corporation
b.	Limited liability	e.	"S" corporation
c.	"S" corporation	f.	Limited liability

8.
a.	vertical merger	d.	horizontal merger
b.	leveraged buyout	e.	conglomerate merger
c.	acquisition	f.	taking a firm private

9. This description identifies several of the benefits of owning a franchise. One of the first in this case is the fact that KFC is a nationally recognized name, which almost guarantees an established customer base. That helps to reduce the risk of failing. KFC provides management training and pays for part of it. They offer advice with opening the store, for such things as advertising, for such things as layout and interior decor. They offer financial advice also and give the franchisee a feel for what the initial costs are going to be. The franchisee can take advantage of a national advertising campaign, while still advertising on a local basis so they are able to meet local needs.

    The drawbacks stem from the franchise fee, which could be relatively high for a nationally recognized franchise, and adds to the initial cost of opening. Further, a royalty rate must be paid on a regular basis to KFC, which takes away part of your profits, and the franchisee must contribute to a national advertising fund. Your menu items are limited to what the franchisor tells you, and you must get permission to offer anything different, so you are closely regulated in terms of the menu, as well as interior decor.

Learning Goals 1, 2, 3

10. a. The landscape/lawn care firm could start out as a sole proprietorship or partnership. There may be no great need for capital to start out with, so there would be no need to incorporate. A partnership may be an advantage because of the amount of labor involved, in order to build the business and do more than one job in a day. Another possibility would be to be a sole proprietor and hire workers to help.

    b. A small manufacturer of component parts would likely do best as a corporation, primarily due to the capital investment required and the need for a variety of skills such as marketing, manufacturing, engineering and so on. There is also the potential for liability in a manufacturing setting, and a corporate structure would protect the owners. This may initially be a closed corporation or even an "S" corporation.

    c. If you want to get into the fast food business, one of the easiest ways would be to investigate owning a franchise. Some fast food franchises are among the fastest growing franchises in the country, and the industry is very competitive. A "guaranteed" market would be a definite plus! The drawback is the initial expense, but if you can come up with the money a franchise may be the best way to go.

    d. The construction/remodeling business again could be a sole proprietorship or partnership. There is a definite need for several people to be working, so you could either hire workers to work for you, or find a partner who can help in the business. The investment in tools may be substantial which may be another indication of the need for a partner.

Learning Goal 6

11. Based upon the description in the text it appears that Ocean Spray is the kind of cooperative set up to give members more economic power as a group than they would have as individuals. The members of the cooperative are cranberry growers who initially formed in order to expand their market, and the cooperative has grown since its inception to a large organization with many different products, while remaining a cooperative.

PRACTICE TEST

MULTIPLE CHOICE

1.	d	14.	a
2.	a	15.	c
3.	c	16.	b
4.	d	17.	b
5.	a	18.	d
6.	b	19.	a
7.	b	20.	c
8.	d	21.	d
9.	b	22.	a
10.	d	23.	b
11.	a	24.	a
12.	d	25.	b
13.	a		

TRUE–FALSE

1.	F	11.	T
2.	T	12.	T
3.	T	13.	F
4.	F	14.	F
5.	T	15.	T
6.	T	16.	T
7.	F	17.	T
8.	F	18.	F
9.	T	19.	T
10.	T	20.	T

CHAPTER 6 – ENTREPRENEURSHIP AND STARTING A SMALL BUSINESS

LEARNING GOALS

After you have read and studied this chapter, you should be able to:

1. Explain why people are willing to take the risks of entrepreneurship, list the attributes of successful entrepreneurs, describe the benefits of entrepreneurial teams and intrapreneurs, and explain the growth of home-based and Web-based businesses.
2. Discuss the importance of small business to the American economy and summarize the major causes of small-business failures.
3. Summarize ways to learn about how small businesses operate.
4. Analyze what it takes to start and run a small business.
5. Outline the advantages and disadvantages small businesses have in entering global markets.

LEARNING THE LANGUAGE

Listed here are important terms found in this chapter. Choose the correct term for each definition and write it in the space provided.

Affiliate marketing	Market
Business plan	Micropreneurs
Enterprise zones	Service Corps of Retired Executives (SCORE)
Entrepreneurial team	Small business
Entrepreneurship	Small Business Administration (SBA)
Incubators	Small-business investment company program (SBIC)
Intrapreneurs	Venture capitalists

1. A _____ consists of people with unsatisfied wants and needs who have both the resources and willingness to buy.

2. Governments try to attract private business investment to specific geographic areas known as _____ by offering lower taxes and other government support.

3. A group of experienced people from different areas of business who join together as a(n) _____ form a managerial team with the skills needed to develop, make, and market a new product.

4. A _____ is independently owned and operated, not dominant in its field of operation, and meets certain standards of size in terms of employees or annual receipts.

5. Individuals or companies known as _____ invest in new businesses in exchange for partial ownership of those businesses.

6. Centers called_____ offer new businesses low-cost offices with basic business services.

7. The SBA office known as the _____ has volunteers from industry, trade associations, and education who counsel services for small businesses at no cost, except for expenses.

8. _____ is accepting the risk of starting and running a business.

9. Creative people known as _____ work as entrepreneurs within corporations.

10. A _____ is a detailed written statement that describes the nature of the business, the target market, the advantages the business will have in relation to competition, and the resources and qualifications of the owners.

11. The program through which private investment companies are licensed by the Small Business Administration to lend money to small businesses is called the _____.

12. _____ are entrepreneurs willing to accept the risk of starting and managing the type of business that remains small, lets them do the kind of work they want to do, and offers them a balanced lifestyle.

13. The U.S. government agency called the _____ advises and assists small businesses by providing management training and financial advice and loans.

14. An internet-based marketing strategy in which a business rewards individuals or other businesses (affiliates) for each visitor or customer sent to its web site is known as _____

ASSESSMENT CHECK

Learning Goal 1

Why People Take the Entrepreneurial Challenge

1. What are four reasons why people become entrepreneurs?

    a. _____

    b. _____

    c. _____

    d. _____

2. Five desirable attributes for entrepreneurs are:

    a. _____

    b. _____

    c. _____

    d. _____

    e. _____

3. You may have a business idea that is a good opportunity if:

   a. _____

   b. _____

   c. _____

   d. _____

4. Why might entrepreneurial teams be better than an individual entrepreneur?

5. Describe a micropreneur and how he or she differs from an entrepreneur.

6. Describe the reasons for the growth of home-based businesses

   a. _____

   b. _____

   c. _____

   d. _____

7. Identify 5 challenges faced by the owners of home-based businesses.

   a. _____

   b. _____

   c. _____

   d. _____

   e. _____

8. If you are interested in getting into a home office, you should focus on:

   a. _____ instead of _____

   b. _____ instead of _____

   c. _____ instead of _____

   d. _____ instead of _____

   e. _____ instead of _____

9. How "big" are Web based businesses?

10. What must Web-based businesses do to be successful?

11. Describe affiliate marketing. What is a widget, and how does it work?

12. Describe a shopping widget operator, such as Lemonade Stand.

13. What is the difference between an entrepreneur and an intrapreneur? What is the idea behind intrapreneurs?

14. What was part of the intention of the Immigration Act of 1990? What are investor visas?

15. In addition to investor visas, what are two ways governments could encourage entrepreneurship?

   a. _____

   b. _____

16. What kinds of services are offered by incubators? How do they help businesses survive?

Getting Started In Small Business

17. What are three criteria used by the SBA to classify a business as "small"?

   a. _____

   b. _____

   c. _____

18. How is it that a business that employs 1,500 people, or has revenues of $22 million, be considered small?

19. What are some statistics that illustrate the impact of small business on the American economy?

   a. _____

   b. _____

   c. _____

   d. _____

   e. _____

   f. _____

   g. _____

20. What are two advantages small business owners believe they have over big business?

21. What is the failure rate of small business? Why are the statistics misleading?

22. a. If you want to be both independent and rich, you need to go after: _____

   b. In general the easiest businesses to start are: _____

   c. In general the easiest businesses to keep alive are: _____

   d. In general the businesses that can make you rich are: _____

Learning Goal 3

Learning About Small-Business Operations

23. What are three ways to learn about small business?

    a. _____

    b. _____

    c. _____

24. What will other small business owners tell you when you talk to them about running your own business?

    a. _____

    b. _____

    c. _____

    d. _____

25. What is the "rule of thumb" about getting experience in small business? How do you get this experience?

26. Three factors used to determine the value of a business are:

    a. _____

    b. _____

    c. _____

Learning Goal 4

Managing a Small Business

27. What two management functions are of primary concern when you are first starting your business? What three functions are of concern after the start-up, when managing the business?

28. A business plan is: _____

_____

29. List the tips for small business owners who want to borrow money from a bank.

a. _____

b. _____

c. _____

d. _____

e. _____

f. _____

g. _____

30. List the information that generally should be included in a business plan.

a. _____

b. _____

c. _____

d. _____

e. _____

f. _____

g. _____

h. _____

i. _____

j. _____

31. What are two software programs that can help with writing a business plan?

32. List several sources of small business funding.

   a. _____

   b. _____

   c. _____

   d. _____

   e. _____

   f. _____

   g. _____

   h. _____

   i. _____

   j. _____

33. According to the text, the most common source of funding is _____.

34. Describe an angel investor.

35. What is peer-to-peer lending?

36. What is one potential drawback with using venture capital?

37. If you're a very small company, which funding source are you more likely to use, venture capital or an angel investor? Why?

38. What are microloans and what criteria are used to award microloans?

39. A Small Business Investment Company can help small businesses from defaulting on loans by

_____

_____

40. Describe a Small Business Development Center, and how they help small businesses.

41. Three important factors for success in your small business are:

a. _____

b. _____

c. _____

42. Once you have identified your market and its needs, you must:

_____

43. What is one of the greatest advantages small businesses have over larger businesses?

44. What three criteria are critical for a small business owner with regard to managing employees?

a. _____

b. _____

c. _____

45. How do employees of small businesses often feel about their jobs? Why?

46. What are the challenges in small businesses regarding promotion and delegating authority?

47. Small business owners say they need the most assistance in the area of _____.

48. Computers can help a small business owner in the area of accounting by:

_____

_____

_____

49. How can an accountant help in managing a small business?

50. What are five areas in which you may need assistance as a small business owner?

    a. _____   d. _____

    b. _____   e. _____

    c. _____

51. In what ways can a lawyer help a small business owner?

52. In what areas will a marketing research study help a small business owner?

    a. _____

    b. _____

    c. _____

53. Would an Internet site be important if you aren't planning to sell products online?

54. How would a small business owner benefit from the advice of a commercial loan officer and an insurance agent?

55. Describe some important sources of information for small business owners.

a. _____

b. _____

c. _____

d. _____

e. _____

f. _____

g. _____

h. _____

Learning Goal 5

Going International: Small-Business Prospects

56. In general, what is the level of small businesses involvement in the global market place?

57. What are four hurdles small businesses face in the international market?

a. _____

b. _____

c. _____

d. _____

58. Small businesses have advantages over large business in the international market because:

a. _____

b. _____

c. _____

d. _____

CRITICAL THINKING EXERCISES

Learning Goal 1

1. Eric is a young man with a vision. He sees himself as heading up a large corporation someday, a company that he has started and helped to grow. He has basically supported himself since he was fifteen, and has, at the age of 20, already started and sold 2 successful small businesses. Right now he is going to college full time because he feels that getting an education will be beneficial to him in the long run. He is supporting himself partially with the money he received from the sale of his last business. He intends to start yet another business as soon as he graduates.

    Eric's most recent business was in a fairly competitive market in the area in which he lives. He says that while he received some encouragement from a few friends, for the most part they all said he was crazy to work as hard as he was working. But Eric says he just felt that he "had to do things my own way" and built his business to become the second largest of its type in the area.

    How does Eric portray the entrepreneurial attributes your text identifies?

Learning Goals 2, 3

2. Eric seems to have beaten the odds already. What do you think Eric would tell you about success (or failure) and how to learn to be a successful small business owner?

3. Now, fast forward a few years. Eric has graduated from school, and is ready to start his new business. He has never applied for a bank loan, and has come to you for advice on how to continue beat the odds. What will you tell him?

4. Maria Ruiz has a degree in business, but at this point in her business career has decided to stay home with her small children. Maria would like to start a small home-based business helping other small business owners write business plans, and contracting with other, larger business, in writing grant proposals. What would you tell Maria about home-based businesses and the challenges she will face?

Learning Goals 3, 4

5. After planning and financing, the functions necessary to be successful in running your small business include:

Knowing your market	Keeping efficient records
Managing employees	Looking for help

Read the following situation, keeping in mind what you have learned about operating successful small businesses. Do you think this small business will "beat the odds?"

Dave and Kevin worked together as sales representatives for a clothing manufacturer in Michigan. They were successful, but were interested in working on their own, and developed a plan for a partnership as manufacturer's representatives selling clothing and hats to their current customers, using a supplier network they would develop. While they were working full time, Dave and Kevin spent 6 months finding backers and lining up suppliers, and got a feel for which of their current customers they could count on later. They casually consulted with an accountant and a lawyer.

Finally they decided they were ready, and opened up under the name of Premium Incentives, Inc. Here is the situation on the day Premium Incentives opened:

* They each worked at home.

* They had promises, but no written contract from two suppliers to lend them a total of $100,000 over a one year period in return for all their business.

* They decided not to do a business plan, as they already had financing.

* Dave's wife agreed to do the bookkeeping as a favor. She had a degree in business, but not in accounting. However she had a full time job and a three-year-old child and was expecting another child in 5 months.

* They hired sales representatives to help with sales outside their home state, and planned to pay them on commission.

* They set up a price schedule designed to under-cut their competitors by a significant amount.

After two months in business, Dave and Kevin were still hopeful, but disappointed. They had made $5000 in sales, but hadn't yet been paid, as the product hadn't been delivered to the customers, and they had over $3,000 in start-up expenses. This would not have been a problem had the suppliers come through on their promises to finance Premium Incentives. However, one of the suppliers, after reconsidering, decided not to lend them any money, and the second dropped his offer down to $5000 a month for six months, with repayment beginning in the seventh month. Since Premium Incentives, Inc. did not have a written contract, they had no legal recourse. Dave and Kevin didn't worry too much about repaying the loan, as they figured they still had four months to build up the business. The problem was, their customers weren't buying as much as Dave and Kevin had anticipated, and they weren't sure what to do to find new customers.

Dave's wife was having problems keeping up with the books, so Dave began spending several days a week working on that, in addition to trying to sell. His wife suggested they develop some way of billing a customer, then re-billing if they hadn't paid within 15 days. Dave and Kevin disagreed about what to do, and eventually did nothing. They did finally hire a bookkeeper after several months of doing the books themselves. They continued to struggle with not knowing when a customer was going to pay, and therefore had no idea how much income they were going to have each month.

What do you think? What did Dave and Kevin do right? What did they do wrong? What are their chances of success?

Learning Goal 4

6. A. Draw up a list of the types of consultants whose services you may need in starting and managing your small business.

a. _____   e. _____

b. _____   f. _____

c. _____   g. _____

d. _____

B. What other sources of information are available?

a. _____   d. _____

b. _____   e. _____

c. _____   f. _____

Learning Goal 5

7. Chad Lane is the owner of a small software business based in California. Chad is interested in growing his business, but he has seen that the market in the U.S. has become very competitive, and the technology market as a whole has slowed considerably. He is considering the possibilities of "going global" with his small business, and would like to explore some international opportunities. What would you tell him as his advisor?

PRACTICE TEST

MULTIPLE CHOICE — Circle the best answer

Learning Goal 1

1. Entrepreneurs take the risk of starting a business for all of the following reasons except:
   a. they want independence.
   b. they like the challenge and the risk.
   c. they want to make money for themselves.
   d. they want to work less.

2. Steve Jacobie is an entrepreneur to the max. Steve has started three businesses, two of which he sold for a great deal of money. He is now involved in running his third business, with plans to sell it shortly and start yet another one. When commenting on his success as an entrepreneur, he says that once an idea comes to him, he just can't wait to start working on it and bring it to reality, and that is what he focuses on. Which of the traits of successful entrepreneurs does this suggest is characteristic of Steve?
   a. Action-oriented
   b. Self nurturing
   c. Self-directed
   d. Tolerant of uncertainty

3. An entrepreneurial team is:
   a. a group of people who work within a corporation to launch new products.
   b. a group of experienced people who join together to develop and market a new product.
   c. a group from the Small Business Administration which consults with small business owners.
   d. a group of managers who get together to find creative solutions to problems.

4. Federico Romero is a business owner who works from home as a freelance video producer. He really enjoys his work, but isn't looking to "set the world on fire" with his company. He just wants to make a good living and spend time with his family when he can. Federico would be classified as a(n)
   a. entrepreneur.
   b. intrapreneur.
   c. micropreneur.
   d. venture capitalist.

5. An incubator is:
   a. A U.S. government agency that advises and assists small businesses.
   b. A program through which private investment companies licensed by the S.B.A. lend money to small businesses.
   c. A center that offers new businesses low-cost offices with basic business services.
   d. A specific geographic area to which governments try to attract private businesses by a variety of means.

6. Which of the following is among the challenges faced by those with home based businesses?
   a. Computer technology
   b. Managing time
   c. Changes in social attitudes
   d. New tax laws

7. Affiliate marketing is:
   a. an internet-based marketing strategy in which a business rewards individuals or other businesses for sending visitors to their website.
   b. a social networking strategy.
   c. a marketing strategy for developing business plans that will work for many types of related businesses.
   d. a strategy for marketing similar, or complementary, types of businesses on the Internet.

Learning Goal 2

8. Which of the following is a false statement about small business?
   a. Small businesses account for more than 50 percent of G.D.P.
   b. The vast majority of non-farm businesses in the U.S. are considered small.
   c. The first job for most Americans will probably not be in a small business.
   d. The majority of the country's new jobs are in small business.

9. A small business:
   a. must have fewer than 100 employees to be considered small.
   b. is considered small relative to other businesses in its industry.
   c. cannot be a corporation.
   d. should be an S corporation.

10. Miriam Njunge wants to start a small business importing some products from her native Kenya. Before she starts, some good advice to Miriam would be:
   a. talk to others who have been or are in the import business.
   b. get a loan right away.
   c. find a business to buy as soon as possible.
   d. incorporate immediately.

11. In measuring the value of a small firm, which of the following would not be included?
   a. What the business owns.
   b. What the business earns.
   c. What makes the business unique.
   d. What products the business sells globally.

Learning Goal 3

12. The primary concerns when first starting your business are:
   a. marketing and accounting.
   b. planning and human resources.
   c. financing and planning.
   d. financing and marketing.

13. A business plan for a new business does not need to include:
   a. a marketing plan.
   b. a discussion of the purpose of the business.
   c. a description of the company background.
   d. the name of the lending bank.

14. What are the primary sources of funding for entrepreneurs?
    a. personal savings and individual investors
    b. finance companies and banks
    c. the Small Business Administration and banks
    d. former employers and the Economic Development Authority

15. For a market to exist there must be potential buyers:
    a. and a product that is safe and inexpensive.
    b. who have a willingness and the resources to buy.
    c. and stores which are willing to carry the product.
    d. who are looking for a bargain.

16. According to the text, one of the drawbacks of using venture capital is that:
    a. venture capital firms won't give the small business owner any advice.
    b. they don't know your customers.
    c. venture capital firms may ask for a stake in your business.
    d. the venture capital firm asks for very high interest rates.

Learning Goal 4

17. Small business owners often say that the most important assistance they need is in
    a. marketing.
    b. accounting.
    c. planning.
    d. manufacturing.

18. SCORE is:
    a. A U.S. government agency that advises and assists small business by providing management training and financing.
    b. A program through which private investment companies lend money to small businesses.
    c. An SBA service with 13,000 volunteers who provide counseling services for small businesses free, except for expenses.
    d. A group of individuals or companies that invest in new businesses in exchange for partial ownership of those businesses.

Learning Goal 5

19. Small businesses have an advantage over large business in international trade in all these ways except:
    a. They can begin shipping faster.
    b. Their prices are usually lower.
    c. Overseas buyers like dealing with individuals rather than large bureaucracies.
    d. They can provide a wide variety of services.

20. There are many reasons why small business owners don't go international. Which of the following is not one of those reasons?
    a. They don't know how to get started.
    b. Financing is often difficult to find.
    c. Paperwork is often overwhelming.
    d. The market doesn't have great potential.

TRUE–FALSE

Learning Goal 1

1. _____ One benefit of encouraging entrepreneurship is job creation.

2. _____ Entrepreneurs will sometimes look for opportunities by determining what customers <u>don't</u> need.

3. _____ One of the easier elements of working at home is that it is easier to find customers, because you can start in your own neighborhood.

4. _____ A Web-based business will be more successful if it offers the same products available in local stores at better prices.

Learning Goal 2

5. _____ The Immigration Act of 1990 created investor visas which allow 10,000 people to come to the U.S. if they invest $1 million in an enterprise that creates 10 jobs.

6. _____ The majority of new jobs in the United States are created by big business.

7. _____ Many of the businesses with the lowest failure rates require advanced training to start.

8. _____ Small business owners report that their greatest advantages over big companies are their more personalized customer service and the ability to respond quickly to opportunities.

9. _____ The Small Business Administration reports that a vast majority of small business failures are the result of poor management.

Learning Goal 3

10. _____ An effective business plan should catch the reader's interest right away.

11. _____ Angel investors will ask for a stake in your business in exchange for the cash to start up.

12. _____ The SBA offers a lot of advice, but no financial assistance to small business owners.

13. _____ Small business owners could consider borrowing from a potential supplier.

14. _____ A market is basically anyone who wants to buy your product.

Learning Goal 4

15. _____ Employees of small businesses are often more satisfied with their jobs than counterparts in big business.

16. _____ Most small businesses can't afford to hire experts as employees, so they need to turn to outside assistance for help.

17. _____ It is best to stay away from other small business owners for counsel, as they are likely to use your ideas before you can get started.

18. _____ It is not necessary to obtain legal advice when operating a small business, as it is unlikely that your business will be involved in legal matters.

Learning Goal 5

19. _____ The growth potential for small businesses internationally is minimal.

20. _____ One of the major hurdles for a small business in going international is cultural differences.

You Can Find It on the Net

If you are interested in starting your own small business, the Small Business Administration can help. Go the to Small Business Administration Web site (www.sbaonline.sba.gov) Find the following information about the SBA services available in your area.

1. In what areas does the S.B.A. offer assistance, in general?

2. What is the address and phone number of the SBA office nearest you?

3. Are there any SBA sponsored special events scheduled in your area? If so, what are they?

4. Is there a Small Business Development Center in your area? Where?

5. What are your local financing resources?

6. What kind of financing resources are available in your state?

7. What types of training programs are offered by the S.B.A. in your state?

8. Find the home page for your state. Usually, the home page of your state will be www.*postal abbreviation for your state*.gov. For example, for Michigan, the home page is www.mi.gov. For California, it is www.ca.gov. Use a search engine and type in the name of your state and the words "home page"

   What types of incentives, services and help are offered to businesses in your state?

ANSWERS

LEARNING THE LANGUAGE

1.	Market	8.	Entrepreneurship
2.	Enterprise zones	9.	Intrapreneurs
3.	Entrepreneurial team	10.	Business plan
4.	Small business	11.	Small Business Investment Company program (SBIC)
5.	Venture capitalists	12.	Micropreneurs
6.	Incubators	13.	Small Business Administration (SBA)
7.	Service Corps of Retired Executives (SCORE)	14.	Affiliate marketing

ASSESSMENT CHECK

Learning Goal 1

Why People Take the Entrepreneurial Challenge

1. Four reasons people become entrepreneurs are:
   a. Opportunity
   b. Profit
   c. Independence
   d. Challenge

2. Five desirable attributes for entrepreneurs are:
   a. Self-directed
   b. Self-nurturing
   c. Action-oriented
   d. Highly energetic
   e. Tolerant of uncertainty

3. You may have a business idea that is a good opportunity if:
   a. It fills customer needs.
   b. You have the skills and resources to start a business.
   c. You can sell the product at a price customers can pay and still make a profit.
   d. You can get your product to customers before competitors beat you to the market.
   e. You can keep the business going.

4. An entrepreneurial team may be better than an individual entrepreneur because a team can combine creative skills with areas such as marketing and production skills from the beginning. A team can ensure better cooperation and coordination between functions of a business.

5. Many micropreneurs are home-based business owners who are interested in simply enjoying a balanced lifestyle while doing the kind of work they want to do. While micropreneurs can be happy if their companies remain small, an entrepreneur may be committed to growing his or her business.

6. The reasons for the growth of home-based businesses are:
   a. Computer technology allows home-based businesses to look and act like their corporate competitors.
   b. Corporate downsizing has led many to venture out on their own.
   c. Social attitudes have changed.
   d. New tax laws have loosened restrictions regarding deductions for home offices.

7. Challenges for home-based businesses include:
   a. Getting new customers
   b. Managing time
   c. Keeping work and family tasks separate
   d. Abiding by city ordinances
   e. Managing risk

8. Home-based business owners should focus on:
   a. finding opportunity instead of security.
   b. getting results instead of following a routine.
   c. earning a profit instead of a paycheck.
   d. trying new ideas instead of avoiding mistakes.
   e. long-term vision instead of a short-term payoff.

9. Web based businesses have experienced a great deal of growth. In 2007 online retail sales reached $165.9 billion, approximately 8% of all retail sales. Online sales grew nearly six times faster than total retail sales.

10. Web-based businesses have to do more than offer the same merchandise customers can buy at local stores. They must offer unique products and services.

11. Affiliate marketing is an internet based marketing strategy in which a business rewards individuals or other businesses for each visitor or customer the affiliate sends to its web site.

    A widget is an application that links your page on a social network such as MySpace to a seller's site. Whenever anyone clicks on the widget, which is an image of seller's product), and buys that product, the seller pays you a commission.

12. Once an e-tailer is partnered with a shopping widget such as Lemonade Stand, the e-retailer provides Lemonade Stand access to product information and images. Lemonade Stand then funnels that information through its web site so users can select which products they would like to appear in the widget product galleries on their web sites, social network pages, or blogs. Widget users get commissions on sales generated through the widgets. Using a widget operator such as Lemonade Stand saves users from having to register as an affiliate with multiple sellers.

13. While entrepreneurs are risk takers who have started their own businesses, intrapreneurs are creative people who work as entrepreneurs within corporations. The idea is to use existing human, financial and physical resources to launch new products and generate new profits.

14. Part of the intention of the Immigration Act of 1990 was to encourage more entrepreneurs to come to the United States. The act created a category of "investor visas" that allows 10,000 people to come to the U.S. each year if they invest $1 million in an enterprise that creates or preserves 10 jobs.

15. The government could have a significant effect on entrepreneurship by:
    a. creating enterprise zones, which are specific geographic areas to which governments attract business investment by offering lower taxes and other government support.

    b. offering tax breaks to businesses that make investments to create jobs.

16. Incubators are centers that offer new businesses low cost offices with basic business services such as accounting, legal advice, and secretarial help. Incubators help companies survive because they provide assistance in the early stage of a businesses' development.

Getting Started in Small Business

17. A small business is one that is:
    a. independently owned and operated.
    b. not dominant in its field of operation.
    c. meets certain standards of size in terms of employees or annual receipts.

18. A small business is considered small relative to the industry it is in. If it still meets the criteria listed above, a $22 million business would still be considered small. In manufacturing a company can have 1,500 employees and still be considered small.

19. a. There are 26.8 million small businesses in the U.S.
    b. Of all nonfarm businesses, 97% are considered small.
    c. Small businesses account for more than 50% of GDP.
    d. Nearly 750,000 businesses are started every year.
    e. Small businesses generate 60-80% of the new jobs each year.
    f. Small businesses employ about half of all private-sector employees.
    g. About 80% of workers find their first jobs in small businesses.

20. Small businesses owners believe their advantages over large businesses are: more personal customer service and their ability to respond quickly to opportunities.

21. The Monthly Labor Review reports that 56% of new businesses don't last four years. A study by an economist indicates that the failure rate is only 18 percent over the first 8 years. However, the statistics can be misleading because when small business owners went out of business to start new and different businesses, they were included in the business failure statistics. Also, when a business changes its form of ownership from a partnership, for example, to a corporation, it was included in the statistics, as were retirements.

22. a. If you want to be both independent and rich, you need to go after growth.

    b. In general the easiest businesses to start are the ones that tend to have the least growth and the greatest failure rate.

    c. In general the easiest businesses to keep alive are the difficult ones to get started.

    d. In general the businesses that can make you rich are the ones that are both hard to start and hard to keep going.

Learning Goal 3

Learning About Small Business Operations

23. Three ways to learn about small business are:
    a. learn from others.
    b. get some experience.
    c. take over a successful firm.

24. When you talk to others about starting a small business, they:
    a. will tell you location is critical.
    b. tell you not to start without enough money.
    c. warn you about the problems of finding and retaining good workers.
    d. will suggest that you hire a lawyer and an accountant.

25. The rule of thumb is: have three years' experience in a comparable business. You can get this experience by working for a small business owner, and eventually learning the business well enough to allow the owner to take off weekends and holidays, and take a vacation. After working for several years and learning as much as you can about the business, make an offer to take over the management of the business.

26. Three factors used to determine the value of business are:
    a. what the business owns.
    b. what it earns.
    c. what makes it unique.

Learning Goal 4

Managing a Small Business

27. The two management functions of primary concern are planning and financing. The three important functions after the startup are knowing your customers (Marketing), managing your employees (Human resource development), and keeping records (Accounting)

28. A business plan is a detailed written statement that describes the nature of the business, the target market, the advantages the business will have over competition, and the resources and qualifications of the owner. It forces a small business owner to be specific about products they intend to offer.

29. Tips for small business owners wanting to borrow money are:
    a. pick a bank that serves small businesses.
    b. have a good accountant prepare a complete set of financial statements and personal balance sheet.
    c. make an appointment before going to the bank.
    d. go to the bank with an accountant and all necessary financial information.
    e. demonstrate good character.
    f. ask for all the money you need.
    g. be specific.
    h. be prepared to personally guarantee the loan.

30. The information that should generally be included in a business plan includes:
    a. Cover letter.
    b. Executive Summary of proposed venture.
    c. Company background.
    d. Management team.
    e. Financial plan.
    f. Capital required.
    g. Marketing plan.
    h. Location analysis.
    i. Manufacturing plan.
    j. Appendix which includes marketing research and other information about the product.

31. Two software programs that can help with writing a business plan are Business Plan Pro and MiniPlan.

32. Sources of small business funding include:
    a. Personal savings.
    b. Relatives.
    c. Former employers.
    d. Banks.
    e. Finance companies.
    f. Venture capitalists.
    g. Small Business Administration.
    h. Farmers Home Administration.
    i. Economic Development Authority.
    j. Minority Business Development Agency.

33. According to the text, the most common source of funding is friends and family.

34. Angel investors are private individuals who invest their own money in potentially hot companies before they go public.

35. Peer-to-peer lending is a form of individual investing. Web sites match people who want money with people who are willing to lend it.

36. The potential drawback with venture capital is that these companies will often ask for as much as 60% ownership in your business. You could lose control of your business.

37. If you're a very small company you don't have a very good chance of getting venture capital. Since the failure of early Web start-ups, venture capitalists are willing to invest less are willing to invest in a business and they expect more return on their investment. You will stand a better chance of finding an angel investor.

38. The microloan program provides very small loans and technical assistance to small business owners. These loans are awarded on the basis of belief in the borrowers' integrity and the soundness of their business ideas.

39. A Small Business Investment Company can help small businesses from defaulting on loans by identifying a business's trouble spots early, giving entrepreneurs advice, and rescheduling payments.

40. Small Business Development Centers are funded jointly by the federal government and individual states and are usually associated with state universities. SBDCs can help a small business owner evaluate the feasibility of their idea, develop the business plan and complete the funding application, all of which is free of charge.

41. Three important factors for success in your small business are:
    a. knowing your customers.
    b. managing your employees.
    c. keeping efficient records.

42. Once you have identified your market and its needs, you must fill those needs by offering top quality at a fair price with great service.

43. One of the greatest advantages that small businesses have over larger ones is the ability to know their customers better and to adapt quickly to their changing needs.

44. Three criteria critical for small business owners regarding managing employees are:
    a. hiring
    b. training
    c. motivating employees

45. Employees of small companies are often more satisfied with their jobs than their counterparts in big business. Often they find their jobs more challenging, their ideas more accepted, and their bosses more respectful.

46. Entrepreneurs who have built their companies often feel compelled to promote employees who have been with them from the start, even when those employees aren't qualified as managers. There is also sometimes the idea that you must promote, or can't fire, someone because they're family, and this can hinder growth

47. Small business owners say they need the most assistance in the area of accounting.

48. Computers can help a small business owner in the area of accounting by simplifying recordkeeping, and by enabling the business owner to follow sales, expenses and profits. A computer system can also help with inventory control, customer records and payroll.

49. An accountant can help make decisions such as whether to buy or lease equipment and whether to own or rent a building. Further, an accountant can help with tax planning, financial forecasting, choosing sources of financing, and writing requests for funds.

50. Small business owners have learned they need help with
    a. legal advice
    b. tax advice
    c. accounting advice
    d. marketing
    e. finance

51. Lawyers can help with such areas as partnership agreements, leases, contracts, and protection against liabilities.

52. Marketing research can help you determine
    a. where to locate
    b. whom to select as your target market
    c. what would be an effective strategy for reaching the market.

53. Your business will benefit from a presence online even if you don't directly sell online. For example, a restaurant could feature their menu and daily specials, the head chef's credentials, and photos of the restaurant.

54. A commercial loan officer can help a small business owner design an acceptable business plan, offer financial advice and lend money when necessary. An insurance agent will explain all the risks associated with a small business and how to cover them most efficiently with insurance and other means.

55. Important sources of information for small business owners are:
    a. the Service Corps of Retired Executives (SCORE)
    b. local colleges which may have business professors who will advise small businesses
    c. other small-business owners
    d. local chambers of commerce
    e. the Better Business Bureau
    f. national and local trade associations
    g. the business reference section of the library
    h. and many small-business related sites on the Internet

Learning Goal 5

Going International: Small Business Prospects

56. According to the U.S. Department of Commerce only about a third of small businesses now export, but half are expected to engage in global trade by 2018. Small and medium-sized business accounted for 99 percent of the growth in exporting in recent years.

57. Four hurdles in the international market are:
    a. Financing is difficult to find
    b. would-be exporters don't know how to get started
    c. Potential global business people do not understand cultural differences
    d. The bureaucratic paperwork can be overwhelming

58 Small businesses have advantages over big businesses, because
    a. Overseas buyers enjoy dealing with individuals rather than large corporate bureaucracies
    b. Small companies can begin shipping faster
    c. Small companies provide a wide variety of suppliers
    d. Small companies can give more personal service and more undivided attention

CRITICAL THINKING EXERCISES

Learning Goal 1

1. The text mentions that desirable entrepreneurial attributes include being self-directed, self-nurturing, action-oriented, highly energetic, and tolerant of uncertainty. Eric demonstrates these characteristics in several ways. He is self-directed in that he had the discipline not only to build 2 businesses, but to leave those businesses when he decided that he wanted to go on to college. He has been self-supporting for a number of years, and so most likely is quite tolerant of uncertainty, and probably felt quite comfortable with that element of risk in starting his own businesses. He continued to work while his friends told him he was "crazy for working that hard" so it seems that he doesn't depend on other people's approval i.e. he's self-nurturing, and appears to be pretty energetic. He must be action oriented, able to build his "dream into a reality" by taking an idea and creating a successful business.

2. Eric seems to lend validity to the questionable failure statistics the text refers to. He has beaten the odds twice, and it would seem that the odds of failure may have been lower than traditionally reported.

    Eric may tell you that you need to talk to people who have already started their own businesses and get their advice. They can give you valuable information about the importance of location, finding good workers, and having enough capital to keep you going.
    He may also suggest that you work for a successful entrepreneur and get some experience in the fields in which you're interested.

    Another idea is to take over a firm that has already been successful. (That's what the <u>buyers</u> of Eric's most recent firm decided to do!) A strategy may be to work for the owner for a few years, then offer to buy the business through profit sharing or an outright purchase.

3. I would tell Eric to be prepared. First, have a well-written business plan already prepared. Pick a bank that serves small businesses, have an accountant prepare complete financial statements, including a personal balance sheet and take all the financial information with you to the bank, along with the business plan. Make an appointment with the loan officer, and ask for exactly what you need. Be prepared to personally guarantee the loan.

    Eric could also work with the Small Business Administration to determine if he qualifies for some of their loan programs. Small Business Investment Companies also lend money to small businesses meeting their criteria. Further options include Small Business Development Centers and angel investors.

4. Maria could be considered a micropreneur, interested in balancing her family life with her work life. Home-based businesses have experienced a great deal of growth in recent years as access to computer technology has expanded and social attitudes have changed.

    Maria will face challenges as a home-based business owner. Finding new customers could be more difficult, and she will have to become a great time manager while balancing work and caring for her small children. One idea for Maria will be to develop a web site for her business to be better able to compete with larger businesses and to get the word out to potential customers.

    Maria could create a network of contacts through family, friends and community connections to encourage referrals, and use affiliate marketing to further the growth of her small business.

Learning Goals 3, 4

5. Dave and Kevin followed one of the suggestions in the text for successfully starting a business - they worked for someone else in the same field before starting out on their own. They knew their customers, and by all indications the market was there with the resources to buy what Dave and Kevin were selling. They had no employees to manage because they were using independent sales representatives. As is typical in some small business partnerships, Dave and Kevin couldn't agree on some issues.

    Keeping efficient records seems to be a real weakness. Dave's wife didn't really have the skill or time to do the books. Hiring a bookkeeper was a good idea. Perhaps the bookkeeper can suggest an effective billing method and a simple computer system that will simplify recordkeeping.

Although Dave and Kevin had funding, it appears to have been very "casual", and not very well thought out. They made no plan to repay the supplier's loan, which was to come due in 4 months. They didn't look for any help, and so ran the risk of running into legal as well as financial problems. Since they decided not to do a business plan, they don't seem to have been very well organized. They had no marketing plan, and no effective strategy for reaching customers other than those they started out with. They appear to have made many of the mistakes the text mentions being causes for small business failure, i.e. poor planning and inadequate financial management.
(Ed. note: The company "limped along" for about three years before Dave and Kevin began to disagree on how to proceed. They were sued by the supplier for non payment of the loan, and eventually the business dissolved. Each partner went out on their own. Neither is still in business.)

Learning Goal 4

6. A. There are a number of outside consultants that a small business owner can go to for help in starting and managing their businesses, for example:

    a. Accountant
    b. Lawyer
    c. Marketing research service
    d. Commercial loan officer
    e. Insurance agent
    f. Other business owners
    g. Business professors

    B. Other sources of information include:

    a. Chambers of Commerce
    b. Better Business Bureau
    c. National and local trade associations
    d. Library business sections
    e. online sources such as Findforms.com
    f. SCORE

Learning Goal 5

7. The international market provides a lot of growth potential for a small business. The global market may especially be a good idea for Chad if he sees a softening in the domestic market. As a small business owner he has several advantages over larger businesses because he can deal with his customers personally and he can start providing his product immediately.

    There are several hurdles to overcome in the international market, especially if Chad is inexperienced. Cultural differences for the product may not be a problem for software, but sales techniques will vary from those in the United States. In addition, the paperwork in developing an international market can be overwhelming. There are several places available to Chad to find information, including the SBA, the Commerce Department, export management companies, and export trading companies.

PRACTICE TEST

MULTIPLE CHOICE

1.	d	11.	d
2.	a	12.	c
3.	b	13.	d
4.	c	14.	a
5.	c	15.	b
6.	b	16.	c
7.	a	17.	b
8.	c	18.	c
9.	b	19.	b
10.	a	20.	d

TRUE–FALSE

1.	T	11.	F
2.	T	12.	F
3.	F	13.	T
4.	F	14.	F
5.	T	15.	T
6.	F	16.	T
7.	T	17.	F
8.	T	18.	F
9.	T	19.	F
10.	F	20.	T

CHAPTER 7 – MANAGEMENT AND LEADERSHIP

LEARNING GOALS

After you have read and studied this chapter, you should be able to:

1. Describe the changes occurring today in the management function.
2. Describe the four functions of management.
3. Relate the planning process and decision making to the accomplishment of company goals.
4. Describe the organizing function of management.
5. Explain the differences between leaders and managers, and describe the various leadership styles.
6. Summarize the five steps of the control function of management.

LEARNING THE LANGUAGE

Listed below are important terms found in the chapter. Choose the correct term for the definition and write it in the space provided.

Autocratic leadership	Internal customers	Planning
Brainstorming	Knowledge management	PMI
Conceptual skills	Leading	Problem solving
Contingency planning	Management	Staffing
Controlling	Middle management	Strategic planning
Decision making	Mission statement	Supervisory management
Enabling	Objectives	SWOT analysis
External customers	Operational planning	Tactical planning
Free-rein leadership	Organization chart	Technical skills
Goals	Organizing	Top management
Human relations skills	Participative (democratic) leadership	Vision

1. A _____ is a planning tool used to analyze an organization's strengths, weaknesses, opportunities, and threats.

2. Individuals and units within the firm called _____ receive services from other individuals or units.

3. _____ are specific short- term statements detailing how to achieve the organization's goals.

4. The process of _____ involves developing detailed, short-term statements about what is to be done, who is to do it, and how it is to be done.

5. Finding the right information, keeping the information in a readily accessible place, and making the information known to everyone in the firm is known as _____.

6. The level of management that includes general managers, division managers, and branch and plant managers who are responsible for tactical planning and controlling is called _____.

7. The process of _____ means choosing among two or more alternatives.

8. An individual who demonstrates _____ makes managerial decisions without consulting others.

9. The management function of _____ includes designing the structure of the organization, and creating conditions and systems in which everyone and everything work together to achieve the organization's goals and objectives.

10. A _____ is an encompassing explanation of why the organization exists and where it's trying to head.

11. When an individual uses _____, managers and employees work together to make decisions.

12. _____ is the process of determining the major goals of the organization and the policies and strategies for obtaining and using resources to achieve those goals.

13. The management function of _____ includes hiring, motivating, and retaining the best people available to accomplish the company's objectives.

14. Skills that involve the ability to perform tasks in a specific discipline or department are considered _____.

15. The leadership style known as _____ involves managers setting objectives and employees being relatively free to do whatever it takes to accomplish those objectives.

16. The management function of _____ involves anticipating trends and determining the best strategies and tactics to achieve organizational goals and objectives.

17. The highest level of management, consisting of the president and other key company executives who develop strategic plans is called _____.

18. When a manager does _____, he or she is in the process of preparing alternative courses of action that may be used if the primary plans don't achieve the objectives of the organization.

19. A(n) _____ is a visual device that shows relationships among people and divides the organization's work: it shows who is accountable for the completion of specific work and who reports to whom.

20. _____ is the process used to accomplish organizational goals through planning organizing, leading, and controlling people and other organizational resources.

21. _____ involve the ability to picture the organization as a whole and the relationship among its various parts.

22. The management function of _____ involves establishing clear standards to determine whether or not an organization is progressing toward its goals and objectives, rewarding people for doing a good job, and taking corrective action if they are not.

23. Creating a vision for the organization, and guiding, training, coaching, and motivating others to work effectively to achieve the organization's goals and objectives is called _____.

24. The level of management known as _____ includes managers who are directly responsible for supervising workers and evaluating their daily performance.

25. Broad, long-term statements known as _____ are accomplishments an organization wishes to attain.

26. _____ means giving workers the education and they need to make decisions.

27. When a manager is doing _____ he or she is setting work standards and schedules necessary to implement the company's tactical objectives.

28. Dealers, who buy to sell to others, and ultimate customers, or end users, who buy products for their own personal use are called _____.

29. The _____ is an outline of the fundamental purposes of the organization.

30. Skills that involve communication and motivation, called _____ enable managers to work through and with people.

31. In a _____, all the pluses for a solution are listed in one column, all the minuses in another and the interesting implications in a third column.

32. When individuals are involved in _____, they are coming up with as many solutions to a problem as possible in a short period of time with no censoring of ideas.

33. _____ is the process of solving the everyday problems that occur: it is less formal than the decision-making process and usually calls for quicker action.

34. Presenting company facts and figures in a way that is clear and apparent to all stakeholders is commonly known as _____

ASSESSMENT CHECK

Learning Goal 1

Manager's Roles are Evolving

1. Describe how today managers have changed.

Functions of Management

2. The four functions of the management process are:

   a. _____   c. _____

   b. _____   d. _____

3. Identify the activities performed in each of the management functions.

   <u>Function</u>   <u>Activities</u>

   a. _____   a. _____

                                  b. _____

                                  c. _____

                                  d. _____

   b. _____   a. _____

                                  b. _____

                                  c. _____

                                  d. _____

   c. _____   a. _____

                                  b. _____

                                  c. _____

                                  d. _____

                                  e. _____

   d. _____   a. _____

                                  b. _____

                                  c. _____

                                  d. _____

4. In planning the trend today is _____

   _____

5. In organizing, many of today's organizations are being designed around: _____

_____

6. What must organizations do in order to please the customer at a profit?

7. In leading, the trend today is: _____

_____

8. Controlling basically means measuring _____

_____

Learning Goal 3

Planning: Creating a Vision Based On Values

9. Distinguish between a "vision" and a goal.

10. List the areas a meaningful mission statement should address:

   a. _____

   b. _____

   c. _____

   d. _____

   e. _____

   f. _____

11. A mission statement becomes _____

_____

12. What is the difference between goals and objectives?

13. What two fundamental questions are answered in the planning process?

    a. _____

    b. _____

14. What questions are answered as a part of the SWOT analysis?

    a. _____

    b. _____

    c. _____

    d. _____

    e. _____

    f. _____

    g. _____

    h. _____

    i. _____

    j. _____

    k. _____

15. What does S.W.O.T. stand for?

16. What are four forms of planning?

    a. _____   c. _____

    b. _____   d. _____

17. Policies are: _____

    Strategies are: _____

18. At the strategic planning stage, the company decides:

    a. _____

    b. _____

    c. _____

19. Why is strategic planning becoming more difficult? What are some companies doing in response?

20. What activities are included in tactical planning? At what level of management is tactical planning usually done, compared to strategic planning?

21. How is operational planning different from strategic planning? At what level of management is operational planning done?

22. Why is it wise to make contingency plans?

23. In terms of planning leaders of market-based companies want to: _____

    _____

24. What are the 7 D's of the decision making process?

    a. _____

    b. _____

    c. _____

    d. _____

    e. _____

    f. _____

    g. _____

25. What is the difference between problem solving and decision making?

26. Describe two problem solving techniques used by companies.

Organizing: Creating a Unified System

27. What are the three levels of management?

    a. _____ b. _____ c. _____

28. What are the responsibilities of a

    CEO: _____

    COO: _____

    CFO: _____

    CIO/CKO: _____

29. List examples of positions found in middle management. What has happened to some middle management positions?

30. What is another name for supervisory management?

31. Describe the three categories of skills managers should have.

    a. _____

    b. _____

    c. _____

32. How do the various levels of management differ in the skills needed?

33. What makes staffing so critical today?

Learning Goal 5

Leading: Providing Continuous Vision and Values

34. Describe the difference between management and leadership.

35. What are four things leaders must do?

    a. _____

    b. _____

    c. _____

    d. _____

36. Describe the important aspects of:

    Autocratic leadership: _____

    _____

    Participative leadership: _____

    _____

    Free rein leadership: _____

    _____

37. Which leadership style is best?

38. How do traditional leaders differ from progressive leaders? How is a manager's role changing as a result?

39. What is the difference between empowerment and enabling? How is enabling the key to the success of empowerment?

40. What are the two steps in developing a knowledge management system? What is the key to a successful knowledge management system?

Learning Goal 6

Controlling

41. List the five steps in the control process

    a. _____

    b. _____

    c. _____

    d. _____

    e. _____

42. Standards must be:

    a. _____   b. _____   c. _____

43. The criterion for measuring success in a customer-oriented firm is: _____

    _____

44. Other than your answer to the above question, identify other criteria for measuring organizational effectiveness.

CRITICAL THINKING EXERCISES

Learning Goal 1

1. Re read the first section of this chapter, "Managers' Roles are Evolving". If you have a job or an internship, (or if you used to have a job) evaluate your manager's actions using the description of management behavior in this section. For example, does your manager tell you what to do, or does he or she place more emphasis on training you to make decisions on the job? Does management emphasize teamwork and cooperation? Has this manager been with the company for a long time, or has he or she moved around from one company to another? Is your manager a skilled communicator, team player, planner, coordinator, organizer?

Learning Goal 2

2. There are four functions of management:

Planning	Leading
Organizing	Controlling

    Read the following examples and identify which leadership function the manager is performing.

    a. _____ Grant Wimmer is concerned about his newest employee, Peter Wong. In looking over his sales reports, Grant sees that Peter hasn't been performing well and has only met his sales goals once in the past 6 months. Grant is thinking about ways to help Peter improve his sales performance

    b. _____ John Bradford is a manager for a firm in the technology industry. John feels it is vital for him to monitor the changes in the industry and look for opportunities presented by those changes. If he sees a major trend emerging, John sets an objective to learn more about it and to determine ways for his company to participate in the trend.

    c. _____ Elvira Mihalek is a manager who spends a lot of time with her employees helping them to attain their goals. She looks for ways to motivate them, makes sure they are trained well, and gives them a great deal of freedom to do their jobs in the best way for them, while still working to achieve the goals of the organization.

    d. _____ Phil Ardmore is focused on how his company can better serve their customers. He is constantly looking for ways he can design jobs and his department in the best way to be as flexible as possible to meet the needs of their customers.

3. Below are examples that illustrate the planning function for an automotive manufacturer. Match the statement with the proper term:

Mission statement   Objectives
Goals   Vision

a. _____ To assemble and distribute automotive products worldwide and achieve market share leadership.

b. _____ Introduce a hybrid version of a current model within the next three years to U.S., Canadian, and European markets.

c. _____ To be the premier auto company in North America in the world by 2015. The purpose of this company is to build cars and trucks that people will buy, will enjoy driving, and will want to buy again.

d. _____ Our vision is to be the world leader in transportation products and related services. In order to achieve this vision, we recognize that many issues must be addressed and many goals attained. It is imperative that economic, environmental and social objectives be integrated into our daily business objectives and future planning activities so that we can become a more sustainable company.

4. Strategic and Tactical planning provide the framework for the planning process. Contingency planning provides alternative plans of action.

Eric Benoit wants to start his own business making a product he has invented for the automotive industry. It's a windshield design that automatically darkens when the car is in the sun, then lightens when the car is in the shade, or as it gets later in the day. The technology is the same as that used in some eyeglass lenses. The windshield can be installed in the factory, but can also be installed by dealers, or by windshield repair/replacement companies, at any time after the manufacture of the car. The product's brand name, and the name of Eric's company is "Sun-2-Shade".

Complete the following for Eric's new company:

Mission Statement:

a. Strategic plan

b. Tactical plan

c. Contingency plan

5. Using the information in your text and in the Spotlight on Small Business, do a brief SWOT analysis for Sun-2-Shade. In other words, what do you believe may be the strengths, weaknesses, opportunities and threats for this company in the coming years?

Learning Goal 4

6. Identify two individuals at your college or university, or at your place of employment at each level of management. Can you draw a simple organization chart? With some research, you may be able to find an organizational chart for your school or your company.

   a. Top   _____

              _____

   b. Middle   _____

              _____

   c. Supervisory   _____

              _____

7. There are many specific skills needed by various levels of management:

   Technical skills   Managing diversity
   Human relations skills   Decision-making
   Conceptual skills

   For each of the following situations, indicate the management level and the skills being used or described.

   A. Alice Burling is concerned about Bob Mailing's sales performance. In their meeting, Alice and Bob agree there's a problem. Alice listens carefully to Bob while he explains the situation in his territory, and after asking some questions, Alice shows Bob how to handle things differently. After the meeting, Alice completes a schedule assigning new accounts to various salesmen in her department. Later, with one of the sales people, Alice makes a sales call to a particularly important customer.

       a. Management level _____

       b. Skills _____

B. In a typical week in her office, Maria works on a long range forecast for a new product the company is considering, and decides to implement a new program to encourage communication and idea exchange between division heads. She appoints several division heads to formulate a plan for implementation. She schedules most meetings, but leaves time open for interruptions and unplanned meetings with subordinates.

    a.   Management level _____

    b.   Skills _____

C. In reviewing weekly production reports, Joel Hodes notices a drop in overall production from last month. He works for several days on an incentive plan he thinks will push production back up to the company's objectives and still maintain high morale. He then calls a meeting with the line supervisors. After getting their responses and suggestions, Joel revises and implements the plan in his plant.

    a.   Management level_____

    b.   Skills_____

Learning Goal 5

8. You have been hired to be a supervisor in the Sun-2-Shade plant where they are going to make the self-darkening windshields, referred to in a previous exercise. Your workers are well educated and highly skilled. How do you intend to lead and organize these employees? How will your leading (or directing) differ from Eric's, the top manager?

9. Effective leadership styles range along a continuum based upon the amount of employee involvement in setting objectives and making decisions. The three leadership styles are called:

Autocratic   *Participative (Democratic)*   *Free rein*

Which of those styles are being illustrated in the following situations?

A. Production workers complain about having to punch a time clock each day.

    a. _____   "Too bad, I'm not getting rid of it!"

    b. _____   "Let's get a committee together and see if we can come up with some alternatives to using the time clock."

B. A university sees a need for some action to be taken to reverse declining enrollment trends.

   a. _____ "Let's form a committee of faculty and administrators to study the problem and give recommendations on how to solve the problem."

   b. _____ "The objective for each division is to increase enrollment by 10% for the next school year. Each division is free to take whatever action is appropriate for their area in order to reach the objective."

C. A manager notices that an employee consistently turns in work past the deadline.

   a. _____ "Bob, your work has been late three times this month. This is a problem. How can we work together to solve it?"

   b. _____ "Bob, your work has been late three times this month. One more time and you will be disciplined. Two times and you're fired. Got it?"

10. Sun-2-Shade, the company that makes self-darkening windshields for the automotive industry, has been in business for several months and you have just been assigned to re-organize the production department. Eric Benoit, the CEO, knows that he will need inventory if things go as planned. Production is very slow right now but there are some orders to fill. Money, however, is tight. All the production workers are peers (none are supervisors), but there is one member of the group who appears to be the informal leader. The workers are paid by the hour, and they are well paid by normal standards.

You have some ideas about how to increase production without increasing costs. One idea, for example, is to change the method of paying workers from hourly to by how much they produce. The way you have it figured, the workers would have to produce more to make the same income. Another way is to set up individual workstations to cut down on the amount of socializing you have seen going on.

While you are confident these ideas, and others you have thought of, are the best solutions, you aren't sure how to implement the changes. You do know that this will be a test of your management and leadership skills.

a. How would you go about developing alternatives and implementing changes you believe are necessary to increase productivity and save money?

b. What leadership style do you think you used in developing your solution? Why?

11. "The control system's weakest link tends to be the setting of standards." Standards must be: specific, attainable, and measurable.

Improve the way the following vague standards are written:

a. "Increase sales" _____

b. "Get a degree" _____

c. "Be a better manager" _____

PRACTICE TEST

MULTIPLE CHOICE — Circle the best answer

Learning Goal 1

1. Managers today:
   a. closely supervise highly skilled workers who would like to "do their own thing."
   b. emphasize teamwork and cooperation, and act as coaches, rather than "bosses."
   c. have to become specialists in one or two functional areas.
   d. have to function as intermediaries between workers and unions.

2. The financial crisis of 2008–2009 created problems for companies because:
   a. managers had to cut jobs and lay off many workers.
   b. managers found too many options for financing as banks looked for more customers.
   c. it was difficult to find workers to fill jobs in plants that had been modernized.
   d. management moved away from the team concept to an emphasis on discipline and order giving as more workers refused to leave jobs.

Learning Goal 2

3. Kajori is a manager for a small software firm. This week, Kajori is focusing on researching some new applications in the computer industry that could present opportunities for her firm. Kajori is involved in the _____ function of management.
   a. organizing
   b. planning
   c. leading
   d. controlling

4. "We believe in creating loyal customers by providing a superior experience at a great value. We are committed to direct relationships, providing the best products and services based on standards-based technology, and outperforming the competition with value and a superior customer experience." This statement is a part of Dell's:
   a. objectives.
   b. strategy.
   c. mission statement.
   d. goal.

5. H. Ameneggs is working on a project to determine his company's strengths and weaknesses by looking at the economy, technology, the competition, social, and other changes that are affecting his firm. He is looking to identify some opportunities his company can take advantage of in the new economy. H. is also concerned about some things he has identified that inhibit his company's growth. H. is working on.
   a. Setting objectives.
   b. A mission statement.
   c. Contingency planning.
   d. A SWOT analysis.

6. A(n) _____is a specific short-term statement detailing how to achieve _____.
   a. mission statement/goals
   b. goal/objectives
   c. goal/the mission statement
   d. objective/goal

7. Maria Mainini is in the middle of setting her plan for the next year. She knows the company has the goal of increasing market share in the Northeast, so she has developed a plan for expanding the advertising budget for the next year and adding at least one more sales person to cover the larger territories. Maria is involved in:
   a. Contingency planning.
   b. Strategic planning.
   c. Tactical planning.
   d. Operational planning.

8. Which of the following employees of the local hardware store, Hammerhead, would most likely be involved in strategic planning?
   a. Joe Hartley – department head.
   b. Annelise Oswalt – advertising manager.
   c. Elliot Nessy – President and CEO.
   d. Manny Martinez – chief accountant.

9. Which of the following is not part of the seven Ds of decision making?
   a. Define the situation.
   b. Develop alternatives.
   c. Determine if the alternatives are possible.
   d. Decide which alternative is best.

10. In the process of problem solving, managers sometimes use the technique of _____, which involves listing all the minuses of a solution in one column, all the plusses in another, and the implications in a third.
    a. PMI
    b. brainstorming
    c. strategic planning
    d. SWOT analysis

11. General managers, division managers, plant managers and college deans are all a part of:
     a.   supervisory management.
     b.   middle management.
     c.   top management.
     d.   first-line management.

12. Harold is a supervisor in a small automotive shop. He spends a lot of his time training some workers, while helping others solve some of the problems they have in doing their jobs. He also runs the diagnostic machine. Harold spends time on:
     a.   technical skills.
     b.   mechanical skills.
     c.   human relations skills.
     d.   conceptual skills.

13. Which of the following is a false statement?
     a.   Companies are looking at the best way to organize to respond to the needs of customers.
     b.   General consensus is that larger companies are more responsive to customer needs than smaller companies.
     c.   Many large firms are being restructured into smaller, customer-focused units.
     d.   Companies are organizing so that customers have more influence, not managers.

14. The management function of _____ includes hiring, motivating and retaining the best people to accomplish the company's objectives.
     a.   planning
     b.   staffing
     c.   controlling
     d.   leading

15. Which of the following is not characteristic of a leader?
     a.   A leader has a vision and rallies others around the vision.
     b.   A leader will establish corporate values.
     c.   A leader will emphasize corporate ethics.
     d.   A leader will always attempt to keep things from changing.

16. When a manager uses democratic leadership, he or she will
     a.   work with employees to make decisions together.
     b.   set objectives and allow employees to be relatively free to do what it takes to accomplish them.
     c.   give employees direction, and be sure that they are doing their job the way the manager wants them to.
     d.   make managerial decisions without consulting employees.

17. At Schwinn, the bicycle manufacturer, managers of the various new departments were told, "Go out and shape the department the way you want. You have total freedom." That is an example of:
     a.   effective delegating.
     b.   free rein leadership.
     c.   decision making.
     d.   technical skills.

18. The first step in developing a knowledge management system is:
    a. find answers to questions from the SWOT analysis.
    b. determine what knowledge is most important.
    c. setting goals and developing action plans.
    d. establishing performance standards.

Learning Goal 6

19. Measuring performance relative to objectives and standards is part of _____
    a. decision making.
    b. using technical skills.
    c. directing.
    d. controlling.

20. Which step in the control process is considered to be the weakest?
    a. Setting clear standards
    b. Monitoring and recording results
    c. Communicating results to employees
    d. Taking corrective action

21. Which of the following statements is stated most effectively as a control standard?
    a. Cut the number of finished product rejects.
    b. Empower employees to make more decisions next year.
    c. Praise employees more often this month.
    d. Increase sales of our top end product from 2000 in the first quarter to 3000 during the same period by the year 2010.

TRUE-FALSE

Learning Goal 1

1. _____ Today progressive managers are being educated to tell people what to do and to watch over the new type of workers.

2. _____ Because employees tend to stay at the same company for most of their careers, managers don't have a need to earn the trust of their employees.

Learning Goal 2

3. _____ Planning in businesses today could include planning teams, which help monitor the environment, find opportunities and watch for challenges.

4. _____ Robert is a manager in a large hospital. Because the hospital is so big, Robert has been trying to find ways to make sure that the needs of the patients and other customers of the hospital are always met. He has looked at creating small teams on his floor that will each work to find ways to please the customers. This is an example of the organizing function of management.

Learning Goal 3

5. _____ A mission statement outlines a company's fundamental purpose.

6. _____ Operational planning answers the questions "What is the situation now?" and "Where do we want to go?"

7. _____ A SWOT analysis begins with an analysis of the company's profitability.

8. _____ The first step in decision making is to describe and collect the kind of information needed to make the decision.

Learning Goal 4

9. _____ Today staffing is a critical part of organizational success.

10. _____ The difference between managers and leaders is that a leader creates the vision, the manager carries it out.

11. _____ Top managers will spend their time developing tactical level plans.

12. _____ The skills needed by managers are different at different levels of management.

Learning Goal 5

13. _____ Enabling means giving employees the authority (the right) to make decisions on their own.

14. _____ Generally, there is one best leadership style to which all leaders should adhere.

15. _____ Autocratic leadership will be effective in emergencies or when absolute followership is needed.

16. _____ Progressive leaders are less likely than traditional leaders to give specific instructions to employees.

17. _____ Knowledge management tries to keep people from "re-inventing the wheel", or duplicating the work of gathering information, every time a decision needs to be made.

Learning Goal 6

18. _____ The first step in the control process is to monitor and record performance results.

19. _____ The criteria for measuring success in a customer-oriented firm is customer satisfaction of both internal and external customers.

20. _____ External customers include the ultimate customer, also known as the "end user".

You Can Find It On the Net

This is really a collection of several exercises – pick and choose!

Visit www.businessweek.com or www.inc.com and search for leadership related articles. What topics are new in the leadership area? Topics will change over time. How do the topics covered in the articles reinforce the material related in our text?

Click on http://www.impactfactory.com/ and then click on leadership. Scroll down to "leadership quiz". Do you have what it takes to be a good leader?

Alternatively click on http://crs.uvm.edu/gopher/nerl/personal/Assess/b.html
And take the quiz Assessment of leadership qualities and skills.

Go to the website listed below:
http://www.quintcareers.com/SWOT_Analysis.html

Do a SWOT analysis for yourself, following the instructions listed.

ANSWERS

LEARNING THE LANGUAGE

1.	SWOT analysis	13.	Staffing	25.	Goals
2.	Internal customers	14.	Technical skills	26.	Enabling
3.	Objectives	15.	Free rein leadership	27.	Operational planning
4.	Tactical planning	16.	Planning	28.	External customers
5.	Knowledge management	17.	Top management	29.	Mission statement
6.	Middle management	18.	Contingency planning	30.	Human relations skills
7.	Decision making	19.	Organization chart	31.	PMI
8.	Autocratic leadership	20	Management	32.	Brainstorming
9.	Organizing	21.	Conceptual skills	33.	Problem solving
10.	Vision	22.	Controlling	34.	Transparency
11.	Participative (democratic) leadership	23.	Leading		
12.	Strategic planning	24.	Supervisory management		

ASSESSMENT CHECK

Learning Goal 1

Manager's Roles are Evolving

1. Today's managers emphasize teams and team building, they create drop-in centers, team spaces and open work areas. They tend to guide, train, support, motivate, and coach employees rather than to tell them what to do. Modern managers will emphasize teamwork and cooperation rather than discipline and order giving. In general, management is experiencing a revolution.

    Today's managers are also younger, more are female, and fewer were educated at elite universities. In the future managers are more likely to be working in teams and assuming new roles in the firm, taking a leadership role in adapting to climate change.

Learning Goal 2

Functions of Management

2. The four functions of the management process are:
    a. planning
    b. organizing
    c. leading
    d. controlling

3. <u>Function</u>

    a. Planning

    <u>Activities</u>

    a. Set goals
    b. Develop strategies to reach goals
    c. Determine resources needed
    d. Set standards

b.	Organizing	a.	Allocate resources, assign tasks establish procedures
		b.	Create structure
		c.	Recruit, select, train, develop employees
		d.	Effective placement of employees
c.	Leading	a.	Guiding and motivating employees to work effectively
		b.	Give assignments
		c.	Explain routines
		d.	Clarify policies
		e.	Provide performance feedback
d.	Controlling	a.	Measure results against objectives
		b.	Monitor performance relative to standards
		c.	Reward outstanding performance
		d.	Take corrective action

4. In planning the trend today is to have <u>planning teams</u> to help monitor the environment, find business opportunities, and watch for challenges.

5. In organizing, many of today's organizations are being designed around pleasing the customer at a profit.

6. In order to please the customer at a profit, the organization must remain flexible and adaptable because customer needs change and organizations must change too.

7. In leading, the trend today is to empower employees, giving them as much freedom as possible to become self-directed and self-motivated. In smaller firms the role of managers is often telling employees exactly what to do. In most large modern firms, however, managers no longer tell people exactly what to do because often knowledge workers and others know how to do their jobs better than the manager.

8. Controlling basically means measuring whether what actually occurs in an organization actually meets the organization's goal.

Learning Goal 3

Planning: Creating a Vision Based On Values

9. Goals are broad, long-term accomplishments that an organization wants to reach. A vision is greater than a goal; it's the larger explanation of why the organization exists and where it's trying to head.

10. A meaningful mission statement should address:
    a. The organization's self concept
    b. Company philosophy/Goals
    c. Long-term survival
    d. Customer needs
    e. Social responsibility
    f. Nature of product or service

11. A mission statement becomes the foundation for setting goals and selecting and motivating employees.

12. Goals are the broad, long-term accomplishments an organization wishes to obtain. Objectives are specific, short-term statements detailing how to achieve the goals that have been set.

13. Two fundamental questions answered in the planning process are:
    a. What is the situation now?
    b. How can we get to our goal from here?

14. The questions answered by a SWOT include:
    a. What is the situation now?
    b. What is the state of the economy and other environments?
    c. What opportunities exist for meeting people's needs?
    d. What products and customers are most profitable?
    e. Who are our major competitors?
    f. What threats are there to our business?
    g. What external success factors affect the industry?
    h. How does our firm measure up to other firms?
    i. What are our social objectives?
    j. What are our personal development objectives?
    k. What can we do to survive and prosper during a recession?

15. S.W.O.T. stands for Strengths, Weaknesses, Opportunities, Threats

16. Four forms of planning are:
    a. Strategic   c. Operational
    b. Tactical   d. Contingency

17. Policies are broad guidelines for action
    Strategies determine the beast way to use resources

18. At the strategic planning stage, the company decides:
    a. which customers to serve
    b. what products or services to sell
    c. the geographic areas in which the firm will compete.

19. Strategic planning is becoming more difficult because changes are occurring so fast that plans set for even months in the future may quickly become obsolete. Therefore, some companies are making shorter-term plans that allow for quick responses to the market.

20. Tactical planning is the process of developing detailed, short-term strategies about what has to be done, who will do it and how it is to be done. Managers or teams of managers at lower levels of the organization do this type of planning, whereas strategic planning is done at top levels of management.

21. Whereas strategic planning looks at the organization as a whole, operational planning focuses on specific supervisors, department managers, and individual employees. The operational plan is the department manager's tool for daily and weekly operations. Operational planning is done by the department manager, and his/her tool for daily and weekly operations.

22. It is wise to have alternative plans of action because the environment changes so rapidly. Contingency plans are needed in anticipation of those changes.

23. In terms of planning leaders of market based companies want to stay flexible, listen to customers, and seize opportunities when they come, whether they are planned or not.

24. The 7 D's of the decision making process are:
    a. Define the situation
    b. Describe and collect needed information
    c. Develop alternatives
    d. Develop agreement among those involved
    e. Decide which alternative is best
    f. Do what is indicated (implement solution)
    g. Determine whether the decision was a good one and follow up

25. Problem solving is less formal than decision making and usually calls for quicker action to resolve everyday issues.

26. Two problem solving techniques are brainstorming and PMI. Brainstorming means coming up with as many solutions as possible in a short period of time with no censoring of ideas. PMI means listing all the pluses (P) in one column, the minuses (M) in another, and the implications (I) in a third.

Learning Goal 4

Organizing: Creating a Unified System

27. The three levels of management are:
    a. supervisory or first-line
    b. middle
    c. top

28. CEOs are responsible for introducing change into an organization.

    The COO is responsible for putting those changes into effect. His or her tasks include structuring, controlling, and rewarding to ensure that people carry out the leader's vision.

    The CFO is responsible for obtaining funds, budgeting, collecting funds, and other financial matters.

    The CIO/CKO is responsible for getting the right information to other managers.

29. Middle management positions include general managers, divisional mangers, branch managers, plant managers and at a college, deans. Many firms have eliminated some middle managers through downsizing.

30. Supervisory managers are also known as first-line managers because they're the first level above workers.

31. Three skills managers must have are:
    a. technical skills involve the ability to perform tasks in a specific discipline.
    b. human relations skills involve communication and motivation, and those associated with leadership, coaching, morale building, delegating, training and development, and help and support.
    c. conceptual skills are needed in planning, organizing, controlling systems development, problem analysis, decision making, coordinating, and delegating.

32. First line managers need to be skilled in all three areas, but most of their time is spent on technical and human relations tasks. They spend little time on conceptual tasks. Top managers need to use few technical skills. Almost all of their time is devoted to human relations and conceptual tasks.

33. Staffing is critical because recruiting good employees is an important part of organizational success. It is especially important today in the Internet and high-tech areas. Firms with the most innovative and creative workers can go from start-up to major competitor with leading companies in a very short time.

Learning Goal 5

Leading: Providing Continuous Vision and Values

34. One difference between managers and leaders is that managers strive to create order and stability while leaders embrace and manage change. Leadership is creating a vision for others to follow, establishing corporate values and ethics, and transforming the way the organization does business. Good leaders motivate workers and create the environment for workers to motivate themselves, while management is the carrying out of the vision.

35. Four things leaders must do are:
    a. Communicate a vision and rally others around the vision.
    b. Establish corporate values.
    c. Promote corporate ethics.
    d. Embrace change.

36. a. Autocratic leadership involves making managerial decisions without consulting others. Such a style is effective in emergencies and when absolute followership is important.

    b. Participative or Democratic leadership consists of managers and employees working together to make decisions. This type of leadership usually increases job satisfaction.

    c. Free rein leadership involves managers setting objectives and employees being relatively free to do what it takes to accomplish those objectives. More and more firms are adopting this style of leadership with some employees. The traits needed by managers in such organizations include warmth, friendliness, and understanding.

37. Research indicates that successful leadership depends on what the goals and values of the firm are, who is being led and in what situation. Different leadership styles may be successful depending on the people and the situation and a leader may use different styles with different employees. There is no such thing as a leadership trait that is effective in all organizations.

38. Traditional leaders give explicit instructions to workers, telling them what to do to meet the goals and objectives of the organization. This is called directing. Progressive leaders are less likely than traditional leaders to give specific instructions to employees. They are more likely to empower employees to make decisions on their own. In cooperation with employees, managers will set up teams that will work together to accomplish goals. The manager's role is becoming less that of a boss and director and more that of a coach, assistant, counselor, or team member.

39. Empowerment means giving employees the authority and responsibility to respond quickly to customer requests. Enabling is the term used to describe giving workers the education and tools they need to assume their new decision-making powers.

40. The two steps to developing a knowledge management system include determining what knowledge is most important, and then setting out to find answers to those questions. The key to success is learning how to process information effectively and turn it into knowledge that everyone can use to improve processes and procedures.

Learning Goal 6

Controlling

41. The steps in the control process are:
    a. Establish clear performance standards.
    b. Monitoring and recording actual performance.
    c. Comparing results against plans and standards.
    d. Communicating results and deviations to the employees involved.
    e. Taking corrective action when needed.

42. Standards must be:
    a. specific.
    b. attainable.
    c. measurable.

43. The criterion for measuring success in customer-oriented firms is customer satisfaction of both internal and external customers.

44. Other criteria of organizational effectiveness may include the firm's contribution to society and its environmental responsibility. Traditional measures of success are usually financial. These are still important, but they're not the whole purpose of the firm. The purpose of the firm today is to please, employees, customers, and other stakeholders.

CRITICAL THINKING EXERCISES

Learning Goal 1

1. Your answer will of course be determined by your own experience. The key is to look at how your manager fits into the new style of management, or if he or she is more traditional. If you work for a small firm, it may be that your manager acts in a more traditional manner, for example. But, if the company you work for is a larger organization, management styles may be different.

Learning Goal 2

2. a. Controlling
    b. Planning
    c. Leading
    d. Organizing

Learning Goal 3

3. a. Goals
    b. Objectives
    c. Mission statement
    d. Vision

4. Eric has a big job ahead of him. There are many possible responses to this question, but an example might be:

    Mission statement: Sun-2-Shade's mission is to make and develop products for the automotive industry. We are committed to helping our employees develop their potential and encourage their creativity and energy. We intend to continually create value for our customers by forming long lasting partnerships with our customers and suppliers, and to exceed our customer's expectations.

    a. Strategic plan – Become the supplier of self-darkening windshield for automobiles within the next 5 years, with a 25% market share. Become the major supplier for self-darkening windshields to the automotive aftermarket.

    b. Tactical plan – Contact the production and/or engineering managers of the major automobile manufacturers and sell them on the product within the next 12 months. Develop a sales program to present to automotive aftermarket dealers, such as windshield repair companies.

    c. Contingency plan - If the automakers are not interested right now, begin focusing on the automotive after-market, to sell product as an add-on.

5. A suggested SWOT analysis for Sun-2-Shade could contain:

Strengths:	Young, creative workforce Energetic CEO
Weaknesses:	New company Finding financing sources
Opportunities:	Increasing interest in "luxury" options for automobiles Increasing household incomes Increased interest in products that make life more pleasant
Threats:	Competition from other companies utilizing this technology

    These are <u>only suggestions</u>. You may have come up with additional ideas!

Learning Goal 4

6. There are many variations for answering this question, depending upon your school or company. Some possibilities for a school are:

   a. Top Managers – Chancellor, President, Provost
   b. Middle – Dean of Instruction, Executive Dean, Associate Dean
   c. Supervisory – Lab supervisor, Department chair, Business manager

   The organization chart may look like this:

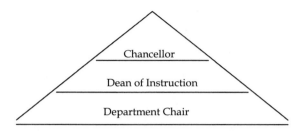

7. A. a. Supervisory level
      b. Human relations, technical skills

   B. a. Top management
      b. Decision making, conceptual skills

   C. a. Middle management
      b. Human relations skills, technical skills, decision making, conceptual skills

Learning Goal 5

8. As a manager of educated and skilled workers you are less likely to be giving specific instructions to your employees. Instead, you may give them the authority to make decisions, which will allow them to respond quickly to any customer requests. In all likelihood, you will set up a team approach for the plant, using self-managed work teams if possible. Your job will be more that of a coach and team member, allowing for more participation in decision-making and more flexibility for the workers.

   Eric, as the top manager of the company, will be concerned with a broader view of where he wants the company to go. As a first line manager, your job will be more specific, and your goals and objectives more specific than those Eric has outlined for the entire company. So your directions to subordinates, to the extent you will give them direction, will be more specific.

9. A. a. Autocratic
      b. Participative

   B. a. Participative
      b. Free rein

   C. a. Participative
      b. Autocratic

10. Your answers will vary, as each of you will have your own individual style. However, review the material in this section of the chapter. Would a team-based approach be appropriate for this group? Could you use a participative management style? Did you consider getting opinions from the workers about what they see as a method to increase production without raising costs? Did you ask for advice? Are you making an effort to both empower and enable your employees?

11. a. Increase sales of Product X by 10% in the next 6 months.
    b. Get a Bachelor's Degree in Business in 4 years.
    c. Spend 3 hours a week reading management articles or books. Praise employees twice a week. Ask for employee input or suggestions monthly.

PRACTICE TEST

MULTIPLE CHOICE

1.	b	12.	a
2.	a	13.	b
3.	b	14.	b
4.	c	15.	a
5.	d	16.	a
6.	d	17.	b
7.	c	18.	b
8.	c	19.	d
9.	c	20.	a
10.	a	21.	d
11.	b		

TRUE - FALSE

1.	F	11.	F
2.	F	12.	T
3.	T	13.	F
4.	T	14.	F
5.	T	15.	T
6.	F	16.	T
7.	F	17.	T
8.	F	18.	F
9.	T	19.	T
10.	T	20.	T

CHAPTER 8 – ADAPTING ORGANIZATIONS TO TODAY'S MARKETS

LEARNING GOALS

After you have read and studied this chapter, you should be able to:

1. Outline the basic principles of organization management.
2. Compare the organizational theories of Fayol and Weber.
3. Evaluate the choices managers make in structuring organizations.
4. Contrast the various organizational models.
5. Identify the benefits of inter-firm cooperation and coordination.
6. Explain how restructuring, organizational culture, and informal organizations can help businesses adapt to change.

LEARNING THE LANGUAGE

Listed below are important terms found in the chapter. Choose the correct term for each definition and write it in the space provided.

Benchmarking	Flat organization structure	Organizational (or corporate) culture
Bureaucracy	Formal organization	Real time
Centralized authority	Hierarchy	Restructuring
Chain of command	Informal organization	Span of control
Core competencies	Inverted organization	Staff personnel
Cross-functional self managed teams	Line organization	Tall organization structure
Decentralized authority	Line personnel	Transparency
Departmentalization	Matrix organization	Virtual corporation
Digital natives	Networking	
Economies of scale		

1. Groups of employees from different departments who work together on a long- term basis are called _____.

2. A _____ is a system in which one person is at the top of the organization and there is a ranked or sequential ordering from the top down of managers who are responsible to that person.

3. Using communications technology and other means to link organizations, or _____, allows them to work together on common objectives.

4. Redesigning an organization so that it can more effectively and efficiently serve its customers is known as _____.

5. Widely shared values within an organization, or the _____, provide unity and cooperation to achieve common goals.

6. The _____ is the system of relationships and lines of authority that develop spontaneously as employees meet and form relationships, and lines of authority outside the formal organization.

7. Those functions that the organization can do as well as or better than any other organization in the world are called _____.

8. A _____ is an organization with many layers of managers who set rules and regulations and oversee all decisions.

9. An organization in which decision-making authority is maintained at the top level of management at the company's headquarters utilizes _____.

10. In a(n) _____ contact people are at the top and the chief executive officer is at the bottom of the organization chart.

11. The _____ refers to the optimum number of subordinates a manager supervises or should supervise.

12. The line of authority that moves from the top of the hierarchy to the lowest level is called the _____.

13. Employees known as _____ are part of the chain of command that is responsible for achieving organizational goals.

14. When a company is using _____, it is comparing its practices, processes, and products against the world's best.

15. When decision-making authority is delegated to lower-level managers more familiar with local conditions than headquarters' management could be, a company is said to have _____.

16. A _____ has few layers of management and a broad span of control.

17. Dividing organizational functions into separate units is commonly called _____.

18. The _____ is the structure that details lines of responsibility, authority, and position and is shown on the organizational chart.

19. A _____ is one in which specialists from different parts of the organization are brought together to work on specific projects but still remain part of a traditional line and staff structure.

20. Employees known as _____ advise and assist line personnel in meeting their goals.

21. The concept of _____ describes a situation in which companies can reduce their production costs if they can purchase raw materials in bulk, so the average cost of goods goes down as production levels increase.

22. An organizational structure in which the pyramidal organization chart would be quite tall because of the various levels of management would be called a _____.

23. A _____ is one that has direct two-way lines of responsibility, authority, and communication running from the top to the bottom of the organization, with all people reporting to only one supervisor.

24. The present moment or the actual time in which something takes place is called _____.

25. The term _____ is used to describe young people who grew up using the Internet.

26. A _____ is a temporary, networked organization made up of replaceable firms that join the network and leave it as needed.

ASSESSMENT CHECK

Learning Goal 1

Everyone's Organizing

1. According to the text the key to success for organizations is: _____

   _____

2. Describe:

   a. Division of labor: _____

   b. Job specialization: _____

3. Structuring an organization consists of:

   a. _____

   b. _____

   c. _____

   d. _____

   e. _____

   f. _____

4. What does an organization chart show?

5. What has created so much change in organizations?

Learning Goal 2

The Changing Organization

6. Identify and briefly describe 10 of Fayol's "principles" of organizing:

    a. _____

    b. _____

    c. _____

    d. _____

    e. _____

    f. _____

    g. _____

    h. _____

    i. _____

    j. _____

7. The process of rule making often led to _____

8. Identify four characteristics of Max Weber's bureaucracy.

    a. _____

    b. _____

    c. _____

    d. _____

9. How do workers today differ from those during the time that Weber was writing, and how did that affect management?

10. In a company with many layers of management, what is the process for an employee to introduce a work change? What did Weber mean by the term "bureaucrat"?

11. When employees have to ask their manager for permission to make a change _____

    _____.

12. How are companies reorganizing to make customers happy?

Learning Goal 3

Decisions to Make in Structuring Organizations

13. What are the advantages and disadvantages of centralized authority?

Advantages   Disadvantages

a. _____   a. _____

b. _____   b. _____

c. _____   c. _____

d. _____   d. _____

14. What are the advantages and disadvantages of decentralized authority?

Advantages   Disadvantages

a. _____   a. _____

b. _____   b. _____

c. _____   c. _____

d. _____   d. _____

15. Why does span of control narrow at higher levels of the organization?

16. What is the trend in today's organizations regarding span of control?

17. Compare span of control in tall and flat organizational structures.

18. Why can flat structures respond more readily to customer demands?

19. What are the advantages and disadvantages of the traditional functional structure?

Advantages

a. _____

b. _____

c. _____

Disadvantages

a. _____

b. _____

c. _____

d. _____

e. _____

20. What are five methods of grouping, or departmentalizing, workers?

a. _____

b. _____

c. _____

d. _____

e. _____

21. The decision about which way to departmentalize depends on _____

_____.

22. A hybrid form of departmentalization is being used when _____

_____,

Learning Goal 4

Organization Models

23. Name four types of organizational structures.

a. _____

b. _____

c. _____

d. _____

24. What are the disadvantages of a line organization, for a larger organization?

a. _____

b. _____

c. _____

d. _____

25. What is the difference between line and staff personnel?

26. In a matrix system, a product manager can: _____

    _____

    This is important in industries in which the emphasis is on _____

    _____

27. What are the advantages and disadvantages of a matrix structure?

    Advantages:

    a. _____

    b. _____

    c. _____

    d. _____

    Disadvantages:

    a. _____

    b. _____

    c. _____

    d. _____

28. A potential problem with the teams created by matrix management is _____

    _____

    An answer to the disadvantage of the teams created by matrix management is: _____

    _____

29. Describe the characteristics of cross-functional teams.

30. Why should cross functional teams include customers, suppliers and distributors?

Managing the Interactions Among Firms

31.   What is meant by the concept of transparency?

32.   How have the networking, real time and the concept of transparency, changed the way information is shared between organizations?

33.   What is the result of those changes on organizational design and structure?

34.   How does benchmarking lead to outsourcing, and ultimately to a firm's core competencies?

Adapting to Change

35.   Why is introducing change in an organization difficult?

36.   How are companies using the Internet to help adapt to changes?

37.   Illustrate and describe an inverted organization.

38.   What is a manager's job in an inverted organization?

39. How does the inverted organization support front line personnel? How does this change the requirements for front-line personnel?

40. How is the culture of an organization reflected?

41. Describe the kind of organizational cultures that the best organizations have, including the key to a productive culture.

42. What are two organizational systems that all companies have?

a. _____   b. _____

43. What is a drawback of the formal organization? What is a benefit of the formal organization?

44. What is the drawback of the informal organization? What is the benefit?

45. Describe the importance of the "grapevine" in the organization.

46. How have managers' views toward the informal organization changed in the new more open organizations?

CRITICAL THINKING EXERCISES

Learning Goal 1

1. Consider an organization with which you are familiar. This could be the school you attend, or the company you work for, or a charitable organization with which you have worked. Can you identify the manner in which this organization is "organized"?
How is the work divided? Are there teams? Is the organization departmentalized? Are the positions of authority clear? What are the various types of tasks that need to be accomplished? Are there clear procedures for doing work? Is there an organization chart?

Learning Goal 2

2. Many organizations today have been organized around principles developed by <u>Henri Fayol</u> and <u>Max Weber</u>. Read the following and determine whose ideas are being described.

   a. _____ Introduced several "principles" of organizing.

   b. _____ Believed workers should think of themselves as coordinated teams, and that the goal of the team is more important than individual goals.

   c. _____ Promoted a bureaucratic organization.

   d. _____ Believed that large organizations demanded clearly established rules and guidelines, which were to be precisely followed.

   e. _____ Wrote that each worker should report to only one boss.

   f. _____ Said that managers should treat employees and peers with respect.

   g. _____ Wrote that functions are to be divided into areas of specialization such as production, marketing and so on.

   h. _____ Believed in written rules, decision guidelines and detailed records.

   i. _____ Said that staffing and promotions should be based solely on qualifications.

   j. _____ Proposed that an organization should consist of three layers of authority: top managers, middle managers, and supervisors.

   k. _____ Believed the less decision-making employees had to do, the better.

   l. _____ Believed that managers have the right to give orders and expect obedience.

3. You are a manager for Sun-2-Shade, a company that makes a self-darkening windshield for automobiles using the same technology that is used for prescription eyeglasses. Sun-2-Shade is a small company right now, with just a few workers. Eric is the CEO and founder of the company. You are the plant manager. The customers for Sun-2-Shade for right now are automobile manufacturers. Do you think a centralized or decentralized authority structure would be most effective? Why?

4. As companies are moving away from traditional methods of organizing, and taking different perspectives regarding span of control, how are companies changing in the area of centralization versus decentralization, and tall versus flat organizational structures?

5. There are a number of ways companies have tried to departmentalize to better serve customers:

Product   Customer group   Process
Function   Geographic location

The hybrid structure is an organization that has used several forms of departmentalization.

Match each of the following to the correct form:

a. _____   General Motors has the Chevrolet and Buick, divisions, each employing separate staffs for design, engineering, product development and so on.

b. _____   At the highest corporate levels, G.E. has a corporate strategic planning staff, production staff, human resources staff, technical resources staff and finance staff.

c. _____   Apple Computer, in manufacturing the Mac Computer System, begins with an assembly line that makes the logic board; another line makes the analog board. Once assembled, the boards go through diagnostic tests before being assembled into a computer unit.

d. _____   When Wendy's made the decision to expand into the European market, the company created a separate European division.

e. _____   Most banks have commercial loan officers who deal only with business customers and consumer loan specialists for personal loans.

6. There are 4 types of organizational structures:

    Line   Matrix
    Line and Staff   Cross-functional self-managed teams

    Read below brief descriptions of several companies and decide which form of organizational structure would be most suitable for each.

    a. _____ A small company, Dynalink, is in the biotechnology industry. Competition is fierce, and new product development is of highest importance. The field is changing and growing so rapidly that new product ideas must come fast and furious. The firm employs highly skilled, very creative people.

    b. _____ Another small firm is Cleanem Up, a dry cleaning establishment, with one owner and one store. They are located in a suburban area and have a loyal clientele. The store is known for its quality and courteous service.

    c. _____ Wells Industries is a medium sized firm employing about 1500 people. Wells makes a variety of business- related products such as stationary, forms, and so forth. They have a good sales force, which knows the product very well. While this is a fairly competitive industry, new product development happens as the need arises, such as when firms went from sophisticated word processing machines to even more sophisticated computerized office management.

    d. _____ Mitsubishi wants to develop a new luxury car to compete with Lexus, Infiniti, and others. Time is important, as they want to enter the market within 18 months.

Learning Goals 4, 5

7. How will cross functional self managed teams impact organizational designs of the future?

8. How does the inverted organizational structure relate to the other kinds of changes we have read about in this chapter, such as wider spans of control, decentralization, cross functional teams, outsourcing, benchmarking, and so on?

9. What is the relationship between leadership style, the organizational structure (such as tall vs flat organizations, span of control, delegation, teams) and the creation of an organizational culture?

Learning Goals 1–5

10. Think about the organizational design of the school you are attending, or an organization with which you are familiar, such as where you work. Can you identify the "hierarchy"? Identify how many layers of management come between the front-line workers and the highest level of management. Are there separate departments for various functions (instruction, bookstore, and so on)? Are there rules and regulations that seem to keep workers organized and are meant to make the organization run efficiently? (Hint - perhaps your instructor will have a copy of the organizational chart for your school, or your manager may have one for the company for which you work.)

11. Sun-2-Shade is in a growth state and Eric, the CEO and founder, wants to be sure to build on a good foundation. The product is a windshield that darkens automatically when your car goes into a sunny area, much like the eyeglasses. This is a small company, with a educated and well trained workers, and Eric is very concerned about customer service. What suggestions can you give Eric about organizational design, knowing what you already know about the company and its employees?

PRACTICE TEST

MULTIPLE CHOICE — Circle the best answer

Learning Goal 1

1. The first step in the process of organizing a business is to:
   a. determine the work that needs to be done.
   b. divide people into teams.
   c. grouping workers into departments based on skills or expertise.
   d. develop an organization chart.

2. The process of setting up individual departments to do specialized tasks is called:
   a. division of labor.
   b. job specialization.
   c. departmentalization.
   d. planning.

Learning Goal 2

3. The evolving business environment has made _____ a critical managerial function.
   a. controlling employees
   b. managing change
   c. finding new employees
   d. division of labor

4. The principle of _____ means that each person should know to whom they report, and that managers should have the right to give orders and expect others to follow.
   a. unity of command
   b. division of labor
   c. order
   d. hierarchy of authority

Learning Goal 3

5. Robin Banks is in a supervisor for a large, bureaucratic organization on the West Coast. According to the views of a bureaucratic organization, this means that Robin should:
   a. be included on decision making when decisions affect her workers.
   b. do her work and let middle and upper level managers do the decision making.
   c. try to get her workers organized into cross-functional teams.
   d. have a wide span of control.

6. A manager's span of control:
   a. can narrow as subordinates need less supervision.
   b. will narrow as the manager gets to higher levels in the organization and work becomes less standardized.
   c. will decrease as employees become more professional.
   d. is generally the same in most organizations.

7. Who Dunnit is a new firm that makes murder mystery games for sale in retail stores and through catalogs. The company has very few management positions, and most everybody pitches in when they need to, to get the job done. It is really a "team" effort, with very few layers of management. Who Dunnit is an example of a:
   a. tall organization.
   b. bureaucratic organization.
   c. centralized organization.
   d. flat organization.

8. Dewey, Cheatum, and Howe is a car company that makes four models, a hybrid sport utility, a sports car, a four door sedan, and a compact car. Workers at Dewey basically work on only one type of vehicle, and separate marketing and product development processes are designed for each type of vehicle, to better serve the customers for each type of vehicle. Dewey, Cheatum, and Howe is departmentalized by:
   a. product.
   b. function.
   c. process.
   d. customer.

9. In order to more quickly respond to customer needs, Hewlett Packard is changing it's organizational structure to give more authority and responsibility to field managers located across the country. These managers spend time with customers and know what the customers need right away. It appears that H-P is moving toward a _____ structure.
   a. more decentralized
   b. more centralized
   c. more bureaucratic
   d. more traditional

Learning Goal 4

10. The form of organizational structure that is most flexible, and allows the organization to take on new projects without adding to the organizational structure is the:
    a. Line.
    b. Line and staff.
    c. Matrix.
    d. Cross-functional self managed team.

11. Maria Escobar works as an attorney for a large East Coast consulting firm. Maria's job is to act as an advisor to the consultants, to be sure that they do not confront any legal issues when they are working at the various clients' job sites. Maria's position would be classified as a _____ position.
    a. line
    b. middle management
    c. first line
    d. staff

12. Banana Computers is restructuring, and intends to implement cross-functional teams.
    All of the following *are likely to* serve on a cross-functional team <u>except</u>:
    a. a Banana engineer.
    b. an employee of Peelit, Inc. one of Banana's competitors.
    c. an employee of Monkeyshine, one of Banana's suppliers.
    d. a Banana salesperson.

13. One of the advantages of the matrix organization is:
    a. It is less costly.
    b. It can result in creative solutions to problems.
    c. There is less need for interpersonal skills because there is constant communication.
    d. It is a long term solution to problems.

Learning Goal 5

14. When a firm is rating its processes and products against the best in the world, the firm is practicing:
    a. total quality management.
    b. outsourcing.
    c. their core competencies.
    d. benchmarking.

15. An auto assembly plant in suburban Detroit is "connected" to its seat supplier in a way that the seat supplier has the information it needs to schedule its production to coordinate with the production of cars at the plant. The seat supplier knows, for example, that B. Goode's cherry red compact with tan leather interior is scheduled for production, so that it can make sure that the correct seats are in the process when the car is made. This type of system is known as:
    a. a cross functional team.
    b. a virtual corporation.
    c. Transparency.
    d. Benchmarking

Learning Goal 6

16. In an inverted organization, the managers' job is to:
    a. maintain direct contact with customers.
    b. direct and closely monitor employee performance.
    c. look for the best ways to outsource functions.
    d. assist and support sales personnel and other employees who work directly with customers.

17. When IBM changed its organizational design, the company gave more authority to lower level employees, to become more flexible in responding to customer needs. The company broke down barriers between functions, and ended top-down management. This process is known as:
    a. creating an informal organization.
    b. changing span of control.
    c. restructuring.
    d. becoming more bureaucratic.

18. Which of the following would not be used to describe a company with a positive corporate culture?
    a. Emphasizes service to others, especially customers.
    b. People enjoy working together to provide good products at reasonable prices.
    c. Less need for policy manuals, formal rules and procedures.
    d. Closer supervision of employees.

19. The corporate structure shown on the organizational chart, which details lines of responsibility, is known as the:
    a. informal structure.
    b. bureaucratic structure.
    c. formal structure.
    d. grapevine.

20. Mr. Bilko is the one to see in the company when there is something you need. He will obtain what you need quickly, and can avoid the red tape that often delays action. Mr. Bilko is the one to see if you need advice or help. Mr. Bilko is an important member of the firm's:
   a. purchasing deportment.
   b. informal structure.
   c. formal structure.
   d. bureaucratic structure.

TRUE–FALSE

Learning Goal 1

1. _____ Many U.S. firms have been reorganizing in an effort to adjust to the changing business climate.

2. _____ Structuring an organization consists of devising a division of labor, setting up teams or departments to do specific tasks and assigning responsibility and authority to people.

Learning Goal 2

3. _____ A bureaucratic organizational system is a good when workers are relatively well educated and trained to make decisions.

4. _____ It has basically been proved that an organization with many rules, procedures and policies is more effective because employees can respond quickly to problems by simply referring to a rule or policy guideline.

5. _____ To make customers happier, some companies are reorganizing to give upper management the primary power to make more decisions and to have strict rules and regulations.

Learning Goal 3

6. _____ A company that must focus on regional or global differences in customer tastes should use decentralized authority.

7. _____ Today's rapidly changing markets tend to favor centralization of authority, so decisions can be made quickly.

8. _____ The trend today is to expand the span of control as organizations reduce the number of middle managers.

9. _____ An organization with many layers of management, such as the U.S. Army or a large corporation, is a good example of a flat organization.

10. _____ The decision about which way to departmentalize depends greatly on the nature of the product and the customers served.

11. _____ Firms should not use more than one form of departmentalization.

Learning Goal 4

12. _____ Human resource management and legal advising are examples of staff positions in a manufacturing firm.

13. _____ Companies that create cross-functional self-managed teams empower the teams to make decisions on their own without seeking the approval of management.

14. _____ One of the advantages of the matrix form of organizing is that it gives managers flexibility in assigning people to projects

Learning Goal 5

15. _____ When a company can't perform a certain function as well as the best, the company may outsource that function, in order to concentrate on the functions at which they are the best.

16. _____ Cross functional teams should definitely not include customers or suppliers, as they could leak sensitive product information to competitors.

17. _____ The term "digital natives" is used to describe young people who have grown up with the Internet.

Learning Goal 6

18. _____ In general, an organizational culture cannot be negative.

19. _____ The informal organization in most organizations is not particularly powerful.

You Can Find It on the Net

Visit the website   http://www.organizedchange.com/index.htm

Click on Teams and Facilitation

What is meant by 360 degree feedback?

What kinds of groups are defined?

Click on "Ten Commonly Asked Questions".

What are some indicators of poor teamwork?
What are the group causes of poor teamwork?
What are the organizational causes of poor teamwork?
What can be done to encourage teamwork?

What types of seminars and training does this company provide that corresponds to the material related in this and previous chapters?

ANSWERS

LEARNING THE LANGUAGE

1.	Cross-functional self managed teams	10.	Inverted organization	19.	Matrix organization
2.	Hierarchy	11.	Span of control	20.	Staff personnel
3.	Networking	12.	Chain of command	21.	Economies of scale
4.	Restructuring	13.	Line personnel	22.	Tall organization structure
5.	Organizational (or corporate) culture	14.	Benchmarking	23.	Line organization
6.	Informal organization	15.	Decentralized authority	24.	Real time
7.	Core competencies	16.	Flat organization structure	25.	Digital natives
8.	Bureaucracy	17.	Departmentalization	26.	Virtual corporation
9.	Centralized authority	18.	Formal organization		

ASSESSMENT CHECK

Learning Goal 1

Everyone's organizing

1. According to the text the key to success for organizations is remaining flexible and adapting to the changing times. Often that means going back to basic organizational principles.

2. a. Division of labor refers to dividing up tasks among workers.
   b. Job specialization is dividing tasks into smaller jobs.

3. Structuring an organization consists of:
   a. devising a division of labor.
   b. setting up teams or departments to do specific tasks.
   c. assigning responsibility and authority to people.
   d. allocating resources.
   e. assigning specific tasks.
   f. establishing procedures for accomplishing organizational objectives.

4. An organization chart shows relationships among people: who is accountable for the completion of specific work and who reports to whom.

5. The change in organizations is due to the changing business environment—more global competition, a declining economy, faster technological change, and pressure to do more about the environment. Consumer expectations have also changed, and consumers expect the highest quality products and fast, friendly service at a reasonable cost.

The Changing Organization

6. a. Unity of command—reporting to only one boss.
   b. Hierarchy of authority—workers should know to whom they report.
   c. Division of labor—functions are divided into areas of specialization.
   d. Subordination of individual interests to the general interest—team work.
   e. Authority—managers have the right to give orders and power to enforce obedience.
   f. Degree of centralization—The amount of decision making power given to top management.
   g. Clear communication channels—worker should be able to easily contact each other.
   h. Order—people and materials should be in the proper location.
   i. Equity—managers should treat employees with respect and justice.
   j. Esprit de corps—a spirit of pride and loyalty should be created.

7. The process of rule making often led to rigid organizations that didn't always respond quickly to consumer requests.

8. Four characteristics of Weber's bureaucracy are:
   a. Job descriptions.
   b. Written rules, decision guidelines and detailed records.
   c. Consistent procedures, regulations and policies.
   d. Staffing and promotions based on qualifications.

9. Workers during Weber's time were much less educated and trained than today's workers. Weber felt that a firm would do well if employees would do what managers told them to do. The less decision making employees had to do, the better.

10. In a company with many layers of management, if employees want to introduce work changes, they ask a supervisor, who asks a manager, who asks a manager at the next level up, and so on. Eventually a decision is made and passed down from manager to manager until it reaches the employee. Decisions can take weeks or months to be made.

    Weber used the term bureaucrat to describe a middle manager whose function it was to implement top management's orders.

11. When employees have to ask their manager for permission to make a change, the process may take so long that customers become annoyed. This can happen in both large and small organizations. Since customers want efficient, quick service, slow service is not acceptable.

12. To make customers happy, organizations are giving employees more power to make decisions on their own and to please the customer no matter what.

Learning Goal 3

Decisions to Make in Structuring Organizations

13. Centralized authority

Advantages	Disadvantages
a. Greater management control	a. Less responsiveness to customers
b. More efficiency	b. Less empowerment
c. Simpler distribution system	c. Interorganizational conflict
d. Stronger brand/corporate image	d. Lower morale away from headquarters

14. Decentralized authority

   Advantages

   a. Better adaptation go customer wants
   b. More empowerment of workers
   c. Faster decision making
   d. Higher morale

   Disadvantages

   a. Less efficiency
   b. Complex distribution system
   c. Less top-management control
   d. Weakened corporate image

15. At levels where work is standardized, span of control can be broad. The appropriate span gradually narrows at higher levels of the organization because work becomes less standardized and managers need more face-to-face communication.

16. The trend is to expand the span of control by reducing the number of middle managers and hiring more educated and talented lower level employees.

17. In a tall organization there are many levels of management, and span of control is small. In a flat organization, there are fewer layers of management, and the span of control gets broader.

18. A flat structure can respond more readily to customer demands because lower-level employees have authority and responsibility for making decision s, and managers can be spared some day-to-day tasks.

19. The advantages and disadvantages of the traditional functional structure are:

   Advantages

   a. Skills can be developed in depth and employees can progress as skills are developed.
   b. Economies of scale because resources can be centralized.
   c. Coordination with the function.

   Disadvantages

   a. Lack of communication among departments.
   b. Employees identify with the department and not with the corporation as a whole.
   c. Response to change is slow.
   d. People trained too narrowly.
   e. People in the same department tend to think alike—groupthink.

20. Five methods of grouping, or departmentalizing, workers are:
   a. Product
   b. Function
   c. Customer group
   d. Geographic location
   e. Process

21. The decision about which way to departmentalize depends upon the nature of the product and the customers served.

22. A hybrid form of departmentalization is being used when companies use a combination of departmentalization techniques.

Learning Goal 4

Organization Models

23. Four organizational structures are:
    a. Line organizations.
    b. Line and staff organizations.
    c. Matrix-style organizations.
    d. Cross-functional self-managed teams.

24. In a large business, a line organization may have the disadvantages of
    a. being too inflexible.
    b. having too few specialists.
    c. having long lines of communication.
    d. being unable to handle complex decisions necessary in a large organization.

25. The difference between line and staff personnel is authority. Line personnel have formal authority to make policy decisions. Staff personnel have the authority to advise the line personnel and make suggestions, but they can't make policy changes themselves.

26. In a matrix system a product manager can borrow people from different departments to help design and market new product ideas.

    This is important in industries where competition is stiff, and the life cycle of new ideas is short, and where the emphasis is on new product development, creativity, special projects, rapid communication, and interdepartmental teamwork.

27. The advantages and disadvantages of a matrix structure are:

    Advantages

    a. Flexibility in assigning people to projects.
    b. Encourages cooperation among departments.
    c. Can produce creative solutions to problems.
    d. Allows for efficient use of resources.

    Disadvantages

    a. Costly and complex.
    b. Can cause confusion among employees as to where their loyalty belongs.
    c. Requires good interpersonal skills and cooperative managers and employees.
    d. Temporary solution to long term problem.

28. A potential problem with teams created by matrix management is that the project teams are not permanent. After a problem is solved or a product developed, the team breaks up, so there is little opportunity for cross-functional training.

    An answer to the disadvantage of the temporary teams created by matrix management is to develop permanent teams and to empower them to work closely with suppliers, customers, and others to quickly and efficiently bring out new, high-quality products while giving great service.

29. Cross-functional teams consist of groups of employees from different departments who work together on a long term basis. These teams are empowered to make decisions without having to seek the approval of management. Barriers between functions fall when these interdepartmental teams are created.

30. When cross functional teams include customers, suppliers and distributors it goes beyond the boundaries of the organization, and market information can be shared.

Learning Goal 5

Managing the Interactions Among Firms

31. Transparency occurs when a company is so open to other companies that electronic information is shared as if the companies were one company.

32. Organizations are so closely linked via networking that each organization knows what the others are doing, in real time. Since data is so readily available to organizational partners, companies are so open to one another that the solid walls between them have become transparent. Because of this integration, two companies can now work together so closely that they operate as two departments within one company.

   Most organizations are no longer self-sufficient or self-contained. Many modern organizations are part of a vast network of global businesses. An organizational chart showing what people do within any one organization may not be complete because the company is actually part of a larger system of firms.

33. Organizational structures tend to be flexible and changing. Experts from one company may work for one company one year, and another the next year. Organizations deal with each other on a temporary basis and the ties between organizations are no longer permanent. These are often called virtual corporations because they are made up of replaceable firms or individuals that join the network and leave it as needed.

34. Benchmarking demands that organizations compare each function against the best in the world. If an organization can't do as well as the best in a particular area, it often will try to outsource the function to an organization that is the best. Outsourcing is assigning various functions to outside organizations. When a firm has completed the outsourcing process, the remaining functions are the firm's core competencies, which are functions that the organization can do as well as, or better than, any other organization in the world.

Learning Goal 6

Adapting To Change

35. Introducing change in an organization is difficult because managers and employees may have a tendency to "get stuck" in their old ways, and resist the efforts to change.

36. The Internet has created new opportunities to ask customers questions and provide them with information. Companies are coordinating the efforts of traditional departments with their Internet staff to create easy-to-manage interactions. Companies are also training older employees to be more tech savvy to become familiar with social networking sites such as Facebook and Twitter as well as other applications.

37.

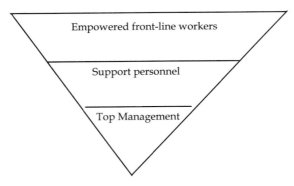

An inverted organization has contact people at the top and the chief executive officer at the bottom. There are few layers of management.

38. A manager's job in an inverted organization is to assist and support front line people, not boss them around.

39. Companies based upon an inverted organization structure support front-line personnel with internal and external databases, advance communication systems and professional assistance.

This means that front line personnel have to be better educated, better trained and better paid than in the past.

40. The culture of an organization is reflected in stories, traditions, and myths.

41. The best organizations have cultures that emphasize service to others, especially customers. The atmosphere is one of friendly, concerned, caring people who enjoy working together to provide a good product at a reasonable price. Those companies have less need for close supervision of employees, and fewer policy manuals, organization charts and formal rules, procedures and controls.

These companies stress high moral and ethical values such as honesty, reliability, fairness, environmental protection, and social involvement. The key to a productive culture is mutual trust.

42. All companies have a(n)
   a. formal organization   b.   informal organization

43. The drawback of the formal organization is that it is often too slow and bureaucratic to enable an organization to adapt quickly. The benefit of a formal organization is that it provides helpful guidelines and lines of authority to follow in routine situations.

44. The drawback of the informal organization is that it is often too unstructured and emotional to allow careful, reasoned decision-making on critical matters. But the informal organization is very effective in generating creative solutions to short-term problems and providing a feeling of camaraderie and teamwork among employees.

45. The grapevine is the nerve center of the informal organization. It is the system through which unofficial information flows between employees and managers. Key people in the grapevine have considerable influence.

46. In more traditional organizations, managers and employees were often at odds, and the informal structure often hindered management. In the new, more open organizations, managers and employees work together and the informal structure is viewed as an asset that promotes harmony among workers and establishes a positive corporate culture.

CRITICAL THINKING EXERCISES

Learning Goal 1

1. Obviously the answer to these questions will depend upon the organization you are evaluating. A college or university for example, will be divided by various functions that have to do with either administration or student issues. Then there will be the various academic departments, such as Accounting, Marketing and Finance. The lines of authority will be visible through department chair and dean positions. There are usually very clear procedures in colleges and universities for things such as applying for financial aid, obtaining on-campus housing, and registering for classes. In general, an academic institution will be very organized, and is often a good example of a bureaucracy.

Learning Goal 2

2. a. Fayol   e. Fayol   i. Weber
    b. Fayol   f. Fayol   j. Weber
    c. Weber   g. Fayol   k. Weber
    d. Weber   h. Weber   l. Fayol

Learning Goal 3

3. Sun-2-Shade is very small with a customer base where most of the needs are similar. In other words, there is no need to customize products to meet different regional needs, only shapes and sizes for different automobile brands. This company could use centralized authority because it is small and decision-making can still be made quickly. Employees probably have easy access to Eric, the founder and CEO of the company, who may want to retain control over his new company for the time being.

4. Changes in the areas we have been discussing are closely related to the changes we are seeing in the area of decision making. As spans of control widen and non-traditional ways of grouping workers emerge, decision-making is being delegated to lower levels of management, or even to non-management levels. Cross functional Self-managed teams, which are at the "lowest levels" of the organization, for example, are being given decision-making authority. Today's rapidly changing markets and differences in consumer tastes are favoring a more decentralized structure, flatter organizational structures, with wider spans of control and a team based structure.

5. a. Product and function (hybrid)   d. Geographic location
    b. Function   e. Customer group
    c. Process

Learning Goal 4

6. a. The best answer is most likely a matrix system.
    b. Line.
    c. Line and staff.
    d. Cross-functional self-managed teams.

7. Cross functional self managed teams will have a major impact on organizational designs of the future. Companies will be linked with customers, suppliers, and distributors through these teams, often through virtual corporations, creating an integrated system of firms working together to create products and services designed to quickly and exactly meet customers needs. Firms designed in such a manner will have a real competitive edge over corporations that are more traditional in their organizational structure.

8. These organizational changes are focused on designing the organization with meeting the needs of the customer as the most important objective. Inverted organizations empower front-line workers, who deal directly with the customers, and provide them with the information and support to satisfy customers. There is a focus on customer service and an emphasis on the firm's core competencies, outsourcing the functions at which the company is less proficient. Those functions that are not outsourced are benchmarked against the best in the world. The Internet makes it possible for firms to link with suppliers and customers to bring the "voice of the customer into the organization. The common theme is customer service.

9. The best organizations have positive corporate cultures that emphasize service to customers, have a relaxed atmosphere and concerned employees who enjoy working together to provide the best product at the best price. Companies that have good organizational cultures have less need for close supervision of employees, organization charts and formal rules, procedures and controls. That would indicate broad spans of control, empowered employees, flatter organizations, and a participative leadership style. Employees who need minimal supervision will flourish in self-managed teams, and there is mutual trust between workers and management.

10. There will obviously be many different answers to this question. A typical hierarchy in a community college for example may be President, Dean of Instruction, Associate Deans, Department Chairs, and faculty for instruction. For non-instruction areas, there may be Associate Deans, Directors, and non-management positions. There are often many layers of management between the lowest levels and the higher levels, and functional areas are well defined. There will be similar kinds of structures in a company.

11. How you would design the organization is up to you. Many of the ideas presented in the chapter will be helpful. This is a small company, so a line organization might be appropriate. We noted earlier that the workers are well educated and trained and don't need a lot of supervision, so close monitoring could prove to be counter-productive. There doesn't seem to be an immediate need for new product development, so a matrix structure wouldn't be necessary. The emphasis on customer service has been apparent throughout the chapter, so however you design the company, the focus should be on whatever design will most effectively help the company to meet customer needs using such tools as the Internet, to develop strong ties with both customers and suppliers.

PRACTICE TEST

MULTIPLE CHOICE

1.	a	11.	d
2.	c	12.	b
3.	c	13.	b
4.	d	14.	d
5.	b	15.	c
6.	b	16.	d
7.	d	17.	c
8.	a	18.	d
9.	a	19.	c
10.	c	20.	b

TRUE-FALSE

1.	T	11.	F
2.	T	12.	T
3.	F	13.	T
4.	F	14.	T
5.	F	15.	T
6.	T	16.	F
7.	F	17.	T
8.	T	18.	F
9.	F	19.	F
10.	T		

CHAPTER 9 – PRODUCTION AND OPERATIONS MANAGEMENT OF GOODS AND SERVICES

LEARNING GOALS

After you have read and studied this chapter, you should be able to:

1. Describe the current state of U.S. manufacturing and what manufacturers have done to become more competitive.
2. Describe the evolution from production to operations management.
3. Identify various production processes and describe techniques that improve productivity, including computer aided design and manufacturing, flexible manufacturing, lean manufacturing, and mass customization.
4. Describe operations management planning issues including facility location, facility layout, materials requirement planning, purchasing, just-in-time inventory control and quality control.
5. Explain the use of PERT and Gantt charts to control manufacturing processes.

LEARNING THE LANGUAGE

Listed below are important terms found in the chapter. Choose the correct term for each definition and write it in the space provided.

Assembly process	Form utility	Process manufacturing
Computer-aided design (CAD)	Gantt chart	Production
Computer- aided manufacturing (CAM)	Intermittent process	Production management
Computer integrated manufacturing (CIM)	ISO 9000	Program evaluation and review technique (PERT)
Continuous process	ISO 14000	Purchasing
Critical path	Just-in-time (JIT) inventory control	Quality
Enterprise resource planning (ERP)	Lean manufacturing	Six Sigma quality
Facility layout	Mass customization	Statistical process control (SPC)
Facility location	Materials requirement planning (MRP)	Statistical quality control (SQC)
Flexible manufacturing	Operations management	Telecommuting

1. A bar graph showing production managers what projects are being worked on and what stage they are in at any given time is called a _____.

2. A quality measure known as _____ allows only 3.4 defects per million opportunities.

3. A computer application called _____ is a newer version of MRP, and combines the computerized functions of all the divisions and subsidiaries of the firm, such as finance, materials requirement planning, human resources, and order fulfillment, into a single integrated software program that uses a single database.

4. A production process called the _____ puts together components into a finished product.

5. The term _____ is used to describe all the activities managers do to help their firms create goods.

6. Some managers use the process known as _____ to continually monitor all phases of the production process to assure that quality is being built into the product from the beginning.

7. The use of computers in the design of products is called _____.

8. A concept known as _____ means tailoring products to meet the needs of individual customers.

9. A specialized area in management called _____ converts or transforms resources into goods and services.

10. The function in a firm that searches for quality material resources, finds the best suppliers and negotiates the best price for goods and services is known as _____.

11. The term _____ refers to the physical arrangement of resources in the production process.

12. The use of computers in the manufacturing of products is known as _____.

13. Consistently producing what the customer wants while reducing errors before and after delivery to the customer is known as _____.

14. The value added by the creation of finished goods and services, or _____ , refers to the value added, for example, by taking silicon and making computer chips or putting services together to create a vacation package.

15. The production process known as _____ physically or chemically changes materials.

16. Designing machines to do multiple tasks so that they can produce a variety of products is called _____.

17. _____ is the production of goods using less of everything compared to mass production.

18. In a PERT network, the _____ is the sequence of tasks that takes the longest time to complete.

19. A computer application called _____ uses sales forecasts to make sure the needed parts and materials are available at the right time and place.

20. Uniting computer-aided design with computer-aided manufacturing is called _____.

21. Production processes known as _____ have long production runs that turn out finished goods over time.

22. The common name given to quality management and assurance standards is _____.

23. The process of _____ consists of taking statistical samples of product components at each stage of the production process and plotting those results on a graph. Any variances from quality standards are recognized and can be corrected if beyond the set standards.

24. When a minimum of inventory is kept on the premises, and parts, supplies and other needs are delivered just in time to go on the assembly line, the company is using _____.

25. The process of _____ is selecting a geographic location for a company's operations.

26. A method called _____ means analyzing the tasks involved in completing a given project, estimating the time needed to complete each task, and identifying the minimum time needed to complete the total project.

27. _____ is the creation of finished goods and services using the factors of production: land, labor, capital, entrepreneurship and knowledge.

28. A(n) _____ is a production process in which the production run is short and the machines are changed frequently to make different products.

29. A collection called _____ identifies the best practices for managing an organization's impact on the environment.

30. Working from home via computer and modem is known as _____.

ASSESSMENT CHECK

Learning Goal 1

Manufacturing and Services in Perspective

1. Describe the current state of manufacturing in the U.S. compared to the beginning of this decade. Is the U.S. still a manufacturing based economy?

2. What are 7 areas American manufacturers and service organization do to maintain a competitive edge in the world marketplace?

a. _____

b. _____

c. _____

d. _____

e. _____

f. _____

g. _____

Learning Goal 2

From Production to Operations Management

3. What is the difference between production management and operations management?

4. What is the focus of operations management in the service sector?

5. What has become the quality standard in the services industry?

Learning Goal 3

Production Processes

6. What are the three basic requirements of production, according to Andrew Grove?

a. _____

b. _____

c. _____

7. What is the difference between process manufacturing and assembly process?

8. What is the difference between a continuous production process and an intermittent process, in manufacturing?

9. Why do many manufacturers today use intermittent processes?

10. The ultimate goal of operations management is to _____

_____

11. What four major developments have radically changed the production process in the United States?

a. _____   c. _____

b. _____   d. _____

12. What is made possible with the use of CAD/CAM?

13. What is CIM and what is the benefit?

14. How can flexible manufacturing reduce labor costs?

15. How does a company become "lean"?

16. What are the characteristics of lean companies?

   a. _____

   b. _____

   c. _____

   d. _____

   e. _____

17. What are some examples of how companies have used mass customization?

Learning Goal 4

Operations Management Planning

18. What are the problems solved by operations management planning?

   a. _____   d. _____

   b. _____   e. _____

   c. _____   f. _____

19. One strategy in selecting a facility location is to find a location that _____

   _____.

20. What do brick and mortar stores have to do to compete with services offered over the Internet?

21. List the major considerations in the site selection process.

   a. _____

   b. _____

   c. _____

   d. _____

   e. _____

   f. _____

   g. _____

h. _____

i. _____

22. What is the key reason why firms move their plants?

23. Other key reasons that firms move their production facilities include:

    a. _____

    b. _____

24. In reducing time to market, what do manufacturers need?

25. What is the benefit, for companies, of locating close to their suppliers?

26. Why do businesses build factories in foreign countries? What do U.S. firms consider in choosing a site in a foreign country?

27. Identify the quality of life questions that firms consider in the facilities location process.

28. Describe the concept of "interfirm process", as it relates to operations management.

29. What impact is technology having on facilities location?

30. How do manufacturing and services differ with respect to facilities layout?

31. What's the difference between an assembly line layout and a modular layout?

32. Describe:

    a. A process layout:

    b. A fixed position layout:

33. How is ERP different from MRP?

34. What are the results from using ERP?

35. How is the purchasing function different today from the past?

36. What is required in order for a JIT (just-in-time inventory) program to work effectively? What problems could be encountered?

37. JIT systems make sure the: _____

    _____.

38. What problems resulted when quality control was conducted at the end of the production line?

    a. _____

    b. _____

    c. _____

39. a. Six sigma quality detects _____.

b. Statistical quality control is the process used to _____

_____.

c. Statistical process control reduces the need for _____

_____.

40. What are the seven key areas in which a company must show quality in order to qualify for the Baldrige Awards?

a. _____   e. _____

b. _____   f. _____

c. _____   g. _____

d. _____

41. Name the two major criteria for earning the Baldrige Awards.

a. _____

b. _____

42. Describe the International Organization for Standardization.

43. What do the new ISO 9004: 2000 standards require?

44. Why is ISO certification so important for U.S. firms?

45. What is the difference between ISO 9000 and ISO 14000?

46. What are the requirements for ISO 14000 certification?

Control Procedures: PERT and Gantt charts

47.　List the four steps in designing a PERT chart:

a.　_____

b.　_____

c.　_____

d.　_____

48.　Why is it "critical" to identify the critical path?

49.　What is the difference between a Gantt Chart and a PERT Chart?

50.　How can a manager use a Gantt Chart?

CRITICAL THINKING EXERCISES

Learning Goal 1

1.　We have been reading throughout the text of the move toward a global marketplace, and the need for U.S. firms to make changes to be competitive. How are production processes and productivity fundamental to the process?

Learning Goal 2

2. Why has the term "production management" been changed to "operations management"? What are some examples of operations management?

Learning Goal 3

3. In manufacturing, two types of manufacturing processes are:

    a) process manufacturing , which is changing materials.
    b) assembly process which is putting together components.

    In addition, production processes are either: continuous or intermittent

    Match the correct type of production process to each of the following, according to the description:

    a. _____   The steel industry never shuts down its ovens.

    b. _____   In the furniture industry, a store will sell custom designed furniture and pass the order on to the manufacturer, who then custom makes each piece.

    c. _____   The Ford Mustang is assembled piece by piece along an assembly   line.

    d. _____   In the steel industry, ore is melted down, poured into forms, and then cooled.

4. How can CAD/CAM be related to mass customization?

5. You have learned in earlier chapters that one advantage small businesses often have over larger, less flexible companies is the ability to move quickly to serve the needs of their markets and provide more customized service. As increasing numbers of large businesses implement the modern production techniques discussed in this chapter, what potential impact could this have on small businesses?

6. Five radically different production techniques have emerged in recent years:

Just-in-time inventory control   Mass customization
Flexible manufacturing   Lean manufacturing

Distinguish the differences between each technique in the following:

a. _____ At the Harley Davidson motorcycle plant in York Pennsylvania the suppliers are electronically linked to the Harley plant and parts go straight from the delivery truck to the assembly floor. There is no inventory storage area in the plant.

b. _____ Volvo uses modular construction in their plants, where workers are grouped into autonomous teams working on mobile assembly platforms that carry the cars to the workers. Each worker has been trained to do a whole cluster of tasks. This system enabled Volvo to build quality cars with fewer workers in more space efficient plants, and has reduced the number of hours need to assemble a car.

c. _____ You can design your own athletic shoes at nike.com, personalize your M&Ms at mm.com and even custom design your own Mini Cooper because of today's production technology.

d. _____ At Dynalink Industries, 15 machines are used to make, test and package component parts for stereo and quadraphonic sound systems. The parts are never touched by human hands.

Learning Goal 4

7. Businesses may choose to locate close to where the buying power for their product is located, where labor is inexpensive and/or skilled, where land and other resources are inexpensive and readily available, close to their markets or where quality of life is high.

Evaluate the area in which you live based on the site-selection criteria discussed in the text. Does your area have an advantage in the variables considered for site selection? If so, which ones? Are you located close to markets? What could you say to convince a producer or service business to locate in your area? In some areas there will be an organization that addresses these very issues. In St. Louis, Missouri, for example, the Regional Chamber and Growth Association (www.stlrcga.org) addresses many of the site selection factors for the St. Louis region.

8. How has increased global competition forced U.S. firms to "rethink" quality?

9. Sun-2-Shade, a company that makes self-darkening windshields for automobiles, is beginning to gear up for production. It has 2 main product lines: a windshield that is designed to be installed during the automotive assembly process, and an "after-market" product, to be sold in auto parts stores, which can be installed by companies that repair and install windshields after manufacture. These windshields are made from a lightweight, specially formulated plastic. Sun-2-Shade buys the raw material from a plastic supplier. The plastic is melted down and poured into molds, which are then allowed to cool. The windshields are then transformed into the self-darkening type windshield using proprietary processes. For added durability the last stage of manufacturing applies a scratch resistant hard coat to all windshields. The process is similar for both product lines, with some alterations needed for the retail version. What type of production process is Sun-2-Shade likely to be using? How can the company ensure their product is available when the assembly plant needs it, and when the retailer wants to sell it?

Learning Goal 5

10. PERT, Critical Path and Gantt charts are control measures used to ensure that products are manufactured and delivered on time.

   Draw a PERT Chart for cooking and serving a breakfast of 3-minute eggs, buttered toast and coffee and identify the critical path.

PRACTICE TEST

MULTIPLE CHOICE — Circle the best answer

Learning Goal 1

1. What statement is most accurate in describing the trend in manufacturing in the United States?
   a. The U.S. is expected to become a manufacturing based economy.
   b. Traditional manufacturing techniques have proved to be the most efficient and effective.
   c. Jobs in the U.S. manufacturing have declined significantly.
   d. Foreign competition has not affected U.S. manufacturers.

2. When looking at how American manufacturers have regained a competitive edge, which of the following would <u>not</u> be included?
   a. Reducing product quality to keep costs low.
   b. Relying on the Internet to unite companies.
   c. Practicing continuous improvement.
   d. Focusing on customers.

3. The United States has:
    a. has begun to focus on lower quality products in order to provide the lowest priced products to customers.
    b. has seen a change in manufacturing from operations management to production management.
    c. become a service based economy.
    d. begun to see a major resurgence in U.S. manufacturing jobs.

4. New production techniques have:
    a. been difficult and costly to implement, and so have been largely ignored.
    b. made it possible to custom-make products for individual buyers.
    c. have been implemented primarily by foreign manufacturers.
    d. have not been shown to be effective in making U.S. manufacturers competitive.

5. _____ is a specialized area in management that converts or transforms resources into goods and services and includes the areas of inventory management, quality control, production scheduling, follow-up services and more.
    a. Lean manufacturing
    b. CAD/CAM
    c. Flexible manufacturing
    d. Operations management

Learning Goal 3

6. Paul Klabber designs and makes custom wood furniture. The process Paul uses in his business is an example of a(n):
    a. assembly process.
    b. intermittent process.
    c. analytic system.
    d. continuous process.

7. Quon Ho believes that there must be a way to cut down on the amount of resources his company uses in the production process. Quon feels that the company uses more space, tools and time to make their product than is necessary. Quon should examine the benefits of:
    a. lean manufacturing.
    b. CAD/CAM.
    c. mass customization.
    d. facilities layout.

8. _____ makes it possible to custom-design products to meet the needs of small markets with very little increase in cost.
    a. CAD/CAM
    b. Site selection
    c. Production management
    d. Process manufacturing

9. Which of the following is <u>not</u> considered a strong reason for companies to move production facilities from one area to another?
    a. availability of cheap labor
    b. cheaper natural resources
    c. the level of unemployment in a geographic area
    d. reducing the time it takes to deliver products to the market

10. Sun-2-Shade is beginning to see some competition for their self-darkening windshield. In order to remain competitive, Sun-2-Shade must be sure to:
    a. replace all workers with automated equipment.
    b. move all manufacturing to foreign countries.
    c. train all salesmen in aggressive selling techniques.
    d. keep the costs of manufacturing down.

11. Quantum Industries is a maker of component parts in heating and cooling ventilation systems. The company is looking for a site on which to build a new production facility. They are considering areas that have adequate rail access, and are at the hub of major highways. Quantum's major consideration appears to be:
    a. inexpensive resources.
    b. time to market.
    c. access to cheap land.
    d. finding low cost labor.

12. The idea of facility layout is to:
    a. make it easy for workers to find their work stations.
    b. have offices, machines, and storage areas in the best position to enable workers to produce goods and services for their customers.
    c. ensure that the building meets all building codes for the area in which they are located.
    d. facilitate the assembly line process.

13. The U.S. award that recognizes firms that meet customer needs, produce high quality products and have high quality internal operations, is known as:
    a. ISO 9000 standards.
    b. The Customer Excellence Award.
    c. The Malcolm Baldrige National Quality Award.
    d. ISO 14000 standards.

14. One reason ISO 9000 standards are so important is that:
    a. they must be met in order to win any quality awards.
    b. most free trade agreements require that these standards be met.
    c. meeting these standards will automatically increase worker productivity.
    d. companies that want to do business with the EU must be certified by ISO standards.

15. Many companies are moving from a(n) _____ , in which workers do only a few tasks at a time to a _____ , in which teams of workers combine to produce more complex units of the final product.
    a. modular layout; assembly line layout
    b. intermittent process; continuous process
    c. assembly line layout; modular layout
    d. continuous process; process manufacturing

16. Tony Ruggali is in the process of opening a new restaurant. Tony wants to be sure that his new place The Fresh Place, always has the freshest ingredients, and will always be known for being the "freshest place in town." He also wants to devote most of the space in the restaurant to tables for diners, not for storing products. Tony could make use of:
    a. analytic production.
    b. Gantt charts.
    c. Just in time inventory control.
    d. mass production.

17. Sun-2-Shade wants to link its resource planning and manufacturing with its suppliers in order to develop a more integrated system. Sun-2-Shade could use:
    a. enterprise resource planning.
    b. continuous process manufacturing.
    c. PERT charts.
    d. total quality control.

18. _____ is the process managers use to continually monitor al phases of the production process to ensure that quality is being built into the product from the beginning.
    a. Six sigma quality
    b. Statistical process control (SPC)
    c. Statistical quality control (SQC)
    d. Process manufacturing

Learning Goal 5

19. A _____ is a bar graph that shows which projects are being worked on and how much has been completed.
    a. PERT chart
    b. flexible manufacturing system
    c. Gantt chart
    d. CAD/CAM system

20. Hector Lopez is a production supervisor at the local cucumber processing plant. Hector is looking at a chart that illustrates for him the sequence of tasks involved in processing the cukes. He is especially interested in the sequence of tasks that take the longest time to complete. Hector is interested in the:
    a. Gantt chart.
    b. total quality management process.
    c. critical path.
    d. lean manufacturing process.

TRUE-FALSE

Learning Goal 1

1. _____ One thing American manufacturers have done to regain a competitive edge has been to incorporate more rigid management styles.

2. _____ The United States is still a leader in industries such as nanotechnology, biotechnology, and other areas.

3. _____ As the U.S. service sector grows, managers will become more occupied with service productivity, and with blending services and manufacturing through the Internet.

4. _____ Global competition has had little effect on American manufacturers.

Learning Goal 2

5. _____ Operations management is a specialized area in management that converts resources into goods and services.

6. _____ Operations management focuses primarily on manufacturing, as it doesn't really apply in the service sector.

7. _____ Delighting customers by anticipating their needs has become the quality standard for most service businesses.

Learning Goal 3

8. _____ Form utility is the value added by placing goods and services in areas easily accessible to your customers.

9. _____ The ultimate goal of manufacturing and process management is to provide high-quality goods and services instantaneously in response to customer demand.

10. _____ Computer integrated manufacturing (CIM) unites computer aided design machines with computer aided manufacturing machines.

11. _____ Flexible manufacturing systems are so flexible that a special order, even a single item can be produced without slowing down the manufacturing process.

12. _____ Mass customization is a means of manufacturing small batch products using mass production techniques.

Learning Goal 4

13. _____ Quality of life issues are generally not important when firms are considering site locations.

14. _____ Enterprise Resource Planning is a way of integrating functions within a single firm.

15. _____ Operations management is becoming an interfirm process where companies work together to design, produce, and ship products to customers.

16. _____ Facility layout is not an important factor in the services industry.

17. _____ The Internet has transformed the purchasing function.

18. _____ Six Sigma quality control standards allow for no defects whatsoever.

Learning Goal 5

19. _____ A Gantt computer program will allow a manager to trace the production process minute by minute to determine which tasks are on time and which are behind.

20. _____ The critical path in a PERT network is the group of activities that must be completed in order for the project to be successful.

You Can Find It on the Net

We have studied some of the ideas of lean manufacturing in this chapter. To learn more, visit www.leanstrategies.com

What are the key strategies of "lean" companies?

What are "lean customer relationships"? How do you create them?

What are the areas to consider in lean order fulfillment?

What do lean supply chains do, and what areas are important?

What must a company do to have lean product development?

ANSWERS

LEARNING THE LANGUAGE

1.	Gantt chart	11.	Facility layout	21.	Continuous process
2.	Six Sigma quality	12.	Computer aided manufacturing (CAM)	22.	ISO 9000
3.	Enterprise resource planning (ERP)	13.	Quality	23.	Statistical process control (SPC)
4.	Assembly process	14.	Form utility	24.	Just in time inventory control (JIT)
5.	Production management	15.	Process manufacturing	25.	Facility location
6.	Statistical quality control (SQC)	16.	Flexible manufacturing	26.	Program evaluation and review technique (PERT)
7.	Computer aided design (CAD)	17.	Lean manufacturing	27.	Production
8.	Mass customization	18.	Critical path	28.	Intermittent process
9.	Operations management	19.	Materials Requirement Planning (MRP)	29.	ISO 14000
10.	Purchasing	20.	Computer integrated manufacturing (CIM)	30.	Telecommuting

ASSESSMENT CHECK

Learning Goal 1

Manufacturing and Services in Perspective

1. Jobs in manufacturing have been declining in the last years, and unemployment could reach double digits in the manufacturing sector. However, from 2001 until the collapse in 2007, manufacturing output rose 4 percent per year, and the United States was still the world's leading manufacturer, accounting for 25 percent of all goods produced in the world each year.

    The U.S. is no longer manufacturing based. About 70 percent of G.D.P. and 85 percent of jobs now come from the service sector.

2. Manufacturers today have emphasized:
    a. Focusing on customers.
    b. Maintaining close relationships with suppliers and other companies to satisfy customer needs.
    c. Practicing continuous improvement.
    d. Focusing on quality.
    e. Saving on costs through site selection.
    f. Relying on the Internet to unite companies.
    g. Adopting new manufacturing techniques.

From Production to Operations Management

3. Production management is the term used to describe all the management activities that help firms create goods. Operations management is a specialized area in management that converts or transforms resources into goods and services. It includes inventory management, quality control, production scheduling, follow-up services, and more.

4. Operations management in the service sector is all about creating a good experience for those who use the service.

5. The quality standard in the services industry has become delighting the customers by anticipating their needs.

Learning Goal 3

Production Processes

6. According to Andrew Grove, the three basic requirements of production are:
    a. Build and deliver products in response to demands of a customer at a scheduled delivery time.
    b. Provide an acceptable quality level.
    c. Provide everything at the lowest possible cost.

7. Process manufacturing physically or chemically changes materials, such as the process used to change sand into glass. Assembly process puts components together, such as in the assembly of an automobile.

8. A continuous process is one in which long production runs turn out finished goods over time, as in the chemical industry. An intermittent process is an operation where the production run is short and the machines changed frequently to product different products, as in custom made furniture.

9. Many manufacturers use intermittent processes because the use of computers, robots, and flexible manufacturing processes make it possible to make custom-made goods almost as fast as mass-produced goods were once made.

10. The ultimate goal of operations management is to provide high-quality goods and services instantaneously in response to consumer demand.

11. Four major developments that have changed the production process in the United States are:
    a. Computer aided design and manufacturing.
    b. flexible manufacturing.
    c. lean manufacturing.
    d. mass customization.

12. CAD/CAM has made it possible to custom-design products to meet the needs of small markets with very little increase in cost. A manufacturer can program the computer to make a simple design change, and that change can be incorporated directly into the production line.

13. Computer integrated manufacturing, CIM, is software that unites CAD with CAM. It can reduce the amount of time needed to program machines by as much as 80% and thus reduces the cost of manufacturing.

14. Flexible manufacturing allows manufacturers to design machines to do multiple tasks so that they can produce a variety of products. Products and changes are made without any labor, thus reducing labor costs.

15. A company becomes lean by continuously increasing the capacity to produce high quality goods while decreasing its need for resources.

16. Characteristics of lean companies are:
    a. They take half the human effort.
    b. They have half the defects in the finished product or service.
    c. They require one-third the engineering effort.
    d. They use half the floor space for the same output.
    e. They carry 90 percent less inventory.

17. Companies in both the manufacturing and the service sector are using mass customization. GNC stores for example feature machines that allow shoppers to custom design several products. Other companies provide custom made books, custom greeting cards and custom fitted shoes and clothes. In the service sector there are customized insurance policies, fitness programs, and vacation packages

Learning Goal 4

Operations Management Planning

18. The problems solved by operations management planning include:
    a. facility location
    b. facility layout
    c. materials requirement planning
    d. purchasing
    e. inventory control
    f. quality control

19. One strategy in selecting a facility location is to find a location that makes it easy for customers to access your service and to maintain a dialogue about their needs. This strategy is being used by flower shops and banks when they locate facilities in supermarkets, McDonald's in Wal-Mart and gas stations.

20. In order for brick and mortar stores to compete with Internet shopping they have to choose good locations and offer outstanding service to those who come to the store.

21. The major considerations in the site selection process are:
    a. labor costs.
    b. availability of resources, including labor.
    c. access to transportation that can reduce time to market.
    d. proximity to suppliers.
    e. proximity to customers.
    f. low crime rates.
    g. quality of life for employees.
    h. cost of living.
    i. the ability to train or retrain the local workforce.

22. A key reason why producers move their plants is the availability of inexpensive labor, or the right kind of skilled labor.

23. Other key reasons for moving production facilities include:
    a. inexpensive resources.
    b. to reduce the time-to-market.

24. In reducing time to market, manufacturers need sites that allow products to move through the system quickly, at the lowest costs, so they can be delivered rapidly to customers. Access to transportation is critical, and information technology is important, so companies look for areas with the most advanced information systems.

25. The benefit of locating close to suppliers is that it cuts the cost of distribution and makes communication easier.

26. Companies choose to locate in foreign counties in order to get closer to international customers. U. S. firms consider whether they are near to transportation facilities so that raw materials and finished goods can be moved quickly and easily.

27. Quality of life questions include: Are there good schools nearby? Is the weather nice? Does the local community welcome new businesses? Do the chief executive and other key managers want to live there?

28. Companies are creating new relationships with suppliers over the Internet so that operations management is becoming an "interfirm" process, where companies work together to design, produce, and ship products to customers. Many manufacturing companies are developing new Internet-focused strategies that will enable them and others to compete more effectively. The changes are having a dramatic effect on operations managers who have to adjust from a one-firm system to an interfirm environment.

29. Information technology is giving firms and employees more flexibility in the choice of locations. This allows for telecommuting, and companies that no longer need to locate near sources of labor will be able to move to areas where land is less expensive and the quality of life may be higher.

30. In manufacturing facilities layout depends on the processes that are to be performed. The physical arrangement must be designed to most efficiently produce goods and services for customer.
    For services, the layout is designed to help the consumer find and buy what they need. Often this means helping consumers to find and buy things on the Internet. Some stores have added kiosks that enable customers to search for goods on the Internet and place the order from the store.

31. An assembly line layout is one in which workers do only a few tasks at a tine. A modular layout is one in which teams of workers combine to produce more complex units of the final product.

32. a. process layout is one in which similar equipment and functions are grouped together. The order in which the product visits a function depends on the design of the item.
    b. A fixed position layout allows workers to congregate around the product to be completed.

33. MRP allows manufacturers to make sure that needed parts and materials are available at the right place and the right time. ERP is the newest variation of MRP. Enterprise resource planning is a computer-based production and operations system that enables multiple firms to manage all of their operations on the basis of a single, integrated set of corporate data.

34. The results from using ERP is shorter time between orders and payment, less staff to do ordering and order processing, reduced inventories, and better customer service for all firms involved.

35. In the past, manufacturers tended to deal with many different suppliers. Today manufacturers are relying more heavily on one or two suppliers because so much information is shared that firms don't want to have so many companies knowing their business. Thus, the relationship between suppliers and manufacturers is much closer than ever before. The Internet has significantly reduced the cost of purchasing items.

36. To work effectively, the JIT process requires excellent coordination with carefully selected suppliers who are electronically connected.
   JIT runs into problems when suppliers are located at some distance from their customers. Weather may delay shipments for example.

37. JIT systems make sure the right materials are at the right place at the right time at the cheapest cost toe meet both customer and production needs.

38. In the past quality control was often done at the end of the production line in the quality control department. The problems that resulted were:
   a. There was a need to inspect other people's work. This took extra people and resources.
   b. If errors were found, someone would have to correct the mistake or scrap the product. This is costly.
   c. A customer who found the mistake could be dissatisfied and buy from someone else.

39. a. Six sigma quality detects potential problems before they occur.
   b. Statistical quality control is the process used to continually monitor all processes in the production process to assure that quality is being built into the product from the beginning.
   c. Statistical process control reduced the need for having a quality control inspection at the end of a production line because mistakes are caught much earlier in the production process.

40. To qualify for a Baldrige Award, a firm must show quality in:
   a. leadership.
   b. strategic planning.
   c. customer and market focus.
   d. information and analysis.
   e. human resources focus.
   f. process management.
   g. business results.

41. The two major criteria for earning the Baldrige Awards are
   a. whether customer wants and needs are met.
   b. customer satisfaction ratings are better than the competition.

42. The International Organization for Standardization is a worldwide federation of national standards bodies from more than 140 countries that set the global measures for the quality of individual products. It is a non-governmental organization established to promote the development of world standards to facilitate the international exchange of goods and servies.

43. ISO 9004: 2000 standards require that a company determine what customer needs are, including regulatory and legal requirements. There must also be communication arrangements to handle issues like complaints. Other standards involve process control, product testing, storage, and delivery.

44. ISO certification is important for U.S. firms because the European Union is demanding that companies that want to do business with the EU be certified by ISO standards.

45. ISO 9000 is the name given to quality management and assurance standards. ISO 14000 is a collection of the best practices for managing an organization's impact on the environment. It does not prescribe a performance level like ISO 9000 does.

46. The requirements for ISO 14000 include having an environmental policy, having specific improvement targets, conducting audits of environmental programs, and maintaining top management review of the processes.

Learning Goal 5

Control Procedures: PERT and Gantt charts

47. The four steps involved in developing a PERT chart include:
    a. Analyze and sequence tasks that need to be done
    b. Estimate the time needed to complete each task
    c. Draw a PERT network illustrating the 2 previous steps
    d. Identify the critical path

48. The critical path in a PERT chart identifies the sequence of tasks that takes the longest time to complete. It is critical because a delay in the time needed to complete this path would cause the project or production run to be late.

49. A PERT chart analyzes the tasks involved in completing a given project, estimating the time needed to complete each task, and identifying the minimum time needed to complete the total project. It is a complex project that is done by computer.
    A Gantt chart is used to measure production progress using a bar chart that shows what projects are being worked on and how much has been completed at any given time.

50. With a Gantt chart, a manager can trace the production process minute by minute to determine which tasks are on time, and which are behind so that adjustments can be made to stay on schedule.

CRITICAL THINKING EXERCISES

Learning Goal 1

1. Production is the creation of goods and services using the factors of production, while productivity measures how <u>efficiently</u> the goods and services have been created. To be competitive in world markets, manufacturers must keep the cost of production low while production must be relatively high. The fundamental question is: How does a producer keep costs low and still produce high quality products that satisfy customer needs? In other words, how do manufacturers increase productivity?

   U.S. manufacturers have emphasized areas such as: focusing on customers, maintaining close relationships with suppliers and other companies, focusing on quality, practicing continuous improvement, saving on costs through site selection, relying on the Internet to unite companies, and adopting new manufacturing techniques to increase productivity and regain a competitive edge in the global marketplace.

2. The term production has changed to operations to reflect the fact that the United States has become a service-based economy, and the term "operations" reflects both goods and services production. Operations management is a specialized area of management, and includes inventory management, quality control, production scheduling and more. An example of operations management in goods manufacturing is an automotive plant, where operations management transforms raw materials, human resources, parts, supplies, and other resources into automobiles. In a college, operations management takes inputs such as information, professors, supplies, buildings and so on and creates a process of education.

Learning Goal 3

3. a. continuous   c. assembly process
    b. intermittent assembly process   d. process manufacturing

4. CAD/CAM is the integration of computers into the design and manufacture of products. This process has enabled manufacturers to tailor products to meet the needs of individual consumers at very little or no extra cost. A simple design change can be incorporated directly into the production line. It is what has enabled Nike to offer "custom made" athletic footwear at very little additional cost. CAD/CAM systems have revolutionized the production process and have essentially <u>created</u> and allowed for the concept of mass customization.

5. As bigger businesses increase the use of sophisticated manufacturing technology, they will be able to meet the changing needs of their markets much more quickly. This weakens one advantage small businesses have had, which has been the ability to adapt quickly to changing customer markets. Additionally, big businesses are now able to customize their product, enabling them to meet the needs of smaller target markets, traditionally a stronghold for smaller businesses.

6. a. Just-in-time inventory control   c. Mass customization
    b. Lean manufacturing   d. Flexible-manufacturing system

Learning Goal 4

7. The area in which you live may meet a number of important criteria. Look for a population that may be willing to work hard for less pay, such as new immigrants. What kind of skilled labor is available in your area? Is your state a "right to work" state or a heavily unionized state? That affects labor costs. Are you in a rural, suburban or urban area? That affects the availability and costs of land.

   If you live in a large urban area, such as Chicago, New York, or Los Angeles, businesses may be attracted because that's where their customers are. However land is more expensive, so a large production facility may not be built there. There may be lots of opportunity for a service-based business to locate in that area. Government support will vary from one area to another, in the form of tax incentives and zoning laws.

8. If U.S. firms want to remain competitive in today's global environment, they must focus on quality issues the same way that European and Asian countries have done. As we have read in earlier chapters these countries are often able to produce high quality goods at low prices. Further ISO standards have provided a common denominator of business quality around the world. U.S. firms have begun to realize that in order to be competitive, they must not only compete with, but also cooperate with, international firms to continue to serve global markets with the highest quality products and services at the lowest possible prices.

   U.S. firms have adopted programs such as Six Sigma, SQC and SPC to both reduce costs and ensure high quality products for their customers

Learning Goals 3, 4

9. It sounds like Sun-2-Shade uses the process manufacturing system to create the product, as they mold the plastic used for the windshields into a product to meet their needs. This would most likely be an intermittent process, as the machines or molds may need to be changed depending upon the style of automobile for which they are making the windshield. This can be done entirely by using a flexible manufacturing system.

   Sun-2-Shade needs to keep track of its own inventory, as well as that of the auto assembly plants and their retail customers. Enterprise resource planning is a sophisticated computer-based operations system that would link Sun-2-Shade with their suppliers, as well as with their customers. With this system, Sun-2-Shade could track the availability of the plastic they need from their supplier. They could monitor their own inventory to ensure adequate stock at crucial times, and be sure that their customers have what they need when they need it to keep production flowing smoothly, and sales at the retail level from slacking off.

   Sun-2-Shade must also consider locating their plant(s) near the plants assembling the cars installed with their windshield. This is especially important for any automotive assembly plant using JIT systems.

Learning Goal 5

10. To cook a breakfast of 3-minute eggs, buttered toast and coffee, a PERT chart may look like this:

The critical path is the brewing and pouring of the coffee, as it takes the longest time to complete.

254

PRACTICE TEST

MULTIPLE CHOICE

1.	c	11.	b
2.	a	12.	b
3.	c	13.	c
4.	b	14.	d
5.	d	15.	c
6.	b	16.	c
7.	a	17.	a
8.	a	18.	c
9.	c	19.	c
10.	d	20.	c

TRUE-FALSE

1.	F	11.	T
2.	T	12.	F
3.	T	13.	F
4.	F	14.	T
5.	T	15.	T
6.	F	16.	F
7.	T	17.	T
8.	F	18.	F
9.	T	19.	T
10.	T	20.	F

CHAPTER 10 – MOTIVATING EMPLOYEES

LEARNING GOALS

After you have read and studied this chapter, you should be able to:

1. Explain Taylor's theory of scientific management.
2. Describe the Hawthorne studies and their significance to management.
3. Identify the levels of Maslow's hierarchy of needs and apply them to employee motivation.
4. Distinguish between motivators and hygiene factors identified by Herzberg.
5. Differentiate among Theory X, Theory Y and Theory Z.
6. Describe the key principles of goal setting theory, expectancy, reinforcement, and equity theories.
7. Show how managers put motivation theories into action through such strategies as job enrichment, open communication, and job recognition.
8. Show how managers personalize motivation strategies to appeal to employees across the globe and across generations.

LEARNING THE LANGUAGE

Listed below are important terms found in the chapter. Choose the correct term for each definition and write it in the space provided.

Equity theory	Intrinsic reward	Motivators
Expectancy theory	Job enlargement	Principle of motion economy
Extrinsic reward	Job enrichment	Reinforcement theory
Goal-setting theory	Job rotation	Scientific management
Hawthorne effect	Management by objectives (MBO)	Time-motion studies
Hygiene factors	Maslow's hierarchy of needs	

1. Herzberg's theory of motivating factors called _____ , cause dissatisfaction if missing, but do not motivate employees if increased.

2. The theory that positive and negative reinforcers motivate a person to behave a certain way is called _____ .

3. Begun by Frederick Taylor, _____ are studies of which tasks must be performed to complete a job and the time needed to do each task.

4. A(n) _____ is the personal satisfaction you feel when you perform well and complete goals.

5. A system of goal setting and implementation known as _____ involves a cycle of discussion, review, and evaluation of objectives among top and middle-level managers, supervisors, and employees.

6. A job enrichment strategy known as _____ involves combining a series of tasks into one assignment that is challenging and interesting.

7. A(n) _____ is something given to you by someone else as recognition for good work, including pay increases, praise and promotions.

8. A motivational strategy that emphasizes motivating the workers through the job itself is called _____.

9. Herzberg's theory of motivating factors known as _____ cause employees to be productive and give them satisfaction.

10. _____ is the idea that setting ambitious but attainable goals can motivate workers and improve performance if the goals are accepted, accompanied by feedback and facilitated by organizational conditions.

11. The _____ refers to the tendency for people to behave differently when they know they are being studied.

12. Known as _____ this is a job enrichment strategy involving moving employees from one job to another.

13. Victor Vroom's _____ indicates that the amount of effort employees exert on a specific task depends on their expectations of the outcome.

14. The study of workers to find the most efficient way of doing things and then teaching people those techniques is known as _____.

15. _____ is the idea that employees try to maintain equity between inputs and outputs compared to others in similar positions.

16. Frank and Lillian Gilbreth developed the _____ which is the theory that every job can be broken down into a series of elementary motions.

17. The theory of motivation called _____ is based on unmet human needs from basic physiological needs to safety, social, and esteem needs to self-actualization needs.

ASSESSMENT CHECK

Learning Goal 1

The Value of Motivation

1. What is meant by the term "engagement" in terms of workers motivation? Why is it important to have "engaged" workers?

2. What did Taylor believe were the ways to improve productivity?

    a. _____

    b. _____

    c. _____

3. What three elements were basic to Scientific Management?

    a. _____

    b. _____

    c. _____

4. Taylor measured worker output by conducting _____.

5. Henry Gantt developed _____

_____

6. What contribution did Frank and Lillian Gilbreth make to the field of Scientific Management?

7. Scientific management viewed workers as _____

_____

8. How are the ideas of Scientific Management being used today?

Learning Goal 2

Elton Mayo and the Hawthorne Studies

9. What problem was revealed during the initial Hawthorne experiments?

10. Why did the experimenters believe the Hawthorne Experiments were a failure after the second series of experiments?

11. Describe three conclusions drawn from the Hawthorne Experiments:

    a. _____

    b. _____

    c. _____

12. To what does the term "the Hawthorne Effect" refer?

13. How did research, and assumptions about employees, change after the Hawthorne Experiments?

Learning Goal 3

Motivation and Maslow's Hierarchy of Needs

14. Describe the five need levels on Maslow's Hierarchy:

    a. _____

    b. _____

    c. _____

    d. _____

    e. _____

15. According to Maslow, what happens when a need is satisfied?

16. Many of the world's workers struggle to meet what kinds of needs?

17. What kind of work environment must U.S. firms create to compete successfully?

Herzberg's Motivating Factors

18. What did Herzberg's research find were the most important factors that motivate workers?

a. _____   h. _____

b. _____   i. _____

c. _____   j. _____

d. _____   k. _____

e. _____   l. _____

f. _____   m. _____

g. _____   n. _____

19. Factors that motivated workers clustered around _____.

20. According to Herzberg what do workers want from the job?

21. In Herzberg's study, the absence of _____

could cause _____

but _____.

22. Identify Herzberg's motivators:

a. _____

b. _____

c. _____

d. _____

e. _____

23. List Herzberg's hygiene factors.

    a. _____

    b. _____

    c. _____

    d. _____

    e. _____

24. Herzberg's motivating factors lead to what conclusion about the best way to motivate employees?

Learning Goal 5

McGregor's Theory X and Theory Y

25. Identify the assumptions of a Theory X manager:

    a. _____

    b. _____

    c. _____

    d. _____

26. What are the natural consequences of a Theory X manager's attitudes?

27. What are the assumptions of a Theory Y manager?

    a. _____

    b. _____

    c. _____

    d. _____

    e. _____

    f. _____

    g. _____

28. How do the Theory Y manager's attitudes affect behavior toward employees?

29. Empowerment gives employees _____

   _____.

30. For empowerment to be a motivator, management should follow these steps:

   a. _____

   b. _____

   c. _____

31. List the major elements of Ouchi's "Type J" management approach, based on Japanese culture.

   a. _____   e. _____

   b. _____   f. _____

   c. _____   g. _____

   d. _____

32. According to William Ouchi, the American management approach, or Type A involves:

   a. _____   e. _____

   b. _____   f. _____

   c. _____   g. _____

   d. _____

33. Describe Theory Z, and its major elements.

   a. _____   e. _____

   b. _____   f. _____

   c. _____   g. _____

   d. _____

34. According to the text an appropriate management style is _____

   _____.

Learning Goal 6

Goal-Setting Theory and Management By Objectives

35. Goals can motivate workers and improve performance if the goals are:

   a. _____

   b. _____

   c. _____

36. The four things a manager does in an MBO program are:

   a. _____

   b. _____

   c. _____

   d. _____

37. Describe the difference between "helping" and "coaching".

38. Problems arise when management uses MBO as a strategy for _____

   _____.

Meeting Employee Expectations: Expectancy Theory

39. According to expectancy theory, what are three questions employees ask before exerting maximum effort to a task?

   a. _____

   b. _____

   c. _____

40. According to expectancy theory what are the steps to improving employee performance?

   a. _____

   b. _____

   c. _____

   d. _____

   e. _____

Reinforcing Employee Performance: Reinforcement Theory

41. In the words of reinforcement theory, motivation is the result of _____ _____.

42. Positive reinforcements are _____.

    Negative reinforcement includes _____.

43. What is meant by the term "extinction" in reinforcement theory?

Treating Employees Fairly: Equity Theory

44. What are the basic principles of Equity theory?

45. How do people behave when they perceive an inequity?

46. Equity judgments are based on _____.

    Workers are going to feel rewards are inequitable when _____ _____.

    Organizations deal with this by_____.

    The best remedy is: _____.

Learning Goal 7

Putting Theory Into Action

47. In a job enrichment motivational strategy, work is assigned _____ _____.

48. Describe the five characteristics of work important in affecting individual motivation and performance.

    a. _____

    b. _____

    c. _____

    d. _____

    e. _____

49. What is job simplification?

50. Discuss the difference between job enlargement and job rotation.

51. Procedures for encouraging open communication include:

   a. _____

   b. _____

   c. _____

   d. _____

   e. _____

   f. _____

   g. _____

52. How can managers "re-invent work"?

53. What are some things companies can do to celebrate and reward work well done, and improve employees' spirits?

Learning Goal 8

Personalizing Motivation

54. What makes motivating workers today complicated?

55. Describe the difference between a "high context" culture and a "low-context culture".

56. How will generational differences between baby boomers and Generation X affect motivation?

57. Millennials tend to share the following characteristics:

    a. _____

    b. _____

    c. _____

    d. _____

    e. _____

    f. _____

    g. _____

    h. _____

    i. _____

    j. _____

    k. _____

58. In business, it is likely that motivation will come from _____
_____.

59. In order to motivate workers managers will need to give them:

    a. _____

    b. _____

    c. _____

CRITICAL THINKING EXERCISES

Learning Goal 1

1. Extrinsic and intrinsic rewards are important aspects of motivation for workers, as well as for students! Think about the job you currently hold, or a job you would like to have in the future, or alternatively, about your "job" as a student. Identify some of the extrinsic rewards that are specific to your job, or to you as a student. What intrinsic rewards do you find in those jobs?

Learning Goals 1, 2

2. Early management studies were conducted by:

    Frederick Taylor – Scientific Management
    Frank and Lillian Gilbreth – Motion economy
    Elton Mayo – Hawthorne Experiments

    Read the following and indicate which ideas are being described.

    a. _____ Conducted a series of experiments designed to measure the effect of working conditions on worker productivity.

    b. _____ These studies became the basis for human-based management.

    c. _____ Created time-motion studies to measure output over time.

    d. _____ Discovered that worker productivity could increase despite adverse conditions.

    e. _____ Believed the way to improve productivity was to scientifically study the most efficient ways to perform each task, determine the one "best way" to do things, then teach people those methods.

    f. _____ The principle of motion economy was based on his theory.

    g. _____ Developed the principle of scientific management.

    h. _____ Discovered that when workers are involved in planning and decision-making, the workers are more motivated.

    i. _____ Found that workers were motivated in an informal atmosphere where they could interact with supervisors.

    j. _____ Believed people would be motivated primarily by money.

k. _____ Identified the tendency for people to behave differently when they know they are being studied.

l. _____ Developed the idea that every job could be broken down into a series of elementary motions, which could then be analyzed to make it more efficient.

m. _____ His findings lead to new assumptions about employees, including the idea that pay is not the only motivator for workers.

3. How did Taylor and other proponents of Scientific Management view workers? How does that compare to Mayo's Hawthorne Studies?

Learning Goal 3

4. The principle behind Maslow's ideas is that only unmet needs are motivators, and that needs could be arranged in a hierarchy.
   Complete the illustration shown below, and give two examples for each need level, where appropriate.

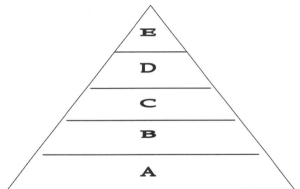

A. _____   D. _____

   1. _____   1. _____

   2. _____   2. _____

B. _____   E. _____

   1. _____   1. _____

   2. _____   2. _____

C. _____

   1. _____

   2. _____

5. Read the following statements, and determine which need on Maslow's Hierarchy is being described.

    a. _____ Ryan Raley gets home from school and immediately raids the refrigerator.

    b. _____ Jan Stahl joins as many campus organizations as she can fit into her schedule.

    c. _____ Bill Cook wins "Zone Manager of the Month" in his sales office, in recognition of his outstanding performance.

    d. _____ Wendy Armstrong, a 33 year old student with severe cerebral palsy, receives her bachelor's degree, a lifelong dream.

    e. _____ A union contract negotiator makes sure that layoffs will be made on the basis of seniority.

6. In developed countries, people seek to fill social, self-esteem, and self-actualization needs at work. Give two actions that a company or a manager could take to fill each of these higher level needs. What would motivate <u>you</u>?

    a. Social

    b. Self-esteem

    c. Self-actualization

Learning Goal 4

7. Workers at Universal Industries are among the best paid in the industry. Their factories are clean and workers seem to get along well with one another. "The bosses are okay" one worker is quoted as saying, "but they sure do hang around us a lot". The union has made sure that everyone has a secure position. Management at Universal is aware that their competitive position is in jeopardy, as several foreign firms have been making inroads into their market. Management is also aware that while it doesn't seem that there are problems with the workers, they don't seem to be motivated. Using Herzberg's theory of motivators and hygiene factors, discuss what the problem may be and what could be done to solve it.

Learning Goal 5

8. McGregor observed that managers had two different attitudes toward workers, which led to different management styles. He called these styles Theory X and Theory Y.

    Which type of manager would make each of the following statements?

    a. _____   "Joe is pretty good at solving these kinds of problems. Let's get his input on this."

    b. _____   "Ann, I know you'd like that promotion. Keep up the good work and I think you'll be the next new product manager."

    c. _____   "Tell that secretary that if she values her job, she'll keep those coffee breaks down to 15 minutes!"

    d. _____   "I think that secretary takes long coffee breaks because she gets her work done so quickly and then doesn't have much to do. She's been asking about working on the new product project. I'll talk to her about it and see what she thinks."

    e. _____   "Ann, new product managers have to work a lot of weekends and evenings. If you think you want that job, you'll have to prove to me you're willing to work those extra hours."

    f. _____   "Joe you need to do exactly what I tell you to fix the problem in your department. This needs to be done my way!"

9. Think back to Chapter 7, in which leadership styles are discussed. What kind of leadership style would a Theory X manager use most often? Theory Y? Why?

Learning Goal 6

10. Review MBO programs described in the text. How do you think an MBO program fits into the ideas of Maslow and Herzberg? What are some potential problems with MBO?

11. Think about expectancy theory and how it works for you. What is something you really want? How likely is it that you can reach the goal? Will the hard work be worth the effort? For example:

What kind of job do you want as a career? (or, go back and review the exercise you completed in Chapter 7 on planning, when you were asked to write out some long range and short range goals for yourself)

What do you need to do to get that kind of job? Is it possible to get that job if you exert the effort?

What intrinsic and extrinsic benefits will you get from this kind of job?

12. You are a manager of entry-level workers in an office of about 15 people. You have an employee who is consistently late for work, as often as 2 times per week. This is a problem because this individual is responsible for answering phones from both internal and external customers, and he has often missed important phone calls. Using reinforcement theory, how would you try to solve the problem with this employee, whose work is excellent, when he is there? You don't want to fire this person, because it would be costly and difficult to replace him.

13. Hal Yard is in marketing with a major manufacturer of sailboats. He has been happy with his job since he started there 3 years ago. He has received several raises, and has always gotten very good reviews. He is in line for a good promotion, which he should know about soon. Hal recently went to lunch with a new co-worker, Donna Telli. Donna just got her degree at night school, and this is her first "real" job. During the course of their conversation, Donna mentioned her starting salary, which is only $50 per month lower than Hal's!
How would you feel if you were Hal? Why? What would you do? What theories of motivation may come into play here?

Learning Goal 7

14. Four job design strategies are:

job enrichment   job enlargement
job simplification   job rotation

Which of the following is being illustrated in each of the following examples?

a. Employees at Published Image, a financial newsletter, are combined into a team so that one team has the entire responsibility of selling, writing, proofing, editing and distributing the newsletter to their own group of clients. While each member will specialize in a certain area, each member of the team knows enough about all the jobs to get the product out.

_____

b. New zone managers at Ford Motor Company move from one job to another during their training program, to familiarize themselves with the operations of the district sales office. _____

c. At the Pasta House Company restaurant, you are either an expediter, a host, a busser or a server. The job lines don't cross, and are distinct from one another. _____

d. At the Hosin Manufacturing Company, production is such that each worker makes an entire motor, instead of working only on separate parts. _____

15. Keeping in mind the five characteristics of work important in affecting motivation and performance, design an "enriched" job for publishing campus newsletters or for another area with which you are familiar.

Learning Goals 2–8

16. Things have really been happening at Sun-2-Shade, a company that manufactures self-darkening windshields. Lots of changes have been made and it would seem like things ought to be going smoothly. However, there are problems with the workers, and you just can't figure out what's wrong. People don't seem to be motivated, although they are being paid well. You have been in charge, made the decisions you thought were best for the company and the workers, and have even pitched in and shown people how you want things done from time to time. Everybody has their own job, and they know exactly how it's supposed to be done. You have heard some people complain that their job is boring, but you know that the way you have shown them is the best way to get things done. People come in late, and sometimes seem to actually resent your help! Most of the employees of this company are close to your age (Gen Xers and Millennials). You would really like the employees of this company to feel like they are a team. How will you solve this problem?

PRACTICE TEST

MULTIPLE CHOICE — Circle the best answer

Learning Goal 1

1. Time and motion studies, methods of work and rules of work were all part of the ideas of _____.
    a. Maslow's hierarchy of needs.
    b. Herzberg's two-factor theory.
    c. Taylor's scientific management.
    d. The Hawthorne Experiments.

2. Scientific Management viewed people largely as _____.
    a. Machines that needed to be programmed.
    b. Individuals who had specific needs that were filled at work.
    c. Workers in groups who needed to be self managed.
    d. Important contributors to management decision-making.

3. Frederick Taylor believed the best way to improve worker productivity was to:
   a. scientifically determine the most efficient way to perform a task and then teach people.
   b. design jobs to be interesting and challenging.
   c. determine people's needs at work and find ways to meet those needs.
   d. give people the authority to make decisions.

Learning Goal 2

4. Which of the following was identified by the Hawthorne Experiments?
   a. Workers were motivated primarily by money.
   b. traditional scientific management principles are the most effective way to improve productivity.
   c. It was not important to involve workers in the planning of the experiment.
   d. Workers though of themselves as a social group and enjoyed the atmosphere of a special room.

5. The tendency for people to behave differently when they know they're being studied is referred to as:
   a. Maslow's Hierarchy
   b. The Hawthorne effect
   c. Motivating factors
   d. Theory X

Learning Goal 3

6. The need for feel a part of a group, for love and acceptance is part of the _____ need on Maslow's hierarchy.
   a. self-actualization
   b. social
   c. esteem
   d. physical

7. Harry Leggins has worked for Shavem Industries for a number of years. He has just been passed over for promotion, again, and is considering leaving his employer because it seems that his managers don't appreciate his abilities. The only problem is that he really likes his co-workers, and they have an undefeated softball team. Harry is concerned with filling:
   a. esteem needs.
   b. social needs.
   c. self-actualization needs.
   d. safety needs.

8. According to Maslow's theory, when a need is satisfied:
   a. the need disappears, and will not re-appear.
   b. another, higher level need emerges and motivates a person to satisfy that need.
   c. it will continue to motivate a person, but not as strongly.
   d. we are content, and will continue to work, but will only be motivated by more money.

Learning Goal 4

9. According to Herzberg, workers felt that good pay and job security
   a. are the most important motivators for most workers.
   b. were important for participative management.
   c. provided a sense of satisfaction, but did not motivate them.
   d. were the best way to keep jobs interesting and to help them achieve their objectives.

10. Herzberg's hygiene factors include:
    a. achievement.
    b. salary.
    c. work itself.
    d. recognition.

11. Herzberg's theories conclude that:
    a. money is the number one motivator.
    b. motivation comes primarily from good working conditions.
    c. the absence of good working conditions has little to no effect on job satisfaction.
    d. the best ways to motivate employees is to make their jobs interesting, recognize achievement and add responsibility.

Learning Goal 5

12. At Flo Valley Manufacturing workers are encouraged to find their own solutions to problems, and to implement their solutions when practical. They work with little supervision because management feels they are committed workers, and that the workers are pretty creative. Flo Valley reflects a(n) _____ attitude about workers.
    a. Theory X
    b. autocratic
    c. scientific
    d. Theory Y

13. _____ emphasizes life time employment, collective decision making and individual responsibility for the outcome of decisions.
    a. Theory Z
    b. Theory X
    c. Theory Y
    d. Theory M

14. Douglas McGregor said that managers with a Theory X attitude believed:
    a. workers prefer to be directed.
    b. people seek responsibility.
    c. people will use imagination in problem solving.
    d. workers like work.

Learning Goal 6

15. According to the text, setting ambitious but attainable goals can motivate workers and improve performance if:
    a. people know what is expected of them.
    b. the goals are not too ambitious.
    c. employees are engaged in helping to set the goals.
    d. there is a definite time frame for completing the goals.

16. The central idea of MBO is that:
    a. managers need to set realistic goals for employees.
    b. employees need to motivate themselves.
    c. job satisfaction comes from the ability to learn new skills.
    d. employees must be closely supervised, and giving them goals will help to achieve that.

17. In terms of expectancy theory, which of the following is not one of the questions employees will ask themselves before committing a maximum effort toward a task?
    a. Can I accomplish this task?
    b. Is the reward worth the effort?
    c. Will the task include negative feedback?
    d. If I do accomplish the task, what is the reward?

18. Reinforcement theory is based on the idea that:
    a. positive and negative reinforcers motivate a person to behave a certain way.
    b. perceptions of fairness and how those perceptions affect employees' willingness to perform.
    c. the way managers go about motivating people at work depends on their attitudes toward workers.
    d. attainable goals will lead to high levels of motivation under certain conditions.

19. According to equity theory, when workers perceive an inequity, they will
    a. try to reestablish an equitable feeling in a number of ways.
    b. always reduce their efforts in the future.
    c. always increase their effort in the future.
    d. generally be mistaken in their perceptions.

Learning Goal 7

20. At the NOVA car manufacturing company, workers are grouped into self-managed teams, which are responsible for completing a significant portion of the automobile. Unlike the typical assembly plant, the car stops along the way, and the team completes their portion of the car before the vehicle moves on. The team is given the freedom to decide who does which job, and they receive constant feedback from the company. NOVA is using a job strategy of:
    a. job rotation.
    b. job enlargement.
    c. job enrichment.
    d. job simplification.

21. The strategy of making work interesting and motivating employees by moving them from one job to another is called:
    a. job enlargement.
    b. job simplification.
    c. job rotation.
    d. job enrichment

22. The degree to which a job has a substantial impact on the work of others in the company is called:
    a. skill variety.
    b. task identity.
    c. autonomy.
    d. task significance

23. To create an atmosphere of "us working together" and encourage open communication, managers should do everything but:
    a. provide feedback.
    b. eliminate separate facilities for managers.
    c. develop precise job descriptions so that everyone knows what to do.
    d. reward all upward communication, even if the discussion is negative.

Learning Goal 8

24. Generation X managers:
    a. may tend to focus more on results than on hours in the workplace.
    b. will tend to be inflexible.
    c. will have narrower viewpoints than their predecessors.
    d. will most likely closely supervise their workers, especially the Generation Y workers.

25. Lee Kwon is a Korean worker who has been transferred by his company to the United States for 6 months to negotiate a supplier contract. Lee is having some problems understanding how to do business in the U.S. He has tried to get to know his U.S. co-workers, but feels re-buffed when they prefer to just get down to business and get things done. The problem could be due to the fact that Lee is from a(n) _____ , and his U.S. co-workers are more comfortable with doing business differently.
    a. informal culture.
    b. high context culture.
    c. company that does not encourage communication
    d. low context culture

TRUE–FALSE

Learning Goal 1

1. _____ The satisfaction you feel when you have finished a term paper and done a good job is an example of an extrinsic reward.

2. _____ Frank and Lillian Gilbreth developed the principle of motion economy and therbligs.

3. _____ The ideas of Frederick Taylor and Scientific Management were good for their time, but are no longer being implemented in today's workplace.

Learning Goal 2

4. _____ The problem with the initial experiments of the Hawthorne Study was that the productivity of the experimental group actually decreased when lighting was changed.

5. _____ The Hawthorne Experiments led to new assumptions about workers, including that pay was not a strong motivator.

6. _____ One of the conclusions of the Hawthorne Experiments was that workers were more motivated because the felt their ideas were respected and that they were involved in decision making.

Learning Goal 3

7. _____ According to Maslow, satisfied needs will continue to motivate most individuals.

8. _____ Self-actualization needs on Maslow's Hierarchy refer to the need for recognition, acknowledgement and self respect.

9. _____ Herzberg's research results showed that the most important factors that motivate workers were a sense of achievement and earned recognition.

10. _____ Pay is included in the list of Herzberg's motivators.

Learning Goal 5

11. _____ A Theory Y manager believes that employees should be involved in both defining problems and in designing the solutions.

12. _____ Today, fierce competition is forcing Japanese companies to move away from their traditional ways of conducting business.

Learning Goal 6

13. _____ Goal-setting theory is based on the notion that workers will be more motivated if they know they have a goal in terms of the amount of money they will earn if they do a certain amount of work.

14. _____ The best way to implement MBO programs is to make sure that managers set goals in cooperation with everyone in the organization.

15. _____ In reinforcement theory positive reinforcements are rewards such as praise, recognition, or a pay raise.

16. _____ The basic principle of expectancy theory is that workers try to maintain equity when they compare what they expect to gain to people in similar situations.

Learning Goal 7

17. _____ Job rotation strategy is one in which work is assigned to individuals so that they have the opportunity to complete an identifiable task from beginning to end.

18. _____ A type of job enrichment is job enlargement, which combines a series of tasks into one challenging and interesting assignment.

19. _____ The concept of re-inventing work involves respecting workers, rewarding good work, developing worker skills and decentralizing authority.

20. _____ One procedure for encouraging open communication in an organization is to create a culture that rewards listening.

Learning Goal 8

21. _____ Delphi is an automotive vendor doing a significant amount of business in Asia. The company, based in the U.S. is looking for a way to motivate their Asian employees, and has decided to give the same kinds of merchandise awards they give their employees in the U.S., as a way to make the Asian workers feel accepted. According to the text, this is most likely the best way to motivate the Asian workers.

22. _____ A constant in business is that motivation comes from external punishments or rewards.

You Can Find It On the Net

Visit the web site www.accel-team.com/motivation   What motivation theories that have been discussed in this chapter can you identify from these pages?

How does what is noted compare to what is discussed in your text?

What is the "take" on money as a motivator?

How does the article indicate job design can be used to motivate?

Sometimes we wonder what companies can do to create a motivated workforce in the "real world". Go to the Fortune Magazine web site www.fortune.com . Link to the magazine's list of America's Most Admired Companies, the best place to work, the top 100 companies to work for in the United States and look through the articles that you are able to link to. What do you think makes the companies listed good places to work?
(If you are unable to access this link at home, you may go to your school or public library, and they should have the proper passwords or subscriber access.)

ANSWERS

LEARNING THE LANGUAGE

1.	Hygiene factors	7.	Extrinsic reward	13.	Expectancy theory
2.	Reinforcement theory	8.	Job enrichment	14.	Scientific management
3.	Time-motion studies	9.	Motivators	15.	Equity theory
4.	Intrinsic reward	10.	Goal setting theory	16.	Principle of motion economy
5.	Management by objectives (MBO)	11.	Hawthorne effect	17.	Maslow's hierarchy of needs
6.	Job enlargement	12.	Job rotation		

ASSESSMENT CHECK

Learning Goal 1

The Value of Motivation

1. The term engagement is used to describe employees' level of motivation, passion and commitment. Engaged or motivated employees work with passion and feel a connection to their company. Workers who are "disengaged" have "checked out."

2. The way to improve productivity according to Taylor was to
   a. scientifically study the most efficient way to do things
   b. determine the one best way
   c. teach people those methods

3. Three elements basic to Taylor's approach are:
   a. time   b. methods   c. rules of work

4. Taylor measured worker output by conducting *time and motion studies.*

5. Henry Gantt developed charts which managers use to plot the work of employees a day in advance down to the smallest detail.

6. Frank and Lillian Gilbreth used Taylor's ideas to develop the principle of motion economy, which showed that every job could be broken down into a series of elementary motions called a therblig.

7. Scientific management viewed people largely as machines that needed to be programmed. There was little concern for psychological or human aspects of work.

8. Today, some of Taylor's ideas are still being implemented. Some companies still place more emphasis on conformity to work rules than on creativity, flexibility, and responsiveness. UPS is a modern example of Scientific Management at work today.

Learning Goal 2

Elton Mayo and The Hawthorne Studies

9. Elton Mayo and his colleagues wanted to test the degree of lighting associated with optimum productivity, a traditional scientific management study. The problem with the initial experiments was that productivity of the experimental group compared to other workers doing the same job went up regardless of whether the lighting was bright or dim.

10. The second series of experiments added a number of other environmental factors to the experiment, such as temperature and humidity. Productivity went up with each experiment. No matter what the experimenters did, productivity went up thus proving the initial ideas were invalid.

11. Three conclusions drawn from the Hawthorne Experiments are:
    a. People in work groups think of themselves as a social group.
    b. Involving employees in decision-making motivates them.
    c. Job satisfaction increases with a friendly atmosphere and additional compensation.

12. The Hawthorne Effect refers to the tendency of people to behave differently when they know they're being studied.

13. After the Hawthorne Experiments, the emphasis of research shifted away from Taylor's scientific management to a new human-based management. Mayo's findings led to new assumptions about employees, and found that money was a relatively ineffective motivator. That change led to many theories about the human side of management.

Learning Goal 3

Motivation and Maslow's Hierarchy of Needs

14. The five need levels on Maslow's Hierarchy are:
    a. Physiological – basic survival needs, such as the need for food, water and shelter
    b. Safety – the need to feel secure at work and at home
    c. Social – the need to feel loved, accepted and part of a group
    d. Esteem – the need for recognition and acknowledgement from others, self respect and sense of status or importance
    e. Self-actualization – the need to develop one's fullest potential

15. Maslow believed that people are motivated to satisfy unmet needs. When one need is satisfied another, higher level need emerges, and a person will attempt to satisfy that need. Needs that have been satisfied do not provide motivation.

16. In many parts of the world, workers struggle to meet the basic needs, such as the physiological and safety needs. In countries such as the United States, lower level needs do not dominate, and workers seek to satisfy higher level needs such as social, esteem and self actualization.

17. To compete successfully, U.S. firms must create a work environment that includes goals such as social contribution, honesty, reliability, service, quality, dependability, and unity for all levels of employees.

Learning Goal 4

Herzberg's Motivating Factors

18. Herzberg's research found that the most important factors that motivated workers are:
    a. sense of achievement
    b. earned recognition
    c. interest in the work
    d. opportunity for growth
    e. opportunity for advancement.
    f. importance of responsibility
    g. peer and group relationships
    h. pay
    i. supervisor's fairness
    j. company policies and rules
    k. status
    l. job security
    m. supervisor's friendliness
    n. working conditions

19. Herzberg noted that the factors that motivated workers clustered around job content.

20. Workers like to feel that they contribute. They want to earn recognition and feel their jobs are important. They want responsibility and want recognition for that responsibility by having a chance for growth and advancement. They also want their jobs to be interesting.

    Herzberg also noted that factors having to do with job environment were not considered motivators by workers. This includes pay, which workers feel gives them a sense of satisfaction, but does not motivate.

    Herzberg's motivators had to do with job content, and caused employees to be productive and gave them satisfaction. Hygiene factors (or maintenance factors) had to do with job environment, and could cause dissatisfaction if missing, but would not motivate employees if these factors were increased.

21. According to Herzberg, the absence of good pay, job security, and friendly supervisors could cause dissatisfaction, but their presence did not motivate.

22. Herzberg's motivators are:
    a. The work itself
    b. Achievement
    c. Recognition
    d. Responsibility
    e. Growth and advancement

23. Hygiene factors are:
    a. Company policy and administration
    b. Supervision
    c. Working conditions
    d. Interpersonal relations
    e. Salary

24. Herzberg's motivating factors led to the conclusion that the best way to motivate employees is to make the job interesting, help them to achieve their objectives, and recognize that achievement through advancement and added responsibility.

Learning Goal 5

McGregor's Theory X and Theory Y

25. The assumptions of a Theory X manager are:
    a. The average person dislikes work and will avoid it if possible.
    b. The average person must be forced, controlled, directed or threatened with punishment to make them work.
    c. The average worker prefers to be directed, wants to avoid responsibility, has little ambition and wants security.
    d. Primary motivators are money and fear.

26. As a result of his or her attitudes, a Theory X manager will watch people closely, telling them what to do and how to do it. Motivation will take the form of punishment for bad work, rather than reward for good work. Workers are given little responsibility, authority, or flexibility.

27. The assumptions of a Theory Y manager are:
    a. The average person likes work, and feels it is as natural as play or rest.
    b. The average person naturally works toward goals to which they are committed.
    c. How committed a person is to goals depends on the rewards for achieving them.
    d. Under certain conditions, the average person accepts and seeks responsibility.
    e. People are capable of creativity, cleverness, and imagination.
    f. The average person's intellectual potential is only partially used in industry.
    g. People are motivated by a variety of rewards, unique to each worker.

28. A Theory Y manager will emphasize a relaxed atmosphere, in which workers are free to set objectives, be creative, be flexible, and go beyond the goals set by management. A key factor in this environment is empowerment.

29. Empowerment gives employees the ability to make decisions and the tools to implement the decisions they make.

30. For empowerment to be a motivator, management should:
    a. Find out what problems people think are in the organization.
    b. Let them design the solutions.
    c. Get out of the way and let them put the solutions into action.

31. The elements of Type J management include:
    a. life-time employment
    b. consensual decision making
    c. collective responsibility
    d. slow evaluation and promotion
    e. implied control mechanisms
    f. nonspecialized career paths
    g. holistic concern for employees

32. The American management approach, or Type A involves:
    a. short term employment
    b. individual decision making
    c. individual responsibility
    d. rapid evaluation and promotion
    e. explicit control mechanisms
    f. specialized career paths
    g. segmented concern for employees

33. Theory Z blends the characteristics of Type J and Type A. This approach involves
    a. long-term employment,
    b. collective decision-making
    c. individual responsibility for the outcome of decisions
    d. slow evaluation and promotion
    e. moderately specialized career paths
    f. implicit, informal control, with explicit formalized control
    g. holistic concern for the employee, including the family

34. According to the text, the appropriate management style is one that fits the culture, the situation, and the specific needs of the organization.

Learning Goal 6

Goal-Setting Theory and Management by Objectives

35. Goals can motivate workers and improve performance if the goals are:
    a. accepted.
    b. accompanied by feedback.
    c. facilitated by organizational conditions.

36. The four things a manager does in an MBO program are:
    a. Set goals in cooperation with everyone in the organization.
    b. Commit employees to the goals.
    c. Monitor results.
    d. Reward accomplishments.

37. Helping means working with the subordinate and doing part of the work if necessary. Coaching means acting as a resource—teaching guiding, and recommending- but not participating actively or doing the task.

38. Problems arise when management uses MBO to force managers and workers to commit to goals that are not mutually agreed upon, but are instead set by top management.

Meeting Employee Expectations: Expectancy Theory

39. Before exerting maximum effort employees will ask:
    a. Can I accomplish the task?
    b. If I do accomplish it, what's my reward?
    c. Is the reward worth the effort?

40. To improve employee performance, managers should:
    a. Determine what rewards are valued by employees.
    b. Determine the employee's desired performance standard.
    c. Ensure performance standards are attainable.
    d. Guarantee rewards are tied to performance.
    e. Be certain rewards are considered adequate.

Reinforcing Employee Performance: Reinforcement Theory

41. In the words of reinforcement theory, motivation is the result of the carrot-and-stick approach, reward and punishment. Individuals act to receive rewards and avoid punishment.

42. Positive reinforcements are rewards such as praise, recognition, or a pay raise.

    Negative reinforcement includes reprimands, reduced pay, layoff or firing.

43. Extinction is what happens when a manager tries to stop undesirable behavior by not responding to it. The hope is that the unwanted behavior will eventually become extinct.

Treating Employees Fairly: Equity Theory

44. Equity theory has to do with perceptions of fairness and how those perceptions affect employees' willingness to perform. The basic principle is that workers try to maintain equity between inputs and outputs compared to people in similar positions. It is based on the perceptions of fairness and how those perceptions affect employees' willingness to perform.

45. When workers perceive an inequity, they will try to reestablish fairness. They reduce effort or rationalize differences, for example. Or, if you believe you have benefited from the inequity, you may increase your effort to justify the higher reward or rationalize by saying "I'm worth it!"

46. Equity judgments are based on perceptions.

Workers are going to feel rewards are inequitable when they overestimate their own contributions, as happens often. So they will feel that any rewards given out for performance are inequitable.

Organizations try to deal with this by keeping salaries secret, but that can make things worse.

The best remedy is clear and frequent communication.

Learning Goal 7

Putting Theory Into Action

47. In a job enrichment strategy, work is assigned so individuals can complete an identifiable task from beginning to end. They are held responsible for successful completion of the task.

48. The characteristics of work important in affecting individual motivation and performance are:
   a. Skill variety – The extent to which a job demands different skills.
   b. Task identity – The degree to which the job requires doing a task with a visible outcome from beginning to end.
   c. Task significance – The degree to which the job has a substantial impact on the lives or work of others in the company.
   d. Autonomy – The degree of freedom, independence, and discretion in scheduling work and determining procedures.
   e. Feedback – The amount of direct and clear information that is received about job performance.

49. Job simplification produces task efficiency by breaking down a job into simple steps and assigning people to each of those steps.

50. Job enlargement combines a series of tasks into one assignment that is more challenging, interesting, and motivating. Job rotation also makes work more interesting, but does so by moving employees from one job to another.

51. Procedures for encouraging open communication include:
   a. Create an organizational culture that rewards listening by creating places for employees to talk, and by providing feedback, adopting employee suggestions and rewarding upward communication.
   b. Train supervisors and managers to listen.
   c. Use effective questioning techniques.
   d. Remove barriers to open communication such as separate facilities for management.
   e. Avoid vague and ambiguous communication, such the passive voice, and terms like "possibly" and "perhaps".
   f. Make it easy to communicate with open facilities, and organizational activities which allow employees at all levels to mix.
   g. Ask employees what is important to them by using "stay interviews".

52. Re-inventing work means companies must focus on respecting workers, providing interesting work, rewarding good work, developing workers' skills, allowing autonomy ,decentralizing authority and rewarding good work.

53. To celebrate and reward work well done, companies can provide advancement opportunities, and recognize positive actions to help employees fee valued. Many companies have raised employees' spirits without raising paychecks by offering family trips to theme parks for a day, various kinds of perks, days off to work for charities, and various kinds of employee recognition programs. Sometimes workers will be inspired by the offer of a small equity stake or stock options in the company.

Learning Goal 8

Personalizing Motivation

54. Managers will have to get to know each worker personally and tailor the motivational effort to the individual. This is true because different employees respond to different managerial and motivational styles. Motivating workers is made more complicated by the increase in global business and the fact that managers now work with employees from many different cultures and from different generations. Different cultures and members of different generations experience motivational approaches differently.

55. In a "high-context" culture, workers build personal relationships, and develop group trust before focusing on tasks. In a "low-context" culture workers often view relationship building as a waste of time that diverts attention from the task.

56. Baby boomer managers will need to learn to be flexible with their Generation X employees, or risk losing them. Generation X employees will need to use their enthusiasm for change and streamlining to their advantage.

57. Millennials tend to share the following characteristics:
    a. impatient
    b. skeptical
    c. blunt and expressive
    d. image driven
    e. inexperienced
    f. adaptable
    g. tech savvy
    h. able to grasp new concepts
    i. practiced at multi-tasking
    j. efficient
    k. tolerant

58. In business it is likely that motivation will come from the job itself rather than from external punishments or rewards.

59. In order to motivate workers managers will need to give them:
    a. the right tools.
    b. the right information.
    c. the right amount of cooperation.

CRITICAL THINKING EXERCISES

Learning Goal 1

1. Of course your answer will be specific to your personality. Some extrinsic rewards for you could be pay, but other others might be a chance to play on a softball team with a group of co-workers you enjoy.

   The intrinsic rewards you could get as a student, for example could he satisfaction from completing a paper, or the sense of camaraderie from playing on your school's softball team.

Learning Goals 1, 2

2. a. Elton Mayo – Hawthorne experiments
   b. Hawthorne studies
   c. Taylor
   d. Hawthorne studies
   e. Taylor
   f. Gilbreth
   g. Taylor
   h. Hawthorne experiments
   i. Hawthorne experiments
   j. Taylor
   k. Hawthorne experiments
   l. Gilbreth
   m. Hawthorne experiments

3. Taylor and the other proponents of scientific management viewed people largely as machines which, properly programmed, could perform at a high level of effectiveness. Time and motion specialists studied every move a worker made, and standardized every motion. The most important tools were a stopwatch and observation.

   Although the Hawthorne studies grew out of Taylor's research, they came to a very different conclusion. Mayo began by studying environmental effects on worker productivity, with the idea of determining the degree of lighting associated with optimum productivity. When productivity increased regardless of the amount of illumination, a second series of experiments was conducted. When those experiments had similar results, Mayo guessed that some human or psychological factor was involved. When workers were interviewed about their feelings Mayo recognized that people were motivated at work by a relaxed atmosphere, being involved in decision-making, and by being in a social group as well as by additional compensation.

   The Hawthorne Studies, then, recognized the human and psychological factors that impact worker productivity. This was different from scientific management, which ignored the human aspect of work.

Learning Goal 3

4. The examples you give will be different from these but you get the idea.

   A. Physiological
      1. Food
      2. Rest
   B. Safety
      1. Locks on your doors
      2. Job security
   C. Social
      1. Belonging to a club
      2. Family life
   D. Self-esteem
      1. Winning an award
      2. Getting a desired promotion
   E. Self-actualization
      1. Accomplishing a goal
      2. Getting an "A" in a difficult class

5. a. Physiological   d. Self-actualization
   b. Social   e. Safety
   c. Self-esteem

6. a. To fill social needs companies could sponsor baseball teams, hold picnics, implement self-managed work teams
   b. Esteem needs can be met by recognition programs, recognizing an employee's achievement in a company newsletter, allowing employees to participate in decision-making
   c. To help fill self-actualization needs, companies could offer tuition assistance programs, provide job training, allow people to set their own goals, implement self-managed work teams, provide appropriate rewards for accomplishing objectives.

Learning Goal 4

7. From Herzberg's perspective, it looks like management and the union both have been concentrating on hygiene factors, while ignoring those factors that would motivate workers to greater productivity. The workers are apparently satisfied, as there are no problems, according to management. This means that the workers are content with pay, supervision, working conditions and interpersonal relations, as is indicated throughout the story. If management wants motivated workers, they should continue what they are doing now, but also find ways to give workers a sense of achievement, make the work more interesting, give workers more responsibility, a chance for growth and advancement. According to Herzberg, these are factors which will motivate workers.

Learning Goal 5

8. a. Y   d. Y
   b. Y   e. Y
   c. X   f. X

9. A Theory X manager would most likely use an autocratic style of leadership. When a manager believes that workers prefer to be told what to do, and do not want to assume responsibility, they are not likely to involve workers in decision making. A Theory X manager will make decisions, then announce the decision to his/her workers.

   A Theory Y manager is more likely to use a more democratic or participative leadership style. Employee input will be important to a Y manager, who believes that people are creative and seek responsibility. In essence Theory Y empowers employees to reach their potential. A Theory Y manager may also lean toward a laissez-faire leadership style.

Learning Goal 6

10. MBO programs could fill upper level needs on Maslow's hierarchy and serve as motivators in Herzberg's terms, by giving workers responsibility, a chance for growth and helping them to meet their own personal goals. Involvement of employees in setting goals is a key because it focuses on the participative management aspects of MBO, which is the type of leadership or management style these theories support. This motivates employees by making them feel part of the team.

   Potential problems with MBO programs often stem from the way the programs are implemented. The important element of employee involvement is lost when management uses MBO as a strategy for forcing managers and workers to commit to goals that are not mutually agreed on, but set by top management

11. The answer to this question will depend on what your goals are, and how hard you are willing to work to reach them. The level of motivation you feel will be determined, according to expectancy theory, by how strongly you value what you say your goals are, and whether or not you feel like you can "make the grade", or get the kind of job you want. And lastly, in the end, your level of motivation will be determined by whether or not you feel that the effort would actually be worth it.

12. In reinforcement theory you have a number of options available to solve the problem with this employee. You could reprimand the employee for being late and threaten pay reduction if he continues to be late. That would be "punishment". You could publicly praise him when he shows up on time, which is using positive reinforcement, and withhold the praise when he is late, a form of extinction. The strategy you use will depend on your style.

13. If you were Hal, you may feel like there is an inequity in your level of compensation compared to Donna's. This is equity theory at work! After all, she is new, and you have been a good employee for three years. What you would do will depend upon your own view of how big the inequity is. You may choose to talk to your boss, work harder to get promoted and recognized, work a little less for a while, rationalize the inequity in some way, or take the afternoon off!

    This could involve Maslow's Hierarchy, and Herzberg's theories in addition to equity theory.

Learning Goal 7

14. a. job enrichment   c. job simplification
    b. job rotation   d. job enlargement

15. An "enriched" job would include skill variety, task identity, task significance, autonomy and feedback. For publishing a newsletter, you could create self-managed teams, with each team member trained to do all the jobs necessary to get the newsletter out on deadline: editing, proofing, research, layout, selling advertising, fielding questions. The team members will be responsible for deciding which member will do what job, what the deadline needs to be, how to coordinate with the other teams, and will evaluate their own performance. This meets all the criteria identified

Learning Goals 2–8

16. How you would solve these problems is really up to you. It's a matter of personal style. However, there are some suggestions. You may want to sit down with these people and find out exactly what they think the problem is, or even if they recognize that there is a problem. It will help to listen to them, ask for their suggestions about how to solve the problems and implement those suggestions.

    It sounds like you have been making most of the decisions yourself, and not generally trusting these workers to be responsible. In other words, sounds like you have used a Theory X approach focusing on Herzberg's hygiene factors as a way to increase productivity. This may be appropriate in some instances, these workers may prefer less direction and "bossing" and more "coaching". You can act as a resource, teaching, guiding and recommending, but not actively participate in doing work. Allow them to decide the most appropriate way of designing their jobs. Programs such as job enlargement may be appropriate, or job rotation. You may also consider self-managed teams.

    Since these employees are younger, you will need adapt your style to fit the needs of your (and their) generation. Since Gen Xers are good at collaboration and consensus building, including them on the problem solving would use their strengths to your advantage. Job enlargement strategies seem custom made for these multi-tasking generations. They need the stimulation of challenges. Plus, think about ways to make your company a fun place to work!

    Many of the programs and theories described in this chapter may provide the solution to your problems.

PRACTICE TEST

MULTIPLE CHOICE

1.	c	14.	a
2.	a	15.	c
3.	a	16.	b
4.	d	17.	c
5.	b	18.	a
6.	b	19.	a
7.	a	20.	c
8.	b	21.	c
9.	c	22.	d
10.	b	23.	c
11.	d	24.	a
12.	d	25.	b
13.	a		

TRUE–FALSE

1.	F	12.	T
2.	T	13.	T
3.	F	14.	T
4.	F	15.	T
5.	T	16.	F
6.	T	17.	F
7.	F	18.	T
8.	F	19.	T
9.	T	20.	T
10.	F	21.	F
11.	T	22.	F

CHAPTER 11 – HUMAN RESOURCE MANAGEMENT: FINDING AND KEEPING THE BEST EMPLOYEES

LEARNING GOALS

After you have read and studied this chapter, you should be able to:

1. Explain the importance of human resource management and describe current issues in managing human resources.
2. Illustrate the effects of legislation on human resource management.
3. Summarize the five steps in human resource planning.
4. Describe methods companies use to recruit new employees and explain some of the issues that make recruitment challenging.
5. Outline the six steps in selecting employees.
6. Illustrate employee training and development methods.
7. Trace the six steps in appraising employee performance.
8. Summarize the objectives of employee compensation programs and describe various pay systems and fringe benefits.
9. Explain scheduling plans managers use to adjust to workers' needs.
10. Describe the ways employees can move through a company: promotion, reassignment, termination, and retirement.

LEARNING THE LANGUAGE

Listed below are important terms found in the chapter. Choose the correct term for the definition and write it in the space provided.

Affirmative action	Job analysis	Online training
Apprentice programs	Job description	On-the-job training
Cafeteria-style fringe benefits	Job sharing	Orientation
Compressed workweek	Job simulation	Performance appraisal
Contingent workers	Job specifications	Recruitment
Core time	Management development	Reverse discrimination
Flextime plan	Mentor	Selection
Fringe benefits	Networking	Training and development
Human resource management	Off-the-job training	Vestibule training

1. The set of activities called _____ are used to obtain a sufficient number of the right people at the right time.

2. The written summary of the minimum qualifications required of a worker to do a particular job is called the _____.

3. A work schedule known as _____ gives employees some freedom to choose when to work, as long as they work the required number of hours.

4. Employment activities designed to "right past wrongs" by increasing opportunities for minorities and women are known as _____.

5. Training programs known as _____ involve a period during which a learner works alongside an experienced employee to master the skills and procedures of a craft.

6. The process of _____ is the training and educating of employees to become good managers and then monitoring the progress of their managerial skills over time.

7. Known as _____ these include sick-leave pay, vacation pay, pension plans, and health plans that represent additional compensation to employees beyond base wages.

8. Discrimination against whites or males in hiring or promoting is called _____.

9. An experienced employee known as a(n) _____ is one who supervises, coaches and guides lower-level employees by introducing them to the right people and generally acts as their organizational sponsor.

10. The process of determining human resource needs is called _____ , and involves recruiting, selecting, developing, motivating, evaluating, compensating, and scheduling employees to achieve organizational goals.

11. A _____ is a work schedule that allows an employee to work a full number of hours per week but in fewer days.

12. A _____ is a study of what is done by employees who hold various job titles.

13. The process of _____ involves establishing and maintaining contacts with key managers in and outside the organization and using those contacts to weave strong relationships that serve as informal development systems.

14. The process of gathering information and deciding who should be hired, under legal guidelines, for the best interests of the individual and the organization is known as _____.

15. A training program known as _____ consists of internal and external programs and occurs away from the workplace to develop a variety of skills or to foster personal development.

16. A _____ is a summary of the objectives of a job, the type of work to be done, the responsibilities and duties, the working conditions and the relationship of the job to other functions.

17. The _____ refers to the period when all employees are expected to be at their job stations.

18. An arrangement known as _____ is one whereby two part-time employees share one full-time job.

19. The program known as _____ is one where the employee learns by doing, or watches others for a while and then imitates them.

20. _____ includes all attempts to improve employee performance by increasing an employee's ability to perform. Part focuses on short-term skills, part on long-term abilities.

21. The activity known as _____ introduces new employees to the organization; to fellow employees, to their immediate supervisors, and to the policies, practices and objectives of the firm.

22. A _____ is an evaluation in which the performance level of employees is measured against established standards to make decisions about promotions, compensation, training or termination.

23. A type of training known as _____ is done in schools where employees are taught on equipment similar to that used on the job.

24. A program called _____ is a fringe benefits plan that allows employees to choose the benefits they want up to a certain dollar amount.

25. A training method that uses equipment that duplicates job conditions and tasks so that trainees can learn skills before attempting them on the job is _____.

26. Employees known as _____ includes part-time workers, temporary workers, seasonal workers, independent contractors, interns, and co-op students.

27. _____ is a program in which employees complete classes via the Internet.

ASSESSMENT CHECK

Learning Goal 1

Working With People is Just the Beginning

1. List the functions of human resource management.

   a. _____   e. _____

   b. _____   f. _____

   c. _____   g. _____

   d. _____   h. _____

2. Why has human resource management received increased attention in recent years? What is making the area more challenging?

3. What challenges are facing the human resources area?

a. _____

b. _____

c. _____

d. _____

e. _____

f. _____

g. _____

h. _____

i. _____

j. _____

k. _____

Learning Goal 2

Laws Affecting Human Resource Management

4. What does Title VII of the Civil Rights Act of 1964 prohibit?

5. What is the EEOC and what powers does the EEOC have?

6. How did affirmative action programs result in charges of reverse discrimination?

7. The Civil Rights Act of 1991 _____

_____.

8. Who does the Vocational and Rehabilitation Act of 1973 protect?

9. What does the ADA require?

10. "Accommodation" means: _____.

    Accommodations include: _____

    _____.

11. In 2008 Congress passed the Americans with Disabilities Amendments Act which _____

    _____.

12. The Age Discrimination in Employment Act:

13. Identify four important aspects of the impact of legislation on human resource management.

    a. _____

    b. _____

    c. _____

    d. _____

Learning Goal 3

Determining A Firm's Human Resources Needs

14. List the steps in human resource planning:

    a. _____   d. _____

    b. _____   e. _____

    c. _____

15. What information is included in a human resources inventory?

16. What's the difference between a job description and job specifications?

17. How will future supply of employees change?

18. What information must be addressed in a human resources strategic plan?

Learning Goal 4

Recruiting Employees From a Diverse Population

19. What are the reasons why recruiting has become more challenging?

    a. _____

    b. _____

    c. _____

20. Five methods of *internal* recruiting include:

    a. _____

    b. _____

    c. _____

    d. _____

    e. _____

21. Benefits of recruiting from within include:

    a. _____

    b. _____

22. Your text lists 21 sources of external recruiting. What are seven of them?

a. _____

b. _____

c. _____

d. _____

e. _____

f. _____

g. _____

Learning Goal 5

Selecting Employees Who Will Be Productive

23. List the six steps in selecting employees:

a. _____

b. _____

c. _____

d. _____

e. _____

f. _____

24. Describe the automated program "Workforce Acquisition". What benefits does it provide?

25. What do employment tests measure?

The tests should be directly related to: _____.

26. Why are background checks important?

27. How do states vary in their requirements regarding employment or pre-employment physical exams?

28. What is the benefit to the firm of a trial, or probationary, period?

29. What are the reasons that firms hire contingent workers?

30. What are the positives and negatives of being a contingent worker?

31. How are the background of contingent workers and the jobs they fill, changing?

Learning Goal 6

Training and Developing Employees for Optimum Performance

32. What is the difference between training and development?

33. What are three steps taken in the process of creating training and development programs?

    a. _____

    b. _____

    c. _____

34. Describe an employee orientation program.

35. When is on-the- job training the easiest to implement?

36. What types of jobs would you train for in an apprenticeship?

What job classification comes after apprenticeship?

How will apprenticeship programs change?

37. Off-the-job training is expanding to include what other types of training?

38. What are the benefits of online training, or distance learning?

39. How does job simulation differ from vestibule training and when would this type of training be used?

40. Describe these types of management development programs:

On-the-job coaching:

Understudy positions:

Job rotation:

Off-the-job courses and training:

41. What are three reasons for companies to develop mentoring and networking programs for women and minorities in the workplace?

    a. _____

    b. _____

    c. _____

Learning Goal 7

Appraising Employee Performance to get Optimum Results

42. What kinds of decisions are based upon a performance appraisal?

43. What are the steps followed in a performance appraisal?

    a. _____

    b. _____

    c. _____

    d. _____

    e. _____

    f. _____

44. Performance standards must be:

    a. _____

    b. _____

    c. _____

45. Describe the 360-degree review type of performance appraisal.

Learning Goal 8

Compensating Employees: Attracting and Keeping the Best

46. Why are compensation and benefit packages being given special attention today?

47. What objectives can be accomplished by a well-managed compensation and benefit program?

   a. _____

   b. _____

   c. _____

   d. _____

   e. _____

48. Describe the various types of pay systems:

   a. _____

   b. _____

   c. _____

   d. _____

   e. _____

   f. _____

   g. _____

   h. _____

49. What happens when team pay is based on individual performance?

50. Describe a skill based pay system for teams, including the drawbacks.

51. Describe a gain sharing system of compensation for teams.

52. Where does individual compensation fit into these team-based plans?

53. What are some of the benefits included in fringe benefits packages?

   How big a part of companies' compensation plans are fringe benefits?

54. Describe "soft benefits".

55. Why have companies implemented cafeteria-style fringe benefits packages? What is the key to offering these types of plans?

56. The cost of administering benefits programs has become so great that a number of companies

   _____

   _____

Learning Goal 9

Scheduling Employees to Meet Organizational and Employee Needs

57. Flextime plans are designed to _____

   _____.

58. What are the disadvantages of flextime?

59. What is a disadvantage of a compressed work week?

60. What are the benefits to working at home for workers?

   For employers?

61. The benefits to job sharing include:

   a. _____

   b. _____

   c. _____

   d. _____

   e. _____

62. What are some disadvantages to job sharing for employers?

Learning Goal 10

Moving Employees Up, Over, and Out

63. Four ways of moving employees through the organization are:

   a. _____   c. _____

   b. _____   d. _____

64. What are the benefits of promotion from within a company?

65. Why is it more common now for employees to move over to a new position, rather than move up?

66. Why are companies hesitant to hire or re-hire workers full time, even when an economy is booming?

67. Describe the doctrine of "employment at will".

How has the "employment at will" doctrine changed?

68. What is a "golden handshake"?

69. What are two advantages of early retirement programs, over laying off employees?

70. Why would an organization want to learn about an employee's reason for leaving, and how can the organization get the information?

CRITICAL THINKING EXERCISES

Learning Goals 1, 2

1. Six functions of human resource management are:

Human resource planning	Training and development
Recruitment	Evaluation
Selection	Compensation

   You have read in previous chapters of the changing structure of American business and about population trends occurring in the United States. In this chapter, we read about the challenges in human resource management.

   For each of the following, identify at least one area of human resource management that could be affected, and how companies are affected or how companies could respond to the change.

	AREA AFFECTED	COMPANY RESPONSE
a. Shortages of trained workers	_____	_____ _____ _____
b. Increases in single parent and two-income families	_____	_____ _____ _____

c. Changing attitudes toward
   work   _____   _____
                                                    _____
                                                    _____

d. Concern over family and
   work issues   _____   _____
                                                    _____
                                                    _____
e. Complex laws   _____   _____
                                                    _____
                                                    _____

Learning Goal 2

2. How have changes in the "make-up" of the workforce—more immigrants, more minorities, more women, and so on, affected corporations from a legal perspective?

Learning Goal 3

3. Five steps in human resource planning are:

   Prepare a human resource inventory
   Prepare a job analysis
   Assess future human resource demand
   Assess future supply
   Establish a strategic plan

   Match the correct step to each of the following:

   a. _____   A large West Coast two-year college recently required its clerical staff to identify all the tasks involved in their jobs and to show how each job related to the other areas of their department.

   b. _____   Ford periodically requests employees to update information in their personnel file, for such things as recent courses taken, recent training programs and other employee information.

   c. _____   General Motors anticipates that its plant managers will need to develop updated skills in new management techniques as technology changes.

d. _____ A major automotive company makes arrangements with a local college for on-site training for its plant managers, and arranges to retrain workers at state-sponsored retraining programs.

e. _____ The human resource manager of a large East Coast firm gets statistics on the educational background of the graduating MBA classes of several East Coast colleges, including two schools with a large minority enrollment and two high tech schools.

Learning Goal 4

4. Be observant! Look around you and observe how many different methods that firms are using to recruit employees. Are newspapers, radio, signs in windows, college placement office, job fairs, offering internships? What ways would you use to look for a job, and "be recruited" to apply? How many Internet recruiting sites can you find?

Talk to a person in charge of recruiting for the company where you work. What methods does the company use? What challenges has your manager found in finding qualified personnel?

Learning Goal 5

5. A typical selection process may involve six steps:

Complete application	Background investigations
Initial and follow-up interviews	Physical exams
Employment tests	Trial periods

Match each of the following to the correct step in the selection process:

a. _____ Contributes to the high cost of turnover but enables a firm to fire incompetent employees after a certain period of time.

b. _____ Helps a firm to determine the information about an employee that is pertinent to the requirements of the job. Legal guidelines limit what companies can ask.

c. _____ An investigation of pervious work records and school records, and follow-up on recommendations.

d. _____ These have been criticized because of charges of cultural discrimination. They are most often used to measure specific job skills.

e. _____ Used to screen applicants after the application form has been reviewed. Gives the company an opportunity to assess communication skills.

f. _____ A major controversy in this step is pre-employment drug testing to detect drug or alcohol abuse, and AIDS screening.

6. Sun-2-Shade is a company that makes self-darkening windshields for the automobile industry. The company needs the human resources manager to begin developing some job descriptions, identify the various skills needed to perform the different jobs in the company and to start to develop a recruitment and selection process. Select at least one job that will be a part of Sun-2-Shade's organization; write a job description, job specifications, and develop a plan for recruiting and selecting job candidates.

Learning Goal 6

7. Firms have several types of training programs available:

Employee orientation   Vestibule training
On-the-job training   Job simulation
Apprentice programs   Management development
Off-the-job training

Match the correct type of training program to each situation described:

a. _____   Before Tom Hershberger went to work for a construction firm, he had a lot of training on how to use the heavy equipment he was assigned to.

b. _____   Bill Martin is a plumber. Before he became a journeyman, he had to work for several years alongside another plumber to learn the skills and procedures for the job.

c. _____   Maria Alvarez went on a sales call her second day on the job. She basically "learned by doing."

d. _____   Scott Toblin is learning to fly the newest, and largest, commercial aircraft, a 797. Before he takes it up in the air, he will work the control panel, and "land" on the runways of virtually every airport in the United States, all while staying right on the ground.

e. _____ Bernie Breen spent three weeks at a seminar learning effective communications and human relations skills for his job as a middle manager in a major corporation.

f. _____ In his first day on the job, Hong Nyu was introduced to several department managers, studied a corporate brochure describing all the company's products and saw a video of the history of his company. He was even assigned a mentor.

8. The text discusses networking, and its importance in business. How could networking become even more important in the future, and how can you start now to develop a "network"?

Learning Goal 7

9. You are the newly appointed sales manager for Sun-2-Shade, and your job is to develop a new appraisal system that is effective and objective. This is the first real test of your skills as a manager. What, specifically, do you think you should do? In other words, what kinds of things will you include on an appraisal form, and then what will you do after that's completed?

10. Right now at Sun-2-Shade, you have a salesman who doesn't seem to be performing the way she should. You know something must be done. This is the second real test of your management skills. How will you handle this situation?

Learning Goal 8

11. Basic pay systems include:

Salary systems	Bonus plans
Hourly wage	Profit-sharing
Piecework	Gain sharing
Commission plans	Stock options

Give a suggested pay system for each situation described below. Your suggestion can be a combination of systems:

a. _____ A sales job that includes a variety of non selling functions such as advising, keeping records and setting up displays.

b. _____ An assembly line operation in which each worker completes several tasks before the product moves to the next station.

c. _____ An office manager just starting out with new office equipment designed to increase productivity.

d. _____ The president of a small firm that makes computer chips.

e. _____ A worker in a garment factory, making shirts.

f. _____ A manager with specific goals to meet in his department, and who has been with the company for several years.

12. How can a company ensure that their benefits programs meet the needs of a changing workforce? Why is that important?

13. Changing workforces mean changing schedules for many companies and their employees. Some alternative work schedules are:

Job sharing   Compressed work weeks
Flextime plans   In-home work

What kind of program is being described:

a. _____ This type of program can give an employee a break, and lets them sleep in once in a while!

b. _____ At Renovation Capital, employees work 35 hours in 4 days for each week in May, giving everyone a three day weekend.

c. _____ At St. Lukes Hospital, Julie Andersen works as an accountant every morning, and Mary Krull takes over each afternoon.

d. _____ Felicia Hill has a fax, modem, and a computer that she carries with her wherever she goes, but she doesn't have an office!

e. _____ Some of the benefits of this schedule include a reduction in absenteeism and tardiness, because people can handle their other duties in off hours.

f. _____ With this program, Juan and Elena Morena can schedule their days so that one of them is home to see their children off in the morning, and the other is home when the children come home from school.

g. _____ One of the disadvantages of this program is the need to hire, train and supervise twice as many people.

h. _____ Gil Pfaff likes this schedule, because it allows him to avoid the heavy morning traffic during his commute to work.

i. _____ Manager David Whitsell likes this program because he has found workers who take advantage of it are often more productive and its easier for him to schedule people into peak demand periods for his department.

j. _____ Debbie Rhodes schedules doctor's appointments on days when she comes in early and leaves early.

Learning Goal 10

14. How have the changes in the workforce and in the workplace, discussed in this and other chapters, affected the ways companies move employees around?

PRACTICE TEST

MULTIPLE CHOICE — Circle the best answer

Learning Goal 1

1. A firm's ultimate resource is:
   a. the amount of start-up capital.
   b. it's employees
   c. stock price
   d. relationship with its customers

2. Among the challenges faced by human resource managers are:
   a. An oversupply of people trained to work in growth areas.
   b. Fewer laws to direct the actions of human resources managers.
   c. Continued downsizing that is taking a toll on employee morale, and increased demand for temporary workers.
   d. Fewer older workers, and too many of them want to retire, making it difficult to fill their jobs.

Learning Goal 2

3. Title VII of the Civil Rights Act:
   a. requires that disabled applicants be given the same consideration for employment as people without disabilities.
   b. prevents businesses from discrimination against people with disabilities on the basis their physical or mental handicap.
   c. prohibits discrimination in hiring, firing, and other areas on the basis of race, religion, creed, sex or national origin.
   d. gives the victims of discrimination the right to a jury trail and punitive damages

4. The law that requires employers to give disabled applicants the same consideration for employment as people without disabilities is the:
   a. Age Discrimination in Employment Act.
   b. Equal Employment Opportunity Act.
   c. Civil Rights Act.
   d. Americans with Disabilities Act.

5. Which of the following is an accurate statement of the effect laws have had on human resources management?
   a. Court cases have demonstrated that it is legal to go beyond providing equal rights and to provided special employment and training to correct past discrimination.
   b. Employers must have lawyers on staff to ensure compliance with the laws.
   c. Companies can require employees to retire at a certain age, regardless of the job they hold.
   d. Reverse discrimination has been proved to be irrelevant in most situations.

Learning Goal 3

6. A job analysis will provide information about:
   a. whether or not the labor force is paid adequately.
   b. what is done by various employees who fill different job titles.
   c. the strategic plan for recruiting, selecting training and development.
   d. education, capabilities, training and specialized skills to determine if the company' s labor force is technically up-to-date.

7. "Clerical worker, with responsibilities for answering phones, greeting clients, filing for human resources department. Some weekends required." This is an example of a:
   a. job analysis.
   b. job specification.
   c. job description.
   d. human resource inventory.

Learning Goal 4

8. Which of the following is <u>not</u> included in a list of reasons why recruiting has become difficult?
   a. Sometimes people with necessary skills aren't available.
   b. The number of available recruiting tools has begun to shrink.
   c. The emphasis on participative management makes it important to hire people who fit in with the corporate culture.
   d. Some companies have policies that make it difficult to recruit.

9. According to the text, the greatest advantage of hiring from within is:
   a. it is quick.
   b. it requires less training.
   c. it helps maintain employee morale.
   d. it keeps the firm from having an oversupply of workers trained in certain areas.

Learning Goal 5

10. What is the first step in the selection process?
    a. Obtaining a completed application form.
    b. Contacting an employment agency.
    c. Background investigation.
    d. Interviews.

11. Background investigations:
    a. are no longer legal.
    b. help identify which candidates are most likely to succeed.
    c. include an investigation of skills.
    d. are not good predictors of who will be successful.

12. Employment tests must:
    a. be directly related to the job.
    b. measure only specific skills.
    c. be conducted in the initial job interview.
    d. in general be avoided, because of legal issues.

Learning Goal 6

13. Internal and external programs to develop a variety of skills and to foster personal development away from the job is called:
    a. an apprentice program.
    b. vestibule training.
    c. off-the-job training.
    d. employee orientation.

14. Armin is a manager in a major tool company. He is currently being given a number of assignments in various areas of the company so that he can see how various operations work within his company. This example of _____ will help him to succeed in the company.
    a. Understudy positions
    b. On-the-job coaching
    c. Job enlargement
    d. Job rotation

Learning Goal 7

15. Decisions about promotions, compensation, additional training, or firing are all based on:
    a. going through the appropriate training program.
    b. having the right selection process in place.
    c. performance evaluations.
    d. legal considerations

16. At Big Bear Industries, manager reviews include information from the managers' boss, as well as the manager's subordinates and peers. This would be considered:
    a. a peer review
    b. a 360-degree review.
    c. the most effective way to get rid of poor managers.
    d. an unnecessary step in the evaluation process, and is disappearing as a performance appraisal technique.

Learning Goal 8

17. Henry Aguerra is interested in making a lot of money. He is a very good salesperson. People tell him he could sell sand to Saudi Arabia! He is a very hard worker, and is willing to work a lot of hours to make the kind of money he wants. Henry should most likely look for the kind of job that is paid :
    a. on salary with overtime.
    b. by commission.
    c. with profit sharing.
    d. in a situation with team based compensation.

18. Studies of compensation for teams have shown that:
    a. it is recommended that pay should be based on team performance.
    b. team based pay programs are pretty well developed and need not be changed.
    c. team members should be compensated as individuals.
    d. it is important to compensate the team, but also to reward outstanding individuals on the team.

19. Fringe benefits:
    a. include pay, as well as items such as executive dining rooms and country club memberships.
    b. are usually set, and won't change over time.
    c. Is relatively easy for a company to administer, once benefits have been determined.
    d. are expensive for companies, and account for as much as 30 percent of payroll today.

20. Maria Hernandez is a single parent with a child in elementary school. Maria loves her schedule because she can go in any time that is convenient for her, as long as she is there during the core hours of 10 a.m. to noon. Maria apparently enjoys a schedule known as:
    a. job sharing.
    b. flextime.
    c. a compressed workweek.
    d. home based work.

21. Among the disadvantages, or challenges, of telecommuting, or home based work is:
    a. reduced productivity for the organization.
    b. makes job performance appraisal more difficult.
    c. reduces the amount of time available for work for the employee.
    d. increases the amount of office politics as workers who have to come in are jealous of those who work at home.

Learning Goal 10

21. The effect of downsizing and the resulting flatter corporate structures is that:
    a. fewer layers of management make it more difficult for employees to be promoted to higher levels of management.
    b. companies are now scrambling to re-hire those workers who were laid off.
    c. a decrease occurs in the level of complexity of managing human resources.
    d. less need to adhere to employment law.

22. Many companies are hesitant to hire or re-hire workers full time because:
    a. employee morale declines when former workers are re-hired at higher rates of pay.
    b. it makes promotion decisions more difficult.
    c. the cost of terminating employees is high in terms of training costs and various legal costs and considerations.
    d. they will eventually have to fund a golden handshake for the workers when they retire.

TRUE–FALSE

Learning Goal 1

1. _____ Qualified labor is more scarce today, which makes recruiting and selecting more difficult.

2. _____ Human resource management has become so important that it is no longer a function of just one department, but a function of all managers.

Learning Goal 2

3. _____ Legislation and legal decisions have had little effect on human resource management.

4. _____ The EEOC is charged with enforcing affirmative action programs.

5. _____ A key concept of Title VII of the Civil Rights Act of 1964 is accommodation in the workplace.

Learning Goal 3

6. _____ Because technology changes so rapidly, training programs should not be started too long before the skills are needed, in case the skills become outdated.

7. _____ Because of retiring baby boomers, virtually all types of jobs will be difficult to fill in the future.

Learning Goal 4

8. _____ Recruiting qualified workers may be difficult for small businesses because they may not be able to offer the sort of compensation that attracts qualified workers.

9. _____ In recruiting, it is important to look for individuals who are skilled, but less important that they fit in with the culture, as skilled workers will quickly learn how to fit in.

Learning Goal 5

10. _____ The application form and the initial interview are good ways for a company to find out about an applicant's family and religious backgrounds.

11. _____ According to the Americans with Disabilities Act, medical tests cannot be given just to screen out individuals

Learning Goal 6

12. _____ A well designed training program can lead to higher retention rates and increased productivity.

13. _____ It is important for companies to take the initiative to develop female and minority managers because it is a key to long-term profitability.

14. _____ Off-the-job training consists of training in classrooms with equipment similar to that used on the job so employees learn proper methods and safety procedures.

Learning Goal 7

15. _____ Discussing the results of a performance evaluation with the employee should be avoided because it's important to let an employee "sink or swim" in a job.

16. _____ A 360 degree performance review includes employees, peers, subordinates, and managers.

Learning Goal 8

17. _____ While compensation and benefits packages are important to keep employees, these programs play little role in attracting qualified employees.

18. _____ Soft benefits include things such as on-site haircuts and shoe repair and free breakfasts.

Learning Goal 9

19. _____ One benefit of job sharing has been reduced absenteeism and tardiness.

20. _____ Some companies have found that telecommuting has helped the company to save money.

21. _____ While early retirement programs are a more expensive strategy of downsizing than laying off employees, it can increase the morale of remaining employees.

22. _____ Learning why an employee leaves a company is not especially valuable information for a company to determine.

You Can Find It On the Net

The Web site www.workforceonline.com is a comprehensive Human Resources site that provides a considerable amount of information about a wide variety of topics. These topics will vary over time.

What "Features" topics did you find? How do they relate to what we have learned in this chapter?

What topics were in the "News" portion? What additional information is provided beyond what has been discussed in this chapter?

What new ways are companies finding to recruit employees?

What topics are listed under the following areas:
    Compensation and Benefits
    HR Management
    Recruiting and Staffing
    Training and Development

ANSWERS

LEARNING THE LANGUAGE

1. Recruitment	10. Human resource management	19. On-the-job training
2. Job specifications	11. Compressed work week	20. Training and development
3. Flextime plans	12. Job analysis	21. Orientation
4. Affirmative action	13. Networking	22. Performance appraisal
5. Apprentice programs	14. Selection	23. Vestibule training
6. Management development	15. Off-the-job training	24. Cafeteria-style benefits
7. Fringe benefits	16. Job description	25. Job simulation
8. Reverse discrimination	17. Core time	26. Contingent workers
9. Mentor	18. Job sharing	27. Online training

ASSESSMENT CHECK

Learning Goal 1

Working With People Is Just the Beginning

1. The functions of human resource management include:
   a. Determining human resource needs
   b. Recruiting
   c. Selecting
   d. Developing
   e. Motivating
   f. Evaluating
   g. Compensating
   h. Scheduling

2. Human resource management has received greater attention recently because the U.S. economy has experienced a major shift from manufacturing to service industries and high tech industries that require highly technical job skills. This means that workers must re-train for new, more challenging jobs.
   This makes the job of human resources more challenging since qualified workers are scarcer, which makes recruiting and retaining people more important and more difficult.

3. Challenges facing the human resources area are:
   a. Shortages of people trained to work in growth areas.
   b. A large population of skilled and unskilled workers from declining industries who are unemployed or underemployed and need retraining.
   c. A growing percentage of new workers who are undereducated and unprepared for jobs in the contemporary business environment.
   d. A shortage of workers in skilled trades due to retirement of aging baby boomers.
   e. Increasing numbers of single parent and two-income families who need programs like job sharing, maternity leave, and career advancement programs.
   f. Changing employee attitudes toward work with leisure having a greater priority.
   g. A declining economy with an effect on morale and a resulting increasing demand for contingency workers.
   h. Challenges from an overseas labor pool who will accept lower wages.
   i. Increased demand for benefits tailored to the individual.
   j. Growing concern for issues such as health care, elder care and employment for people with disabilities.
   k. A decreased sense of employee loyalty resulting in higher turnover and increased costs.

Learning Goal 2

Laws Affecting Human Resource Management

4. Title VII of the Civil Rights Act of 1964 prohibits discrimination in hiring, firing, compensation, apprenticeships, training, terms, conditions, or privileges of employment based on race, religion, creed, sex, national origin or age.

5. The EEOC, the Equal Employment Opportunity Commission is a regulatory agency created by the Civil Rights Act in 1964 and strengthened by the Equal Opportunity Act of 1972. Specifically, the EEOC has the power to issue guidelines for acceptable employer conduct in administering equal employment opportunity, enforce mandatory record-keeping procedures and insure that mandates are carried out.

6. Charges of reverse discrimination primarily resulted from the interpretation of affirmative action laws. Reverse discrimination charges have occurred when companies have been perceived as unfairly giving preference to women or minority groups in hiring and promoting, when following affirmative action guidelines.

7. The Civil Rights Act of 1991 expanded the remedies available to victims of discrimination. Now victims have the right to a jury trial and punitive damages.

8. The Vocational Rehabilitation Act of 1973 extended protection from discrimination to people with any physical or mental disability.

9. The Americans with Disabilities Act of 1990 requires that disabled applicants be given the same consideration for employment as people without disabilities. Companies must make "reasonable accommodations" to people with disabilities.

10. Accommodation means treating people according to their specific needs.

    Accommodations include putting up barriers to isolate people readily distracted by noise, reassigning workers to new tasks, and making changes in supervisors' management styles.

11. In 2008 Congress passed the Americans with Disabilities Amendments Act which overturned Supreme Court Decisions that had reduced protections for certain people with disabilities such as diabetes, epilepsy, heart disease, and cancer.

12. The Age Discrimination in Employment Act protects individuals who are 40 hears of age or older from employment discrimination based on age. Additionally, the law outlawed mandatory retirement in most organizations, unless evidence shows the ability to perform a particular job diminishes with age or poses a danger to society.

13. Four important aspects of the impact of legislation on human resource management are:
    a. Employers must know and act in accordance with the legal rights of all groups in the workplace.
    b. Legislation affects all areas of human resource management.
    c. It is clear that it is sometimes legal to go beyond providing equal rights for minorities and women to provide special employment and training to correct past discrimination.
    d. New court cases and legislation change human resource management almost daily which makes it important to keep current.

Learning Goal 3

Determining A Firm's Human Resources Needs

14.   a.   Prepare a human resource inventory of the organization's employees.
         b.   Prepare job analyses, job descriptions, and job specifications.
         c.   Assess future demand.
         d.   Assess future supply.
         e.   Establish a strategic plan.

15.   A human resources inventory includes ages, names, education, capabilities, training, specialized skills and other information pertinent to the organization, such as languages spoken. This information reveals whether or not the labor force is technically up to date and thoroughly trained.

16.   In brief, the job description is about the job, and job specifications are about the person who does the job.

17.   There are likely to be increased shortages of some skills in the future, like computer and robotic repair workers, and an oversupply of other types of skills like assembly line workers.

18.   A human resources strategic plan must address recruiting, selecting, training and developing, appraising, compensating, and scheduling the labor force.

Learning Goal 4

Recruiting Employees From a Diverse Population

19.   Recruiting has become more challenging because:
         a.   Some organizations' have policies that demand promotions from within, or other policies that make recruiting and keeping employees difficult or subject to restrictions.
         b.   The emphasis on culture, teamwork, and participative management makes it important to hire the right kind of people.
         c.   Sometimes people with the necessary skills are not available, and so workers must be hired and trained internally.

20.   Five methods of internal recruiting include:
         a.   Transfers
         b.   Promotions
         c.   Employee recommendations
         d.   Retrained employees
         e.   Department reorganizations

21.   The benefits of recruiting from within include:
         a.   It is less expensive.
         b.   It helps maintain employee morale.

22. The list can include:
    a. Public and private employment agencies
    b. personal applications
    c. College placement bureaus
    d. Management consultants
    e. New graduates
    f. Former employees
    g. Part-time applicants

    The complete list is in Figure 11-3 in your text.

Learning Goal 5

Selecting Employees Who Will Be Productive

23. a. Obtaining a complete application form   d. Background investigations
    b. Initial and follow-up interviews   e. Physical exams
    c. Employment tests   f. Establishing trial periods

24. Workforce Acquisition is an automated program used to make the application process more effective and efficient. An applicant sits at a computer and answers questions about job experience, time available and personality. A report e-mailed to the hiring manager indicates whether or not to interview the applicant.

    Workforce Acquisition can significantly cut the amount of time needed to process applications, eliminates interview hours and reduces turnover.

25. Employment tests measure basic competencies in specific job skills, and help evaluate applicants' personalities and interests.

    The employment test should be directly related to the job.

26. Background checks are important because it is so costly to hire, train, and motivate people. These checks help to identify which candidates are most likely to succeed in a given position.

27. In some states, physical exams can be given only after an offer of employment has been accepted. Other states allow pre-employment physical exams, but they must be given to everyone applying for the same position.

28. During a trial period, a person can prove his or her worth to the firm. After the trial period, a firm has the right to discharge an employee based upon performance evaluations, so it is easier to fire inefficient or problem employees.

29. A varying need for employees is the most common reason for hiring contingent workers. Other reasons include situations when full time employees are on leave, there is a peak demand for labor, or quick service to customers is a priority. Companies in areas where there are qualified contingent workers available and in which jobs require minimum training are most likely to consider contingency workers.

30. Contingent workers are often offered full-time positions, and because they are told there is a possibility of full time employment they are often more productive than permanent workers.

    As contingent workers they receive few health, vacation and pension benefits. They also tend to earn less than permanent workers.

31. Experts say temps are filling openings in an increasingly broad range of jobs. Increasing numbers of contingent workers are educated professionals.

Learning Goal 6

Training and Developing Employees for Optimum Performance

32. Training is short-term skills oriented, while development is long-term career oriented.

33. Three steps in the process of creating training and development programs are:
    a. Assessing the needs of the organization and the skills of the employees to determine training needs.
    b. Designing the training activities to meet the needs.
    c. Evaluating the effectiveness of the training.

34. During an employee orientation program, new employees will be introduced to fellow employees and to their immediate supervisors, and learn about the policies, practices and objectives of the firm. Orientation programs included everything from informal talks to formal activities that last a day or more and include visits to various departments and required reading of handbooks.

35. On- the-job training is the easiest kind of training to implement when the job is relatively simple, such as clerking in a store, or repetitive, such as cleaning carpets.

36. As an apprentice, you would train for a skilled craft, such as a bricklaying or plumbing. Workers who successfully complete an apprenticeship earn the classification of journeyman. In the future, there are likely to be more but shorter apprenticeships programs to prepare people for skilled jobs in changing industries. This is a result of baby boomers retiring.

37. Off-the-job training is expanding to include further formal education, such as a Ph.D. and personal development in areas such as time management, stress management, health and wellness and other areas.

38. The benefit of online training or distance learning is that it gives large numbers of employers the ability to provide consistent content tailored to specific training needs at convenient times.

39. Job simulation is the use of equipment that duplicates job conditions and tasks so trainees can learn skills before attempting them on the job. It differs from vestibule training in that simulation attempts to duplicate the *exact* conditions that occur on the job. This kind of training is used to train astronauts, airline pilots, and others who must learn difficult procedures off the job.

40. a. On-the-job coaching—means that a senior manager will assist a lower-level manager by teaching them the needed skills and providing direction, advice, and feedback.

    b. Understudy positions—are a successful way of developing managers. Selected employees work as assistants to higher-level managers and participate in planning and other managerial functions until they are ready to assume such positions themselves.

    c. Job rotation—is used so that managers can learn about different functions of the organization. Managers are given assignments in a variety of departments to get a broad picture of the organization, which is necessary to their success.

    d. Off-the-job courses and training—occurs when managers periodically go to schools or seminars for a week or more to more fully develop technical and human relations skills. In these courses they learn the latest concepts and create a sense of camaraderie as they live, eat, and work together in a college-type atmosphere.

41. Companies taking the initiative to develop female and minority managers understand that:
    a. grooming women and minorities for management positions is a key to long term profitability.
    b. the best women and minorities will become harder to attract and retain in the future.
    c. more women and minorities at all levels means that businesses can better serve female and minority customers.

Learning Goal 7

Appraising Employee Performance to get Optimum Results

42. Decisions about promotions, compensation, additional training or firing are all based on performance appraisals.

43. a   Establish performance standards
    b. Communicate the standards
    c. Evaluate performance
    d. Discuss results with employees
    e. Take corrective action
    f. Use the results to make decisions

44. Performance standards must be:
    a. understandable.
    b. subject to measurement.
    c. reasonable.

45. The 360-degree review calls for feedback from superiors, subordinates and peers. The goal is to get an accurate and comprehensive idea of the worker's abilities.

Learning Goal 8

Compensating Employees: Attracting and Keeping the Best

46. Compensation and benefits packages have become a main marketing tool used to attract qualified employees. At the same time, employee compensation is one of the largest operating costs for many organizations, and the firm's long-term survival may depend on how well it can control employee costs, and optimize employee efficiency.

47. A well managed compensation and benefit program can meet objectives such as:
    a. Attracting the kind of people the organization needs.
    b. Providing employees with incentives
    c. Keeping valued employees from leaving
    d. Maintaining a competitive position in the marketplace
    e. Providing employees a sense of financial security through insurance and retirement benefits

48. a. Salary systems—fixed compensation computed on weekly, biweekly, or monthly pay periods.
    b. Hourly wage or daywork—wage based on the number of hours or days worked, used for most blue-collar and clerical workers.
    c. Piecework—wage based on the number of items produced rather than by the hour or day.
    d. Commission plans—pay based on some percentage of sales, often used to compensate sales personnel.
    e. Bonus plans—extra pay for accomplishing or surpassing certain objectives. Two forms of bonuses are monetary and cashless.
    f. Profit sharing plans—share of the company's profits over and above normal pay.
    g. Gain-sharing plans—annual bonuses paid based on achieving specific goals such as quality or customer service measures, and production targets.
    h. Stock Option plans—the right to purchase stock in the company at a specific price over a specific period of time.

49. A study of team pay found that when pay is based on individual performance it erodes team cohesiveness and makes the team less likely to meet its goals as a collaborative effort.

50. Skill-based pay is related to the growth of the individual and of the team. Base pay is raised when team members learn and apply new skills. The drawbacks of the skill-based pay system are that the system is complex and that it is difficult to correlate skill acquisition and profit gains.

51. In a gain sharing system bonuses are based on improvements over previous performance.

52. Outstanding team players who go beyond what is required and make an outstanding individual contribution to the firm should be separately recognized for their additional contribution. A way to avoid alienating recipients who feel team participation was uneven is to let the team decide which members get what type of individual award.

53. Fringe benefits include sick-leave pay, vacation pay, pension plans, and health plans. They can also include recreation facilities, company cars, country club memberships, discounted massages, special home-mortgage rates, paid and unpaid sabbaticals, day care services and executive dining rooms, dental care, eye care, elder care, legal counseling, mental health care and shorter work weeks.

    Fringe benefits account for approximately 30 percent of payrolls today.

54. "Soft benefits" include such things as on-site haircuts and shoe repair, concierge services and free breakfasts that help workers maintain the balance between work and family life.

55. Firms offer cafeteria-style fringe benefits to address the growing demand for different kinds of benefits. Today employees are more varied and need different kinds of benefits.

    The key to cafeteria-style benefits is choice, where individual needs can be met.

56. The cost of administering benefits programs has become so great that a number of companies hire outside companies to run their employee benefits plans. This saves money and helps companies avoid the growing complexity and technical requirements of the plans.

Learning Goal 9

Scheduling Employees to Meet Organizational and Employee Needs

57. Flextime plans are designed to allow employees to adjust to demands on their time, and to have freedom to adjust when they work, as long as they work the required number of hours.

58. One disadvantage of flextime is that it doesn't work in assembly-line processes where everyone must work at the same time, or for shift work. In addition, managers often have to work longer days to be able to assist and supervise employees. Flextime can make communication more difficult, as certain employees may not be at work when you need to talk to them. Further, some employees could abuse the system, and that could cause resentment.

59. A disadvantage to a compressed workweek is that some employees get tired working such long hours, and productivity could decline.

60. Workers who work at home can choose their own hours, interrupt work for childcare and other tasks, and take time out for personal reasons.

    Home based work can be a cost saver for employers

    A full list of benefits and challenges of home based work can be found in Figure 11-7

61. Benefits to job sharing include:
    a. employment opportunities to those who cannot or prefer not to work full-time.
    b. a high level of enthusiasm and productivity.
    c. reduced absenteeism and tardiness.
    d. ability to schedule people into peak demand periods.
    e. retention of experienced employees who might have left otherwise.

62. The disadvantages to job sharing include having to hire, train, motivate and supervise twice as many people and to prorate some fringe benefits.

Learning Goal 10

Moving Employees Up, Over and Out

63. Four ways of moving employees through an organization are:
    a. Promotions   c. Terminations
    b. Reassignment   d. Retirement

64. Many companies find that promotion from within the company improves employee morale. Promotions are also cost-effective because the promoted employees are already familiar with the corporate culture and procedures.

65. Because of flatter corporate structures it is more common for workers to move over to a new position than to move up to a new position. Such transfers allow employees to develop and display new skills and to learn more about the company overall.

66. One reason that companies are hesitant to hire or rehire workers full time because the cost of terminating employees is very high in terms of lost training costs and possible damages and legal fees for wrongful discharge suits. That's why many companies are using temporary employees or outsourcing certain functions.

67. "Employment at will" is an old doctrine that meant that managers had as much freedom to fire workers as workers had to leave voluntarily.
Most states now limit the "at will" doctrine to protect employees from wrongful firing. Companies can no longer fire someone who has exposed a company's illegal actions (whistleblowers), refused to violate a law. This has restricted management's ability to terminate employees as it has increased workers' rights to their jobs. Employees who are members of a minority or other protected group also may have protections under equal employment law.

68. Golden handshakes are financial incentives such as one-time cash payments, used to entice older and more expensive workers to retire.

69. Two advantages of early retirement programs are increased morale of surviving employees and greater promotion opportunities for younger employees.

70. Learning about an employee's reasons for leaving can help to prevent the loss of other good employees. One way to learn the reasons why people leave a company is to have a third party conduct an exit interview. Web-based systems can get the information without a face-to-face interview.

CRITICAL THINKING EXERCISES

Learning Goals 1, 2

1.

		AREA	COMPANY RESPONSE
a.	Shortages of trained workers	Training Recruitment	Training programs, aggressive recruiting programs
b.	Increases in single-parent and two income families	Compensation	Companies will need to look at income; offering day care; continuing to offer cafeteria style benefits will be especially important as companies experience shortages of trained workers.
c.	Changing attitudes about work	Planning	Need to look at flextime and compressed work weeks to meet needs of future workers.

| d. | Concern over family and work issues | Planning Compensation | Companies will begin to offer programs to help employees cope with issues regarding eldercare and day care; develop workplace violence policies and continue to provide opportunities for people with disabilities |
| e. | Complex laws | Recruitment Selection Compensation | These laws will require companies to look at their policies regarding hiring, promotion and termination, including application forms, and interview questions |

Learning Goal 2

2. As the workforce becomes more culturally diverse, laws protecting minorities from discrimination will be carefully monitored. These areas have become very complex, and a diverse workforce makes enforcement even more complex. However, as more women and minorities with the necessary skills enter the workforce, compliance with these laws may actually become less an issue than in the past.

    A major issue has been providing equal opportunity for people with disabilities. Companies are finding that making structural accommodations is less difficult than understanding the difference between the need to be accommodating and the need to be fair to all employees. As the workforce ages, age discrimination may become an issue.

Learning Goal 3

3. a. Job analysis
    b. Human resource inventory
    c. Assess future human resource demand
    d. Establish a plan
    e. Assess future supply

Learning Goal 4

4. You will probably notice a number of ways that companies are trying to recruit new employees. One good reason to develop a "network" is that employers often use current employees to find new hires. The newspaper, especially on Sundays, may have several pages of employment opportunities. On your college campus, there may be signs in windows, ads in the college newspaper, ads on electronic bulletin boards among a myriad of other ways that companies are using to look for qualified employees. You may also visit a web site such as Monster.com and investigate the methods used on this recruiting website. Additionally, your college may have an Employer Recruitment site, on which students can post resumes to be screened by potential employers.

    Managers will describe many challenges in finding qualified personnel. A common theme will probably be finding people willing to work for the pay the company can afford to offer.

Learning Goal 5

5. a. Trial periods
    b. Complete application
    c. Background investigations
    d. Employment tests
    e. Initial and follow up interviews
    f. Physical exams

6. Your answer will depend upon what kind of job you have chosen. There are many different jobs which will be a part of Sun-2-Shade: Sales, production, marketing, accounting, and clerical, to name a few.

    For a sales job, a job description may be:

    > "Sales for a small manufacturing company, calling on automotive manufacturers and/or automotive after market dealers. Sales territory will be primarily based on geographic location. Duties will include sales calls; follow up reports, working directly with production manager, direct input into marketing program development. Compensation will be salary plus commission.
    >
    > Skills required include familiarity with electronic communication equipment, teamwork skills, good oral and written communications skills, presentation skills, and a Bachelor's degree, preferably in marketing or a related area."

    You may make use of any of the recruiting tools listed in the text. Good sources may include current employees, local colleges, a local professional marketing organization, or using an Internet recruiting tool. The selection process should include several interviews, in particular with the people with whom the sales person will work, such as the production manager, other marketing people, and other members of the team he/she will work with.

Learning Goal 6

7. a. Vestibule training   d. Job simulation
    b. Apprenticeship   e. Management development
    c. On-the-job training   f. Employee orientation

8. As corporations downsize, and layers of management "thin out" your network of co-workers, friends and professional associations could become especially important. To get the kind of job that meets your needs, you may have to do a lot of searching. To "move up the ladder" in the face of declining numbers of management positions, you may have to find the right mentor.

    In college, you can begin to develop a network in a number of ways. If there are student chapters of professional business organizations, such as The American Marketing Association or The American Management Association for example, you could take advantage of student membership rates and attend monthly meetings and meet people already working in the field. Your professors may have contacts in the area you are interested in, also. Further, you could begin a series of "informational interviews". Make appointments with managers in corporations you may have an interest in working for in the future, and find out exactly what kind of skills they are looking for, what kinds of jobs they think will be available in the future and a little bit about the company. Lastly, network with your fellow students. You never know who may be the future CEO of the company you're dying to work for!

9. The first thing you need to do in developing this appraisal system is decide exactly what elements of the salespersons' jobs will be included in the system. For example, you will probably include: sales volume, number of sales calls, number of sales compared to number of sales calls (called the closing ratio), dollar amount per sale, number of units per sale, sales expenses, average dollar volume per customer, and so on. You will also have to determine what time frame will be used for evaluations, for example, six months or a year. After that, you will want to decide what is an acceptable and reasonable standard for each of those areas - i.e. how many sales calls per month is enough? What's an acceptable dollar amount per sale? What is an acceptable sales volume in the given period? Lastly, these standards must be communicated to each salesperson, explained clearly and precisely. Each individual must know exactly what is expected of him or her.

10. How you would deal with an employee who is not performing well is a matter of individual style. However there are a number of suggestions to make the process more effective. The most important thing to do first is to discuss the problem with the employee and determine what is causing the problem. There may be a problem in her territory, family problems that took her away from work or inadequate support from the company. Figure 11-4 gives you some specific suggestions about conducting an effective appraisal. It will be important to get agreement from the employee that there is a problem, and suggestions from her about how to take corrective action. It may be a good idea to give her a period of time to improve, and then re-evaluate.

Learning Goal 8

11. These are some <u>suggested</u> answers:
    a. Salary or salary plus commission, gain sharing
    b. Hourly wages plus profit sharing
    c. Salary plus bonus for meeting objectives, gain sharing
    d. Salary plus profit sharing, or bonus for meeting profit objective
    e. Piecework, plus profit sharing
    f. Salary, plus gain sharing or stock options

12. To counter growing demands for more individualized benefits, companies have begun to offer cafeteria-style benefits. The key to this type of program is providing enough choices so that employees can meet their varied needs, while still maintaining cost effectiveness. These types of programs are particularly important in light of the predicted difficulty in finding skilled employees. These programs are also important to retain good quality workers.

Learning Goal 9

13.
    a. Flextime
    b. Compressed work week
    c. Job sharing
    d. In home work
    e. Job sharing
    f. Flextime
    g. Job sharing
    h. Flextime
    i. Job sharing
    j. Flextime

14. As downsizing has created flatter organizational structures, there are fewer opportunities for employees to be promoted. To keep morale from sagging, and to keep employees productive, it is common today for companies to reassign workers rather than move them up. This kind of transfer allows employees to develop and display new skills. Downsizing has also forced companies to struggle with layoffs and terminations. Many companies are reluctant to rehire permanent workers because of the high cost involved. Legislation has also made firing more difficult, in light of wrongful discharge lawsuits, and some companies find it more cost effective to use contingent workers to replace permanent workers when the need arises.

As an alternative to layoffs, companies have offered early retirement to entice older employees to resign, and allow younger workers to move up. As the workforce gets older, these programs will enable companies to reduce the number of older, more expensive workers. However, if skilled workers are in short supply, companies may need experienced workers, and could reconsider offering early retirement plans.

PRACTICE TEST

MULTIPLE CHOICE

1.	b	12.	a
2.	c	13.	c
3.	c	14.	d
4.	d	15.	c
5.	a	16.	b
6.	b	17.	b
7.	c	18.	d
8.	b	19.	d
9.	c	20.	b
10.	a	21.	a
11.	b	22.	c

TRUE–FALSE

1.	T	12.	T
2.	T	13.	T
3.	F	14.	F
4.	T	15.	F
5.	F	16.	T
6.	F	17.	F
7.	F	18.	T
8.	T	19.	T
9.	F	20.	T
10.	F	21.	T
11.	T	22.	F

CHAPTER 12 – DEALING WITH EMPLOYEE-MANAGEMENT ISSUES AND RELATIONSHIPS

LEARNING GOALS

After you have read and studied this chapter, you should be able to:

1. Trace the history of organized labor in the United States.
2. Discuss the major legislation affecting labor unions.
3. Outline the objectives of labor unions.
4. Describe the tactics used by labor and management during conflicts and discuss the role of unions in the future.
5. Assess some of today's controversial employee-management issues such as executive compensation, pay equity, child care and elder care, drug testing, and violence in the workplace.

LEARNING THE LANGUAGE

Listed below are important terms found in the chapter. Choose the correct term for the definition and write it in the space provided.

Agency shop agreement	Givebacks	Right-to-work laws
American Federation of Labor	Grievance	Secondary boycott
Arbitration	Industrial unions	Sexual harassment
Bargaining zone	Injunction	Shop stewards
Certification	Knights of Labor	Strike
Closed shop agreement	Lockout	Strikebreakers
Collective bargaining	Mediation	Union
Congress of Industrial Organizations	Negotiated labor-management agreement (labor contract)	Union security clause
Cooling-off period	Open shop agreement	Union shop agreement
Craft union	Primary boycott	Yellow-dog contract
Decertification		

1. The _____ is the range of options between the initial and final offer that each party will consider before negotiations dissolve or reach an impasse.

2. A period of time known as the _____ is a period when workers in a critical industry return to their jobs while the union and management continue negotiations.

3. The process known as _____ is one by which workers take away a union's right to represent them.

4. A charge by employees that management is not abiding by the terms of the negotiated labor-management agreement is called a _____.

5. This tactic, known as a _____ , is an attempt by management to put pressure on unions by closing the business.

6. A tactic called a _____ occurs when the union encourages both its members and the general public not to buy the products of a firm involved in a labor dispute.

7. An employee organization known as _____ has the main goal of representing members in employee-management bargaining about job-related issues.

8. A clause in a labor-management agreement that says employers may hire nonunion workers who are not required to join the union but must pay a union fee is called an _____.

9. Under _____ a third party, called a mediator, encourages both sides to continue negotiating and often makes suggestions for resolving the dispute.

10. Known as _____ this includes unwelcome sexual advances, requests for sexual favors, and other conduct of a sexual nature that creates a hostile work environment.

11. A _____ was a type of contract that required employees to agree as a condition of employment not to join a union; prohibited by the Norris-LaGuardia Act in 1932.

12. _____ are union officials who work permanently in an organization and represent employee interests on a daily basis.

13. A provision in a negotiated labor-management agreement known as a _____ stipulates that employees who benefit from a union must either officially join or at least pay dues to the union.

14. An organization known as the _____ consisted of craft unions that championed fundamental labor issues; founded in 1886.

15. Concessions made by union members to management or gains from labor negotiations given back to management to help employers remain competitive and thereby save jobs are called _____.

16. Under this type of agreement, known as a(n) _____ workers in right to work states have the option to join or not join the union, if one exists in their workplace.

17. Workers who are hired to do the jobs of striking employees until the labor dispute is resolved are called _____.

18. The formal process of a union becoming recognized by the NLRB as the bargaining agent for a group of employees is called _____.

19. Labor organizations called _____ consist of unskilled and semi-skilled workers in mass production industries such as automobiles and mining.

20. This clause in a labor-management agreement called a _____ , indicates that workers do not have to be members of a union to be hired, but must agree to join the union within a prescribed period.

21. The process known as _____ is where union representatives, and management form a labor-management agreement, or contract, for workers.

22. The first national labor union was the _____ , and was formed in 1869.

23. A _____ is an attempt by labor to convince others to stop doing business with a firm that is the subject of a primary boycott; prohibited by the Taft-Hartley Act.

24. The agreement to bring in an impartial third party to render a binding decision in a labor dispute is called _____.

25. The clause in a labor-management agreement known as a _____ specified that workers had to be members of a union before being hired; it was outlawed by the Taft-Hartley Act.

26. A _____ is an agreement that sets the tone and clarifies the terms under which management and labor agree to function over a period of time.

27. Legislation that gives workers the right, under an open shop, to join or not join a union if it is present is called _____.

28. A union strategy known as a _____ means that workers refuse to go to work; the purpose is to further workers' objectives after an impasse in collective bargaining.

29. The _____ is the union organization of unskilled workers that broke away from the AFL in 1935 and rejoined it in 1955.

30. An organization of skilled specialists in a particular craft or trade is a _____.

31. A(n) _____ is a court order directing someone to do something or to refrain from doing something.

ASSESSMENT CHECK

Learning Goal 1

Employee-Management Issues

1. Why did workers originally form unions?

2. Labor unions were largely responsible for:

   a. _____

   b. _____

   c. _____

   d. _____

   e. _____

   f. _____

3. Why has union strength declined in the last 2 decades?

4. Most historians agree that today's unions are an outgrowth of: _____

   _____

   _____

5. Formal labor organizations date back to _____

6. How did the Industrial Revolution impact the formation and growth of unions?

7. The first national labor organization was the: _____

   Its intention was to: _____

8. What was the AFL and why did the AFL limit membership?

9. Why was the CIO formed?

10. How was the AFL-CIO created?

Learning Goal 2

Labor Legislation and Collective Bargaining

11. Five major pieces of labor-management legislation are:

    a. _____

    b. _____

    c. _____

    d. _____

    e. _____

12. The major elements of the Norris LaGuardia Act are that it:

   a. _____

   b. _____

   c. _____

13. What are the major provisions of the Wagner Act (National Labor Relations Act)?

14. The NLRB provides _____

   _____

15. How would the Employee Free Choice Act benefit unions?

16. What did the Fair Labor Standards Act do for workers?

17. What act did the Taft-Hartley Act amend, and what does Taft-Hartley permit and prohibit?

18. What are the major elements of the Landrum-Griffin Act?

Learning Goal 3
Objectives of Organized Labor

19. How have the objectives of organized labor shifted with social and economic trends?

20. List the general topics covered in labor-management agreements.

a. _____   g. _____

b. _____   h. _____

c. _____   i. _____

d. _____   j. _____

e. _____   k. _____

f. _____

21. Distinguish between:

Union security clause:

Union shop agreement:

Agency shop agreement:

Closed shop agreement:

Open shop agreement:

22. What areas will be the focus of union negotiations in the future?

a. _____   d. _____

b. _____   e. _____

c. _____   f. _____

Resolving Labor-Management Disagreements

23. What are generally the sources of grievances?

a. _____   d. _____

b. _____   e. _____

c. _____

24. In the negotiation process, when does mediation become necessary? What is the job of a mediator?

25. How does arbitration differ from mediation?

Learning Goal 4

Tactics Used in Labor-Management Conflicts

26. What are the tactics used by <u>labor</u> (unions) in labor-management disputes?

    a. _____   c. _____

    b. _____   d. _____

27. What are the possible effects of a strike?

28. What is picketing and what is the purpose of picketing?

29. Why are public safety workers often prohibited from striking? What action is often taken as an alternative?

30. The tactics available to management in labor-management disputes are:

    a. _____   c. _____

    b. _____

31. Under what conditions might management seek an injunction?

    a. _____

    b. _____

    c. _____

32. For a court to issue an injunction management must: _____

    _____.

33. New issues that affect labor-management relations include:

    a. _____

    b. _____

    c. _____

    d. _____

34. What is the state of union membership today?

35. How will unions have to change in order to grow in the future?

36. How are unions assisting management today?

Learning Goal 5

Controversial Employee-Management Issues

37. What is the central issues regarding executive compensation today?

38. What is the controversy surrounding using stock options as a form of compensation for CEOs?

39. What did management consultant Peter Drucker say regarding the level of executive compensation?

40. How does the pay of U.S. executives compare to executive pay in other countries? What may be an explanation for the difference?

41. Describe the issue of pay equity.

42. What explains the disparity between women's pay and men's pay, and how is the disparity changing?

43. In evaluating sexual harassment, a person's conduct on the job could be considered illegal if:

    a. _____

    b. _____

44. What is the difference between "quid pro quo" sexual harassment and "hostile environment" harassment?

45. What is a problem with implementing harassment policies?

    What could companies do to help prevent lawsuits?

46. Child care issues raise the concerns of employers for two key reasons:

    a. _____

    b. _____

47. What controversial questions surround child care in the public and private sector?

    a. _____

    b. _____

    c. _____

48. List five kinds of programs companies are providing to help with child care concerns.

    a. _____

    b. _____

    c. _____

    d. _____

    e. _____

49. What conditions illustrate why the issue of elder care has become important in today's workplace?

50. What programs can businesses offer to employees dealing with elder care responsibilities?

51. What is expected to happen to the cost to companies of elder care issue in the United States?

52. What is the loss to business due to substance and alcohol abuse? What have companies done in response?

53. Describe the impact of workplace violence in the workplace.

54. What actions have firms taken to deal with the growing threat of workplace violence?

CRITICAL THINKING EXERCISES

Learning Goal 1

1. How do the issues that concerned the early crafts unions before and during the Industrial Revolution issues compare with modern day work issues?

Learning Goal 2

2. Five major pieces of legislation which have had an impact on the development of labor unions are:

    Norris-LaGuardia Act 1932
    National Labor Relations Act (Wagner Act) 1935
    Fair Labor Standards Act 1938
    Labor-Management Relations Act (Taft-Hartley Act) 1947
    Labor-Management Reporting and Disclosure Act (Landrum-Griffin Act) 1959

    Identify which act is being discussed in each of the following:

    a. _____   Texas, Florida, Georgia, Iowa, Kansas and 17 other states have passed right-to-work laws under this act.

    b. _____   The AFL-CIO and Teamsters file financial reports every year with the U.S. Department of Labor.

    c. _____   Union members picketed the Price Chopper grocery stores to protest the stores' use of non-union labor.

    d. _____   A retail store in Michigan is prevented from getting an injunction against a worker who is trying to organize a union.

    e. _____   Workers at a General Motors plant in Ohio went on strike, forcing closings at another plant that needed parts supplied by the striking plant.

    f. _____   A grocery store in Illinois carries products produced by a company the AFL-CIO is striking. Under this law, the AFL-CIO cannot call for a boycott of the grocery store.

    g. _____   Voter fraud was alleged in the election of a UAW union official, and is being investigated.

    h. _____   In an attempt to avoid a strike, union and management officials in the aeronautical industry begin negotiating a year in advance of the end of the current contract.

    i. _____   In July, 2009 the federal minimum wage was increased to $7.25 an hour.

Learning Goal 3

3. There are four types of union agreements:

closed shop   union shop

agency shop   open shop

Identify each of the following:

a. _____ When Tom Oswalt worked in an automotive factory for the summer in Michigan, he chose not to join the local union. However, he was still required to pay a fee to the union under a union-security clause.

b. _____ After the Wagner Act was passed, unions sought security with this type of agreement. With passage of the Taft-Hartley Act in 1947, however, these types of shops were made illegal.

c. _____ When Peter Tobler went to work at Tyson Foods in Springdale, Arkansas, he was not required to join the union, and did not have to pay any fees to the union.

d. _____ Gary Reese took a job with the Saint Louis plant of InBev-Anheuser-Busch in August. He had until October to join the union.

Learning Goals 2, 3

4. Several years ago, the National and American League baseball players went on strike, and ended the baseball season for the year without playoffs or the World Series. While player representatives continued to negotiate with team owners, (sporadically) the strike was still not resolved by the opening of the season in the spring of the following year. Even then- President Bill Clinton could not convince the owners and players to come to the bargaining table and talk to one another. What options are available to labor and management for resolving agreements, which could have been used before the players went on strike, or while they were on strike?

Learning Goal 4

5. When the collective bargaining process breaks down, both management and labor have specific tactics available to them to reach their objectives.

Management	**Labor**
Injunction	Strike
Lockout	Picketing
Strikebreakers	Primary boycotts
	Secondary boycotts

Match the tactic being used in each of the following descriptions:

a. _____ In the past, members of various unions have mounted campaigns to persuade consumers not to shop at Wal-Mart, because Wal-Mart does not use union labor.

b. _____ When contract negotiations broke down, the owners of the national hockey clubs refused to allow players to play, and delayed the start of the season by several weeks.

c. _____ While the hockey players were being prevented from working, the baseball players were refusing to work!

d. _____ In order to start a season anyway, the baseball club owners hired replacement players, bringing many up from the minor leagues.

e. _____ During a strike against producers members of the American Federation of Musicians of the United States and Canada attempted to raise public awareness and sympathy for their cause by gathering outside Broadway theaters in New York City carrying signs outlining their grievances.

f. _____ To prevent a sympathy strike by its machinists, United Airlines obtained a court order making it illegal for the machinists to strike during a strike by the flight attendants.

g. _____ Although it is illegal, the employees of an airline threatened this action against the railways in sympathy with the railroad strikers.

6. What might be the unions' role in the concepts we have discussed in previous chapters, such as self-managed teams, continuous improvement, and so on?

Learning Goal 5

7. What justifications can you state for the high level of executive pay in the United States?

8. What are the negative aspects of the high level of executive pay in the United States?

9. The issue of pay equity centers on comparing the value of jobs traditionally held by women with the value of jobs traditionally held by men. What do comparisons of "men's jobs" with "women's jobs" show? How are things changing?

10. As more women have entered the workforce, the issue of sexual harassment has become increasingly visible. What are the problems surrounding this issue, and what are companies doing about it?

11. What are the issues surrounding:

Child care:

Eldercare:

Drug testing:

Violence in the workplace:

PRACTICE TEST

MULTIPLE CHOICE — Circle the best answer

Learning Goal 1

1. Workers originally formed unions:
   a. as social organizations.
   b. to protect themselves from intolerable work conditions and unfair treatment.
   c. as a way to increase job security.
   d. to have the rights to strike and to picket.

2. Most historians agree that today's union movement is an outgrowth of:
   a. the Great Depression.
   b. the Civil War.
   c. the Industrial Revolution.
   d. the Revolutionary War.

3. The AFL was an organization:
   a. of crafts unions.
   b. that promoted social, labor and economic issues.
   c. who's intention was to gain significant political power.
   d. that was one large union, encompassing workers in all trades areas.

Learning Goal 2

4. When Joe Kerr began working at his local bakery, he felt there was a need for the workers to sit down with management and talk about some of the problems facing the workers at their job. Joe found out there was a union representing the bakery workers, but that management didn't take them seriously, and refused to sit down with the union and negotiate. After some research Joe found out that under the _____ , workers had the right to expect management to negotiate with them.
   a. Norris-LaGuardia Act
   b. Wagner Act
   c. Fair Labor Standards Act
   d. Taft-Hartley Act

5. Marriette Rene lives in Alabama and works in a factory making heating and air conditioning equipment. When she first got the job, she was afraid she was going to have to join a union, but soon found out that Alabama is a right-to-work state, and she can't be required to join. This is because the _____ permits states to pass laws prohibiting compulsory union membership.
   a. Taft-Hartley Act
   b. Landrum-Griffith Act
   c. Norris LaGuardia Act
   d. Wagner Act

Learning Goal 3

6. When Dave Sutton went to work for a printing shop, he thought he was going to have to join the union representing the shop. However on his first day of work he was told that while there was a union representing the workers, he was not *required* to join, and he didn't have to pay any dues to the union if he chose not to join. Dave works in a(n) _____ shop.
   a. union
   b. agency
   c. closed
   d. open

7. The sources of grievances are generally
   a. overtime rules, promotions and layoffs.
   b. money and company policies.
   c. hours worked, other employees and contract negotiations.
   d. items to be included in contract negotiations.

8. A bargaining zone is:
   a. the location in which negotiations take place.
   b. a type of legislation that gives workers the right to join or not join a union.
   c. a contract that requires employees to agree not to join a union as a condition of employment.
   d. the range of options between the initial and final offer that each party will consider before negotiations dissolve.

9. When baseball players went on strike, an individual was brought in to help resolve the dispute between management and players. This third party was involved to make suggestions, but legally could not make any decisions about how the players dispute should be settled. This is an example of:
   a. arbitration.
   b. grievance.
   c. mediation.
   d. a bargaining zone.

Learning Goal 4

10. When organized labor encourages its members not to buy products made by a firm in a labor dispute, it is encouraging a:
    a. strike.
    b. primary boycott.
    c. secondary boycott.
    d. injunction.

11. Which of the following is a tactic used by management in a labor dispute?
    a. picketing
    b. strikes
    c. boycotts
    d. injunction

12. Union membership has:
    a. continued to grow as companies face worker discontent with overseas outsourcing.
    b. been steady in the last decades, and is expected to grow very slowly in the next 10 years.
    c. been steadily declining for many years.
    d. has declined to near zero, and unions most likely will disappear in the next 10 years.

13. For unions to grow in the future, they will have to:
    a. continue to grant givebacks to management.
    b. begin to organize foreign workers in overseas markets.
    c. adapt to a more culturally diverse, white collar workforce.
    d. take up the fight against continuous improvement and employee involvement.

Learning Goal 5

14. When compared to their European counterparts, U.S. corporate executives:
    a. are making considerably more than executives in other countries.
    b. are being paid much less than their counterparts, considering how much more they work.
    c. are compensated better when times are good, but worse when the company isn't doing as well.
    d. are at about the same level in terms of compensation.

15. The issue of pay equity deals with:
    a. paying equal wages to men and women who do the same job.
    b. equal pay for different jobs that require similar levels of training and education or skills.
    c. assuring that men and women have equal opportunity in the job market.
    d. ensuring that executive pay is not more than 20 times the pay of the lowest paid worker.

16. Which of the following is not included in a discussion of behavior that would be considered sexually harassing?
    a. An employee must submit to a certain behavior as a condition of employment.
    b. Submission or rejection of a behavior is used as a basis for employment decisions.
    c. A behavior interferes with job performance or creates a hostile working environment.
    d. Reporting of a behavior results in job dismissal.

17. Which of the following is true regarding the issue of child-care for workers?
    a. Federal child-care assistance has declined considerably.
    b. A major question is who should pay for child-care services.
    c. A majority of major companies provide some kind of child- care services.
    d. Parents have made it clear they will compromise on the issue of child- care.

18. Companies have responded to requests for assistance in child-care with all of the following except:
    a. discount arrangements with national child care chains.
    b. vouchers that offer payment toward the kind of child care the employee prefer.
    c. on-site child-care centers.
    d. increases in the number of allowable sick leave days for employees to use when a child is ill.

19. Elder care issues in the United States:
    a. will continue to grow and become more costly as higher executives and managers begin to deal with the care of elderly parents and relatives.
    b. has become less important as many women stay at home and can take on the care of elderly parents and relatives.
    c. is becoming easier for companies to address.
    d. have been addressed by many companies in the form of elder care programs and benefits.

20. Which of the following is included as a major issue which companies will have to address in the coming years?
    a. executive compensation
    b. union growth and power
    c. child care
    d. violence in the workplace

TRUE–FALSE

Learning Goal 1

1. _____ Labor unions were largely responsible for the establishment of minimum-wage laws, overtime rules, worker's compensation, severance pay, and more.

2. _____ The CIO, Congress of Industrial Organizations, grew out of the Knights of Labor.

3. _____ In the early part of the last century (the 1900s), it was common for workers to have an 80 hour work week.

4. _____ The Taft-Hartley Act outlawed contracts forbidding union activities.

5. _____ The minimum wage was established by the Fair Labor Standards Act.

6. _____ Under the Wagner Act, labor was granted the right to collectively bargain, but was expected to bargain in good faith.

7. _____ In a decertification campaign, workers take away a union's right to represent them.

Learning Goal 3

8. _____ A union security clause stipulates that union workers with seniority will be the last workers to be laid off.

9. _____ Under an agreement called an agency shop, companies can hire nonunion workers, who are not required to join the union, but who must pay a special union fee.

10. _____ In right to work states, workers may choose not to join a union, even if one exists to represent them in their work place.

11. _____ In the process of arbitration, an impartial third party will make a binding decision in a labor dispute.

Learning Goal 4

12. _____ Many states prohibit strikes by people in jobs such as police officers or fire fighters.

13. _____ "Just cause" must be shown when a union wants to go on strike.

14. _____ Unions have begun to assist management in training workers, redesigning jobs and helping to recruit and train workers who need special help to adapt to the job requirements of the new economy.

15. _____ A "cooling off" period requires that management must allow 30 days after a contract dispute before requiring that labor go back to the bargaining table.

Learning Goal 5

16. _____ In the past, the primary explanation for the disparity between men and women's pay has been that women often aren't as educated as men.

17. _____ "Quid pro quo" harassment exists when the employees submission to such conduct is made either explicitly or implicitly a term or condition of employment.

18. _____ The issue of elder care is expected to decline in importance in coming years.

19. _____ A key reason that child-care issues are important to companies today is that absences related to child care cost them billions of dollars annually.

20. _____ Individuals who use illegal drugs are more likely to be involved in workplace accidents and to file a worker's compensation claim.

You Can Find It on the Net

Let's take a look at the issues unions are considering in the 21st century. Visit the AFL-CIO website at **www.aflcio.org**

How are the topics featured related to what the text indicates are key issues for today's unions?

Click on the "Corporate Watch" link, then on "Executive Paywatch" and scroll down to the CEO and You link. This link will show you how much your pay would be if you were a CEO. How much would you be making today if you were the CEO? Pick a company and find out what the CEO of that company made.

Enter one of the blogs and give your opinion about the topics that interest you on this page.

Go to www.uaw.org At the time of this writing the U.S. automotive companies were in serious financial trouble—Chrysler had declared bankruptcy, and General Motors was close to doing the same.

How is the UAW addressing these problems?

What is the UAW saying about how they can help the U.S. economy recover?

ANSWERS

LEARNING THE LANGUAGE

1.	Bargaining zone	12.	Shop stewards	22.	Knights of Labor
2.	Cooling off period	13.	Union security clause	23.	Secondary boycott
3.	Decertification	14.	American Federation of Labor (AFL)	24.	Arbitration
4.	Grievance	15.	Givebacks	25.	Closed shop agreement
5.	Lockout	16.	Open shop agreement	26.	Negotiated labor management agreement
6.	Primary boycott	17.	Strikebreakers	27.	Right-to-work laws
7.	Unions	18.	Certification	28.	Strike
8.	Agency shop agreement	19.	Industrial unions	29.	Congress of Industrial Organizations (CIO)
9.	Mediation	20.	Union shop agreement	30.	Craft union
10.	Sexual harassment	21.	Collective bargaining	31.	Injunction
11.	Yellow dog contract				

ASSESSMENT CHECK

Employee-Management Issues

Learning Goal 1

1. Workers originally formed unions to protect themselves from intolerable work conditions and unfair treatment from owners and managers. They also wanted to secure some say in the operations of their jobs.

2. Labor unions were largely responsible for:
   a. the establishment of minimum wage laws
   b. overtime rules
   c. workers' compensation
   d. severance pay
   e. child labor laws
   f. job safety regulations

3. It is suggested that the reasons for the decline in union strength/membership are global competition, shifts from manufacturing to service and high-tech industries, growth in part-time work, and changes in management philosophies. Others believe that the membership decline is related to labor's success in seeing the issues it has promoted become law.

4. Most historians agree that today's unions are an outgrowth of the economic transition caused by the Industrial Revolution. Workers who went from agricultural jobs to factory jobs found that strength through unions could lead to improved job conditions, better wages and job security.
   The Industrial Revolution changed the economic structure of the United States.

5. Formal labor organizations date back to the time of the American Revolution, as early as 1792.

6. The Industrial Revolution changed the economic structure of the United States. Productivity increases from mass production and job specialization made the U.S. a world economic power.

   This growth brought problems for workers in terms of expectations, hours of work, wages and unemployment. Workers who failed to produce lost their jobs. People had to go work when they were ill or had family problems. Hours of work were expanded, and an 80-hour work week was not uncommon. Wages were low, and the use of child labor was widespread.

7. The first national labor union was the Knights of Labor.

   The intention of the Knights of Labor was to gain significant political power and eventually restructure the entire U.S. economy.

8. The American Federation of Labor, AFL, was an organization of craft unions that championed fundamental labor issues.

   The AFL limited membership to skilled workers assuming they would have better bargaining power in getting concessions from employers.

9. The Congress of Industrial Organizations broke away from the AFL, and was formed to organize both craftspeople and unskilled workers.

10. The AFL and the CIO merged in 1955 after each organization struggled for leadership for several years.

Learning Goal 2

Labor Legislation and Collective Bargaining

11. a. Norris-LaGuardia Act 1932
    b. National Labor Relations Act (Wagner Act) 1935
    c. Fair Labor Standards Act 1938
    d. Labor Management Relations Act (Taft-Hartley Act) 1947
    e. Labor Management Reporting and Disclosure Act (Landrum-Griffin Act) 1959

12. The major elements of the Norris-LaGuardia Act are that it
    a. Prohibited courts from issuing injunctions against nonviolent union activities.
    b. Outlawed contracts forbidding union activities.
    c. Outlawed yellow dog contracts.

13. The Wagner Act (National Labor Relations Act) gave employees the right to form or join labor organizations, and the right to collectively bargain in good faith with employers who were obligated to meet at reasonable times. It also gave workers the right to engage in strikes, picketing, and boycotts. The act prohibited certain unfair labor practices by management, and established the National Labor Relations Board. It also provided workers with a clear process to remove a union as its workplace representative.

14. The NLRB provides guidelines and offers legal protection to workers that seek to vote on organizing a union to represent them in the workplace. This process is called certification.

15. The Employee Free Choice Act would benefit unions in that it would make I easier for unions to organize workers. The legislation would replace the secret ballot now used with card check, whereby workers would approve union representation by simply signing a card.

16. The Fair Labor Standards Act set a minimum wage and maximum basic hours for workers.

17. The Taft-Hartley Act amended the Wagner Act. It permitted states to pass right to work laws, and set up methods to deal with strikes affecting national health and safety. The act also prohibits secondary boycotts, closed- shop agreements, and featherbedding.

18. The Landrum-Griffin Act amended the Taft-Hartley Act and the Wagner Act. It guaranteed individual rights of union members in dealing with their union, and required annual financial reports to be filed with the U.S. Department of Labor. One goal of this act was to clean up union corruption.

Learning Goal 3

Objectives of Organized Labor

19. The primary objectives of labor unions in the 1970s were additional pay and additional benefits. In the 1980s the focus shifted to issues related to job security and union recognition. In the 1990s and early 2000s, the focus was again on job security due to global competition and outsourcing.

20. The general topics covered in labor-management agreements are:
    a. Management rights
    b. Union recognition
    c. Union security clause
    d. Strikes and lockouts
    e. Union activities and responsibilities
    f. Wages
    g. Hours of work and time-off policies
    h. Job rights and seniority principles
    i. Discharge and discipline
    j. Grievance procedures
    k. Employee benefits, health and welfare

21. Union security clause: Stipulates that employees who reap benefits from a union must either officially join or at least pay dues to the union.

    Union shop agreement: Workers do not have to be members of a union to be hired for a job, but must agree to join the union within a prescribed period of time.

    Agency shop agreement: Employers may hire nonunion workers, who are not required to join the union, but must pay a special union fee or pay regular union dues.

    Closed shop agreement: Specified that that workers had to be members of a union in order to be hired. This practice was outlawed by the Taft-Hartley Act.

    Open shop agreement: Gives workers the option to join or not join a union when one is present in the workplace.

22. In the future unions will focus on
    a. child and elder care
    b. worker retraining,
    c. two-tiered wage plans
    d. offshore outsourcing
    e. employee empowerment
    f. integrity and honesty testing

Resolving Labor-Management Disagreements

23. Sources of grievances are:
    a. overtime rules
    b. promotions
    c. layoffs
    d. transfers
    e. job assignments

24. Mediation becomes necessary if labor-management negotiators aren't able to agree on alternatives within the bargaining zone. The mediator evaluates facts in a dispute and makes *suggestions* for resolving the dispute.

25. In arbitration, an impartial third party will render a binding decision in the labor dispute. A mediator can only make a suggestion.

Learning Goal 4

Tactics Used in Labor-Management Conflicts

26. Tactics used by labor in labor-management disputes are:
    a. Strikes
    b. Picketing
    c. Boycotts
    d. Work slowdowns

27. A strike attracts public attention to a labor dispute and at times causes operations in a company to slow down or totally shut down. Strikes can lead to a resolution of a dispute, but have also led to violence and extended bitterness. Few labor disputes lead to a strike today.

28. When strikers picket, they walk around the outside of the organization carrying signs and talking with the public and the media about the issues in a labor dispute. Unions also use picketing as an informational tool before going on strike.

    The purpose is to alert the public about an issue that is stirring labor unrest even though no strike has been voted.

29. Workers such as police officers or fire fighters are prohibited because of the potential for economic and social problems if those workers go off the job. As an alternative, many workers will engage in "sick-outs", sometimes known as the "blue flu", which is when workers arrange in groups to be absent from work and claim illness as the reason.

30. Tactics available to management in labor-management disputes include:
    a. Lockouts
    b. Injunctions
    c. Use of strikebreakers

31. Management might seek an injunction to
    a. order striking workers back to work.
    b. limit the number of pickets that can be used during a strike.
    c. deal with actions that could be detrimental to the public welfare.

32. For a court to issue an injunction management must show "just cause", such as the possibility of violence or the destruction of property.

33. New issues that affect labor-management relations include:
    a. increased global competition.
    b. advancing technology.
    c. offshore outsourcing.
    d. the changing nature of work.

34. Membership in unions has declined from a peak of almost 36% in 1945 to just 12.4% today, and only 7.6% of workers in the private sector are unionized. Union membership varies by state. The largest union today is the National Education Association.

35. For unions to grow, they will have to include white collar, female, and foreign born workers.

36. Unions are helping management in training workers, redesigning jobs, and assimilating the new workforce. They are helping to recruit and train foreign workers, unskilled workers, and others who may need special help in adapting to the job requirements of the new economy.

Learning Goal 5

Controversial Employee-Management Issues

37. The central issue regarding executive compensation seems to be the level of executive pay. The average CEO of a major corporation makes 180 times the average hourly worker's pay.

    There is also considerable frustration about the fact that some CEOs are forced to resign due to poor performance, yet are still give considerable compensation upon leaving.

38. Stock options account for a major portion of executive pay, and a problem arises when executives are compensated with stock options even when the company doesn't meet expectations.

39. Management consultant Peter Drucker suggested that CEOs should not earn much more than 20 times as much as the company's lowest paid employee.

40. European executives typically earn about 40 percent of what U.S. CEOs make. One explanation for the difference between the pay of American CEOs and that of European chief executives is that European companies often have workers who sit on the board of directors. Since boards set executive pay, this could be a reason why pay is less for European executives.

41. Pay equity goes beyond the concept of equal pay for equal work. Pay equity revolves around the concept of "comparable worth", the idea that people in jobs that require similar levels of education, training, or skills should receive equal pay. It centers on comparing jobs that have traditionally been held by women with those that have traditionally been held by men.

42. In the past the primary explanation for the pay disparity between men and women was that women only worked a portion of their available years once they left school, whereas men worked all of those years. This explanation no longer applies. Now the explanation is that many working women devote more time to their families and so opt for lower paying jobs.

    Studies have found that earnings of women with a college degree earn today close to what men earn.

43. Conduct can be considered sexually harassing if:
    a. an employee's submission to such conduct is made either explicitly or implicitly a term of employment or is the basis for employment decisions.
    b. the conduct interferes with a worker's job performance or creates an intimidating, hostile or offensive work environment.

44. "Quid pro quo" harassment could be a threat such as "go out with me or you are fired", for example. This explicitly creates a term or condition of employment.

    A "hostile environment" is created when an individual's conduct interferes with a worker's job performance or creates an intimidating or offensive work environment. A key term is "unwelcome", which refers to behavior that would offend a reasonable person.

45. A major problem with implementing harassment policies is that workers and managers often know that a policy exists but have no idea what it says. Many companies have also set up rapid, effective grievance procedures and reacted promptly to allegations of harassment.

    Companies could offer management training, and require sexual harassment workshops for all employees, which can be done on the Internet.

46. Child-care issues are important to employers today because:
    a. It is estimated that child care related absences already cost American businesses billions of dollars each year
    b. They raise the question of who should pay for child care services.

47. The questions surrounding child care today concern:
    a. responsibilities for child-care subsidies.
    b child care programs.
    c. parental leave.

48. Companies have responded to the need for safe, affordable day care by providing:
    a. Discount arrangements with national child care chains.
    b. Vouchers that offer payments toward whatever child care the employee chooses.
    c. Referral services that help identify quality child care facilities.
    d. On-site child care centers.
    e. Sick-child care centers.

49. The issue has become important because the workforce in the U.S. is aging, and many workers are going to confront the problem of how to care for older parents. The number of households with at least one adult providing elder care has dramatically increased in the last two decades and is expected to continue to grow.

    Current estimates suggest that companies are presently losing $11 billion a year in reduced productivity, absenteeism, and turnover from employees who have responsibilities with aging parents.

50. Companies can allow employees to move to flextime, telecommuting, part-time employment or job sharing. Certain companies offer employees employee assistance programs or elder care management services. However, few companies offer any type of elder care benefits programs.

51. It is expected that costs to companies will rise as more experience and high ranking employees become involved in caring for older parents and relatives. Estimates are that costs could go as high as $25 billion annually. Companies already realize that transfers and promotions are often out of the question for employees whose parents need ongoing care. The problem will continue to exist well into the 21st century.

52. Approximately 40 percent of industrial injuries and fatalities can be linked to alcohol consumption. Individuals who use drugs are three and a half times more likely to be involved in workplace accidents and five times as likely to file a worker's compensation claim. According to the U.S. Department of Labor drug use costs U.S. companies $276 billion in lost work, health care costs, crime traffic accidents and other expenses, and over $140 billion in lost productivity annually.

    In response, over 70% of major companies now test workers and job applicants for substance abuse.

53. There is a growing trend toward violence in the workplace. Workplace homicides account for 16 percent of all workplace deaths and are the number one cause of death for women in the workplace. One in six violent crimes in the U.S. occurs at work.

54. Many firms have begun to hold focus groups for employee input, have hired managers with strong interpersonal skills, and employed skilled consultants to deal with the growing employee/management issue of workplace violence.

CRITICAL THINKING EXERCISES

Learning Goal 1

1. The development of crafts unions, beginning in 1792 came about to discuss work issues such as pay, hours, conditions and job security. The Industrial Revolution led to changes, and problems for workers in terms of productivity, hours of work, wages and unemployment. If you failed to produce, you lost your job. Hours worked increased to as many as 80 hours per week. Wages were low and the use of child labor was common.

   Unions today are focusing on job security and union recognition, just as the early crafts unions did. However, union negotiators today have also begun to address such issues as global competition, drug testing, benefits such as day care and elder care, violence in the workplace and employee stock ownership programs.

Learning Goal 2

2. a. Taft-Hartley
   b. Landrum-Griffin
   c. Wagner Act
   d. Norris-LaGuardia
   e. Wagner Act
   f. Taft-Hartley Act
   g. Landrum-Griffin
   h. Wagner-Act
   i. Fair Labor Standards Act

Learning Goal 3

3. a. Agency shop
   b. Closed shop
   c. Open shop
   d. Union shop

Learning Goals 2, 3

4. There are three options available for resolving these disputes. The players union could have filed grievances against the owners before going on strike, in an attempt to resolve their differences without putting an end to the season. Either side could have brought in a mediator, before or during the strike. The mediator's job is to make suggestions for resolving the dispute. Lastly, arbitration could have been used. In arbitration, the parties agree to bring in a third party to make a binding decision, a decision that both parties must adhere to. The arbitrator must be acceptable to both parties. (In fact, in this case, an arbitrator was discussed between the players and the owners, but neither side could agree on the choice of an arbitrator!)

Learning Goal 4

5. a. Primary boycott   e. Picketing
    b. Lockout   f. Injunction
    c. Strike   g. Secondary boycott
    d. Strikebreakers

6. The role of unions is likely to be much different from that of the past. Union leadership is aware of the need to be competitive with foreign firms. Unions have taken a leadership role in introducing such concepts as continuous improvement, constant innovation and employee involvement programs. In the future, unions will help management in training, work design such as self-managed teams, and in recruiting and training foreign workers, unskilled workers and others.

Learning Goal 5

7. U.S. executives are responsible for billion dollar corporations. They often work 70 or more hours per week. Many can show stockholders that they have turned potential problems into profitable success. Further, many top performers in sports, movies and entertainment are paid large sums, so is it therefore out of line that CEOs of major corporations should be compensated in the same way? Furthermore, there is not a plentiful supply of seasoned, skilled professionals to manage large corporations, especially through the difficult times we have experienced in the early 2000s.

8. The drawbacks of the high level of pay are most noticeable when an executive makes staggering sums, while the financial performance of the company may be lagging. Some question the compensation paid to a departing CEO whose performance forced them to resign their job involuntarily. Stakeholders could certainly question these practices in a business. In comparison to our global competitors, U.S. executives earn substantially more than their counterparts. In the U.S. the average CEO earns 180 times what the average hourly worker earns, while in Europe the CEOs of large corporations earn, comparatively, quite a bit less.

9. A comparison of jobs traditionally held by men with jobs traditionally held by women would show that women earn about 80 percent of what men earn, thought the differences vary by profession, job experience and tenure and the person's level of education. In the past, disparities could be explained by the fact that women only worked 50 to 60 percent of their available years after they left school, whereas men worked all of those years. As fewer women left the work force for an extended period, this changed. Another explanation for the disparity may be that many women try to work as well as care for families, and thus do not move ahead in their careers as quickly as men. Others opt for lower paying jobs that are less demanding.
    In today's knowledge based economy, it appears that women will compete with men, financially, in such areas as health care, telecommunications and knowledge technology.

10. The major question surrounding the issue of sexual harassment is the fact that while managers and workers may know that their company has a sexual harassment policy they don't know what it says. Conduct becomes illegal when: 1) an employee's submission to such conduct is made either explicitly or implicitly a term of employment, or an employee's submission to or rejection of such conduct is used as the basis of employment decisions affecting the worker's status or 2) the conduct interferes with a worker's job performance or creates an unhealthy atmosphere.

    Companies are becoming more sensitive to comments and behavior of a sexual nature. Suggestions are more management training, and mandatory sexual harassment workshops for all employees.

11. The issue of <u>child-care</u> will remain a concern in the 21st century. There are questions surrounding who should pay for child care, and around the cost of absences related to child care. The number of companies that offer child-care is growing, and some have begun to provide such benefits as discount arrangements with child-care chains, vouchers, referral services, on-site daycare and sick-child centers.

The <u>elder care</u> issue has arisen because the workforce of the U.S. is aging. Older workers are more likely to be concerned with finding care for elderly parents than with finding day care for children. Businesses do not seem to be responding to the need for elder care as quickly as they could, even though it is estimated that elder-care givers cost employers billions of dollars in lost output and replacement costs.

Companies feel that <u>alcohol and drug abuse</u> is a serious problem in the workplace because so many workers are involved. Drug testing is growing at a rapid pace.

<u>Violence in the workplace</u> is a growing trend. Still, many companies don't offer formal training for dealing with prevention of violence in the workplace, because managers feel the issue is overblown by the media.

PRACTICE TEST

MULTIPLE CHOICE

1.	b	11.	d
2.	c	12.	c
3.	a	13.	c
4.	b	14.	a
5.	a	15.	b
6.	d	16.	d
7.	a	17.	b
8.	d	18.	d
9.	c	19.	a
10.	b	20.	b

TRUE–FALSE

1.	T	11.	T
2.	F	12.	T
3.	T	13.	F
4.	F	14.	T
5.	T	15.	F
6.	T	16.	F
7.	T	17.	T
8.	F	18.	F
9.	T	19.	T
10.	T	20.	T

CHAPTER 13 – MARKETING: HELPING BUYERS BUY

LEARNING GOALS

After you have read and studied this chapter, you should be able to:

1. Define marketing and apply the marketing concept to profit and nonprofit organizations.
2. Describe the four Ps of marketing.
3. Summarize the marketing research process.
4. Show how marketers use environmental scanning to learn about the changing marketing environment.
5. Explain now marketers apply the tools of market segmentation, relationship marketing, and the study of consumer behavior.
6. Compare the business-to-business market and the consumer market.

LEARNING THE LANGUAGE

Listed below are important terms found in the chapter. Choose the correct term for the definition and write it in the space provided.

Benefit segmentation	Marketing	Product
Brand name	Marketing concept	Promotion
Business-to-business (B2B) market	Marketing mix	Psychographic segmentation
Consumer market	Marketing research	Relationship marketing
Customer relationship management (CRM)	Market segmentation	Secondary data
Demographic segmentation	Mass marketing	Target marketing
Environmental scanning	Niche marketing	Test marketing
Focus group	One-to-one marketing	Volume, or usage segmentation
Geographic segmentation	Primary data	

1. A word, letter or group of words or letters is a _____ that differentiates one seller's goods and services from those of competitors.

2. All the techniques sellers use to motivate people to buy products or services are called _____.

3. Dividing the marketing by cities, counties, states, or regions is known as _____.

4. All individuals and organizations that want goods and services to use in producing other goods and services or to sell, rent or supply goods to others is known as the _____.

5. The process known as _____ is being used when an organization tests products among potential users.

6. Information that has already been compiled by others and published in journals and books or made available online is called _____.

7. A _____ is any physical good, service or idea that satisfies a want or need plus anything that would enhance the product in the eyes of a consumer, such as a brand.

8. The process of _____ is dividing the market by age, income, and education level.

9. A three-part business philosophy called the _____ involves (1) a customer orientation, (2) a service orientation, and (3) a profit orientation.

10. A _____ is a small group of people who meet under the direction of a discussion leader to communicate their opinions about an organization, its products, or other given issues.

11. The process known as _____ calls for finding small, but profitable market segments and designing or finding products for them.

12. The ingredients that go into a marketing program are called the _____ and include product, price, place, and promotion.

13. The process known as _____ is marketing toward those groups (market segments) an organization decides it can serve profitably.

14. The activity called _____ is the analysis of markets to determine opportunities and challenges, and to find the information needed to make good decisions.

15. The process of _____ means dividing the market by determining which benefits of the product to talk about.

16. The _____ consists of all the individuals or households that want goods and services for personal consumption or use.

17. The process of _____ is defined by the activity, set of institutions, and processes for creating, communicating, delivering, and exchanging offerings that have value for customers, clients, partners and society at large.

18. _____ calls for learning as much as possible about customers and doing everything you can to satisfy them, or even exceed their expectations with goods and services over time.

19. The process of dividing the total market into several groups whose members have similar characteristics is called _____.

20. Data referred to as _____ , are data that you gather yourself, not from secondary sources such as books and magazines.

21. The marketing strategy known as _____ has the goal of keeping individual customers over time by offering them products that exactly meet their requirements.

22. The process of _____ is identifying the factors that can affect marketing success.

23. Dividing the market by using a group's values, attitudes and interests is _____.

24. _____ is dividing market by usage (volume of use).

25. Developing a unique mix of goods and services for each individual customer is called _____.

26. _____ is the term used to describe developing products and promotions to please large groups of people.

ASSESSMENT CHECK

Learning Goal 1

What is Marketing?

1. Whereas in the past marketing was focused on helping the seller sell, today, much of marketing is instead about _____.

    This is often accomplished by buyers using _____.

    Wise marketers are cultivating customer relationships using _____.

2. The four eras defined in the evolution of marketing are:

    a. _____

    b. _____

    c. _____

    d. _____

3. Describe the general philosophy of business during the production era.

4. How was the selling era different from the production era?

5. Describe the three parts of the marketing concept.

    a. _____

    b. _____

    c. _____

6. The idea of customer relationship management is to _____

    _____.

7. How well are marketers doing with regard to customer relationship management?

8. Give some examples of how non-profit organizations use marketing.

Learning Goal 2

The Marketing Mix

9. Managing the controllable parts of the marketing process involves:

   a. _____

   b. _____

   c. _____

   d. _____

10. List the steps in the marketing process.

    a. _____   f. _____

    b. _____   g. _____

    c. _____   h. _____

    d. _____   i. _____

    e. _____

11. What is "concept testing"?

12. Identify some of the factors involved in setting an appropriate price for a product.

13. What are marketing intermediaries?

14. List six promotion techniques:

    a. _____   d. _____

    b. _____   e. _____

    c. _____   f. _____

15. Relationship building with customers includes: _____

    _____

Learning Goal 3

Providing Marketers with Information

16. What are three things which marketing research helps to determine?

    a. _____

    b. _____

    c. _____

17. What are the four steps of the marketing research process?

    a. _____

    b. _____

    c. _____

    d. _____

18. Distinguish between primary and secondary data.

19. What are six general sources of secondary data?

    a. _____   d. _____

    b. _____   e. _____

    c. _____   f. _____

20. Which data should be gathered first, primary or secondary? Why?

21. Why or when will a company use primary data?

22. What are the sources of primary data?

    a. _____

    b. _____

    c. _____

    d. _____

    e. _____

    f. _____

    g. _____

    h. _____

23. What the important aspects of analyzing the data collected in the market research process?

24. If the results of the actions taken based on market research are not as expected, what can the company do?

Learning Goal 4

The Marketing Environment

25. What are the factors included in an environmental scan?

    a. _____   d. _____

    b. _____   e. _____

    c. _____

26. How has the use of the Internet changed global marketing?

27. What are the most important technological changes in marketing? Why?

28. What are some sociocultural trends that marketers must monitor?

29. How has the Internet affected competition for "brick and mortar" companies?

30. How does marketing change with a change in the economy?

31. What determines if a product is a business-to-business product or a consumer product? What is the difference between them?

Learning Goal 5

The Consumer Market

32. Why do companies use market segmentation?

33. What kind of segmentation is being used when we:

   a. Segment by what benefits a customer prefers? _____

   b. Segment by where people live?   _____

   c. Segment by age, income, or education?   _____

   d. Segment by a group's values, attitudes or interests?   _____

   e. Segment by how much a customer uses?   _____

34. What is the difference between niche marketing and one-to-one marketing?

35. Describe what is meant by the "long tail" theory.

36. The mass marketer tries to sell the same products to : _____

    using: _____

37. The goal of relationship marketing is to: _____

38. How has technology aided in the development of relationship marketing?

39. List the steps in the consumer decision-making process.

    a. _____

    b. _____

    c. _____

    d. _____

    e. _____

40. Describe the four types of influences on the consumer decision-making process.

    a. _____

    b. _____

    c. _____

    d. _____

41. In the area of consumer behavior, what are:

    Learning: _____

    _____

    Reference group: _____

    _____

    Culture: _____

    _____

    Subculture: _____

    _____

    Cognitive dissonance: _____

    _____

The Business-To-Business Market (B2B)

42.   What types of organizations are included in the B2B market?

   a.   _____

   b.   _____

   c.   _____

   d.   _____

43.   Why do business-to-business marketing strategies differ from consumer marketing strategies?

44.   What are six factors that make business-to-business marketing different from consumer marketing?

   a.   _____

   b.   _____

   c.   _____

   d.   _____

   e.   _____

   f.   _____

CRITICAL THINKING EXERCISES

Learning Goal 1

1.   Todd Whitman was a full-time student at a community college in the St. Louis area. In addition to going to school, Todd also worked for a company out of Idaho (Todd's home state) that made ice cream. As Todd tells it: "Alan Reed owns a potato farm in Idaho. He was looking for another market for his potatoes when he realized that the chemical make up of the potato was such that it could be used in making a tasty ice cream without using any sugar - i.e. a sugar free ice cream. He figured there had to be a market for that kind of product, one made without any artificial products to sweeten, so he made a few batches and tried it on his friends, without telling them it was made from potatoes." He called the ice cream Al and Reed's. This is where Todd came in. While in St. Louis, Todd's job was to attempt to get the product sold to St. Louisans. His employer shipped him a few gallons (as much as he could hold in his home freezer). Todd started trying to sell Al and Reed's to local grocery store chains, and ultimately got one of them to carry the ice cream in a couple of stores on a trial basis. He also brought some samples in to his Introduction to Business class, after persuading his teacher to allow a taste test. The product went over well, until the students found out it was made from potatoes!

Todd continued his promotional efforts with grocery stores, calling on them whenever he could. He left promotional pamphlets that explained the concept and production of ice cream made from potatoes, and offered the stores discounts for buying in volume.

a. Did Todd and Alan Reed use the marketing concept? Did Alan learn about customer needs? Which of the eras described in the evolution of marketing do you think Todd and Alan exemplify?

b. What steps in the marketing process did Todd and Alan Reed take?

c. What potential problem might they encounter with this product? How could Todd and Alan use the last step of the marketing process to overcome the problem?

d. Identify the product, promotion and place variables in this situation. What price do you think they should charge? Why?

Learning Goals 2, 3, 4

2. Sun-2-Shade is a revolutionary automotive product. Using technology available from the eyewear industry Eric, our entrepreneur, had created a car windshield that automatically darkens in the sun and lightens when in the shade or on a cloudy day. Now is the time to begin developing a marketing plan for our product.

a. What need did Eric see when he came up with the idea of Sun-2-Shade?

b. Who/what do you think should be Sun-2-Shade's customers?

c. How could concept testing have helped Sun-2-Shade?

d. Conduct an environmental scan for Sun-2-Shade.

e. Could Sun-2-Shade make use of one-to-one marketing?

Learning Goal 3

3. Marketing research is conducted to determine the needs of the market and the best ways to fill those needs.

   Using the four steps outlined in your book, suggest a market research project that might be of use to Sun-2-Shade.

   a. _____

   b. _____

   c. _____

   d. _____

Learning Goal 4

4. The major segmentation variables are:

   Geographic   Psychographic   Volume
   Demographic   Benefit

   Listed below are various products. Identify a target market for each product, then list the segmentation variable that could be used to identify that target market. There could be more than one target market for some products.
   Example:
   Head and Shoulders Shampoo:
   Target market: People with dandruff
   Variables: Benefit, health

   a. Toyota Prius automobile

   b. Nike footwear

   c. McDonalds

   d. Campbell's nacho cheese soup

5. Chad Allen turned on his c.d. player to listen to music while he was studying, and all he heard was a loud buzzing coming from his speakers. "Oh no! Now what?" thought Chad. Well Chad found the problem, and realized that the system was shot. "Well, we've got to have music for the party coming up in two weeks, so I'm going to have to get a new player," Chad said to his roommate on the way to class. He looked through the ads in the Sunday paper, and saw several sales at a couple of different stores. He spent part of the weekend, and part of a few days the following week researching different component pieces on the Internet, comparing each for price and sound quality and talking to sales people about which system was the best value. A couple of friends gave Chad their opinions of the brands, based on their experience with the specific brand Chad was looking at. Chad knew this brand was a good one, because his sister had purchased it last year. He bought the new system the following weekend, before the sale went off. He felt somewhat uneasy at how much he had spent, but when he saw an ad for that same system in an upscale magazine for $100 more, he felt better.

    Identify the steps in the decision making process that Chad took, and what factors influenced his decision, using the figure in your text.

Learning Goals 5, 6

6. Let's continue helping Sun-2-Shade to develop a marketing plan:

    a. Who would you choose as Sun-2-Shade's target market?

    b. If you were to choose the consumer market, what are some variables that you would want to consider?

    c. How would marketing your product to a business market differ from marketing the product to the consumer market?

370

7. Would you classify Sun-2-Shade product as a consumer good or as a business good? What characteristics of the business-to-business market will affect Sun-2-Shade's marketing efforts, and how?

8. Determine whether the following describes a consumer or a business-to-business product.

    a. Monsanto buys apples to sell in its company cafeteria. _____

    b. Jeff Walter buys a lawn mower for his lawn mowing business _____

    c. Darlene Knott buys a lawn mower to mow her lawn. _____

    d. Marti Galganski buys apples for her daughter's lunch. _____

PRACTICE TEST

MULTIPLE CHOICE — Circle the best answer

Learning Goal 1

1. When Maritza Toros opened her Mexican restaurant in a fashionable suburb of Kansas City, she believed that the most important element of her success would be advertising. She made sure that a significant portion of her budget was devoted to advertising in local papers, sent out coupons and really focused on the promotional aspects of the restaurant. Which of the four eras of marketing does it seem that Maritza emphasized?
    a. production era
    b. sales era
    c. marketing era
    d. customer relationship management

2. Which of the following would not be included in a discussion of the marketing concept?
    a. A customer orientation
    b. Service orientation
    c. Profit orientation
    d. A cost orientation

3. Learning as much as possible about customers and doing everything you can to satisfy them and exceed their expectations is:
    a. customer relationship management.
    b. marketing management.
    c. market segmentation.
    d. Promotion

4. Which of the following would be considered when discussing the marketing mix variables?
    a. determining production schedules
    b. financing the acquisition of new machinery
    c. minimizing the cost of producing the product
    d. setting a price for the product

5. When McDonald's considered adding pizza to their menu, the company made pizza available in some of their typical markets, to determine customer reactions. That process is called:
    a. promotion.
    b. test marketing.
    c. outsourcing.
    d. concept testing

6. Intermediaries are:
    a. consumers who are in the middle of the consumer decision making process.
    b. advertising agencies responsible for developing the advertising campaign for a new product.
    c. companies responsible for developing products to sell to businesses.
    d. organizations that are in the middle of a series of organizations that distribute goods from producers to consumers.

Learning Goal 3

7. Marketing research helps determine all but which of the following?
    a. how distribution needs will change
    b   what customers have purchased in the past
    c. what changes have occurred to change what customers want
    d. what customers are likely to want in the future

8. What is the first step in the marketing research process?
    a. analyze data
    b. collect data
    c. define the problem
    d. develop potential solutions

9. When Sun-2-Shade needed some information about the potential market for their product, the marketing team looked to the Internet to find industry trends, and to look at the market for eyewear products, which uses the same technology that is used in their self-darkening windshield. The type of information the marketing team was using is:
    a. secondary data.
    b. surveys.
    c. primary data.
    d. focus groups.

Learning Goal 4

10. Louis Chang is in a marketing position for Pro Performance, Inc, a consulting firm. One of Pro Performance's customers is hoping to find new markets for their existing products, as well as opportunities for products they are considering developing with some of their existing technologies. To help with this process Pro Performance should consider conducting:
    a. some marketing mix evaluations.
    b. a competitor evaluation.
    c. an environmental scan
    d. an evaluation of the strengths of the customer's finances.

11. The increase in the number of older Americans has created a growing demand for nursing homes, health care, continuing education and more. This is as a result of the changes in the _____ factors in the environment.
    a. sociocultural
    b. economic
    c. technological
    d. competitive

12. Which of the following products would be considered as the "business to business" market?
    a. classes at a university for a college freshman
    b. pens and pencils for that student
    c. books for the class
    d. a computer for the instructor to use while teaching the class

Learning Goal 5

13. Johnson and Johnson targets children with Sesame Street bandages, and GM targets women for their Chevy Cobalt vehicle. These are examples of:
    a. benefit segmentation.
    b. volume segmentation.
    c. psychographic segmentation.
    d. demographic segmentation.

14. We FlyU Anywhere is a travel agency that specializes in creating exotic trips to unusual destinations for their clients. They will create a "designer" vacation just for you. The most accurate description for the kind of marketing this travel agency is using would be:
    a. Niche marketing.
    b. One-to-one marketing.
    c. Customer Relationship marketing.
    d. Stakeholder marketing.

15. The company that makes the Nautica brand licensed with the Stride-Rite company to make an athletic shoe to compete with Nike. The company wants the shoe to be used for athletics, not worn just for style. Nautica is making use of:
    a. market analysis.
    b. market segmentation.
    c. niche marketing.
    d. one-to-one marketing.

16. At one time, companies developed products and promotions to please large groups of people, and tried to sell as many products to as many people as possible. This is known as:
    a. relationship marketing.
    b. a consumer orientation.
    c. forming a community of buyers.
    d. mass marketing.

17. Kelly Butler is looking for a new car. Kelly is an aspiring lawyer, and she is looking for a car that will help her to project that "lawyer "image. Kelly is influenced by:
    a. a cultural influence.
    b. a reference group.
    c. cognitive dissonance.
    d. the consumer market.

18. After Kelly bought her car, she realized just how much money she had spent! She spent some time wondering if she had made the right decision. Kelly seems to be suffering from:
    a. cognitive dissonance.
    b. consumer behavior.
    c. self-doubt.
    d. psychological influences.

Learning Goal 6

19. Which of the following is most descriptive of the business-to-business market?
    a. the business to business market has a larger number of customers than the consumer market
    b. business to business promotions tend to focus on advertising that can reach a large number of companies
    c. business to business buyers are generally more rational that consumer buyers
    d. business markets tend to be geographically scattered

20. Marketing strategies for the business-to-business market:
    a. differ from consumer marketing strategies because the nature of the buyers is different
    b. are basically similar to the consumer market, because business buyers are consumers
    c. are not concerned with relationship marketing techniques
    d. are concerned with the same types of influences as those in the consumer market.

TRUE-FALSE

Learning Goal 1

1. _____ The idea of customer relationship management is to enhance customer satisfaction and stimulate long-term customer loyalty.

2. _____ Non profits for the most part do not need to make use of marketing techniques.

Learning Goal 2

3. _____ Coupons rebates and cents-off deals are part of the promotion variable of the marketing mix.

4. _____ Test marketing refers to the development of an accurate description of your product and then testing it by asking people whether the idea appeals to them.

5. _____ Setting an appropriate price includes considering the cost involved in producing, promoting, and distributing the product.

Learning Goal 3

6. _____ To keep costs lower, it is best to use secondary data first, when possible, in the market research process.

7. _____ Socio-cultural factors such as population growth and changing demographics may affect some marketers, but are not important for most organizations.

8. _____ If the economy begins to fall on hard times, about the only thing marketers can do is to cut production and wait for better times.

Learning Goal 4

9. _____ Environmental scanning primarily involves considering the effects of weather patterns on a consumer's buying behavior.

10. _____ Because the consumer's buying behavior is different when shopping "brick and mortar" stores, there really is no competition between brick and mortar and Internet retailers.

Learning Goal 5

11. _____ The process of dividing the total market into several groups is called target marketing.

12. _____ An example of psychographic segmentation is dividing the market by whether or not your customers live in cities or in suburban areas.

13. _____ The Big and Tall Men's stores, which cater to men who are of certain heights and weights, is an example of a company using niche marketing.

14. _____ Relationship marketing leads away from mass production toward more custom-made goods and services.

Learning Goal 6

15. _____ The reason for distinguishing between consumer markets and the business to business market is because the strategies for reaching the markets are different, because the buyers are different, and the number of B2B buyers is relatively small.

16. _____ The business-to-business market is smaller than the consumer market in terms of the number of buyers, but large, in terms of the size of the buyers.

17. _____ Business to business sales tend to be less direct than consumer sales, because business buyers use more middlemen.

You Can Find It on the Net

Rollerblade's Web site contains a lot of information about a variety of areas. Visit this site at www.rollerblade.com

Does Rollerblade's Web site help the company strengthen the relationship it has with its customers?

How does the site attempt to create new relationships with new customers?

How do the elements of Rollerblade's Web site reflect their target market? Be specific.

Does Rollerblade invite comments from visitors to its Web site? If so, how does this affect its attempt to build positive relationships with its customers?

ANSWERS

LEARNING THE LANGUAGE

1. Brand name	10. Focus group	19. Market segmentation
2. Promotion	11. Niche marketing	20. Primary data
3. Geographic segmentation	12. Marketing mix	21. Relationship marketing
4. Business-to-business market	13. Target marketing	22. Environmental scanning
5. Test marketing	14. Marketing research	23. Psychographic segmentation
6. Secondary data	15. Benefit segmentation	24. Volume segmentation
7. Product	16. Consumer market	25. One-to-one marketing
8. Demographic segmentation	17. Marketing	26. Mass marketing
9. Marketing concept	18. Customer relationship Management (CRM)	

ASSESSMENT CHECK

Learning Goal 1

What is Marketing?

1. Whereas in the past marketing was focused on helping the seller sell, today, much of marketing is instead about *helping the buyer to buy*.

   This is often accomplished by buyers using the Internet to do searches for the information about the products they want to buy.

   Wise marketers are cultivating customer relationships using blogs and social networking sites such as MySpace and Facebook.

2. The four eras defined in the evolution of marketing are:
   a. production era
   b. selling era
   c. marketing concept era
   d. customer relationship era

3. The general philosophy of business during the production era was "Produce as much as you can because there is a limitless market". This was due to the combined factors of limited production capability and vast demand for products. The goals of business centered on production because most goods were bought as soon as they became available so there was a need for greater and greater production.

4. The selling era came about because businesses developed mass-production techniques, and production capacity often exceeded market demand so the philosophy turned from producing to selling. This is directly opposite from the production era. The business philosophy turned from an emphasis on production to an emphasis on selling, and most companies emphasized both selling and advertising.

5. The three parts of the marketing concept were:
    a. A customer orientation, which is to find out what customers want and provide it for them.
    b. A service orientation, making sure everyone in the organization has the same objective of customer satisfaction.
    c. A profit orientation, which is focusing on the goods and services that will earn the firm a profit and enable it to survive and expand.

6. The idea of customer relationship management is to enhance customer satisfaction and stimulate long-term customer loyalty.

7. The degree of consumer dissatisfaction that exists, especially with services, shows that marketers have a long way to go to create customer satisfaction and loyalty.

8. Marketing is used in many ways by non-profit organizations. Charities use marketing to raise funds or to obtain other resources. For example, the Red Cross uses promotion to encourage people to donate blood. Schools use marketing to attract new students and churches use marketing to attract new members and raise funds. Politicians use marketing to get votes and states use marketing to attract businesses and tourists. Many organizations use marketing to promote environmental causes.

Learning Goal 2

The Marketing Mix

9. Managing the controllable parts of the marketing process involves:
    a. designing a want satisfying <u>product.</u>
    b. setting a <u>price</u> for the product.
    c. placing the product in a <u>place</u> where people will buy it.
    d. <u>promoting</u> the product.

10. The steps in the marketing process are:
    a. Find opportunities
    b. Conduct research
    c. Identify a target market
    d. Design a product to meet the need, based upon research results
    e. Do product testing
    f. Determine a brand name, design a package and set a price
    g. Select a distribution system
    h. Design a promotional program
    i. Build a relationship with your customers

11. In concept testing, an accurate description of a product is developed, and then people are asked whether the concept appeals to them.

12. Setting a price depends on a number of factors. In a competitive market, it is wise to set a price close to your competitors. The costs involved in producing, distributing, and promoting the product must also be considered. If you want to create an image of quality, you might price the product higher.

13. Marketing intermediaries are organizations are in the middle of a series of organizations that distribute goods from producers to consumers. Another name for them is middlemen.

14. Six promotion techniques are:
    a. advertising
    b. personal selling
    c. public relations
    d. publicity
    e. word of mouth
    f. sales promotion

15. Relationship building with customers includes responding to suggestions from consumers and post purchase service.

Learning Goal 3

Providing Marketers with Information

16. Marketing research helps to determine:
    a. what customers have purchased in the past
    b. what situational changes have occurred to change what customers want
    c. what customers are likely to want in the future

17. The four steps of the marketing research process are:
    a. Define the question and determine the present situation
    b. Collect data
    c. Analyze the research data
    d. Choose the best solutions

18. Primary data are statistics and information not previously published that you gather on your own through observation, surveys, and personal interviews or focus groups. Secondary data are previously published reports and research from journals, trade associations, the government, information services and others.

19. General sources of secondary data are:
    a. Government Publications
    b. Commercial Publications
    c. Magazines
    d. Newspapers
    e. Internal sources
    f. General sources

20. Secondary data should be gathered first, because it is less expensive to obtain than primary data.

21. Companies will use primary data when additional, in-depth information is needed because secondary data may not provide all the information managers need to make decisions.

22. Sources of primary data are:
    a. Interviews
    b. Surveys
    c. Observation
    d. Personal interviews
    e. Focus groups
    f. Online surveys
    g. Customer Comments
    h. Letters from customers

23. The data collected in the research process must be turned into useful information. Good interpretation of the data collected can help a company find useful alternatives to specific marketing challenges. After analyzing the data, market researchers determine alternative strategies and make recommendations as to which strategy may be best and why.

24. If the results of the actions taken based on market research are not as expected, the company can take corrective action and conduct new studies in the ongoing attempt to provide consumer satisfaction at the lowest cost. So, marketing is a continuous process

Learning Goal 4

The Marketing Environment

25. The factors included in an environmental scan include:
    a. global   c. sociocultural   e. economic
    b. technological   d. competitive

26. Using the Internet, businesses can more easily reach and have a dialogue with the world's customers.

27. The most important technological changes in marketing also involve the Internet and include consumer databases, blogs, and social networking. Using these sources, companies can develop products and services that more closely match the needs of consumers.

28. Marketers must monitor sociocultural trends such as population growth, and changing demographics such as the growing population of older people and the shifting ethnic nature of the American population.

29. Brick and mortar companies must be aware of new competition from the Internet. Consumers can now search literally all over the world for the best prices through the Internet so brick and mortar stores must adjust their pricing, delivery, and services accordingly.

30. When an economy is growing, there is a demand for expensive products. When the economy slows, marketers have to adapt by offering products that are less expensive or more tailored to consumers with modest incomes.

31. The buyer's reason for buying and the end use of the product determine whether a product is considered a consumer product or an industrial product. The consumer market consists of individuals or households that want goods and services for personal consumption. The business-to-business market consists of individuals and organizations that want goods and services to use in producing other goods and services or for other business purposes.

Learning Goal 5

The Consumer Market

32. Consumer groups differ in age, education level, income and taste, and a business can't usually fill the needs of every group. So the company must decide what groups to serve, and develop products and services specially tailored to meet their needs. Dividing the total market into groups with similar characteristics is called market segmentation.

33. a. benefit
    b. geographic
    c. demographic
    d. psychographic
    e. volume

34. Niche marketing is the process of finding small but profitable market segments and designing or finding products for them. One-to-one marketing means developing a unique mix of goods and services for each individual customer.

35. The "long tail" theory explains how companies selling more products with lower demand can easily compete with, or even surpass, those solely dependent upon big sellers.

36. The mass marketer tries to sell the same products to as many people as possible, using mass media, such TV, radio, and newspapers.

37. The goal of relationship marketing is to keep individual customers over time by offering them new products that exactly meet their requirements.

38. Technology enables sellers to work with individual buyers to determine their wants and needs and to develop goods and services specifically designed for them.

39. The steps in the consumer decision-making process are:
    a. Problem recognition
    b. Information search
    c. Alternative evaluation
    d. Purchase decision
    e. Postpurchase decision (cognitive dissonance)

40. a. Marketing mix influences - product, price, promotion, place
    b. Sociocultural influences - Reference groups, family, social class, culture, subculture
    c. Situational influences - Type of purchase, social surroundings, physical surroundings, previous experience
    d. Psychological influences - Perception, attitudes, learning, motivation

41. a. Learning involves changes in an individual's behavior resulting from previous experiences and information
    b. A reference group is the group that an individual uses as a reference point in the formation of his or her beliefs, attitudes, values or behavior.
    c. Culture is the set of values, attitudes, and ways of doing things that are passed down from one generation to another in a society.
    d. Subculture is the set of values, attitudes and ways of doing things that result from belonging to a certain ethnic group, religious group, racial group or other group with which one identifies.
    e. Cognitive dissonance is a type of psychological conflict that can occur after a purchase, particularly a major purchase.

The Business-To-Business Market (B2B)

42. The business to business (B2B) market includes
     a. manufacturers
     b. intermediaries such as retailers
     c. institutions like hospitals and schools
     d. the government.

43. The strategies of business-to-business marketing differ from consumer marketing strategies because business buyers have their own decision making process.

44. The factors that make business-to-business different from consumer marketing are:
     a. The number of customers in the B2B market is relatively few
     b. The size of business customers is relatively large
     c. B2B markets tend to be geographically concentrated
     d. Business buyers generally are more rational than ultimate consumers are
     e. B2B sales tend to be direct
     f. B2B sales are based on *selling*, where as consumer promotions are based more on advertising.

CRITICAL THINKING EXERCISES

Learning Goal 1

1. a. From the story, it doesn't sound as if Al found an opportunity to fill a need for a sugar free ice cream and then found a way to develop it, which would be the first part of the marketing concept. There also doesn't appear to be a concern for customer satisfaction, other than to make sure the consumers liked the product. It sounds more like he had extra potatoes and needed to find a novel way to sell them! This exemplifies the production era when the main marketing concern was distribution and storages. The difference today in the business environment is the level of demand and the competition.

    b. Alan recognized the need for a sugar free ice cream. At least he thought he did. We don't know how much research he did on the actual demand for a sugar free ice cream. He did test the concept by making small batches and testing it with his friends. He made the product in small batches at first. Todd did some research in his business class. You could say the concept testing was combined with the test marketing stage or that St. Louis served as a test market. The brand name stemmed from the originator's name, Alan Reed (Al and Reed's). The marketing middlemen are Todd, and then the grocery stores, which finally agreed to sell the product through Todd's efforts. Promotion was done primarily through pamphlets and personal selling by Todd. There is no mention made of any effort to build a relationship with the customer.

    c. Probably the biggest potential problem is the negative reaction to the product. It could be that consumers will not be attracted to ice cream made from potatoes, and would wonder about the taste. (The students actually liked the taste of the ice cream until they found out it was made from potatoes!) By talking with consumers, grocery store managers (who are consumers, too, and must be convinced) Todd and Alan may have found ways to overcome the perception that ice cream made from potatoes must taste terrible.

d. <u>Product</u>—sugar free ice cream made from potatoes

   <u>Promotion</u>—personal selling, such as Todd taking the ice cream to the grocery store. They also offered discounts to the grocers, which could be seen as a form of promotion.

   <u>Place</u>—Todd's efforts were to place the product in the grocery store

   <u>Price</u>—how much would you pay for this product? Would it be considered a premium product? Often sugar free versions of products are a little higher in price than the regular product. Would you pay $5 per gallon?

Learning Goals 2, 3, 4

2. a. This may be a situation where Eric is creating a need! Since the windshield would keep cars cooler on hot, sunny days, this kind of product could be popular in areas that are sunny for a good part of the year, like the Southwest, for example. However, it has potential for any area of the country.

    b. There is a potential for two types of customers, the automotive manufacturers, for installation as an option in new cars, and the after-market dealers, like auto supply stores, for people who want the product to be installed later. There will still be a need for a retailer of some kind, to install the windshield. So another potential customer would be companies that repair damaged windshields.

    c. Asking people if they need a product such as this would have given Eric a feel for what demand might have been. He would have to be sure to ask the right questions of the right people to get an accurate idea. He could have given prototypes to friends, or potential customers, for use, to "field test" or test market the product.

    d. The <u>Social</u> environment consists of trends and population shifts. A trend toward higher end, more luxury-type cars, contributes to a positive outlook for Sun-2-Shade's product. An aging population, with a stronger interest in health and comfort also makes for a positive outlook for the company.

       Since this type of equipment could possibly be offered only in certain kinds of cars, <u>economic</u> factors such as disposable income, and unemployment, would affect demand for the cars, and thus for Sun-2-Shade'sproduct. The company may have to overcome a perception that this product is a prestige product, which could affect demand. In a slowing economy Sun-2-Shade will need to focus on the advantages their product offers, and be sure to downplay the fact that a self-darkening windshield will be more expensive. This also could have an impact globally, as foreign economies are slow. When economies are growing, Sun-2-Shade can take advantage of a prestige image, if that is what they want to create.

       With a rapidly expanding <u>global </u>market, there may be possibilities outside the United States, as well as potential competition. Sun-2-Shade will have access to foreign manufacturers with manufacturing facilities here as well.

       Right now, it doesn't seem that Sun-2-Shade appears to have much direct <u>competition,</u> so the company may have an advantage. There are no "brick and mortar" store selling this product.

       <u>Technology</u> has affected Sun-2-Shade simply by virtue of the fact that the process for creating the windshield has only been in existence for a few years. Further, new high-tech production techniques will help Sun-2-Shade to produce more products with fewer people at a lower cost. Also, technology will enable Sun-2-Shade to reach global customers.

e. Can Sun-2-Shade adopt a one to one marketing strategy? Basically, the product must be made to suit many different models of car, with different windshield sizes and shapes. The product is "custom made" for "customized marketing." The possibility exists for allowing customers to choose the color of their windshield.

Learning Goal 3

3. a. Sun-2-Shade may want to determine what kind of demand there will be for their product in the next five years. They may want to find out if their primary market should be younger or older drivers, and relate that to the type of car being driven. They may also want to determine if there are other markets they could enter. For example, over-the-road truckers could make use of this product, but it may have to be of a different size and shape to fit onto a semi. Another potential market is the automotive manufacturers, who could make the windshield an option for certain of their models. Market research could determine the potential for this type of business market.

   b. Collecting secondary data for the automotive market may be easily done to determine potential demand for autos and their product in the automotive market. Trade journals and government publications would provide sales forecasts for the type of cars Sun-2-Shade is targeting. The truck market may require some primary research, such as focus groups or some kind of survey, possibly distributed through the mail, or directly to truckers in some way.

   c. Analysis of the data may indicate there is a big market for the product for the truck market. Alternatively, it may indicate that sales are predicted to go flat or decline for the kinds of cars Sun-2-Shade has targeted, or for the automotive industry in general. This would indicate that the company may want to target a different car segment, or another market altogether.

   d. Choosing the best solution would be to choose the market that will be the most profitable for Sun-2-Shade and still meet the needs of their stakeholders.

4. Sample Answers:
   a. Toyota Prius
      Target market — People with a need for a second, smaller car, environmentalists, commuters looking for a car with very high fuel economy
      Variables — Could be demographic, such as age, income, family life cycle
      Could also be benefit, since the Prius is fuel efficient

   b. Nike
      Target market — Teenagers, boys and girls, interested in sports
      Variables — Demographic — sex, age and Psychographic — interests, self image

   c. McDonalds
      Target market — Families with young children
      Variables — Demographic — family life cycle, age, income, and Psychographic — lifestyle

   d. Campbell's nacho cheese soup
      Target market — Consumers in the west and southwest
      Variables — Geography — region Demographic — nationality, or Culture

5. Problem recognition came when Chad realized his system couldn't be fixed. Chad searched for information through the newspaper ads, and also by going to the stores and talking to salespeople. He was evaluating the alternatives by comparing each component piece for value and sound. When he finally made his purchase, he felt "cognitive dissonance," uneasy as to how much he spent, until he saw an ad for the same brand at a more expensive price.

Along the way, several factors influenced Chad's decision. He spoke to friends, which could be considered a reference group. Family may have been an influence, as Chad's sister has the same brand. There was a cultural influence as well, just from the fact that Chad felt the importance of having a new c.d. system for his party, rather that using a less expensive alternative. The price variable of the marketing mix was an influence, as the system was on sale. You could consider the psychological influence of learning, as Chad's friends had learned that this was a good brand through experience, and passed that information along. You may have thought of other influences as well.

Learning Goals 5, 6

6. Keep in mind these are suggested answers, and you may come up with a totally different plan.

   a. We have mentioned two target markets for Sun-2-Shade- the original equipment automotive market, to be installed as cars are assembled, and a consumer market, through auto parts stores perhaps. A third market, which is complementary to the original automotive market, is car windshield installation and repair companies. You may have decided on another way to approach the market.

   b. If you chose the consumer market, variables could include: Income, because the owners who would be interested may own cars that are higher end. With research you may find out that age could be a consideration. Geography may be a consideration, in that this product may especially appeal to consumers where the weather stays hot and sunny much of the year. Benefits sought could also be a variable. This is where research can really come in handy.

   c. To market to the business-to-business market, Sun-2-Shade must focus on personal selling, in a very concentrated market. The automotive industry has few domestic producers, but there are several foreign manufacturers with production facilities here in the United States. You would have to focus on quality, be able to meet the volume required to sell to the business market, and meet delivery requirements that may include dealing with a just-in-time inventory control system. This would require a sophisticated production and delivery system on the part of Sun-2-Shade.

7. Sun-2-Shade's product could be classified as both a consumer product and a product for the business-to-business market. If Eric sells the windshield through after market auto equipment retailers, the product would be considered a consumer good, in general. In attempting to reach the automotive manufacturers, Eric is developing a business-to-business marketing relationship.

The characteristics of the business-to-business market listed in your book will affect Sun-2-Shade in a number of ways. First, the primary market is the automotive industry, so there will be relatively few customers compared to the consumer market. Those car manufacturers are very large corporations, among the largest in the world, each with significant buying power. The domestic car market, at least, is concentrated in one geographic area. If Eric were to try to appeal to buyers for foreign manufacturers, he would have to do some more traveling. These buyers will consider Eric's product based on the "total product offer," including how much more marketable Sun-2-Shade will make <u>their</u> product, in addition to factors such as quality and price. If the customer is the auto industry, Eric won't need to use wholesalers or retailers, marketing middlemen, he will sell directly to the car companies. For the consumer market, he will have to use at least a retail distribution center.

8. a. Business   c. Consumer
    b. Business   d. Consumer

PRACTICE TEST

MULTIPLE CHOICE

1.	b	11.	a
2.	d	12.	d
3.	a	13.	d
4.	d	14.	b
5.	b	15.	b
6.	d	16.	d
7.	a	17.	b
8.	c	18.	a
9.	a	19.	c
10.	c	20.	a

TRUE–FALSE

1.	T	10.	F
2.	F	11.	F
3.	T	12.	F
4.	F	13.	T
5.	T	14.	T
6.	T	15.	T
7.	F	16.	T
8.	F	17.	F
9.	F		

CHAPTER 14 – DEVELOPING AND PRICING GOODS AND SERVICES

LEARNING GOALS

After you have read and studied this chapter, you should be able to:

1. Describe a total product offer.
2. Identify the various kinds of consumer and industrial goods.
3. Summarize the functions of packaging.
4. Contrast brand, brand name, and trademark, and the value of brand equity.
5. Explain the steps in the new-product development process.
6. Describe the product life cycle.
7. Explain various pricing objectives and strategies.

LEARNING THE LANGUAGE

Listed below are important terms found in the chapter. Choose the correct term for the definition and write it in the space provided.

Brand	Everyday low pricing (EDLP)	Product screening
Brand association	Generic goods	Psychological pricing
Brand awareness	High-low pricing strategy	Shopping goods and services
Brand equity	Industrial goods	Skimming price strategy
Brand loyalty	Knockoff brands	Specialty goods and services
Brand manager	Manufacturers' brand names	Target costing
Break-even analysis	Penetration strategy	Total fixed costs
Bundling	Price leadership	Total product offer
Commercialization	Product analysis	Trademark
Competition-based pricing	Product differentiation	Unsought goods and services
Concept testing	Product life cycle	Value
Convenience goods and services	Product line	Variable costs
Dealer (private) brands	Product mix	

1. The process used to determine profitability at various levels of sales is called _____.

2. The method of pricing known as a _____ is when a product is priced low to attract many customers and discourage competitors.

3. The strategy of _____ involves setting prices that are higher than EDLP stores, but having many special sales where the prices are lower than competitors.

4. A _____ consists of everything that consumers evaluate when deciding whether to buy something; also called a value package.

5. The degree to which customers are satisfied, like the brand, and are committed to further purchases is called _____.

6. A theoretical model called the _____ shows what happens to sales and profits for a product class over time; stages are introduction, growth, maturity and decline.

7. A strategy known as _____ is one in which a new product is priced high to make optimum profit while there is little competition.

8. A brand that has been given exclusive legal protection for both the brand name and the pictorial design is called a _____.

9. The linking of a brand to other favorable images is called _____.

10. Products identified as _____ are used in the production of other products and are sometimes called business goods or B2B goods.

11. Conducting a _____ involves making cost estimates and sales forecasts to get a feeling for the profitability of new product ideas.

12. A _____ is a name, symbol, or design (or combination thereof) that identifies the goods or services of one seller or group of sellers and distinguishes them from those of competitors.

13. The process of _____ calls for taking a product idea to consumers to test their reactions.

14. Products called _____ are products that the consumer wants to purchase frequently with a minimum of effort.

15. Grouping two or more products together and pricing them as a unit is known as _____.

16. Products called _____ don't carry the manufacturer's name, but carry a distributor or retailer's name instead.

17. Products with unique characteristics and brand equity are perceived as having no reasonable substitute. The consumer puts forth a special effort to purchase these products, called _____.

18. How quickly or easily a given brand name comes to mind when a product category is mentioned is _____.

19. A group of products known as the _____ are physically similar or are intended for a similar market.

20. Nonbranded products called _____ usually sell at a sizable discount compared to national or private-label brands.

21. Designing a product so that it satisfies customers and meets the profit margins desired by the firm is called _____.

22. Products known as _____ are products that consumers are unaware of, haven't necessarily thought of buying, or find that they need to solve an unexpected problem.

23. Consumers buy _____ only after comparing value, quality, price, and style and from a variety of sellers.

24. A combination of factors called _____ includes awareness, loyalty, perceived quality, images and emotions people associate with a brand name.

25. The brand names of manufacturers that distribute a product nationally are called _____.

26. Costs known as _____ change according to the level of production.

27. Consumers want a good quality product at a fair price, so they calculate the _____ of a product by looking at the benefits, and subtracting the costs to see if benefits exceed the costs.

28. Illegal copies of national brand-names goods are known as _____.

29. A _____ has direct responsibility for one brand or one product line; called a product manager in some firms.

30. The process of _____ is designed to reduce the number of new-product ideas being worked on at any one time.

31. Known as _____ these are all the expenses that remain the same no matter how many products are sold.

32. Promoting a product to distributors and retailers to get wide distribution and developing strong advertising and sales campaigns to generate and maintain interest in the product among distributors and consumers is called _____.

33. The creation of real or perceived product differences is called _____.

34. The practice of _____ is setting prices lower than competitors and then not having any special sales.

35. The term _____ is used to describe the combination of product lines offered by a manufacturer.

36. The procedure of _____ is one by which one or more dominant firms set the pricing practices that all competitors in an industry follow.

37. A pricing strategy called _____ is based on what all the other competitors are doing. Price can be set at, above, or below competitor's prices.

38. Pricing goods and services at price points that make the product appear less expensive is known as _____.

ASSESSMENT CHECK

Learning Goal 1

Product Development and the Total Product Offer

1. To satisfy consumers today marketers and managers must _____

    _____.

    Organizations must constantly monitor _____

    _____.

2. What are the factors that make up the total product offer?

    a. _____   g. _____

    b. _____   h. _____

    c. _____   i. _____

    d. _____   j. _____

    e. _____   k. _____

    f. _____   l. _____

3. Why does a company develop a variety of total product offers?

4. What is the difference between a product line and a product mix?

Learning Goal 2

Product Differentiation

5. How does a marketer create a perception of product differentiation?

6. List the four different classes of consumer goods and services. Give an example of each kind.

    a. _____

    b. _____

    c. _____

    d. _____

7. What are three things important to marketers of convenience goods?

    a. _____   c. _____

    b. _____

8. Describe the characteristics of shopping goods.

9. Why will consumers put forth a special effort to purchase a specific brand name when purchasing specialty products? How are these goods marketed?

10. What are the best ways to promote:

     Convenience goods:

     Shopping goods:

     Specialty goods:

     Unsought goods:

11. What determines into which class a product falls? Can one consumer good be classified in several ways?

12. What distinguishes a consumer good from an industrial (or B2B) good?

Can a good be classified as both?

How would the marketing be different?

13. In discussing industrial goods, describe:

Installations: _____

Capital items: _____

Accessory equipment: _____

Learning Goal 3

Packaging Changes the Product

14. Identify the functions of packaging.

a. _____

b. _____

c. _____

d. _____

e. _____

f. _____

g. _____

15. What are three ways in which packaging can change a product?

a. _____

b. _____

c. _____

16. Describe RFID in packaging.

17. Why is packaging carrying more of the promotional burden today than in the past?

18. In bundling, or combining goods and services into one package, what is the consideration marketers must be aware of, with regard to price?

Learning Goal 4

Branding and Brand Equity

19. What is the difference between a brand, brand name and a trademark?

20. How does a brand name benefit buyers and sellers?

For the buyer a brand name:

a. _____

b. _____

c. _____

For the seller brand names:

a. _____

b. _____

c. _____

d. _____

21. How does a manufacturer's brand name become a generic brand?

22. Describe three important components of brand equity.

a. _____

b. _____

c. _____

23. What is the key to creating perceived quality?

24. What are brand preference and brand insistence?

25. How can a company create brand associations?

26. What are the responsibilities of a brand manager?

Learning Goal 5

The New Product Development Process

27. What are the odds that a product will be successful?

28. What are four reasons for product failure?

a. _____   c. _____

b. _____   d. _____

29. Identify the steps in the new product development process.

a. _____   d. _____

b. _____   e. _____

c. _____   f. _____

394

30. What are important sources of new product ideas?

    a. _____   c. _____

    b. _____

31. List the criteria used for product screening.

    a. _____

    b. _____

    c. _____

32. In the product analysis step of the new product development process, what happens to products that don't meet established criteria?

33. What questions are answered by concept testing?

    a. _____

    b. _____

    c. _____

    d. _____

    e. _____

34. What are two important elements of the marketing effort during commercialization?

    a. _____

    b. _____

Learning Goal 6

The Product Life Cycle

35. What are the four stages of the product life cycle?

    a. _____   c. _____

    b. _____   d. _____

36. Do all products follow the traditional stages of the product life cycle in the same pattern?

37. Different stages in the product life cycle call for _____

38. Identify the marketing strategies for the Marketing Mix variables in each stage of the Product Life Cycle by completing the following chart:

	Product	Price	Place	Promotion
Introduction				
Growth				
Maturity				
Decline				

39. What happens to sales, profits, and competitors during each of the stages in the Product Life Cycle?

	Sales	Profits	Competitors
Introduction			
Growth			
Maturity			
Decline			

Learning Goal 7

Competitive Pricing

40. What are five pricing objectives?

a. _____   d. _____

b. _____   e. _____

c. _____

41. Describe a "loss leader" in pricing.

42. Pricing objectives should be influenced by:

43. Discuss the important considerations in cost-based pricing.

44. What are the important elements of target costing?

45. What is the major price consideration when evaluating competition based pricing?

46. Define the break-even point. What is the formula for determining a break-even point?

47. What are some of the expenses included in:

    fixed costs:

    variable costs:

48. What are six pricing strategies other than competition based, cost based, and demand based?

    a. _____   d. _____

    b. _____   e. _____

    c. _____   f. _____

49. What pricing strategy is being used when the company:

    a. _____ Sets prices high to make optimum profit when there is little competition?

    b. _____ Sets prices higher than those at stores, using EDLP, but has special sales?

    c. _____ Prices products at points that make them appear less expensive?

    d. _____ Prices products low to attract customers and discourage competition?

    e. _____ Groups products together and prices them as a unit?

    f. _____ Sets prices lower than competitors and usually doesn't have sales.

50. What is the main idea behind EDLP?

51. What is the problem with a high-low pricing strategy?

52. Describe demand oriented pricing.

53. How is the Internet affecting pricing?

54. In using non-price competition, what aspects of their products will firms tend to stress?

CRITICAL THINKING EXERCISES

Learning Goal 1

1. When people buy a product, they evaluate and compare on several dimensions:

   For each product below, identify some of the dimensions that may influence the buyer.

   a. Bicycle _____

   _____

   b. Toothpaste _____

   _____

   c. A new suit _____

   _____

Learning Goal 2

2. The two major product classifications are consumer goods and services and industrial goods and services.

    a. Classify the following products:

        1. Milk _____

        2. Steel _____

        3. Tickets to the Olympics _____

        4. Dry cleaners _____

        5. Diesel engines _____

        6. Flashlight batteries _____

        7. Auto repair _____

        8. Heart surgeon _____

        9. Management consultant _____

        10. Winter coat _____

    b. Consumer goods and services are further classified as either: convenience, shopping, specialty or unsought. Indicate the correct class for each of the **consumer** items you identified above.

        1. _____   5. _____

        2. _____   6. _____

        3. _____   7. _____

        4. _____

3. Marketing strategies will change depending upon the category of the product. Identify the most appropriate way to market:

    a. a new car model—

    b. a marketing consulting firm—

    c. banking services—

    d. a funeral home—

Learning Goal 3

4. Packaging is carrying the promotional burden for products more than ever, and performs a number of functions: attract attention, describe contents, explain benefits, provide information, indicate price, value, and uses, and protect goods. Evaluate the importance of packaging, which function(s) may be the most important and how well the packaging performs those functions for the following:

   a. Lunch meat (like bologna) _____

   _____

   b. Children's cereal (like Froot Loops) _____

   _____

   c. Potato chips (like Pringles) _____

   _____

Learning Goals 1, 2, 3

5. You are in conference with the marketing manager of Sun-2-Shade, and are still in the process of developing a marketing plan. Sun-2-Shade is a company that manufactures automobile windshields that self-darken in the same manner as some eyewear, automatically darkening in the sun, and going back to light in the shade, on a cloudy day or in the evening.

   In evaluating the windshield to be produced by Sun-2-Shade, you want to know what features customers might consider when purchasing Sun-2-Shade from an auto parts store or an after-market windshield installation and repair company. Are the same things going to be important if the main customers are the auto manufacturers? What additional or different features might manufacturers consider?

   Just before your meeting, you jotted down these questions you feel need to be answered in order to create an effective marketing plan:

   a) What is the total product offer?

   b) How can we differentiate the product?

   c) How would Sun-2-Shade be classified?

   d) Will packaging be an important consideration for Sun-2-Shade?

6. a. Are you a brand loyal consumer? What products can you name for which you will only purchase a certain brand? What level of brand loyalty would you consider your type of purchase pattern? What factors have influenced your decision to only buy that brand?

   b. What is the first brand name that comes to mind when you think of?

      1. digital camera _____

      2. milk _____

      3. MP3 player _____

      4. a sports car _____

      5. soft drink _____

   Why do you think it was more likely that you could think of a national brand for some of these products, but not for others?

   c. Why is it a problem for a manufacturer when their brand name becomes generic?

7. You have just been named as a product manager for Nestle-Purina. Your manager has told you that your primary objective is to develop new products and bring them to market. This is your first day on the job! How will you accomplish the objectives your boss has given you?

8. The product life cycle is a model of what happens to classes of products over time. It consists of four stages. Draw and label the illustration outlined below.

9. There are different marketing strategies used in each stage of the product life cycle. Using your text, give a specific example of a marketing strategy from one of the four P's that could be used for the following products.

MARKETING STRATEGY

a. Introduction   Global Positioning Systems

       _____

       _____

       _____

b. Growth   Digital cameras

       _____

       _____

       _____

c. Maturity   Fast food

       _____

       _____

       _____

d. Decline   DVD players

       _____

       _____

       _____

Learning Goal 7

10. Among the objectives that firms use in setting prices are:

Achieve a target profit	Increase sales
Build traffic	Create an image
Achieve greater market share	Social objectives

Match the correct pricing objective to each of the following statements.

a. _____ Kroger's advertises large eggs at 10 cents a dozen.

b. _____ Nestle Purina changes a price that gives them a 25% profit on dog food, higher than they need. Consumers are willing to pay the high price for this particular dog food.

c. _____ Farmers in Arkansas receive subsidies on their grain products, so they can keep their prices artificially low. This keeps prices on derivative products low enough for a larger market to purchase.

d. _____ Retailers, facing several dismal Christmas seasons in a row, slashed prices on a wide variety of merchandise several years in a row.

e. _____ Movado watches sell from $500 and up in the retail stores that carry the brand.

f. _____ If you go to Midas Muffler with a bid from a competitor, Midas will meet that price in order to keep your business.

11. a. How many units will Sun-2-Shade have to sell to break even if their fixed costs are $1,200,000, the price (revenue from each unit) is $500 and the variable cost per unit is $100 per unit?

b. How much profit will Sun-2-Shade make if they sell 5,000 units?

c. What would the break-even point (the number of units which need to be sold in order to break even) be if Sun-2-Shade raised their price to $600? _____

d. The marketing department has said that at a price of $600, Sun-2-Shade would be able to sell about 2000 units. Should they raise their price? Why or why not?

12. After determining which pricing objectives fit with the firm's objectives, a business can use any of several different strategies.

Skimming   Bundling
Penetration   Psychological pricing
High-low pricing   Demand oriented pricing
Everyday low pricing (EDLP)

Match the correct pricing strategy to each of the following:

a. _____ Home theater systems can run as high as $100,000 or more and there are only a few companies offering the systems.

b. _____ Hotel and motel prices in Breckenridge Colorado are higher from October to May, times which Breckenridge would describe as their peak season.

c. _____ Larry Dietzel, a real estate agent, advised his clients to price their home at $199,900 when they listed with his agency.

d. _____ Carl Godwin is just starting out in the home remodeling and construction business. When he makes a bid, it is generally significantly lower than the bids of any of his competition, as Carl wants the business.

e. _____ Chad Stahr is a home do-it-yourself guy. He most often shops at Lowes, because although they usually don't run sales, he knows the store will be the lowest price around on the tools he needs.

f. _____ When the Mays family took a trip to Europe, they went to Uniglobe travel, where the travel agent worked out a trip for them that included airfare, hotels and some of the special tours that they were interested in taking, all for one price.

g. _____ A major retailer in St. Louis charges "full retail" for most of the clothing lines, but has regular "special holiday" sales, during which they lower their prices considerably.

PRACTICE TEST

MULTIPLE CHOICE—Circle the best answer

Learning Goal 1

1. Which of the following would <u>not</u> be included in the total product that consumers consider when they purchase a product?
    a. Price
    b. Image created by advertising
    c. Brand name
    d. Buyer's income

2. Proctor and Gamble produces a wide variety of products including air fresheners, baby and child care, household cleaners, prescription drugs, and paper products. This would be Proctor & Gamble's:
    a. product mix.
    b. product depth.
    c. product width.
    d. product line.

Learning Goal 2

3. Companies that distribute bottled water, like Evian or Aquafina, have the challenge of making a product that looks the same from one company to another appear to have qualities unique to that brand. Companies create these perceived differences using
    a. consumer goods classification.
    b. the product life cycle.
    c. the product mix.
    d. product differentiation.

4. Small businesses often have an advantage in product differentiation because
    a. they have fewer products, so they can spend more time working on them.
    b. they are more flexible in adapting to customer wants and needs.
    c. larger businesses aren't interested in getting close to the consumer.
    d. larger businesses don't have to differentiate their products.

5. Which of the following would be considered a specialty good/service?
    a. toothpaste
    b. funeral services
    c. washing machine
    d. Rolex watch

6. The best way to promote products like clothes and shoes is to emphasize:
    a. location of stores.
    b. advertising in specialty magazines.
    c. price differences, quality differences or some combination of the two.
    d. a web site where customers can place orders.

7. When a manufacturer buys a laptop computer for employees use at work, the computer would be considered a:
   a. business good.
   b. specialty good.
   c. consumer good.
   d. shopping good.

8. The factory that Sun-2-Shade, a manufacturer of self-darkening windshields, is building on the outskirts of Denver is an example of a(n) _____ type of business good.
   a. installation
   b. accessory equipment
   c. production
   d. support

Learning Goal 3

9. Because products are often being sold in self-service outlets, rather than by salespersons:
   a. brand names have become less important.
   b. packaging has become more important, as a way to promote the product.
   c. the popularity of generic products has declined.
   d. packaging has become less important, because consumers want to see what they are buying.

10. A relatively new type of packaging technology is _____, which is a way of tracking products using a chip to send out signals telling the company where the product is at all times.
    a. bundling
    b. trademark tracking
    c. radio frequency identification chip (RFID)
    d. digital packaging

Learning Goal 4

11. The Jolly Green Giant would be an example of a:
    a. brand name.
    b. generic name.
    c. trademark.
    d. knockoff brand.

12. Rollerblade is working to make sure that when people refer to inline skating, they don't use the name Rollerblade to refer to the sport. Rollerblade is afraid that their brand name will become a:
    a. generic good.
    b. knockoff brand.
    c. private brand.
    d. trademark.

13. Each time you purchase toothpaste, you will only buy Close 'n Brite, a toothpaste guaranteed to give you fresh breath and whiter teeth. If the store is out of this brand you will make a point of going to a different store to buy that product. This is an example of _____
    a. brand equity.
    b. brand awareness.
    c. brand preference.
    d. brand insistence.

14. The process of taking a product idea to consumers to test their reactions is known as:
    a. test marketing.
    b. product screening.
    c. concept testing.
    d. business analysis.

15. Most new product ideas come from:
    a. research and development.
    b. employees.
    c. competitors.
    d. suppliers.

16. Soho Bottling makes natural soft drinks and started in a kitchen in Brooklyn New York. When the company entered the commercialization stage of the new product development process, they knew they would have to:
    a. decide what stage of the product life cycle the product was in.
    b. determine the appropriate bundling strategy.
    c. do the appropriate concept testing.
    d. promote the product to distributors and retailers to get wide distribution.

Learning Goal 6

17. The importance of the product life cycle is that:
    a. different stages in the product life cycle call for different marketing strategies.
    b. most brands follow the same pattern in the product life cycle.
    c. all products go through the product life cycle in the same length of time.
    d. in the growth stage, marketers will differentiate their product from competitors.

18. Sony and other makers of high definition television sets have made the prices of these products more competitive, have increased the number and kinds of stores in which they are available, have offered a variety of choices, and are advertising extensively. These products are in the _____ stage of the product life cycle.
    a. introduction
    b. growth
    c. maturity
    d. decline

Learning Goal 7

19. Schnucks grocery stores promotes milk, eggs and other daily essentials at low prices in order to attract consumers to the store. This would be an example of the pricing objective of:
    a. increasing sales
    b. increasing market share
    c. building traffic
    d. create an image

20. When Sony considers how to price a new product, they determine what price they think their customers will pay, and then identify what profit the company needs. From there they determine the features they can offer on this product. This method of determining price is known as:
    a. demand oriented pricing.
    b. cost based pricing.
    c. target costing.
    d. value pricing.

21. If fixed costs are $100,000, variable cost per unit is $40, and the selling price is $60, how many units must be sold for the firm to break even?
    a. 10,000
    b. 1,000
    c. 2500
    d. 5000

22. When Nintendo entered the video game market with the Wii, they priced the product lower than the Sony video game in order to capture a large share of the market quickly.
    This strategy is called a:
    a. penetration strategy.
    b. EDLP.
    c. high-low pricing strategy.
    d. skimming strategy.

23. Upscale retailers, such as Nordstrom's, feature customer service as their significant point of difference, and use that difference to compete with less expensive stores. This is known as:
    a. upscale competition.
    b. nonprice competition.
    c. market force competition.
    d. service competition.

TRUE–FALSE

Learning Goal 1

1. _____ In today's market, marketers must learn to listen to consumers and adapt to a constantly changing market.

2. _____ To create an attractive value package an organization must always begin with a low price.

3. _____ It is often easier for larger companies to establish a close relationship with customers because they have representatives in most parts of the country.

Learning Goal 2

4. _____ An example of a convenience good would be a candy bar.

5. _____ Products can be classified as either a consumer or business product, but not as both.

6. _____ Marketing strategies are generally very similar from one stage in the Product Life Cycle.

Learning Goal 3

7. _____ One major function of packaging is that it should attract the buyer's attention.

8. _____ Travelocity offers vacations that include the flight, hotel, and a rental car for a certain price. This practice is known as bundling.

9. _____ Brand loyalty means that your product comes to mind when a product category is mentioned.

10. _____ An example of a dealer, or private, brand would be Cherokee, sold exclusively in Target stores nationwide.

Learning Goal 5

11. _____ A brand manager, or product manager, has the responsibility for all the elements of the marketing mix for one brand or product line.

12. _____ Making cost estimates and sales forecasts is part of the product analysis stage of the new product development process.

Learning Goal 6

13. _____ Sales of a product peak late in the growth stage of the product life cycle.

14. _____ Most products go through the stages in the product life cycle in only a few months.

Learning Goal 7

15. _____ A firm will pursue only one pricing strategy at a time.

16. _____ Pricing objectives generally will have no effect on the other marketing mix variables.

17. _____ The break-even point is the point where sales revenue is equal to profits.

18. _____ When movie theaters charge lower rates for children, and companies give discounts to senior citizens, they are using demand oriented pricing.

19. _____ Most pricing depends upon what the competition is charging.

20. _____ Marketers won't generally compete on product attributes other than price.

You Can Find It On the Net

Tommy Hilfiger is a major manufacturer of clothing for, perhaps, people of all ages. What image do you have of the Tommy name? Who do you think wears their clothes? Now, visit their web site at www.tommyhilfiger.com

How does the web site reinforce the Tommy Hilfiger brand name and image? Give examples to support your answer.

How does Tommy appear to differentiate their product from a major competitor, such as Abercrombie and Fitch? (**www.abercrombie.com**)

Compare the Abercrombie web site to Tommy's. Are they targeting the same market? Why or why not?

Where do you think Tommy Hilfiger is on the Product Life Cycle? What suggestions can you give to extend their product life cycle?

ANSWERS

LEARNING THE LANGUAGE

1. Break-even analysis	14. Convenience goods and services	27. Value
2. Penetration strategy	15. Bundling	28. Knockoff brands
3. High-low price strategy	16. Dealer (private) brands	29. Brand manager
4. Total product offer	17. Specialty goods and services	30. Product screening
5. Brand loyalty	18. Brand awareness	31. Total fixed costs
6. Product life cycle	19. Product line	32. Commercialization
7. Skimming price strategy	20. Generic goods	33. Product differentiation
8. Trademark	21. Target costing	34. Everyday low pricing (EDLP)
9. Brand association	22. Unsought goods and services	35. Product mix
10. Industrial goods	23. Shopping goods and services	36. Price leadership
11. Product analysis	24. Brand equity	37. Competition based pricing
12. Brand	25. Manufacturer's brand names	38. Psychological pricing
13. Concept testing	26. Variable costs	

ASSESSMENT CHECK

Learning Goal 1

Product Development and the Total Product Offer

1. To satisfy consumers today marketers and managers must learn to listen and to adapt constantly to changing market demands.

   Organizations must constantly monitor changing consumer wants and needs, adapt products, policies, and services accordingly.

2. a. Price
   b. Store surroundings
   c. Guarantee
   d. Brand name
   e. Service
   f. Speed of delivery
   g. Convenience
   h. Internet access
   i. Image created by advertising
   j. Package
   k. Buyer's past experience
   l. Reputation of producer

3. A company develops a variety of product offers because different consumers want different total product offers.

4. Product lines are groups of products that are similar or are intended for a similar market. They usually face similar competition. A product mix is the combination of all product lines that a company has available for sale.

411

Learning Goal 2

Product Differentiation

5. Marketers use a creative mix of pricing, advertising and packaging to create a unique, attractive image to differentiate their products.

6. The four different classes of consumer goods and services are:
   a. Convenience — bread
   b. Shopping — appliances
   c. Specialty — expensive watches, such as a Rolex
   d. Unsought — emergency car towing

7. Three things important to marketers of convenience goods are:
   a. location
   b. brand awareness
   c. image

8. Comparisons of shopping goods are based on the quality, price, and style from a variety of sellers. Shopping goods are sold largely through shopping centers so that consumers can shop around and compare. Because consumers compare, marketers can emphasize price differences, quality differences, or some combination of the two.

9. Specialty goods and services have a perceived value for the customer, have no reasonable substitute, and as a result, consumers will put forth a special effort to purchase a specific brand name.

   Specialty goods are often marketed through specialty magazines and through the Internet.

10. The best ways to promote:

    Convenience goods is to make them readily available and to create the proper image.

    Shopping goods is to create an appeal based on a combination of price, quality and service.

    Specialty goods is to reach special market segments though advertising.

    Unsought goods is to rely on personal selling and some kinds of advertising.

11. Whether a good or service falls into a particular class depends on the individual consumer. For example, what is considered a shopping good for one consumer could be a specialty good for another. So any good can conceivably be classified into any of the categories.

12. Consumer goods are purchased for personal consumption, while industrial (or business) goods are products used in the production of other products.

    A product can be classified as both a consumer and/or an industrial good depending upon the end use of the product.

    The marketing varies by how the good is classified. If a computer, for example, is bought as a consumer good, it would be sold through a store and promoted through advertising. If it was bought by a business for business uses, the computer would likely be sold through personal selling or the Internet.

13. <u>Installations</u> are major capital equipment such as new factories and heavy machinery.

   <u>Capital items</u> are expensive products that last a long time.

   <u>Accessory equipment</u> consists of capital items that are not quite as long lasting or as expensive as installations.

Learning Goal 3

Packaging Changes the Product

14. The functions of packaging are:
   a. Attract the buyer's attention
   b. Protect the goods inside, stand up under handling and storage be tamperproof and deter theft
   c. Be easy to open and use
   d. Describe and give information about the contents of the product
   e. Explain the benefits of the product
   f. Provide information on warranties and any warnings
   g. Give an indication of price, value, and uses

15. Packaging changes the product by changing its
   a. visibility   c. attractiveness
   b. usefulness

16. RFID stands for radio frequency identification chips. These chips are attached to products and send out signals telling a company where products are at all times. The advantages RFID has include the fact that more information can be carried in the chips, items don't have to be read one at a time, and items can be read at a distance.

17. Packaging is carrying more of the promotional burden than in the past because many products that were once sold by sales persons are now being sold in self service outlets, and the package has been given more sales responsibility.

18. In bundling, or combining goods and services into one package, marketers must not include so much that the price gets too high.

Learning Goal 4

Branding and Brand Equity

19. A *brand* is a name, symbol, or design, or a combination of those, that identifies the goods or services of one seller and distinguishes them from competitors. A *brand name* is the part of the brand that is a word, letter or group of words or letters comprising a name, and a *trademark* is a brand that has been given exclusive legal protection for the brand name and the pictorial design.

20. For the buyer, a brand name:
   a. assures quality
   b. reduces search time
   c. and adds prestige to purchase.

   For a seller, brand names:
   a. facilitate new-product introductions
   b. help promotions efforts
   c. add to repeat purchases
   d. differentiate products so that prices can be set higher.

21. A brand name can become generic when a name becomes so popular, so identified with the product that it loses its brand status and become the name of the product category. Examples include aspirin, nylon, escalator, and zipper.

22. a. The core of brand equity is *brand loyalty*. A loyal group of customers represents substantial value to the firm.
    b. Another part of brand equity is *brand awareness*, which is built by advertising and event sponsorships
    c. A third element is *perceived quality* which is an important part of brand equity. A product that is perceived as having better quality than its competitors can be priced accordingly.

23. The key to creating a perception of quality is to identify what consumers look for in a high-quality product and then to use that information in every message the company sends out. Factors influencing the perception of quality include price, appearance and reputation.

24. Consumers develop brand preference when they prefer one brand over another. This happens when companies use effective promotion that focuses on quality, price, appearance and reputation. When consumers reach the point of brand insistence, the product becomes a specialty good, and consumers will go out of their way and pay a premium for that brand.

25. Brand associations can be created by linking your brand to other product users, to a popular celebrity, to a particular geographic area, or to competitors.

26. The responsibilities of a brand manager include all the elements of the marketing mix: product, price promotion and place.

Learning Goal 5
The New Product Development Process

27. The odds that a new product will fail are high. Over 80% of products introduced in any year fail to reach their business objectives.

28. Reasons that products fail include:
    a. products don't deliver what they promise
    b. poor positioning
    c. too few differences from competitors
    d. poor packaging

29. The steps in the new product development process are:
    a. Idea generation
    b. Screening
    c. Product analysis
    d. Development
    e. Testing
    f. Commercialization

30. Three important sources of new product ideas are:
    a. employees
    b. research and development
    c. suppliers

31. Criteria used for screening include:
   a. whether the product fits in well with present products,
   b. has good profit potential,
   c. is marketable.

32. Products that don't meet established criteria in the product analysis phase of the new product development process are withdrawn from consideration.

33. Questions answered by concept testing include:
   a. Do customers see the benefit of this product?
   b. How frequently would they buy it?
   c. At what price?
   d. What features do they like and dislike?
   e. What changes would they make?

34. Two important elements for the marketing effort during commercialization are:
   a. promoting the product to distributors and retailers to get wide distribution.
   b. developing strong advertising and sales campaigns to generate and maintain interest.

Learning Goal 6

The Product Life Cycle

35. The stages of the product life cycle include:
   a. Introduction   c. Maturity
   b. Growth   d. Decline

36. Not all individual products follow the life cycle, and even particular brands may act differently. Some may never get beyond the introduction stage, while others may stay in the introduction stage for years. Some products become classics and never enter decline.

37. Different stages in the product life cycle call for different marketing strategies.

38.

	Product	**Price**	**Place**	**Promotion**
Introduction	Offer market-test product; keep product mix small	Skimming or penetration price strategy	Selective distribution; wholesalers	Advertising and sales promotion to stimulate primary demand
Growth	Improve product	Adjust price to meet competition	Increase distribution	Competitive advertising
Maturity	Product differentiation	Further price reductions	Intensify distribution	Emphasize brand name and product benefits and differences
Decline	Cut product mix	Consider price increases	Drop some outlets	Reduce advertising

39.

Life Cycle Stage	Sales	Profits	Competitors
Introduction	Low sales	Losses	Few
Growth	Rapidly rising sales	Profits peak	Growing number
Maturity	Peak sales	Declining profits	Stable number, then declining
Decline	Falling sales	Profits fall to losses	Numbers decline further

Learning Goal 7

Competitive Pricing

40. Five pricing objectives include:
    a. Achieve a target return on investment or profit
    b. Build traffic
    c. Achieve a greater market share
    d. Create an image
    e. Further social objectives

41. A loss leader is a product which is priced at or below cost to attract people to a store.

42. Pricing objectives should be influenced by other marketing mix variable decisions, such as product design, packaging, branding, distribution and promotion.

43. Companies often develop cost accounting systems to measure production costs, add in profit, and come up with a price. The question is whether the price will be satisfactory to the market.

44. Target costing is demand based. This means that a product will be designed so that it satisfies customers and meets the firm's desired profit margins. To use target costing, the firm will estimate the selling price people would be willing to pay for a product and subtract the desired profit margin. The result is the target cost of production.

45. Competition based pricing is a strategy based on what the competition is charging. The price can be at, above or below the competition. It depends on customer loyalty, perceived differences in the product, and the competitive climate.

46. The break-even point is the point where revenues from sales equal all costs. The formula is:

$$\text{Break even point} = \frac{\text{Fixed costs}}{\text{Price per unit} - \text{variable cost per unit}}$$

47. <u>Fixed costs</u>: include rent and insurance which don't vary with the level of production.

    <u>Variable costs</u> include expenses for materials and the direct cost of labor used in making goods. These costs vary with the level of production.

48. Six pricing strategies other than competition-based, cost-based and demand based include:
    a. skimming strategy
    b. penetration strategy
    c. everyday low pricing (EDLP)
    d. high-low pricing
    e. bundling
    f. psychological pricing

49. a. skimming
    b. high-low
    c. psychological
    d. penetration
    e. bundling
    f. everyday low pricing

50. The main idea behind everyday low pricing is to have consumers come to the store whenever they want a bargain, rather than wait until there is a sale.

51. The problem with a high-low pricing strategy is that it teaches consumers to wait for sales, thus cutting into profits.

52. Demand oriented pricing is used when price is set on the basis of consumer demand rather than cost or some other calculation. An example is movie theaters with low rates for children or companies offering discounts for senior citizens.

53. Customers can now compare prices of many goods and services on the Internet, and can get lower prices on many items. Price competition is going to heat up with the Internet, as more customers have access to price information from around the world. As a result, nonprice competition will increase.

54. Firms using nonprice competition will stress product images and consumer benefits such as comfort, style, convenience, and durability.

CRITICAL THINKING EXERCISES

Learning Goal 1

1. a. In the purchase of a bicycle, a consumer may evaluate the product in terms of price, guarantee, reputation of the producer, brand name, past experience, and on the service the retailer may provide. Other considerations would be how the buyer will use the product (mountain biking vs. street), the brand image and durability

   b. In buying toothpaste, a purchaser may look at price, package, image created by advertising, brand name and the buyers' past experience. They will also consider the benefit for which they are buying – fluoride, whiter teeth and so on.

   c. For a new suit, the dimensions may be fit, style, price, store surroundings, image of the store, brand name, guarantee, and past experience with that brand.

Learning Goal 2

2. a.
1. Consumer	6. Consumer	
2. Industrial	7. Consumer	
3. Consumer	8. Consumer	
4. Consumer	9. Industrial	
5. Industrial	10. Consumer	

   b.
   1. Milk – Convenience
   2. Tickets to the Olympics – Specialty
   3. Dry Cleaners – Probably convenience service but could be shopping service
   4. Flashlight batteries – Convenience
   5. Auto repair – Unsought
   6. Heart Surgeon – Unsought
   7. Winter coat – Shopping

3. a. A car is a shopping good, so the best way to market this product would be to ensure customers that they are getting a good quality product at a good price. A car dealer may want to promote the services they offer customers, such as extended hours for getting a car serviced, or free oil changes for the life of the car.

   b. A marketing consulting firm sells a specialty service. This type of service would best be marketed through a business oriented magazine, or a newspaper such as the Wall Street Journal. A good website will also be important.

   c. Banking services are considered to be convenience service. A bank will need to be conveniently located, near potential customers. It is important for the bank to make services available on the Internet while still ensuring privacy and safety for its customers.

   d. A funeral home's services would be considered unsought goods. This type of product requires advertising, but locally, like in the newspaper and the Yellow Pages to bring people to the door. Once a family contacts the funeral home, effective personal selling is a must.

Learning Goal 3

4. a. For lunchmeat like bologna, the primary consideration would be protecting the product from spoiling, and enabling the buyer to see what they are getting. The price or uses won't be listed on the package, but the package may need to attract the buyer's attention, as it is a crowded market. The main problem with the package is that once it is opened, most lunchmeat packages don't easily close, so the product gets stale quickly.

   b. For a children's cereal, the most important variable would be attracting the children's attention! For the parent, nutrition information would be important to include on the package. Further, keeping the product fresh would be important. For the most part, most kids' cereals do a great job of attracting children's attention, and by law must provide nutrition information on each box. As with the lunchmeat, the problem with most of theses packages is that once they are opened, they are difficult to re-close, and the cereal can turn stale quickly.

   c. One of the considerations for potato chips is protection from damage, as chips break easily. In fact, that consideration was one of the factors Proctor & Gamble looked at when they introduced Pringles. The package needs to attract attention, as it is a crowded market. Most companies have not found a good way of keeping chips from breaking, and the same old problem arises: once they are opened, the package doesn't close very well, and the product can get stale quickly.

Learning Goals 1, 2, 3

5. a. The total product offer for Sun-2-Shade could include convenience, image, and comfort while driving. An additional benefit is that the car interior stays cooler in the summer while parking in a sunny area. Customers will also consider price, service (what happens if the windshield gets scratched?) and the image Sun-2-Shade could create through effective advertising. These are just suggestions – you may have thought of several more possible answers.

   b. Sun-2-Shade's product is unique. It is the only company to offer this type of product up to this point. It would likely be considered a luxury type product. You could differentiate the product by giving it an image of not only convenience, but of the "ultimate," the kind of auto accessory that everyone needs to have in today's image-conscious world. You could create the perception that this product isn't merely a luxury, but a <u>necessity</u>. Advertising could be aimed at the end consumer, with the idea of people asking for the product when they go to the dealership to buy the car.

   The main consideration for an auto manufacturer will be price, how much it will add to the sticker price of the car, guarantee, and speed of delivery and reputation of Sun-2-Shade. The ease of installation is also important.

c. Sun-2-Shade's product would be classified as a consumer good, when we are aiming our marketing strategy at the end consumer, and as a B2B good when we are marketing toward the auto manufacturers. It could be positioned as either a shopping good or a specialty good for the consumer market.

d. Packaging won't be an important variable for Sun-2-Shade other than for shipping to the retailers for installation for the after-market.

6. a. Your answer to the first part of this question will be unique to you. Many consumers are brand loyal to personal care items such as deodorant or toothpaste, but that isn't always the case. You may only wear a certain brand of jeans because they fit you well or you like the style. The influences on brand loyalty for those products would be advertising, and knowing that the product meets their needs. Some people are loyal to certain car brands. Those influences could include advertising, perceived quality, price, reputation and product features.

b. You could come up with a ready answer for a digital camera (Kodak or Olympus), a sports car (Ford Mustang) and a soft drink (Pepsi or Coke) and MP3 player (iPod) but not perhaps for milk. The reasons for this come from brand awareness and advertising the manufacturers of these products have done. Some manufacturers simply dominate the market, like Ford and the sports car market, or Apple for MP3 players. Other markets are so competitive and there are so many brand names and price points that it is difficult to develop a high level of brand awareness, let alone brand insistence. The markets for some products like milk and dairy products may be dominated by private or local brands.

c. The problem with a brand name becoming generic is that the producer must then come up with a new brand name, and begin the process of developing brand awareness and brand loyalty all over again.

7. As a new product manager, you will need to start with generating ideas from many different sources. You will would investigate your competitors, and try to generate ideas from your own company personnel.

Once enough ideas have been generated, you would then have to screen them for profitability and potential. Any product ideas not meeting the criteria the company has set will be dropped from further analysis.

The next step will be to develop a product concept. If you develop a new premium pet food for example, as a concept, then you may need to create a prototype to test with consumers and their pets. During that step you would make sure pets like the product, determine how much people might be willing to pay for a premium pet food, how people will view this product, and what flavors the pet prefers.

If the product tests well, you would take it to market through your traditional retailers, or perhaps through the Internet. You may choose to offer the product through pet stores rather than the grocery stores, to reinforce the idea of a premium product.

8.

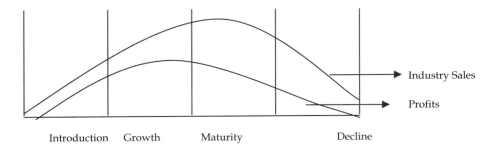

| Introduction | Growth | Maturity | Decline |

9. Possible answers

a. High price; Promote as a necessity for driving safety in upscale publications; stress need and uses for product

b. Change advertising to change product image; Add distribution outlets; Decrease price, or give price "deals."

c. Add new menu items, such as healthier versions of standard items; Look for new target markets; price deals

d. Reduce advertising; Limit the product variations; eventually consolidate distribution outlets

Learning Goal 7

10. a. Build traffic   d. Increase sales
    b. Achieve a target profit   e. Create an image
    c. Social objectives   f. Achieve a greater market share

11. a. The number of units Sun-2-Shade would have to sell to break even is 3,000.

$$\frac{1,200,000}{\$500 - \$100} = 3,000 \text{ units}$$

b. The break-even point is 3,000 units, so any unit sold beyond 3,000 will generate profits. If the company sells 5,000 units, profits will be generated by 2,000 of those units.

Price per unit = $500
Variable cost per unit = $100
Profit per unit = $400

400 x 2000 = $800,000 profit

c. If Sun-2-Shade raised their price to $600, the break-even point would be 2,400 units.

$$\frac{\$1,200,000}{\$600 - \$100} = 2,400 \text{ units}$$

d. No, they should not raise their price to $600. If they will break even at 2,400 but can only sell 2,000 units at that price, they will be losing money.

12. a. Skimming pricing   e. Everyday low pricing (EDLP)
    b. Demand pricing   f. Bundling
    c. Psychological pricing   g. High-low pricing
    d. Penetration pricing

PRACTICE TEST

MULTIPLE CHOICE

1.	d	13.	d
2.	a	14.	c
3.	d	15.	b
4.	b	16.	d
5.	d	17.	a
6.	c	18.	b
7.	a	19.	c
8.	a	20.	c
9.	b	21.	d
10.	c	22.	a
11.	c	23.	d
12.	a		

TRUE–FALSE

1.	T	11.	T
2.	F	12.	T
3.	F	13.	F
4.	T	14.	F
5.	F	15.	F
6.	F	16.	F
7.	T	17.	F
8.	T	18.	T
9.	F	19.	F
10.	T	20.	F

CHAPTER 15 – DISTRIBUTING PRODUCTS

LEARNING GOALS

After you have read and studied this chapter, you should be able to:

1. Explain the concept of marketing channels and their value.
2. Demonstrate how intermediaries perform the six marketing utilities.
3. Identify the types of wholesale intermediaries in the distribution system.
4. Compare the distribution strategies retailers use.
5. Explain the various kinds of nonstore retailing.
6. Explain the various ways to build cooperation in channel systems.
7. Describe logistics and outline how intermediaries manage the transportation modes and storage of goods.

LEARNING THE LANGUAGE

Listed below are important terms found in the chapter. Choose the correct term for the definition and write it in the space provided.

Administered distribution system	Inbound logistics	Rack jobbers
Agents/brokers	Information utility	Retailer
Cash-and-carry wholesaler	Intensive distribution	Reverse logistics
Channel of distribution	Intermodal shipping	Selective distribution
Contractual distribution system	Logistics	Service utility
Corporate distribution system	Marketing intermediaries	Supply chain (or value chain)
Direct marketing	Materials handling	Supply-chain management
Direct selling	Merchant wholesalers	Telemarketing
Drop shippers	Outbound logistics	Time utility
Electronic retailing	Place utility	Wholesaler
Exclusive distribution	Possession utility	
Freight forwarder		

1. The area of logistics called _____ brings raw materials, packaging, other goods and services, and information from suppliers to producers.

2. A marketing intermediary known as a _____ sells to other organizations.

3. A(n) _____ is a distribution system in which producers manage all the marketing functions at the retail level.

4. The movement of goods within a warehouse, from warehouses to the factory floor, and from the factory floor to various workstations is _____.

5. The function of _____ involves planning, implementing, and controlling the physical flow of materials, final goods, and related information from points of origin to the point of consumption to meet customer requirements at a profit.

6. The distribution strategy known as _____ puts products into as many retail outlets as possible.

7. The sale of goods and services by telephone is called _____.

8. A firm adds value to products through _____ by having them where people want them.

9. The use of _____ includes using multiple modes of transportation to complete a single long distance movement of freight.

10. The process of managing the movement of raw materials, parts, work in progress, finished goods, and related information through all the organizations involved in the supply chain; managing the return of such goods, if necessary; and recycling materials when appropriate is called _____.

11. The distribution strategy known as _____ sends products to only one retail outlet in a given geographic area.

12. Providing fast, friendly service during and after the sale and teaching customers how to best use products over time is considered to be _____.

13. The whole set of marketing intermediaries in the _____ includes wholesalers and retailers that join together to transport and store goods in their path from producers to consumers.

14. A _____ is an organization that sells to ultimate consumers.

15. A distribution system called a _____ is one in which all the organizations in the channel of distribution are owned by one firm.

16. A distribution strategy that sends products to only a preferred group of retailers in an area is called _____.

17. An organization adds value called _____ to products by opening two-way flows of information between marketing participants.

18. Organizations called _____ assist in moving goods and services from producers to businesses (B2B) and from businesses to consumers (B2C) users.

19. Wholesalers known as a _____ furnish racks or shelves full of merchandise to retailers, display products, and sell on consignment.

20. A _____ is an organization that puts many small shipments together to create a single large shipment that can be transported more cost-effectively to the final destination.

21. Wholesalers called _____ solicit orders from retailers and other wholesalers and have the merchandise shipped directly from a producer to a buyer.

22. Wholesalers that serve mostly smaller retailers with a limited assortment of products are _____.

23. Marketing intermediaries called _____ bring buyers and sellers together and assist in negotiating an exchange but don't take title to the goods.

24. Adding value to products by making them available when they're needed is called _____.

25. The concept of _____ is doing whatever is necessary to transfer ownership from one party to another, including providing credit, delivery, installation, guarantees, and follow-up service.

26. The function of _____ refers to managing the flow of finished products and information to business buyers and ultimate consumers.

27. In a _____ , members are bound to cooperate through contractual agreements.

28. Independently owned firms called _____ take title to the goods they handle.

29. Selling to consumers in their homes or where they work is called _____.

30. Selling goods and services to ultimate consumers over the Internet is known as _____.

31. The _____ consists of the sequence of linked activities that must be performed by various organizations to move goods from the sources of raw materials to ultimate consumers.

32. Any activity known as _____ directly links manufacturers or intermediaries with the ultimate consumer.

33. Bringing goods back to the manufacturers because of defects or for recycling materials is called _____.

ASSESSMENT CHECK

Learning Goal 1

The Emergence of Marketing Intermediaries

1. Channels of distribution help ensure: _____

   _____.

2. Why do we need marketing intermediaries?

3. Describe how marketing intermediaries create exchange efficiency in the distribution system.

4. Discuss the "value versus the cost" of intermediaries. In other words, is it cheaper to avoid intermediaries?

5. What are three basic points to remember about middlemen?

   a. _____

   b. _____

   c. _____

Learning Goal 2

Utilities Created by Intermediaries

6. List six utilities created by intermediaries.

   a. _____   d. _____

   b. _____   e. _____

   c. _____   f. _____

7. What kind of organization creates form utility? How is it created?

8. How does an intermediary add:

   time utility _____

   _____

   place utility _____

   _____

   possession utility _____

   _____

   information utility _____

   _____

   service utility _____

   _____

9. Which of the utilities is becoming the most important utility for retailers? Why?

Learning Goal 3

Wholesale Intermediaries

10. What is the difference between a "retail sale" and a "wholesale sale"?

11. Distinguish between these merchant wholesalers:

    a. full-service wholesalers:

    b. limited-function wholesalers:

12. Identify the functions a full service wholesaler will perform

    a. _____

    b. _____

    c. _____

    d. _____

    e. _____

    f. _____

    g. _____

    h. _____

13. Three types of limited service wholesalers are:

    a. _____

    b. _____

    c. _____

14. Describe how rack jobbers operate.

15. How does a cash and carry wholesaler function?

16. How does a drop shipper operate?

17. How are agents and brokers different from merchant wholesalers?

18. What is the difference between and agent and a broker?

19. Describe the difference between manufacturer's agents and sales agents.

20. Describe the role of a broker.

Learning Goal 4

Retail Intermediaries

21. Distinguish between the various types of retailers.

    a. _____

    b. _____

    c. _____

    d. _____

    e. _____

    f. _____

    g. _____

    h. _____

22. Describe the three retail distribution strategies:

    a. Intensive distribution:

    b. Selective distribution:

    c. Exclusive distribution:

Learning Goal 5

Nonstore Retailing

23. What are six types of non-store retailing?

    a. _____   d. _____

    b. _____   e. _____

    c. _____   f. _____

24. What are the "battles", or challenges, of e-tailing?

    a. _____

    b. _____

    c. _____

    d. _____

25. What kinds of customer service problems have electronic retailers experienced? How are they trying to improve the customer service problems?

26. How are brick and mortar stores using electronic retailing? What will be needed in the future?

27. Traditional retailers have learned that selling on the Internet calls for: _____

_____.

28. Companies use telemarketing to: _____.

29. The benefit of vending machines is: _____

    _____.

    The benefits of kiosks and carts are: _____

    _____.

30. What kinds of products are sold using direct selling? How is direct selling changing?

31. Describe multilevel marketing.

32. What are two attractions of multilevel marketing for employees?

    a. _____

    b. _____

33. What are some forms of direct marketing?

    a. _____   c. _____

    b. _____   d. _____

34. Why has direct marketing become so popular?

35. What has been the impact of interactive video on direct marketing?

Learning Goal 6

Building Cooperation in Channel Systems

36. What is the benefit to a manufacturer of a corporate distribution system?

37. Identify the characteristics of the three types of contractual distribution systems.

    a.   Franchise systems:

    b.   Wholesaler sponsored chains:

    c.   Retail cooperatives:

38. What functions does the producer take on in an administered distribution system? Why do retailers cooperate?

39. How does a supply chain compare to a channel of distribution?

40. How do supply chain systems "pay for themselves"?

    a.   _____

    b.   _____

    c.   _____

41. What is meant by the term "value chain"?

Learning Goal 7

Logistics: Getting Goods To Consumers Efficiently

42. Discuss the problems and complexities of shipping from one country to another.

43. What are "factory processes"?

44. What is meant by the term "third party logistics"?

45. Name six criteria used to evaluate transportation modes.

   a. _____   d. _____

   b. _____   e. _____

   c. _____   f. _____

46. List five transportation modes used to transport products, in order of volume.

   a. _____   d. _____

   b. _____   e. _____

   c. _____

47. What does the term "piggyback" mean in shipping?

48. In what situation would a company use a freight forwarder?

   Other than combining shipments, what functions may a freight forwarder offer?

49. What is the benefit of using trucks for shipping?

50. Often the least expensive way to ship is: _____.

   The drawback to this form of shipping is: _____.

51. What are "fishyback" and "birdyback" forms of distribution?

52. What kinds of products are primarily shipped using pipelines?

53. The fastest way of shipping is: _____.

    The drawback to this form of shipping is: _____.

54. What is an intermodal marketing company?

55. What do the costs of storage include?

56. Distinguish between:

    storage warehouses:

    distribution warehouses:

57. Describe RFID technology.

CRITICAL THINKING EXERCISES

Learning Goal 1

1. What do you think is the channel of distribution for:

   a.   cars   b.   soft drinks   c.   business forms (like blank invoices)

2. Joe Dell and his friend Woody were complaining as they were shopping for suits about how expensive they seemed to be. "Man" said Joe, "if we just had one of those outlet malls where we could avoid the "middleman "we'd be better off. That outlet store down at the Lake of the Ozarks is always advertising about how much lower their prices are because they get shipments direct from the manufacturer. Wouldn't it be a better deal if we just didn't have to deal with these expensive stores?" Woody replied: "Well Joe, I understand what you mean, but in my marketing class we've talked about marketing intermediaries, or middlemen, and they're not as bad as you think! Besides, if you go to an outlet store, you're still using a middleman!" What did Woody mean?

Learning Goal 2

3. Marketing intermediaries add value to products by creating six utilities:

Form   Possession
Time   Information
Place   Service

Match the correct response to each example:

a. _____ St. Luke's Hospital sponsors a "pediatric party" every Saturday for its young patients to show what will happen while they are in the hospital for surgery.

b. _____ Although it is a division of a larger retailing company, Macy's, a large department store, offers its own credit card.

c. _____ Many colleges are offering classes in the late afternoon, and on weekends to meet the needs of a diverse student body.

d. _____ McDonald's restaurants can be found in some Wal-Mart superstores, where you can order your meal from the Wal-Mart check-out counter.

e. _____ St. Louis Community College offers classes on three different campuses, as well as on the Internet, to provide convenience for their students.

f. _____ At Dierbergs, a grocery chain, the butcher will cut steaks to your specifications from their meat display.

4. Sun-2-Shade manufactures self-darkening windshields for automobiles. Their main customers are likely to be the automobile manufacturing companies. (For more information on this company, look at previous chapters.) The company is looking at its distribution function, and you and the marketing manager must make a proposal soon. In general, what kind of marketing intermediaries should the company consider? How does the classification of Sun-2-Shade as either a shopping good, a specialty good, or a business good affect the answer to this question? What will the channel of distribution look like? Is there a need for a marketing intermediary if the company targets primarily the automotive manufacturers? What kind of utilities will our customers find most important?

Learning Goal 3

5. There are several types of wholesalers:

   Full-service

   Limited Service (Function), which includes: *Rack jobbers, Cash and carry wholesalers and Drop shippers*

   Agents and Brokers, which include: *manufacturer's agents and sales agents*

   Identify the correct type of wholesaler with the following:

   a. _____ These wholesalers have begun selling to the public in larger stores, and have begun to allow their customers to use credit cards, although traditionally customers were required to pay cash.

   b. _____ Jim Stoeppler represents a number of companies that manufacture various components of certain kinds of uniform, such as a hat manufacturer and a shirt maker.

   c. _____ L'Eggs are displayed in the store on a rack. When the product is sold, the company shares the profit with the retailer.

   d. _____ Homedics is a wholesaler that stores thousands of different products for their customers. They offer credit and will ship products within 24 hours of receiving an order. They often offer deals to their customers, and have recently expanded their sales and marketing force to include some market research function.

   e. _____ Peabody Coal will sell their product to this wholesaler, who will then make arrangements for the coal to be shipped from the mine to an AmerenUE facility in southern Missouri.

f. _____ Larry Jackson owns a commercial real estate company in suburban Seattle. His company will connect potential buyers with sellers and negotiate the contracts. After the deal is done, Larry is no longer involved with either party.

g. _____ Maria Alvarez loves being self-employed. She sells for a small textile company that is based in North Carolina, and acts as their sales force for the entire East Coast and the Midwest. However, she is not an employee of the textile company.

Learning Goal 4

6. The three types of retail distribution strategies are:

Intensive distribution
Selective distribution
Exclusive distribution

Which strategy would likely be used for:

a. Chewing gum _____   d. Tickets to the Olympics _____

b. Athletic shoes _____   e. Designer snow skis _____

c. Potato chips _____   f. Winter coats _____

Learning Goal 5

7. There are several types of nonstore retailing:

Electronic retailing   Direct selling
Telemarketing   Multilevel marketing
Vending machines, kiosks and carts   Direct marketing

Determine which is being described in each of the following:

a. _____ Catalogs, telemarketing, and on-line shopping all help to make this form of retailing very convenient for consumers.

b. _____ In Japan, everything from bandages and face cloths to salads and seafood are sold in machines located in airports, movie theaters and other public places.

c. _____ Lingerie, artwork, baskets, jewelry and plastic bowls are sold at "parties" held at a customer's home or work place.

d. _____ Companies "reach out and touch someone" using this form of marketing, to supplement or replace in-store selling and supplement online retailing.

e. _____ Retailers like this form of retailing, as it lends an outdoor marketplace atmosphere to the mall in which they are located.

f. _____ Using this form of retailing, a new salesperson's job is to sell the products provided by the company and to recruit several people who will use the product and recruit others to sell and use the product.

g. _____ Traditional "brick and mortar" stores are beginning to use this type of non-store retailing.

Learning Goal 6

8. A further look at Sun-2-Shade's distribution system shows the need to consider the kind of cooperation necessary for us to create an efficient system.

In what kind of distribution system (corporate, contractual or administered) will Sun-2-Shade take part? Can you describe what their supply chain might look like? What are the important aspects of Sun-2-Shade's supply chain management?

Learning Goal 7

9. Think back to what we have learned in previous chapters about marketing and meeting the needs of our customers, as well as what we have learned in this chapter. What forces have created the change over the years to return the focus of marketing to the area of logistics?

10. Five basic modes of transportation are:

Railroad   Ship (water)
Truck   Airplane
Pipeline

A. Using the figure in your text, determine which mode of transportation would likely be used in the following situations when:

1. _____ Speed of delivery is the most important criterion, and cost is not a essential element.

2. _____ There is a need to serve multiple locations fairly quickly.

3. _____ Products are bulky, cost is a major consideration and speed of delivery is not an essential element.

4. _____ There is a need for constant or steady delivery to a minimal number of locations; speed of delivery is not important.

5. _____ There are multiple locations, bulky products, and cost and speed of delivery are of equal but moderate importance.

B. Which do you think would be the best choice of transportation mode for Sun-2-Shade? Why?

PRACTICE TEST

MULTIPLE CHOICE — Circle the best answer

Learning Goal 1

1. A(n) _____ brings buyers and sellers together and assist in negotiating a sale, but don't take title to goods.
   a. retailer
   b. channel of distribution
   c. supply chain
   d. agent or broker

2. Which of the following statements is accurate regarding marketing intermediaries?
   a. Intermediaries add cost to products, but not value.
   b. Intermediaries perform some functions cheaper and faster than manufacturers.
   c. The functions performed by marketing intermediaries are easily eliminated.
   d. Intermediaries have never performed their job efficiently, that's why they are being eliminated.

Learning Goal 2

3. In some areas of the country, Wal-Mart stays open 24 hours a day, most days of the year. This is an example of:
   a. service utility.
   b. place utility
   c. time utility.
   d. possession utility.

4. _____ utility is rapidly becoming the most important utility for many retailers as they face competition from direct marketing form s of retailing, such as the Internet or catalogs.
   a. Place
   b. Form
   c. Time
   d. Service

Learning Goal 3

5. The major difference between wholesalers and retailers is that:
   a. retailers sell only in certain parts of the country, while wholesalers are nationwide.
   b. wholesale organizations are generally more profitable than retail organizations.
   c. retailers sell goods to consumers for their personal use, and wholesalers sell to businesses for their use.
   d. retailers sell to final consumers, while wholesalers sell to another member of the channel of distribution, not final consumers.

6. Sam's Club sells to retailers, but doesn't offer transportation. Sam's will also allow a final consumer to shop, but charges an annual fee, and they have begun to allow customers to use credit, but the store will not deliver. Sam's is an example of a:
   a. rack jobber.
   b. freight forwarder.
   c. drop shipper.
   d. cash and carry wholesaler.

7. Cindy Murphy wants to get into fashion merchandising. Because of the risks involved in high fashion, and how quickly fashions go out of date, Cindy doesn't want to start a company in which she has title to the clothing. Cindy will have to rule out which of the following in her choice of business?
   a. broker
   b. agents
   c. merchant wholesaler
   d. manufacturer's agent

Learning Goal 4

8. Borders, Lowe's Hardware and Office Max are stores that offer wide selections of a product category at competitive prices. These stores can be so price competitive that they will drive out smaller businesses. These stores are known as:
   a. discount stores.
   b. supermarkets.
   c. supercenters.
   d. category killers.

9. After a few years of relying on the Internet to market their product, management at The Flying Noodle, a pasta company, has decided that it is time to get their product into the supermarket. This kind of basic pasta product will do best with:
   a. selective distribution.
   b. intensive distribution.
   c. exclusive distribution.
   d. nonstore retailing distribution.

Learning Goal 5

10. Which of the following is most accurate regarding electronic retailing?
    a. Most brick and mortar retailers can get away without going online.
    b. Selling on the Internet has meant that the distribution function has gotten less complicated.
    c. Electronic retailers are considered to be good at handling customer complaints.
    d. Brick and mortar stores are going online so that customers can pick and choose which shopping technique suits them best.

11. One of the fastest growing forms of nonstore retailing is:
    a. vending machines.
    b. telemarketing.
    c. direct marketing.
    d. multilevel marketing.

12. One successful nonstore retailer today is called Team. This company sells MonaVie, a relatively expensive fruit juice that is packaged in a wine bottle. Sales people for MonaVie earn commissions on their own sales, create commissions for the "upliners" who recruited them, and receive commissions from the "downliners" they have recruited. MonaVie operates in the area of

    _____.
    a. direct selling.
    b. direct marketing.
    c. multilevel marketing.
    d. a corporate distribution system.

Learning Goal 6

13. Midas Muffler, Baskin-Robbins, and other franchisors are examples of a:
    a. corporate distribution system.
    b. contractual distribution system .
    c. retail cooperative.
    d. administered distribution system.

14. Compared to a channel of distribution, a supply chain:
    a. is longer, because it includes links from suppliers.
    b. is shorter, because it doesn't include the manufacturer.
    c. is similar to a channel of distribution, but includes totally different members.
    d. is considered another form of wholesaling.

15. Which of the following is true of supply chain management systems?
    a. They are shorter than the average channel of distribution.
    b. Virtually any company that participates has benefited from lower costs.
    c. The can help to make a company more responsive to market changes.
    d. They create a more efficient method of production.

Learning Goal 7

16. Logistics is:
    a. the moving of goods within the warehouse, and within a factory.
    b. the process of changing raw materials and parts and other inputs into finished goods.
    c. planning, implementing, and controlling the physical flow of materials, final goods, and related information from points of origin to points of consumption.
    d. an effort to make sure that all of the organizations in a channel of distribution are owned by one firm.

17. Third party logistics refers to:
    a. bringing goods back to the manufacturers because of defects or to recycle.
    b. the use of outside firms to help move goods.
    c. managing the flow of finished products to business buyers and ultimate consumers.
    d. the movement of goods within a warehouse, from warehouses to the factory floor and from the factory floor to various workstations.

18. Dave Klein is a produce farmer in northern California. His major customers are grocery stores in the Midwest. Dave's product will only last for about 2 weeks after it has been picked, so Dave is concerned with getting his product to his customers quickly, but also needs to be aware of the cost of shipping, as produce is a perishable item. He ships almost daily when his produce is in season. Which form of shipping is Dave MOST likely to use?
    a.   trucks
    b.   ships
    c.   air
    d.   rail

19. When Hans Kaupfmann bought his car while on a trip to Germany, he wasn't sure how it would be shipped. The dealer assured him that many people buy cars and have them shipped to overseas destinations. The dealer explained that it's a smooth transition from land to sea and back to land, by trucking the car to the port, loading the entire truck trailer on to the ship, then trucking again to the destination. This process is known as:
    a.   piggyback.
    b.   fishyback.
    c.   bi-modal transportation.
    d.   transatlantic transportation.

20. A _____ gathers, then redistributes products.
    a.   distribution warehouse
    b.   storage warehouse
    c.   full-service wholesaler
    d.   drop shipper wholesaler

TRUE–FALSE

Learning Goal 1

1. _____   A channel of distribution consists of marketing intermediaries who join together to store and transport goods in their path from producer to consumer.

2. _____   Generally, it is much less expensive and much faster when we can avoid the use of a marketing intermediary and go straight to the producer.

3. _____   Marketing intermediaries can be eliminated but their activities can't.

Learning Goal 2

4. _____   Form utility is typically provided by producers rather than intermediaries.

5. _____   When Lowe's makes arrangements for a refrigerator to be delivered to the buyer's home, they are providing time utility.

Learning Goal 3

6. _____   Merchant wholesalers do not buy what they sell; they primarily match buyers with sellers.

7. _____   A sales agent, or manufacturer's agent, can represent several companies.

Learning Goal 4

8. _____ Exclusive distribution would be used by a producer of a product such as skydiving equipment.

9. _____ The most appropriate distribution strategy for products such as appliances or furniture would be selective distribution.

Learning Goal 5

10. _____ One of the challenges of electronic retailing is providing customer service and keeping customers.

11. _____ Mall owners prefer not to have kiosks and carts located in the mall because they are too much competition for the traditional mall stores.

12. _____ Multilevel marketing is not a good way to make money, because it costs too much to get into.

Learning Goal 6

13. _____ In a corporate distribution system, a retailer signs a contract to cooperate with a manufacturer.

14. _____ The primary concern of supply chain managers is keeping costs down, regardless of anything else.

15. _____ Supply chain management enables companies to carry lower levels of inventory and improve customer service.

Learning Goal 7

16. _____ Today, logistics is as much about the movement of information as it is about the movement of goods.

17. _____ A major issue in marketing in the future will be how to ship goods to other countries in the fastest way possible and still keep costs low.

18. _____ A smaller manufacturer may make use of a freight forwarder because they don't ship enough product to fill a railcar or truck.

19. _____ Intermodal shipping uses multiple modes of transportation to complete a single long-distance movement of freight.

20. _____ A distribution warehouse hold products for a relatively long time, until they can be distributed to the appropriate retailer or customer.

You Can Find It on the Net

Compare shopping on the Internet to shopping in a store. Visit www.cduniverse.com or www.amazon.com and check out the prices of three of your favorite c.d.'s.

How do the prices compare to the price you pay in the store? (You may have to actually visit the store to determine this!)

How much does shipping add to the price of the c.d.'s?

How does the web site encourage you to buy the product?

What problems do you see with shopping for music over the Internet?

How does the web site overcome those problems?

ANSWERS

LEARNING THE LANGUAGE

1.	Inbound logistics	12.	Service utility	23.	Agents/brokers
2.	Wholesaler	13.	Channel of distribution	24.	Time utility
3.	Administered distribution system	14.	Retailer	25.	Possession utility
4.	Materials handling	15.	Corporate distribution system	26.	Outbound logistics
5.	Logistics	16.	Selective distribution	27.	Contractual distribution system
6.	Intensive distribution	17.	Information utility	28.	Merchant wholesalers
7.	Telemarketing	18.	Marketing intermediaries	29.	Direct selling
8.	Place utility	19.	Rack jobbers	30.	Electronic retailing
9.	Intermodal shipping	20.	Freight forwarder	31.	Supply chain (or value chain)
10.	Supply chain management	21.	Drop shippers	32.	Direct marketing
11.	Exclusive distribution	22.	Cash and carry wholesaler	33.	Reverse logistics

ASSESSMENT CHECK

Learning Goal 1

The Emergence of Marketing Intermediaries

1. Channels of distribution ensure communication flows and the flow of money and title to goods. They also help ensure that the right quantity and assortment of goods will be available when and where needed.

2. Marketing intermediaries perform marketing tasks like transporting, storing, selling, advertising, and relationship building faster and cheaper than most manufacturers could.

3. Marketing intermediaries create exchange efficiency in the distribution system by reducing the number of transactions necessary to get the product to the buyer. Marketing intermediaries are perform these functions faster and more cheaply than a manufacturer could.

4. Some people believe that if they could get rid of the intermediary they could reduce the cost of what they buy. However, if we got rid of a retailer, for example, we may be able to buy a product for a little less but we would still have to drive further and spend more time looking for the product. The value of intermediaries is that they make products available to us at times and places that are convenient for us. That often outweighs the cost they add to the product.

5. Three basic points to remember about middlemen include:
   a. Marketing intermediaries can be eliminated, but their activities cannot.
   b. Intermediaries have survived because they have performed functions faster and cheaper than others.
   c. Intermediaries add cost, but the cost is usually offset by the value they create.

Learning Goal 2

Utilities Created by Intermediaries

6. The six utilities created by intermediaries are:
   a. Form
   b. Time
   c. Place
   d. Possession
   e. Information
   f. Service

7. Form utility is added by various organizations, such as butchers, farmers, or food processors. Form utility is created by taking raw materials and changing their form so that they become useful products.

8. Intermediaries add:
   Time utility to products by making them available when they're needed, like a retailer which is open 24 hours a day.

   Place utility by having products where people want them, in a convenient place.

   Possession utility by doing whatever is necessary to transfer ownership from one party to another, including providing credit. Activities include delivery, installation, guarantees, and follow-up service.

   Information utility by opening two-way flows of information between marketing participants. Newspapers, sales people, libraries, web sites, and government publications are all information sources made available by intermediaries.

   Service utility by providing fast, friendly service during and after the sale and by teaching customers how to best use products.

9. Service utility is becoming the most important utility for retailers, because without personal service they could lose business to electronic marketing or direct marketing.

Learning Goal 3

Wholesale Intermediaries

10. A *retail sale* is a sale of goods and services to <u>consumers</u> for their own use. A *wholesale sale* is the sale of goods and services to <u>businesses and institutions</u> for use in the business or for resale.

11. a. Full-service wholesalers perform all distribution functions.
    b. Limited function wholesalers perform only selected functions.

12. The functions a full service wholesaler will perform include:
    a. Provide a sales force
    b. Communicate manufacturer's advertising deals and plans
    c. Maintain inventory for producer
    d. Arrange or undertake transportation
    e. Provide capital by paying cash or quick payment
    f. Provide suppliers with marketing information
    g. Granting credit to customers
    h. Assume risk by taking title

13. Three types of limited service wholesalers are:
    a. rack jobbers
    b. cash- and- carry wholesalers
    c. drop shippers

14. Rack jobbers furnish racks or shelves full of merchandise to retailers, display products and sell on consignment. They keep title to goods until they are sold and share the profits with the retailers.

15. A cash-and-carry wholesaler serves mostly smaller retailers with a limited assortment of products. Traditionally, retailers went to such wholesalers, paid cash, and carried the goods back to their stores. Today, some stores allow retailers and others to use credit cards for purchases.

16. A drop shipper solicits orders from retailers and other wholesalers and has the merchandise shipped directly from a producer to a buyer. They own the merchandise but don't handle, stock or deliver it. That is handled by the producer.

17. Agents and brokers never own the products they distribute. Usually they do not carry inventory, provide credit, or assume risks. While merchant wholesalers earn a profit from the sale of goods, agents and brokers earn commissions or fees based upon a percentage of the sales revenue.

18. An agent maintains long-term relationships with the people they represent, whereas a broker is usually hired on a temporary basis.

19. A manufacturer's agent may represent one or several manufacturers in a specific territory, as long as the suppliers are not competitors. A sales agent represents a single producer in a larger territory.

20. A broker has no continuous relationship with a buyer or seller. Once the broker negotiates a contract between a buyer and a seller, their relationship ends.

Learning Goal 4

Retail Intermediaries

21. The various types of retailers are:
    a. Department stores—sell a wide variety of products in separate departments
    b. Discount stores—sell many different products at prices below department stores
    c. Supermarkets— sell mostly food with other nonfood items like paper products
    d. Warehouse clubs—sell food and general merchandise in very large facilities; may require membership
    e. Convenience stores—sell food and other often needed items at convenient locations
    f. Category killers—sell a huge variety of one type of product; dominates a category of goods
    g. Outlet stores—sell general merchandise directly from the manufacturer at a discount
    h. Specialty stores—sell a wide selection of goods in one category

22. a. Intensive distribution—puts products into as many outlets as possible. Products that need intensive distribution include convenience goods.

    b. Selective distribution—the use of only a preferred group of the available retailers in an area. Manufacturers of shopping goods use this type of distribution.

    c. Exclusive distribution—the use of only one retail outlet in a given geographic area. Auto makers and producers of specialty goods use this.

Nonstore Retailing

23. Six types of nonstore retailing are:
    a. Electronic retailing
    b. Telemarketing
    c. Vending machines, kiosks and carts
    d. Direct selling
    e. Multilevel marketing
    f. Direct marketing

24. The major challenges of e-tailing are:
    a. getting customers
    b. delivering the goods
    c. providing helpful service
    d. keeping customers

25. Electronic retailers have had problems with handling complaints, accepting returns, and providing personal help. Some sites are trying to improve customer service by adding help buttons that you can click on to get almost instant assistance from a real person.

26. Traditional retailers are going online, so that now customers can pick and choose which shopping form they prefer. Companies that want to compete in the future will probably need both a store presence and an online presence to provide consumers with all the options they want.

27. Traditional retailers have learned that selling on the Internet calls for a new kind of distribution system. Both traditional retailers and Internet retailers have to develop new distribution systems to meet the demands of today's Internet-savvy shoppers.

28. Companies use telemarketing to supplement or replace in-store selling and to complement online selling.

29. The benefit of vending machines is their location in areas where people want convenience items, such as airports, office buildings, schools and service stations.

    The benefits of kiosks and carts are that they have lower costs than stores. Therefore they can offer lower prices on certain items. Mall owners often like them because they are colorful and create a marketplace atmosphere. Customers enjoy interactive kiosks because they dispense coupons and provide information when buying products.

30. Major users of direct selling include cosmetics, and vacuum cleaner manufacturers. Other businesses are using direct selling for lingerie, artwork, plants and candles sold at home parties. Because so many buyers work outside the home during the day, many of the sellers are sponsoring parties at workplaces or in the evenings and on weekends.

31. Multilevel marketing sales people work as independent contractors. They earn commissions on their own sales and create commissions for the "upliners" who recruited them. In multilevel marketing, an "upliner" is an individual who has recruited others to sell for them. The "downliners" are the people who have been recruited to sell.

32. The main attractions of multilevel marketing for employees are:
    a. great potential for making money
    b. low cost of entry

33. Direct marketing includes:
    a. direct mail
    b. catalog sales
    c. telemarketing
    d. on-line marketing

34. Direct marketing has become popular because shopping from home or work is more convenient for consumers than going to the store. Consumers can shop in catalogs and free-standing advertising supplements in the newspaper and then buy by phone, by mail, or by computer.

35. Direct marketing changed when consumers became more involved with interactive video. Producers now provide information on a c.d. or on websites that consumers can access. Companies that use these tools have become major competitors for those who market using paper catalogs.

Learning Goal 6

Building Cooperation in Channel Systems

36. If the manufacturer owns the retail firm it can maintain control over its operations.

37. Franchise systems - the franchisee agrees to all of the rules, regulations, and procedures established by the franchisor. This results in consistent quality and level of service.

    Wholesaler-sponsored chains - each store signs an agreement to use the same name, participate in chain promotions and cooperate as a unified system of stores, even though each store is independently owned and managed.

    Retail cooperatives - the arrangement is much like a wholesaler-sponsored chain except it's initiated by the retailers. The same cooperation is agreed to, and the stores remain independent.

38. In an administered distribution system the producer manages all of the marketing functions at the retail level. This includes display, inventory control, pricing, and promotion. Retailers cooperate with producers in administered distribution systems because they get so much help for free.

39. A supply chain is longer than a channel of distribution because it includes suppliers to manufacturers whereas the channel of distribution begins with manufacturers. Channels of distribution are part of the supply chain.

40. A supply chain pays for itself from:
    a. inventory savings,
    b. customer service improvement
    c. responsiveness to market changes

41. The term "value chain" is just another word for a supply chain. This term may be used because such systems are so effective and efficient.

Logistics: Getting Goods To Consumers Efficiently

42. When shipping from country to country the major questions are how to ship goods in the fastest way possible and still keep costs low. This is especially challenging when shipping bulky merchandise such as cars. It is sometimes impossible to use trucks or trains because the goods have to travel over water. Shipping by air is often prohibitively expensive. The last source is by ship. The questions are how to get goods to the ship and from ship to buyer, as well as handling trade duties and taxes.

43. Factory processes change raw materials and parts and other inputs into outputs, such as finished goods.

44. Third party logistics is the term used to describe the use of outside firms to help move goods from here to there. It is part of a larger trend toward outsourcing.

45. Six criteria used to evaluate transportation modes are:
     a. Cost
     b. Speed
     c. On-time dependability
     d. Flexibility in handling products
     e. Frequency of shipments
     f. Reach

46. Five transportation modes used in transporting products, listed by volume are:
     a. Railroad
     b. Trucks
     c. Pipeline
     d. Water transportation
     e. Air

47. A piggyback system means that a truck trailer is detached from the cab of a truck, loaded onto a railroad flatcar and taken to a destination where is will be offloaded, attached to a truck and driven to customers' plants.

48. A company would use a freight forwarder when it doesn't ship enough goods to fill a railcar or truck. The freight forwarder can combine many small shipments to create a single large shipment that can be transported cost-effectively, by either truck or train.

     Other than shipping, a freight forwarder may offer warehousing, customer assistance, and other services along with pickup and delivery.

49. A benefit of using trucks for shipping is that trucks are able to reach more destinations than other forms of transportation because a truck can deliver door to door.

50. Often the least expensive way to ship is water transportation.
     The drawback is that water transportation is so slow.

51. Fishyback and birdyback forms of distribution are similar to piggyback. In fishyback, the truck trailer is loaded onto ship, and re-connected to the truck cab at the destination. With birdyback, the trailer is loaded onto an airplane.

52. Pipelines are used primarily to transport water, petroleum and petroleum products.

53. The fast way of shipping is by air.

     The drawback of shipping by air is that it is very expensive.

54.   Services that specialize in intermodal shipping are known as intermodal marketing companies.

55.   The costs of storage include the cost of the storage warehouse (distribution facility) and its operation plus movement of goods within the warehouse.

56.   Storage warehouses – store products for a relatively long time, such as seasonal goods, like snow shovels and lawnmowers.

      Distribution warehouses – are facilities used to gather and redistribute products.

57.   RFID technology tags merchandise so that it can be tracked from the time it's loaded off the supplier's docks to when the customer buys the product. This is the latest in tracking technology.

CRITICAL THINKING EXERCISES

Learning Goal 1

1.   The channel of distribution for

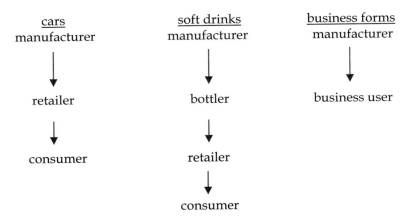

2.   What Woody was trying to tell Joe is that, first, the outlet store is a type of middleman, called a retailer. Further, retailers and the other type of middlemen, wholesalers, add many things to a product that would be difficult to replace. In the first place, Joe would have to drive to wherever the suit he chose was manufactured, if he were to really avoid a middleman. That could be as far away as the Far East! The retailer is much closer. Secondly, if he decided to have the manufacturer ship the suit to him, he would have to pay for shipping the suit to his home, which could be expensive. He would have to contact the manufacturer during working hours, which for a manufacturer would probably be Monday - Friday, between 8a.m. and 5 p.m. Then he would have to try it on, and figure out any alterations, perhaps ship the suit back to be altered, or find someone to alter it for him. Further, Joe would not be able to see the suit before it was sent, or would have to spend hours looking through the manufacturer's warehouse looking through hundreds of suits (that is after having traveled to the Far East in the first place...)

     In short, middlemen provide value through adding convenience such as transportation and storage, and enable us to shop for and find exactly what we want, at times convenient for us with far less effort. Therefore, while middleman organizations can be eliminated, their functions cannot.

Learning Goal 2

3. a. Information
   b. Possession
   c. Time

   d. Place and possession
   e. Place
   f. Form

Learning Goals 1, 2, 3

4. If Sun-2-Shade targets primarily the auto industry, the company will not necessarily need a wholesaling middleman, unless it uses some kind of a broker in lieu of employing a sales force. The channel of distribution will look like one of these two suggestions:

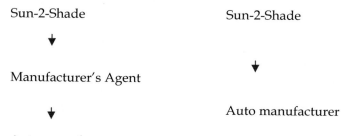

The most important utility for the end consumer may be information utility, as the consumer may need to know more about the product. Place utility is important, but is affected by our classification of Sun-2-Shade as either a shopping good or specialty good or a business good. This affects the kind of store we will choose, as shopping goods may be found in several kinds of stores and specialty goods will be found in fewer, different kinds of stores.

For the auto manufacturers, time and place utility will be important, as they will need the product delivered when they need it, where they need it.

Learning Goal 3

5. a. Limited service: cash and carry
   b. Manufacturer's agent
   c. Limited service: rack jobber
   d. Full service

   e. Limited service: drop shipper
   f. Broker
   g. Sales agent

Learning Goal 4

6. a. Intensive
   b. Selective
   c. Intensive

   d. Exclusive
   e. Exclusive
   f. Selective

Learning Goal 5

7. a. Direct marketing
   b. Vending machines
   c. Direct selling
   d. Telemarketing

   e. Kiosks, carts
   f. Multilevel marketing
   g. E-tailing

8. Sun-2-Shade will be an integral part of an automaker's supply chain, and will want to be linked electronically to their customers. Sun-2-Shade's supply chain will include suppliers of raw materials as well as the auto manufacturers. The critical element of their supply chain management system will be to coordinate the receipt of the raw materials needed to make the windshield and the process of manufacturing, with the orders coming in from customers. This process is known as outbound logistics.

   Sun-2-Shade won't be using retailers right away, since the company will most likely be focusing on the automakers at first. When it does begin to sell to retailers, it will become part of yet a different supply chain.

Learning Goal 7

9. As we have learned in earlier chapters the focus today is on meeting the needs of our customers in every way possible. But the idea of meeting customer needs goes beyond developing need-satisfying products, and today extends to meeting our customers demands for quick delivery at reasonable prices. This includes our global as well as domestic customers. We can meet customer demands for high quality, reasonably price products, delivered when we want them, by focusing on logistics and supply chain management. Focusing on these important areas of marketing will ensure that products are stored, delivered, handled and shipped in the most cost efficient manner. As customer demands have increased, so has the focus on planning, implementing, and controlling the physical flow of materials, final goods and related information from points of origin to points of consumption to meet customer requirements – in other words, logistics.

10. A.
    1. Air   4. Pipeline
    2. Truck   5. Railroad
    3. Water

    B. The best transportation mode for Sun-2-Shade would probably be by truck to both the auto manufacturers and the retailers. For auto manufacturers, which are located a considerable distance from Sun-2-Shade's production facility, a combination of rail and truck could be used for flexibility, number of deliveries, and speed. The major problem with trucks is the cost, but it serves the other needs best.

PRACTICE TEST

MULTIPLE CHOICE

1.	d	11.	c
2.	b	12.	d
3.	c	13.	b
4.	d	14.	a
5.	d	15.	d
6.	d	16.	c
7.	c	17.	b
8.	d	18.	a
9.	b	19.	b
10.	a	20.	a

TRUE-FALSE

1.	T	11.	F
2.	F	12.	F
3.	T	13.	F
4.	T	14.	F
5.	F	15.	T
6.	F	16.	T
7.	T	17.	T
8.	T	18.	T
9.	T	19.	T
10.	T	20.	F

CHAPTER 16 – USING EFFECTIVE PROMOTIONAL TECHNIQUES

LEARNING GOALS

After you have read and studied this chapter, you should be able to:

1. Identify the new and traditional tools that make up the promotion mix.
2. Contrast the advantages and disadvantages of various advertising media, including the Internet.
3. Illustrate the steps of B2B and B2C selling processes.
4. Describe the role of the public relations department and show how publicity fits in that role.
5. Assess the effectiveness of various forms of sales promotion including sampling.
6. Show how word of mouth, email marketing, viral marketing, blogging, and podcasting and mobile marketing work.

LEARNING THE LANGUAGE

Listed below are important terms found in the chapter. Choose the correct term for each definition and write it in the space provided.

Advertising	Product placement	Push strategy
Blog	Promotion mix	Qualifying
Infomercial	Prospect	Sales promotion
Interactive promotion	Prospecting	Sampling
Integrated marketing communication (IMC)	Publicity	Trial close
Personal selling	Public relations (PR)	Viral marketing
Pick economy	Pull strategy	Word-of-mouth promotion
Podcasting		

1. The promotional tool known as _____ stimulates consumer purchasing and dealer interest by means of short-term activities.

2. Paid, nonpersonal communication, or _____ , goes through various media by organizations and individuals who are in some way identified in the advertising message.

3. The management function of _____ evaluates public attitudes, changes policies and procedures in response to the public's requests, and executes a program of action and information to earn public understanding and acceptance.

4. A _____ is a promotional strategy in which heavy advertising and sales promotion efforts are directed toward consumers so that they will request the products from retailers.

5. The step in the selling process referred to as the _____ consists of a question or statement that moves the selling process toward the actual close.

6. The _____ is the combination of promotion tools that an organization uses.

7. A promotional tool that involves people talking about products they have purchased is called _____.

8. In the selling process _____ is making sure that people have a need for the product, the authority to buy and the willingness to listen to a sales message.

9. Researching potential buyers and choosing those most likely to buy is called _____.

10. A technique known as _____ combines all the promotional tools into one comprehensive, unified promotional strategy.

11. An online diary is known as a _____; it looks like a web page but is easier to create and update by posting text, photos, or links to other sites.

12. The form of promotion known as _____ is any information about an individual, product, or organization that's distributed to the public through the media and that's not paid for, or controlled by, the seller.

13. A _____ is the promotional strategy in which the producer uses advertising, personal selling, sales promotion and all other promotional tools to convince wholesalers and retailers to stock and sell merchandise.

14. A full-length TV program devoted exclusively to promoting goods and services is known as a(n) _____.

15. The promotion tool of _____ is the face-to-face presentation and promotion of products and services.

16. The term _____ refers to those consumers who pick out their products from online outlets or who do online comparison shopping.

17. Putting products into TV shows and movies where they will be seen is called _____.

18. A tool named _____ allows marketers to go beyond a monologue, where sellers tried to persuade buyers to buy things, to a dialogue where buyers and sellers can work together to create mutually beneficial exchange relationships.

19. The term _____ is used to describe everything from paying people to say positive things on the Internet to setting up multilevel selling schemes whereby consumers get commissions for directing friends to specific Web sites.

20. A person with the means to buy a product, or _____ also has the authority to buy, and the willingness to listen to a sales message.

21. A promotional tool in which a company lets consumers have a small sample of the product for no charge is called _____.

22. A means of distributing audio and video programs via the Internet is called _____ and it lets users subscribe to a number of files, also known as feeds, and then hear or view the material at the time they choose.

ASSESSMENT CHECK

Learning Goal 1

Promotion and the Promotion Mix

1. What are the tools of the promotion mix?

   a. _____   c. _____

   b. _____   d. _____

2. What is the idea behind Integrated Marketing communication?

3. List the steps in a typical promotion campaign.

   a. _____   d. _____

   b. _____   e. _____

   c. _____   f. _____

Learning Goal 2

Advertising: Informing, Persuading, and Reminding

4. List the various categories of advertising:

   a. _____   f. _____

   b. _____   g. _____

   c. _____   h. _____

   d. _____   i. _____

   e. _____

5. How does the public benefit from advertising?

   a. _____

   b. _____

   c. _____

6. List some of the advantages and disadvantages of each form of advertising media:

	Advantages	Disadvantages
a. Newspapers	_____	_____
	_____	_____
	_____	_____
	_____	_____
b. Television	_____	_____
	_____	_____
	_____	_____
	_____	_____
c. Radio	_____	_____
	_____	_____
	_____	_____
	_____	_____
d. Magazines	_____	_____
	_____	_____
	_____	_____
	_____	_____
e. Outdoor	_____	_____
	_____	_____
	_____	_____
	_____	_____
f. Direct mail	_____	_____
	_____	_____
	_____	_____
	_____	_____

g. Yellow pages   _____   _____

_____   _____

_____   _____

_____   _____

h. Internet   _____   _____

_____   _____

_____   _____

_____   _____

i. Mobile
advertising   _____   _____

_____   _____

7. What is the newest form of product placement?

8. Why are infomercials so successful in selling products?

9. Describe the benefits to corporations of Internet advertising.

10. How has technology improved customer communications?

11. What are the two approaches to advertising in the global market?

a. _____

b. _____

12. Distinguish between "globalism" and "regionalism" in advertising.

Personal Selling: Providing Personal Attention

13. Describe "effective selling." How does technology help the salesperson to be effective?

14. What are the seven steps in the personal selling process?

    a. _____   e. _____

    b. _____   f. _____

    c. _____   g. _____

    d. _____

15. In personal selling, what is the difference between prospecting and qualifying?

16. Where do sales people find prospects?

17. What is involved in the preapproach?

18. What is the objective during the first sales call during the approach stage?

19. What is the main idea when making the presentation?

20. What should the salesperson do in answering objections?

21. What activities are involved in closing a sale?

22. Identify the activities involved in the follow up.

    a. _____

    b. _____

    c. _____

23. According to the text, what are the two goals of a salesperson?

    a. _____

    b. _____

24. How does the role of the salesperson in the B2C (Business to Consumer) sales process differ from that in the B2B (Business to Business) sales process?

25. What does the salesperson do during the presentation in the B2C sales process?

26. During the trial close in B2C selling, a trial close is important, but the sales person must _____

    _____.

27. Why is follow-up important in B2C selling?

Learning Goal 4

Public Relations: Building Relationships

28. Identify the three steps in creating a good public relations campaign.

    a. _____

    b. _____

    c. _____

29. A public relations department maintains close ties with: _____

    _____

30. What are the advantages of publicity over other promotional tools?

    a. _____

    b. _____

    c. _____

31. What are three disadvantages of publicity?

    a. _____

    b. _____

    c. _____

32. One way to see that publicity is handled well by the media is to: _____

    _____.

Learning Goal 5

Sales Promotion: Giving Buyers Incentives

33. List 5 types of B2B sales promotions.

    a. _____   d. _____

    b. _____   e. _____

    c. _____

34. List the various consumer sales promotion techniques.

    a. _____   g. _____

    b. _____   h. _____

    c. _____   i. _____

    d. _____   j. _____

    e. _____   k. _____

    f. _____   l. _____

35. Sales promotion programs are designed to: _____

    _____.

36. The most important *internal* sales promotion efforts are directed at: _____

_____.

37. List the internal sales promotion efforts:

a. _____

b. _____

c. _____

38. What is a virtual trade show, and what is the benefit for dealers and distributors?

39. What is the benefit of sampling as a sales promotion tool?

Learning Goal 6

Word of Mouth and Other Promotional Tools

40. What are 6 additional forms of promotion in addition to the traditional methods?

a. _____   d. _____

b. _____   e. _____

c. _____   f. _____

41. Any activity that encourages people to talk favorably about an organization could be what form of promotion?

42. What are some ways that companies are using viral marketing to create word of mouth promotion?

43. What is one of the best ways to reduce negative word of mouth?

44. What does podcasting allow for?

45. Describe how mobile media is used as a promotion technique.

46. The best way for reaching large groups of consumers with similar traits is _____.

    The best way to sell to large organizations is _____.

    To motivate people to buy now rather than later marketers use _____.

    The most powerful tool is often _____.

47. What is the idea behind a push strategy?

48. What should happen when a pull strategy is successful?

49. Describe a total systems approach to marketing.

CRITICAL THINKING EXERCISES

Learning Goal 1

1. Sun-2-Shade is a company that makes self-darkening windshields for automobiles. (We have worked on this company in previous chapters.) While we haven't yet decided on a promotion mix for Sun-2-Shade, discuss the steps we will we take to create our promotion campaign, as specifically as possible to this point.

Learning Goal 2

2. There is a variety of media available to use for advertising. Using the chart in your text, determine what might be the most appropriate form of advertising media for: (there may be more than one answer for each)

   a. _____ A rock concert at an outdoor theater

   b. _____ Sales at the local mall

   c. _____ Products aimed specifically at women

   d. _____ A local news television show

   e. _____ New type of cell phone

   f. _____ Credit cards

   g. _____ Computer software

   h. _____ A self-darkening windshield for a car/truck

3. No matter what the specific promotion mix will be for Sun-2-Shade, a company that manufactures self darkening windshields for vehicles, there is no doubt that technology will play an important role. How would you incorporate the use of the interactive promotion into the promotion mix for Sun-2-Shade?

Learning Goal 3

4. We're continuing to work on a promotion mix for Sun-2-Shade (see question 1). We know it will include some form of personal selling. Using the seven steps in your text, prepare an outline for a sales presentation to your automotive manufacturing customers.

Learning Goal 4

5. The Fox affiliate in large midwestern city added a news broadcast to its lineup. In order to compete with the larger affiliates, the Fox affiliate (Channel 30) decided to air their program at 9:00 p.m. Before the news broadcast went on the air, the station surveyed viewers regarding their likes and dislikes about the current local news broadcasts. Shortly before the new show was to premiere, the station began promoting the show, the news anchors, and how this show was going to be different from current shows.

    One of the changes the new show made was to avoid, as much as possible, the real "bad news" stories as leads to the broadcast, leaving them until later in the show. They made a point of finding "good news" stories about the city and its inhabitants. They did this because that's what viewers said they wanted. During the broadcast, just before a commercial break, a screen will show with the exact show times of each of the upcoming stories, in response to customer complaints that other stations will use upcoming stories as "hooks" but actually not air the story until much later in the broadcast. In promoting the show, and during the news broadcast, mention is made of the way the station is responding to viewer requests. Further, during the broadcast, the station's telephone number was flashed, and viewers were encouraged to call with complaints, requests, or suggestions.

    How do these actions by the television station demonstrate a "good" public relations program?

Learning Goal 5

6. Identify three main groups that are the main focus of sales promotion efforts, and a technique used to reach each group.

    Group   Technique

    a. _____   _____

    b. _____   _____

    c. _____   _____

7. Continuing with developing the promotion mix for Sun-2-Shade, identify some sales promotion techniques you would use for employees, the B2B market and the B2C market.

8. How do the other elements of the promotion mix affect word of mouth promotion?

    Product _____

    Sales promotion _____

    Advertising _____

    Publicity _____

    Personal selling _____

Learning Goals 1-6

9. Now that we have covered the promotion mix variables, you are an expert in designing an effective promotion campaign. What do you think would be the most effective promotion mix for Sun-2-Shade to use? Will it be more important to use a push or a pull strategy, a combination, or a "total systems" approach? How will you use new tools such as podcasting, blogging and viral marketing?

PRACTICE TEST

MULTIPLE CHOICE—Circle the best answer

Learning Goal 1

1. Non-traditional forms of promotion include:
   a. personal selling and advertising.
   b. social networking and podcasting.
   c. sales promotion and public relations.
   d. public relations and advertising.

2. Sun-2-Shade is a company that makes self-darkening windshields for cars and trucks. Which of the following would <u>not</u> be included as part of Sun-2-Shade's promotion mix?
   a. Designing an interactive Web site for customers to ask questions and order products.
   b. Sponsoring a NASCAR race.
   c. Hiring a sales force to call on automotive customers.
   d. Expanding the product line to include sunglasses custom made to match the customer's windshield colors.

3. The first step in developing a typical promotion campaign is:
   a. define the objectives for each element of the promotion mix.
   b. determine a promotional budget.
   c. identify a target market.
   d. develop a unifying message.

Learning Goal 2

4. Which of the following is a benefit of Internet newspaper advertising, according to the text?
   a. Inexpensive global coverage.
   b. Can target specific audiences.
   c. High visibility and repeat exposures.
   d. Good coverage of local markets.

5. Product placement refers to:
   a. paying to put products into TV shows and movies where they will be seen.
   b. the location of products on a grocery store shelf.
   c. the image the product has in the mind of the consumer.
   d. the location of the product at any given point in the channel of distribution.

6. Which media would be best if you are interested in targeting a specific audience, need flexibility, have a local market and don't have a lot of money to spend?
   a. The Internet
   b. Television
   c. Outdoor
   d. Radio

7. Garden.com's website includes a forum where people can chat with each other to ask questions about gardening problems and interests. This is known as:
   a. the company's marketing mix.
   b. interactive promotion.
   c. blogging.
   d. mobile marketing.

8. In personal selling, the relationship must continue for a long time, as the salesperson responds to new requests for information from current customers. This is an important part of the _____ step in personal selling.
    a. prospecting
    b. closing
    c. follow-up
    d. presentation

9. What is the first step in the B2B personal selling process?
    a. Approach
    b. Make presentation
    c. Prospect and Qualify
    d. Preapproach

10. Which of the following is true regarding personal selling today?
    a. Automation has had a big impact on personal selling with the use of high-tech hardware and software.
    b. The objective of an initial sales call is to make a sale immediately.
    c. Big customers should always be treated with more care than small ones.
    d. It is more difficult to find customers in the business-to-business market than in the consumer market.

11. The first formal step in the B2C personal selling process is:
    a. Approach.
    b. Make presentation.
    c. Prospect and qualify.
    d. Preapprach.

12. Which of the following is the first step in developing a good public relations program?
    a. Listen to the public
    b. Inform people of the fact you're being responsive
    c. Develop policies and procedures in the public interest
    d. Advertise in a way that promotes positive word of mouth.

13. It is the responsibility of the public relations department to:
    a. work closely with marketing to develop an appropriate advertising campaign.
    b. have a presence at trade shows and conventions.
    c. maintain close ties with the media, community leaders, government officials and other corporate stakeholders.
    d. develop an effective sales presentation format.

14. Gary Fordham works for a major firm, writing news releases about new products the company intends to introduce. He has just finished writing an article about their latest innovation, and has released this to his contacts at the major newspapers across the company, hoping they will carry the story in their business sections. Gary is working in the area of:
    a. sales promotion.
    b. institutional advertising.
    c. publicity.
    d. blogging.

15. When Mary Lynn went to the grocery store last week, she took with her several coupons she had received in the mail that week. While at the store, Mary Lynn was offered samples of several food items and she actually bought a few of those, using the in-store coupons. She also bought a particular brand of toothpaste, because the tube came with a free toothbrush. Mary Lynn is taking advantage of:
    a. viral marketing.
    b. sales promotion.
    c. advertising.
    d. publicity.

16. Which of the following is most accurate regarding sales promotion efforts?
    a. Sales promotion efforts are aimed first at employees, then dealers, then at the end consumer.
    b. Sales promotion is generally aimed only at the final consumer.
    c. Sales promotion programs are designed to take the place other, more expensive promotion efforts.
    d. Sales promotion efforts are designed to create long-term relationships.

17. One of the best ways to reduce negative word of mouth is to:
    a. mount an aggressive publicity campaign to refute any bad events surrounding your product.
    b. take care of consumer complaints quickly and effectively.
    c. run continuous positive advertising campaigns.
    d. motivate your sales force and give them information to overcome bad publicity.

18. Viral marketing is
    a. An Internet based form of notification of a potential computer virus.
    b. A term used to describe promotional efforts such as paying people to say positive things about your product on the Internet.
    c. A system in which consumer can access company information on their own and supply information about themselves in an ongoing dialogue.
    d. A function that evaluates public attitudes and executes a program of action and information to earn public understanding.

19. Podcasting refers to:
    a. a means of distributing audio and video programs via the Internet that lets users subscribe to a number of files and then hear or view the material at the time they choose.
    b. an online diary that looks like a web page.
    c. a promotional tool that involves people telling other people about products they have purchased.
    d. putting products into television shows and movies where they will be seen.

20. The city of San Antonio has made an effort to develop promotional materials for travel agents and bus tour companies that are within a 300-mile radius of the city. City officials are hopeful that these efforts will encourage tourism in the area when agents suggest the city to their clients. San Antonio is making use of a:
    a. push strategy.
    b. pull strategy.
    c. segmentation strategy.
    d. targeting strategy.

TRUE–FALSE

Learning Goal 1

1. _____ Integrated marketing communication combines all the promotional tools into a comprehensive and unified promotional strategy.

2. _____ Promotion techniques are only used by profit making organizations.

Learning Goal 2

3. _____ One of the benefits of Internet advertising is that marketers can reach the people they most want to reach, which are consumers researching products in which they are interested.

4. _____ In global advertising, the evidence supports the theory that promotional strategies should be implemented worldwide with few changes for a consistent message.

5. _____ The current trend in promotion is to build relationships with customers over time.

Learning Goal 3

6. _____ The follow up step in personal selling is the least important.

7. _____ The objective during an initial sales call is to make a sale, or get a commitment to a sale.

8. _____ Selling is a process of establishing relationships, not just selling goods and services.

Learning Goal 4

9. _____ One of the advantages of publicity is that the company has control over how the media will use the story.

10. _____ An important step in the development of a good public relations program is to inform your customers that you have been responsive to their needs.

Learning Goal 5

11. _____ Sales promotion can be used as an attempt to keep salespeople enthusiastic about the company and the product.

12. _____ Event marketing means sponsoring events such as rock concerts or being at various events to promote your products.

Learning Goal 6

13. _____ Viral marketing includes paying customers to say positive things on the Internet, including using Twitter or setting up multilevel selling schemes.

14. _____ When using a pull strategy, advertising and sales promotion efforts are directed at consumers.

15. _____ When designing a promotion mix, one should keep in mind that large groups of consumers are usually most efficiently reached through advertising.

16. _____ The term pick economy refers to those consumers who pick out their products from online outlets or who do online comparison shopping.

You Can Find It On the Net

You can visit virtually any web site to observe how companies implement the techniques we have discussed in this chapter. Here are a few suggestions.
Visit www.gap.com

Do they attempt to create a dialogue with the customer? How?

How do they attempt to develop a relationship with you, the customer?

Visit www.cduniverse.com

What sales promotion techniques does cduniverse now use?

How does cduniverse make their website "user friendly"?

How does cduniverse promote to their buyers, or create a dialogue with their users?

Track the sites you visit over a few days. Can you remember the advertising you saw?

Think back to the ads you may have seen while visiting various Internet sites. How many do you remember? What products were they selling? How effective do you think Internet advertising is?

ANSWERS

LEARNING THE LANGUAGE

1. Sales promotion	9. Prospecting	16. Pick economy
2. Advertising	10. Integrated marketing communication (IMC)	17. Product placement
3. Public relations (PR)	11. Blog	18. Interactive promotion
4. Pull strategy	12. Publicity	19. Viral marketing
5. Trial close	13. Push strategy	20. Prospect
6. Promotion mix	14. Infomercial	21. Sampling
7. Word-of-mouth promotion	15. Personal selling	22. Podcasting
8. Qualifying		

ASSESSMENT CHECK

Learning Goal 1

Promotion and the Promotion Mix

1. The tools of the promotion mix are:
   a. Personal selling
   b. Advertising
   c. Sales promotion
   d. Public relations

2. The idea of integrated marketing communication is to use all the promotional tools and company resources to create a positive brand image and to meet the strategic marketing and promotional goals of the firm.

3. The steps in a typical promotion campaign include:
   a. Identify a target market
   b. Define the objectives for each element
   c. Determine a budget
   d. Develop a unifying message
   e. Implement the plan
   f. Evaluate effectiveness

Learning Goal 2

Advertising: Informing, Persuading, and Reminding

4. The various categories of advertising are:
   a. Retail advertising
   b. Trade advertising
   c. Business-to-business advertising
   d. Institutional advertising
   e. Product advertising
   f. Advocacy advertising
   g. Comparison advertising
   h. Interactive advertising
   i. Online advertising

5. The public benefits from advertising because:
   a. ads are informative.
   b. it provides us with free TV and radio because advertisers pay for the production costs.
   c. advertising also covers the major costs of producing newspapers and magazines.

6. The advantages and disadvantages of each form of advertising media are:

		Advantages	Disadvantages
a.	Newspapers	Good local coverage ads placed quickly high acceptance; ad can be clipped and saved	Ads compete with other features; poor color; ads get thrown away
b.	Television	Sight, sound, motion reaches all audiences; high attention with no competition	High cost; short exposure time; takes time to prepare ads
c.	Radio	Low cost; can target specific audiences; flexible; good for local marketing	People may not listen; short exposure time; audience can't keep ad
d.	Magazines	Target specific audiences; good use of color; long life ad can be clipped and saved	Inflexible; ads must be placed weeks before publication; cost is relatively high
e.	Outdoor	High visibility and repeat exposures; low cost; local market focus	Limited message, low selectivity of audience
f.	Direct mail	Best for targeting specific markets; very flexible; ad can be saved	High cost; consumer rejection as junk mail; must conform to postal regulations
g.	Yellow pages	Great coverage of local markets; widely used by consumers; available at point of purchase	Competition with other ads; cost may be too high for very small businesses
h.	Internet	Inexpensive global coverage; available at any time; interactive	Relatively low readership
i.	Mobile ad	Great reach among younger shoppers	Easy to ignore, avoid

7. The newest form of product placement is to put virtual products into video games.

8. Infomercials allow the seller to show the product in detail, which helps the product to sell itself. They allow for testimonials and for showing the customer how the product actually works, and allow for the use of drama, demonstration, graphics, and other advertising tools.

9. When marketers advertise on sites such as Yahoo they can reach the people they most want to reach. The goal is to get customers and potential customers to a Web site where they can learn more about the company and its products. When customers go to the web site, the company can provide information and interact with the customer, so Internet advertising becomes a means to bring customers and companies together.

   Online advertising also enables advertisers to see how many people have clicked on a commercial and how much of it each potential customer has read or watched.

10. Through online videos, chat rooms, and other services, companies are "promoting to" to "working with" customers. Marketers want to build relationships with customers over time. That means carefully listening to what consumers want, tracking their purchases, providing them with better service, and giving them access to more information.

11. The two approaches to advertising in the global market are:
    a. to develop a promotional strategy that can be implemented worldwide
    b. to design promotions that are targeted at specific countries and or regions

12. Globalism is the idea of producing one ad for everyone in the world, and regionalism is to develop specific ads for each country and /or for specific groups within a country.

Learning Goal 3

Personal Selling: Providing Personal Attention

13. Effective selling is a matter of helping others to satisfy their wants and needs. Sales people can use the Internet, portable computers, pagers, and other technology to help customers search the Internet, design custom-made products, look over prices, and generally do everything it takes to complete the order.

14. The steps in the personal selling process are:
    a. Prospect and qualify
    b. Preapproach
    c. Approach
    d. Make presentation
    e. Answer objections
    f. Close sale
    g. Follow-up

15. Prospecting involves researching potential buyers and choosing those most likely to buy. To qualify people means to make sure that they have a need for the product, the authority to buy, and the willingness to listen to a sales message. People who meet these criteria are called prospects.

16. Sales people find prospects at trade shows, the company website, and people at companies who were recommended to you by others who use your company's product.

17. Before making a sales call, the sales representative must do further research, which is done during the preapproach. As much as possible should be learned about customer's wants and needs. All that information should be stored in a database.

18. The objective of an initial sales call is to give an impression of professionalism, create rapport, build credibility, and to start a relationship.

19. During the sales presentation, the idea is for the sales representative to match the benefits of his or her value package to the client's needs. The presentation can be tailored to the customer's needs.

20. A sales person must anticipate objections the prospect may raise and determine proper responses. Think of questions as opportunities for creating better relationships. You are there to resolve the doubts the customer has.

21. Closing techniques include a trial close, which helps finalize the sales. The final step is asking for the order and showing the client where to sign.

22. The follow-up includes:
    a. handling customer complaints
    b. making sure that the customer's questions are answered
    c. supplying what the customer wants.

23. The goals of a salesperson are to:
    a. help the buyer buy
    b. make sure the buyer is satisfied after the sale.

24. In both B2B and B2C sales, knowing the product comes first. However, in retail sales the salesperson does not have to do much prospecting or qualifying. Also, retail salespeople don't usually have to go through a preapproach step.

    The first formal step in the B2C sales process then is the approach. The idea is to show the customer that you are there to help and that you are friendly, and knowledgeable. You also need to discover what the customer wants.

25. During the presentation in the B2C selling process you show customers how the products you have meet their needs. You answer questions that help the customer choose the right product for them.

26. During the trial close in B2C selling a trial close is important, but the sales person must know the difference between being helpful and being pushy. Often a customer needs to spend some time thinking about the purchase.

27. After- sale follow-up is an important but often neglected step in B2C sales. If the product is supposed to be delivered, the salesperson should follow up to be sure it is delivered on time. The same is true if the product has to be installed.

Learning Goal 4

Public Relations: Building Relationships

28. The three steps in creating a good public relations campaign are:
    a. Listen to the public
    b. Change policies and procedures
    c. Inform people that you're being responsive to their needs

29. A public relations department maintains close ties with the media, community leaders, government officials, and other corporate stakeholders.

30. The advantages of publicity over other promotional tools are:
    a. stories are published for free.
    b. it may reach people who would not read an advertisement.
    c. it's more believable than advertising.

31. Three disadvantages of publicity are:
    a. The company has no control over how or when the media will use the story.
    b. The story may be altered, and could end up not as positive as the original.
    c. Once a story has run, it won't be repeated.

32. One way to see that publicity is handled well by the media is to establish a friendly relationship with media representatives, being open with them when they seek information.

Learning Goal 5

Sales Promotion: Giving Buyers Incentives

33. Five types of B2B sales promotion are:
    a. Trade shows
    b. Portfolios for salespeople
    c. Deals (price reductions)
    d. Catalogs
    e. Conventions

34. The various consumer sales promotion techniques are:
    a. Coupons
    b. Cents-off promotions
    c. Sampling
    d. Premiums
    e. Sweepstakes
    f. Contests
    g. Bonuses (Buy one, get one free)
    h. Catalogs
    i. Demonstrations
    j. Special events
    k. Lotteries
    l. In-store displays

35. Sales promotion programs are designed to supplement the other promotion mix variables by creating enthusiasm for the overall promotional program.

36. The most important internal sales promotion efforts are directed at salespeople and other customer-contact people.

37. Internal sales promotion efforts include:
    a. sales training
    b. development of sales aids like flip charts, audiovisual displays and videotapes
    c. participation in trade shows where sales people can get leads

38. A virtual trade show is a trade show on the Internet. This allows customers to see many products without leaving the office, and the information is available 24 hours a day.

39. Sampling is a quick effective way of demonstrating a product's superiority at the time when consumers are making a purchase decision.

Learning Goal 6

Word of Mouth and Other Promotional Tools

40. Additional forms of promotion include:
    a. word of mouth
    b. viral marketing
    c. blogging
    d. Podcasting
    e. E-mail promotions
    f. Mobile media

41. Any activity that encourages people to talk favorably about an organization could be word of mouth promotion.

42. Companies have begun to create word of mouth by paying people to go into Internet chat rooms and talk favorably about various products and services. The term for this and other forms of Internet word of mouth promotion is <u>viral marketing</u>. Companies are creating word of mouth through sending testimonials, and paying commissions for sending people to specific Web sites.

43. One of the best ways to reduce the effects of negative word of mouth is to take care of consumer complaints quickly and effectively.

44. Podcasting allows you to become your own newscaster, and gives broadcast radio and television programs a new distribution method.

45. With mobile media marketers make use of the cell phone, using text messaging to promote sweepstakes, send customers news or sports alters, and give them company information.

46. The best way for reaching large groups of consumers with similar traits is advertising.

    The best way to sell to large organizations is personal selling.

    To motivate people to buy now rather than later marketers use sales promotion, like sampling, coupons, discounts, special displays, and premiums.

    The most powerful tool is often word of mouth.

47. The idea of a push strategy is to push the product through the distribution system to the stores.

48. In a pull strategy, heavy advertising and sales promotion efforts are directed toward consumers so they'll request the products from retailers. If it works, consumers will go to the store and order the products. Seeing demand, the storeowner will then order them from the wholesaler. The wholesaler in turn will order from the producer. The idea is to pull products down through the distribution system.

49. A total systems approach to marketing is when promotion is a part of supply chain management. In such cases retailers would work with producers and distributors to make the supply chain as efficient as possible. Then a promotional plan would be developed for the whole system. The idea would be to develop a value package that would appeal to everyone.

CRITICAL THINKING EXERCISES

Learning Goal 1

1. a. The first step in developing a promotion campaign is to <u>identify a target market</u>. We have discussed several possibilities in previous chapters: specifically the automotive manufacturers and the after market, which could consist of windshield installation and repair companies.

    b. The second step is to <u>define the objectives for each element of the marketing mix</u>. The overall goal will be to create awareness of the product, and to inform both the target market, the automotive industry, and ultimate consumers. The company may depend on consumers to go to the dealers to ask for the product. Here are some examples.

    Personal selling — this form of promotion will be an important tool, because this product will require that some detailed information be provided to the buyer. This will be focused on the main target market — the automotive industry.

    Advertising — This may be important for the consumer market to create awareness and to inform them of the benefits. Since there are no competitors at this point, Sun-2-Shade will not have to focus on brand awareness quite yet. The company could also create awareness by using product placement in movies, to illustrate the product's qualities. How about James Bond?

    Public relations — The company can make use of public relations to enhance the goal of creating awareness. The company could sponsor any number of activities designed to introduce automakers to the product.

    Sales promotion — This form of promotion may be more important to focus on later in the promotion campaign. But for right now, again to create awareness, Sun-2-Shade could give away sunglasses which use the technology the company is using for the windshields, along with information indicating that with their product, there is no need to take sunglasses on and off all the time.

    We may also want to consider forms of promotion that are outside the traditional methods, such as email, mobile promotions, social networking pages such as Facebook, podcasting and others.

    c. The third step is to <u>determine a promotional budget</u>. This will determine how much can be spent on each method of promotion. The amount we can spend on promotion will depend on how much revenue we have, or anticipate that we will have, generated.

    d. The fourth step is to <u>develop a unifying message.</u> The message in the campaign could be one of luxury and convenience, along with other benefits you may have identified.

    e. The fifth step, <u>implement the plan,</u> will coordinate all the elements of the promotion effort. This means making sure that all of our promotional efforts will send the same message.

    f. Lastly, <u>evaluate effectiveness</u> is to measure the results, which depends upon clearly written objectives.

Learning Goal 2

2. a. Radio
    b. Newspaper, radio
    c. Magazines, Internet sites aimed at women Product placement
    d. Outdoor, local TV, radio
    e. Mobile marketing, product placement, email ads
    f. Direct mail, TV
    g. Magazines
    h. Newspaper, direct mail, Web site

3. The Internet is changing organizations' approach to customers, creating an environment in which a company will work with, rather than promote to, their customers. Sun-2-Shade will need to create a relationship with customers by listening to what they want in terms of product and service, and giving them access to information. This will require a web site to be interactive so customers can talk to the company, and even to each other, ask questions and get as much information as possible. Links to the auto manufacturers that offer our product could be incorporated as well.

Learning Goal 3

4. A sales presentation for Sun-2-Shade will have to begin with prospecting. Which carmakers are you going to target? Are you going to go after just one carmaker, or several? Initially, you will probably be wise to begin with just one. The question then becomes which maker to go after. After research, you may be able to make that decision more easily.

Then, the preapproach will call for learning as much as possible about the products your customer sells. Which models will be the best suited for Sun-2-Shade? What's the production volume on those models? What's the competition doing? How could Sun-2-Shade benefit your customer?

Making the approach will involve making an appointment with the <u>right person</u>, the decision-maker. You will need to look professional, and have a prototype of the product with you; in other words, drive one of their car models equipped with your windshield to the sales call. Come prepared with questions geared to help you find out what they may be looking for.

During the presentation, you will have to show the carmaker how Sun-2-Shade will make their cars better than the competition. You could discuss the benefits of convenience, luxury, having something the competition doesn't have. You could come prepared with visuals demonstrating how Sun-2-Shade works on any model. This can be done with a computer graphics program, or with Power Point presentations.

You will also want to know something about who your customer's customers are, in order to be able to demonstrate how Sun-2-Shade will appeal to them. Objections will have to be overcome by showing how easily Sun-2-Shade works with their cars, again by driving a car (one of their models of course) with Sun-2-Shade installed, and taking the customer for a ride to demonstrate the Sun-2-Shade luxury.

Eventually you will have to close the sale, by asking to make Sun-2-Shade an available option, or asking your customer to put Sun-2-Shade in some of their cars. Finally, always be available for questions, "hand-holding," and problems that may arise. Keep in mind that this process will take a lot of time, and won't be accomplished in one sales call.

5. It sounds like the station really wanted to know what people thought of their programming, and what people wanted in a news program. The first step of a good public relations program is to do research to evaluate public attitudes, which is exactly what the station did, by researching the market before the premier, and by publishing the station's phone numbers and encouraging viewers to call. The station also seems to have responded by avoiding, as much as possible, the "bad news" stories as lead ins, which is in the public interest, especially as the broadcast is at 9:00 p.m. when it is possible that older children could be watching. They also seem to have avoided the scandalous stories upon which many TV news programs seem to have thrived. This is also illustrated by the fact that they tell the viewers exactly when a news story will air, allowing viewers to change the channel if children are likely to be watching a story that parents don't want them to see, for example. Lastly, during the broadcast and in their advertising they are mentioning the specific ways in which they have responded to viewer requests, which is the third step in a good public relations program.

Learning Goal 5

6. Suggested answers:

Group	Technique
a. Salespeople	Sales training, conventions, trade shows
b. Dealers	Catalogues, trade shows , "deals"
c. Customers	Coupons, sweepstakes, displays, samples

7. Sales promotion is the tool that stimulates interest by means of short-term activities. Sales promotion can take place both internally and externally. The most important internal sales promotion efforts are directed at sales people, and other customer contact people.

For sales people: The sales force needs to be fully informed about the process used to make these windshields. This will help in overcoming any objectives the customers will have. To aid in the presentations to the automakers, it will be extremely important to have product samples, even a car with the windshield installed, as mentioned earlier. The sales force could allow a company decision maker to drive the car for 24 hours to demonstrate how well the process works.

Dealers/Intermediaries: The intermediaries that are important to win over in this case are car dealerships. They will be an extremely important group because they will basically serve as the sales force to the ultimate consumer. They can reach dealers at trade shows, but it will be vital also for Sun-2-Shade to have an interactive website for car dealers to visit. Sun-2-Shade could sponsor contests for dealers. For example, if a dealer sells a certain number of cars with the windshield installed, the dealer wins a prize like a trip to the Caribbean. Each dealership sales person would also be eligible to win cash prizes, for example, if they sell a certain number of cars with the windshield.

Consumers: The goal is to make the ultimate consumer aware of this product, both in terms of what its benefits are, and what car models can be equipped with it. If they go to a dealership that has ordered cars with the windshield installed, they will be able to "sample" the product. But how do we make them aware enough to ask to see the windshield in the first place? For one thing, Sun-2-Shade must be installed in cars that are shown at consumer tradeshows, the annual auto shows held in major cities each year. Demonstrations at car shows and in the dealership will be important. Advertising will drive this effort so the customer is aware of the product in the first place. Some time later, Sun-2-Shade could offer a coupon for 50% off an after market installation of a windshield when the customer buys an installed windshield.

8. <u>Product</u> – A good product will generate positive word of mouth because customers will be happy with the product and pass the word along.

    <u>Sales promotion</u> – Techniques such as special events and contests often create positive word of mouth promotion

    <u>Advertising</u> – When an advertisement is easily remembered or funny it will often create positive word of mouth. A good technique is to advertise to people who already use your product.

    <u>Publicity</u> – A news story can create word of mouth by stimulating the public's interest in the product.

    <u>Personal selling</u> – A good sales person can help the customer to develop a positive image of the product, thus creating positive word of mouth.

Learning Goals 1-6

9. Your response to this question will really depend upon whom you have selected as you primary target market. Assuming you have decided to go after the automotive manufacturers as your primary market, then most likely your promotion mix will include lots of personal selling, some advertising in the form of brochures, perhaps, aimed at the car dealerships who will be selling the cars with your product installed. It should also include a well-designed web site, with interactive features. If your research has been done, and a need for this kind of product has been established, you could design a public relations campaign <u>for the auto manufacturer,</u> indicating that the company listened to your need for a product like Sun-2-Shade, then made the product in response.

    However, reaching the consumer will also be important, as you want the customer to be familiar with your product, and to ask for the product at the dealership. As mentioned earlier, you should have your own web site, with attractive graphics and interactive sales techniques. You may be able to advertise on-line, on Web sites that appeal to an affluent market, for example, which may be more likely to purchase your product for their car. You may also consider direct marketing, such as order forms in upscale magazines.

    An important part of your advertising strategy may be to place your product on cars that are shown in feature movies. With this kind of promotion, the customer will see the product "in action".

    By sponsoring strategically selected newscasts, podcasting may work to expose consumers to your product who may then go to their dealer and request your product. You could use viral marketing by finding current customers and paying them to go into automotive chat rooms to make positive remarks about Sun-2-Shade's products. These same consumers could be involved in creating their own blog and talking about the benefits they have gained by using your product.

    Most likely you will use a combination of a push and pull strategy for the product. You will be using primarily a push strategy if you are aiming primarily at the automotive manufacturers. A combination will be most effective if you are aiming at the consumer market. Probably the best approach, once you are an established company, will be to work with your customers, retailers and develop a value package that will appeal to everyone, the manufacturers, retailers and consumers.

PRACTICE TEST

MULTIPLE CHOICE

1. b
2. d
3. c
4. a
5. a
6. d
7. b
8. c
9. c
10. a
11. a
12. a
13. c
14. c
15. b
16. a
17. b
18. b
19. a
20. b

TRUE–FALSE

1. T
2. F
3. T
4. F
5. T
6. F
7. F
8. T
9. F
10. T
11. T
12. T
13. T
14. T
15. F
16. T

CHAPTER 17 – UNDERSTANDING ACCOUNTING
AND FINANCIAL INFORMATION

LEARNING GOALS

After you have read and studied this chapter, you should be able to:

1. Demonstrate the role of financial information and accounting plays for a business and for its stakeholders.
2. Identify the different disciplines within the accounting profession.
3. List the steps in the accounting cycle, distinguish between accounting and bookkeeping. and explain how computers are used in accounting.
4. Explain how the major financial statements differ.
5. Demonstrate the application of ratio analysis in reporting financial information.

LEARNING THE LANGUAGE

Listed below are important terms found in the chapter. Choose the correct term for the definition and write it in the space provided.

Accounting	Depreciation	Liquidity
Accounting cycle	Double-entry bookkeeping	Managerial accounting
Accounts payable	Financial accounting	Net income or net loss
Annual report	Financial statement	Notes payable
Assets	Fixed assets	Operating expenses
Auditing	Fundamental accounting equation	Owner's equity
Balance sheet	Government and not-for-profit accounting	Private accountant
Bonds payable	Gross profit (gross margin)	Public accountant
Bookkeeping	Income statement	Ratio analysis
Cash flow	Independent audit	Retained earnings
Certified internal auditor (CIA)	Intangible assets	Revenue
Certified management accountant (CMA)	Journal	Statement of cash flows
Certified public accountant (CPA)	Ledger	Tax accountant
Cost of goods sold (cost of goods manufactured)	Liabilities	Trial balance
Current assets		

1. A yearly statement called the _____ states the financial condition, progress, and expectations of an organization.

2. A company's _____ is the difference between cash coming in and cash going out of a business.

3. Items known as _____ can or will be converted into cash within one year.

4. An accounting system called _____ is used for organizations whose purpose is not generating a profit but serving ratepayers, taxpayers, and others according to a duly approved budget.

5. Assets that are relatively permanent, or _____ include items such as land, buildings and equipment.

6. A_____ is the record book or computer programwhere accounting data are first entered.

7. Long term liabilities that represent money lent to the firm that must be paid back are _____.

8. The amount of the business that belongs to the owners minus any liabilities owed by the business is the formula for _____.

9. A _____ is a summary of all the data in the account ledgers to show whether the figures are correct and balanced.

10. An accountant known as a(n) _____ is trained in tax law and is responsible for preparing tax returns or developing tax strategies.

11. The ease with which an asset can be converted into cash is its _____.

12. A(n) _____ is an evaluation and unbiased opinion about the accuracy of a company 's financial statements.

13. Accounting used to provide information and analyses to managers inside the organization to assist them in decision-making is called _____.

14. A concept called _____ is a system of writing every business transaction in two places.

15. An accountant called a _____ passes a series of examinations established by the American Institute of Certified Public Accountants

16. The economic resources, or things of value, owned by the firm are called _____.

17. _____ are current liabilities or bills the company owes to others for merchandise or services purchased on credit but not yet paid for.

18. A firm's _____ is how much the firm earned by buying, or making, and selling merchandise.

19. Accounting information and analyses prepared for people outside the organization is _____.

20. _____ is revenue left over after all costs and expenses, including taxes, are paid.

21. The financial statement called a _____ reports the financial condition of a firm at a specific time and is composed of three major accounts: assets, liabilities and owner's equity.

22. An accountant who works for a single firm, government agency, or nonprofit organization is called a(n) _____ ,

23. The recording, classifying, summarizing and interpreting of financial events and transactions, called _____ provides management and other interested parties the information they need to make good decisions.

24. A company's _____ is the value of what is received from goods sold, services rendered and other financial sources.

25. The job of reviewing and evaluating the records used to prepare the company's financial statements is called _____.

26. A _____ is the summary of all transactions that have occurred over a particular period.

27. The six-step procedure called the _____ results in the preparation and analysis of the major financial statements.

28. A type of expense called the _____ is a measure of the cost of merchandise sold or cost of raw materials and supplies used for producing items for resale.

29. A _____ is one who provides accounting services to individuals or businesses on a fee basis.

30. Accounts known as _____ indicate what the business owes to others (debts).

31. A specialized accounting book known as a _____ is one in which information from accounting journals is accumulated into specific categories and posted so managers can find all the information about one account in the same place.

32. A _____ is a professional accountant who has met certain educational and experience requirements, passed a qualifying exam in the field, and been certified by the Institute of Certified Management Accountants.

33. The recording of business transactions is called _____

34. The _____ shows a firm's profit after costs, expenses and taxes; it summarizes all of the resources that have come into the firm, all the resources that have left the firm and the resulting net income.

35. _____ is the systematic write-off of the cost of a tangible asset over its estimated useful life.

36. Long-term assets that are relatively permanent are known as _____ and include patents, and copyrights that have no real physical form but do have value.

37. The financial statement called a _____ reports cash receipts and disbursements related to a firm's three major activities: operations, investment, and financing.

38. A _____ is an accountant who has a bachelor's degree 2 years of internal auditing experience, and has passed an exam administered by the Institute of Internal Auditors.

39. Assets equal liabilities plus owner's equity is the _____ and is the basis for the balance sheet.

40. Costs involved in operating a business, such as rent, utilities, and salaries are called _____.

41. The assessment of a firm's financial condition and performance, or _____ is done through calculations and interpretations of financial ratios developed from the firm's financial statements.

42. The accumulated earnings from a firm's profitable operations that were kept in the business and not paid out to stockholders in dividends are _____.

43. Short-term or long-term liabilities, or _____ , are those that a business promises to repay by a certain date.

ASSESSMENT CHECK

Learning Goal 1

The Role of Accounting Information

1. Why is it important to know something about accounting?

2. Financial transactions include:

    a. _____

    b. _____

    c. _____

    d. _____

3. What are two purposes of accounting?

    a. _____

    b. _____

4. Who are the users of accounting information?

    a. _____

    b. _____

    c. _____

    d. _____

Accounting Disciplines

5. List the five key working areas of accounting.

   a. _____

   b. _____

   c. _____

   d. _____

   e. _____

6. Identify the areas with which managerial accounting is concerned.

   a. _____

   b. _____

   c. _____

   d. _____

   e. _____

7. How does financial accounting differ from managerial accounting?

8. Answers to financial questions such as profitability, and about debt and liabilities are answered in the company's _____

9. What are some accounting services public accountants may provide for their clients ?

   a. _____

   b. _____

   c. _____

10. What does it indicate when financial reports are prepared in accordance with GAAP?

11. Describe the Sarbanes-Oxley Act.

12. Internal audits are conducted to guarantee_____

_____

13. A Tax accountant is responsible for:

a. _____

b. _____

14. Who are the primary users of government and not-for-profit accounting information? What do the users of this information want to ensure?

Learning Goal 3

The Accounting Cycle

15. How do accountants differ from bookkeepers?

16. List the six steps in the accounting cycle

a. _____

b. _____

c. _____

d. _____

e. _____

f. _____

17. What is the benefit of double-entry bookkeeping?

18. What is the difference between a journal and a ledger?

19. How have computers helped in the accounting process?

a. _____

b. _____

c. _____

d. _____

e. _____

Learning Goal 4

Understanding Key Financial Statements

20. Describe the three key financial statements

a. _____

b. _____

c. _____

21. The difference between the financial statements can be summarized this way:

22. The fundamental accounting equation is:

_____ = _____ + _____

23. How do you calculate your net worth, or equity?

24. Assets include _____

_____

25. Describe "goodwill" as an asset.

26. In what order are assets listed on a balance sheet?

27. Describe the three categories of assets on a balance sheet.

   a. _____

   b. _____

   c. _____

28. What is the difference between current liabilities and long-term liabilities?

29. Describe:

   a. Accounts payable:

   b. Notes payable

   c. Bonds payable

30. How is "equity" calculated? What is shareholder's equity?

31. What is a capital account?

32. An income statement

   a. summarizes: _____

   _____

   b. reports the firm's operations over _____

   _____

33. What is the formula for developing an income statement, according to GAAP?

34. What is the difference between:

   a. revenue and sales?

   b. between gross sales and net sales?

35. Costs that make up cost of goods sold include:

36. How does gross margin differ between a service firm and a manufacturing firm?

37. Describe the two categories of operating expenses.

38. What is the "bottom line"?

39. Describe the three major activities for which cash receipts and disbursements are reported on a statement of cash flows.

   a. _____

   b. _____

   c. _____

40. What questions may be answered by a statement of cash flows?

   a. _____

   b. _____

   c. _____

   d. _____

41. How would you describe a poor, or negative, cash flow?

42. How do cash flow problems start?

Analyzing Financial Performance using Ratios

43. Financial ratios provide key insights into how a firm compares to other firms in the same industry in what key areas?

    a. _____   c. _____

    b. _____   d. _____

44. What do liquidity ratios measure?

45. Two key liquidity ratios are:

    a. _____

    b. _____

46. The formula for the current ratio is as follows:

47. The current ratio is compared to:

    a. _____

    b. _____

48. The formula for the acid test ratio is:

49. To what kinds of firms is the acid test ratio important?

50. What do leverage ratios measure?

51. What is the formula for the debt to equity ratio, and what does it measure?

52. What does it mean if a firm has a debt to equity ratio above 100%?

53. What do profitability ratios measure?

54. What are three profitability ratios?

   a. _____

   b. _____

   c. _____

55. What is the difference between Basic EPS and diluted EPS?

56. What is the formula for determining Basic Earnings Per Share?

57. What is the formula for return on sales and for what do firms use this ratio?

58. What is the formula for return on equity? What does it measure?

59. What do activity ratios measure?

60. What is the formula for inventory turnover? What does it measure?

61. What is meant by inventory turnover ratios that are:

   a. lower than average?

   b. higher than average?

CRITICAL THINKING EXERCISES

Learning Goals 1,2

1. Match the following terms with the descriptions below. Some of these terms are describing general areas of accounting, others are similar but more specific, so use your text to help you to differentiate the terms!

    Annual report
    Auditing
    Certified internal auditor
    Certified management accountant (CMA)
    Certified public accountant (CPA)
    Financial accounting

    Tax accountant
    Independent audit
    Managerial accounting
    Private accountant
    Public accountant

    a. _____ Markus Larsen works for a mid-sized, publicly held company. He is responsible for the preparation and analysis of financial information for people and organizations outside the firm.

    b. _____ Jim Hopson has his own small accounting firm. He provides business assistance to his clients in a number of ways. Most recently he helped a small business by designing an accounting system for the firm, and helped them select the correct software to use to get them started.

    c. _____ Bob Glenn is majoring in accounting, but plans to specialize in this area, as he enjoys preparing budgets and checking to determine if costs for departments are within the budget. Bob also feels that with growing emphasis on global competition, outsourcing, and organizational cost cutting the job market for this area of accounting may be very strong.

    d. _____ Harry Winston prepares tax returns for his company, and develops strategies to minimize the company's tax burden.

    e. _____ Nancy Hoffman works for Monsanto on a full time basis to help the company keep accurate financial information.

    f. _____ Hector Perez's job is to guarantee that proper accounting procedures and financial reporting are being carried on within the company. For this job Hector not only examines the financial health of a company but looks into organizational efficiencies and effectiveness.

    g. _____ Kimberly Chung recently passed a series of examinations to meet the state's requirement for education and experience, and she can now work as a private or public accountant in this type of position in accounting.

    h. _____ Irena Manovich is involved with this type of accounting, which is concerned with measuring and reporting costs of production, marketing and other functions, preparing budgets, checking to see that units are staying within budgets and designing strategies to minimize taxes.

i. _____ In his job as a public accountant for a major accounting firm, Ryan Deiker performs this job, which is to determine if a firm has prepared its financial statements according to accepted accounting principles.

j. _____ As a stockholder in Microsoft, Gary Ford receives this document each year. Gary has noticed that more information is going into this yearly report, as pressure builds from stakeholders.

k. _____ Because internal financial controls are very important for firms, Eric Minette, who is a private accountant, ensures that proper accounting procedures and financial reporting are being carried out within the company for which he works.

Learning Goal 3

2. Sun-2-Shade is a new company that manufactures self-darkening windshields for automobiles. The company is doing very well! They need a bookkeeper to help them with their paperwork, and an accountant. You have been given the task of writing a brief job description for each job. How would you write the job description for each?

Bookkeeper –

Accountant –

3. The Accounting Cycle is as follows:

1) analyze documents
2) record transactions in journals
3) post to ledgers
4) trial balance
5) prepare financial statements
6) analyze financial statements

Identify which of the following activity is being described in each statement.

a. _____ Joan Perez has finished analyzing and categorizing original documents, and is getting ready for the next step in the accounting cycle, which will be this activity.

b. _____ Joan is summarizing all the data, to check that all the information is correct

c. _____ The accountant for Joan's company is getting ready to evaluate the financial condition of the firm from the financial statements.

d. _____ Joan is just beginning the bookkeeping process, and is in the process of dividing the firms transactions onto categories such as sales documents, purchasing receipts and shipping documents.

e. _____ While Joan has prepared the journals, this step is often done by computer.

f. _____ Once the summary statements show that all the information is correct, then the accountant will do this, in accordance with generally accepted accounting principals, so that she can analyze them.

Learning Goal 4

4. a. Two key financial statements are the <u>balance sheet</u> and the <u>income statement.</u>
Indicate whether each of the following accounts would be found on a balance sheet or an income statement.

1.	_____ Cash	11.	_____ Notes payable
2.	_____ Retained earnings	12.	_____ Accounts receivable
3.	_____ Accounts payable	13.	_____ Equipment
4.	_____ Interest expense	14.	_____ Advertising expense
5.	_____ Rent expense	15.	_____ Wages expense
6.	_____ Property	16.	_____ Supplies expense
7.	_____ Commission revenue	17.	_____ Utilities expense
8.	_____ Gross sales	18.	_____ Cost of goods sold
9.	_____ Common stock	19.	_____ Inventories
10.	_____ Supplies expense	20.	_____ Gross Profit

b. Identify the current assets and list them in order of their liquidity.

1. _____

2. _____

3. _____

5. The balance sheet reports the financial condition of a firm at a specific time. The basic formula for a balance sheet is:

Assets = Liabilities + Owner's Equity

Total assets consist of current, fixed and intangible assets

Total liabilities consist of current and long-term liabilities

Owner's Equity consists of various types of stock and retained earnings

Using the following list of accounts, construct an accurate balance sheet for Sun-2-Shade, Inc.

BE CAREFUL! Not all of the accounts listed will be used for the balance sheet.

SUN-2-SHADE, INC.
List of accounts

Accounts payable	$25,000	Utilities	$12,000
Net sales	$600,000	Supplies	$3700
Accounts receivable	$110,000	Investments	$45,000
Depreciation expense	$4000	Rent	$35,000
Inventories	$62,000		
Advertising	$28,000		
Wages and salaries	$125,000		
Notes payable (current)	$15,000		
Rental revenue	$3000		
Cost of goods sold	$313,000		
Property, plant, equipment	$200,000		
Cash	$18,000		
Retained earnings	$165,000		
Accrued taxes	$40,000		
Long-term debt	$60,000		
Common stock	$130,000		

SUN-2-SHADE, INC.
BALANCE SHEET
Year ending December 31, 20___

6. The income statement reports all the revenues and expenses of a firm for a specific period of time. The basic formula for an income statement is:

Revenue – Cost of goods sold = Gross profit (gross margin)
Gross profit – operating expenses = Net income (loss) before taxes
Net income before taxes – taxes = Net income (loss)

Using the previous list of accounts construct an accurate income statement for Sun-2-Shade. For purposes of illustration, assume a 28% tax rate on income.
Be careful! Not all the accounts listed will appear on an Income Statement!

SUN-2-SHADE, INC.
INCOME STATEMENT
Year ending December 31, 200_

7. Cash flow problems arise when a firm has debt obligations that must be met before cash from sales is received.

   Prepare a personal cash flow statement for two weeks. Include all projected income and all projected cash disbursements (payments) How's your cash flow?

Cash flow forecast	Week one	Week two
Projected income (Include all sources of income)	_____	_____
Projected "outgo" (Include all expenses)	_____	_____
Surplus (Deficit)	_____	_____

Learning Goal 5

8. Liquidity ratios measure a firm's ability to pay short-term debt. *Using the balance sheet and income statement you calculated earlier :*

   a. Calculate the current ratio for Sun-2-Shade

   b. Calculate the acid-test ratio for Sun-2-Shade

   c. What shape does Sun-2-Shade appear to be in?

9. Leverage ratios refer to the degree to which a firm relies on borrowed money for its operations.

   a. Calculate the Debt to owner's equity ratio for Sun-2-Shade

   b. If the industry average is .75, how does Sun-2-Shade compare?

10. Profitability ratios measure how effectively the firm is using its resources.

    a. If Sun-2-Shade has approximately 30,000 shares of common stock outstanding, what is their Basic Earnings per share?

    b. Calculate their Return on sales.

    c. What is Return on Equity?

11. Activity ratios measure the effectiveness of the firm in using the available assets.

   a. If the average inventory for Sun-2-Shade is 70,000, what is the inventory turnover rate?

   b. If the industry average is 3.5, what does that indicate for Sun-2-Shade?

PRACTICE TEST

MULTIPLE CHOICE – Circle the best answer

Learning Goal 1

1. Which of the following describes an activity associated with accounting?
   a. establishing a channel of distribution and supply chain
   b. forecasting demand for a new product
   c. developing strategies for entering new markets
   d. summarizing and interpreting company financial information

2. The purpose of accounting is to:
   a. allow for government tracking of business activities.
   b. make sure a business is paying its taxes.
   c. help managers evaluate the financial condition of the firm .
   d. provide a method of spending money wisely.

Learning Goal 2

3. The type of accounting that is concerned with providing information and analyses to managers within the organization is called:
   a. financial accounting.
   b. managerial accounting.
   c. auditing.
   d. tax accounting.

4. Jim Hopson is an accountant who works for a number of businesses as a "consultant." He has helped to design an accounting system, provides accounting services, and has analyzed the financial strength of many of his clients. Jim is working as a:
   a. private accountant.
   b. certified management accountant.
   c. certified internal auditor.
   d. public accountant.

5. This legislation created new government reporting standards for publicly traded companies.
   a. The Public Company Oversight Act
   b. The Robinson-Patman Act
   c. The Sarbanes-Oxley Act
   d. The Clayton Act

6. If you were working as a bookkeeper, the first action you would take is:
   a. record transactions into a ledger.
   b. develop a trial balance sheet.
   c. prepare an income statement.
   d. divide transactions into meaningful categories.

7. A specialized accounting book in which information is accumulated into specific categories and posted so managers can find all information about one account in the same place is a:
   a. ledger.
   b. journal.
   c. trial balance sheet.
   d. double entry book.

8. Which of the following is true of the use of computers in accounting?
   a. Computerized accounting systems are primarily used only in large corporations.
   b. Computers have been programmed to make financial decisions on their own.
   c. Computers can free up accountants to do important tasks, such as financial analysis.
   d. Computerized accounting systems have actually made the accounting process slightly more complicated because of the need to understand the software.

Learning Goal 4

9. The _____reports the firm's financial condition at a specific time.
   a. income statement
   b. cash flow statement
   c. statement of stockholder's equity
   d. balance sheet

10. Which of the following would be considered a current asset?
    a. accounts payable
    b. accounts receivable
    c. copyrights
    d. buildings

Use the information below to answer questions 11 and 12:

Net sales	$30,000
Total Assets	16,000
Taxes	2,300
Cost of goods sold	12,500
Total Liabilities	8,000
Operating expenses	3,200

11. Net income is:
    a. 14,000.
    b. 17,500.
    c. 14,300.
    d. 12,000.

12. Equity is:
    a. 16,000.
    b. 24,000.
    c. 8,000.
    d. can't determine from information given.

13. Which of the following assets would be considered to be the most liquid assets?
    a. current assets
    b. fixed assets
    c. intangible assets
    d. long-term assets

14. Gross profit (gross margin) is equal to:
    a. Gross sales minus net sales.
    b. Operating expenses minus taxes.
    c. Revenue minus cost of goods sold.
    d. Cost of goods sold minus operating expenses.

15. Mary Jane Ashton is in accounting for the small manufacturing firm by which she has been employed for several years. She is currently in the process of preparing the company's statement of cash flow. When she is done, this statement will show:
    a. net income after taxes.
    b. gross profit.
    c. total owner's equity.
    d. cash inflow and cash outgo from operations.

Learning Goal 5

16. Financial ratios
    a. are used to calculate profits from one year to the next
    b. are a poor indicator of a company's financial condition
    c. are only used by independent auditors
    d. are helpful to use in analyzing the actual performance of a company

17. The calculation for the current ratio is:
    a. net income divided by net sales.
    b. net income after taxes divided by number of common shares outstanding.
    c. cost of goods sold divided by average inventory.
    d. current assets divided by current liabilities.

18. Which kind of ratio is used to determine the ability of a firm to pay its short-term debts?
    a. activity ratios
    b. profitability
    c. debt
    d. liquidity

19. A debt to equity ratio of over 100% would mean:
    a. the company has more debt than equity.
    b. the company has more equity than debt.
    c. by comparison with other firms, the company is probably in good shape.
    d. the company is in too much debt, and should restructure.

20. Earnings per share, return on sales and return on equity are all :
    a. activity ratios.
    b. profitability ratios.
    c. liquidity ratios.
    d. debt ratios.

TRUE–FALSE

Learning Goal 1

1. _____ Understanding accounting is primarily important only if you are planning on working in the field.

2. _____ Financial transactions include buying and selling goods, acquiring insurance and using supplies.

Learning Goal 2

3. _____ Financial accounting is used to provide information and analyses to managers within the firm to assist in decision making.

4. _____ Dave Daschle works for Lawson Allen, an accounting firm that provides accounting services to individuals or businesses on a fee basis. Dave would be considered a private accountant

5. _____ An annual report is a yearly statement of the financial condition, progress and expectations of the firm.

6. _____ A tax accountant will perform the internal audits for a firm in order to determine what a firm's tax liability will be.

7. _____ The primary users of government accounting information are individuals and groups that want to ensure that the government is fulfilling its obligations.

Learning Goal 3

8. _____ The practice of writing every transaction in two places is known as double entry bookkeeping

9. _____ Trial balances are derived from information contained in ledgers.

10. _____ Computerized accounting systems assist in making financial information readily available whenever the organization needs it.

Learning Goal 4

11. _____ The fundamental accounting equation is assets = liabilities - owner's equity

12. _____ The "bottom line" is shown in the balance sheet.

13. _____ Cash flow is generally not a problem for companies that are growing quickly.

14. _____ Revenue can be generated from activities other than sales.

15. _____ Retained earnings are accumulated earnings from the firms profitable operations that were kept in the business.

16. _____ The four types of financial ratios include liquidity, debt, profitability and activity ratios.

17. _____ The higher the risk involved in an industry, the lower the return investors expect on their investment.

18. _____ There are two forms of earnings per share, basic and diluted.

You Can Find It on the Net

Do you know what your personal balance sheet looks like? For a way to find out, visit the web site at
http://financialplan.about.com/
Click on the Personal finance link, then budgets and follow to the budgeting worksheets. Use this worksheet to develop your own personal financial statements. Any surprises? What's your net worth? Would you be a good risk for a business loan, or to get involved in franchising, as the web site describes? Why or why not?

ANSWERS

LEARNING THE LANGUAGE

1.	Annual report	16.	Assets	30.	Liabilities
2.	Cash flow	17.	Accounts payable	31.	Ledger
3.	Current assets	18.	Gross margin (gross profit)	32.	Certified Management Accountant (CMA)
4.	Government and not-for-profit accounting	19.	Financial accounting	33.	Bookkeeping
5.	Fixed assets	20.	Net income or net loss	34.	Income statement
6.	Journal	21.	Balance sheet	35.	Depreciation
7.	Bonds payable	22.	Private accountant	36.	Intangible assets
8.	Owner's equity	23.	Accounting	37.	Statement of cash flows
9.	Trial balance	24.	Revenue	38.	Certified Internal Auditor (CIA)
10.	Tax accountant	25.	Auditing	39.	Fundamental accounting equation
11.	Liquidity	26.	Financial statement	40.	Operating expenses
12.	Independent audit	27.	Accounting cycle	41.	Ratio analysis
13.	Managerial accounting	28.	Cost of goods sold (cost of goods manufactured)	42.	Retained earnings
14.	Double entry bookkeeping	29.	Public accountant	43.	Notes payable
15.	Certified Public Accountant (CPA)				

ASSESSMENT CHECK

Learning Goal 1

The Role of Accounting Information

1. You have to know something about accounting if you want to succeed in business. It's almost impossible to run a business without being able to read, understand, and analyze accounting reports and financial statements.

2. Financial transactions include
   a. buying and selling goods and services
   b acquiring insurance
   c. paying employees
   d. using supplies.

3. Two purposes of accounting are:
   a. to help managers evaluate the financial condition and operating performance of the firm
   b. to report financial information to people outside the firm such as owners, creditors, suppliers, employees, investors, and the government.

4. Users of accounting information include:
   a. government agencies, such as the IRS
   b. other regulatory agencies
   c. stockholders, creditors, financial analysts and suppliers
   d. managers of the firm.

Learning Goal 2

Accounting Disciplines

5. The five key working areas of accounting are:
   a. Managerial accounting
   b. Financial accounting
   c. Auditing
   d. Tax accounting
   e. Government and not-for-profit accounting

6. Managerial accounting is concerned with:
   a. measuring and reporting costs of production, marketing, and other functions
   b. preparing budgets(planning)
   c. checking whether or not units are staying within their budgets (controlling)
   d. designing strategies to minimize taxes.

7. Financial accounting differs from managerial accounting because the information and analyses are for people outside the organization.

8. Answers to financial questions such as profitability, and about debt and liabilities are answered in the company's annual report.

9. Some accounting services public accountants may provide for their clients include:
   a. providing business assistance by designing an accounting system for a firm
   b. helping to select the correct computer and software to run the system
   c. analyzing the financial strength of an organization .

10. The independent Financial Accounting Standards Board defines what are *generally accepted accounting principles* that accountants must follow. If financial reports are prepared "in accordance with GAAP" , users know the information is reported according to standards agreed on by accounting professionals.

11. The Sarbanes-Oxley Act created new government reporting standards for publicly traded companies, following the scandals involving companies such as WorldCom, Enron and Tyco. The act also created the Public Company Accounting Oversight Board (PCAOB) which is charged with overseeing the American Institute of Certified Public Accountants.

12. Internal audits are conducted to guarantee that the company is carrying out proper accounting procedures and financial reporting.

13. A tax accountant is responsible for:
    a. preparing tax returns
    b. developing tax strategies.

14. The primary users of government accounting information are citizens, special interest groups, legislative bodies, and creditors. These users want to ensure that government is fulfilling its obligations and making the proper use of taxpayers' money.

Learning Goal 3

The Accounting Cycle

15. Accountants classify and summarize the data provided by bookkeepers. They interpret the data and report them to management. They also suggest strategies for improving the financial condition and progress of the firm.

16. The steps in the accounting cycle are:
    a. Analyze source documents, such as sales documents, purchasing receipts and shipping documents.
    b. Record transactions into journals
    c. Post journal entries into ledgers
    d. Prepare a trial balance
    e. Prepare financial statements: income statement, balance sheet, and statement of cash flows
    f. Analyze financial statements

17. It is possible that a bookkeeper could make a mistake when recording financial transactions. In double entry bookkeeping, two entries in the journal and the ledgers are required for each company transaction. The entries can be double checked to make sure that there have been no mistakes.

18. A *ledger* is a specialized accounting book in which information from accounting *journals* is accumulated into specific categories and posted so managers can find all the information about one account in the same place.

19. Computers
    a. have simplified the accounting process
    b. have made financial information available whenever the organization needs it
    c. can free up accountants to do more important tasks such as financial analysis.
    d. can address the specific needs of small businesses.
    e. can help make accounting work less monotonous.

Learning Goal 4

Understanding Key Financial Statements

20. a. Balance sheets report the firm's financial condition on a specific date.
    b. Income statements summarizes revenues, cost of goods, and expenses, for a specific period of time, and highlights the total profit or loss the firm experienced during that period.
    c. The Statement of cash flows provides a summary of money coming into and out of the firm that tracks a company's cash receipts and cash payments.

21. The difference between the financial statements can be summarized this way: The balance sheet details what the company owns and owes on a certain day. The income statement indicates what a firm sells its products for and what its selling costs are over a specific period of time. The statement of cash flows highlights the difference between cash coming in and cash going out of a business.

22. The fundamental accounting equation is: <u>Assets</u> = <u>Liabilities</u> + <u>Owner's equity</u>

23. To calculate your net worth, you would add up everything you own – cash, property, money owed to you; in other words, all your assets. From that you would subtract the money you owe to others, your liabilities, such as credit card debt, IOUs, current car loan, and student loans, for example. That figure tells you your net worth, or equity.

24. Assets include productive, tangible items such as equipment, buildings, land, furniture, fixtures, and motor vehicles that help generate income, as well as intangibles of value such as patents or copyrights.

25. Goodwill represents the value attached to factors such as a firm's reputation, location, and superior products. It is included on a balance sheet when one firm acquires another and pays more for it than the value of its tangible assets.

26. Assets on a balance sheet are listed in order of their liquidity, which refers to how fast an asset can be converted into cash.

27.   a. Current assets are items that can or will be converted into cash within one year. Current assets include cash, accounts receivable, and inventory.
  b. Fixed assets are long-term assets that are relatively permanent such as land buildings and equipment. They are often referred to as property, plant and equipment on a balance sheet.
  c. Intangible assets are long-term assets that have no physical form but have value. Examples include patents, trademarks, copyrights, and goodwill.

28. Liabilities are what the business owes to others. Current liabilities are payments due in one year or less; long-term liabilities are payments not due for one year or longer.

29.   a. Accounts payable is money owed to others for merchandise and/or services purchased on credit but yet not paid. If you have a bill you haven't paid, you have an account payable.
  b. Notes payable are short-term or long-term loans that have a promise for future payment
  c. Bonds payable are money loaned to the firm that it must pay back.

30. The value of things you own, <u>assets</u>, minus the amount of money you owe others, <u>liabilities</u>, is called <u>equity</u>. The value of what stockholders own in a firm minus liabilities is called <u>stockholders equity.</u>

31. Businesses that are not incorporated identify the investment of the sole proprietor or partner(s) through a capital account. For them, owner's equity means the value of everything owned by the business less any liabilities of the owners, such as bank loans.

32. The income statement
  a. summarizes all of the resources, called revenue, that have come into the firm from operating activities, money resources used, expenses incurred, and resources left after covering expenses.
  b. reports the firm's financial operations over a particular period of time, usually a year, a quarter of a year or a month.

33. The formula for an income statement is:
Revenue
<u>– Cost of Goods Sold</u>
Gross Margin
<u>–Operating Expenses</u>
Net Income before Taxes
<u>–Taxes</u>
= Net income (or loss)

34. a. Revenue is the value of what is received for goods sold, services rendered, and other financial sources. Most revenue comes from sales, but there could be other sources of revenue such as rents received, money paid to the firm for use of its patents, interest earned, and so forth.
    b. Gross sales are the total of all sales the firm completed. Net sales refer to sales minus returns, discounts, and allowances.

35. The cost of goods sold includes the purchase price plus any freight charges paid to transport goods plus any costs associated with storing the goods. In other words, all the costs of buying and keeping merchandise for sale are included in the cost of goods sold.

36. It's possible in a service firm that there may be no cost of goods sold; therefore, net revenue could equal gross margin. In a manufacturing firm, it is necessary to estimate the cost of goods manufactured.

37. Two categories of operating expenses are selling and general expenses. Selling expenses are related to the marketing and distribution of the firm's goods or services, such as salaries for salespeople, advertising and supplies. General expenses are administrative expenses of the firm, such as office salaries, depreciation, insurance and rent.

38. The "bottom line" is the net income or net loss the firm incurred from operations.

39. The three major activities for which cash receipts and disbursements are reported on a statement of cash flows include:
    a. Operations – cash transactions associated with running the business
    b. Investments – cash used in or provided by the firm's investment activities
    c. Financing – cash raised from new debt or new equity capital, or cash used to pay expenses, debts or dividends

40. Questions answered by a statement of cash flows may be:
    a. how much cash came into the business from current operations, in other words, from buying and selling goods and services?
    b. Was cash used to buy stocks, bonds or other investments?
    c. Were some investments sold that brought in cash?
    d. How much money came into the firm from issuing stock?

41. A poor, or negative, cash flow indicates that more money is going out of the business than is coming in from sales or other sources of revenue.

42. Cash flow problems start when, in order to meet the demands of customers, more and more goods are bought on credit. Similarly, more and more goods are sold on credit. This can go on until the firm uses up all the credit it has with banks that lend it money. When the firm requests money from the bank to pay a crucial bill the bank refuses the loan because the credit limit has been reached. All other credit sources may refuse a loan as well. The company needs to pay its bills or else its creditors could force it into bankruptcy.

Learning Goal 5

Analyzing Financial Performance using Ratios

43. Firms provide key insights into how a firm compares to other firms in the same industry in the key areas of:
    a. liquidity
    b. debt
    c. profitability
    d. overall business activity

44. Liquidity ratios measure the company's ability to pay its short-term debts. Short-term debts are expected to be repaid within one year and are of importance to the firm's creditors who expect to be paid on time.

45. Two key liquidity ratios are:
   a. current ratio
   b. quick ratio

46. Current ratio = $\dfrac{\text{Current assets}}{\text{Current liabilities}}$

47. The current ratio is compared to
   a. competing firms within the industry to measure how the company sizes up to its main competitors.
   b. the previous year to note any significant changes.

48. Acid test ratio = $\dfrac{\text{Cash + marketable securities + receivables}}{\text{Current liabilities}}$

49. This ratio is important to firms with difficulty converting inventory into quick cash.

50. Leverage ratios measure the degree to which a firm relies on borrowed funds in its operations.

51. Debt to equity ratio = $\dfrac{\text{Total liabilities}}{\text{Owner's equity}}$

   This ratio measures the degree to which the company is financed by borrowed funds that must be repaid.

52. A debt to equity ratio of above 100% would show that a firm actually has more debt than equity. It's possible that this firm could be perceived as a risk to both lenders and investors. It's always important to compare ratios to other firms in the same industry because debt financing is more acceptable in some industries.

53. Profitability ratios measure how effectively the firm is using its various resources to achieve profits.

54. Three profitability ratios are:
   a. Earnings per share
   b. Return on sales
   c. Return on equity

55. Basic earnings per share measures the amount of profit earned by a company for each share of outstanding common stock. Diluted EPS measures the amount of profit earned by a company for each share of outstanding common stock, but takes into consideration stock options, warrants, preferred stock and convertible debt securities that can be converted into common stock.

56. Basic earnings per share = $\dfrac{\text{Net Income}}{\text{Number of Common shares outstanding}}$

57. Return on sales = $\dfrac{\text{Net Income}}{\text{Net Sales}}$

Firms use this ratio to see if they are doing as well as the companies they compete against in generating income on sales they achieve.

58. Return on equity = $\dfrac{\text{Net Income}}{\text{Total Owner's Equity}}$

Return on equity measures how much was earned for each dollar invested by owners.

59. Activity ratios measure how effectively management is turning over inventory.

60. Inventory turnover = $\dfrac{\text{Cost of Goods Sold}}{\text{Average Inventory}}$

The inventory turnover ratio measures the speed of inventory moving through the firm and its conversion into sales. Inventory sitting by idly in a business costs money.

61. a. A lower than average inventory turnover ratio often indicates obsolete merchandise on hand or poor buying practices.
     b. A higher than average ratio may signal lost sales because of inadequate stock. An acceptable turnover ratio is generally determined on an industry-by-industry basis.

CRITICAL THINKING EXERCISES

Learning Goals 1,2

1. a. Financial accounting
    b. Public accountant
    c. Certified management accountant (CMA)
    d. Tax accountant
    e. Private accountant
    f. Auditing
    g. Certified public accountant (CPA)
    h. Managerial accounting
    i. Independent audit
    j. Annual report
    k. Certified internal auditor (CIA)

Learning Goal 3

2. BOOKKEEPING JOB DESCRIPTION - The bookkeeper for Sun-2-Shade will be responsible for collecting all original transaction documents, and dividing them into meaningful categories (sales, purchasing, shipping, and so on). The information will be recorded into journals on a daily basis, using the double-entry method. The bookkeeper will also be responsible for recording the information from the journals into ledgers. Must be familiar with computer accounting applications.

    ACCOUNTANT JOB DESCRIPTION - The accountant for Sun-2-Shade will be responsible for classifying and summarizing the data provided by the bookkeeper. He/she will interpret the data, report to management, and suggest strategies for improving the financial condition and progress of the firm. Must be able to suggest tax strategies and be skilled in financial analysis. Must be a Certified Management Accountant.

3. a. Record in journals
   b. Take a trial balance
   c. Analyze financial statements
   d. Analyze source documents
   e. Post to ledgers
   f. Prepare financial statements

Learning Goal 4

4. a.
1.	Balance sheet	11.	Balance sheet
2.	Balance sheet	12.	Balance sheet
3.	Balance sheet	13.	Balance sheet
4.	Income statement	14.	Income statement
5.	Income statement	15.	Income statement
6.	Balance sheet	16.	Income statement
7.	Income statement	17.	Income statement
8.	Income statement	18.	Income statement
9.	Balance sheet	19.	Balance sheet
10.	Income statement	20.	Income statement

   b. 1. Cash
      2. Accounts receivable
      3. Inventories

5.

BALANCE SHEET
SUN-2-SHADE
Year ending December 31, 20 _

Assets
Current assets
Cash	$18,000	
Investments	45,000	
Accounts receivable	110,000	
Inventory	62,000	
Total current assets		**$235,000**
Property, plant and equipment		
(Less accumulated depreciation)		200,000
Total Assets		**$435,000**

Liabilities and Stockholder's equity
Liabilities
Current liabilities		
Accounts payable	$25,000	
Notes payable (current)	15,000	
Accrued taxes	40,000	
Total current liabilities		**$ 80,000**
Long-term Debt		60,000
Total liabilities		**$140,000**

Stockholder's equity
Common stock	$130,000	
Retained earnings	165,000	
Total stockholders equity		**$295,000**
Total liabilities and stockholder's equity		**$ 435,000**

6.

SUN-2-SHADE, INC.
INCOME STATEMENT
Year ending December 31, 200 _

Revenues

Net sales	$600,000	
Rental revenue	3,000	
Total revenues		**$603,000**
Cost of goods sold		313,000
Gross profit		**$290,000**
Operating Expenses		
Wages and salaries	$125,000	
Rent	35,000	
Advertising	28,000	
Depreciation	4,000	
Utilities	12,000	
Supplies	3,700	
Total Operating Expenses		**$207,700**
Net Income Before Taxes		$ 82,300
Less Income Taxes		23,044
Net Income After Taxes		**$ 59,256**

7. Everyone's answer will vary, obviously. The things to look at include your wages for the next two weeks, and any other income you will be receiving within the next two weeks (not including that $10 your friend owes you unless you <u>know</u> they're going to pay you!), and any expenses that will be due within the next two weeks, such as car payments, insurance, rent, groceries, utility bills, cell phone bills, credit card payments, tuition, books, and so on.....

Learning Goal 5

8. a. Current ratio: $\dfrac{\$235,000}{\$80,000} = 2.9$

   b. Acid-test ratio: $\dfrac{\$173,000}{\$80,000} = 2.16$

   c. It seems that Sun-2-Shade is financially sound from the liquidity perspective, as their ratios are above the benchmark of the 2:1 ratio.

9. a. Debt/Owner's equity ratio: $\dfrac{\$140,000}{\$295,000} = .47$

   b. Sun-2-Shade seems to be in very good shape, and could actually afford to take on slightly more debt, according to the industry average.

10. a. Earnings per share: $\dfrac{\$59{,}256}{30{,}000} = \$1.98$ share

b. Return on sales: $\dfrac{\$59{,}256}{\$600{,}000} = 10\%$ approximately

c. Return on equity: $\dfrac{\$59{,}256}{\$295{,}000} = 20.1\%$

11. a. Inventory turnover: $\dfrac{313{,}000}{70{,}000} = 4.47$ times

b. Sun-2-Shade's turnover is high, compared to the industry average. This could indicate that they are running the risk of lost sales from inadequate stock.

PRACTICE TEST

MULTIPLE CHOICE

1.	d	11.	d
2.	c	12.	c
3.	b	13.	a
4.	d	14.	c
5.	c	15.	d
6.	d	16.	d
7.	a	17.	d
8.	c	18.	d
9.	d	19.	a
10.	b	20.	b

TRUE–FALSE

1.	F	10.	T
2.	T	11.	F
3.	F	12.	F
4.	F	13.	F
5.	T	14.	T
6.	F	15.	T
7.	T	16.	T
8.	T	17.	F
9.	T	18.	T

CHAPTER 18 – FINANCIAL MANAGEMENT

LEARNING GOALS

After you have read and studied this chapter, you should be able to:

1. Explain the role and responsibilities of financial managers.
2. Outline the financial planning process and the three key budgets in the financial plan.
3. Explain why firms need operating funds.
4. Identify and describe different sources of short-term financing.
5. Identify and describe different sources of long-term financing

LEARNING THE LANGUAGE

Listed below are important terms found in the chapter. Choose the correct term for the definition and write it in the space provided.

Budget	Finance	Revolving credit agreement
Capital budget	Financial control	Risk/return trade-off
Capital expenditures	Financial managers	Secured bond
Cash budget	Financial management	Secured loan
Cash flow forecast	Indenture terms	Short-term financing
Commercial finance companies	Leverage	Short-term forecast
Commercial paper	Line of credit	Term-loan agreement
Cost of capital	Long-term financing	Trade credit
Debt financing	Long-term forecast	Unsecured bond
Equity financing	Operating (master) budget	Unsecured loan
Factoring	Promissory note	Venture capital

1. Organizations called _____ make short-term loans to borrowers who offer tangible assets as collateral.

2. In a process known as _____ a firm periodically compares its actual revenues, costs and expenses with its budget.

3. Funds need for more than one year (usually 2 to 10 years) are considered _____

4. A line of credit called a _____ is guaranteed but usually comes with a fee.

5. A _____ is a promissory note that requires the borrower to repay the loan in specified installments.

6. A(n) _____ is a loan that is not backed by any specific assets.

7. Managers working as _____ examine financial data prepared by accountants and recommend strategies for improving the financial performance of a firm.

8. Funds known as _____ are raised from operations within the firm or through the sale of ownership in the firm.

9. The _____ is the rate of return a company must earn in order to meet the demands of its lenders and expectations of its equity holders.

10. A written contract or _____ is a promise to pay a supplier a specific sum of money at a definite time.

11. A _____ is a prediction of revenues, costs, and expenses for a period of one year or less.

12. Funds raised through various forms of borrowing that must be repaid are called _____.

13. A(n) _____ is the budget that ties together all of a firm's other budgets and summarizes its proposed financial activities.

14. A _____ is a loan backed collateral, something valuable such as property.

15. A forecast called a _____ predicts cash inflows and outflows in future periods, usually months or quarters.

16. A given amount of unsecured short-term funds, or a _____ is what a bank will lend to a business, provided funds are readily available.

17. A bond backed only by the reputation of the issuer is known as a debenture bond, or a (n) _____.

18. Raising needed funds through borrowing to increase a firm's rate of return is called _____.

19. _____ is the term used to describe the process of selling accounts receivable for cash.

20. A _____ highlights a firm's spending plans for major asset purchases that often require large sums of money.

21. A financial plan that sets forth management's expectations called a(n) _____ allocates the use of specific resources throughout the firm based on those expectations.

22. A _____ is a prediction of revenues, costs and expenses for a period longer than one year, sometimes extending 5 or 10 years into the future.

23. Unsecured promissory notes of $100,000 and up are known as _____ and mature in 270 days or less.

24. The practice of _____ is buying goods and services now and paying for them later.

25. The term _____ refers to funds needed for one year or less.

26. The function in a business called _____ refers to the process of acquiring funds for the firm and manages those funds within the firm.

27. The principle of _____ means the greater the risk a lender takes in making a loan, the higher the interest rate required.

28. A bond issued with some form of collateral is a _____.

29. The terms of the agreement in a bond issue are known as _____.

30. The _____ estimates a firm's cash inflows and outflows in future periods, usually months or quarters.

31. The job of managing the firm's resources so it can meet its goals and objectives is _____.

32. Major investments, or _____, are for long-term assets such as land, buildings, equipment, or intangible assets such as patents, trademarks, and copyrights.

33. Money that is invested in new or emerging companies that are perceived as having great profit potential is known as _____.

ASSESSMENT CHECK

Learning Goal 1

The Role of Finance and Financial Managers

1. What is the difference between an accountant and a financial manager?

2. Two key responsibilities of a financial manager's task are to:

   a. _____

   b. _____

3. Controlling funds includes managing:

   a. _____

   b. _____

   c. _____

4. Is finance important for small business?

5. Describe three of the most common ways for any firm to fail financially.

   a. _____

   b. _____

   c. _____

6. For what activities are financial managers responsible? What are two key components of a financial manager's job?

Learning Goal 2

Financial Planning

7. What is the overall objective of financial planning?

8. What are the three steps involved in financial planning?

   a. _____

   b. _____

   c. _____

9. The long term financial forecast gives top management and operations managers_____

   _____

10. Identify three types of budgets

    a. _____

    b. _____

    c. _____

11. What kinds of spending plans are the focus of the capital budget?

12. How do cash budgets help managers? When is a cash budget prepared?

13. What is the function of an operating budget?

14. How do financial control procedures help managers?

    a. _____

    b. _____

    c. _____

Learning Goal 3

The Need for Operating Funds

15. What are four key areas for which businesses need operating funds?

    a. _____

    b. _____

    c. _____

    d. _____

16. Financial managers must ensure funds are available to meet_____

    _____

17. Describe the time value of money. What is the importance of the time value of money?

18. Why do financial managers try to keep cash expenditures to a minimum?

19. Why do financial managers want to make credit available?

    a. _____

    b. _____

20. What is a problem with offering credit? How do finance manager address the problem?

21. What does inventory control have to do with finance?

22. How do capital expenditures affect a firm's financial plan?

23. A firm can seek to raise needed capital through

   a. _____

   b. _____

   c. _____

Learning Goal 4

Obtaining Short-Term Financing

24. Why do firms need to borrow short-term funds?

   a. _____

   b. _____

   c. _____

25. What are seven sources of short-term financing?

   a. _____   e. _____

   b. _____   f. _____

   c. _____   g. _____

   d. _____

26. Which of these forms is the most widely used source of short term financing? Why?

27. Describe the invoice terms of 2/10 net 30, when using trade credit.

28. Why might a supplier require a promissory note?

29. What steps are recommended when borrowing from family or friends?

    a. _____

    b. _____

    c. _____

30. How much funding for small businesses comes from commercial banks? Why should the business owner keep in close touch with the bank?

31. Describe four types of bank loans.

    a. _____

    _____

    b. _____

    _____

    c. _____

    _____

    d. _____

    _____

32. Discuss a firm's use of commercial finance companies.

33. Describe factoring as a source of funds.

34. What kinds of companies are able to sell commercial paper? What are the benefits of commercial paper?

35. What are the drawbacks of using credit cards as a source of short term funds?

Learning Goal 5

Obtaining Long-Term Financing

36. What are three questions financial managers ask when setting long-term financing objectives?

    a. _____

    b. _____

    c. _____

37. What kinds of purchases are made with long-term capital?

38. What are the two major sources of initial long-term financing?

    a. _____   b. _____

39. Firms can borrow long-term funds by either:

    a. _____

    b. _____

40. What is the tax advantage of a term-loan agreement?

41. What are some drawbacks to a long-term loan?

    a. _____

    b. _____

    c. _____

42. What is the risk/return trade-off?

43. To put it simply a bond is: _____

_____

44. What types of organizations can issue bonds?

a. _____

b. _____

c. _____

d. _____

45. What is another name for a debenture bond?

46. What are the sources of equity financing?

a. _____

b. _____

c. _____

47. The purchasers of stock become: _____

The number of shares of stock available for purchase is determined by: _____

48. What is the term used to describe the first time a company offers to sell its stock to the general public?

49. What is the most favored source of long-term capital? Why?

50. Venture capitalists invest in a business in return for _____

For their investment they expect _____

51. How has the slowdown in the economy affected the venture capital industry?

52. What are the two key jobs of the finance manager, or CFO?

a. _____

b. _____

53. How can a firm use borrowed funds to get a higher rate of return for stockholders, compared to equity funding?

CRITICAL THINKING EXERCISES

Learning Goal 1

1. Among the functions a finance manager performs are:

Planning	Collecting funds (credit management)
Auditing	Controlling funds
Managing taxes	Obtaining funds
Advising top management	Budgeting

Match the correct function to each statement below.

a. _____ Before Sun-2-Shade sends out quarterly financial statements, Debbie Breeze does her job, which is to ensure that no mistakes have been made, and that all transactions have been treated in accordance with established accounting rules and procedures.

b. _____ Joe Saumby determined that his firm's accounts receivable were too high, and developed a more effective collection system.

c. _____ Ann Bizer decided to include money for a new bank of computers in the operating budget.

d. _____ In an effort to generate capital, Gerald McMillian decided that his company should "go public" and make a stock offering.

e. _____ A major automotive company developed a long-range objective of developing a hybrid vehicle, which would cost millions of dollars.

f. _____ In order to monitor expense account spending, many companies require employees to submit a receipt for any expenditure over $25.

g. _____ During a period of high inflation, the Kroger Company changed some of their accounting practices to reduce the company's tax liability.

h. _____ In a report to the CEO and other top managers in his company, Joe Kelley outlined the effect of newly proposed pollution control requirements on the company's long-range profit forecasts.

2. The text identifies three kinds of budgets

    Operating (master) budget   Cash budget
    Capital budget

    Determine which type of budget is being described in each of the following:

    a. _____   St. Louis Community College District projects that $350,000 will be spent for attendance and participation in conferences and seminars.

    b. _____   Kevin Nelson, the finance manager for TNG Enterprises, has just finished work on the budget that will help him to determine how much money the firm will have to borrow for the next year.

    c. _____   At Whitfield School, a fund raising activity helped the school add money to the funds allocated to purchasing computer equipment for student and faculty use.

    d. _____   Phillip Knott is the comptroller for a major electronics firm. At their annual finance meeting, he presented a summary of all the budgets for board approval.

Learning Goal 3

3. Eric is the owner/founder of Sun-2-Shade, a company that manufactures self-darkening windshields for the automotive industry, and Eric is upset! He has just stormed into Sun-2-Shade's finance manager's office "What's going on? I just looked at our inventory levels, and they're lower than what I think we ought to see. Don't we have the money to buy inventory? How are we going to make our orders? And what's the idea of all these credit sales? Visa? MasterCard? And another thing! Why are we always paying our bills at the last minute? Are we that short of cash? " "Hold on" said Bill Whittier, the new finance manager, " things look pretty good to me. We're actually in great shape!" " What? I don't understand!" replied Eric. "You know, I want to look into building a new plant within the next 2 years. Sales are going to continue to go way up. I need to know whether or not we're going to be able to afford it. Right now, it looks as if we are too short of cash. Explain!"

4. There are several sources of short-term funds:

Trade credit   Factoring
Promissory notes   Commercial paper
Family and friends   Credit Cards
Commercial bank loans

Match the correct type of short-term financing to each of the following:

a. _____   A major Midwestern retailer often sells its accounts receivable for cash.

b. _____   Lou Fusz auto network finances its inventories, using the vehicles themselves as collateral for the loans.

c. _____   During a recent recession, Van Nuys Enterprises had some problems paying their bills on time. Afterwards, Van Nuys' suppliers required them to sign a written contract in order for them to buy with credit.

d. _____   Echo Enterprises recently raised some "quick cash" through selling $100,000 promissory notes. Echo agreed to pay the principle plus interest within 90 days of the sale. Monterrey Bay Co. bought Echo's promissory notes as an investment for their extra cash.

e. _____   Kellwood bills its retail customers on a 2/10 net 30 basis.

f. _____   To pay an unexpectedly high liability insurance premium, the owner of a small chemical company borrowed money from his best friend.

g. _____   Dave Flynn has just opened a small business in a suburb of his home town of Atlanta. To promote the business Dave created some color brochures, and determined that it would be cheaper for him to print the brochures himself rather than have the job done at a printer so he purchased a color laser printer with his personal credit card, and charged the business later.

5. There are several kinds of loans:

Unsecured loans   Line of credit
Secured loans (including pledging)   Revolving credit agreement
Inventory financing   Commercial finance companies

Match each type to the following examples:

a. _____   Ternier Steel Company is using their most recent shipment of coal as collateral for a short-term loan.

b. _____   In their commodities brokerage business, Bartholomew Enterprises needs guaranteed loans without having to apply for the loan each time it is needed. They are willing to pay a fee for the guarantee.

c. _____   Rivertown Insurance is having some short-term cash problems. They have substantial accounts receivable which they intend to use as collateral for a loan.

d. _____ Danny Noble Enterprises has been in business for a fairly long time and has a great financial record. When they needed money they went to their banker and applied for the loan without needing to put up collateral.

e. _____ Because they often have a need for short term funds with short notice, Binny and Jones Manufacturing applied to their bank for a "continual" sort of unsecured loan. The bank lends Binny a given amount without Binny having to re-apply each time. While not a guaranteed loan, the funds will be available if Binny's credit limit is not exceeded and the bank has the money available.

f. _____ Because they were considered a credit risk, PPI, Inc. had to pay a higher rate of interest, and pledge their inventory as collateral for the loan. They went to General Electric Capital Services because they couldn't obtain funding from a commercial bank.

Learning Goal 5

6. There are 2 general sources of long-term funds

Debt capital - loans and bonds
Equity capital - stock, retained earnings, venture capital

Match the correct type of financing to each of the following statements:

a. _____ The unsecured form of these are commonly referred to as "debentures."

b. _____ If a firm cannot obtain a long-term loan or can't sell bonds it will turn to this type of financing.

c. _____ Generally the most favored source of long-term capital.

d. _____ These can be either secured or unsecured.

e. _____ For this, a business must sign a term-loan agreement because of the long repayment period.

f. _____ The key word here is "ownership."

g. _____ This source of funds can involve a high degree of risk for companies choosing it and firms providing this type of funding may hold companies to strict standards before investing their capital.

h. _____ Using this source saves the company interest payments, dividends and any underwriting fees, and won't dilute ownership.

i. _____ The terms of agreement are called indenture terms.

j. _____ Good sources of start up capital for new companies, they often want a stake in the ownership of the business.

k. _____ When using this form of financing, a company has a legal obligation to pay interest.

PRACTICE TEST

MULTIPLE CHOICE — Circle the best answer

Learning Goal 1

1. Which of the following is a reason for why businesses fail financially?
    a. Expense controls are too elaborate
    b. Poor use of marketing mix
    c. Undercapitalization
    d. Stock is undervalued

2. Jackie Jones is a finance manager for Pokey Poseys, a wholesale florist. As finance manager, which of the following would be one of Jackie's responsibilities?
    a. preparing financial statements
    b. preparing tax returns
    c. production planning
    d. planning for spending funds on long-term assets, such as plant and equipment

3. Internal audits are important because:
    a. the firm needs to keep a constant look out for employees who may be committing fraud.
    b. internal audits help to make accounting statements more reliable.
    c. they aid in the development of financial statements.
    d. the firm uses the audits to determine desired profits for the following year.

Learning Goal 2

4. Rachael Straub works in finance for a small microbrewery. This week Rachael is working on a budget for the next 12 months. She has been doing research to determine prices for the new equipment they will need in the next 12 months to stay competitive in this market. Which of the steps in financial planning is Rachael involved in?
    a. Develop financial statements for outside investors.
    b. Forecast short- term financial needs.
    c. Establish financial controls.
    d. Develop budgets to meet financial needs.

5. A _____ forecast predicts revenues, costs, and expenses for a period longer than one year.
    a. short-term
    b. long-term
    c. cash flow
    d. revenue

6. Guillermo Reta-Martinez is currently in the process of projecting how much his firm will have to spend on supplies, travel, rent, advertising, and salaries for the coming financial year. Guillermo is working on the _____.
    a. advertising budget.
    b. capital budget.
    c. cash budget.
    d. operating (master) budget.

7. Financial controls are designed to help managers to:
   a. identify variances from the financial plan and take corrective actions.
   b. predict cash inflows in future periods.
   c. manage the day to day cash needs of a business.
   d. develop the appropriate budgets.

Learning Goal 3

8. The time value of money means that
   a. the value of money will fall over time.
   b. it is better to make purchases now, rather than wait until later.
   c. a monetary system will devalue it's money over time.
   d. it is better to have money now, than later.

9. What is the major problem with selling on credit?
   a. A sizeable portion of a firm's assets could be tied up in accounts receivable.
   b. You can't control when customers will pay their bills.
   c. It makes production scheduling more difficult.
   d. Customers who aren't allowed to buy on credit become unhappy.

10. Companies must have a carefully constructed inventory policy in order to:
    a. be able of accept credit cards.
    b. manage available funds and maximize profitability.
    c. increase demand for their products.
    d. reduce the need for long-term funds.

11. Debt financing:
    a. refers to funds raised through various forms of borrowing.
    b. is always more expensive than selling stocks.
    c. refers to funds raised through selling ownership in the firm.
    d. requires that the firm pay interest from after tax profits.

Learning Goal 4

12. Which of the following is a source of short-term funds?
    a. The sale of bonds
    b. The use of trade credit
    c. Venture capital
    d. The use of retained earnings

13. The credit terms 2/10 net 30 means:
    a. The full amount of a bill is due within 2-10 days
    b. Customers will receive a 10 percent discount if they pay in 30 days
    c. A 2 percent discount will be given if customers pay within 30 days
    d. Customers will receive a 2 percent discount if they pay within 10 days

14. Factoring is a term that means:
    a. determining the credit terms for a trade credit agreement.
    b. selling accounts receivable as a way to raise cash
    c. determining whether to use debt or equity financing to raise funds
    d. using a continual line of credit.

15. Commercial finance companies accept more risk than banks, and the interest rates they charge are usually _____than commercial banks.
    a. higher
    b. about the same as
    c. lower
    d. more variable

Learning Goal 5

16. Using equity financing includes _____ as a source of funds
    a. the sale of bonds
    b. the sale of stock
    c. the sale of inventory
    d. the sale of accounts receivable

17. One of the benefits of using debt financing, over equity financing, as a source of long-term funds is that
    a. bonds don't have to be paid back.
    b. the company isn't required to pay interest.
    c. bondholders do not have a say in running the business.
    d. interest is paid after taxes are paid.

18. When a corporation takes out a long-term loan, the company must:
    a. calculate a risk/return tradeoff.
    b. sign a term-loan agreement.
    c. agree to indenture terms.
    d. sell its commercial paper.

19. The most favored source of meeting long-term capital needs is:
    a. selling stock.
    b. venture capital.
    c. selling bonds.
    d. retained earnings.

20. When a major automotive firm decided to purchase one of it's competitors, the firm borrowed a significant portion of the funds it needed to make the purchase. This is known as using:
    a. venture capital.
    b. leverage.
    c. retained earnings.
    d. equity capital.

TRUE–FALSE

Learning Goal 1

1. _____ Financial managers examine the financial data prepared by accountants and make recommendations to top executives about strategies for improving the financial strength of a firm.

2. _____ Financial understanding is important primarily for anyone wanting to major in accounting, but not necessary for others involved in business.

3. _____ Because taxes represent a cash outflow, financial managers are involved in planning tax strategies, and in tax management.

Learning Goal 2

4. _____ The cash budget is often the first budget that is prepared.

5. _____ Financial control means that the actual revenues, costs, and expenses are reviewed and compared with projections.

6. _____ The short-term forecast is the foundation for most other financial plans.

Learning Goal 3

7. _____ Finance managers will sometimes pay bills as late as possible as a way of managing cash for daily operations.

8. _____ One way to decrease the expense of collecting accounts receivable is to accept bank credit cards.

9. _____ Firms may use innovations such as just-in-time inventory control to help reduce the amount of funds tied up in inventory.

Learning Goal 4

10. _____ When suppliers are hesitant to give trade credit to organizations with a poor credit rating, or which have no credit history, they may ask for the customer to sign a promissory note as a condition for obtaining credit.

11. _____ One benefit of borrowing from friends or family is that you don't have to draw up formal papers like you do with a bank loan.

12. _____ It is important for a businessperson to keep close relations with a banker because the banker may be able to spot cash flow problems early and point out problems.

13. _____ A line of credit guarantees a business a given amount of unsecured short-term funds, if funds are available.

14. _____ Long-term capital is generally used to pay for supplies, rent, and travel.

15. _____ Only the federal government can issue bonds.

16. _____ Cost of capital refers to the rate of return a company must earn in order to meet the demands of its lenders and expectations of its stockholders.

You Can Find It On the Net

What are some of the financial considerations of starting and managing your own small business? Visit http://www.bizmove.com/financial.htm and click on the Introduction to Financial Management.

What is the difference in managing finance for small firms compared to big firms?

Go back and click on the Money Sources link

What available sources are listed?

What reasons are there for the need for additional capital?

Go back and click on the How To Reduce Costs link

What suggestions are made about how to reduce the costs of your small business?

ANSWERS

LEARNING THE LANGUAGE

1.	Commercial finance companies	12.	Debt financing	23.	Commercial paper
2.	Financial control	13.	Operating budget	24.	Trade credit
3.	Long-term financing	14.	Secured loan	25.	Short-term financing
4.	Revolving credit agreement	15.	Cash flow forecast	26.	Finance
5.	Term-loan agreement	16.	Line of credit	27.	Risk/return tradeoff
6.	Unsecured loan	17.	Unsecured bond	28.	Secured bond
7.	Financial managers	18.	Leverage	29.	Indenture terms
8.	Equity financing	19.	Factoring	30.	Cash budget
9.	Cost of capital	20.	Capital budget	31.	Financial management
10.	Promissory note	21.	Budget	32.	Capital expenditures
11.	Short-term forecast	22.	Long-term forecast	33.	Venture capital

ASSESSMENT CHECK

Learning Goal 1

The Role of Finance and Financial Managers

1. Financial managers use the data prepared by accountants and make recommendations to top management regarding strategies for improving the health of the firm. It is the equivalent of a lab technician who takes the measures of a person's health (the accountant) and the doctor who interprets the reports (the finance manager).

2. Two key responsibilities of a financial manager's task are to:
   a. obtain funds.
   b. effectively control the use of those funds.

3. Controlling funds includes managing:
   a. the firm's cash.
   b. credit accounts.
   c. inventory

4. Finance is important not matter what the firm's size. The need for careful financial management is a challenge that large and small businesses must face throughout their existence.

5. The three most common ways for any firm to fail financially are:
   a. Undercaptitalization - not enough funds to start with
   b. Poor control over cash flow
   c. Inadequate expense control

6. Financial managers are responsible for seeing that the company pays its bills at the appropriate time and for collecting overdue payments to make sure that the company does not lose too much money to bad debts. Two key components are buying merchandise on credit and collecting payment from customers. They are also involved in tax management and internal audits.

Financial Planning

7. Financial planning involves analyzing short-term and long-term money flows to and from the firm. The overall objective of financial planning is to optimize the firm's profitability and make the best use of its money.

8. Financial planning involves:
   a. Forecasting both short-term and long-term financial needs
   b. Developing budgets to meet those needs
   c. Establishing financial controls

9. The long term financial forecast gives top management and operations managers some sense of the income or profit potential of different strategic plans. It also helps in preparing company budgets.

10. Three types of budgets are:
    a. Operating (master) budgets
    b. Capital budgets
    c. Cash budgets

11. The capital budget highlights the purchase of such assets as property, plant, and equipment.

12. Cash budgets help assist managers in anticipating borrowing, repaying debt, operating expenses, and short-term investments. The cash budget is the last budget prepared.

13. The operating, or master, budget ties together all the firm's other budgets and summarizes a company's proposed financial statements. It is in this budget that the firm determines how much the company will spend on supplies, travel, rent, advertising, salaries and so forth. It is the most detailed budget.

14 Control procedures help managers
   a. identify variances to the financial plan.
   b. take corrective action if necessary.
   c. provide feedback to help identify which accounts, departments and people are varying from the financial plan.

Learning Goal 3

The Need for Operating Funds

15. Four basic financial needs affecting both small and large businesses are:
    a. Managing day-by-day needs of the business   c. Acquiring needed inventory
    b. Controlling credit operations   d. Making capital expenditures

16. Financial mangers muse ensure funds are available to meet daily cash needs without compromising the firm's investment potential.

17. Money has a time value, which means that if someone offered to give you money today or one year from today, you would benefit by taking the money today. You could start collecting interest or invest the money you receive today, and over time, your money would grow. For a firm, the interest earned on investments is important in maximizing the profit the company will gain.

18. Financial managers often try to keep cash expenditures at a minimum to free funds for investment in interest-bearing accounts. It is suggested that finance managers pay bills as late as possible and collect what is owed as fast as possible, and collect what's owed to it as fast as possible.

19. Financial mangers know that making credit available helps
    a. keep current customers happy
    b. attract new customers.

20. The major problem with selling on credit is that as much as 25 percent or more of the business's assets could be tied up in its accounts receivable so the firm has to use some of its available cash to pay for the goods or services already given to customers who bought on credit. As a result financial managers must develop efficient collection procedures.

    Finance managers often develop efficient collection procedures, like offering cash or quantity discounts to buyers who pay their accounts by a certain time. They also scrutinize old and new credit customers to see if they have a history of meeting credit obligations on time.

21. A carefully constructed inventory policy assists in managing the use of the firm's available funds and maximizing profitability. Inventory controls can reduce the funds tied up in inventory. Poorly managed inventory can affect cash flow.

22. The purchase of major assets is important to many businesses. It is critical that companies weigh all the possible options before committing a large portion of its available resources.

23. A firm can seek to raise needed capital through:
    a. borrowing money – debt capital
    b. selling ownership – equity capital
    c. earning profits – retained earnings

Learning Goal 4

Obtaining Short-Term Financing

24. Firms need to borrow short-term funds for:
    a. purchasing additional inventory.
    b. for meeting bills that come due unexpectedly.
    c. to obtain short-term funds when the firm's cash reserves are low.

25. Seven sources of short-term financing are:
    a. Trade credit   e. Factoring accounts receivable
    b. Promissory note   f. Commercial paper
    c. Family and friends   g. Credit cards
    d. Commercial bank loans

26. The most widely used source of short-term funding is trade credit, because it is the least expensive and most convenient form of short-term financing.

27. Terms of 2/10 net 30 means that the buyer can take a 2 percent discount for paying within 10 days. The total bill is due (net) in 30 days if the purchaser does not take advantage of the discount.

28. Some suppliers hesitate to give trade credit to organizations with a poor credit rating, no credit history, or a history of slow payment. In such cases, the supplier may insist that the customer sign a promissory note as a condition for obtaining credit.

29. When borrowing from family or friends:
    a. Agree on specific terms.
    b. Write an agreement.
    c. Pay them back the same way you would a bank loan.

30. Commercial banks fund almost half of small business financing today. It is important for a businessperson to keep in close touch with a banker because the banker may spot cash flow problems early and point out danger areas. Additionally, the banker may be more willing to lend money in a crisis if the businessperson has established a strong, friendly relationship build on openness and trust.

31. Four types of bank loans are:
    a. <u>Secured loans</u> are backed by something of value, which is known as collateral. If the buyer fails to make payment on the loan, the lender may take possession of the collateral.
    b. <u>Unsecured loans don't require the lender to offer collateral. These loans are usually only offered to</u> long standing customers or customers who are financially stable.
    c. <u>A line of credit is</u> a short term unsecured loan that the bank will lend to the business provided the bank has funds available. It is designed to speed up the borrowing process so that the firm doesn't have to apply for a new loan every time it needs funds.
    d. A <u>revolving credit agreement</u> is a line of credit that is guaranteed.

32. Commercial finance companies are used by businesses when the business can't obtain a short term loan from a bank. The commercial finance company will make short-term loans to borrowers with tangible assets such as property, plant and equipment, and will charge higher interest rates than commercial banks, because the commercial credit companies are willing to accept higher degrees of risk.

33. In the process of factoring, a firm sells many of its products on credit to consumers and businesses, creating accounts receivable. Some of these buyers may be slow in paying their bills, causing the company to have a large amount of money due in accounts receivable. A factor is a market intermediary that agrees to <u>buy</u> the accounts receivable from the firm at a discount for cash. It is expensive, but many small businesses, as well as some large businesses use factoring as a source of cash.

34. Commercial paper is unsecured, so only financially stable firms, mainly large corporations, are able to sell it. Commercial paper is a way to get short-term funds quickly and for less than bank interest rates. It is also an investment opportunity for buyers who can afford to put up cash for short periods to earn some interest.

35. The drawbacks of using credit cards as a short term source of funds is that their use can be very risky and costly. Interest rates can be very high, and users must pay penalties if they fail to make payments on time. Credit cards are best used as a last resort.

Obtaining Long-Term Financing

36. Three questions financial managers ask when setting long-term financing objectives are:
    a. What are the long-term goals and objectives of the firm?
    b. What are the financial requirements needed to achieve these goals and objectives?
    c. What sources of long-term capital are available, and which will fit our needs?

37. In business, long–term capital is used to buy fixed assets such as plant and equipment and to finance expansion of the organization.

38. a. debt financing which must be repaid   b. equity financing

39. Firms can borrow funds by either:
    a. getting a loan from a lending institution
    b. issuing bonds

40. A major tax advantage of a term-loan agreement is that the interest paid on the long-term debt is tax deductible.

41. Drawbacks to long term loans include:
    a. long-term loans are often more expensive to the firm than short-term loans, because larger amounts of capital are borrowed.
    b. since the repayment period could be as long as twenty years, the lenders are not assured their capital will be repaid in full so most long-term loans require some form of collateral.
    c. lenders may require certain restrictions on a firm's operations to force the firm to use responsible business practices.

42. The risk/return trade-off is the idea that the greater the risk a lender takes in making a loan, the higher the rate of interest it requires.

43. To put it simply, a bond is like a company IOU with a promise to repay the amount borrowed on a certain date.

44. The types of organizations that can issue bonds are:
    a. federal, state, and local governments
    b. federal government agencies
    c. corporations
    d. foreign governments and corporations.

45. Another name for a debenture bond is an unsecured bond, backed only by the reputation of the issuer.

46. Sources of equity financing are:
    a. selling ownership in the firm in the form of stock.
    b. using retained earnings the firm has accumulated and kept to reinvest in the business.
    c. venture capital.

47. The purchasers of stock become owners in an organization.

    The number of shares of stock available for purchase is determined by the organization's board of directors.

48. The first time a company offers to sell its stock to the general public is called an initial public offering, or an IPO.

49. Retained earnings are usually the most favored source of meeting long-term capital needs, since the company saves interest payments, dividends, and any possible underwriting fees. Retained earnings also create no new ownership in the firm, as stock does.

50. Venture capitalists invest in a business in return for part ownership of the business.

   For their investment they expect higher-than-average returns and competent management performance for their investment.

51. The slowdown in the overall economy reduced venture capital expenditures, and has caused venture capitalists to spend cautiously and hold companies to strict standards before investing their capital.

52. Two key jobs of the finance manager or CFO are:
   a. to forecast the need for borrowed funds
   b. to manage borrowed funds.

53. If a firm's earnings are larger than the interest payments on borrowed funds, then the business owners are realizing a higher rate of return than if they used equity financing.

CRITICAL THINKING EXERCISES

Learning Goal 1

1. a. Auditing   e. Planning
    b. Collecting funds   f. Controlling funds
    c. Budgeting   g. Managing taxes
    d. Obtaining funds   h. Advising top management

Learning Goal 2

2. a. Operating(master) budget   c. Capital budget
    b. Cash budget   d. Operating (master) budget

Learning Goal 3

3. Eric doesn't understand some basic ideas about financial management. Bill needs to explain the financial needs of all businesses: managing daily operations, managing accounts receivable, obtaining needed inventory (including inventory management) and major capital expenditures, and how a finance manager deals with each area.

   One of the first things a finance manager will do is to see that funds are available to meet daily cash needs, without using too much cash and not being able to take advantage of other investments. So, bills are paid at the latest date possible to allow the firm to take advantage of interest-bearing accounts. Sun-2-Shade allows for credit purchases because it helps to keep their customers happy and helps to attract new customers. With effective collection procedures, selling on credit can be a benefit to the firm. It's important to keep inventories at a level necessary to fill orders, but too high an inventory level will tie up funds that could be used elsewhere for investment. Programs like just-in-time inventory help to reduce the amount of funds a firm must tie up in inventory.

There is no way to tell if the firm can afford to build a new plant in two years, but the finance manager will be able to evaluate the various alternatives, such as buying a facility, expanding on a current facility or building their own building.

Learning Goal 4

4. a.   Factoring
    b.   Bank loan (inventory financing)
    c.   Promissory note
    d.   Commercial paper
    e.   Trade credit
    f.   Family and friends
    g.   credit card

5. a.   Inventory financing
    b.   Revolving credit agreement
    c.   Secured loan
    d.   Unsecured loan
    e.   Line of credit
    f.   Commercial credit company

Learning Goal 5

6. a.   Debt financing – bonds
    b.   Equity financing
    c.   Equity financing – retained earnings
    d.   Debt financing – loans, bonds
    e.   Debt financing – loans
    f.   Equity financing – stock
    g.   Equity financing - venture capital
    h.   Equity financing - retained earnings
    i.   Debt financing - bonds
    j.   Equity financing – venture capital
    k.   Debt financing – loans, bonds

PRACTICE TEST

MULTIPLE CHOICE

1.	c	11.	a
2.	d	12.	b
3.	b	13.	d
4.	b	14.	b
5.	b	15.	a
6.	d	16.	b
7.	a	17.	c
8.	d	18.	b
9.	a	19.	d
10.	b	20.	b

TRUE–FALSE

1.	T	9.	T
2.	F	10.	T
3.	T	11.	F
4.	F	12.	T
5.	T	13.	T
6.	T	14.	F
7.	T	15.	F
8.	T	16.	T

CHAPTER 19 – USING SECURITIES MARKETS FOR FINANCING AND INVESTING OPPORTUNTIES

LEARNING GOALS:

After you have read and studied this chapter you should be able to:

1. Describe the role of securities markets and of investment bankers.
2. Identify the stock exchanges where securities are traded
3. Compare the advantages and disadvantages of equity financing by issuing stock, and detail the differences between common and preferred stock.
4. Compare the advantages and disadvantages of obtaining debt financing by issuing bonds and identify the classes and features of bonds.
5. Explain how to invest in securities markets and set investment objectives such as long-term growth, income, cash, and protection from inflation.
6. Analyze the opportunities stocks offer as investments
7. Analyze the opportunities bonds offer as investments.
8. Explain the investment opportunities in mutual funds and exchange-traded funds (ETFs).
9. Describe how indicators like the Dow Jones Industrial Average affect the market.

LEARNING THE LANGUAGE

Listed below are important terms found in the chapter. Choose the correct term for the definition and write it in the space provided.

Bond	Institutional investors	Program trading
Buying stock on margin	Interest	Prospectus
Capital gains	Investment bankers	Securities and Exchange Commission (SEC)
Common stock	Junk bonds	Sinking fund
Debenture bond	Maturity date	Stockbroker
Diversification	Mutual fund	Stock certificate
Dividends	(NASDAQ)	Stock exchange
Dow Jones Industrial Average (the Dow)	Over-the-counter market (OTC)	stocks
Exchange traded funds (ETFs)	Preferred stock	Stock splits
Initial public offering (IPO)		

1. Large investors known as _____ are organizations such as pension funds, mutual funds, insurance companies, and banks that invest their own funds or the funds of others.

2. The _____ is an exchange that provides a means to trade stocks not listed on national exchanges.

3. Evidence of stock ownership is called a _____ and specifies the name of the company, the number of shares it represents, and the type of stock being issued.

4. Trading known as _____ means giving instructions to computers to automatically sell if the price of stock dips to a certain point to avoid potential losses.

5. The most basic form of ownership in a firm is _____, which confers voting rights and the right to share in the firm's profits through dividends, if offered by the firm's board of directors.

6. A _____ is a reserve account in which the issuer of a bond periodically retires some part of the bond principal prior to maturity so that enough capital will be accumulated by the maturity date to pay off the bond.

7. A registered representative who works as a market intermediary known as a _____, buys and sells securities for clients.

8. An organization that is known as a _____ is one whose members can buy and sell securities for companies and investors.

9. The exact date the issuer of a bond must pay the principal to the bondholder is known as the _____.

10. Stock called _____ gives its owner's preference in the payment of dividends and an earlier claim on assets than common stockholders if the business is forced out of business and its assets sold.

11. Specialists called _____ assist in the issue and sale of new securities.

12. The payment the issuer of a bond makes to the bondholders to pay for the use of borrowed money is called _____.

13. A _____ is a bond that is unsecured (i.e. not backed by any collateral.)

14. The process of _____ is the purchase of stocks by borrowing some of the purchase cost from the brokerage firm.

15. The part of a firm's profits that may be distributed to stockholders as either cash payments or additional shares of stock are called _____.

16. A _____ is an action by a company that gives stockholders two or more shares of stock for each one they own.

17. The technique of _____ means buying several different investment alternatives to spread the risk of investing.

18. Shares of ownership in a company are called _____.

19. A _____ is an organization that buys stocks and bonds and then sells shares in those securities to the public.

20. A corporate certificate called a _____ indicates that a person has lent money to a firm.

21. The average cost of 30 selected industrial stocks called the _____ is used to give an indication of the direction of the stock market over time.

22. The _____ is the federal agency that has the responsibility for regulating the various exchanges.

23. A condensed version of economic and financial information called a _____ must be filed with the SEC before issuing stock; it must be sent to potential purchasers of the firm's stock.

24. The _____ is a nationwide electronic system that links dealers across the nation so that they can buy and sell securities electronically.

25. _____ are the positive differences between the purchase price of a stock and its sale price.

26. A (n) _____ is the first public offering of a corporation's stock.

27. High-risk, high-interest bonds are called _____.

28. Collections of stocks that are traded on exchanges are called _____ , and are traded more like individual stocks than like mutual funds.

ASSESSMENT CHECK

Learning Goal 1

The Function of Securities Markets

1. Describe the two major functions of securities markets.

    a. _____

    b. _____

2. Explain the difference between the primary and the secondary markets

3. What functions do investment bankers perform for companies?

    a. _____

    b. _____

4. Give some examples of types of institutional investors

Stock Exchanges

5. Describe the NYSE Euronext.

6. How does trading over the counter (OTC) differ from trading on the NYSE Euronext?

7. The NASDAQ is _____

_____

8. How does the Securities Act of 1933 protect investors?

9. Discuss the provisions of the Securities and Exchange Act of 1934.

    a. _____

    b. _____

    c. _____

    d. _____

10. Insider trading is : _____

_____

    The term "insider" includes: _____

_____

11. How is it possible for Americans to purchase stocks in foreign companies, and for foreigners to purchase stock in American companies?

Learning Goal 3

How Businesses Raise Capital by Selling Stock

12.   What is meant by a stock's par value?

13.   Describe the important elements of dividends.

      a. _____

      b. _____

      c. _____

14.   List the advantages of raising funds through the sale of stock.

      a. _____

      b. _____

      c. _____

15.   Describe the disadvantages of issuing stock.

      a. _____

      b. _____

      c. _____

16.   What are three rights of holders of common stock?

      a. _____

      b. _____

      c. _____

17.   What are the benefits of owning preferred stock?

      a. _____

      b. _____

18. Normally, preferred stockholders do not get_____

    Preferred stock is generally issued with a par value that becomes_____

    _____

19. The special features of preferred stock are that it can be:

    a. _____

    b. _____

    c. _____

Learning Goal 4

How Businesses Raise Capital by Issuing Bonds

20. What legal obligation does a company have when selling bonds?

21. What is meant by the term "principal" when referring to a bond?

22. If a $1,000 bond has an interest rate of 10% and a maturity date of 2030, what does that mean to a bondholder?

23. What is meant by the term "coupon rate" with regard to bonds?

24. What factors affect the interest rate of a bond? Can the rate of interest change, once it has been set?

25. List the advantages of raising long-term capital by selling bonds.

    a. _____

    b. _____

    c. _____

    d. _____

26. What are the disadvantages?

     a. _____

     b. _____

     c. _____

27. Describe the two classes of corporate bonds.

28. Why are sinking funds attractive to firms and investors?

     a. _____

     b. _____

     c. _____

29. What the characteristics of a callable bond, and what is the benefit to a company?

30. What are the features of a convertible bond, and why would an investor convert a bond to common stock?

Learning Goal 5

How Investors Buy Securities

31. What is the process for an individual to invest in stocks and bonds?

32. What is the benefit of trading on-line?

33. What kind of customers use online trading?

34. The first step in any investment program is to: _____

     Other factors to consider are: _____

     _____

35. Describe the five criteria to use when selecting an investment option.

a. _____

b. _____

c. _____

d. _____

e. _____

36. What is the benefit of diversification in a portfolio of stocks and bonds?

Learning Goal 6

Investing in Stocks

37. In the stock market, describe:

Bulls (and a bull market): _____

_____

Bears (and a bear market): _____

_____

38. According to the text, what determines the market price of a stock?

39. Describe:

a. Growth stocks: _____

_____

b. Income stocks: _____

_____

c. Blue chip stocks: _____

_____

d. Penny stocks: _____

_____

40.   What is the difference between a market order and a limit order, when placing an order to buy stock?

41.   What is the difference between a round lot and an odd lot?

42.   Why would a company declare a stock split?

      How does a two-for-one- stock split work?

      How does a stock split benefit an investor?

43.   What is a "margin"? What does a 50% margin rate mean?

44.   What is the downside of buying on margin?

      What is meant by the term "margin call"?

45.   What information is included in a stock quote?

      a.   _____

      b.   _____

      c.   _____

      d.   _____

      e.   _____

Learning Goal 7

Investing in Bonds

46.   What are the best investments for those who desire limited risk and guaranteed income?

47. What are two questions first time corporate bond investors may ask? What are the answers to the questions?

48. What does it mean to sell a bond:

at a discount? _____

at a premium? _____

49. Why are junk bonds considered "junk"?

50. How is the price of a bond quoted?

51. What information is included in a bond quote?

a. _____

b. _____

c. _____

d. _____

e. _____

Learning Goal 8

Investing in Mutual Funds and Exchange-Traded Funds

52. What benefit does a mutual fund offer to an investor?

53. Describe an index fund.

54. What is the difference between a no-load and a load fund?

55. What is the difference between an open-end fund and a closed-end fund?

56. Discuss the primary characteristics of ETFs.

57. What information is contained in a mutual fund quote?

   a. _____

   b. _____

   c. _____

   d. _____

   e. _____

58. What is the net asset value, or NAV and how is it calculated?

Learning Goal 9

Understanding Stock Market Indicators

59. The financial industry used the Dow Jones Industrial Average to _____

_____

60. Do the companies included in the Dow ever change?

61. What is a criticism of the Dow Jones Industrial Average?

   What do many investors prefer to follow instead of the Dow?

62. What happens in a stock market "crash" and how often has it happened?

63. What do analysts many feel has been the cause of the market turmoil in the last two decades??

64 What are curbs and when are they put into effect?

65. What are circuit breakers and when are they put into effect?

66. What is believed to be the cause of the deep decline of 2000-2002?

67. What has happened in the real estate market which has contributed to the financial crisis and market crash of 2008-2009?

68. What should you do when considering investing in today's economic environment?

CRITICAL THINKING EXERCISES

Learning Goal 1

1. Sun-2-Shade is a young company that makes self-darkening windshields for the automotive industry. The financial manager of Sun-2-Shade has convinced management that new capital is needed for future growth. He hasn't yet decided on whether or not to issue stocks or bonds, but he knows that he wants to avoid the difficulty of looking for and marketing to potential investors himself, and prefers to let "experts" perform those functions. How should he go about pursuing this issue?

2. The three major ways stock is traded the United States are:

    NYSE Euronext
    NASDAQ
    OTC

    Match the correct answer to each of the following statements.

    a. _____   The largest stock exchange in the world.

    b. _____   Provides companies and investors with a means to trade stocks not listed on
                         the national exchanges.

    c. _____   Some large companies, like Microsoft are traded on this exchange as well as
                         federal, state and city government bonds.

    d. _____   Lists approximately 3,200 companies, including many technology companies.

    e. _____   Merged with Archipelago, a securities trading company that specializes in
                         electronic trading and recently purchased the second largest exchange in the
                         U.S. the AMEX.

    f. _____   A network of several thousand brokers, who maintain contact with each other
                         and buy and sell securities through a nationwide electronic system.

Learning Goals 3, 4

3. As the finance manager of Sun-2-Shade, Eric the owner has come to you for advice about whether
    or not to issue stock, or bonds to raise new capital. What would you tell him about the advantages
    and disadvantages of each type of security?

4. In discussing stocks, there are several terms with which you need to be familiar:

Stock   Pre-emptive right
Stock certificate   Preferred stock
Dividends   Cumulative preferred stock
Common stock   Callable preferred stock

Match the correct term to each of the following:

a. _____ Carmen Arauz was considering buying this type of stock, but was somewhat concerned about the risk when she learned that as a stockholder of this type, if the firm closed, she would be the last to share in the firm's assets.

b. _____ When her grandson was born, Judi Burton bought 100 shares of her favorite stock, and gave his parents this, as evidence of his ownership, which showed the number of shares owned, the name of the company, and the type of stock.

c. _____ As Judi's grandson Burke grew he received these periodic payments from his stock, which his parents invested for college.

d. _____ When Judi was deciding which kind of stock to purchase, she decided upon this type, because the dividends are fixed and must be paid before other dividends are paid. Further, there are no voting rights with this type of stock.

e. _____ What Burke doesn't have is this, which is the right of the stockholder to purchase new shares when the firm makes a new issue, so that his proportionate ownership in the company is maintained.

f. _____ One of the advantages of Burke's stock is that if the company misses his dividend, the company must pay it before it pays any other, and the missed dividends accumulate.

g. _____ Either common or preferred, this represents ownership in a firm.

h. _____ When Judi Burton bought these shares she made sure her stock didn't have this feature, which would require her grandson Burke to sell his shares back to the corporation.

5. Why do you think Judi Burton decided to buy her grandson Burke preferred stock instead of common stock?

6. In discussing bonds, there are several terms with which you need to be familiar:

Bond   Secured bonds
Interest   Sinking fund
Principal   Callable bond
Maturity date   Convertible bond
Unsecured bonds (debentures)

Match the correct term to each of the following descriptions:

a. _____ Gerry Hoffman will receive this on the date her bond becomes due in the year 2020.

b. _____ Beth Galganski will receive the principle value of her bond on this date.

c. _____ Tom Huff is in finance with Sun-2-Shade. Each quarter Sun-2-Shade puts money in this fund to pay off previously issued bonds, and Tom checks the amount of money the company has in the fund to be sure the company can pay off their bond issue on the maturity date.

d. _____ Because it has declared bankruptcy in the past, and the future is uncertain, General Motors would probably not be able to issue this type of bond.

e. _____ Bonnie Andersen receives $100 per year from her bond because this is a 10% bond.

f. _____ Mobil Oil issued an unsecured one at 14.4 percent due in 2020.

g. _____ TNG Enterprises issued this kind of bond, because they forecasted a decline in interest rates in a few years, and wanted the flexibility of being able to pay off the bond early.

h. _____ Bill Paterson bought this type of bond because he anticipated exchanging it for common stock in the firm later.

i. _____ Caldwell Industries used real estate holdings as collateral for their bonds.

Learning Goal 5

7. Five criteria to use when selecting a specific investment strategy are

Investment risk   Liquidity
Yield   Tax consequences
Duration

Read the following situations and evaluate the criteria in terms of the needs of the potential investors.

a. A young couple wants to invest money to begin a college tuition fund for their 5-year-old child. Since the child has no income, they are going to put the account in his name to avoid taxes.
b. A two-career couple; both anticipate retirement within the next five years.
c. A single person, just graduating from college; just starting a high paying job and wants to build capital. Not concerned about losing money at first.

8. As a potential investor in stocks, there are several terms used in securities trading with which you should be familiar:

Stockbroker	Stock splits
Growth stocks	Round lots
Income stocks	Margin calls
Blue chip stocks	Mutual funds
Penny stocks	ETFs
Market order	Diversification
Limit order	Bulls
Bears	Prospectus
Capital gains	Index fund
Buying on margin	

Match the term that would apply to the following descriptions:

a. _____   In 2006 Monsanto gave its stockholders one additional share of stock for every share they owned. This reduced the price from $80 per share to around $40 per share.

b. _____   Evelyn Minervi likes to dabble in the stock market. Last year she bought a number of stocks of this type, which each sold for $1.45 cents per share, but which were considered fairly risky.

c. _____   Joe Contino works in this job for a major brokerage firm, buying and selling stocks and bonds for his clients.

d. _____   Ron Stahl recently purchased this amount, exactly 100 shares, of Navistar stock.

e. _____   Dexter Inholt wanted to buy 500 shares of Ford at $40, each, but he only had $12,000 to invest, so he borrowed the $8,000 he still needed from his brokerage firm.

f. _____   The stock of General Electric, which pays regular dividends and has had fairly consistent growth in its stock price, is considered this type of stock.

g. _____   Marina Vasquez called her broker and asked him to buy Pepsico stock at the best price he could get, under this type of order.

h. _____   Hong Le believed the stock market was going to take a big jump after the most recent national elections, and purchased the stocks she wanted in anticipation of stock price increases.

i. _____   Lee Kornfeld, a prosperous doctor, has a lot of money invested in the market. He recently called his broker and told her to buy the stock of several firms after the price went down to a certain level under this type of order.

j. _____ Dexter Inholt bought Pfizer stock on margin a few weeks ago. When Pfizer's stock took a slight dip in price, Dexter Inholt got worried that his broker would issue this and would ask him to come up with some money to cover the losses the stock suffered.

k. _____ LaTonya Adams is a first time investor, unfamiliar with the market. She wants to get into the market, but diversify her risk, and invest in lots of firms. Her brother advised her to get into one of these, because then an expert does the research and manages the fund.

l. _____ Because he is investing money for his son's college education, Tim Martin decided to invest in several public utilities, because they offer a high dividend yield for the investment and usually keep up with inflation.

m. _____ The Chesterfield Investment Club always sends for this document, which discloses the financial information of the firms in which the club is interested in investing.

n. _____ Monte McHewie sold many of the stocks he was holding after he heard some economic news that led him to believe prices in the stock market were going to decline soon, indicating this type of market.

o. _____ Lindsey Schopp has a portfolio that consists of 10 percent high-risk growth stocks, 40 percent mutual funds, 30 percent government bonds, and 20 percent commodities. Lindsey has focused on this in creating her portfolio.

p. _____ Casey Argetsinger bought several shares of a relatively new company, for $7.50 per share. The stock paid no dividend, but was in the biotechnology field, and was predicted to grow by 20 percent per year over the next 10 years.

q. _____ When Ben and Casey Miller decided to buy a house, they sold a number of the stocks they had been holding. They found that there was a significant difference between what they paid for the stock, and the price at which they were able to sell it. So much so, that they were able to make a substantial down payment on their new house. This difference in selling prices was called their _____.

r. _____ Chad Mueller is 21 years old, and working at his first job out of college. He knows the value of saving money early, and wants to start investing now in mutual funds. He has decided on this type of fund, one that focuses on certain kinds of stock which covers the whole stock market.

s. _____ Samantha Glenn is a new investor who has decided to try a new way to diversify. Samantha is focusing on this kind of investment, which is a collection of stocks that unlike a mutual fund can be trading throughout the entire trading day, offering Samantha more flexibility than a mutual fund.

9. The managers of Sun-2-Shade are considering whether or not to issue stocks or bonds. Naturally, if the company issues bonds it wants to make sure that the bond is attractive for investors. What are the considerations that the managers need to look at to attract potential investors in their bonds? What will potential investors consider?

Learning Goal 8

10. The financial section of the Wall Street Journal contains stock and bond quotes, the Dow Jones Index and mutual fund quotes. Complete the following exercises, using the Wall Street Journal, or your local newspaper, or online, at a variety of sites, such as www.excite.com , www.yahoo.com www.motleyfool.com or, for mutual funds, at www.morningstar.com .

    a. Get the stock quotes for a company of your choice and get the following information.

        1. What was the actual price of the stock at the close of the day?   _____

        2. What was the net change in dollars?   _____

        3. What was the highest price the stock traded for in the previous year?   _____

        4.   How many shares were traded that day?   _____

        5. What is the company's earnings per share?   _____

        6. What is the P/E ratio for this company?   _____

    Click on Key Statistics for this company.

        7. What was the last dividend paid and when was it paid?   _____

        8. When was the last stock split, and what was the split factor?   _____

b. Go to www.yahoo.com and click on finance. Click on mutual funds.
   Choose a mutual fund and answer the following questions:

   1. What is the net asset value?   _____

   2. Is this a "no load" fund?   _____

   3. What is the fund family?   _____

   4. What is the year to date return?   _____

   5. What is the Morningstar rating?   _____

   6. What is the minimum investment?   _____

c. Look at the Dow Jones Industrial Average during the time your class is studying this chapter. Answer the following questions:

   1. Have stock prices trended up or down over the last 6 months?

   2. What was the highest Dow Jones Industrial Average in the last 6 months?

   3. What was the lowest?

PRACTICE TEST

MULTIPLE CHOICE – Circle the best answer

Learning Goal 1

1. One of the major functions of the securities markets is to:
   a. advertise the sale of stocks and bonds of major corporations.
   b. provide long term funding for corporations.
   c. assist businesses in finding long-term funding to finance business expansion or buying major goods and services.
   d. provide investors with information regarding the value of stock and bond issues offered by major corporations.

2. Which of the following statements is incorrect?
   a. The only time a corporation receives the money from the sale of stock is after the IPO.
   b. The IPO is handled in the secondary market.
   c. The first public offering of a corporation's stock is called an IPO.
   d. Investors buy and sell stocks in the secondary market.

3. An investment-banking firm underwrites a new issue of stocks and bonds by:
   a. buying the entire bond or stock issue a company wants to sell at an agreed discount.
   b. guaranteeing a minimum price in the market for a stock or bond.
   c. selling the entire bond issue for the issuing firm in global markets.
   d. putting up collateral for long term loans, such as bonds.

4. Which stock is the largest electronic stock trading market, and lists such companies as Google, Starbucks, Cisco and Dell?
    a.   NASDAQ
    b.   NYSE
    c.   AMEX
    d.   Chicago exchange

5. When the International Ladies Investment Club is deciding on which stock to purchase, the Club will often request a _____ before making that decision.
    a.   insider report
    b.   income statement
    c.   prospectus
    d.   disclosure statement

6. One of the benefits of trading on-line is that:
    a.   investing on-line is more accurate.
    b.   when you invest on-line you are more likely to make a good decision.
    c.   on-line trading services are less expensive than regular stockbroker commissions.
    d.   insider trading is less likely on-line.

Learning Goal 3

7. One of the disadvantages of issuing stock is that:
    a.   the company is legally obligated to pay dividends.
    b.   stockholders have the right to vote for the board of directors.
    c.   selling stock hurts the condition of the balance sheet since it creates debt.
    d.   Stockholder investments must be repaid.

8. Daddy Warbucks bought his daughter Annie some stock for her birthday. The type of stock Daddy bought has a fixed dividend, and if the dividend isn't paid when it is due, the missed dividend will accumulate and be paid later. Daddy bought Annie
    a.   common stock.
    b.   cumulative preferred stock.
    c.   convertible stock.
    d.   preemptive right stock.

9. Dividends are paid:
    a.   based on the prevailing market price of the stock.
    b.   before a firm pays interest to bondholders.
    c.   as determined by the stockholders.
    d.   from a firm's profits.

Learning Goal 4

10. Which of the following is not accurate when considering the advantages of selling bonds?
    a.   The debt is eventually eliminated when the bonds are paid off.
    b.   Interest on the bonds is not a legal obligation.
    c.   Bondholders have no say in running the firm.
    d.   interest is tax deductible.

11. Issuing a _____ permits a bond issuer to pay off the bond's principal prior to its maturity date.
    a. sinking fund
    b. convertible bond
    c. callable bond
    d. maturity date

12. On the maturity date of a bond, the issuing company will pay:
    a. the bondholder the bond principal in full.
    b. the investment banking firm the sinking fund.
    c. the bondholder the interest accrued for the duration of the bond.
    d. a dividend to the institutional investors.

Learning Goal 5

13. Ramon and Mariel Martinez are in their late 50s and hoping to retire within a few years. Their daughter, Elisa has just begun a new job after graduate school, and is considering investing now for some future needs, maybe a house, or even retirement. What investment advice would you give?
    a. Ray and Mariel should consider a high risk/high return investment, since they need to make as much money as possible before they retire.
    b. Elisa needs to be conservative, because she is young and may lose her job sometime over her career and need the money.
    c. Ray and Mariel should consider more conservative investments, as they want to retire soon.
    d. Ray and Mariel, and Elisa should all consider investing in growth stocks, since the prices of those stocks will rise.

14. Linda Hutton is considering investing in the stock market. Linda wants to be sure to be able to get her money back whenever she wants. Linda is concerned with:
    a. growth.
    b. yield.
    c. tax consequences.
    d. liquidity.

Learning Goal 6

15. Maria Chadwick is interested in investing in the stock of a corporation that pays regular dividends and generates consistent growth in the price of a share. Maria is interested in purchasing
    a. growth stocks.
    b. income stocks.
    c. blue chip stocks.
    d. penny stocks.

16. When the price of a share of U.S. On Line went up to $150 per share, the company declared a 3 for 1 stock split. The price of a share of U.S. On Line stock is now approximately:
    a. $100 per share.
    b. $75 per share.
    c. $50 per share.
    d. $25 per share.

17. Irena Dadiavich bought several shares of Google stock a couple of years ago for around $100. When Irena saw that Google was selling for over $400 a share she decided to sell all of her shares and take the profits to buy a new car. The difference between the price at which Irena bought the stock and the price at which she sold it is called:
    a. a market order
    b. capital gains
    c. a bear market
    d. premium

18. Adam Culbreath wanted to invest in the stock market, but didn't have the entire $10,000 he needed to buy the shares of the company he wanted. Adam does have $7,000, so he decided to borrow the remainder in order to be able to buy the stock he wanted. Adam:
    a. is investing in junk bonds.
    b. is buying on margin.
    c. is completely safe as he can always count on the price of his stock to go up.
    d. is interested in diversification.

19. Which of the following is not included in a stock quote?
    a. The average price for the last year
    b. The last dividend paid per share.
    c. The P/E ratio.
    d. The highest and lowest price the stock has sold for over the past 52 weeks.

Learning Goal 7

20. The best type of bond for an investor who wants low risk is:
    a. a premium bond.
    b. a U.S. government bond.
    c. a discount bond.
    d. a callable bond.

21. A bond that sells for more than face value is called a
    a. premium bond.
    b. U.S. government bond.
    c. discount bond.
    d. callable bond.

22. If the corporate bond price is stated as 89 ½, the price an investor would have to pay is:
    a. $890.50.
    b. $8950.
    c. $895.
    d. $89.50.

Learning Goal 8

23. The benefit of a mutual fund for investors is that
    a. mutual funds help investors to diversify and invest in many different companies.
    b. an investor doesn't have to do as much research.
    c. mutual funds are less expensive than most individual shares of stock.
    d. mutual funds don't charge a commission or up-front fee.

24. An index fund is a mutual fund that:
    a. guarantees dividends
    b. offers a minimum return
    c. only invests in stocks listed on the Dow Jones Industrial Average
    d. invests only in certain kinds of stock.

Learning Goal 9

25. The Dow Jones Industrial Average:
    a. identifies recessions from the last 30 years.
    b. gives an indication of the ups and downs of the stock market over time.
    c. compiles average stock prices of all stocks on the NYSE.
    d. shows the average stock price of 20 stocks for the last year.

26. In the stock market a circuit breaker:
    a. requires that only stocks of certain companies can be traded.
    b. is when a key computer is turned off and program trading is halted.
    c. halts trading for a half hour to two hours when the Dow falls 10, 20, or 30 percent in a day
    d. requires that all stockbrokers register their trades with an SEC advisor.

TRUE–FALSE

Learning Goal 1

1. _____ In the securities markets, the secondary markets handle the sale of previously issued securities between investors.

2. _____ An institutional investor is a large investor who buys the entire bond or stock issues a company wants to sell.

Learning Goal 2

3. _____ The Securities and Exchange Commission is responsible for regulating activities in the various exchanges.

4. _____ Insider trading involves the use of knowledge or information that individuals gain through their position that allows them to benefit unfairly from fluctuations in security prices.

5. _____ Investors in the United States are unable to invest in foreign companies, and vice versa

Learning Goal 3

6. _____ Dividends are declared by a company's board of directors.

7. _____ Common stock normally does not include voting rights.

8. _____ Preferred stock can be convertible to shares of common stock.

Learning Goal 4

9. _____ Bondholders receive one vote for each bond they own in a company.

10. _____ Josh Hayes intends to invest in a bond, but at some point believes it may be beneficial to change that bond over to common stock in the company he is investigating. Josh should consider a convertible bond.

11. _____ A company is legally bound to pay the interest on a bond, but not the principal amount

Learning Goal 5

12. _____ A stockbroker is a registered representative who acts as an intermediary to buy and sell stocks for clients

13. _____ A young person saving for retirement can afford to invest in higher risk stocks than a person who is nearing retirement age.

14. _____ One of the major criteria to consider when investing is duration, which is the amount of time your money is committed to that investment.

Learning Goal 6

15. _____ "Bulls" are investors who believe that stock prices are going to rise, so they buy in anticipation of the increase.

16. _____ Companies may offer a stock split when the price of their stock is too high and the company wants to stock to be more desirable in the market.

17. _____ A market order tells a broker to buy or sell a particular stock at a specific price.

18. _____ One of the items found in a stock quote will be the highest price paid in the last 52 weeks

Learning Goal 7

19. _____ In general, the higher the risk of a bond, the lower the interest rate the issuer must offer in order to keep the price low so it will be attractive to investors.

20. _____ One of the disadvantages of a bond as an investment is that once purchased, it must be held to maturity.

Learning Goal 8

21. _____ Mutual funds are probably the best way for smaller investors to get started.

22. _____ The portfolio strategy, or allocation model refers to a strategy of diversified investment.

23. _____ Buying stock on margin means borrowing stock from a stockbroker, selling it, then buying the stock back at a lower price than what you paid.

Learning Goal 9

24. _____ Many investors believe the Dow is not an accurate measure of stock prices, and prefer to follow a stock index such as Standard and Poors 500.

25. _____ Analysts agree that program trading is responsible for the periods of turmoil the market has experienced since 1987.

You Can Find It On The Net

How much would you have made, or lost, if you had invested in the stock market a year ago? Two years ago? How about 5 years ago?

Go to **www.yahoo.com**, and click on Finance/Quotes. Go down to historical quotes, and follow the instructions. Alternatively, do a search of the yahoo site for historical stock price quotes. This should get you to the correct page.

If you had purchased $1000 of a blue chip stock, such as Coca-Cola, General Electric or IBM exactly one year ago, what would your capital gain, or loss, be as of today? What would the difference be from 5 years ago?

Calculate the same information for a technology related company, such as Cisco, Microsoft or Yahoo.com Would you have a capital gain? How much?

Now, visit an online broker such as www.etrade.com or www.ameritrade.com How do their fees compare to trading online with a discount broker such as Charles Schwab – www.charlesschwab.com, or a traditional broker such as A.G. Edwards www.agedwards.com

ANSWERS

LEARNING THE LANGUAGE

1.	Institutional investors	11.	Investment bankers	20.	Bond
2.	Over the counter market (OTC)	12.	Interest	21.	Dow Jones Industrial Average
3.	Stock certificate	13.	Debenture bond	22.	Securities and Exchange Commission (SEC)
4.	Program trading	14.	Buying stock on margin	23.	Prospectus
5.	Common stock	15.	Dividends	24.	NASDAQ
6.	Sinking fund	16.	Stock split	25.	Capital gains
7.	Stockbroker	17.	Diversification	26.	Initial Public Offering (IPO)
8.	Stock exchange	18.	Stocks	27.	Junk bonds
9.	Maturity date	19.	Mutual fund	28.	Exchange-traded funds (ETFs)
10.	Preferred stock				

ASSESSMENT CHECK

Learning Goal 1

The Function of Securities Markets

1. Two major functions of securities markets are:
   a. to assist businesses in finding long-term funding they need to finance operations, expand their businesses, or buy goods and services.
   b. to give investors a place to buy and sell investments such as stocks and bonds to help build their financial future.

2. The primary market handles the sale of new securities. This is the only time corporations make money on the sale of securities. After the corporation has made its money, the secondary market handles the trading of securities between investors. The proceeds of sales in the secondary market go to the investor selling the stock, not to the corporation whose stock is sold.

3. Investment bankers
   a. help companies prepare the extensive financial analyses necessary to gain SEC approval for stock or bond issues.
   b. underwrite new issues, which means that the investment banker will buy the entire bond or stock issue a company wants to sell at an agreed upon discount and then sell the issue to private or institutional investors at full price.

4. Institutional investors are mutual funds, pension funds, insurance companies and banks. Because they have such large buying power, they are a powerful force in the securities markets.

Learning Goal 2

Stock Exchanges

5. The NYSE Euronext is the world's largest securities exchange. It is a group of stock exchanges in six countries, with 6,500 stocks listed including 78 of the 100 largest companies in the world.

6. The OTC market is a network of several thousand brokers who maintain contact with one another and buy and sell securities through a nationwide electronic system. Trading is conducted between two parties directly, instead of through an exchange like the NYSE Euronext.

7. The NASDAQ is a telecommunications network that links dealers across the nation so they can buy and sell securities electronically. It is the largest U.S. electronic stock trading market.

8. The Securities Act of 1933 protects investors by requiring full disclosure of financial information by firms selling new stocks or bonds. Congress passed this act to deal with the "free-for-all" atmosphere that existed during the Roaring Twenties.

9. The Securities and Exchange Act of 1934:
    a. created the Securities and Exchange Commission.
    b. requires that companies trading on the national exchange must register with the SEC and provide annual updates.
    c. established guidelines companies must follow issuing stocks or bonds to the public
    d. established guidelines to prevent insiders from taking advantage of privileged information.

10. Insider trading is the use of knowledge or information that individuals gain through their position that allows them to benefit unfairly from fluctuations in security prices.

    The term "insider" includes just about anyone with securities information that is not available to the general public.

11. Stock exchanges operate all over the world, and expanded communications and the relaxation of legal barriers enable investors to buy securities from companies almost anywhere in the world through brokers who have access to foreign stock exchanges. Foreign investors can easily invest in U.S. securities because exchanges in foreign countries trade large amounts of U.S. securities. The number of U.S. companies that are listed on foreign stock exchanges is growing.

Learning Goal 3

How Businesses Raise Capital by Selling Stock

12. A stock's par value is a dollar amount assigned to each share of stock by the corporation's charter. Some states use par value as a basis for calculating the state's incorporation charges and fees. Today most companies issue "no-par" stock.

13. Important elements of dividends are:
    a. Dividends are a part of a firm's profits that <u>may</u> be distributed to shareholders.
    b. Dividends are declared by a corporation's board of directors and are generally paid quarterly.
    c. Dividends will be distributed as either cash payments or additional shares of stock.

14. The advantages of raising funds through the sale of stock are:
    a. Because stockholders are owners, they never have to be repaid.
    b. There is no legal obligation to pay dividends.
    c. Selling stock can improve the condition of the balance sheet because it creates no debt.

15. The disadvantages of issuing stock are:
    a. As owners, stockholders can alter the control of the firm, through voting for the board of directors.
    b. Dividends are paid out of after tax profits so are not tax deductible.
    c. Management decision-making can be hampered by the need to keep the stockholders happy.

16. Three rights of common stockholders are:
    a. the right to vote for the board of directors and important issues affecting the company.
    b. to share in the firm's profits though dividends declared by the board of directors.
    c. *preemptive right*, which is the first right to purchase any new shares of common stock the firm decides to issue. This right allows common stockholders to maintain a proportional share of ownership in the company

17. Owners of preferred stock:
    a. have a preference in the payment of dividends.
    b. have a prior claim on company assets if the firm goes out of business.

18. Normally preferred stockholders do not get have voting rights in the firm.

    Preferred stock is generally issued with a par value that becomes the base for a fixed dividend the firm is willing to pay.

19. The special features of preferred stock are that it can be:
    a. Callable, like bonds. This means a company could require preferred stockholders to sell back their shares.
    b. Convertible to common stock.
    c. Cumulative. If one or more dividends are not paid when due, the missed dividends of cumulative preferred stock will accumulate and be paid later.

Learning Goal 4

How Businesses Raise Capital by Issuing Bonds

20. A company that issues bonds has a legal obligation to pay regular interest payments to investors and repay the entire bond principal amount at a prescribed time, called the maturity date.

21. The principal is the face value of a bond, which the issuing company is legally bound to repay in full to the bondholder.

22. A 10% bond with a maturity date of 2030 means that the bondholder will receive $100 in interest per year until the year 2030, when the full principal, most likely $1000, must be repaid. Interest is usually paid in two installments each year.

23. The interest rate paid on bonds is also called the bond's coupon rate.

24. The interest rate paid on a bond varies according to factors such as the state of the economy, the reputation of the company issuing the bond, and the going interest rate being paid by U.S. government bonds or bonds of similar companies. Once an interest rate is set it generally can't be changed.

25. a. Bondholders are not owners of a firm so they have no vote on corporate matters. Management maintains control over the firm's operations.
    b. The interest paid on bonds is tax deductible for the firm.
    c. Bonds are a temporary source of funding. They are eventually repaid, and the debt is eliminated.
    d. Bonds can be repaid before the maturity date if they contain a call provision, and can also be convertible to common stock.

26. a. Bonds are an increase in debt and could adversely affect the firm.
    b. Interest on bonds is a legal obligation. If interest isn't paid, bondholders can take legal action.
    c. The face value of bonds must be repaid at maturity, which could cause cash flow problems.

27. Unsecured bonds, called debentures, are not supported by any collateral. Generally only firms with excellent credit ratings can issue debentures. The other class of bonds, secured bonds, is backed by some tangible asset, or collateral, that is pledged to the bondholder if bond interest isn't paid.

28. Sinking funds are attractive to firms and investors because:
    a. They provide for an orderly retirement of a bond issue.
    b. They reduce the risk of not being repaid, and so make the bond more attractive as an investment.
    c. They can support the market price of a bond because of reduced risk.

29. A callable bond permits the bond issuer to pay off the bond's principal before its maturity date. Callable bonds give companies some discretion in long-term forecasting. The company can benefit if they call in a bond issue that pays a high rate of interest, and re-issue new bonds at a lower rate of interest.

30. A convertible bond is a bond that can be converted into shares of common stock in the issuing company. If the value of the firm's common stock grew in value over time, bondholders can compare the value of the bond's interest with the possibility of a sizable profit by converting to a specified number of common shares.

Learning Goal 5

How Investors Buy Securities

31. To invest in stocks or bonds, you first decide what stock or bond you want to buy. Then you find a stockbroker. The stockbroker will place an order where the bond or stock is traded and negotiate a price. When the transaction is completed, the trade is reported to your broker who notifies you to confirm your purchase. The same procedures are followed if you sell stocks or bonds. Large brokerage firms maintain automated order systems that allow brokers to enter you order the instant you make, so the order can be confirmed in seconds.

32. On-line trading services are less expensive than regular stockbroker commissions.

33. Customers interested in online trading services are primarily those who are willing to do their own research and make their own investment decisions without the assistance of a broker. The leading online brokerage services provide market information but no advice.

34. The first step in any investment program is to analyze your risk tolerance.

    Other factors to consider are your desired income, cash requirements, growth prospects, and hedging against inflation.

35. The five criteria to use when selecting an investment option are:
    a. Investment risk – the chance that your investment could go down in value in the future.
    b. Yield - the rate of return.
    c. Duration – the length of time for which you are committing your assets.
    d. Liquidity – how quickly you can get back your money if you need to.
    e. Tax consequences – how the investment affects your tax situation.

36. Diversification involves buying several different types of investments to spread the risk of investing. With diversification, investors decrease the chance of losing everything they have invested.

Learning Goal 6

Investing in Stocks

37. Bulls are investors who believe that stock prices are going to rise, so they buy stock in anticipation of the increase. When overall stock prices are rising, it is called a bull market.

    Bears are investors who believe that stock prices are going to decline. These investors sell their stocks before they expect prices to fall. When the prices of stocks decline steadily, it is referred to as a bear market.

38. According to the text, the market price of a common stock is dependent upon the overall performance of the corporation in meeting its business objectives.

39. a. Growth stocks are stocks of corporations whose earnings are expected to grow at a rate faster than other stocks. They are often considered risky, but they offer investors the potential for higher returns.
    b. Income stocks offer investors a high dividend yield on their investment.
    c. Blue chip stocks are the stock of high quality companies. They pay regular dividends and generate consistent growth in the company stock price.
    d. Penny stocks sell for less than $2. These stocks are considered high risk investments.

40. A *market order* tells a broker to buy or to sell a sotck immediately at the best price available.
    A *limit order* tells the broker to buy or sell a stock at a specific price, if that price becomes available.

41. Companies and brokers prefer to have stock purchases conducted in *round lots*, which are purchases of 100 shares at a time. Investors often buy stock in *odd lots* which are purchases of less than 100 shares at a time.

42. When investors cannot afford to buy shares of stock in companies selling for a high price, the company may choose to declare a stock split; that is, they issue two or more shares for every share of stock currently outstanding.

    A two-for-one stock split the effect of dropping the price of a share, by half, which giving the investor twice the number of shares. For example, if a stock was selling for $150 and you had one share, after a two for one stock split, you would have two shares, and each share would be valued at about $75.

    This stock split may increase demand for the stock, which may cause the price to go up in the near future.

43. The margin is the portion of the stock's purchase price an investor must pay with their own money. If a margin rate is 50 percent, an investor may borrow 50 percent of the stock's purchase price from a broker.

44. The downside of buying on margin is that investors must repay the credit extended by the broker, plus interest.

    If an investor's account goes down in market value, the broker will issue a margin call, requiring the investor to come up with more money to cover the losses the stock has suffered. If the investor is unable to make the margin call, the broker can legally sell shares of the investor's stock to reduce the broker's chance of loss.

45. A stock quote will contain the following information:
    a. The highest and lowest price the stock traded for that day
    b. The highest and lowest price over the past 52 weeks
    c. Stock's dividend yield
    d. The price/earnings (P/E) ratio
    e. Return on equity

Learning Goal 7

Investing in Bonds

46. For those who desire limited risk and guaranteed income, U.S. Government bonds are a secure investment backed by the full faith and credit of the federal government. Municipal bonds are also secure, and are offered by local governments, and often have advantages such as tax free interest.

47. Two questions first time corporate bond investors have are
    a. "If I purchase a bond, do I have to hold it to the maturity date?" The answer is no. However if you decide to sell your bond before its maturity date, you are not guaranteed to get the face value of the bond.
    b. " How can I assess the investment risk of a particular bond issue?" Standard and Poor's and Moody's Investor Service rate the level of risk of many corporate and government bonds.

48. If your bond does not have features that make it attractive to other investors, you may have to sell your bond at a discount which is a price less than face value

    If the bond is highly valued, you may be able to sell it at a premium which is a price above face value.

49. Standard & Poor's Investment Advisory Service and Moody's Investor Service define junk bonds as those with high-risk and high default rates. If the company can't pay off the bond, the investor is left with a bond that isn't worth more than the paper it's written on.

50. A bond price is quoted as a percentage of $1000.

51. A bond quote in the paper contains
    a. the interest rate
    b. the maturity date
    c. rating
    d. price of the bond
    e. whether the bond is callable

Investing in Mutual Funds and Exchange-Traded Funds

52. The benefit of a mutual fund to an investor is they can buy shares of the mutual fund and share in the ownership of many different companies they could not afford to invest in individually. Thus mutual funds help investors diversify.

53. An index fund is a fund that invests in a certain kind of stocks or bonds, or in the market as a whole. An index fund may focus on large companies, small companies, emerging countries, or real estate.

54. A no-load fund is one that charges no commission to either buy or sell its shares. A load fund would charge a commission to investors.

55. An open-end fund will accept the investment of any interested investors. Closed-end funds offer a specific number of shares for investment. Once the fund reaches its target number, no new investors are admitted into the fund.

56. ETFs resemble both stock and mutual funds in that they are collections of stocks and bonds that are traded on exchanges, but themselves are traded more like individual stocks than like mutual funds. Unlike mutual funds, ETFs can be traded throughout the entire trading day, like individual stocks.

57. The information contained in a mutual fund quote includes:
    a. Name of the fund
    b. Price at which a fund's share can be purchased or sold, called the Net Asset Value (NAV)
    c. year to date rate of return of the fund
    d. Change from the previous day's NAV
    e. Fund's net assets

58. The Net Asset Value, NAV, is the market value of the mutual fund's portfolio divided by the number of shares it has outstanding. The NAV is the price per share of the mutual fund.

Learning Goal 9

Understanding Stock Market Indicators

59. The financial industry uses the Dow Jones Industrial Average to give an indication of the direction of the stock market over time.

60. The companies in the Dow have changed over the years. The Dow started with 12 stocks, and now contains stocks of 30 different companies. The companies included in the Dow have changed over the years when it's deemed appropriate to reflect changes in our economy.

61. Critics of the Dow Jones Average argue that if the purpose of the Dow is to give an indication of the direction of the broader market over time, the 30-company sample is too small to get a good statistical representation.

    Many investors and market analysts prefer to follow stock indexes like the Standard and Poor's 500 that tracks the performance of many more companies. Investors also closely follow the NASDAQ.

62. A stock market crash occurs when the stock market loses a significant part of its value in a single day. The largest crashes occurred in 1929, 1987, and 1997, 2000-2002 and 2008

63. Many analysts believe that program trading was a big cause of the stock market drop in the last two decades. In program trading, investors give computers instructions to automatically sell if the price of their stock dips to a certain price to avoid potential losses.

64. Program trading curbs are put into effect when the Dow moves up or down by a large number of points in one trading day. A key computer is turned off and program trading is halted.

65. Circuit breakers are more drastic restrictions than curbs, and are triggered when the Dow falls 10, 20, or 30 percent in one day. Depending upon the rate of decline and the time of day the circuit breakers will halt trading between a half hour and two hours to give traders a chance to assess the situation. If the Dow drops 30 percent trading closes for the entire day.

66. The deep decline of 2000-2002 is believed to be the bursting of the "dot.com" bubble. A bubble occurs when too many investors drive the price of something unrealistically high.

67. Like the earlier tech bubble, the real estate bubble burst in 2008. Investors believed home prices would increase consistently. Financial institutions reduced lending requirements to make more mortgage loans, homebuilders overbuild, and buyers overspent. The government contributed to the problem by requiring mortgages to be given to low and moderate income buyers with weak credit scores, and without verification of income. These were called *subprime* loan.

   These loans were packaged as securities that were sold to investors. When the real estate market peaked and prices began to fall, many financial institutions were driven into a panic, and some failed.

68. When considering investing today, it is important to diversify your investments and understand the risks of investing. It is also wise to take a long-term perspective. It's important to do research, keep up with the news, and make use of investment resources such as newspapers, magazines, newsletters, the Internet, and TV programs.

CRITICAL THINKING EXERCISES

Learning Goal 1

1. The finance manager of Sun-2-Shade has the opportunity to avoid the difficulties of a new issue by making use of specialists in the securities markets such as investment bankers. These companies will underwrite the new issue, by purchasing the entire issue for a discount. The investment banker will then sell the issue on the open market to either private or institutional investors, such as pension funds, mutual funds, insurance companies, or banks.

Learning Goal 2

2. a. NYSE Euronext
   b. OTC
   c. NASDAQ
   d. NASDAQ
   e. NYSE Euronext
   f. OTC

3. As we learned in previous chapters, one of the jobs of a finance manager is to determine the best way for a firm to raise long-term capital. When deciding which form of long-term funding is best a finance manager will weigh the options of both equity and debt funding.

    You will probably tell Eric that bonds offer several long term financing advantages. Perhaps one of the most important to Eric will be that bondholders are not owners of the firm, so they won't have a vote on corporate matters. So, Eric and his management team will maintain control over the firm. Other benefits include the fact that bond interest is tax deductible, and that eventually the debt will be repaid. If interest rates are high when the bonds are issued, they can be called and re-issued when rates have lowered.

    Conversely, when the firm goes into debt by issuing bonds, there could be an adverse affect on the market's perception of the firm. If for some reason a cash flow problem develops, interest is a legal obligation, and the firm would still have to pay interest, even with a negative cash flow, and provisions have to be made for when the face value has to be paid off. This could also negatively affect cash flow.

    Stocks offer the opportunity for a firm to stay out of debt, and there is no legal obligation to pay dividends. Selling stock can also improve the look of the balance sheet.

    The downside of stock issues is that the structure of ownership changes, and stockholders have the right to vote on the board of directors, and sometimes decisions have to be made with the primary goal of keeping stockholders happy. Eric may not want to give up his ownership control. Another downside is that dividends, if paid, are not tax deductible.

Learning Goal 3

4. a. Common stock
    b. Stock certificate
    c. Dividends
    d. Preferred stock
    e. Pre-emptive right
    f. Cumulative preferred
    g. Stock
    h. Callable preferred

5. While both forms of stock represent ownership, there are several differences between preferred and common stock. First, an owner of common stock has the right to vote, and so can influence corporate policy. Judi probably did not consider this to be important, as Burke was a baby, and wouldn't really be concerned about such things! Further, common stock is considered to be more risky than preferred, because if a company closes, common stockholders share in assets only <u>after</u> bondholders and preferred stockholders. Also, while preferred dividends are fixed, and sometimes accumulate, common stock dividends will only be paid after both bondholders and preferred stockholders receive their interest and dividends. If Judi was interested in starting a "college fund" for Burke, then the preferred stock was a better match for her needs.

Learning Goal 4

6. a. Principal
    b. Maturity date
    c. Sinking fund
    d. Unsecured bond (debenture)
    e. Interest
    f. Bond
    g. Callable bond
    h. Convertible bond
    i. Secured bond

7. a. This couple would probably want a low to moderate risk investment, which will increase their principal over time. Tax consequences will be minimal, at least at first, as the child will have little income in the early years.

(If they opt for an interest or dividend bearing type of account, the child will be earning income, and tax consequences may become a more important consideration). They will choose an investment that will yield a high return over the long run, and liquidity isn't important for now.

b. Since this investment may be for retirement, this couple will probably want a low risk investment, with as high an after-tax yield as they can earn. It will be of short duration, since they plan to retire in five years, and they may want to keep it fairly liquid in case they retire in less than five years. A big factor will be the tax consequences, as they are a two-income family, and are probably in a high tax bracket with few deductions.

c. A young, single person will choose a higher risk investment than the others, because they probably are not concerned with long-term considerations such as retirement. Since they want to build capital, the yield will be important for the short term. This individual may want to keep investments of short duration to make a large return in a few years, when they may want the money as a down payment for a house, for example, and they may want them fairly liquid. Tax consequences will be important, as there are few deductions, and they may be in a relatively high bracket

Learning Goal 6

8. a. Stock split   k. Mutual fund
    b. Penny stocks   l. Income stock
    c. Stockbroker   m. Prospectus
    d. Round lot   n. Bear
    e. Buying on margin   o. Diversification
    f. Blue chip   p. Growth stock
    g. Market order   q. Capital gains
    h. Bull   r. Index fund
    i. Limit order   s. ETFs
    j. Margin call

Learning Goal 7

9. Managers at Sun-2-Shade will have to determine the market's perceived rate of risk for this bond. If the bond is considered risky, as determined by Standard & Poors and Moody's Investors Service, then the interest rate will have to be higher than if it were considered to be a safer investment. Investors will invest in a bond that is considered risky only if the potential return to them is high enough.

Sun-2-Shade will be offering corporate bonds and the face value will most likely be $1,000. Investors will consider how soon the bond matures, the interest rate, and whether or not it has other features that will allow the investor to sell either at a premium or a discount.

10. Your answers for each section will vary according to which companies you choose to study, and when you are studying this chapter. As for the Dow Jones Industrial Averages, stock prices trended upward in the mid-1990s and the average broke 9000 for the first time in early 1998. Stock prices quickly recovered from the drop in October 1997. By late 1999, the Dow Jones Industrial Average hit over 11,000. During the early 2000s the Average varied, and in early 2001, the Dow Jones fell rapidly, plunging to below 10,000. It started a very slow recovery in mid- 2003. In 2008-2009 the market had a steep decline.

PRACTICE TEST

MULTIPLE CHOICE

1.	c	14.	d
2.	b	15.	c
3.	a	16.	c
4.	a	17.	b
5.	c	18.	b
6.	c	19.	a
7.	b	20.	b
8.	b	21.	d
9.	d	22.	c
10.	b	23.	a
11.	c	24.	d
12.	a	25.	b
13.	c	26.	c

TRUE–FALSE

1.	T	14.	T
2.	F	15.	T
3.	T	16.	T
4.	T	17.	F
5.	F	18.	T
6.	T	19.	F
7.	F	20.	F
8.	T	21.	T
9.	F	22.	T
10.	T	23.	F
11.	F	24.	T
12.	T	25.	T
13.	T		

CHAPTER 20 – MONEY, FINANCIAL INSTITUTIONS, AND THE FEDERAL RESERVE

LEARNING GOALS

After you have read and studied this chapter, you should be able to:

1. Explain what money is and what makes money useful.
2. Describe how the Federal Reserve controls the money supply.
3. Trace the history of banking and the Federal Reserve System.
4. Classify the various institutions in the American banking system.
5. Briefly trace the causes of the banking crisis of 2009-2009 and explain how the government protects your funds during such crises.
6. Describe how technology helps make banking more efficient.
7. Evaluate the role and importance of international banking the World Bank and the International Monetary Fund.

LEARNING THE LANGUAGE

Listed below are important terms found in the chapter. Choose the correct term for the definition and write it in the space provided.

Banker's acceptance	Federal Deposit Insurance corporation (FDIC)	Open-market operations
Barter	International Monetary Fund (IMF)	Pension funds
Certificate of deposit (CD)	Letter of credit	Reserve requirement
Commercial bank	M-1	Savings and loan association (S&L)
Credit unions	M-2	Savings Association Insurance Fund (SAIF)
Debit card	M-3	Smart card
Demand deposit	Money	Time deposit
Discount rate	Money supply	World Bank
Electronic funds transfer (EFT) system	Nonbanks	

1. Nonprofit, member-owned financial cooperatives called _____ offer the full variety of banking services to their members.

2. M-2 plus big money deposits like institutional money market funds make up the _____ money supply.

3. The _____ is a percentage of commercial banks' checking and savings accounts that must be physically kept in the bank.

4. The technical name for a savings account is a _____ , for which the bank can require prior notice before the owner withdraws money.

5. A _____ is a promise that the bank will pay some specified amount at a particular time.

6. _____ is anything that people generally accept as payment for goods and services.

7. The interest rate the Fed charges for loans to member banks is the _____.

8. Financial organizations known as _____ accept no deposits, but offer many of the services provided by regular banks include pension funds, insurance companies, commercial finance companies, consumer finance companies and brokerage houses.

9. A time deposit (savings) account called a _____ earns interest to be delivered at the end of the certificate's maturity date.

10. A computerized system known as _____ electronically performs financial transactions such as making purchases, paying bills, and receiving paychecks.

11. The part of the FDIC that insures holders of accounts in savings and loan associations is called the _____.

12. An electronic funds transfer tool known as a _____ serves the same function as checks, in that it withdraws funds from a checking account.

13. The activity called _____ is the direct trade goods and services for other goods and services.

14. A financial institution called a _____ accepts both savings and checking deposits and provides home mortgage loans.

15. The _____ is the amount of money the Federal Reserve Bank makes available for people to buy goods and services.

16. A _____ is a promise by a bank to pay the seller a given amount if certain conditions are met.

17. _____ are amounts of money put aside by corporations, nonprofit organizations, or unions to cover part of the financial needs of members when they retire.

18. A profit-seeking organization that receives deposits from individuals and corporations in the form of checking and savings accounts and then uses some of these funds to make loans is called a _____.

19. The _____ is an independent agency of the U.S. government that insures bank deposits.

20. The buying and selling of U.S. government bonds by the Fed is called _____ and has the goal of regulating the money supply.

21. The _____ includes everything in M-1 plus money that may take a little more time to obtain, such as savings accounts, money market accounts, mutual funds, and certificates of deposit.

22. The technical name for a checking account is a(n) _____ , from which money can be withdrawn anytime on demand by the depositor.

23. The _____ assists the smooth flow of money among nations.

24. The _____ , also known as the International Bank for Reconstruction and Development, is primarily responsible for financing economic development.

25. Money that can be accessed quickly and easily, such as currency, checks, traveler's checks, is called the _____ money supply.

26. A _____ is an electronic funds transfer tool that is a combination credit card, debit card, phone card, driver's license card and more.

ASSESSMENT CHECK

Learning Goal 1

Why Money Is Important

1. What is a "barter exchange"?

2. Describe five characteristics of a "useful" form of money.

   a. _____

   b. _____

   c. _____

   d. _____

   e. _____

3. What is e-cash and how can you use it?

Learning Goal 2

What is the Money Supply?

4. What are M-1, M-2 and M-3, and what is the difference between them? Which is the most commonly used definition?

5. What would happen if the Fed were to make too much money available in the economy?

6. What would happen if the Fed took money out of the economy?

7. Why does the money supply need to be controlled?

8. What does a "falling dollar" mean?

   What does a rising dollar mean?

   What does this mean for the prices of European goods?

9. What makes our dollar "weak" or "strong"?

10. When the economy is strong the demand for dollars: _____

    When the economy is weak the demand for dollars: _____

    So the value of the dollar depends upon: _____

11. What organization is in charge of monetary policy?

12. What are the five major parts of the Federal Reserve System?

a. _____

b. _____

c. _____

d. _____

e. _____

13. What is the primary function of the board of governors?

14. Describe the Federal Open Market Committee.

15. What are some activities of the Federal Reserve?

a. _____

b. _____

c. _____

d. _____

e. _____

f. _____

g. _____

16. The three basic tools the Fed uses to manage the money supply are:

a. _____

b. _____

c. _____

17. Which of the three tools the Fed uses to manage the money supply is:

    a. most commonly used: _____

    b. most powerful: _____

18. Describe what happens in the economy when the Fed *increases* the reserve requirement.

    What is the result of a *decrease* in the reserve requirement?

19. When using open market operations, what actions does the Fed take when it wants to:

    a. decrease the money supply: _____

        _____

    b. increase the money supply: _____

        _____

20. Why is the Fed often called the banker's bank?

21. An increase in the discount rate by the Fed: _____

    _____

    A decrease in the discount rate by the Fed: _____

    _____

22. What is the federal funds rate?

23. Why do banks encourage forms of payment when customers are making purchases outside of their local area?

The History of Banking and the Need for the Fed

24.   Why were colonists forced to use barter for goods?

25.   Why did Massachusetts begin issuing its own paper money?

      Why did this continental currency become worthless?

26.   Land banks were established to _____.

27.   Describe the evolution of the "central bank."

28.   Describe the state of banking by the time of the Civil War.

29.   The Federal Reserve System was designed to_____.

30.   What led to the bank failures of the 1930's?

31.   What actions did congress take in 1933 and 1935 to strengthen the banking system?

Learning Goal 4

The U.S. Banking System

32.   Identify four types of banking institutions.

      a.   _____

      b.   _____

      c.   _____

      d.   _____

33. What kinds of institutions are included in a list of nonbanks?

    a. _____

    b. _____

    c. _____

    d. _____

    e. _____

34. What are two types of customers for commercial banks?

    a. _____

    b. _____

35. How does a commercial bank make a profit?

36. Describe the characteristics of a certificate of deposit (CD) including how interest rates are determined.

37. Identify the services offered by commercial banks in addition to checking (demand deposits) and savings accounts (time deposits):

    a. _____   g. _____

    b. _____   h. _____

    c. _____   i. _____

    d. _____   j. _____

    e. _____   k. _____

    f. _____   l. _____

38. What services are being offered through ATMs?

39. What is another name for savings and loans institutions, and why are they known as such?

40. Why did so many S&Ls fail between 1979 and 1983?

41. In the 1980s The federal government stepped in to strengthen S&Ls by permitting them to:

a. _____

b. _____

c. _____

d. _____

42. What services do credit unions offer their members?

43. What has been the result of competition between nonbanks and banks?

44. What financial services are offered by:

a. Life insurance companies _____

_____

b. Pension funds _____

_____

c. Brokerage firms _____

_____

d. Commercial and consumer finance companies _____

_____

The Current Banking Crisis and How the Government Protects Your Money

45.   Why do some people believe the Fed was responsible for the recent banking crisis?

46.   Describe mortgage backed loans and how they contributed to the crisis.

47.   How did the Fed contribute to the problems created by mortgage backed loans when home values began to decline?

48.   In the end, the blame for the banking crisis can be placed on:

a.   _____

b.   _____

c.   _____

d.   _____

e.   _____

49.   List the three major sources of financial protection

a.   _____

b.   _____

c.   _____

50.   In the case of a bank failure the FDIC : _____

_____

_____

51.   Why were the FDIC and the FSLIC created?

52. How was SAIF formed?

53. What does the NCUA provide for?

Learning Goal 6

Using Technology to Make Banking More Efficient

54. One solution banks have used to reduce the cost of processing checks is to:

    _____

    The most efficient way to transfer funds is: _____

55. The benefit of electronic funds transfer is that: _____

    _____

56. What are "Go-Tags"?

57. How is a debit card different from a credit card?

    What is a drawback of a debit card compared to credit cards?

58. What are payroll debit cards and how do they work?

59. How are smart cards different from other cards?

60. What is:

    a.   direct deposit? _____

    _____

    b.   direct payment? _____

    _____

61. What banking services are available to customers through online banking?

62. Benefits online banks can offer to customers include: _____

    _____

63. How have customers responded to Internet banks? Why?

64. In banking the future seems to be_____

    _____

Learning Goal 7

Leaders in International Banking

65. What three services are offered to banks to help businesses conduct business overseas?

    a.   _____

    b.   _____

    c.   _____

66. What could be the international impact of the Federal Reserve System changing interest rates?

67. The net result of international banking and finance has been: _____

    _____

    _____

    _____

68. The World Bank is primarily responsible for: _____

69. The World Bank now lends most of its money to _____

_____

70. What criticisms have been aimed at the World Bank?

71. What is required by the International Monetary fund?

a. _____

b. _____

c. _____

72. What is the IMF designed to oversee? What is the goal of the IMF?

73. Why is the IMF running out of money?

CRITICAL THINKING EXERCISES

Learning Goals 1,2

1. Using what you have learned in this chapter as well as in other chapters about economics, answer this question: What is the importance of the stability of the value of money, and controlling the money supply in the international marketplace today?

2. Sun-2-Shade is a company that makes self-darkening windshields for the automotive industry. Sun-2-Shade has made it big! The company has done so well here in the U.S. that management is seriously considering expanding into overseas markets. It is your job to research the idea, and you want to begin by helping other top managers understand some of the considerations of "going global." Within the context of the "value" of money compared to other currencies, what are some of the issues you will want to bring up to your managers?

Learning Goal 2

3. The Fed uses three major tools to control the money supply
   Reserve requirement
   Open market operations
   Discount rate

   a. Complete the following chart illustrating how each tool is used, and its effect on the money supply and the economy:

TOOL	ACTION	EFFECT ON MONEY SUPPLY	EFFECT ON ECONOMY
Reserve requirement	Increase reserve requirement	_____	_____
	Decrease reserve requirement	_____	_____
Open market Operations	Buy government securities	_____	_____
	Sell government securities	_____	_____
Discount rate	Increase discount rate	_____	_____
	Decrease discount rate	_____	_____

   b. Identify whether the Federal Reserve would increase or decrease the money supply in the following situations, and what the effect would be .

      1. High unemployment _____

      2. High rates of inflation _____

4. When the Fed regulates the money supply using one of the three tools just mentioned, what happens to interest rates overall?

Learning Goal 3

5. The American banking system has a long history. List the major events that led up to the establishment of the Federal Reserve System, and subsequent events that have affected the American banking system.

a. _____

b. _____

c. _____

d. _____

e. _____

f. _____

g. _____

h. _____

i. _____

j. _____

k. _____

l. _____

Learning Goal 4

6. The American banking system consists of three types of organizations:
Commercial banks
Savings and loans
Credit unions

Match each of the following descriptions to the correct type of institution:

a. _____ Offers interest-bearing checking accounts called share draft accounts at relatively high rates.

b. _____ Also known as thrift institutions.

c. _____ Offer a wide variety of services, to depositors and borrowers, including ATMs, credit cards, short and long term loans, financial counseling, automatic payment of telephone bills, safe deposit boxes, tax deferred individual retirement accounts, overdraft checking account privileges.

d. _____ Since the 1980s have been able to offer higher interest rates, allocate up to 10% of their funds to commercial loans, and offer adjustable rate mortgages.

e. _____ Since they are member owned and non-profit, they are exempt from federal income taxes.

7. How are credit unions different from commercial banks and S&Ls?

8. Describe how nonbanks are becoming an important financial force, and how they compete with traditional banking institutions.

Learning Goal 5

9. Do some research on the housing and banking crisis in your geographic area. How have the decline in housing prices and the resulting banking crisis affected your area? Have housing prices declined in the same proportion as the national decline? What actions have banks in your area undertaken to get your business to try to stay afloat? Have any banks closed in your area as a result of the crisis? (Hint: a quick way to determine what housing prices have done in your area is simply to do a google search, using your city name along with "housing prices". You can also search to get more information about the banking crisis by googling banking crisis, timeline, or any other descriptor that you find interesting.)

10. What is the difference between FDIC, SAIF, and NCUA? Why were the FDIC, and the predecessor to SAIF, (known as the FSLIC) created?

11. In your opinion, with today's economic conditions, and the competitive banking industry, is it still important to have organizations such as the FDIC, SAIF and the NCUA?

Learning Goal 6

12. Compare what you have learned in earlier chapters about the trends in businesses to become more efficient and competitive to the trends in the U.S. banking industry.

Learning Goal 7

13. In previous chapters, we have discussed the global nature of the marketplace, and the need for U.S. businesses to become and stay more competitive. How does what we have learned in those chapters about U.S. business, relate to international banking, and the U.S. banking industry?

PRACTICE TEST

MULTIPLE CHOICE–Circle the best answer

Learning Goal 1

1. Today many people have found that bartering
   a. can be done online.
   b. has been eliminated by the ease of cash transactions.
   c. become more difficult because it's hard to find people with whom to barter.
   d. has become obsolete in most countries.

2. Which of the following would <u>not</u> be included in a list of characteristics of money?
   a. Portability
   b. Divisibility
   c. Stability
   d. Usability

Learning Goal 2

3. In referring to the money supply, which of the following is money that can be accessed quickly and easily , and includes coins and paper money as well as checks?
   a. M-1
   b. M-2
   c. M-3
   d. money supply

4. The term _____ is used to describe the situation of "too much money chasing too few goods."
   a. recession
   b. inflation
   c. deflation
   d. monetary policy

5. When the price of a European coffee maker becomes less expensive to buy here in the United States, you could say that we are experiencing a
   a. falling dollar.
   b. inflated dollar.
   c. rising dollar.
   d. stable dollar.

6. When the Fed increases the reserve requirement,
   a. interest rates will go down.
   b. banks will have more money to lend.
   c. inflation could go up.
   d. banks have less money to lend.

7. The discount rate is:
   a. the amount of money member banks must keep on hand at the Fed.
   b. the interest rate Fed charges for loans to member banks .
   c. the rate the Fed charges for selling bonds.
   d. the interest rate banks charge other banks.

8. Maria Reta-Martinez read a news article that the Fed is buying back government bonds that people are willing to sell. Maria determined that the Fed
   a. is trying to slow down the economy by reducing the money supply.
   b. is trying to raise interest rates to keep the economy from growing too quickly
   c. is trying to combat inflation by taking money out of circulation.
   d. is increasing the money supply in an attempt to stimulate the economy.

Learning Goal 3

9. The bank failures of 1907 and the resulting cash shortage problems led to the creation of
   a. the Federal Reserve System.
   b. the gold standard.
   c. monetary policy.
   d. the money supply.

10. After the stock market crash of 1929, and the resulting bank failures of that time, Congress passed legislation creating:
    a. laws which prevented banks from failing.
    b. the Federal Reserve System.
    c. federal deposit insurance.
    d. nonbanks.

Learning Goal 4

11. The technical name for a savings account is a:
    a. demand deposit.
    b. time deposit.
    c. certificate of deposit.
    d. deposit insurance.

12. Which of the following organizations would be considered a nonbank institution?
    a. the Missouri Public School Retirement System
    b. the Educational Employees Credit Union
    c. Heartland Bank
    d. Southwest Savings

13. Which of the following services would not be offered to customers by commercial banks?
    a. credit cards
    b. inexpensive brokerage services
    c. pension funds
    d. traveler's checks

14. Competition between banks and nonbanks, such as insurance companies and pension funds, has
    a. decreased with the deregulation of the banking industry.
    b. not changed in 50 years, since the creation of the Federal Reserve System.
    c. increased significantly as nonbanks offer many of the services provided by regular banks.
    d. stabilized with the economic crisis of 2008-2009,

15. The Federal Deposit Insurance Corporation insures accounts up to:
    a. $10,000.
    b. $50,000.
    c. $100,000.
    d. $500,000.

16. Funds in savings and loan institutions are protected by:
    a. Federal Deposit Insurance Corporation (FDIC).
    b. National Credit Union Association (NCUA).
    c. Federal Savings and Loan Insurance Corporation (FSLIC).
    d. Savings Association Insurance Fund (SAIF).

Learning Goal 6

17. Smart cards
    a. are a new credit card offered by nonbanks.
    b. combine the functions of credit cards, debit cards, phone cards and other types of cards.
    c. are a form of direct deposit.
    d. allow employers to make direct payments to your creditors.

18. Internet Banking:
    a. are few in number and not expected to grow.
    b. allows customers to do all financial transactions from home.
    c. have higher expenses because they have to hire administrators of the online systems and software designers.
    d. will most likely continue in organizations that offer traditional banking facilities as well as online services.

Learning Goal 7

19. A _____ is a way of conducting business overseas which promises that a bank will pay some specified amount at a particular time, with no conditions imposed.
    a. guarantee a certain exchange rate
    b. offer letters of credit
    c. bankers acceptance
    d. money exchange

20. The organization which is responsible for financing economic development is the:
    a. Federal Reserve Bank.
    b. International Monetary Fund.
    c. World Bank.
    d. Bank of the Americas.

21. The World Bank:
    a. Has come under criticism from environmentalists.
    b. Makes loans only to countries that can afford to make payments of the loans.
    c. Has been praised in developing nations by AIDs activists.
    d. Works with countries to eliminate sweatshops.

TRUE–FALSE

Learning Goal 1

1. _____ The banking system is becoming simpler as the flow of money from one country to another becomes freer.

2. _____ Bartering is still used by buyers and sellers, online as well as face to face in some developing nations.

3. _____ In order to make money more difficult to counterfeit, the U.S. has changed the look of some of the denominations of its paper currency.

Learning Goal 2

4. _____ If there is too much money in the economy, prices will go up because people will bid up the prices of goods and services, causing inflation.

5. _____ There are 15 Federal Reserve Banks.

6. _____ An increase in the reserve requirement would encourage businesses to borrow money and thus stimulate the economy.

7. _____ The most powerful tool used by the Fed to control the money supply is open market operations.

Learning Goal 3

8. _____ Continental currency, the first paper money printed in the United States, became very valuable over the years as the first form of money used in the U.S.

9. _____ The Federal Reserve system was created after the stock market crash of 1929 to help control the run on banks.

Learning Goal 4

10. _____ Commercial banks have two types of customers – borrowers and lenders.

11. _____ A certificate of deposit has a maturity date, and that is when interest is paid.

12. _____ Commercial banks are offering a wider variety of services, such as brokerage services, financial counseling, automatic payment of bills, and IRAs.

13. _____ Nonbanks are becoming more competitive with other financial organizations and are offering many of the same services

Learning Goal 5

14. _____ The only type of institution in which funds are protected by the U.S. government is a commercial bank.

15. _____ The SAIF is part of the FDIC and was originally known as the FSLIC.

16. _____ Bankers are encouraging transactions that utilize an electronic funds transfer system, as EFT reduces costs.

17. _____ Debit cards are the same as smart cards and offer the same functions.

18. _____ Direct deposit is a preauthorized electronic payment into a merchant's account.

Learning Goal 7

19. _____ The result of international banking has been to link the economies of the world into one interrelated system with no regulatory control.

20. _____ The International Monetary Fund has the responsibility of assisting the smooth flow of money among nations.

You Can Find It On The Net

How many U.S. dollars will buy a British pound? We can find out at **www.xe.com/ucc**
Check out this site and find out!

How many U.S. dollars does it take to buy a euro?

How many U.S. dollars will it take to buy a Japanese yen?

How much did your tuition cost in Canadian dollars?

If you are traveling in France, and your hotel costs 600 euros per night, are you staying at the French equivalent of the penthouse at the Ritz, or at a youth hostel?

ANSWERS

LEARNING THE LANGUAGE

1.	Credit unions	10.	Electronic Funds Transfer System (EFT)	19.	Federal Deposit Insurance Corporation (FDIC)
2.	M-3	11.	Savings Association Insurance Fund (SAIF)	20.	Open-market operations
3.	Reserve requirement	12.	Debit card	21.	M-2
4.	Time deposit	13.	Barter	22.	Demand deposit
5.	Banker's acceptance	14.	Savings and Loan Association (S&L)	23.	International Monetary Fund (IMF)
6.	Money	15.	Money supply	24.	World Bank
7.	Discount rate	16.	Letter of credit	25.	M-1
8.	Nonbanks	17.	Pension funds	26.	Smart card
9.	Certificates of deposit (CD)	18.	Commercial bank		

ASSESSMENT CHECK

Learning Goal 1

Why Money Is Important

1. A barter exchange is an service where you can put goods and services into the system and get trade credits for other goods and services you need. It makes it easier to barter because you don't have to find people to barter with, as the exchange does that for you.

2. Five characteristics of a "useful" form of money are:
    a. Portability – money needs to be easy to carry around
    b. Divisibility – different sized coins are made to represent different values
    c. Stability – the value of money is more stable (unlike the value, or prices, of bartered goods)
    d. Durability – Coins last for a long time
    e. Uniqueness – money must be hard to counterfeit or copy, so it must be elaborately designed

3. Electronic, or e-cash is the latest form of money. You can e-mail e-cash to anyone using websites, and make online bill payments.

Learning Goal 2

What is the Money Supply?

4. These terms stand for different definitions of the money supply. M-1 includes coins and paper bills, money that is available by writing checks and money that is held in traveler's checks or money that is easily available to pay for goods and services. M-2 includes all of that, but adds in money held in savings accounts and other forms of savings that is not as readily available. M-2 is M-2 plus big deposits like intuitional money-market funds.

   M-2 is the most commonly used definition of money.

5. If the Fed made too much money available, prices would go up, assuming that the same amount of goods and services were available. People would bid up prices to get what they want, causing inflation. This could be called "too much money chasing too few goods."

6. If money were taken out of the economy prices would go down because there would be an oversupply of goods and services compared to the money available to buy them.

7. The money supply needs to be controlled because this allows us to manage the prices of goods and services. Also, controlling the money supply affects employment and economic growth or decline.

8. A falling dollar means that the amount of goods and services you can buy with a dollar goes down.

   A rising dollar means that the amount of goods and services you can buy with a dollar goes up.

   The prices you pay for a European good would be lower if the American dollar was strong relative to the euro. When the euro gains strength and rises in value against the dollar, the cost of European goods goes up.

9. What makes a dollar weak or strong (falling or rising dollar) is the position of the U.S. economy relative to other economies.

10. When the economy is strong, the demand for dollars is high, and the value of the dollar rises.

    When the economy is weak, the demand for dollars declines, and the value of the dollar falls.

    So, the value of a dollar depends upon a strong economy.

11. The Federal Reserve System (the Fed) is in charge of monetary policy.

12. The Federal Reserve System consists of
    a. The board of governors
    b. The Federal Open Market Operations
    c. 12 Federal Reserve Banks
    d. Three advisory councils
    e. The member banks of the system

13. The primary function of the board of governors is to set monetary policy. The board of governors also administers and supervises the 12 Federal Reserve System banks.

14. The Federal Open Market Committee has 12 voting members and is the policy-making body. The committee is made up of the seven members of the Board of Governors plus the president of the New York Reserve Bank. Four others rotate in from the other Reserve Banks. The advisory councils offer suggestions to the board and the FOMC. The councils represent the various banking districts, consumers, and member institutions, including banks, savings and loans, and credit unions.

15. The Federal Reserve
    a. buys and sells foreign currencies.
    b. regulates various types of credit.
    c. supervises banks.
    d. collects data on the money supply and other economic activity.
    e. determines the level of reserves that must be held by financial institutions.
    f. lends money to member banks.
    g. buys and sells government securities.

16. The three tools the Fed uses to manage the money supply are:
    a. reserve requirements
    b. open-market operations
    c. the discount rate

17. a. The most commonly used tool to manage the money supply is open market operations.
    b. The most powerful tool the Fed uses is the reserve requirement.

18. When the Fed increases the reserve requirement banks have less money to loan, and money becomes scarce. In the long run, this tends to reduce inflation. It is so powerful because of the amount of money affected when the reserve is changed.

    A decrease in the reserve requirement increases the funds available to banks for loans, so banks make more loans, and money becomes more readily available. An increase in the money supply stimulates the economy to achieve higher growth rates but can also create inflationary pressures.

19. a. To decrease the money supply, the federal government sells U.S. government securities to the public. The money it gets as payment is taken out of circulation, decreasing the money supply.

    b. If the Fed wants to increase the money supply, it buys government securities from individuals, corporations, or organizations that are willing to sell.

20. One reason the Fed is called the banker's bank is that member banks can borrow money from the Fed and then pass it on to their customers as loans. The discount rate is the interest rate that the Fed charges for loans to member banks.

21. An increase in the discount rate by the Fed discourages banks from borrowing and consequently reduces the number of available loans, resulting in a decrease in the money supply.

    A decrease in the discount rate encourages member bank borrowing and increases the funds available for loans, which increases the money supply.

22. The federal funds rate is the rate that banks charge each other.

23. When you write a check from out of state, the process becomes much more long and involved than writing a check to a local retailer. It is a complex and costly process, so banks encourage the use of credit cards, debit cards and other forms of electronic transfers.

Learning Goal 3

The History of Banking and the Need for the Fed

24. Strict laws in Europe limited the number of coins that could be brought to the New World by colonists, and besides, there were no banks in the colonies. So, colonists were forced to barter for goods.

25. Massachusetts issued its own paper money in 1690 because the demand for money was so great.

    This money was called continental currency, and it became worthless after a few years because people didn't trust its value.

26. Land banks were established to lend money to farmers.

27. In 1791, Alexander Hamilton persuaded Congress to form a central bank, a bank where banks could keep their funds and borrow funds if needed. It was the first version of a federal bank, but closed in 1811. It was replaced in 1816 because state chartered banks couldn't support the War of 1812. The Central Bank was closed again in 1836.

28. By the time of the Civil War, banking was a mess. Different banks issued different currencies. During the war, coins were hoarded because they were worth more as gold and silver than as coins. The problems with the banking system continued after the Civil War and climaxed in 1907 when people got so nervous about the safety of banks that they withdrew their funds, creating a "run on the banks." People began to distrust the banking system in general.

29. The Federal Reserve System was designed to prevent a repeat of the 1907 banking panic.

30. The stock market crash of 1929 led to bank failures in the early 1930s. The stock market began tumbling, and people ran to the bank to get their money out. In spite of the Federal Reserve, banks ran out of money, and states were forced to close banks.

31. In 1933 and 1935 Congress passed legislation to strengthen the banking system, to further protect us from bank failures. The most important move was to establish federal deposit insurance.

Learning Goal 4

The U.S. Banking System

32. a. Commercial banks
    b. Savings and loan associations
    c. Credit unions
    d. non-banks

33. Institutions included in a list of nonbanks are:
    a. Pension funds
    b. Insurance companies
    c. Commercial finance companies
    d. Consumer finance companies
    e. Brokerage firms

34. Two types of customers for commercial banks are
    a. Depositors
    b. Borrowers

35. A commercial bank uses customer deposits as inputs, on which it pays interest, and invests that money in interest-bearing loans to other customers. Commercial banks make a profit if the revenue generated by loans exceeds the interest paid to depositors plus all other operating expenses.

36. Certificates of deposit deliver interest at the end of the maturity date. The depositor aggress not to withdraw any of the funds until then. They are available for periods of three months up to many years; the longer the CD is to be held, the higher the interest. Interest rates depend on economic conditions and the prime rate at the time of the deposit.

37. Services offered by commercial banks in addition to checking accounts (demand deposits) and savings accounts (time deposits) include:

    a. Credit cards   g. Tax-deferred IRAs
    b. Life insurance   h. Traveler's checks
    c. Brokerage services   i. Trust departments
    d. Financial counseling   j. Overdraft checking account privileges
    e. Automatic bill paying   k. ATMs
    f. Safe-deposit boxes   l. Loans

38. ATMs can dispense maps and directions, phone cards, and postage stamps. They can sell tickets to movies, concerts, sporting events and more. They can show movie trailers, news tickers, and video ads. Some can take orders for flowers and DVDs, and download music and games.

39. S&L's are often known as thrift institutions since their original purpose was to promote consumer thrift, or saving, and home ownership.

40. Between 1979 and 1983 many savings and loan institutions failed for a variety of reasons. The biggest reason may be the fact that capital gains taxes were raised, making investments in real estate less attractive. Investors walked away from their real estate loans, and left S&Ls with property that was worth less than the money the S&L had loaned to the investors. When the property was sold, the S&Ls lost money.

41. In the 1980s the government stepped in to strengthen S&Ls by permitting them to:
    a. offer higher interest rates
    b. allocate up to 10 percent of their funds to commercial loans
    c. offer mortgage loans with adjustable interest rates.
    d. offer banking services such as financial counseling to small businesses, and credit cards.

42. Credit unions offer their members the full variety of banking services: interest-bearing checking accounts at relatively high rates, short-term loans at relatively low rates, financial counseling, life insurance and a limited number of home mortgage loans.

43. The diversity of financial serves and investment alternatives offered by nonbanks has led banks to expand the services that they offer. As competition between banks and nonbanks has increased, the dividing line between them has become less apparent. In fact, banks today are merging with brokerage firms to offer full-service financial assistance.

44. a. Life insurance companies provide financial protection for their policyholders. They invest the funds they receive from policy holders in corporate and government bonds. Recently more insurance companies have begun to provide long-term financing for real estate development companies.

   b. Pension funds are amounts of money put aside by organizations to cover part of the financial needs of members when they retire. A member may begin to collect a monthly draw on the fund upon reaching a certain age. To generate additional income, pension funds invest in low return, but safe corporate stocks or in other conservative investments.

   c. Brokerage firms have traditionally offered services related to investments in various stock exchanges. They have now made inroads into regular banks' domain by offering high-yield combination savings and checking accounts. In addition firms offer checking privileges on accounts. Investors can also get loans from their broker using their securities as collateral.

   d. Commercial and consumer finance companies offer short-term loans to businesses or individuals who either cannot meet other credit requirements or who have exceeded their credit limit and need more funds. These finance companies' interest rates are higher than those of regular banks.

Learning Goal 5

The Current Banking Crisis and How the Government Protects Your Money

45. Some people believe the Federal Reserve is responsible because it kept the cost of borrowing so low that people borrowed more than they could pay. Congress wanted more affordable housing and prodded banks to lend to people with minimal assets

46. Organizations pressured banks to make risky loans. Banks learned they could avoid much of the risk by dividing their portfolios of mortgages up and selling the "mortgage backed loans" to other banks all over the world. The securities seemed safe because they were backed by the homes that were mortgaged, and seemed to be guaranteed by Fannie Mae and Freddie Mac.

   Banks sold many of these securities hoping to make money, and were accused of pushing loans onto naïve customers.

47. The Fed failed in their duties by failing to issue sufficient warnings. When home values began to decline, people began defaulting on their loans and the properties were turned back over to the banks. Since the banks owned the mortgages on the homes, bank profits dropped dramatically, which led to the banking crisis of 2008-2009 and the need for the government to help out the banks.

48. In the end, the blame for the banking crisis can be placed on:
   a. The Federal Reserve System
   b. Congress for promoting questionable loans
   c. Banks for making risky loans and selling mortgage backed securities as safe investments
   d. government regulatory agencies for not doing their job
   e. people who took out loans they couldn't repay

49. a. Federal Deposit Insurance Corporation (FDIC)
   b. Savings Association Insurance Fund (SAIF)
   c. National Credit Union Administration (NCUA)

50. If a bank were to fail, the FDIC would arrange to have its accounts transferred to another bank or pay off depositors up to a certain amount.

51. The FDIC and the FSLIC were started during the 1930s. Many banks and thrifts failed during those years, and people were losing confidence in them. The FDIC and FSLIC were designed to create more confidence in banking institutions.

52. The government placed the FSLIC under the FDIC, in order to get more control over the banking system. When they did that, they gave it a new name, the Savings Association Insurance Fund, or SAIF

53. The NCUA provides up to $100,000 coverage per individual depositor per institution. The coverage includes all accounts, and additional protection can be obtained by holding accounts jointly or in trust.

Learning Goal 6

Using Technology to Make Banking More Efficient

54. One solution banks have used to reduce the cost of processing checks is to issue credit cards. However credit cards also have costs.

    The most efficient way to transfer funds is the electronic exchange of money, rather than the physical exchange of money.

55. The benefit of EFT is that funds can be transferred more quickly and more economically than with paper checks.

56. "Go Tags" are pea-shaped chips with a radio transmitter inside that can stick to a cell phone or ID badge to make payments fast and easy. They are faster than a credit card.

57. A debit card serves the same function as a check, in that it withdraws money directly from a checking account. Debit cards look like credit cards but they function differently. The difference is that you can spend no more than is in your checking account. When a sale is recorded, an electronic signal is sent to the bank, and funds are automatically transferred from your account to the retailer's account. A record of the transaction appears immediately.

    The drawback for debit cards is that they don't offer the same protection in the case of a stolen card. You are liable for everything.

58. Payroll debit cards are a way that some firms pay their workers, and are an alternative for those who don't qualify for a credit or debit card. Employees can access funds in their accounts immediately after they are posted, withdraw them from an ATM, pay bills online or transfer funds to another cardholder.

    The system is cheaper for companies than issuing checks.

59. Smart cards are a combination of credit cards, debit cards, phone cards, and more. The magnetic strip found on other cards is replaced on a smart card with a microprocessor. The card can then store information, including a bank balance. Each merchant can use the information to check the card's validity and spending limits, and the transaction can debit the amount on the card. Some smart cards are used to allow entrance into buildings and secure areas, such as university dorms, to buy items, and serve as ATM cards. Parents can use smart cards to monitor children's transactions.

60. a. Direct deposit credit made directly to a checking or savings account.

   b. A direct payment is a preauthorized electronic payment. A customer signs a form when he or she wants automatic payment to a certain company, and the designated company is authorized to collect funds for the amount of the bill from the customer's account.

61. Online banking services include transferring funds, paying your bills, and checking on account balances. You can apply for a car loan or mortgage online and get a response immediately. You can also buy and sell stocks online.

62. Benefits online banks can offer include better interest rates and lower fees because they do not have the cost of physical overhead traditional banks have.

63. Many consumers are pleased with the savings and convenience, but not all consumers are happy with the service they receive from Internet banks. Many are nervous about the security of banking online. People fear putting their financial information into cyberspace where others may see it. Also, consumers often want to talk to a knowledgeable person when they have banking problems.

64. In banking the future seems to be with traditional banks that offer both online services and brick and mortar facilities.

Learning Goal 7

Leaders in International Banking

65. Banks help businesses conduct business overseas by providing:
   a. letters of credit
   b. banker's acceptances
   c. money exchange

66. If the Federal Reserve decides to lower interest rates, foreign investors can withdraw their money from the United States and put it in countries with higher rates.

   The opposite is also true, so that when the Fed raises interest rates, money could come into the U.S. just as quickly.

67. The net result of international banking and finance has been to link the economies of the world into one interrelated system with no regulatory control. American firms must compete for funds with firms all over the world. Global markets mean that banks don't necessarily keep their money in their own countries. They make investments where they can get the maximum return.

68. The World Bank is primarily responsible for financing economic development.

69. The World Bank now lends most of its money to less-developed nations to improve productivity and help to raise standards of living and quality of life.

70. Environmentalists charge that the World Bank finances projects that damage the ecosystem. Human rights activists argue that the bank supports countries that restrict religious freedoms and tolerate sweatshops. AIDS activists complain that the bank does not do enough to get low-cost drugs to developing nations.

71. The International Monetary fund was established to assist the smooth flow of money among nations. It requires:
    a. members to allow their currency to be exchanged for foreign currencies freely
    b. members to keep the IMF informed about changes in monetary policy
    c. nations to modify those policies on the advice of the IMF to accommodate the needs of the entire membership.

72. The IMF is an overseer of member countries' monetary and exchange rate policies. The IMF's goal is to maintain a global monetary system that works best for all nations and enhances world trade.

73. Recently several countries have asked the IMF for loans partially as a result of the U.S. banking crisis. The agency is thus running out of funds, while facing pressure to forgive debts of countries that can't feed their population.

CRITICAL THINKING EXERCISES

Learning Goals 1, 2

1. The stability of the value of money in the global marketplace is important because if the value of money is not stable, other countries will not accept that money in trade. In other words, if the marketplace believes your money will not be valuable to use, the market will not accept your money as payment for what you want to buy.

    The money supply needs to be controlled in order to control prices, and in part, the American economy. If there is too much money in the economy, prices of goods and services will increase, because demand will be greater than supply. If there is less money, people will not be spending at the same rate, demand correspondingly goes down, and prices will go down. That could result in an oversupply of goods and services, and possibly a recession. What makes a dollar weak or strong is the position of the U.S. economy relative to other economies. When the economy is strong, people want to buy dollars and the value of the dollar rises. The value of the dollar depends on a strong economy.

2. Some of the "money" issues Sun-2-Shade will need to research relate to how strong the American dollar is compared to the currency of the countries in which Sun-2-Shade is interested. If our dollar is weak, or falling, in comparison to the euro, the British pound, the Japanese yen, or others, Sun-2-Shade could be very affordable for their target market. If the American dollar is strong, or rising, the price of Sun-2-Shade's product could be too high for some.

    Further, we would want to know what the forecast might be for the future of the U.S. economy. Is our economy expected to be strong? What are the forecasts for recession, inflation, income growth, both here, and in our target countries?

Learning Goal 2

3. a.

Tool	Action	Effect on Money supply	Effect on Economy
Reserve Requirement	Increase	Decrease	Slows down
	Decrease	Increase	Stimulated
Open market operations	Buy securities	Increase	Stimulated
	Sell securities	Decrease	Slows down
Discount rate	Increase	Decrease	Slows down
	Decrease	Increase	Stimulated

   b. 1. In a situation of high unemployment, the Federal Reserve may increase the money supply, which would have the effect of reducing interest rates. This would be a tool to stimulate the economy and encourage businesses to borrow, which could create jobs.

   2. With high rates of inflation, the Fed may choose to decrease the money supply. This would have the effect of raising interest rates, which may cool the economy and fight inflation.

4. When the Fed takes action to increase the money supply, (either by decreasing the reserve rate, decreasing the discount rate or buying government bonds) interest rates will go down. Think of interest as the price of money. When the supply goes up, the price will generally go down. Correspondingly, if interest rates have declined, demand for goods and services could go up, the economy begins to grow, and inflation may begin to heat up. The opposite effect occurs when the Fed reduces the money supply. Interest rates will rise, which will slow demand for goods and services, which slows economic growth. Inflation will also then slow down, as supply begins to be equal to or exceed demand, and prices will stabilize.

Learning Goal 3

5. a. Paper money established in 1690.
   b. Land banks established to lend money to farmers.
   c. Central bank established in 1781.
   d. Central bank closed in 1811.
   e. Second central bank established 1816
   f. Division between state banks and central bank.
   g. Central bank closed in 1836.
   h. Civil War - banks issuing their own currency.
   i. Cash shortage problems in 1907; banks began to fail.
   j. Federal Reserve System established in 1907 to lend money to banks.
   k. Stock market crash of 1929 and subsequent bank failures in 1930s.
   l. Legislation passed to strengthen banking system, establishing federal deposit insurance in 1933 and 1935.

Learning Goal 4

6. a. Credit unions
   b. Savings and loan
   c. Commercial banks
   d. Savings and loan
   e. Credit union

7. Credit unions offer services similar to banks and S&Ls, but differ in their ownership structure. Credit unions are financial cooperatives, owned by members, while banks and savings and loans are often publicly held corporations. Credit unions are also not for profit institutions, while banks and credit unions are profit-making organizations.

8. Nonbanks are financial institutions that accept no deposits but offer many of the services offered by regular banks. Nonbanks include life insurance companies, pension funds, brokerage firms, commercial finance companies, and corporate financial services. The diversity of financial services and investment alternatives offered by nonbanks has caused banks to expand the services they offer. For example, life insurance companies invest the funds they receive from policyholders in corporate and government bonds. In recent years, more insurance companies have begun to provide long-term financing for real estate development projects. In fact, banks today are merging with brokerage firms to offer full service financial assistance. Pension funds typically invest in corporate stocks and bonds, and government securities. Some large pension funds lend money directly to corporations. Brokerage houses have made serious inroads into regular banks' domain by offering high-yield combination savings and checking accounts. In addition, investors can get loans from their broker.

Learning Goal 5

9. The answers to this will vary of course depending upon where you live. Housing prices in the St. Louis area for example did not decline as dramatically as those nationally.

10. The FDIC is a government agency that protects bank deposits of up to $100,000. In the case of a bank failure, the FDIC would arrange to have your accounts at that bank transferred to another bank, or pay you off up to $100,000. The FDIC covers about 13,000 institutions, which are mostly commercial banks. SAIF insures the accounts of depositors in thrift institutions, or savings and loans. It is part of the FDIC. SAIF was originally called the Federal Savings and Loan Insurance Corporation. NCUA is the agency that protects depositors in credit unions.

   Both the FDIC and the FSLIC were established to protect the deposits of customers, and to create more confidence in the banking industry at a time when many institutions were failing. This was during the Great Depression, and hundreds of banks were failing. To get more control over the banking system, the government placed the FSLIC under the FDIC and gave it the name of The Savings Association Insurance Fund, SAIF.

11. Answers will vary. Economic conditions to consider would be the American economy - are we coming out of the recession? Will we experience a period of inflation? Other factors to consider are the current mortgage and banking crisis and   the competitive factors in the banking industry. With nonbanks performing significantly more banking functions, how are banks competing? How does this affect the banks' profitability? If banks are struggling to stay in business, then insurance on our funds remains an important security.

Learning Goal 6

12. Trends in the banking industry have paralleled changes we have seen in other industries. We have studied how companies have begun putting the customer first, and have streamlined their operations to better satisfy customer's needs at lower costs. Banks have begun to look at customer needs, and have made "one-stop shopping" available for all a customer's financial needs. One company can provide you with credit cards, mortgages, all kinds of insurance, and brokerage services. As the competition increases, costs will go down, benefiting consumers.

Banks have applied updated technology to their services, offering services like debit cards, payroll debit cards, smart cards, direct deposit and direct payment features.

Further, the Internet has made online banking available, in the same way that the Internet has made the purchase of all kinds of products available from Internet stores. The online banking industry has suffered from customer service problems, just like online stores have done, and so, like other retail businesses, we will likely have a combination of online and brick and mortar financial institutions.

Learning Goal 7

13. The U.S. banking system is directly tied to the success of banking and businesses throughout the world. American firms must compete for funds with firms all over the world. If a firm in another country is more efficient than one here in the United States, the more efficient firm will have better access to international funds. Therefore, U.S. businesses must compete not only in the marketplace, but in the financial arena as well.

Further, today's money markets form a global system, and international bankers will not be nationalistic in their dealings. They will send money to those countries where they can get the best return on their money with an acceptable risk. When the Federal Reserve System makes a move to lower interest rates in the U.S., foreign investors may withdraw their money from the U.S. and put it in countries with higher rates. To be an effective player in the international marketplace and financial worlds, the U.S. must stay financially secure and businesses must stay competitive in world markets.

PRACTICE TEST

MULTIPLE CHOICE

1.	a	12.	a
2.	d	13.	c
3.	a	14.	c
4.	b	15.	c
5.	c	16.	d
6.	d	17.	b
7.	b	18.	d
8.	d	19.	c
9.	a	20.	c
10.	c	21.	a
11.	b		

TRUE–FALSE

1.	F	11.	T
2.	T	12.	T
3.	T	13.	T
4.	T	14.	F
5.	F	15.	T
6.	F	16.	T
7.	T	17.	F
8.	F	18.	F
9.	F	19.	T
10.	F	20.	T

BONUS CHAPTER A – WORKING WITHIN THE LEGAL ENVIRONMENT

LEARNING GOALS

After you have read and studied this chapter, you should be able to:

1. Define business law, and distinguish between statutory and common law, and explain the role of administrative agencies.
2. Define tort law and explain the role of product liability in tort law.
3. Identify the purposes and conditions of patents, copyrights, and trademarks.
4. Describe warranties and negotiable instruments as covered in the Uniform Commercial Code.
5. List and describe the conditions necessary to make a legally enforceable contract, and describe the possible consequences if such a contract is violated.
6. Summarize several laws that regulate competition and protect consumers in the United States.
7. Explain the role of tax laws in generating income for the government and as a method of discouraging or encouraging certain behaviors among taxpayers.
8. Distinguish among the various types of bankruptcy as outlined by the Bankruptcy Code.
9. Explain the role of deregulation as a tool to encourage competition.

LEARNING THE LANGUAGE

Listed here are important terms found in this chapter. Choose the correct term for each definition below and write it in the space provided.

Administrative agencies	Copyright	Patent
Bankruptcy	Damages	Precedent
Breach of contract	Deregulation	Product liability
Business law	Express warranties	Statutory law
Common law	Implied warranties	Strict product liability
Consideration	Involuntary bankruptcy	Taxes
Consumerism	Judiciary	Tort
Contract	Negligence	Uniform Commercial Code (UCC)
Contract law	Negotiable instruments	Voluntary bankruptcy

1. Something of value, one of the requirements of a legal contract, is called _____.

2. _____ refers to government withdrawal of certain laws and regulations that seem to hinder competition.

3. Forms of commercial paper (such as checks) known as _____ are transferable among businesses and individuals and represent a promise to pay a specified amount.

4. Rules, statutes, codes, and regulations called _____ are established to provide a legal framework within which business may be conducted and that are enforceable by court action.

5. The _____ is a comprehensive commercial law, adopted by every state in the United States that covers sales laws and other commercial laws.

6. Specific representations by the seller that buyers rely on regarding the goods they purchase are called _____.

7. A _____ is a wrongful act that causes injury to another person's body, property, or reputation.

8. The legal process of _____ is one by which a person, business, or government entity unable to meet financial obligations is relieved of those obligations by a court that divides any assets among creditors, allowing creditors to get at least part of their money and freeing the debtor to begin anew.

9. A _____ is a document that protects an individual's rights to materials such as books, articles, photos, and cartoons.

10. State and federal constitutions, legislative enactment, treaties of the federal government, and ordinances (written laws) are known as _____.

11. _____ are guarantees legally imposed on the seller.

12. A social movement known as _____ seeks to increase and strengthen the rights and powers of buyers in relation to sellers.

13. A _____ occurs when one party fails to follow the terms of a contract.

14. A legally enforceable agreement between two or more parties is a _____.

15. A document called a _____ gives inventors exclusive right to their inventions for 20 years.

16. The body of law known as _____ comes from decisions handed down by judges and is also known as "unwritten law."

17. A set of laws called _____ specify what constitutes a legally enforceable agreement.

18. Legal procedures called _____ are initiated by a debtor.

19. The part of tort law known as _____ holds businesses liable for harm that results from the production, design, sale, or use of products they market.

20. Federal or state institutions and other government organizations created by Congress or state legislatures with delegated power to pass rules and regulations within their mandated area of authority are known as _____.

21. The branch of the government called the _____ oversees the legal system through the court system.

22. Bankruptcy procedures filed by a debtor's creditors are a(n) _____.

23. Federal, state and local governments raise money through _____.

24. The monetary settlement awarded to a person who is injured by a breach of contract is known as _____.

25. Decisions judges have made in earlier cases, or _____, guide the handling of new cases.

26. In tort law, behavior is called _____ when it causes unintentional harm or injury.

27. Legal responsibility for harm or injury caused by a product regardless of fault is known as _____.

ASSSESSMENT CHECK

Learning Goal 1

The Case for Laws

1. What is the difference between criminal law and civil law?

2. The judiciary governs the activities and operations of business including:

   a. _____

   b. _____

   c. _____

   d. _____

   e. _____

3. Discuss the difference between statutory and common law.

4. Why is common law often referred to as unwritten law? How does precedent relate to common law?

5. What do we mean when we say that administrative agencies hold quasi-legislative, quasi-executive and quasi-judicial powers?

Learning Goal 2

Tort Law

6. What is the difference between an intentional tort and negligence?

7. Can a company be held liable for damages from a defective product even if the company didn't know of the defect?

8. What impact has the rule of strict liability had on businesses?

Learning Goal 3

Legally Protecting Ideas: Patents, Copyrights, and Trademarks

9. The standard of "obviousness" when referring to patents means that _____

_____.

10. What are your chances of receiving a patent?

   How much will you spend in fees over the life of a patent?

11. Are foreign companies eligible to file for U.S. patents?

12. What is required by the American Inventor's Protection Act?

   Why was this act passed?

   What is a submarine patent?

13. How long does a patent last compared to copyright protection?

14. What are the provisions of the Copyright Act of 1978?

15. What are the rights of the holder of a copyright?

What happens if a work is created by an employee in the course of a job?

16. What is the definition of a trademark?

How long does a trademark last?

Learning Goal 4

Sales Law: The Uniform Commercial Code

17. What are the areas of law covered by the Uniform Commercial Code?

a. _____   f. _____

b. _____   g. _____

c. _____   h. _____

d. _____   i. _____

e. _____

18. Describe the difference between express and implied warranties.

19. Describe the difference between a full and a limited warranty.

20. What are four conditions that must be met by a negotiable instrument?

a. _____

b. _____

c. _____

d. _____

21. What is considered an "endorsement" with regard to negotiable instruments?

617

Learning Goal 5

Contract Law

22.   A contract is legally binding if:

     a.   _____

     b.   _____

     c.   _____

     d.   _____

     e.   _____

     f.   _____

23.   An offer becomes legally binding only when: _____.

24.   The principle of mutual acceptance means that: _____

    _____.

25.   How is a person determined to be competent to enter a contract?

26.   When does a contract become illegal and not enforceable?

27.   What kind of contracts must be put in writing?

28.   Describe three results of a breach of contract.

     a.   _____

     b.   _____

     c.   _____

29   Identify three elements that should be present in a contract.

     a.   _____

     b.   _____

     c.   _____

Learning Goal 6

Promoting Fair and Competitive Practices

30. What are four important pieces of pro-competitive federal legislation?

    a. _____

    b. _____

    c. _____

    d. _____

31. What two things does the Sherman Act forbid?

    a. _____

    b. _____

32. The Clayton Act prohibits:

    a. _____   c. _____

    b. _____   d. _____

33. Describe:

    a. exclusive dealing

    b. a tying contract

    c. an interlocking directorate

34. Discuss the major elements of the Federal Trade Commission Act.

35. What areas does the FTC cover?

36. The Robinson Patman Act prohibits: _____.

    The Robinson-Patman Act applies to: _____

    _____.

    The act specifically outlaws: _____

    _____.

Laws to Protect Consumers

37. List the major consumer protection laws and their major provision

    a. _____

    b. _____

    c. _____

    d. _____

    e. _____

    f. _____

    g. _____

    h. _____

    i. _____

    j. _____

    k. _____

    l. _____

Learning Goal 7

Tax Laws

38. Traditionally governments have used taxes primarily as: _____

    _____.

39. What is the purpose of a sin tax?

40. A tax credit is: _____.

41. The major bases of tax revenue are:

    a. _____

    b. _____

    c. _____

42. The federal government receives its largest share of taxes from: _____.

States and local governments make extensive use of: _____.

School districts general depend upon: _____.

43. Tax policies are important considerations when:

a. _____

b. _____

44. What area of sales taxes is being debated in Congress?

Learning Goal 8

Bankruptcy Laws

45. Identify the three major amendments to the bankruptcy code. What do they provide for?

a. _____

_____

b. _____

_____

c. _____

_____

46. What are the provisions of a Chapter 7 bankruptcy?

47. In what order are assets distributed among creditors in a Chapter 7 bankruptcy?

First: _____

Then:

a. _____

b. _____

c. _____

d. _____

e. _____

f. _____

48. What does Chapter 11 bankruptcy allow?

49. What does a Chapter 13 bankruptcy permit? How does this compare to a Chapter 7? How does a Chapter 13 proceed?

Learning Goal 9

Deregulation Versus Regulation

50. The move toward deregulation began because: _____

_____.

51. How has deregulation affected these industries?

Airlines:

Telecommunications:

Banking:

Utilities:

52. Corporate scandals in the early 2000s and the financial market collapse of 2008–2009

have led to: _____

_____.

CRITICAL THINKING EXERCISES

Learning Goal 1

1. Determine if statutory or common law is being described in the following examples.

   a. _____ Joe sued Susan because he was injured while using end tables Susan had given him to prop up his car while working on the muffler. The judge in the case ruled in Susan's favor based upon past cases of implied warranties.

   b. _____ The CEO of a major firm in the electronics industry has refused to sign off on the financial statements for his company because they don't meet his criteria. He is afraid of being held liable for those statements under the Sarbanes-Oxley Act.

   c. _____ Lane Halverson filed bankruptcy under Chapter 13 in October, 2009.

   d. _____ A farmer in the Midwest was sued by his neighbors because his farm animals were so smelly that the neighbors were getting sick. The neighbors sued and the judge ruled in favor of the neighbors after considerable research on similar cases.

Learning Goal 2

2. How has the definition of product liability changed, and how has that affected manufacturers?

Learning Goal 3

3. Eric has developed a new formula for the product his company manufactures, a self-darkening windshield for vehicles. Eric would like to protect this formula because he has just learned that a competitor has recently been using Eric's process. Eric is very busy, and feels like he just doesn't have time to deal with anything complicated right now and that he will probably wait for a while before he decides to do anything about this new formula. What would you advise him about protecting his new product?

Learning Goal 4

4. Determine if the issue described below refers to an express warranty or an implied warranty.

   a. _____ Shirley Glenn got severe food poisoning after eating at a restaurant near her home and sued the restaurant for her medical expenses.

   b. _____ Geraldo Santino bought a drill that worked for 6 months and then quit. The paperwork that came with the drill said that the manufacturer would repair any problems the drill had for 5 years after the purchase, so Geraldo sent the drill to the manufacturer, and received it back within 7 days, fully repaired.

Learning Goal 5

5. A contract will be legally binding if it meets the following conditions:

   An offer is made   Both parties are competent
   There is voluntary acceptance of the offer The contract is legal
   Both parties give consideration   The contract is in proper form

   Given the information below, determine whether each contract is legally binding (assuming other conditions are met) and why or why not.

   a. A resident of Tennessee signs an IOU to a casino in Las Vegas.

   b. You see a newspaper ad for a used car, and after looking the car over, you agree to pay the owner $1000 on the spot, with an oral contract.

   c. A 17-year-old puts a down payment on a new motorcycle.

   d. A student offers to buy your well-used Understanding Business textbook for $10, and you agree.

6. Three actions that can be taken when a breach of contract occurs are:

   Specific performance
   Payment of damages
   Discharge of obligation

   Indicate which action might be taken in each of the following breach of contract situations.

   a. An actor fails to show up for a scheduled theater performance, without prior warning.

   b. A typist working for an author finds that she doesn't have time to finish the manuscript, and quits.

   c. An art dealer fails to deliver a piece of sculpture when promised for an art show.

7. Which of the following major pieces of federal legislation would be associated with each of the situations below?

Sherman Act   Robinson–Patman Act
Clayton Act   Federal Trade Commission Act

a. _____ Prohibits conspiracies in restraint of trade and attempts to monopolize.

b. _____ A greeting card company unsuccessfully attempted to coerce its independently owned distributors into carrying only the products it manufactures.

c. _____ The agency created by this act has conducted three times as many investigations and brought twice as many cases in the 1990s as it did in the 1980s. The legislation prohibits unfair methods of competition in commerce.

d. _____ Prohibits several forms of price discrimination and applies to buyers as well as sellers.

8. Using the list of consumer protection laws in Figure A-4 in your text, identify the law associated with each of the following statements.

a. _____ A package of frozen fish indicates that the fish actually comes from China.

b. _____ Baby cribs are required to have slats close enough together to prevent an infant's head from getting caught between the slats.

c. _____ Fisher-Price was forced to recall a toy that had caused several injuries to young infants.

d. _____ Hershey's was charged with unethical business practices for retrieving information from children on their web site.

e. _____ Visa must notify their cardholders before they are re-instituting a charge that the card holder is disputing.

f. _____ The monthly statement on a Shell credit card indicates a periodic rate per month of 1.5% and an annual percentage rate of 18%.

g. _____ The warranty for a Fisher-Price camera discloses that there is a three-year express warranty, and describes the conditions.

h. _____ A bankruptcy filed several years ago will not show up on a credit report needed for a loan approval.

i. _____ A toy with a mechanical arm is packaged with a warning that it is intended only for children 8 years and older.

j. _____ Anheuser-Busch brought out Michelob Ultra in 2002. The cans and bottles had to have a warning label in a visible place on the container. This is especially important as women are one of the target markets.

k. _____ When Judith Durham buys a box of Snack-Wells cookies, she knows exactly what ingredients are in the cookies and how much fat they contain.

l. _____ When Michael Galganski buys a bag of potato chips, he knows that he is getting 16 oz of chips because that's what the bag indicates even if the bag looks like it contains significantly more than that.

Learning Goal 7

9. As you read in this chapter, the federal government gets most of its revenue from taxes paid on income received by businesses and individuals. Review what you learned about economics in Chapter 2. Why would the government <u>lower</u> taxes during a period of economic difficulties, as was done in the early 2000s? Wouldn't that action tend to reduce government revenues? Why or why not?

Learning Goal 8

10. When persons or businesses file for bankruptcy, they are relieved of their financial obligations by the courts.

Most bankruptcies are filed under one of the following three sections of the act:
          Chapter 7   Chapter 11   Chapter 13

Which section of the bankruptcy law is being invoked in each of the following situations?

a. _____ General Motors Corporation filed for reorganization, and continued operations after declaring bankruptcy.

b. _____ When the fast-food restaurant Jim S. owned failed, he filed for bankruptcy and sold all the assets to pay off his creditors, including his SBA loan.

c. _____ Because of recent revisions in the bankruptcy law, a small dry cleaner was enabled to declare bankruptcy and set up a three year schedule for repayment to his creditors.

Learning Goals 2, 3, 4, 5, 8, 9

11. The types of laws governing business are varied. They include:

Contract law   Bankruptcy law
Sales law (Uniform Commercial Code)   Tort law
Patent law   Deregulation

Match the correct type of business law to each of the following situations.

a. _____ Firestone is being sued by the families of individuals injured by accidents caused by alleged defects in the Firestone tires.

b. _____ A Sears Kenmore washer comes with a 12-month warranty.

c. _____ United Airlines declared itself unable to meet its debt obligations, and filed for Chapter 11 reorganization.

d. _____ The formula for a woman's facial moisturizer is advertised as being protected from duplication until the year 2013.

e. _____ Bob and Dee Slone sued for damages when their building contractor failed to complete the building of their new home.

f. _____ Southwest Airlines was able to take advantage of the opportunities presented when the government stepped away from governing the routes airlines could fly.

Learning Goal 9

12. In the last two decades as your text indicates, several industries have been deregulated, including the telecommunications industry. In the early 1980s in an effort to stimulate competition and give consumers more choices, ATT was forced to divide into several smaller companies, then called the "Baby Bells" which were allowed to compete for phone service with ATT. Since that time the "Baby Bells" have grown up, and are now large corporations. In fact Southwest Bell bought it's former parent, AT&T. With the deregulation of the telecommunications industry in 1996, many options have been opened for phone service. How do you think you as a consumer have benefited from that deregulation?

PRACTICE TEST

MULTIPLE CHOICE — Circle the best answer

Learning Goal 1

1. In Missouri, a law was passed to allow riverboat gambling. The law has been challenged in the legislature several times by different groups. This kind of law is an example of:
   a. common law.
   b. statutory law.
   c. tort law.
   d. liability law.

Learning Goal 2

2. The fact that a company can be held liable for damages or injuries caused by a product with a defect even if the company did not know of the defect at the time of the sale is referred to as:
   a. business law.
   b. negligence.
   c. strict product liability.
   d. implied warranty.

Learning Goal 3

3. A _____ is a document that gives inventors exclusive rights to their inventions for 20 years.
   a. trademark
   b. copyright
   c. express warranty
   d. patent

Learning Goal 4

4. The Uniform Commercial Code covers:
   a. sales law.
   b. bankruptcy law.
   c. product negligence .
   d. contract law.

5. When Chad Holden bought a new lawn mower at his local hardware store, he knew that he could return the product if it broke or didn't function properly because the lawn mower had a(n):
   a. implied warranty
   b. patent
   c. express warranty
   d. copyright

Learning Goal 5

6. Which of the following is most accurate in determining that a contract is legally enforceable?
   a. One of the parties must be over the age of 18
   b. Both parties must agree to the terms of the contract
   c. As long as both parties agree to the terms, an oral contract will be binding in all cases
   d. Both parties must receive money

7. When John Pegg decided he wanted to buy a car, he went looking in the used car ads, and found one in his price range, $3000, from a private seller. John, who is 16, drove the car, and decided he wanted to buy it. What needs to happen to make John's purchase an enforceable contract?
   a. The contract needs to be written up
   b. John needs to find a person older than he, like a parent, to make the contract for him
   c. The seller must wait for 3 days before he can sell it to John
   d. All of the above

8. Billy Joel and Elton John had to cancel a booking for their joint concert in St. Louis because Billy Joel fell ill. If they had not made arrangements to re-book the concert, the cancellation could be considered a breach of contract, and the results could be:
   a. Specific performance.
   b. Payment of damages.
   c. Discharge of obligation.
   d. Could be all of the above.

Learning Goal 6

9. The _____ prohibits exclusive dealing, tying contracts and interlocking directorates.
   a. Clayton Act
   b. Federal Trade Commission Act
   c. Robinson-Patman Act
   d. Interstate Commerce Act

Learning Goal 7

10. The federal government receives most of its revenues from:
    a. individual and corporate income taxes.
    b. sales taxes.
    c. property taxes.
    d. sin taxes.

Learning Goal 8

11. Chapter _____ of the bankruptcy code allows businesses to continue operations while paying a limited portion of their debts.
    a. 7
    b. 11
    c. 13
    d. 22

Learning Goal 9

12. How has deregulation affected business in the U.S.?
    a. Some industries have become more competitive.
    b. Some companies must follow a stricter code of ethics.
    c. Many businesses are raising prices because the government is not controlling them anymore.
    d. Companies are becoming less ethical.

TRUE–FALSE

Learning Goal 1

1. _____ It isn't necessary for business people to know laws governing business, as long as their lawyers understand them.

2. _____ Common law is often referred to as unwritten law.

3. _____ Administrative agencies are allowed to pass rules and regulations in their areas of authority, but cannot hold a hearing if they feel a rule or regulation has been violated.

Learning Goal 2

4. _____ A company can be held liable for injuries resulting from use of their product even if the company had no prior knowledge that the product could be harmful.

5. _____ Negligence is a willful act that results in injury – in other words, the act is intentional.

Learning Goal 3

6. _____ A submarine patent is one that has not yet been granted and is subject to court review.

7. _____ A copyright lasts for the lifetime of the creator of the work, but ends after their death.

Learning Goal 4

8. _____ A full warranty requires a seller to replace or repair a product at no charge if the product is defective.

9. _____ An endorsement is the signature of the payee on the back of a negotiable instrument, such as a check.

Learning Goal 5

10. _____ Any contract for the sale of real property, such as land, must be written.

11. _____ If a breach of contract occurs, the individual who breached the contract will always be required to live up to the contract eventually.

Learning Goal 6

12. _____ The Sherman Act prohibits price discrimination.

13. _____ Exclusive dealing refers to the selling of goods with the condition that the buyer will not buy goods from a competitor.

Learning Goal 7

14. _____ A major tax issue today is that of allowing states to charge sales tax on Internet purchases.

Learning Goal 8

15. _____ In a bankruptcy case, the first thing to be paid will be federal and state taxes.

Learning Goal 9

16. _____ Deregulation has affected most businesses in a positive way, and no businesses have suffered.

You Can Find It On The Net

After learning so much about business, are you interested in starting your own company? Click on   http://www.business.gov/index.html

Select the link "Stay Compliant with Laws. " What areas does this site indicate are of importance to you as a small business owner? Can you see why it is important that as a business person you are familiar with business law?!

ANSWERS

LEARNING THE LANGUAGE

1.	Consideration	10.	Statutory law	19.	Product liability
2.	Deregulation	11.	Implied warranties	20.	Administrative agencies
3.	Negotiable Instruments	12.	Consumerism	21.	Judiciary
4.	Business law	13.	Breach of contract	22.	Involuntary bankruptcy
5.	Uniform Commercial Code (UCC)	14.	Contract	23.	Taxes
6.	Express warranties	15.	Patent	24.	Damages
7.	Tort	16.	Common law	25.	Precedent
8.	Bankruptcy	17.	Contract law	26.	Negligence
9.	Copyright	18.	Voluntary bankruptcy	27.	Strict product liability

ASSESSMENT CHECK

Learning Goal 1

The Case for Laws

1. Criminal law defines crimes, establishes punishments, and regulates the investigation and prosecution of people accused of committing crimes. Civil law involves legal proceedings that do not involve criminal acts. It includes laws regulating areas such as marriage, payment for personal injury and so on.

2. The judiciary governs the activities and operations of business including:
   a. hiring and firing practices
   b. unpaid leave for family emergencies
   c. environmental protection
   d. worker safety
   e. freedom from sexual harassment at work

3. Statutory law is written law, and includes state and federal constitutions, legislative enactments and so forth. Common law is the body of law that comes from decisions handed down by judges which becomes precedent.

4. Common law is referred to as unwritten law because it does not appear in any legislative enactment, treaty, or other such document. Under common law principles, what judges have decided in previous cases is important in deciding current cases. These decisions are called precedent, and they guide judges in handing new cases.

5. Some administrative agencies hold quasi-legislative, quasi-executive and quasi-judicial powers. This means an agency is allowed to pass rules and regulations within its area of authority, conduct investigations in cases of suspected rules violations, and hold hearings when it feels the rules and regulations have been violated. Administrative agencies issue more rulings affecting business and settle more business disputes than courts do.

Learning Goal 2

Tort Law

6. An intentional tort is a *willful* act that results in injury. Negligence deals with *unintentional* behavior that causes harm or injury.

7. Yes, a company can be held liable for damages for a defective product, even if the company didn't know about the defect. The rule of "strict liability" refers to product liability. It is the idea that a company can be liable for damages caused by placing a product on the market with a defect even if the company did not know of the defect at the time of the sale.

8. The rule of strict product liability has caused serious problems for businesses. A number of companies have been forced into bankruptcy due to asbestos litigation, for example. Several other industries, such as the chemical and paint industries, are at risk in the area of product liability. The gun industry, for example, has been accused of damages under the rules of strict product liability, and lawsuits have been filed on behalf of individuals affected by gun violence. McDonalds was named in a suit claiming its food caused obesity.

Learning Goal 3

Legally Protecting Ideas: Patents, Copyrights, and Trademarks

9. The standard of "obviousness" when referring to patents means that a patent cannot be granted for an invention that is an obvious extension of an existing product.

10. Over 60 percent of patent applications are approved.
    Costs will vary depending upon the complexity of the product.

11. Foreign companies are eligible to file for U.S. patents and account for nearly half the U.S. patents issued.

12. The American Inventor's Protection Act requires patent applications to be made public after 18 months regardless of whether a patent has been granted.

    This law was passed in part to address critics that argued some inventors would intentionally delay or drag out a patent application because they expected others to develop similar products or technology.

    When someone else filed for a similar patent, the inventor would claim the patent, which is referred to as a submarine patent and demand large fees for its use.

13. A patent lasts for 20 years. A copyright protects an individual's right to materials for the lifetime of the author or artist plus 70 years and can be passed on to the creator's heirs.

14. The Copyright Act of 1978 gives a special term of 75 years from publication to works published before January 1, 1978 whose copyrights had not expired by that date.

15. The holder of an exclusive copyright may charge a fee to anyone who wishes to use the copyrighted material.

    If a work is created by an employee in the normal course of a job, the copyright belongs to the employer and lasts 95 years from publication or 120 years from creation, whichever comes first.

16. A trademark is a legally protected name, symbol, or design, or combination of those, that identifies the goods or services of one seller and distinguishes them from those of the competition.

   A trademark belongs to the owner forever, so long as it is properly registered and renewed every 10 years.

Learning Goal 4

Sales Law: The Uniform Commercial Code

17. The areas of law covered by the Uniform Commercial Code are:
   a. Sales
   b. Commercial paper
   c. Bank deposits and collections
   d. Letters of credit
   e. Bulk transfers
   f. Warehouse receipts
   g. Bills of lading
   h. Investment securities
   i. Secured transactions

18. An express warranty is often enclosed with the product when purchased. It spells out the seller's warranty agreement. An implied warranty is legally imposed on the seller. It is implied that the product will conform to the customary standards of the trade or industry in which it competes.

19. A full warranty requires a seller to replace or repair a product at no charge if the product is defective. Limited warranties typically limit the defects or mechanical problems that are covered.

20. Negotiable instruments must be:
   a. Signed by the maker
   b. Made payable on demand at a certain time
   c. Made payable to the bearer or to order
   d. Contain an unconditional promise to pay a specific amount of money

21. An endorsement in the area of negotiable instruments is the signature of the payee on the back of the negotiable instrument, such as a check.

Learning Goal 5

Contract Law

22. A contract is legally binding if:
   a. An offer is made
   b. There is voluntary acceptance of the offer
   c. Both parties give consideration
   d. Both parties are competent
   e. The contract is legal (for a legal act)
   f. The contract is in proper form

23. An offer is legally binding only when all other conditions of a contract have been met.

24. The principle of mutual acceptance means that both parties to a contract must agree on the terms of the contract. Even if both agree to the terms, the contract isn't legally binding until the other four conditions are met.

25. In order to be judged competent to enter into a contract, a person must not be under the influence of drugs or alcohol, be of sound mind and be of legal age.

26. A contract covering an illegal act is illegal and not enforceable.

27. An agreement for the sale of goods worth $500 or more must be in writing. Contracts that cannot be fulfilled within one year and contracts regarding real property must also be in writing.

28. Three results from a breech of contract are:
    a. Specific performance i.e. the person may be required to live up to the agreement
    b. Payment of damages
    c. Discharge of obligation, which means to drop the matter

29. A contract does not have to be complicated, but should have the following three elements.
    a. It should be in writing.
    b. mutual consideration is specified.
    c. there is a clear offer and agreement.

Learning Goal 6

Promoting Fair and Competitive Practices

30. a. Sherman Act (1890)
    b. Clayton Act (1914)
    c. Federal Trade Commission Act (1914)
    d. Robinson — Patman Act (1936)

31. The Sherman Act forbids
    a. contracts, combinations or conspiracies in restraint of trade,
    b. actual monopolies or attempts to monopolize any part of trade or commerce.

32. The Clayton Act prohibits
    a. exclusive dealing
    b. tying contracts
    c. interlocking directorates
    d. buying large amounts of stock in competing corporations.

33. a. Exclusive dealing is selling goods with the condition that the buyer will not buy goods from a competitor.
    b. A tying contract requires a buyer to purchase unwanted items in order to purchase the desired items.
    c. An interlocking directorate occurs when a board of directors includes members of the board of competing corporations.

34. The Federal Trade Commission Act prohibits unfair methods of competition in commerce. This act set up the Federal Trade Commission (FTC).

35. The FTC covers competitive issues in a number of different areas, from misleading claims, to telemarketer's practices and funeral pricing. The FTC is now responsible for overseeing mergers and acquisitions in the healthcare, energy, computer hardware, automotive and biotechnology industries.

36. The Robinson-Patman Act prohibits price discrimination.

It applies to both sellers and buyers who knowingly induce or receive an unlawful discrimination in price. It also stipulates that certain types of price cutting are criminal offenses.

It specifically outlaws price differences that substantially weaken competition unless the differences can be justified by lower selling costs. I t also prohibits advertising and promotional allowances unless they are offered to all retailers.

Laws to Protect Consumers

37. The major consumer protection laws are:
    a. Fair Packaging and Labeling Act makes unfair or deceptive packaging or labeling illegal
    b. Child Protection Act removes potentially harmful toys from sale and allows the FDA to pull dangerous products from the market
    c. Truth- in- Lending Act requires full disclosure of all finance charges on credit agreements
    d. Child Protection and Toy Safety Act protects children from toys and other products that contain hazards
    e. Fair Credit Reporting Act requires that consumer credit reports be accurate, relevant and contain recent information and are confidential
    f. Consumer Product Safety Act created an agency to protect consumers from unreasonable risk from consumer products and set safety standards
    g. Magnuson-Moss Warranty-Federal Trade Commission Improvement Act provides for minimum disclosure standards for written product warranties and allows the FTC to interpret rules
    h. Alcohol Labeling Legislation provides for warning labels on liquor for pregnant women
    i. Nutrition Labeling and Education Act requires truthful and uniform nutrition labeling on foods
    j. Consumer Credit Reporting Reform Act increases responsibility of credit issuers for accurate data and requires creditors to verity that disputed data are accurate.
    k. Children's Online Privacy Protection Act gives parents control over what information is collected online from children under 13 and requires Web site operators to keep information obtained from children confidential
    l. Country of Origin Labeling Law requires that product labels on food products sold in the U.S. give the product's country of origin.

Learning Goal 7

Tax Laws

38. Traditionally taxes have been used as a source of funding for government operations and programs. They have also been used as a method of encouraging or discouraging certain behaviors among taxpayers.

39. The purpose of a sin tax is to reduce the use of certain types of products. This is what has happened in the cigarette and alcohol industry.

40. A tax credit is an amount that can be deducted from a tax bill.

41. The major bases of tax revenue are:
    a. income taxes
    b. property taxes
    c. sales taxes

42. The federal government receives its largest share of taxes from income tax. State and local governments make extensive use of sales taxes. School districts general depend upon property taxes.

43. Tax policies are important considerations when:
    a. businesses seek to locate operations
    b. when people are considering where to retire

44. Congress is being petitioned to pass a law permitting states to collect sales taxes from e-commerce transactions.

Learning Goal 8

Bankruptcy Laws

45. Two major amendments to the bankruptcy code include
    a. The Bankruptcy Amendments and Federal Judgeships Act of 1984. This legislation allows a person who is bankrupt to keep part of the ownership in a house, $1,200 in a car, and some other personal property.

    b. The Bankruptcy Reform Act of 1994 amends more than 45 sections of the bankruptcy code and creates reforms that speed up and simplify the process.

    c. The Bankruptcy Abuse Prevention and Consumer Protection Act of 2005 was passed to reduce the total number of bankruptcy filings and to eliminate the perceived ease of filing.

46. Chapter 7 calls for straight bankruptcy, which requires the sale of nonexempt assets. Under federal exemption statutes, a debtor may be able to retain up to $20,200 of equity in a home, up to $3,225 of equity in an automobile, up to $9,850 in household furnishings, and up to $1,225 in jewelry. When the sale of assets is over, the resulting cash is divided among creditors.

47. In a Chapter 7 bankruptcy,
    First creditors with secured claims receive the collateral for their claims, or repossess the claimed asset.
    Then, unsecured claims are paid in this order
    a. Costs involved in the bankruptcy case
    b. Any business costs incurred after bankruptcy was filed
    c. Wages, salaries, or commissions
    d. Employee benefit plan contributions
    e. Refunds to consumers who paid for undelivered products
    f. Federal and state taxes

48. Chapter 11 allows a company to reorganize operations while paying only a limited portion of its debts. Under certain conditions, the company can sell assets, borrow money, and change officers to strengthen its market position.

49. Chapter 13 bankruptcy permits individuals and small business owners to pay back creditors over a period of three to five years. Chapter 13 proceedings are less complicated and less expensive than Chapter 7 proceedings. The debtor files a proposed plan for paying off debts to the court. If the plan is approved, the debtor pays a court appointed trustee in monthly installments, and the trustee pays each creditor.

Learning Goal 9

Deregulation Versus Regulation

50. The move toward deregulation began because there was a concern that there were too many laws and regulations governing business and that these laws and regulations were costing the public money.

51. The most publicized examples of deregulation have been in the airlines and the telecommunications industry.

   a. Airlines: When restrictions were lifted in the airline industry, the airlines began competing for different routes and charging lower prices. New airlines were created to take advantage of new opportunities. Today some argue that the industry needs more government intervention since airlines have lost huge sums of money since 2001.

   b. Telecommunications: Deregulation gave consumers many more options in the telephone service market. There was also a significant increase in retail video competition. Today most households receive many television stations.

   c. Banking: New regulations in the banking and investment industries changed the nature of financial markets and created huge problems. The Fed's reluctance to toughen mortgage regulations contributed to the collapse in the real estate market.

   d. Utilities: California was the first state to deregulate the electric power industry. Since then, the state has had significant problems with the deregulation of the electric power industry. Many states have halted the deregulation process.

52. Corporate scandals in the early 2000s and the financial market collapse of 2008–2009 have led to a further demand for better government regulation and oversight of business operations to protect consumers, workers, and investors.

CRITICAL THINKING EXERCISES

Learning Goal 1

1. a. Common law
   b. Statutory law
   c. Statutory law
   d. Common law

Learning Goal 2

2. At one time, the legal standard for measuring product liability was if a producer knowingly placed a hazardous product on the market. Today, many states have extended product liability to the level of strict liability. Legally this means without regard to fault. Therefore, a company could be liable for damages caused by placing a product on the market with a defect even if the company did not know of the defect at the time of the sale. This has subjected manufacturers to expensive lawsuits.

Learning Goal 3

3. You will probably advise Eric to apply for a patent as soon as possible. A patent will give Eric protection for his new formula for 20 years from the date of the application, which means that his competitor will not be able to copy this new formula anytime soon. You should also let Eric know that once his patent application has been filed he has to make it public within 18 months regardless of whether the patent has been granted.

Learning Goal 4

4. a. implied warranty
   b. express warranty

Learning Goal 5

5. a Yes, this is a binding contract. Although the signer is a resident of Tennessee, he is in Nevada, where gambling is legal.
   b. No, this is not binding. Oral contracts are binding only when the value of the goods is less than $500. It's usually best to get a written contract for the protection of both parties.
   c. No, this is not a binding contract because a minor isn't legally competent to make a contract.
   d. Yes this is a binding contract. The offer was voluntary, so was the acceptance and both parties received consideration.

6. a. Payment of damages
   b. Discharge of obligation
   c. Specific performance

Learning Goal 6

7. a. Sherman Act (1890)
   b. Clayton Act (1914)
   c. Federal Trade Commission Act (1914)
   d. Robinson-Patman Act (1936)

8. a. Country of Origin Labeling Law
   b. Consumer Product Safety Act
   c. Child Protection Act
   d. Children's Online Privacy Protection Act
   e. Consumer Credit Reporting Reform Act
   f. Truth-in-Lending Act
   g. Magnuson-Moss Warranty-Federal Trade Commission Improvement Act
   h. Fair Credit Reporting Act
   i. Child Protection and Toy Safety Act
   j. Alcohol Labeling Legislation
   k. Nutrition Labeling and Education Act
   l. Fair packaging and Labeling Act

9. Your answers will vary. Here are some suggestions to keep you thinking. When the government lowers the tax rate, it should mean that people have more money in their pockets to spend. If the theory holds true, then when people buy goods and services with that extra cash, they increase demand for goods and services, and that should actually increase jobs as companies try to keep up with that demand. When people have jobs they pay taxes, so the reduction in the tax *rate* is made up for by the increase in the number of people working and paying taxes, as well as from companies which experience higher profits. The idea is to create jobs and put people to work so that they will have more money to spend. This will keep tax revenues coming in.

Learning Goal 8

10. a. Chapter 11
    b. Chapter 7
    c. Chapter 13

Learning Goals 2, 3, 4, 5, 8, 9

11. a. Tort law
    b. Sales law (UCC)
    c. Bankruptcy law
    d. Patent law
    e. Contract law
    f. Deregulation

Learning Goal 9

12. Answers will vary, but you may have mentioned such devices as cellular phone service, more options on your land lines, lower prices for example.

PRACTICE TEST

MULTIPLE CHOICE

1.	b	7.	b
2.	c	8.	d
3.	d	9.	a
4.	a	10.	a
5.	c	11.	b
6.	b	12.	a

TRUE–FALSE

1.	F	9.	T
2.	T	10.	T
3.	F	11.	F
4.	T	12.	F
5.	F	13.	T
6.	F	14.	T
7.	F	15.	F
8.	T	16.	F

BONUS CHAPTER B – USING TECHNOLOGY TO MANAGE INFORMATION

LEARNING GOALS

After you have read and studied this chapter, you should be able to:

1. Outline the changing role of business technology.
2. List the types of business information, identify the characteristics of useful information, and discuss how data are stored and mined.
3. Compare the scope of the Internet, intranets, extranets, and virtual private networks as tools in managing information.
4. Review the hardware most frequently used in business.
5. Classify the types of computer software most frequently used in business.
6. Evaluate the human resource, security, privacy and stability issues in management affected by information technology.

LEARNING THE LANGUAGE

Listed below are important terms found in the chapter. Choose the correct term for the definition and write it in the space provided.

Broadband technology	Information systems (IS)	Shareware
Business Intelligence	Information technology (IT)	Virtual private network (VPN)
Cloud-computing	Internet2	Virtualization
Cookies	Intranet	Virus
Data processing (DP)	Network computing systems (Client/server computing)	Web 2.0
Extranet	Public domain software (freeware)	

1. The name for business technology in the 1970s was _____ and included technology that supported an existing business, and was used primarily to improve the flow of financial information.

2. A private data network called a _____ creates secure connections or "tunnels" over regular Internet lines.

3. The private Internet system known as the _____ links government supercomputer centers and a select group of universities; it runs 22,000 times faster than today's public infrastructure and supports heavy-duty applications.

4. A process known as _____ , allows networked computers to run multiple operating systems and programs through one central computer at the same time.

5. A semiprivate network known as a(n) _____ uses Internet technology and allows more than one company to access the same information or allows people on different servers to collaborate.

6. Software that is copyrighted but distributed to potential customers free of charge is called _____.

7. A piece of programming code known as a _____ is inserted into other programming to cause some unexpected and, for the victim, usually undesirable event.

8. Technology called _____ helps companies to do business; includes such tools as automated teller machines (ATMs) and voice mail.

9. Technology known as _____ offers users a continuous connection to the Internet and allows them to send and receive mammoth files that include voice, video, and data much faster than ever before.

10. Computer systems that allow personal computers (clients) to obtain needed information from huge databases in a central computer (the server) are called _____.

11. Technology called _____ helps companies to change business by allowing them to use new methods.

12. Software that is free for the taking is _____.

13. Pieces of information such as registration information or user preferences, known as _____ are sent by a Web site over the Internet to a Web browser that the browser software is expected to save and to send back to the server whenever the user returns to that web site.

14. A company wide network called an _____ is closed to public access, and uses Internet-type technology.

15. _____ is any variety of software applications that takes out useful insights from an analysis of an organization's raw data.

16. A form of virtualization referred to as _____ is one in which a company's data and applications are stored at offsite data centers that are accessed over the Internet (the cloud).

17. The set of tools that allow people to build social and business connections, share information, and collaborate on projects online is _____ and includes blogs, wikis, social-networking sites and other online communities, and virtual worlds.

ASSESSMENT CHECK

Learning Goal 1

The Role of Information Technology

1. What was the primary role and use of data processing?

2. Data are _____

   Information is _____

3. How did Information Systems differ from data processing?

4. What is the role of the CIO in business today?

5. How does IT break time and place barriers to better serve customers?

6. Describe how IT is changing business in:

   a. Organization _____

   b. Operations _____

   c. Staffing _____

   d. New products _____

   e. Customer relations _____

   f. New Markets _____

7. Business Intelligence (BI) activities include:

   a. _____

   b. _____

   c. _____

   d. _____

8. BI helps people focus on _____

Types of Information

9. Describe five types of information.

    a. _____

    b. _____

    c. _____

    d. _____

    e. _____

10. "Infoglut" is _____

11. Referring to information overload, the most important step toward gaining perspective is to:

    _____

    _____

12. Describe four characteristics of useful information.

    a. _____

    b. _____

    c. _____

    d. _____

13. Tips for organizing e-mail and electronic data include:

    a. _____

    b. _____

    c. _____

    d. _____

14. What is a data warehouse, and what is its purpose?

15. What is data mining and what does it do?

16. How does Wal-Mart use data mining to help with sales?

17. What must be done to make data mining successful?

Learning Goal 3

The Road to Knowledge: The Internet

18. How does a firewall work?

19. Applications of an intranet include:

    a. _____

    b. _____

20. How is an intranet different from an extranet?

21. Since the extranet is a semiprivate network, what is a potential problem?

22. One way to increase the probability of total privacy (of an extranet) is to use: _____

    A problems with this method is: _____

23. Describe how a virtual private network solves the problems involved with the use of an extranet, and the benefits of the VPN.

24. How do enterprise portals function?

25. How does broadband technology solve the problems of traffic jams on the Internet?

26. What applications does the Internet2 support?

   a. _____

   b. _____

   c. _____

   d. _____

   e. _____

27. What is a vBNS?

28. In addition to Facebook and MySpace, what are some other social networking sites?

   a. _____

   b. _____

   c. _____

29. What are two challenges for business when they have a social networking site?

   a. _____

   b. _____

30. Using Web 2.0, location-based services are tied to _____

   _____

Learning Goal 4

The Enabling Technology: Hardware

31. What are some hardware components?

   a. _____   d. _____

   b. _____   e. _____

   c. _____   f. _____

32. Identify some examples of wireless information appliances.

33. Describe the major benefits of computer network systems

   a. _____

   b. _____

   c. _____

34. Describe the drawbacks of networks.

35. What have some companies looked into to avoid the drawbacks of computer networking systems?

36. What is the benefit of this thin client network?

37. What is another option for companies looking to avoid problems with networks, besides thin client networks? What is the benefit?

38. Virtualization is cost effective and convenient because _____

   _____

39. Cloud computing has the benefit of _____

   but commits businesses to _____

Learning Goal 5

Software

40. What are six major business uses of software?

   a. _____   d. _____

   b. _____   e. _____

   c. _____   f. _____

Effects of Information Technology on Management

41. Identify the major issues arising out of the growing reliance on information technology:

a. _____   c. _____

b. _____   d. _____

42. What impact has technology had on organizational structures?

43. What are the benefits of telecommuting for companies?

a. _____

b. _____

c. _____

44. What are the benefits of telecommuting for employees?

Telecomm uniting is most successful among what kinds of workers?

45. What are some drawbacks to telecommuting?

a. _____

b. _____

c. _____

46. What is a "nanobot"? Describe these workers.

47. Secure information is at risk from:

a. _____

b. _____

c. _____

48. How are computer viruses spread?

49. What is an MSSP?

50. Describe "phishing" and the way to avoid the problems associated with that acitivity.

51. Since September 11, security officials are most worried about: _____

52. What could be the impact of cyber terrorists?

53. What is the function of the Critical Infrastructure Protection Board?

54. What is the purpose of the Critical Infrastructure Information Act of 2002?

55. What are some of the privacy issues that arise from the use of technology?

56. What information does a cookie contain, and what does it do?

57. What is spyware?

58. To prevent your computer from receiving cookies you can: _____

_____

59. What is causing computer glitches?

    a. _____

    b. _____

    c. _____

    d. _____

    e. _____

    f. _____

CRITICAL THINKING EXERCISES

Learning Goal 1

1. Trace the development of business technology from the 1970's to the 1980's to the present.

2. We have read in previous chapters of the need to meet increasing global competition, and of the movement toward customized products and marketing. How does information technology change business to make those jobs possible?

3. Review Figure B.1 in your text. How has information technology changed your school, or your place of employment in each of these areas?

4.   What is one of the biggest problems with the age of information technology in terms of managing the information? How can business people overcome this problem? How have you, as a student, experienced the problem?

5.   Help! You are swamped by the data, reports, facts, figures, and tons of paper and E-mail being sent to you! It's your job as a low level sales employee to manage the dissemination of all this "stuff" and make sure it makes sense to everyone who gets it. In other words, your job is to manage all that information! What can you do to make this information useful?

Learning Goal 3

6.   Compare Intranets and Extranets. Do you know a company that has an intranet? How is it used? What are the applications in this company?

Learning Goal 4

7.   Are you "evolved"? What kinds of computer hardware do you use? What kinds of hardware do your friends use? How do you keep up with your friends? What kind of computerized instruction do you have in your classes?

8. Five major uses for software include:

Writing (word processing)   Presenting information visually (Graphics)
Manipulating numbers (spreadsheets)   Communicating
Filing and retrieving data (databases)   Accounting

Match the application being used to the following examples:

a. _____   Richard Bolt uses this software to record his students' grades, average the grades and total the grades at the end of the semester. It's easy to change scores if an error is made, because the computer will automatically recalculate averages and totals when the new score is recorded.

b. _____   Ray Smith uses Outlook Express to send and retrieve messages from work.

c. _____   Steve Nicholson is a marketing manager who uses this type of software to keep track of all his sales people. He has all the information regarding territories, sales quotas, expenses, sales calls and more right at his fingertips.

d. _____   Ryan Charles used this software to create a more interesting report for his science project. After he had finished writing the report, he created a pie chart and a bar chart to illustrate the findings of his research.

e. _____   Lin Brinkman works in a law office. Whenever there is a need for a certain kind of document for a specific case, all Lin has to do is pull the document up on her screen and insert the relevant information.

f. _____   Elizabeth Dean creates the financial statements for her small business each month with Peachtree, a software which makes the process much easier.

Learning Goal 6

9. What has happened to organizational structures and methods of work as a result of the increased use of technology?

10. What are some of the security and privacy issues that are important to recognize with the increasing use of information technology?

PRACTICE TEST

MULTIPLE CHOICE — Circle the best answer

Learning Goal 1

1. In the 2000s, as technology became more sophisticated, knowledge technology became better known as _____.
   a. data processing.
   b. business intelligence.
   c. information systems.
   d. information technology.

2. Technology has changed business in a variety of ways. In terms of customer relations technology has enabled companies to:
   a. reduce the number of customer service representatives.
   b. create virtual offices so customers don't have to go to the store with complaints
   c. solve customer problems instantaneously using company databases.
   d. reduced the number of customer complaints by as much as 50%.

Learning Goal 2

3. A problem managers have with the rapid advance of information technology has been:
   a. the skyrocketing cost of information.
   b. the hardware and software products available can't keep up with the expansion of information.
   c. the increased layers of management.
   d. information overload, with the huge amount of information available.

4. The most important step toward gaining perspective in dealing with infoglut is to:
   a. identify your key goals then eliminate information that doesn't relate to the goals.
   b. get as much information as you can, then sift through it.
   c. limit the information you retrieve by limiting your search to only certain websites.
   d. look for a system which will handle the information more readily.

5. Wal-Mart uses data mining to:
   a. track customer purchases.
   b. store customer information such as addresses and which stores they frequent.
   c. organize files and track payroll information.
   d. customize each store offerings on the basis of local demand.

Learning Goal 3

6. At MEMC Electronics, employees can update their addresses, submit requisitions, timesheets and payroll forms online. The company's system is closed to public access, but all employees have access. MEMC is using an _____
   a. intranet.
   b. extranet.
   c. internet.
   d. electronic data interchange system.

7. A(n) _____ is a private data network that creates secure connections or "tunnels" over regular Internet lines.
   a. enterprise portal
   b. virtual private network
   c. broadband
   d. wireless information appliance

8. A system that runs 22,000 times faster than a traditional modem and supports heavy-duty applications is known as:
   a. broadband technology
   b. Web2
   c. an extranet
   d. Internet 2

Learning Goal 4

9. _____ includes, mobile phones, printers and scanners and personal digital assistants.
   a. Software
   b. Multimedia
   c. Extranets
   d. Hardware

10. In recent years, businesses have moved from:
    a. network computing systems to mainframe systems.
    b. client/server computing to network computing systems.
    c. database systems to information processing.
    d. mainframe systems to network computing systems.

11. Which of the following is a benefit of networks?
    a. unnecessary information is deleted from the system
    b. saves time and money
    c. customers can access information more quickly
    d. companies can see their products more clearly

12. This technology stores a company's data and applications at offsite data centers accessed over the Internet.
    a. virtualization
    b. VPN
    c. knowledge technology
    d. cloud computing

Learning Goal 5

13. Which of the following projects would be best suited to a spreadsheet program?
    a. Personalizing a standardized letter to clients.
    b. Recording the sales figures from several different stores, and calculating profits.
    c. Updating lists and schedules, keeping track of inventory.
    d. Making a presentation more appealing with sound clips, video clips, and clip art.

14. For workers, perhaps the most revolutionary effect of computers and increased use of the Internet is
    a. the amount of information which has been made available to managers.
    b. the ability to allow employees to work from home.
    c. the spread of viruses.
    d. the amount of personal information available and people who can access it.

15. Which of the following is <u>not</u> considered a benefit of telecommuting?
    a. It saves money by retaining valuable employees during long leaves.
    b. It involves less travel time and cost.
    c. It can increase productivity.
    d. It avoids isolation of workers.

16. In the movie The Matrix - Reloaded, a rebel group breaks into government computers and accesses some very sensitive information. The term to describe this group would be:
    a. hackers.
    b. viruses.
    c. cookies.
    d. computer illiterates.

17. Computer security today
    a. has become much easier with better encrypting software.
    b. is more complicated than ever with smart phones, social networks, and online games becoming targets for hackers.
    c. is only a concern for major corporations.
    d. is primarily a small business problem because small businesses can't often afford computer security systems.

18. Today, corporate and government security officials are most worried about:
    a. inoculating computers from viruses.
    b. cyberterrorism.
    c. privacy issues.
    d. consumers' fears of using credit cards on the Internet.

19. Which of the following is <u>untrue</u> reagarding concerns about privacy issues and the Internet?
    a. Hackers can easily trap and read your messages.
    b. Companies can track employee emails.
    c. The Internet makes personal information very easy to retrieve.
    d. Cookies allow you to protect your computer from hackers using spyware.

20. Instability in technology:
    a. continues to have a major impact on business
    b. exists primarily in companies that have not upgraded their technology.
    c. is not a problem with improved hardware systems.
    d. is not a problem in the United States, but impacts U.S. businesses because the problem exists in developing nations with which the U.S. does business.

TRUE–FALSE

Learning Goal 1

1. _____ The role of information technology has changed as technology has evolved.

2. _____ Information technology creates organizations and services that are independent of location.

3. _____ Electronic communications can provide companies with substantial time savings.

Learning Goal 2

4. _____ With the increased use of the Internet, information has become easier to manage

5. _____ One type of information available to businesses today is data that indicate the personal preferences of customers.

6. _____ One way to organize electronic files is to save related materials which utilize multiple software programs under the same name.

7. _____ Data mining is looking for hidden patterns in a data warehouse.

Learning Goal 3

8. _____ An extranet is a company wide network which is closed to everyone outside the specific company using the intranet.

9. _____ Broadband technology offers users a continuous connection to the Internet.

10. _____ Social networking sites like Facebook and MySpace use the Internet2 because of its massive computing capabilities.

Learning Goal 4

11. _____ A computer network will help a company file, store and access data more easily.

12. _____ A thin client network allows software changes and upgrades to be made only on a server, so it saves money.

Learning Goal 5

13. _____ Business people most frequently use software for such things as word processing and manipulating numbers, among other uses.

14. _____ Database programs are basically the electronic equivalent of an accountant's worksheet plus features such as math functions, statistical data analysis and charts.

Learning Goal 6

15. _____ Computers have allowed organizations to eliminate middle management functions and flatten organizational structures.

16. _____ Computer security has gotten simpler today with new security programs.

You Can Find It On the Net

As we have discussed in this chapter, there is a lot of information on the web for just about any topic you can imagine. Let's find out what some of the employment statistics are for computer related occupations.

Visit the Bureau of Labor Statistics at **www.bls.gov**. (Talk about Information Overload!)

Scroll down to the Occupations link, and then to the Occupational Outlook Handbook link, then look at Professional.

What is the employment total for Computer and Mathematical occupations?

What is the mean salary?

Return to the main page, and look in the Occupational Outlook Handbook A-Z Index for computer related jobs and investigate some of the jobs listed.

Which did you find that are declining? Why?

Which are expected to grow? Why?

ANSWERS

LEARNING THE LANGUAGE

1.	Data processing	7.	Virus	13.	Cookies
2.	Virtual private network	8.	Information systems	14.	Intranet
3.	Internet2	9.	Broadband technology	15.	Business intelligence
4.	Virtualization	10.	Network computing systems (client/server computing)	16.	Virtualization
5.	Extranet	11.	Information technology	17.	Web 2.0
6.	Shareware	12.	Public domain software		

ASSESSMENT CHECK

Learning Goal 1

The Role of Information Technology

1. The primary role of data processing was to support existing business by improving the flow of financial information.

2. Data are raw, unanalyzed and unorganized facts and figures.
   Information is processed and organized data managers can use for decision making.

3. Information Systems went from supporting business to actually doing business. Customers began to interact with the business through such means as ATMs and voice mail.

4. The role of the CIO is to help the business use technology to communicate better with others while offering better services and lower costs.

5. IT created organizations and services that are independent of location. Being independent of location brings work to people and allows businesses to conduct business around the globe 24 hours a day.

6. IT is changing business in:
   a. <u>Organization</u> by breaking down corporate barriers and sharing information instantly
   b. <u>Operations</u> by shrinking cycle time, reducing defects and cutting waste
   c. <u>Staffing</u> by eliminating layers of management and cutting employees
   d. <u>New products</u> by cutting development cycles by feeding comments to development teams quickly
   e. <u>Customer relations</u> by solving customer problems instantly
   f. <u>New Markets</u> by enabling online businesses to reach customers to which they wouldn't otherwise have access.

7. Business Intelligence (BI) activities include:
   a. data mining
   b. online analytical process
   c. querying
   d. reporting

8. BI helps people focus on deciding how to react to problems and opportunties.

Learning Goal 2

Types of Information

9. Five types of information are:

    a. Business process information – all transaction data gathered from business transactions.
    b. Physical-world observations – result form the use of which has to do with where people and items are located.
    c. Biological data – identification from physical scans such as fingerprinting, and use of biometric devices.
    d. Public data – free data available from people using the internet email and instant messaging.
    e. Data indicating preferences or intentions – left by Internet shoppers.

10. Infoglut is an overabundance of data.

11. The most important step toward gaining perspective on information overload is to identify the four or five key goals you wish to reach, then eliminating the information that is not related to those priorities.

12. Four characteristics of useful information include:
    a. Quality – information is accurate and reliable.
    b. Completeness – enough information to allow you to make a decision but not so much as to confuse the issue
    c. Timeliness – information must reach managers quickly
    d. Relevance – different managers have different needs

13. Tips for organizing e-mail and electronic data include:
    a. Use your e-mail program's organizing tools to create folders
    b. Use consistent file names across multiple software programs
    c. Use online backup services.
    d. Use desktop search software

14. A data warehouse is storage of data on a single subject over a specific period of time. The purpose of a data warehouse is to get data out so that it is useful information.

15. Data mining is a technique that looks for hidden patterns and previously unknown relationship among the data.

16. Wal-Mart customizes each store offerings on the basis of local demand, keeping it suppliers informed about how each of the products in the stores is selling and what managers anticipate will sell next.

17. The success of data mining depends upon access to data to mine in the first place. Multiple data storage systems must be integrated in some way before the data can be connected.

Learning Goal 3

The Road to Knowledge: The Internet, Intranets Extranets and Virtual Private Networks

18. A firewall consists of hardware or software or both that prevents unauthorized outsiders from accessing their sites, and allows only authorized users access to the intranet.

19. Intranet applications include
    a. allowing employees to update their addresses
    b. submit company forms

20. An intranet operates only within a company. An extranet is a semiprivate network that uses Internet technology so that more than one company can access the same information or so people on different servers can collaborate.

21. Since the extranet is a semiprivate network there is a potential for hackers to gain unauthorized access.

22. One way to increase the probability of total privacy of an extranet is to use a dedicated line.

    A problem with this method is that a dedicated line is expensive.

23. A virtual private network solves the problem of extranet privacy by creating secure connections, or "tunnels," over regular Internet lines. The idea is to give the company the same capabilities as dedicated lines at a much lower cost. Companies can use public lines securely. This allows for on-demand networking, and an authorized user can join the network for any desired function at any time, for any length of time, while keeping the corporate network secure.

24. Portals serve as entry points to resources such as e-mail, financial records, schedules, and employment and benefits files. Portals identify users and allow them access to areas of the intranet based upon their roles as customers, suppliers, employees, etc. They make information available in one place so users don't have to deal with several different Web interfaces.

25. Broadband technology solves the Internet traffic jam problem by offering users a continuous connection to the Internet, and allowing them to send and receive large files faster than before.

26. The Internet 2 supports heavy-duty applications such as:
    a. videoconferencing
    b. collaborative research
    c. distance education
    d. digital libraries
    e. full-body simulation environments known as tele-immersion.

27. vBNS, or very high speed Backbone Network Service links government supercomputer centers and a select group of universities.

28. In addition to Facebook and MySpace, other social networking sites are:
    a. LinkedIn for professionals to post resumes and develop business relationships
    b. PatientsLikeMe which lets member share experiences of illnesses and network with people affected by the same ailments.
    c. Ning.com allows users to create their won social networking site

29. Two challenges for businesses when they have a social networking site are:
    a. employee productivity may go down
    b. a single disparaging remark on a social networking forum can have negative effects on the company's reputation.

30. Using Web 2.0, location-based services are tied to devices that can track a user's whereabouts and suggest places like restaurants or shops in the area. This technology is now available in your cell phone.

Learning Goal 4

The Enabling Technology: Hardware

31. Hardware components include
    a. computers,
    b. mobile phones
    c. printers
    d. scanners
    e. fax machines
    f. personal digital assistants

32. Wireless information appliances include PDAs, smart phones, netbooks and in-dash computers for cars.

33. A computer network system:
    a. Saves time and money
    b. Provides easy links to other areas of the company.
    c. Allows employees to see complete information

34. Maintaining a large number of desktop computers can be expensive. Computing costs and productivity losses go up as you upgrade and troubleshoot equipment and software and train employees to use it.

35. Some companies have looked at a hybrid of mainframe and network computing systems. In this model, applications and data reside on a server that handles the processing needs for all the client machines on the network. The PCs lack the possessing power to handle applications on their own. This is called a thin-client network.

36. With a thin client network, software changes and upgrades only need to be made on the server, so the cost is lower.

37. Another option to networks is to rent software and hardware access by way of the Internet on an as-needed basis.

38. Virtualization is cost effective and convenient because the centralized storage system gives companies ready access to update system software and fix problems.

39. Cloud computing has the benefit of universal accessibility and hassle-free data management but commits businesses to an escalating payment system just to access their own data.

Learning Goal 5

Software

40. The six major business uses of software are:
    a. Writing–word processing
    b. Manipulating numbers–spreadsheets
    c. Filing and retrieving data–databases
    d. Presenting information visually–graphics
    e. Communicating–email and instant messaging
    f. Accounting

Learning Goal 6

Effects of Information Technology on Management

41. The major issues arising out of the growing reliance on information technology are:
    a. human resource changes
    b. security threats
    c. privacy concerns
    d. stability

42. Computers often eliminate middle management functions and flatten organizational structures.

43. The benefits of telecommuting for companies include:
    a. reduces travel time
    b. often increases productivity
    c. saving money with smaller less expensive office space.

44. Workers with disabilities will be able to be gainfully employed, and men and women with small children will be able to stay home. Employees can work extra hours at home rather than at work, and this may help to improve morale and reduce stress.

    Telecommuting is most successful among workers who are self-starters, who don't have home distractions and whose work doesn't require face-to-face interaction with coworkers

45. Some of the drawbacks could include:
    a. consistent long-distance work gives workers a feeling of being left out of the office loop.
    b. loss of the energy people can get through social interaction.
    c. the intrusion that working at home makes into the personal life.

46. A "nanobot" is the term used to describe mobile workers how Nearly Autonomous, Not in the office, are doing Business in their Own Time Staff.

    These workers are highly skilled, high achievers who need personal freedom in their jobs. They must be technologically self-sufficient, and have the maturity to use their autonomy in the best interest of their employers and clients. They must have personal networks, knowledge and experience to handle tasks, situations, and problems on their own.

47. Secure information is at risk from:
    a. hackers who break into computers
    b. employees who steal the information
    c. companies which lose it through incompetence, poor gatekeeping or bad procedures

48. Computer viruses are spread by downloading infected programming over the Internet or by sharing an infected disk.

49. An MSSP is a managed security services provider which can install and manage firewalls, VPNs, vulnerability management, Web filtering and anti-spam, security intelligence services and wireless and mobile functions.

50. Phishing is an online security threat. A scammer will embellish an email with a stolen logo from a well-known brand, which makes a message look authentic. Messages will often state "account activation required" or "Your account will be canceled if you do not verify". 'When victims click the link they are sent to a phony Web site that takes personal data which is used to commit fraud.

The best way to avoid the problem is to open a new window and go to a web site directly, rather than accessing the account through email.

51. Since September 11, corporate and government security officials are most worried about cyberterrorism.

52. Cyber terrorists could shut down the entire communications, money supply, electricity and transportation systems.

53. The Critical Infrastructure Protection Board is a part of the Office of Homeland Defense. It was created to devise a plan for improving the security of America's infrastructure. In order to do this, the agency needs the cooperation of businesses across the country.

54. The Critical Infrastructure Information Act of 2002 provides that critical infrastructure information which is voluntarily submitted a covered federal agency is exempt from disclosure under the Freedom of Information Act. This was necessary because while the participation of businesses is critical to success of anti-terrorism efforts, businesses are hesitant to provide information because they are afraid that customers will lose faith in the business if they are aware of breaches in security.

55. The increase of technology creates major concerns about privacy. E-mail can easily be "snooped", and companies routinely monitor their employees' use of e-mail. As more personal information is stored in computers, Web surfers have access to all sorts of personal information about individuals.

56. A cookie contains your name and password that the Web site recognizes the next time you visit the site so that you don't have to re-enter the same information every time you visit. Other cookies track your movements around the Web and then blend that information with their databases and tailor the ads you receive accordingly.

57. Spyware is software that can be installed on your computer without your knowledge which can infect your system with viruses and track your online behavior.

58. To prevent your computer from receiving cookies you can use P3 to set up your browser to communicate only with Web sites that meet certain criteria.

59. Experts say that computer glitches are combinations of
    a. human error
    b. computer error
    c. malfunctioning software
    d. overly complex equipment
    e. bugs in systems
    f. naïve executives who won't challenge consultants or in-house specialists.

CRITICAL THINKING EXERCISES

Learning Goal 1

1. In the 1970's, business technology was known as data processing. It was used primarily to <u>support</u> the existing business, to improve the flow of financial information. In the 1980's, the name changed to information systems, and the role changed from supporting business to <u>doing</u> business. Customers interacted with the technology in a variety of ways. Businesses have shifted to using new technology and new methods of doing business, and the role of information technology has become to <u>change</u> business. Today the role of a Chief Information Officer is to help the business use technology to communicate better with others while offering better service and lower costs.

2. "In the old days" customers had to go to a business during business hours to meet their needs for consumer products, and employees had to "go to the office" to work. We went to the bank for a loan. Businesses decided *when* and *where* we did business with them. Information technology has changed all that. Information technology allows businesses to deliver products and services whenever and wherever it is convenient for the customer. Companies can go global much more easily, and can open global markets more quickly.

    Even further, IT has enabled businesses to become better and faster at serving customer needs by reducing product development times, getting customer feedback quickly, allowing companies to make changes in products easily and quickly, allowing companies to solve customer problems instantly by using databases, reducing defects, cutting expensive product waste. This has allowed businesses to become more customer oriented and thus more competitive in a global marketplace.

3. These are just some examples of how Information technology has changed many schools. You may have lots of other examples:
    <u>Organization:</u> Students can get grades over the net, find out school schedules, find out who is teaching certain courses, e-mail assignments to teacher, get syllabi and other course information. Teachers can enter grades online.
    <u>Operations:</u> Students can register online, and order books online.
    <u>Staffing:</u> With online registration and payments, the need for office personnel may be reduced.
    <u>New products:</u> Online courses are offered at many schools in many different academic areas.
    <u>Customer relations:</u> Students can communicate with instructors, and vice versa via e-mail with questions and problems.
    <u>New markets:</u> With online courses, schools can reach students who wouldn't ordinarily attend a particular school, or who may not attend at all, without the online access.

Learning Goal 2

4. One of the biggest problems of information technology is the overwhelming amount of information available. Today business people are deluged with information from voice mail, the Internet, fax machines, and e-mail. Businesspeople refer to this information overload as "infoglut."

    As a student you may note several areas where information overload could be a problem. For example, in searching for a college you had a base of thousands of schools from which to choose. Most likely all, or most, of these schools have websites full of information about their programs, campus and so on. You made your selection based upon your goals, or criteria, such as geography, finances, programs, entrance requirements and many other possibilities.

5. The first thing you need to do is to improve the quality of the information by combining the facts and figures and so on into something that is meaningful. Put sales reports together and summarize weekly or monthly figures. Note any trends in sales over a given period, and double check for accuracy in all the information you use. (Quality)

    Secondly, you will need to make sure that you are using the latest sales reports, and double-check your figures. Since you will be sending this information to various sales managers, check to be sure that you have included all the data needed to give the managers an accurate picture of how sales are going and why. You don't need to include anything that may not be relevant, such as reports from committees or other areas that don't pertain to sales. (Completeness)

    In addition, you need to work fast! If a sales person is not meeting quotas, a few weeks is too long to wait to find out why. With E-mail, your reports can be sent out almost as soon as they're finished. (Timeliness)

    Lastly, be sure that the sales reports you are sending are appropriate to the management level at which they'll be received. Lower level managers will need inventory information perhaps, but not industry trends. Middle level managers may want your sales forecasts based upon past trends, but not vacation schedules for various salespeople. (Relevance)

Learning Goal 3

6. An intranet is a company-wide network closed to public access, which uses internet-type technology. An extranet is a semiprivate network that uses Internet technology so more than one company can access the same information, or so people on different servers can collaborate. One of the most common uses of extranets is to extend an intranet to outside customers.

    You may find any number of examples of how this operates where you work or go to school, from filing forms online to email.

Learning Goal 4

7. You may be surprised at how much, or how little, computer hardware impacts your life, without realizing it. Many students of traditional college age have given up "traditional" phone calls in favor of text messaging on their mobile phones. You may be in classes with an instructor using a wireless laptop to aid in instruction or showing examples of ads on YouTube, and you may keep track of your assignments using a PDA on which you have stored your friend's phone numbers and e-mail addresses. You may have an MP3 player with video capability to download your favorite movies, or you may listen to podcasts. The possibilities are endless.

Learning Goal 5

8. a. Spread sheet – to store and manipulate numbers
    b. Communicating – to send and retrieve messages
    c. Database – to store and organize information
    d. Graphics – to make a pictorial presentation
    e. Word processing for writing
    f. Accounting

9. Computers have often enabled businesses to eliminate middle management functions, and thus flatten organization structures. Perhaps the most revolutionary effect of computers and the increased use of the Internet and intranets may be the ability to allow employees to stay home and do their work from there, or telecommute. Using computers linked to the company's network, workers can transmit their work to the office and back easily, either from home, or from their virtual office.

10. One problem today is hackers, who break into computer systems for illegal purposes. Today, computers not only make all areas of the company accessible, but also allow access to other companies with which the firm does business. Another security issue involves the spread of computer viruses over the Internet. Viruses are spread by downloading infected programming over the Internet or by sharing an infected disk. A major concern is a problem with privacy as more and more personal information is stored in computers and people are able to access all sorts of information about you. One of the key issues in the privacy debate is: isn't this personal information already public anyway?

PRACTICE TEST

MULTIPLE CHOICE

1.	b	11.	b
2.	c	12.	d
3.	d	13.	b
4.	a	14.	b
5.	d	15.	d
6.	a	16.	a
7.	b	17.	b
8.	d	18.	b
9.	d	19.	d
10.	d	20.	a

TRUE–FALSE

1.	T	9.	T
2.	T	10.	F
3.	T	11.	T
4.	F	12.	T
5.	T	13.	T
6.	T	14.	F
7.	T	15.	T
8.	F	16.	F

BONUS CHAPTER C – MANAGING RISK

LEARNING GOALS

After you have read and studied this chapter, you should be able to:

1. Identify the environmental changes that have made risk management important.
2. Explain the four ways of managing risk and distinguish between insurable and uninsurable risk.
3. Define insurance policies and explain the law of large numbers and the rule of indemnity.
4. Discuss the various types of insurance that businesses can buy to manage risk.

LEARNING THE LANGUAGE

Listed here are important terms found in this chapter. Choose the correct term for each definition below and write it in the space provided.

Claim	Law of large numbers	Rule of indemnity
Health maintenance organizations (HMOs)	Mutual insurance company	Self-insurance
Health savings accounts (HSAs)	Preferred provider organizations (PPOs)	Speculative risk
Insurable interest	Premium	Stock insurance company
Insurable risk	Pure risk	Uninsurable risk
Insurance policy	Risk	

1. A _____ is a type of insurance company owned by stockholders.

2. A written contract known as a(n) _____ is between the insured and an insurance company that promises to pay for all or part of a loss.

3. The _____ says that an insured person or organization cannot collect more than the actual loss from an insurable risk.

4. The threat of loss with no chance of profit is called _____.

5. The _____ is a principle which states that if a large number of people are exposed to the same risk, a predictable number of losses will occur during a given period of time.

6. A chance of either profit or loss is called _____.

7. The chance of loss an entrepreneur takes of losing time and money on a business that may not prove to be profitable is commonly called _____.

8. A _____ is a type of insurance company owned by its policyholders.

9. Health care organizations known as _____ require members to choose from a restricted list of doctors.

10. The fee charged by an insurance company for an insurance policy is a _____.

11. A(n) _____ is one that no insurance company will cover.

12. The practice of setting aside money to cover routine claims and buying only "catastrophe" policies to cover big losses is called _____.

13. A(n) _____ is a risk that the typical insurance company will cover.

14. Health care organizations similar to HMOs except that they allow members to choose their own physicians for a fee are called _____.

15. The possibility of the policyholder to suffer a loss is called _____.

16. Tax-deferred accounts known as _____ are linked to low-cost, high deductible health insurance policies.

17. The insured person sends a statement of loss called _____ to the insurance company to request payment.

ASSESSMENT CHECK

Learning Goal 1

Understanding Business Risks

1. What is ERM?

2. What are the goals of ERM?

   a. _____

   b. _____

   c. _____

Learning Goal 2

Managing Risk

3. Describe the two kinds of risk.

   a. _____

   _____

   b. _____

   _____

4. The kind of risk of most concern to business people is: _____

5. List four methods businesses use to manage pure risk.

   a. _____   c. _____

   b. _____   d. _____

6. What are of examples of how can a firm reduce risk?

   a. _____

   b. _____

   c. _____

7. _____ to threats is critical to risk management

8. How do some companies avoid risk?

9. Self-insurance is most appropriate when: _____

10. What does it mean for a company to "go bare" with self-insurance, and what is the risk?

11. What is a BOP?

12. Describe four kinds of uninsurable risk.

   a. _____

   b. _____

   c. _____

   d. _____

13. Identify the guidelines used to evaluate whether or not a risk is insurable.

    a. _____

    b. _____

    c. _____

    d. _____

    e. _____

    f. _____

Learning Goal 3

Understanding Insurance Policies

14. What makes the acceptance of risk possible for insurance companies is: _____

_____

15. How are appropriate premiums for each policy determined?

16. Today, many insurance companies are charging high premiums not for expected losses but for _____

17. Can a person purchase more than one policy to cover the same risk? Explain.

Learning Goal 4

Insurance Coverage for Various Kinds of Risk

18. What are three types of insurance to cover losses?

    a. _____

    b. _____

    c. _____

19. What are four major options for health insurance?

    a. _____   c. _____

    b. _____   d. _____

20. What are the features of an HMO?

21. What are some complaints about HMOs?

22. What are some characteristics of a PPO?

23. Why do most businesses and individuals choose to join an HMO or a PPO?

24. Describe the features of a health savings account.

25. A major benefit to you of health saving accounts is_____

_____

26. Describe disability insurance.

27. Who provides worker's compensation and what does it guarantee?

28. Who does professional liability insurance cover?

   What is another name for this type of insurance?

29. What is product liability insurance?

30. To ensure those left behind will be able to continue the business, entrepreneurs often buy _____

31. What should you do about insurance coverage if you have a home-based business?

32. What are the issues involved in risk management and the environment?

CRITICAL THINKING EXERCISES

Learning Goal 1

1. The "environment" changes so rapidly that it is difficult to identify all the changes that could affect a business in terms of risk management. Evaluate the company for which you work, or a company with which you are familiar. What is happening today in the environment (you remember this from chapter 1 - the economic and legal, technological, competitive, social, global business environments)? How do the changes you have identified increase the necessity for risk management for this firm? What actions can the firm take to minimize the risk of loss from these changes?

Learning Goal 2

2. Businesses have four options to avoid losses stemming from pure risk situations.

Reduce the risk   Buy insurance to cover the risk
Avoid the risk   Self-insure against the risk

Read the following situations, and determine which option the firm is choosing in each case. Use each option only once.

a. _____   The president of an asbestos removal firm in Merriam, Kansas closed his firm for four months.

b. _____   A group of 27 accounting firms formed its own insurance company to insure themselves.

c. _____   Workers and visitors on construction sites are required to wear hard hats.

d. _____   Senoret Chemical Company experienced a 1600% increase in its liability coverage premium.

3. Many variables determine which risks are insurable. Using your text, determine which of the following situations would constitute an insurable risk.

a. _____ TNG Enterprises would like to buy insurance to cover loss of computer equipment from power surges and possible spills.

b. _____ Gilmores, Inc. a retail store in Kalamazoo, wanted to insure against losses occurring when a competitor, Hudsons, implemented an aggressive marketing campaign.

c. _____ MEMC wants to buy insurance to cover losses created by a breakdown of their robotic and computer driven manufacturing systems.

d. _____ PPI, a small manufacturing firm, wants to insure themselves against losses created by damage from a fire set accidentally.

e. _____ Residents in Morgan City, Louisiana, East Lansing, Michigan and Valley Park, Missouri want to buy flood insurance.

f. _____ Residents of Morgan City, Louisiana, however, face a high risk of flooding, because the Mississippi River is cutting a new tributary through that city, and floods regularly.

g. _____ Boeing has extensive contracts with the government to build fighter planes. The company wants insurance to cover losses that may occur if Congress cuts the defense budget by over 20%.

Learning Goal 3

4. Eric owns a company that makes self-darkening windshields for vehicles, Sun-2-Shade. He is aware of the risks of owning a business, and is considering various insurance plans. Eric would like to make sure that he won't incur any losses, and so is thinking about buying policies from two different companies just to make sure that not only will he be covered, but could make money while the company was down. Eric figures that he will be able to make claims on both policies if something happens, and even make money when both companies pay on the claim. As Eric's advisor, what would you tell him about this plan?

5. You are a small business owner, currently working out of your home and you are concerned about the kinds of insurance that you should carry for your business. Currently, your business consists of yourself, and 3 employees. You have turned to a small business consultant to advise you. What do you think the consultant will say about the need for insurance?

PRACTICE TEST

MULTIPLE CHOICE — Circle the best answer

Learning Goal 1

1. Risk management has become an important concern for businesses today because:
    a.   insurance companies have done such a good job of marketing their products
    b.   rapid environmental changes are becoming a major source of risk for companies.
    c.   companies want to insure themselves against potential losses.
    d.   lawyers have made insurance claims a part of a company's legal strategic plan.

2. An enterprise risk management program has as one of its goals:
    a.   define which risks the program will manage.
    b.   eliminate the risk of doing business.
    c.   insure the company from environmental disasters.
    d.   spread the risk of doing business over time.

Learning Goal 2

3. When Macy's orders inventory for the Christmas season, the company has to predict what their customers will want to buy that season. The kind of risk being described is
    a.   speculative risk.
    b.   pure risk.
    c.   insurable risk.
    d.   self-insurance

4. It is when a company has several widely distributed facilities that _____ is the most appropriate.
    a.   reducing the risk
    b.   avoiding the risk
    c.   self-insurance
    d.   finding another company to take the risk

5. An insurable risk is one in which:
   a. the loss is a specific amount.
   b. the loss is not accidental.
   c. the risk is dispersed.
   d. the policyholder has no insurable interest.

Learning Goal 3

6. The law of large numbers states that:
   a. a large number of people must make claims before an insurance company will begin to pay out.
   b. if a large number of people are exposed to the same risk, a predictable number of losses will occur during a given period of time.
   c. items that will be covered by an insurance policy must not be above a certain amount, i.e. the large number which is set by actuaries.
   d. if losses from an occurrence are large enough, and insurance company will turn the policies over to a reinsurance company.

7. The idea that an insured person or organization cannot collect more than the actual loss from an insurable risk is called the:
   a. law of large numbers.
   b. rule of indemnity.
   c. disability insurance
   d. insurable interest.

Learning Goal 4

8. A type of insurance that requires members to choose from a restricted list of doctors is called a:
   a. health maintenance organization.
   b. preferred provider organization.
   c. disability insurance.
   d. medical savings account.

9. Disability insurance
   a. replaces all your income if you become disabled.
   b. starts immediately after your disability.
   c. is required from employers.
   d. replaces a portion of your income.

10. If a person is injured when using a product and sues the manufacturer, the company is covered by
    a. workers compensation.
    b. disability insurance.
    c. product liability insurance.
    d. business interruption insurance.

11. Which of the following is true of worker's compensation insurance?
    a. It guarantees payment of wages, medical care, and rehabilitation services for employees who are injured on the job.
    b. Only employers in right to work states are required to provide worker's compensation insurance.
    c. The insurance does not provide benefits to the survivors of workers who die as a result of work-related injuries.
    d. The cost of insurance is standard in any industry.

12. Business concern about damage to the environment:
    a. is primarily restricted to companies in the United States.
    b. is declining as companies add more insurance coverage as part of their strategic plans.
    c. has become a global issue because of concerns over issues such as climate changes.
    d. is primarily a concern of companies in the European Union and Eastern Europe.

TRUE–FALSE

Learning Goal 1

1. _____ An enterprise risk management system includes determining how risk management efforts will be coordinated across the firm.

2. _____ New legislation is being passed in some areas which aims to lessen some risk so companies can obtain insurance coverage at a reasonable price.

Learning Goal 2

3. _____ A firm can reduce risk by establishing loss prevention programs such as fire drills, health education and accident prevention programs.

4. _____ Pure risk is the threat of loss with no chance for profit.

5. _____ When a company "goes bare" in terms of insurance, the company is getting the bare minimum insurance coverage from its insurance provider.

6. _____ One type of risk that cannot be covered is loss from accidental injury.

Learning Goal 3

7. _____ The rule of indemnity states that you can have two insurance policies to cover the same risk of loss.

8. _____ A stock insurance company is one that insures the risk of being a stockholder.

Learning Goal 4

9. _____ One of the complaints about an HMO is that members can't choose their own doctors.

10. _____ Health savings accounts are tax-deferred accounts that allow you to save money for future medical expenses.

11. _____ Many professionals other than doctors and lawyers are buying malpractice insurance which is also known as professional liability insurance.

12. _____ Most homeowner's insurance policies have adequate protection for a home based business.

13. _____ Workers' compensation insurance guarantees payment of wages for employees injured on the job, but will not cover medical expenses, as those should be covered by medical insurance programs.

14. _____ Concerns about the environment stem from issues such as global warming and hazards from nuclear power plants.

You Can Find It on the Net

Visit the website **http://www.rmmag.com/** which is the website for Risk Management magazine.

What are the major concerns addressed in the current issue of the magazine? How do those concerns reflect what we have discussed in this chapter?

What is the RIMS?

Visit the home page of the insurance company you currently use for car, homeowners, or other insurance policies. What types of products does this company offer?   Use this company's website to determine if you have adequate insurance to cover your needs.

Can this company insure your small business? What kinds of business insurance do they offer for your small business?

ANSWERS

LEARNING THE LANGUAGE

1.	Stock insurance company	7.	Risk	13.	Insurable risk
2.	Insurance policy	8.	Mutual insurance company	14.	Preferred Provider Organization (PPO)
3.	Rule of indemnity	9.	Health maintenance organizations (HMOs)	15.	Insurable interest
4.	Pure risk	10.	Premium	16.	Medical savings accounts (MSAs)
5.	Law of large numbers	11.	Uninsurable risk	17.	Claim
6.	Speculative risk	12.	Self insurance		

ASSESSMENT CHECK

Learning Goal 1

Understanding Business Risks

1. ERM is an enterprise risk program, designed by executives for their companies.

2. The goals of an ERM can include:
   a. defining which risks the program will manage.
   b. what risk management processes, technologies, and investments will be required.
   c. how these efforts will be coordinated across the firm.

Learning Goal 2

Managing Risk

3. a. <u>Speculative risk</u> involves a chance of either profit or loss. It includes the chance the firm takes to make extra money by buying new machinery, acquiring more inventory and making other decisions in which the probability of loss may be relatively low and the amount of loss is known. An entrepreneur takes speculative risk on the chance of making a profit.

   b. <u>Pure risk</u> is the threat of loss with no chance for profit. It involves the threat of fire, accident or loss. If such events occur, a company loses money, but if the events do not occur, the company gains nothing.

4. The kind of risk of most concern to business-people is pure risk.

5. Firms can manage risk by
   a. Reducing the risk
   b. Avoiding the risk
   c. Self-insure against the risk
   d. Buy insurance against the risk

6. Examples of reducing risk include:
    a. A firm can reduce risk by establishing loss-prevention programs such as fire drills, health education, safety inspections, equipment maintenance, and accident prevention programs.
    b. Retail stores use mirrors, video cameras, and other devices to prevent shoplifting.
    c. Manufacturers have safety devices to protect workers from injury.

7. Quick response is critical to risk management.

8. Companies avoid risk by not accepting hazardous jobs and by outsourcing shipping and other functions. For example, the threat of lawsuits has driven away some drug companies from manufacturing vaccines, and some consulting engineers refuse to work on hazardous sites. Some companies are losing outside members of their boards of directors for lack of liability coverage. Many companies have cut back on their investments to avoid the risk of financial losses.

9. Self insurance is most appropriate when a firm has several widely distributed facilities.

10. When a company "goes bare" the company is paying claims straight out of its budget. This is a very risky strategy for a company. The risk is that the whole firm could go bankrupt over one claim if the damages are high enough.

11. A BOP is a business ownership policy. This is a package that includes property and liability insurance, and reduces the cost of insurance.

12. Four kinds of uninsurable risk include:
    a. Market risks (from price changes, style changes, new products)
    b. Political risks (from war or government restrictions)
    c. Personal risks (from loss of job)
    d. Risks of operation (strikes or inefficient machinery)

13. An insurable risk is evaluated using the following criteria
    a. The policyholder must have an insurable interest.
    b. The loss must be measurable.
    c. The chance of loss should be measurable.
    d. The loss should be accidental.
    e. The risk should be dispersed.
    f. The insurance company can set standards for accepting risk.

Learning Goal 3

Understanding Insurance Policies

14. What makes the acceptance of risk possible for insurance companies is the law of large numbers.

15. Appropriate premiums for insurance policies are determined by using the law of large numbers. Once the insurance company predicts the number of losses likely to occur, it can determine the appropriate premiums for each policy it issues against that loss.
The premium is supposed to be high enough to cover expected losses and still earn a profit for the firm.

16. Today many insurance companies are charging higher premiums not for expected losses but for the costs they anticipate from the increasing number of court cases and high damage awards.

17. A person can't buy two insurance policies and collect from both for the same loss. You cannot gain from risk management you can only minimize losses

Learning Goal 4

Insurance Coverage for Various Kinds of Risk

18. Three types of insurance include:
    a. property and liability
    b. health
    c. life insurance

19. Four major options for health insurance are:
    a. health care providers, such as Blue Cross/Blue Shield,
    b. health maintenance organizations (HMOs)
    c. preferred provider organizations (PPOs)
    d. medical savings accounts (MSAs)

20. HMOs offer a full range of health care benefits. Emphasis is on helping members stay healthy instead of on treating illnesses. Members do not receive bills and do not have to fill out claim forms for routine service. HMOs employ or contract with doctors, hospitals and other systems of health care and members must use those providers. HMOs are less expensive than comprehensive health insurance providers.

21. Members complain about not being able to choose doctors or to get the care they want or need. Some physicians complain that they lose some freedom to do what is needed to make people well and that they often receive less compensation than they feel is appropriate for the services they provide.

22. Preferred provider organizations contract with hospitals and doctors, but do not require members to choose only from those physicians. Members can use outside provides, for which they pay more. Members pay a deductible before the PPO will pay any bills. When the plan does pay, members usually have to pay part of the bill. This payment is called co-insurance.

23. Most individuals and businesses choose to join a PPO or an HMO because they can cost as much as 80 percent less than individual health insurance policies.

24. With a health savings account, you or your employer put part of the money currently spent on health insurance into a health savings account. You would use the money only for needed health care services. At the end of the year you get to keep the money you don't spend in the account for future medical coverage.

25. One major benefit to you of a health saving account is that the money grows tax-free until you take it out.

26. Disability insurance replaces part of your income if you become disabled and unable to work. Usually, before you can begin collecting there is a period of time you must be disabled. The premiums for such insurance vary depending on your age, occupation, and income.

27. Workers compensation insurance guarantees payment of wages, medical care, and rehabilitation services for employees who are injured on the job. Employers in all states are required to provide this type of insurance. This insurance also provides benefits to the survivors of workers who die as a result of work-related injuries.
    The cost of the insurance varies by the category of business; higher risk jobs cost more to insure than lower risk types of jobs.

28. Professional liability insurance covers people who may be found liable for professional negligence, such as lawyers, doctors, dentists, mortgage brokers, and real estate appraisers.

   This is also known as malpractice insurance.

29. Product liability insurance provides coverage against liability arising out of products sold.

30. To ensure those left behind will be able to continue the business, entrepreneurs often buy life insurance that will pay partners and others what they need to keep the firm going.

31. Homeowner's policies usually don't have adequate protection for a home-based business, so you may need to add an endorsement, or rider, to increase the coverage.
   If clients visit your office and or if you receive deliveries regularly, you may need home-office insurance, which protects you from slip and fall lawsuits and other risks associated with visitors. More elaborate businesses may need other kinds of insurance.

32. Risk management goes beyond the protection of individuals and businesses from known risk. It now means evaluating the worldwide risks and prioritizing these risks so that international funds can be spent where they will do the most good.

CRITICAL THINKING EXERCISES

Learning Goal 1

1. Your answers to this question will vary. However, some suggestions as to how to minimize risk may include developing an enterprise risk management program for the company, to determine what risks pose the greatest danger to the company, and how to manage those risks.

Learning Goal 2

2. a. Avoid risk
   b. Self-insure against the risk
   c. Reduce the risk
   d. Buy insurance to cover the risk.

3. a. Yes, companies can buy insurance against the loss of computer equipment.
   b. No, this would be an uninsurable risk.
   c. No, a company cannot insure against inefficient machinery or machinery that breaks down or doesn't work.
   d. Yes you can insure against fire damage.
   e. Yes, probably, unless the occurrence of loss has been too high.
   f. No, most likely because the probability of flooding in Morgan City is too high.
   g. No this would be a "political risk" and is uninsurable.

Learning Goal 3

4. While it is understandable that Eric would be concerned about taking care of losses his business may experience, the rule of indemnity will prevent Eric from filing claims with two different insurance companies for the same incident. The rule of indemnity states that an insured person or organization can't collect more than the actual loss from an insurable risk. If a company carries two policies, the two insurance companies would calculate any loss and divide the reimbursement.

Learning Goal 4

5. As a small business owner located in your home, you will need to have a regular homeowner's policy, but there will be additional coverage that you should consider.

    You may need a rider to cover business equipment, and if customers or clients call on you, you may need home office insurance. If you manufacture items at your home business, you should consider a business owner policy. Depending upon the type of business you own, you may want to consider professional liability insurance or product liability insurance.

    Since you have employees, you may want to check into offering other insurance coverage for them. Employers often offer life insurance, disability insurance, retirement plans, and health insurance.

    You will probably be required to offer worker's compensation insurance. The cost of worker's compensation insurance will be determined by your company's safety record, its payroll and the types of hazards faced by your workers.

PRACTICE TEST

MULTIPLE CHOICE

1.	a	7.	b
2.	b	8.	a
3.	a	9.	d
4.	c	10.	c
5.	c	11.	b
6.	b	12.	c

TRUE-FALSE

1.	T	8.	F
2.	T	9.	T
3.	T	10.	T
4.	T	11.	T
5.	F	12.	F
6.	F	13.	F
7.	F	14.	T

BONUS CHAPTER D – MANAGING PERSONAL FINANCES

LEARNING GOALS

After you have read and studied this chapter, you should be able to:

1. Outline the six steps for controlling your assets
2. Explain how to build a financial base including investing in real estate, saving money, and managing credit.
3. Explain how buying the appropriate insurance can protect your financial base.
4. Outline a strategy for retiring with enough money to last a lifetime.

LEARNING THE LANGUAGE

Listed below are important terms found in this chapter. Choose the correct term for the definition and write it in the space provided.

401(k) plan	Executor	Term insurance
Annuity	Individual Retirement Account (IRA)	Umbrella policy
Contrarian approach	Roth IRA	Variable life insurance
Executor	Social Security	Whole life insurance
Disability insurance	Tax deferred contributions	Will

1. Pure insurance protection for a given number of years is _____.

2. A (n) _____ is a tax-deferred investment plan that enables you and your spouse to save part of your income for retirement. A traditional one allows people who qualify to deduct from their reported income the money they put into an account.

3. A contract to make regular payments to a person for life or for a fixed period is a(n) _____.

4. The term _____ is used to describe the Old-Age, Survivors, and Disability Insurance Program established in 1935.

5. Insurance referred to as _____ invests the cash value of the policy in stocks or other high yielding securities.

6. Life insurance that combines pure insurance and savings is _____.

7. Buying stock when everyone else is selling, or vice versa is called the _____.

8. A document referred to as a(n) _____ names the guardian for your children, states how you want your assets distributed, and names the executor for your estate.

9. A savings plan called a _____ is one that allows you to deposit pretax dollars and whose earnings compound tax free until withdrawal, when the money is taxed at ordinary income tax rates.

10. A broadly based insurance policy called a (n) _____ saves you money because you buy all your insurance from one company.

11. Insurance that pays part of the cost of a long-term sickness or an accident is _____.

12. A(n) _____ is a person who assembles and values your estate, files income and other taxes, and distributes assets.

13. A(n) _____ is one where you don't get up-front deductions on your taxes, but the earnings grow tax fee and are also tax free when they are withdrawn.

14. _____ are retirement account deposits for which you pay no current taxes, but the earnings gained are taxed as regular income when they are withdrawn at retirement.

ASSESSMENT CHECK

Learning Goal 1

The Need for Personal Financial Planning

1. What are the important elements of money management?

   a. _____

   b. _____

   c. _____

   d. _____

2. How do the lifetime earnings of a typical full-time worker with a college degree compare to the earnings of an individual with a high school diploma?

3. What are six steps you can take today to get control of your finances?

   a. _____

   b. _____

   c. _____

   d. _____

   e. _____

   f. _____

4. What is the process for developing a <u>personal balance sheet</u>?

5. What are the steps in developing a <u>personal income statement</u>?

6. What's the best way to keep track of expenses?

7. How is running a household's finances like running a small business?

8. The first thing to do with the money remaining after you pay your monthly expenses is:

   _____

   This is true because: _____

   _____

9. What's a good way to plan for large purchases, such as a car?

10. The best way to save money is to _____

11. For what types of things should you borrow money?

12. Most financial experts advise that you should have how many months of earnings for contingencies?

Building Your Financial Base

13. How can you accumulate capital?

14. In terms of building a financial base, a great strategy for couples is to _____

    _____

15. The rule of thumb for buying a house is _____

    _____

16. What are the investment benefits of buying a home?

    a. _____

    b. _____

    c. _____

17. What are the tax benefits of home ownership?

18. The key element to getting an optimum return on a home is: _____

19. One of the worst places to keep long-term investments is: _____

    This is because: _____

20. One of the best places to invest over time has been: _____

21. When is the best time to buy stocks?

    What is the term used to describe this kind of investing?

22. What are three reasons why credit cards are an important element in a personal financial system?

    a. _____

    b. _____

    c. _____

23. If you finance a purchase using a credit card, what will it do to the total cost of your purchase, when compared to paying cash, if you don't pay off the balance each month?

24. The danger of a credit card is: _____

    _____

25. What kind of card is better for people who have a problem paying the balance each month?

Learning Goal 3

Protecting Your Financial Base: Buying Insurance

26. Three types of life insurance are:

    a. _____

    b. _____

    c. _____

27. How much insurance do you need?

28. Multiyear level-premium insurance is: _____

    _____

29. Explain whole life insurance.

    What is a universal life policy?

30. What is the difference between a fixed and a variable annuity?

31. One of the more popular alternatives to traditional health insurance is _____

32. What is the danger of not having health and disability insurance?

33. What is meant by guaranteed replacement cost when referring to homeowners insurance?

34. What is an insurance rider?

Learning Goal 4
Planning Your Retirement

35. Describe the problems surrounding the Social Security system.

36. Maintaining Social Security may require:

    a. _____

    b. _____

    c. _____

    d. _____

37. Why is a traditional IRA a good deal for an investor?

38. The earlier you start saving: _____

    _____

39. What is the basic difference between a Roth IRA and a traditional IRA?

40. In taking money out of an IRA it's important to know that: _____

    _____

41. Describe a simple IRA.

42. What are the benefits of 401(k) plans?

    a. _____

    b. _____

    c. _____

43. Describe the characteristics of 401(k) plans.

44. Who is a Keogh plan for?

45. What is the advantage of a Keogh plan?

46. How is a Keogh plan like an IRA?

47. A CFP is: _____

    _____

48. What is a one-stop financial center, financial supermarket?

49. What areas financial planning cover?

50. Discuss the steps involved in estate planning.

    a. _____

    b. _____

    c. _____

51. Describe a durable power of attorney.

CRITICAL THINKING EXERCISES

Learning Goal 1

1. What is the benefit of investing in an education?

2. The six steps to get control of your finances are:

    Take an inventory of you financial assets
    Keep track of all of your expenses
    Prepare a budget
    Pay off your debts
    Start a savings plan
    Only borrow money to buy assets that have the potential to increase in value

    Do as many of these steps as possible in the time frame of a week. Use a separate sheet of paper so you're not limited by the space provided in this book:

    Inventory of assets: Do you own a car? house? appliances? stocks? savings account? checking account? collectibles?

    Expenses: What do you spend in a day on food? newspapers? travel? supplies?
    What do you spend in a month on food? housing? car payments? utilities?
    Are you spending more than you are earning? Keep a small notebook handy to record all your spending for each day for a week.

Budget: Listing all your sources of revenue, determine how much you can spend in a month. Set up accounts for money you are going to pay to yourself, for savings, and for major purchases you will want to make sometime in the future as well as for items which may not be paid every month, but will come due eventually, like car or life insurance. Can you spend less than you are making?

Pay off your debts: Can you pay off your credit cards, if you have them? Are there any other debts that can be paid off now?

Start a savings plan: In your budget, did you pay yourself first?

Identify those loans that were for articles which will *depreciate* in value (educational loans don't count! Your education will help you accumulate capital in the long run!)
It's not easy, is it?!

Learning Goal 2

3. "The principle is simple: To accumulate capital, you have to earn more than you spend."

    A. Take a few minutes to think about the way you spend money (beyond money for tuition, books and other school related items.) Using your text for suggestions, list some ways in which you could begin to accumulate capital for the future:

        1. _____

        2. _____

        3. _____

        4. _____

    B. Investigate the real estate market in your area. Determine the amount by which home prices in your area have appreciated (or depreciated) in the last 5 years. You can probably find a source for this information in your campus library or on the Internet.

    C. Let's assume you have found a house in your area for $110,000. What are the mortgage interest rates in your area for a 30-year, fixed rate mortgage? With a $10,000 down payment, what will your monthly mortgage payments be? To get this information, go to http://financialplan.about.com and click on the mortgage link. Scroll until you find the mortgage calculator.

        If, over time, inflation averages 3 percent, how long will it take for the value of your house to double? (Hint: remember the rule of 72, in chapter 2) You can also use the web site listed above to determine the impact of inflation on the prices of goods and services you may be interested in.

    D. Interest on mortgage payments is tax deductible. Assume that you are in the 28% tax bracket and that the payments on your house are $1,200 per month. What is your real cost?

4. Credit cards are a helpful tool to the financially careful buyer. If you have credit cards, you are probably aware of the advantages:

    Useful for identification
    Helpful to keep track of purchases
    Convenient, in place of cash

    You may also be aware of the disadvantages, primarily high interest rates and the convenience of purchasing something you cannot afford.

    A. If you have credit cards, figure the amount you spent last month using each card, and for what purchases. What is the interest rate on your cards? Did you make purchases you would not have made without the card?

    B. Look at the budget you developed earlier. Do you have an account for credit card payments? Did you budget to pay the entire amount, or only a portion of the bill?

    C. Look at your recent credit card statements. How much did you pay in interest on credit card accounts over the last six months? The last year? That is the amount by which you could have increased your capital account.

Learning Goal 3

5. Consider your lifestyle today and evaluate the kind of insurance needs you have. Are you single or married? Do you have children? If you are married does your spouse work? Are you both, or either one, covered by health insurance? Do you rent an apartment or a house, or do you have a mortgage? If you are married, what would happen to your financial situation if one of you was unable to work?

Learning Goal 4

6. A. Why should you invest in an IRA as a young person?

    B. Again, using the rule of 72, if you invest $1,000 in something that earns 10 percent interest, how long would it take to double the amount?

    C. How much would your $1000 be worth in 15 years, if you are earning 10 percent?

7. Compare and contrast a Keogh, 401(k) and an IRA.

PRACTICE TEST

MULTIPLE CHOICE — Circle the best answer

Learning Goal 1

1. When planning for the future, an investment in a college education will:
    a. provide you with new ideas.
    b. give you a chance to learn about different ways of life.
    c. improve your earning potential.
    d. guarantee a certain type of job.

2. Jerry and Jane are having a discussion about their finances. They are wondering what to do about the amount of money they are spending, how to control their financial situation as well as how to reach their financial goals. One technique to help them would be to:
    a. prepare a budget.
    b. do an asset inventory.
    c. develop an income statement.
    d. quit spending money on anything but the bare basics.

3. The first step in taking control of your finances should be:
    a. keep track of all your expenses.
    b. prepare a budget.
    c. pay off your debts.
    d. take an inventory of your assets.

4. When developing a personal balance sheet, which of the following would not be on a list of personal assets?
    a. a bicycle
    b. car
    c. savings account
    d. mortgage

5. The <u>first</u> thing you should do when you have extra money is:
    a. pay cash for a car.
    b. start a savings plan.
    c. pay off your debts.
    d. put a down payment on a house

6. In terms of borrowing money, the advice is to:
   a. borrow money to buy a car to take advantage of interest tax deductions.
   b. borrow money to invest in the stock market because historically the stock market pays the best returns.
   c. borrow money to pay off credit cards because the interest will be lower on a loan than on the credit cards.
   d. borrow money only to buy assets that have the potential to increase in value or generate income

Learning Goal 2

7. To accumulate capital you have to:
   a. get the highest paying job you can find.
   b. live frugally and invest the money you accumulate.
   c. borrow money and invest.
   d. buy assets which appreciate in value.

8. One of the best investments a person can make is in:
   a. a home.
   b. cars.
   c. credit cards.
   d. an apartment.

9. From a financial standpoint it is best to buy:
   a. a large home in a neighborhood where homes are less expensive.
   b. a small home in a great neighborhood.
   c. the smallest home in the least expensive neighborhood.
   d. the largest home in the most expensive neighborhood you can afford.

10. Other than a home, one of the best places to invest over time has been:
    a. a bank or savings and loan.
    b. car ownership.
    c. the stock market.
    d. apartment buildings.

11. The contrarian approach to investing is:
    a. to stay out of the market no matter what the experts are saying.
    b. to buy when others are selling.
    c. to only buy mutual funds, contrary to the belief that the money to be made is in individual stocks.
    d. to invest predominantly in the bond market when others are investing in the stock market.

12. One of the dangers of a credit card is that:
    a. it is difficult to keep track of purchases.
    b. it can be an inconvenience carrying too many credit cards around.
    c. merchants won't accept credit cards as a form of identification.
    d. consumers may buy goods they wouldn't normally buy if they had to pay cash.

Learning Goal 3

13. _____ life insurance is the type in which some part of the money you pay goes toward pure insurance and another part toward savings.
   a. A fixed annuity
   b. Whole
   c. Variable
   d. Term

14. Guaranteed replacement cost in homeowners insurance means that:
   a. the insurance company guarantees they will replace the lost items for you.
   b. the insurance company guarantees they will pay the current value of a lost item.
   c. the insurance company will pay you what it costs to replace the items.
   d. the insurance company will pay you something for lost items, but the amount can't be determined, so they guarantee an average of market value.

Learning Goal 4

15. Social Security:
   a. will continue to grow in benefits in the future.
   b. will not provide you with ample funds for retirement.
   c. will require workers to retire early.
   d. will take the place of traditional IRAs in the future.

16. An advantage of Keogh plan is that:
   a. there is no penalty for early withdrawal.
   b. participants can invest up to $40,000 per year.
   c. there is no limit to how much can be invested.
   d. anyone can open this type of retirement plan.

17. The invested money in a traditional IRA account:
   a. is taxed as you go along.
   b. is not taxed.
   c. is subject to double taxation.
   d. is not taxed until it is withdrawn.

18. One of the benefits of a Roth IRA is that
   a. contributions aren't taxed.
   b. earnings grow tax free.
   c. you can take the money out before the age of 59 ½ without penalty.
   d. you can invest up to $12,000 a year.

19. Financial planners will:
   a. advise you on a proper mix of IRAs, stocks and so on.
   b. help to negotiate salaries with employers.
   c. create durable powers of attorney for their clients.
   d. open investment accounts for you.

20. Which of the following is not included as a step in the financial planning process?
   a. Select a guardian for minor children.
   b. Prepare a durable power of attorney.
   c. Develop an investment plan.
   d. Prepare a will.

TRUE–FALSE

Learning Goal 1

1. _____ In developing an income statement for yourself, your pay check would be considered as revenue.

2. _____ One of the best ways to keep track of your expenses is to record what you spend as you go through the day.

3. _____ It could be said that running a household is similar to running a small business.

4. _____ The statistics indicate that a majority of the population in the U.S. has accumulated enough money by retirement to live comfortably.

5. _____ The first steps to accumulating capital are finding employment and living frugally.

6. _____ It's not necessary to save for large purchases such as a car or home, since the purchase price will be so high that you will have to borrow money anyway.

Learning Goal 2

7. _____ One of the investment benefits of owning a home is that it is a way of forced savings.

8. _____ While it is a good investment, home ownership generally provides no tax advantages.

9. _____ The bank is probably the best place to keep savings, because it is a safe investment.

10. _____ The contrarian approach to investing is to buy when the market is low and sell when it is high.

11. _____ When managing credit card debt, it is important not to pay off the balance each month in order to build a credit history.

Learning Goal 3

12. _____ Other than life insurance, you should also carry health, disability, and auto insurance policies.

13. _____ The reason to carry life insurance is for protection from the risks of loss of income.

Learning Goal 4

14. _____ One of the benefits of a 401(k) plan is that employers often match part of your deposit.

15. _____ A tax deferred investment means that taxes on your money are deferred until you can afford to pay them.

16. _____ One step in estate planning is to prepare a will.

You Can Find It On The Net

There are two things a college student would like to have more of: Time and Money! Well, we all have the same amount of time, but we vary in how much money we have. All of us can find ways to use and spend our money more effectively.

To learn more about this, go to the site **http://financialplan.about.com** . Using the search function, search the site for "budgets for college students". You should come up with a budget worksheet for college students. This budget worksheet can be printed out and completed. Did you find any surprises?

To get further advice from this site, click on the "Money by Stage or Life age" link, and then on whichever age grouping applies to you. What advice did you find? How many of this site's suggestions are you already following?

ANSWERS

LEARNING THE LANGUAGE

1.	Term insurance	6.	Whole life insurance	11.	Disability insurance
2.	Individual Retirement Account (IRA)	7.	Contrarian approach	12.	Executor
3.	Annuity	8.	Will	13.	Roth IRA
4.	Social Security	9.	401(k) plan	14.	Tax deferred contributions
5.	Variable life insurance	10.	Umbrella policy		

ASSESSMENT CHECK

Learning Goal 1

The Need for Personal Financial Planning

1. Important elements of money management include:
   a. earning money
   b. learn to spend wisely
   c. save money
   d. insure against risk

2. The lifetime earnings of a full time worker with a bachelor's degree is significantly higher than those of an individual with just a high school degree.

3. Six steps you can take to get control of your finances are:
   a. Take an inventory of your financial assets
   b. Keep track of all your expenses
   c. Prepare a budget
   d. Pay off your debts
   e. Start a savings plan
   f. If you have to borrow money, only borrow it to buy assets that have the potential to increase in value.

4. The process for developing a <u>personal balance sheet</u> begins with the fundamental accounting equation: *assets = liabilities + owner's equity.*

   This process starts with listing your assets, such things as a TV, DVD, computer, and so on. Your assets are evaluated on their current value, not the purchase price.

   If you have debts, list them. Subtract debts from your assets to get your net worth.

5. In developing a <u>personal income statement</u>, begin with revenue, which is everything you take in from your job, investments and so on. You subtract all your costs and expenses to get net income or profit.

6. The best way to keep track of expenses is to list everything you spend as you go through the day. That list is your journal. At the end of the week, record your journal entries into a record book or computerized accounting program. Develop certain categories, or accounts, to make the task easier and more informative. Be sure to keep a *detailed* record.

7. Running a household takes the same careful record keeping, the same budgeting process and forecasting, the same control procedures and the same need to periodically borrow funds to run a household's finances as it does to run a small business.

8. The first thing to do with the money remaining after you pay your monthly expenses is to pay off your debts.

   This is true because it is better to pay off a debt that costs 18 percent or more than to put the money in a bank account that earns a very low rate of interest.

9. A good way to plan for large purchases such as a car is to save some money each month in a separate account. Then when it comes time to make the purchase, you'll be able to make a significant down payment so that you can reduce finance charges.

10. The best way to save money is to pay yourself first. That is, take your paycheck, take out money for savings, and then plan what to do with the rest.

11. You should only borrow money to buy assets that have the potential to increase in value or generate income, or to cover the most unexpected expenses.

12. Most financial experts advise that you should have six months of earnings for contingencies

Learning Goal 2

Building Your Financial Base

13. To accumulate capital, you have to live frugally and earn more than you spend. The necessary lifestyle is one of sacrifice, not luxury.

14. In terms of building a financial base, a great strategy for couples is to live on one income and to save the other.

15. The rule of thumb for buying a house is " don't buy a home that costs more than two and a half times your annual income.

16. The investment benefits of buying a home include:
    a. A home is an investment you can live in
    b. Payments are relatively fixed, and as your income rises, payments get easier to make
    c. It is a good way to force yourself to save

17. Interest on mortgage payments and real estate taxes are tax deductible. During the first few years, almost all the mortgage payments go for interest on the loan so almost all the early payments are tax deductible.

18. The key element to getting the optimum return on a home is a good location. A home in the "best part of town", near schools, shopping and work is usually a sound financial investment.

19. One of the worst places for young people to keep long-term investments is in a bank or savings and loan.

    This is because interest paid on savings accounts is relatively low compared to other investment choices, such as the stock market.

20. One of the best places to invest over time has been the stock market. The stock market has historically paid a higher rate of return than other investment choices.

21. The best time to buy stocks is when stock prices are low.

    This is called a contrarian approach.

22. Three reasons why credit cards are an important element in a personal financial system are:
    a. Credit cards are needed as a form of identification
    b. They are a way to keep track of purchases
    c. Credit cards are convenient

23. If you finance a large purchase with a credit card, you may end up spending more than if you pay with cash, because of the finance charges on a credit card. It is important to pay the balance in full each month.

24. The danger of a credit card is that too often, consumers are tempted to make purchases they would not make if they had to pay cash or write a check, and pile up debt as a result.

25. For people who have a problem paying the balance of their card it is better to have a debit card which don't let you spend more than you have in the bank.

Learning Goal 3

Protecting Your Financial Base: Buying Insurance

26. Three types of life insurance are:
    a. Term insurance
    b. Whole life insurance
    c. Variable life insurance

27. Newsweek magazine suggests that a family should have 7 times the family income plus $100,000 for college.

28. Multiyear level-premium insurance is a term insurance policy that guarantees you'll pay the same premium for the life of the policy.

29. With whole life insurance some part of the money you pay for the insurance goes toward pure insurance and another part goes toward savings, so you are buying both insurance and a savings plan.

    A universal life policy is a form of whole life insurance that lets you choose how much of your payment should go to insurance and how much to investments.

30. An annuity is a contract to make payments to a person for life or for a fixed period. A fixed annuity is an investment that pays the policy holder a specified interest rate. A variable annuity provides investment choices identical to mutual funds.

31. One of the more popular alternatives to traditional health insurance is a health savings account.

32. It is dangerous financially not to have health insurance. Hospital costs are too high to risk financial ruin by going uninsured. It is a good idea to supplement health insurance policies with disability insurance that pays part of the cost of a long-term sickness or an accident. Your chances of becoming disabled at an early age are much higher than your chances of dying from an accident.

33. Guaranteed replacement cost means that the insurance company will give you whatever it costs to buy all of the insured items new, rather than the depreciated cost of the items.

34. A rider on an insurance policy will cover expensive items that may not be covered under a regular homeowners or renter's policy.

Learning Goal 4

Planning Your Retirement

35. The problems surrounding the Social Security system stem from the fact that the number of workers paying into social security is declining, but the number of people retiring and living longer is increasing dramatically.

36. Maintaining Social Security may require
   a. reducing benefits
   b. encouraging people to retire later
   c. reduced cost of living adjustments
   d. higher social security taxes.

37. A traditional IRA is a good deal for people who qualify because the invested money isn't taxed when the money is invested. That means fast and good returns.

38. The earlier you start saving the better because your money has a chance to double and double again. For example if you save $4000 a year for 35 years in an IRA and earn 11 percent a year, you will accumulate savings of more than $1.5 million.

39. People who invest in a Roth IRA don't get up-front deductions on their taxes like they would with a traditional IRA, but earnings grow tax free and are tax free when they are withdrawn.

   So, traditional IRAs offer tax savings when they are deposited and Roth IRAs offer tax savings when they are withdrawn.

40. In taking money out of an IRA it's important to know that you can't take the money out of either type of IRA until you are 59 ½ years old without paying a 10 percent penalty.

41. A simple IRA can be offered by companies with fewer than 100 employees. Employees of these companies can contribute up to $11,000 of their income annually compared with the $5,000 limit of regular IRAs. This makes for a good employee benefit for smaller companies.

42. The benefits of 401(k) plans are
   a. The money you put in reduces your present taxable income
   b. Tax is deferred on the earnings
   c. Employers often match part of your deposit

43. With a 401(k) plan you can usually select how the money in the plan is invested: stocks, bonds, and in some cases real estate. The money invested in a 401k should be diversified, and not put into only one company.

44. A Keogh plan is for small business people who don't have the benefit of a corporate retirement system. This can be an alternative for doctors, lawyers, real estate agents, artists, writers and other self-employed people.

45. The advantage of Keogh plans is that participants can invest up to $40,000 per year.

46. A Keogh plan is like an IRA because funds aren't taxed until they are withdrawn, nor are the returns they earn. As with an IRA account, there is a 10 percent penalty for early withdrawal. Also, funds may be withdrawn in a lump sum or spread out over the years like an IRA.

47. A CFP is a certified financial planner. This person will have completed a curriculum on 106 financial topics and a 10-hour exam.

48. A one-stop financial center, or financial supermarket provides a wide variety of financial services ranging from banking services to mutual funds, insurance, tax assistance, stocks, bonds, and real estate.

49. Financial planning covers all aspects of investing all the way to retirement and death. A financial planner can steer you into the proper mix of IRAs, stocks, bonds, real estate and so on.

50. The steps involved in estate planning include:
    a. Select a guardian for your minor children
    b. Prepare a will
    c. Prepare a durable power of attorney

51. A durable power of attorney gives an individual you name the power to take over your finances if you become incapacitated. A similar document for health care delegates power to a person named to make health decisions for you if you are unable to make such decisions yourself.

CRITICAL THINKING EXERCISES

Learning Goal 1

1. History has shown that an investment in education has paid off regardless of the state of the economy. We have studied in previous chapters about the need for constant updating. This includes education! Statistics show that a person with an undergraduate degree earns about twice as much as someone with only a high school diploma.

2. Obviously, everyone will have different answers. This is primarily to get you started on the road to good personal financial planning. It is important to take a look at how you spend your money, what areas need to be curtailed, what kinds of assets you have been able to accumulate, whether or not you are spending less than you earn, your debts and credit card bills, and so on.

Learning Goal 2

3. A. This is another section where each individual will have varied answers. Some suggestions may include: living at home while going to school, buying used books, keep clothing allowances to a minimum, walking or riding a bike when you can, eating at home, or if you are in a house or apartment, making meals at home. For students returning to school after being out for a while, the methods of accumulating capital will be different - and you may already have discovered ways of your own!

    B. Prices in different parts of the country vary widely. Some areas that have been hit by unemployment may have seen a decline in the price of homes. Other areas may have seen above average increases.

    C. Using the rule of 72 you can calculate how long it will take for the value of any asset to double. In this case, the rate of inflation is 3 percent. 72 divided by 3 = 24. So the value of a $110,000 house will double to $220,000 in 24 years. If you have a 30-year mortgage, your house will be almost paid off, and you will have a $220,000 asset. (If you put money in a savings account in a bank and earn 3% interest, it will take 24 years for the savings to double, if you don't make any additional deposits. That's how the rule of 72 works.)

    D. In this example, with a house payment of $1200, and a 28% tax bracket, you can calculate your real cost by multiplying $1200 × .28, which equals $336. Subtract $336 from $1200 and your real cost will be $864 with an interest deduction.

4. Your answers will vary. If you have no credit cards yet, use this information to make good decisions about whether to apply for a credit card, and how to use it.

Learning Goal 3

5. Your answers to this exercise will be determined by what your situation is. If you are married and have children your insurance needs will be different from someone who is younger and/or unmarried.

Learning Goal 4

6. A. An IRA is a good deal for a young investor, because the invested money is not taxed. When you put money into an IRA you save in taxes. If you continue to invest in an IRA, you will have a significant amount of money by the time you retire. The earlier you start, the better. For example if you start putting $2,000 a year in an IRA between the ages of 23–28 at 12% interest, you would have *invested* only $12,000, but even if you never add another penny by the time you are 65 you will have almost $900,000, because of compounded interest. If you continued nonstop from age 23 until age 65, you would have almost $2 million.

    B. 72 divided by 10 = 7.2 years. Your $1,000 would double to $2,000 in 7.2 years.

    C. If your money doubles every 7.2 years, in approximately 15 years your money will have doubled twice, to $4,000.

7. The money invested in an IRA is not taxed. Earnings are not taxed until you take them out when you retire, presumably when you are at a lower tax rate. The money cannot be taken out until the age of 59 ½ without paying a penalty. An IRA is for workers to use as a supplement to a company-sponsored retirement plan and Social Security. It is not connected with your employer. A 401(K) plan is offered by employers, who will often match your contribution. Further, you can borrow the funds from a 401(K), whereas that isn't an option in an IRA.

The Keogh plan is for small business people who do not have the benefit of a corporate retirement system, whereas the 401(K) is a company sponsored program. The benefit over an IRA is that the maximum amount that can be invested is much greater.

A Keogh is like an IRA and the 401(K) in that the funds are not taxed, nor are the earnings, and there is a penalty for early withdrawal. All these plans are designed to protect people from the decline in the value of the Social Security system.

PRACTICE TEST

MULTIPLE CHOICE

1.	c	11.	b
2.	a	12.	d
3.	d	13.	b
4.	d	14.	c
5.	c	15.	d
6.	d	16.	b
7.	b	17.	d
8.	a	18.	b
9.	b	19.	a
10.	a	20.	c

TRUE-FALSE

1.	T	9.	F
2.	T	10.	T
3.	T	11.	F
4.	F	12.	T
5.	T	13.	T
6.	F	14.	T
7.	T	15.	F
8.	F	16.	T